KH Blocker MD
October 1982

INTERNATIONAL JOURNAL OF PSYCHOANALYTIC PSYCHOTHERAPY

International Journal of Psychoanalytic Psychotherapy

Edited by ROBERT LANGS, M.D.
and the Editorial Board

Volume Nine
1982–83

NEW YORK • JASON ARONSON • LONDON

With this issue, the IJPP becomes the official journal of the *Society for Psychoanalytic Psychotherapy*. The Society is dedicated to the development, teaching, learning, and researching of sound psychotherapeutic modalities. The IJPP will continue to represent the best work available in the field. Readers interested in membership in the Society should write to Marylee Miller, Secretary, The Society for Psychoanalytic Psychotherapy, c/o The Lenox Hill Hospital Psychotherapy Program, 100 East 77th Street, New York, NY 10022.

Robert Langs, M.D.
Editor-in-Chief

JOURNAL POLICY

All manuscripts should be submitted in triplicate and double-spaced on white bond paper. The title page of each article must contain the author's full name and address, academic affiliation, date of submission, and a 150-page word summary of the article's contents. Charts and tables must be on separate pages keyed to the manuscript. Headings, which should be brief, follow the style used in this journal. Footnotes and references, also following the style of the Journal, should be listed separately triple-spaced at the end of the article.

Submit all manuscripts to Joan Langs, managing editor, 425 East 58th Street, New York, New York 10022.

It is with deep regret that we report the death of Dr. John Klauber during the summer of 1981. Dr. Klauber will be sorely missed as a fine individual and colleague, as a sagacious editor of this journal, and as a creative and gifted contributor to the psycho-analytic literature. We are pleased to publish here one of his final efforts, a lasting reflection of his thoughtfulness, humanity, and originality.

Contributors

Reprint request addresses are in italics.

Z. ALEXANDER AARONS, M.D., F.A.C.P. is on the attending staff of the Mount Zion Hospital Department of Psychiatry in San Francisco. He has been a Visiting Professor of Psychiatry at the University of Manitoba School of Medicine, and also a Professorial Lecturer in Psychiatry at the University of Nevada. He is currently in private practice in psychoanalysis in Carmel. *24705 Crestview Circle/Carmel, CA 93923*

RUTH ABRAHAM, Ph.D. is Staff Psychologist at Ralph K. Davies Medical Center in San Francisco. She is currently in private practice in San Francisco. *2477 Washington Street/San Francisco, CA 94115*

GERALD ADLER, M.D. is a Training and Supervising Analyst at the Boston Psychoanalytic Society and Institute, and Director of Medical Student Education in the Department of Psychiatry at Massachusetts General Hospital. He is also a Lecturer in Psychiatry at Harvard Medical School. *Massachusetts General Hospital/Boston, MA 02114*

FRANCIS BAUDRY, M.D. is an Associate Professor of Clinical Psychiatry at Montefiore Hospital in New York, and a Lecturer at the New York Psychoanalytic Institute. *9 East 96th Street, New York, NY 10028*

JAMES BEATRICE, M.S. is a doctoral student at the California School of Professional Psychology in San Diego. He is currently in private practice in San Diego. *13464 Portofino Drive/Del Mar, CA 92014*

STAVROULA BERATIS, M.D. is an Assistant Professor of Psychiatry at the University of Patras Medical School, and a Clinical Assistant Professor of Psychiatry at Albert Einstein School of Medicine. She is a member of the American and International Psychoanalytic Associations. *University of Patras School of Medicine/Department of Psychiatry/Patras, Greece*

ANNI BERGMAN, is a faculty member in Clinical Psychology at the City University of New York, and a Senior Research Scientist at the Margaret S. Mahler Psychiatric Research Foundation. *Reprints of the article co-authored by Ms. Bergman can be obtained from Margaret Chernack.*

K. H. BLACKER, M.D. is a Professor and Vice Chairman in the Department of Psychiatry at the University of California, Davis, School of Medicine, and a Training and Supervising Analyst at the San Francisco Psychoanalytic Institute. *University of California Davis Medical Center/2315 Stockton Boulevard/Sacramento, CA 95817*

HILDE BRUCH, M.D. is Professor Emeritus of Psychiatry at Baylor College of Medicine. *Department of Psychiatry/Baylor College of Medicine/Texas Medical Center/Houston, TX 77030*

DAN H. BUIE, M.D. is a Training and Supervising Analyst at the Boston Psychoanalytic Society and Institute, and an Associate Professor of Psychiatry at Tufts University School of Medicine. *38 Cliff Road/ Wellesley Hills, MA 02181*

MARGARET CHERNACK is a Psychology Intern at the Long Island Jewish Hospital Hillside Medical Center. *175-39 Dalny Road, #6H/Jamaica, New York 11432*

M. DONALD COLEMAN, M.D. is a Senior Member of the Visiting Staff at Jacobi Hospital in the Bronx, and an Assistant Clinical Professor of Psychiatry at the Albert Einstein School of Medicine. He is a member of the New York and Westchester Psychoanalytic Societies, and is currently in private practice in Mamaroneck, New York. *1030 Greacen Point Road/Mamaroneck, NY 10543*

ROBERT M. DORN, M.D., F.A.C.Pn., F.A.C.P. is Professor of Psychiatry, and Chief of the Division of Child, Adolescent, and Family Psychiatry, in the Department of Psychiatry, University of California, Davis, and former Training and Supervising Analyst for the Los Angeles Psychoanalytic Society and Institute. *Department of Psychiatry/ University of California, Davis/2315 Stockton Blvd./Sacramento, CA 95817*

SUSANNA ISAACS ELMHIRST, M.D., F.R.C.P., F.R.C. Psych. is a Consultant Child Psychiatrist at the London Child Guidance Training Center and Physician-in-Charge of the Children's Department at the London Institute of Psychoanalysis. She is also a Training Analyst at the London Institute of Psychoanalysis. *Child Guidance Training Center/120 Belsize Lange/London, England MW3 5BA*

DENNIS FARRELL, M.D. is a faculty member of the San Francisco Psychoanalytic Institute and an Associate Clinical Professor of Psychiatry at the Langley Porter Psychiatric Institute, University of California, San Francisco. *Langley Porter Psychiatric Institute/401 Parnassus Avenue/San Francisco, CA 94143*

ROBERT M. GALTATZER-LEVY, M.D. is a psychiatrist in private practice on the attending staff of the Michael Reese Hospital Psychosomatic and Psychiatric Institute. He is a Lecturer in Psychiatry at the University of Chicago, and a faculty member of the Child and Adolescent Psychoanalytic Psychotherapy Program at the Chicago Institute for Psychoanalysis. *55 East Washington Street/Room 1819/Chicago, IL 60602*

ELEANOR GALENSON, M.D. is an Attending Psychiatrist at Mount Sinai Hospital, and a Clinical Professor of Psychiatry at Mount Sinai School of Medicine. She is also a member of the New York Psychoanalytic Institute. *9 East 96th Street/New York, NY 10028*

STANLEY GREBEN, M.D., F.R.C.P. (C) is Psychiatrist-in-Chief at Mount Sinai Hospital in Toronto, and Professor of Psychiatry and Senior Departmental Consultant for Training in Individual Psychotherapy at the University of Toronto Department of Psychiatry. He is a member of the Canadian Psychoanalytic Society and a Training Analyst at the Canadian Psychoanalytic Institute. *Room 931/600 University Avenue/ Toronto, Ontario M5G 1X5/Canada*

LESLIE S. GROH, Ph.D. has concentrated on the treatment of borderline and psychotic children, adolescents, and adults. He served on the faculty of the Menninger School of Psychiatry as a psychotherapy supervisor for six years. He is currently in private practice in Los Angeles.

MARTIN GREENE, D.S.W. is a faculty member of the Lenox Hill Hospital Psychotherapy Program, and a Professor at the Adelphi University School of Social Work. He is also Co-director of Psychotherapy Training Associates. He is currently in private practice in Great Neck, New York. *6 Grace Avenue/Great Neck, NY 11021*

JAMES S. GROTSTEIN, M.D. is an Associate Clinical Professor of Psychiatry at the University of California, Los Angeles, and an Attending Staff Physician at Cedars-Sinai Medical Center. He is also a Training and Supervising Analyst at the Los Angeles Psychoanalytic Institute and Society, and Director of the Interdisciplinary Group for Advanced Studies in Psychotic, Borderline and Narcissistic Disorders. *9777 Wilshire Boulevard/Beverly Hills, CA 90212*

MARDI J. HOROWITZ, M.D. is a Professor of Psychiatry and Director of the Center for the Study of Neuroses at the University of California, San Francisco, and a faculty member at the San Francisco Psychoanalytic Institute. *Langley Porter Psychiatric Institute/401 Parnassus Avenue/San Francisco, CA 94143*

MICHAEL F. HOYT, Ph.D. is an Assistant Clinical Professor of Medical Psychology at the Langley Porter Psychiatric Institute, University of California, San Francisco, and Staff Psychologist at Kaiser-Permanente Hospital and Medical Center in Hayward, California. *Kaiser-Permanente Medical Center Department of Psychiatry/27400 Hesperian Boulevard/Hayward, CA 94545*

M. MASUD R. KHAN is a member of the Institute of Psychoanalysis, London, Director of the Sigmund Freud Copyrights, and Foreign Editor of the *Nouvelle Revue de Psychoanalyse*. He is former editor of the International Psycho-Analytical Library, and currently a Consultant Associate Editor for the *International Journal of Psycho-Analysis* and the *International Review of Psycho-Analysis*. *Flat 7/24 Palace Court/London W2 4HU/England*

JOHN KLAUBER (deceased August 11, 1981), D.M., B.Ch. Oxon., F.R.C. Psych., F.B.P.S. was Freud Professor Elect at University College London, and President of the British Psychoanalytic Society. *Reprints of Dr. Klauber's article may be obtained from Jason Aronson Inc./111 Eighth Avenue/New York, NY 10011*

HENRY KRYSTAL, M.D. is a Professor of Psychiatry at Michigan State University and a Lecturer at Michigan Psychoanalytic Institute. *702 Northland Medical Building/Southfield, MI 48075*

JOHN T. MALTSBERGER, M.D. is a staff member at Massachusetts General Hospital. He is a Lecturer in Psychiatry at Harvard Medical School and a faculty member of the Boston Psychoanalytic Institute. *72 Chestnut Street/Boston, MA 02108*

JOYCE McDOUGALL, M.A., D.Ed. is a Supervisory and Training Analyst at the Paris Psychoanalytic Society. *4 Rue Monge/75005 Paris, France.*

W.W. MEISSNER, S.J., M.D. is Staff Psychiatrist at Massachusetts Mental Health Center in Boston, and Clinical Professor of Psychiatry at Harvard Medical School. He is also a Supervising and Training Analyst for the Boston Psychoanalytic Institute. *6 Sumner Road/Cambridge, MA 02138*

ROBERT MILLER, M.D. is Associate Clinical Professor of Psychiatry at Albert Einstein College of Medicine. *37 Riverside Drive, Apt. 14B/New York, NY 10023*

CECIL MUSHATT, M.D., M.Sc. is Senior Staff Member in Psychiatry at University Hospital in Boston, and a Psychiatrist at Beth Israel Hospital. He is Associate Professor of Psychiatry at Boston University School of Medicine and also a Lecturer in Psychiatry at Harvard University. *1093 Beacon Street/Brookline, MA 02146*

WAYNE A. MYERS, M.D. is an Associate Attending Psychiatrist and Clinical Associate Professor at Cornell University Medical Center. He is also a Supervising Analyst at the Columbia University Center for Psychoanalytic Training and Research. *1385 York Avenue, Apartment 17G/New York, NY 10021*

JOEL PARIS, M.D., F.R.C.P.(C) is Director of Education at Sir Mortimer B. Davis–Jewish General Hospital in Montreal. He is an Associate Professor of Psychiatry at McGill University, and Psychiatrist-in-Charge for McGill University's Student Health Service. *Institute of Community and Family Psychiatry/4333 Chemin Cote Ste-Catherine/Montreal, Quebec H3T 1E2*

JAMES O. RANEY, M.D. is a Clinical Assistant Professor of Psychiatry at the University of Washington School of Medicine, and a faculty member of the Seattle Psychoanalytic Association. He is currently in private practice in Seattle. *1932 First Avenue, Suite 906/Seattle, Washington 98101*

DAVID ROSENFELD, M.D. is a Training Psychoanalyst and Professor of Psychopathology for the Buenos Aires Psychoanalytic Society. *Pacheco de Melo 2864 6°A/(1425) Buenos Aires, Argentina*

HAROLD F. SEARLES, M.D. is a Supervising and Training Analyst in the Washington Psychoanalytic Institute. He is a former President of the Washington Psychoanalytic Society, and is currently in full-time private practice in psychoanalysis and psychotherapy. *Suite 623 W Bethesda Air Rights Building/7315 Wisconsin Avenue/Washington, D.C. 20814*

EDWARD R. SHAPIRO, M.D. is Director of the Adolescent and Family Treatment and Study Center and Associate Psychiatrist at McLean Hospital. He is an Assistant Clinical Professor of Psychiatry at Harvard Medical School and a faculty member of the Boston Psychoanalytic Institute. *Adolescent and Family Treatment and Study Center/115 Mill Street/Belmont, MA 02178*

OZZIE SIEGEL, Ph.D. is a faculty member and supervisor of the Lenox Hill Hospital Psychotherapy Program, and an Assistant Clinical Professor at Adelphi University Institute of Advanced Psychological Studies. He is currently in private practice in psychoanalytic psychotherapy. *6 Grace Avenue/Great Neck, NY 11021*

AUSTIN SILBER, M.D. is a Clinical Professor of Psychiatry at New York University Medical Center, and a Training and Supervising Analyst at the Psychoanalytic Institute at New York University Medical Center. *245 East 87th Street/New York, NY 10028*

SYDNEY SMITH, Ph.D., formerly Chief Psychologist at the Menninger Foundation, is now the Dean for Academic and Professional Affairs at the California School of Professional Psychology in San Diego. He is Co-editor of *Psychoanalytic Inquiry* and Associate Editor of *The Bulletin of the Menninger Clinic*, and Senior Instructor at the San Diego Institute for Psychoanalysis. *2356 Rue de Anne/La Jolla, CA 92037*

ROBERT D. STOLOROW, Ph.D. is a Professor of Psychology at Yeshiva University Ferkauf Graduate School and a Visiting Professor for the New York University Postdoctoral Program in Psychoanalysis. *135 East 50th Street/New York, NY 10022*

IAN STORY, Ph.D. is a member of the Clinical Faculty of the Department of Psychiatry, University of California, Los Angeles, and a former member of the Senior Staff and Director of Admissions at Austen Riggs Center. He is currently in private practice in Los Angeles. *Suite 616/ 11665 West Olympic Boulevard/Los Angeles, CA 90064*

C. PHILIP WILSON, M.D. is a psychoanalyst specializing in psychosomatics, and a faculty member at the Columbia and New York University Psychoanalytic Institutes. He is former Chief of Psychosomatics at Brookdale Hospital Center, and current Chairman of the Psychosomatic Workshop of the Psychoanalytic Association of New York, Inc. *1148 5th Avenue/New York, NY 10028*

Table of Contents
International Journal of
Psychoanalytic Psychotherapy
Volume 9

Clinical and Other Problems

Contents

Notes on the Potential Differentiation of Borderline Conditions

W. W. MEISSNER, S.J., M.D.

It is argued that the borderline personality organization as now conceived embraces a spectrum of differentiable diagnostic groupings. Lumping these diagnostic clusters under a single descriptive heading contributes to continuing conceptual ambiguities and theoretical confusion in the understanding of borderline psychopathology. A potential differentiation of borderline entities on clinical grounds is suggested. The bases for discrimination of higher-order borderline conditions versus lower-order conditions are explored. Current accounts of borderline pathology tend to focus on lower-order pathology as characteristic, but do not account for the full range of the borderline spectrum. Other potential discriminations between an hysterical continuum and an obsessional-schizoid continuum are explored. Differential diagnoses suggested include pseudoschizophrenia, psychotic character, borderline personality, and primitive hysteric in the hysterical continuum; schizoid personality, false-self organization, and as-if personality in the schizoid continuum. The syndrome of identity diffusion is also suggested as part of the borderline spectrum.

The borderline conditions have consistently been a source of ambiguity, uncertainty, and difficulty. The history of the concept has been marked by considerable conceptual ambiguity and terminological confusion (Meissner 1978a), finally evolving in the direction of Kernberg's (1966, 1967) descriptive and theoretical clarification. Despite this progress, a significant degree of theoretical diversity and lack of specificity tends to characterize contemporary approaches to the borderline problem (Robbins 1976; Meissner 1978c).

A basic difficulty, which lends confusion and ambiguity to our attempts to clarify and understand borderline pathology is that we may, in fact, be dealing with a heterogeneous group of forms of character pathology. Thus a given description or theoretical account of borderline pathology may refer to one segment of this grouping but be less pertinent to other segments. Other clinical formulations and theoretical accounts may have greater relevance to other forms within the borderline grouping. Perry and Klerman (1978) have recently reviewed diagnostic criteria for borderline diagnoses. They note the lack of agreement over diagnostic criteria, and conclude that either (1) the borderline concept is an illusion; or (2) the borderline concept is adequately defined by common criteria that would apply across the borderline spectrum, such that other distinguishing criteria are nonessential; or (3) there are, in fact, definable subtypes within the borderline group. The first alternative seems regressive, the second is a possible refinement on current trends, and the third (favored by these authors) is congruent with the intentions of the present study, which aims at some initial diagnostic discriminations that may suggest directions of further differentiation and empirical validation of diagnostic categories.

In previous efforts, the present author has addressed the conceptual (Meissner 1978a) and theoretical (Meissner 1978c) ambiguities that plague efforts to come to terms with the complexities of borderline conditions. It has been argued that the borderline conditions offer a heterogeneous spectrum of levels and degrees of pathological personality functioning that can be traced along several important parameters, including the quality of object relations, the degree of object constancy, the level of achieved and maintained self-cohesion, the regressive potential, the degree of projective tendency, and levels of ego and superego structuralization (Meissner, in press). Qualitative and quantitative degrees of difference can be described for these parameters that potentially provide the basis for a meaningful diagnostic discrimination. This approach suggests that the borderline conditions form a complex group of differentiable forms of psychopathology consisting of a spectrum of borderline character disorders. The present reflection is an effort to scan the already extant formulations of borderline personality to begin the process of mapping out areas of potential diagnostic differentiation.

There are two outstanding difficulties that would run counter to such an effort. The first is the predominant position of Kernberg (1967, 1975) to the understanding of borderline pathology. His formulation tends to follow a lumping strategy: it provides a general description that embraces without differentiating most of the borderline spectrum (Perry and Klerman's [1978] second option). The success of his contribution makes one feel that to venture beyond it is risky, or that further differentiation is unwise or clinically unfruitful. At the same time, Kernberg's work makes a further clarifying step possible, and he has provided a useful initiative in that very direction by his description of levels of character pathology (Kernberg 1970b).

The second difficulty stems from the traditional analytic aversion to diagnosis. Historically this reflects a long-standing reaction to the classifying obsession of Kraepelinian descriptive psychiatry and to the counteremphasis on psychodynamic and motivational considerations. At one extreme this takes the form of Zilboorg's allegation (Rangell 1955) that there is no such thing as a borderline condition, or that it is useless to try to make such categories (essentially, Perry and Klerman's [1978] first option). Nonetheless, analysts do diagnose and in quite sophisticated ways. The assessment of analyzability is such a complex diagnostic process. Moreover, the current active controversy over the approaches to narcissistic disorders hinges in large measure on a diagnostic discrimination between borderline pathology and narcissistic personality disorder. Here it is argued that analytic diagnosis has been too long neglected and provides an important area of significant analytic study and reflection. The dangers of excessive classification and the rigidity and reification of classificatory schemata are to be avoided.

With these cautions in mind, a tentative reassessment of the borderline conditions is presented to examine the extent to which meaningful diagnostic differentiation can be attempted. Rather than proposing these groupings as discrete entities, they are envisioned as descriptive groupings or clusters that show a certain general clinical consistency, even though there may be a degree of overlap in the concrete cases and a goodly number of cases may show characteristics of more than one grouping. The groupings thus represent differentiable patterns in which borderline character structure is formed in the attempt to deal with a variety of developmental and object-related vicissitudes more or less common to this intermediate range of personality development and function.

DIFFERENTIATION WITHIN THE BORDERLINE SPECTRUM

Pseudoschizophrenias

The first group includes a variety of disorders variously described as pseudoneurotic schizophrenia, borderline schizophrenia or ambulatory schizophrenia, or even latent schizophrenia. These patients have been described most extensively by Hoch and his associates (Hoch and Cattell 1959, Hoch and Polatin 1949, Hoch et al. 1962). They emphasize that these patients reveal primary symptoms that they share with schizophrenia which may be less striking and intense: these include thought and association disorders both of process and content, disorders of affective regulation, and even disorders of sensorimotor and autonomic functioning. They regard this disorder as a form of schizophrenia that is distinguished by its prominent secondary symptoms, which include pan-anxiety, pan-neurosis, and pan-sexuality. The anxiety is diffuse, chronic, intense, and pervasive. The neurotic symptoms are usually multiple, shifting, and confusing; they include obsessions and compulsions, phobias, hysterical manifestations, hypochondriasis, depression, depersonalization, and a variety of apparently neurotic defense mechanisms occurring simultaneously or successively. The obsessions and phobias may often reach delusional proportions. This pan-neurotic picture may include tendencies to acting-out and dramatic or histrionic behavior, or even antisocial and drug-dependent behavior. Sexual organization and functioning is chaotic, both in fact and in fantasy (Hoch and Cattell 1959, Weingarten and Korn 1967).

It should be noted that the thought disorder is a persistent and characteristic feature of pseudoneurotic schizophrenia. On clinical contact the disorder may be more or less evident, but usually can be found on careful observation and mental testing. Primary process and schizophrenic-like thought processes are almost unexceptionally revealed under the influence of sodium amytal and in the use of unstructured projective tests like the Rorschach (Deniker and Quintart 1961). Moreover, the thought disorder is relatively ego-syntonic. It persists even though patients may present a reasonably good social facade and appropriate behavior, and may even have considerable academic or occupational achievement. Often the record of achievement is somewhat erratic, however (Weingarten and Korn 1967). Similar features have been described by Zilboorg (1941, 1956, 1957) regarding what he called "ambulatory schizophenia."

There has been some argument whether the pseudoschizophrenic group should be regarded as essentially psychotic. Hoch and Zilboorg seemed to feel that they were dealing with a form of schizophrenia (Dickes 1974, Kernberg 1967). Kernberg (1967) clearly opts for including these patients in the borderline spectrum. It can be presumed that borderline patients who show schizophrenic symptoms or a schizophrenic outcome would fall in this category (Gunderson et al. 1975). Even in the Hoch group, there was considerable heterogeneity regarding long-term outcome, but there was a high incidence of life-long illness, with nearly 40 percent requiring rehospitalization (often multiple times), 10 percent attempting suicide, and 20 percent developing overt schizophrenic symptomatology. Half of these (10 percent) developed chronic forms of schizophrenia with the typical catatonic, paranoid, and even hebephrenic symptomatology.

Thus it must be concluded that these patients, if not basically schizophrenic, lived on the very border of psychosis. The fragility and vulnerability of the ego in these patients are reflected in the constant susceptibility to drive influences, and the intolerance of and the inability to bind anxiety, which teeters on the brink of traumatic and even catastrophic anxiety. While the defensive organization and symptom patterning can often look neurotic, the symptomatology is generally more severe than would be expected in a neurotic pattern of organization (Dickes 1974) and is not at all effective in binding the underlying anxiety. Thus the anxiety persists, is often incapacitating, and motivates a multiplicity of relatively unsuccessful defensive maneuvers.

In addition to the ego defects, it must be presumed that the constantly shifting pattern of defense and symptomatology reflects not merely shifting configurations of such aspects of functioning, but in addition corresponds to the fragmentation, inner disorganization, and shifting configuration of the patient's self. There is little cohesiveness or stability in the organization of the self, so that whatever tentative configurations are achieved cannot be maintained or stabilized over any significant period of time. Correspondingly, these patients have considerable difficulties in object relationships, which tend to be intensely ambivalent, covering a diffuse and intense primitive rage, chaotically caught up in the flux of the dilemma of intense need and paralyzing fear.

Selective factors undoubtedly operated in the Hoch and Cattell (1959) studies in which the pathology of pseudoneurotic schizophrenia was determined. The patient sample was limited to individuals with severe psychoneurotic symptomatology but who revealed signs of schizophrenic activity on deeper evaluation (Gunderson and Singer 1975). It is little wonder, then, that a significant number of these patients were later to develop frank schizophrenia and that the authors would conclude that they were dealing with a subgroup of schizophrenia.

In sum, then, the pseudoneurotic schizophrenics represent the lowest order of character pathology within the borderline spectrum, bordering on and sharing some characteristics with the psychoses. Essential to the diagnosis are the failure of reality-testing; the diffuse, intense, and chronic anxiety; the multiplicity and shifting variety of symptomatology and defense organization; and the chaotic sexual functioning. These patients have a high potential for regression, but the emergence of primary process and psychotic-like symptoms need not wait upon such regression, since they remain a constant, if often subtle, part of the syndrome. The evidence of primary-process thinking and failures of reality-testing are usually identifiable on clinical examination.

Psychotic Character

The psychotic character was described in some detail by Frosch (1964, 1970). These patients may never actually develop psychotic symptoms, but they have a high capacity for psychotic decompensation under certain circumstances. Such transient regressions may be accompanied by a loss of reality-testing, but they retain the capacity for ready reversibility of the regression so that psychotic episodes remain transient. In these patients the issues remain psychotic, but unlike the pseudoneurotic schizophrenic, these patients have a higher capacity to maintain their functioning on a more or less consistent level during nonregressed periods, so that they remain in reasonably good contact with reality and are relatively more capable of adaptive functioning.

These patients generally have vulnerable egos, but are in a relatively stronger position than the pseudoneurotic schizophrenics who have little capacity to organize in any stable fashion a consistent pattern of defensive organization or neurotic symptomatology. Psychotic characters can achieve this level of organization, but it remains susceptible to regressive pulls at various times. The maintenance of an integrated and cohesive sense of self is a constant difficulty, in that the self is continually threatened with dissolution and disintegration and is plagued by the need to cling to objects as well as the fear of fusing with them. The need–fear dilemma is thus pitched at a near-psychotic level and the implicit threat is psychic death. As a general rule, self-object differentiation is preserved, but remains problematic and tenuous and is frequently blurred or even lost in regressive episodes. Where such ego boundaries become porous and uncertain, there is often a preoccupation with identity problems; this is often the cause in analysis, where regressive pulls tend to increase the dedifferentiation and defusion of ego boundaries. As Frosch (1970) notes, in the analytic situation this may result in tenuous identifications with the analyst that have an "as if" quality, as well as in attempts to increase the sense of differentiation and separation from the analyst, which may take the form of negativism or even of paranoid distortion. In regressive phases the intensity of these fears is buffered by a variety of primitive defenses of a psychotic kind, but even at levels of better functioning the object involvement of these individuals is highly qualified by active use of projective and introjective mechanisms, which tend to lend a paranoid discoloration to object relationships and to intensify the inner feeling of vulnerability and victimization.

In this connection, a particular area of importance for the evaluation of ego functioning is that of the patient's involvement in reality. In general the capacity to relate to the environment, which Frosch breaks down into functions of the relation to reality, the feeling of reality, and the capacity to test reality, is relatively intact, but susceptible to regressive distortion. It is the relative preservation of the capacity to test reality and the ready reversibility of the loss of these functions that distinguishes psychotic character from the psychoses proper.

One young woman came to therapy because of her unstable and often chaotic emotional life, characterized by precipitous depressive episodes that often brought her to the brink of catastrophic panic and suicide. In such phases her world was colored by projective distortions that were transparently derived from her brutalizing, sadistic, and probably paranoid father and her passive, depressed, and withdrawn mother. In therapy, the extent to which her view of the world and the people around her was a direct reflection of old, painful, and disappointing relations with the important objects in her life became quickly apparent. Also apparent was a pervasive looseness of thought patterns and associations that gave her descriptions of confusing and highly tangential quality. It was never clear whether the context of her material was related to an ongoing situation or whether she was at that point addressing herself to old objects, infantile feelings and terrors, old hurts and losses, etcetera. These would phase in and out of her discourse without warning, in a fashion reminiscent of Breuer's description of Anna O.'s shifts into her *condition seconde*. Nonetheless, the patient retained the capacity—at times with some therapeutic clarification, after the therapist had caught on to the subtle shifts that seemed so ego-syntonic for her—to focus back on the reality and to put herself in realistic contact with it.

The combination of an impaired sense of reality with relatively intact reality-testing can result in experiences of depersonalization and derealization (Arlow 1966), not unfamiliar states in the psychotic character. Even where hallucinations or illusions result from regressive states, the psychotic character may maintain a greater distance from the psychotic experience and regard it as ego-alien, and may even be aware that the hallucinatory experience is internally derived. Even outside of regressive episodes, there is a basic orientation to the world based on distrust and tendencies to project and externalize. Such patients will use action or antisocial behavior to deal with intolerable and painful affects, and use projection to reinforce their sense of entitlement to manipulate, exploit, or destroy an environment that does not respond to their intense needs (Adler 1970).

The object relations in such patients are generally on an intense need-gratifying basis that often leads to unrealistic demands. The frustration of these demands leads to the stimulation of intense rage, which often expresses itself in a paranoid form. Thus the relationship with objects is often highly conflictual and intensely ambivalent. Moreover, the superego remains poorly integrated; superego components have undergone little depersonification or abstraction. Rather, superego functioning is carried out in terms of often regressed and archaic superego precursors that remain highly susceptible to forms of externalization and projection. Thus superego integration is highly irregular and reflects multiple lacunae, so that there is a propensity for impulsive acting-out behavior side-by-side with hypercritical and harshly punitive superego attitudes. There is a capacity for guilt and depression, but this seems fragmentary and inconsistent.

One may wonder whether many of the clinical descriptions given of borderline patients in the literature are not more suitable or more specifically congruent with the characteristics of the psychotic character. For example, Adler's (1970) description of the more primitive aspects of patients who overvalue or devalue in therapy; or Greenson's (Rangell 1955) description of chronic borderline states; or Bychowski's (Bychowski 1953, Robbins 1956) discussion of latent psychosis; and the descriptions of borderline disorders in terms of relatively primitive character organization (Kernberg 1970b); or in terms of intense, stormy, and quickly mobilized transference distortions (Brody 1960, Kernberg 1967, 1970a) are all appropriate to the description of the psychotic character. Thus Kernberg's (1967) delineation of borderline personality functioning and deficits can be more suitably applied to these more primitively organized and regression-prone patients than to better organized and better functioning borderline patients described in the following sections.

This primitive characterological organization and the propensity for regression make a striking contrast with the description of the borderline personality that is to follow. Certainly the regressive potential can be found at all diagnostic levels, but the susceptibility to regression is a marked characteristic of borderline and psychotic conditions. Discriminatory lines are difficult to draw, but patients who quickly manifest a tendency to regression in therapy, or whose regression does not remain within the limits of the therapeutic situation but tends to generalize outside of it, should be seen as functioning on the level of the psychotic character. Similarly, one may wonder, as Frosch (1967b) suggests, whether there may not be important differences between patients who continue or return to the analytic work despite the regression and those who leave the analysis on account of it. The former may represent higher levels of borderline organization with sufficient ego-strength to maintain the relationship in the face of regressive vicissitudes, while the latter reflect a lower-order of borderline organization that lacks these basic capacities.

These regressive phenomena contrast with the more gradual and paced regression that one might often see in the borderline personality whose regressive proclivities require considerably more analytic work and therapeutic regression (Zetzel and Meissner 1973) in order to become manifest. Again, this runs counter to the prevailing trend to amalgamate descriptions of borderline pathology. Frosch himself tends to minimize the differences between his own description of the psychotic character and Kernberg's

(1967) description of borderline personality organization. While Kernberg's description may embrace the psychotic character, it tends to override important discriminations that are worth preserving and are clinically significant. The psychotic character demonstrates a regressive fragility that many better integrated borderline personalities do not.

The young woman described above, who falls in the psychotic character group, presented characteristically in the early portion of her therapy with frequent and severe regressive episodes, usually depressive in character. The rapidity with which these episodes would develop out of relatively innocuous precipitants, and the rapidity with which they were resolved following relatively minor therapeutic intervention and clarification or interpretation, were striking. The rapid alternation of such intensely disturbing emotional states, revealing both a high degree of regressive potential and a ready capacity for reconstitution, would point to a diagnosis of psychotic character. The borderline personality as described below would not tend to manifest this pattern.

The regressive propensity of the psychotic character typically reflects early experiences of a survival-threatening kind that have an impact on psychic development. The ego may be left fragmented, poorly integrated, and vulnerable, and thus prone to dedifferentiation under stress of various kinds, particularly those having to do with threat to object relationships. It may be that such tendencies to severe regression may be suspected in the initial contact with the patient, particularly if there are slips of the tongue with more than usual frequency that may reflect the invasion of id impulses and defensive weakening (Frosch 1967a).

Such lapses and discontinuities in the cognitive sphere, resulting in the emergence of primary process in language and thinking, particularly with a more or less bland tolerance for contradictions in thought and action without any need to reconcile or unify them, are characteristic of borderline pathology (Atkin 1974). Kernberg (1967) relates these observations to early mental conflict and the role of splitting as basic to the diagnosis of borderlines. Margaret Little (1966) has also commented in this regard:

> The first appearance of any illness, or the first thing that may lead an analyst to regard a patient as being a borderline psychotic may be a faulty perception, an inaccurate inference or deduction, a failure to use symbols or analogy, the presence of symbolic equation, or other evidence of concrete thinking; or a piece of totally irrational, often irresponsible, behaviour in a person whose ways of perceiving, thinking, and behaving are otherwise quite ordinary, though he may have other symptoms of neurosis. Areas of primary and secondary process thinking can exist side by side, and will be present or absent according to the predominance of survival, pleasure, or reality principles (p. 479).

The difficulty in the initial stages of evaluation of such patients, however, as Zetzel (1971) has noted, is that one cannot tell whether one is dealing with a patient who is presenting symptoms from a regressive borderline state or whether one is seeing the manifestations of more or less consistent personality functioning. Time and experience with the patient, particularly an assessment of the patient's response to effective therapeutic management and the evolution of the object-relations aspects in the transference and alliance, will provide more solid ground for discrimination.

The psychotic character, then, incorporates a condition in which the ego capacities are significantly stronger than in the pseudoschizophrenic group, since they allow the patient, over significant stretches of his or her experience, to maintain a reasonably effective adjustment to his or her work and social environment, and permit him or her to achieve a relatively good degree of effective ego functioning in other areas. However the underlying issues, particularly those having to do with the relationship with objects, are pitched at a more or less psychotic level and share in the psychotic intensity and life and death extremes of psychotic anxiety. What distinguishes the psychotic character is the relative instability of the organization of the self and the ready regression of narcissistic structures to the level of primitive archaic narcissistic formations characterized by grandiosity and excessive idealization. More specifically, psychotic character, in its fragile and still highly vulnerable organization, has a ready potential for regression that affects the effectiveness of ego functioning and precipitates the utilization of psychotic defenses. Moreover, it may be suggested that this differentiated picture of the psychotic character comes closest to the more familiar description of the classic regressive, disorganized, acting-out, and intensely tempestuous borderline patients, particularly those assessed and treated in the hospital setting.

Borderline Personality

The borderline personality, as proposed here, is not equivalent to Kernberg's (1967) description of the borderline personality organization. Kernberg's description applies in some sense to all of the borderline spectrum disorders, including all of the forms proposed in the present study. In perspective in relationship to the previously described entities, the borderline personality consists in progressively less severe and better integrated and organized forms of character pathology. The borderline personality, then, represents a step up in the consistency of organization and capacity for functioning from the psychotic character, even as the psychotic character also represented a step up from the level of the pseudoschizophrenias. In general, then, the expression of the common borderline elements previously described will be on a higher level of differentiation and integration in the borderline personality than that seen in previously described entities.

There are a number of parameters along which the borderline personality can be characterized. Perhaps the most general category has to do with the quality of life style found in such patients. These patients in general share with the other borderline conditions the difficulties in carrying on their daily lives and the task of relating to other human beings. Thus there is a bizarre and often alienated quality to their life style (Giovacchini 1965, Blum 1972). Also in common with other borderline conditions, the borderline personality has a sense of inner emptiness and deep loneliness (Collum 1972, Chessick 1974).

Moreover, there is a peculiar quality to these patients' subjective experience of interpersonal situations. They seem extraordinarily sensitive and responsive to the unconscious fantasies and impulses, as well as primitive superego contents in the significant objects around them. The conscious and intentional ego activity of people around them is held with abiding suspicion and mistrust, as though they were somehow deceptions or malicious tricks, while the id and superego elements seem somehow more genuine. There is also a tendency for these patients to feel that the elements of enduring character style, self-organization, and ego functioning in themselves are somehow unreal or phony (Krohn 1974).

Correspondingly, the dominance of the Oedipal phase is not so clearly seen in these patients (Frijling-Schreuder 1969), with the result that, like Kernberg's (1967) infantile personalities, there is a mixture of pseudohypersexuality with sexual inhibition and sexual provocativeness, which is rather direct or crude or inappropriate, mixed with orally determined exhibitionism and demandingness. The sexual promiscuity in infantile women has a more drifting quality, with little stability in object relationships along with more or less conscious primitive or polymorphous-perverse fantasies. Moreover, there seem to be multiple deviations in all areas of personality functioning, which may be on a different level of disturbance in different areas (Rosenfeld and Sprince 1963). The failure to achieve Oedipal phase dominance means that, in the pathology of these patients, libidinal material can be detected from all phases of libidinal development, leading to an often confused and disturbed picture. Phallic trends are interfered with so that there is a faulty relationship between the operation of the drives and the ego, and the bulk of the libido remains fixed in the oral and anal phase.

The fluidity and variability may express itself in shifting levels of ego organization, which are reflected in a fluctuation between reality orientation and contact with painful aspects of environment to a preoccupation with idiosyncratic fantasies. The ability of the therapist to establish and maintain contact with these patients seems to mitigate the influence of fantasy but, when the alliance weakens or the therapeutic contact is lost, inner stimuli seem to play a more prominent role (Pine 1974).

The general fluidity and lack of phase dominance is related to the propensity to acting-out in borderline conditions. The more flamboyant and particularly destructive forms of acting-out are found in borderline states and may represent an attempt to restore a sense of reality by creating a situation of intense feeling or pain to counter the emptiness and feeling of unreality related to the acute diffusion of identity in the regressive state (Collum 1972). This regressive form of acting-out is more related to the functioning of the psychotic character than to that of the borderline personality. On a more general level of adjustment, however, acting-out in the borderline personality may take the form of externalization by which the patient transposes his or her inner conflicts and difficulties to the outer world and develops a more or less exclusive preoccupation with dealing with them in that external realm. Consequently, there is a constant tendency to blame forces outside the self for one's problems and to assume little or no responsibility. This externalization and blaming often takes the form of subtle projections, particularly in the therapeutic setting (Giovacchini 1972).

The tendency to regression in the borderline personality has already been noted, but it should be noted as well that this tendency is neither so intense nor marked as in the psychotic character. Borderline personalities do undergo brief psychotic experiences, which frequently have a paranoid quality (Gunderson and Singer 1975), and while these regressive episodes may be provoked by drug influences or severe developmental or emotional crises, they are most frequently seen in the borderline personality as a result of progressive developments in the psychotherapeutic relationship. Because of the peculiar sensitivity of borderline object relationships, these patients often show a rapid improvement of function as a response to good therapeutic handling. This is true not only of borderline children (Frijling-Schreuder 1969), but also borderline adults (Zetzel 1971).

When seen in a regressive crisis, borderline personality patients, unlike potentially healthy neurotics, are unable to easily establish a confident relationship with the therapist. Rather magical expectations, the diminished capacity to distinguish between fantasy and reality, episodes of anger and suspicion, and fears of rejection dominate the therapeutic interaction for an extended period. Gradually, however, such patients are able to respond to good therapeutic management and to at least partially relinquish their unrealistic and magical expectations, as well as their fears and suspicions, and are able to establish a workable therapeutic alliance (Zetzel 1971). Even so, as Blum (1972) notes, these patients retain the capacity to control and reverse their regression, turning it to adaptive use.

The difficulties in therapy with these borderline patients may often lie less in transference difficulties than in the therapeutic alliance. Even when the transference neurosis develops unexceptionally, there often remains a tentative, insecure quality to the alliance that rides on an underlying basic mistrust and inability to relate to the therapist as a reliably helpful and benignly well-intentioned object. Subtle misalliances can develop and persist through long stretches of the therapy. One young man came to analysis on account of his fragile self-esteem, depressive concerns, and general dissatisfaction with his life. His analysis unfolded unremarkably with uncovering of much important genetic material and a fairly intense but workable transference neurosis. But as time wore on, real therapeutic gains seemed incommensurate with the level and extent of insight he had gained—as though therapist and patient were caught up in a subtle, pervasive, low-grade, negative therapeutic response. Gradually it became clear that a faulty alliance permeated the analysis. Only then did the degree of guardedness and suspicion become apparent, the abiding conviction that, despite his years of experience in the analysis, somehow the therapist would turn on him, hurt him, reject him, put him down, and make him feel worthless and impotent. Only as these issues came into focus did the more borderline qualities of the patient's manner of relating and his involvement in the analysis become apparent.

Nonetheless, the borderline personality is able to retain a relatively good level of functioning and adaptation to reality. The regression in these patients is more typically seen either as the result of progressive involvement in the therapeutic relationship and increasing susceptibility to regressive pulls, usually in analysis but also frequently enough in psychotherapy or in particularly intense relationships with significant objects outside of the therapy. Thus the borderline personality may be able to retain relatively good and well-functioning relationships with a wide spectrum of other people in his or her environment, but may regress to relatively infantile and destructive, if not maladaptive, involvements with particular objects. This pattern is not uncommon between husbands and wives. It should be noted that the stress that precipitates such regressive states is characteristically one having to do with the vicissitudes of object involvement.

It is in these regressive states that intense affects are often unleashed, usually hostile and destructive or depressed (Gunderson and Singer 1975, Kernberg 1967). The destructive impulses may be turned against the self in forms of self-destructive cutting, self-mutilation, or impulsive suicidal gestures. Such regressive destructive manifestations reflect the organization at a primitive level of the themes of victimization and aggressive destructiveness, which reflect the inner organization of the victim-introject and the corresponding aggressor-introject (Meissner 1978b, Robbins 1976). Although Kernberg (1971) relates such self-destructive tendencies to the predominance of pregenital and oral aggression, these self-destructive tendencies can be manifested or organized into pathological character traits that reflect a more or less self-destructive etiology.

In these cases a more or less structured and self-directed aggression can be reflected in the tendency for negative therapeutic reaction or a tendency to draw pleasure and pride from their self-destructive power, enjoying the defeat of those closest to them, including the therapist. This may be rationalized as a submission to a harsh and demanding value system, often religious but not exclusively so. Kernberg stresses the need to distinguish between unconscious self-defeat as a submission to a sadistic superego from a more conscious affirmation of self-destruction as an ego ideal that calls for the sacrifice of any happiness, success, satisfaction, or rewarding relationships to this ideal. The motif of suffering (victimization) thus plays a prominent role in such patients. This tendency may also reflect a need to defeat oneself as the price for defeating an unconsciously hated or envied helper. The self-destruction, therefore, becomes a triumph over the envied object, and this obviously plays itself out in the negative therapeutic response as a triumph over the therapist. The need to defeat the therapist may also be related to elements of oral envy and the seeking of revengeful destruction of a potential but not fully satisfying source of love and gratification. It should be noted as well that even at more adaptive levels of functioning, in the ways in which the borderline personality patient goes about carrying out his or her daily living experience, ample evidence can be found to identify the elements of victimization and destructive aggressiveness (Meissner 1978b).

Another point to keep in mind in reference to the regressive episodes, both in reference to the borderline personality and even more particularly in reference to the psychotic character, is the quality of the emergent transient psychosis. The regression in some of these patients is characterized by the emergence of schizophrenic symptoms, but in some other cases the regression seems to point in the direction of a more manic-depressive configuration. The existence of such cyclothymic characteristics in at least some borderline personalities (Robbins 1976) raises the question of differential symptomatology that might be expressed on a more characterological level as well. A clinical description of such early subtle signs of a "protomanic personality" has been offered recently by Stone (1976).

It has been customary in the descriptions of borderline pathology to refer to ego defects (Blum 1972, Brody 1960, Maenchen 1968, Masterson 1972) or of ego weakness (Kernberg, 1967). Such defects are quite evident in regressive borderline states, but here the focus is on the question of ego functioning on a more specifically characterological level. On that level, the borderline personality is capable of maintaining a quite adequate functional capacity, but ego apparatuses remain vulnerable and reveal a characteristic instability (Rosenfeld and Sprince 1963). The present author prefers to reserve the terminology of defect and weakness for the lower orders of borderline pathology.

The ego of the borderline personality reflects a certain passivity that is manifested in more or less passive or masochistic behaviors, a sense of ego helplessness, and a difficulty in maintaining a sense of control or capacity to achieve goals. Such individuals often anticipate defeat and may adopt a posture of passivity as a form of minor and often quite subtle characterological level of adjustment, which become marked characteristics of borderline states in periods of regression. Thus the primitive defenses (Rosenfeld and Sprince 1963, Kernberg 1967) are identifiable, but cannot be said at this level of organization to be distinguishable from the use of similar defenses in neurotic personalities or the higher level character disorders. Some more specific comments will be offered later about the interplay of introjection and projection, particularly in reference to object relationships. In general, however, the mobilization of defensive operations has a neurotic quality, so that these patients are capable not only of using higher order defenses including repression, but in the use of lower order defenses remain essentially within the neurotic range. It is only in regressive crises that the full flowering of the primitive defenses, including splitting, primitive idealization, projection, denial, omnipotence, and devaluation, as they have been described for example by Kernberg (1967), are in evidence.

A specific comment can be made about the defensive operation of splitting. The role of splitting in Kernberg's theory is central, since it underlies the factors of ego weakness and the inability to achieve adequate integration of both good and bad self-images and good and bad object-images. This affects the quality of the patient's object relationships, as well as the failure of internal integration that leaves the patient vulnerable to regression. Moreover, Kernberg employs the role of splitting as characteristic of borderline pathology and uses it to discriminate between borderline and neurotic forms of organization, the latter having repression as the central defense mechanism.

While the description of splitting seems, from the point of view of this current view, to have valid application to the lower orders of borderline pathology, and to the organization of psychic experience in regressive states, its applicability to the borderline personality must be taken in a more subtle and refined sense. It has more to do with the characteristic organization of aspects of introjective configurations, particularly the component elements of the victim-introject and the aggressor-introject (Meissner 1978b). In terms of the characterologic organization of the borderline personality, both of these configurations are operative along with others that are better expressed in terms of narcissistic components.

Each configuration can be found to operate alternately in different contexts of the subject's experience without the accompanying tendency for one or another configuration to be more completely repressed as in the case with neurotics. In the neurotic personality, and particularly in forms of character pathology, one can identify these configurations, but usually only after a considerable amount of analytic work and in the context of increasing analytic regression. One or another of the introjective configurations may be more or less available to the patient's conscious awareness, but the others tend to be correspondingly repressed. In the borderline personality, however, these configurations remain relatively unrepressed and are generally much more available and more readily expressed along with the contradictory ego states that accompany them.

Thus a view from the vantage point of introjective organization makes the discrimination between splitting and repression less polar and rests the diagnostic discrimination between the borderline and neurotic forms of personality organization more on the manner in which splitting and repression are utilized, rather than an all-or-none presence or absence of these mechanisms. Nonetheless, Kernberg's statement to the effect that the more these primitive mechanisms of splitting, primitive idealization, projection and projective identification, denial, omnipotence, and devaluation dominate the clinical picture, the more the diagnosis of a borderline condition is warranted and retains its validity, since these mechanisms are characteristically found in the lower-order forms of the borderline spectrum. Where they do in fact come to dominate the clinical picture in the present perspective, one would infer that the patient was one of the lower forms of borderline pathology or was functioning in a regressive state. At the same time, it must be said that in many borderline personalities, as here described, there may be little indication of the operation of such mechanisms in clinical terms, and they may become operative only under special conditions of induced regression.

Something similar can be said about the manifestations of ego weakness. On the characterological level, the lack is relative and results only in a tendency toward more or less direct expression of impulses and a pattern of nonspecific diminishing of impulse control. This relates to the general variability and tendency toward acting-out as reactions to the building-up of psychic tension. Depending on the degree of diminished control, this suggests the necessity for setting limits within the therapy and a general need for the therapist to maintain a more active structuring approach. In general, the impulsivity of relatively nonregressed borderline personality patients is easily managed and is readily responsive to effective therapeutic intervention. If the loss of control is more severe, however, this may reflect a regressive state. The diminution of ego control in such patients has been analogized to an unreliable thermostat; rather than a breakdown in the thermostatic control, it results in relative unpredictable and variable functioning (Ekstein and Wallerstein 1954).

Anxiety tolerance is compromised in the borderline personality, but not to the degree found in the psychotic character and even more extremely in the pseudoschizophrenic. In the latter entities, the anxiety tends to be pitched at a level of severe separation anxiety or even a catastrophic or annihilation anxiety level. The issues for these entities, then, tend to be psychotic in proportion and the anxiety is pitched at a life and death level. In the borderline personality, the issues tend to be generated more on the level of castration and separation anxiety. Such patients may express castration fears and castration motifs, but, particularly in a meaningfully productive and gradually regressive therapeutic context, the issues rapidly become those of loss of love and fear of loss of the object. The description of intense, traumatic, overwhelming fears of disintegration, annihilation, the panicky fear of merging or engulfment, and the fears of inner disintegration and loss of identity (Rosenfeld and Sprince 1963, Maenchen 1968, Frijling-Schreuder 1969) are more closely related to lower levels of borderline pathology or are found more explicitly in transient regressive borderline states even in the borderline personality.

Nonetheless, on the characterologic level, there tends to be a free-floating and diffuse anxiety that exceeds the capacity of multiple symptoms and character structures to bind (Kernberg 1967). The crucial issue is not the degree of anxiety experienced, but rather the extent to which any additional anxiety may lead to an increase of symptoms, acting-out, or may precipitate an ego regression (Kernberg 1967, 1971). In other words, the borderline personality retains a capacity for signal anxiety, even though that anxiety may be pitched at a level of separation concerns; he or she only retreats to a traumatic level or a level of annihilation anxiety in which the relationship to the potentially lost object is based on incorporation in regressive states (Little 1966). In these terms, then, the presence and capacity for signal anxiety, even though it be diffuse and chronic, can be an optimistic prognostic indicator (Kernberg 1971).

The lack of sublimatory channels should be regarded less as a lack than as a variably expressed capacity that depends very much on circumstance. Kernberg (1967, 1971) notes the difficulty in evaluating this capacity particularly in relation to the capacity for creative achievement and the ability to invest oneself in an activity or profession beyond the mere satisfaction of narcissistic needs. The borderline personality often seems compromised in this regard, but where such creativity or artistic expressiveness can be tapped, these patients often prove capable of high degrees of productive effort and creativity. It is extremely difficult, however, to tease out of such forms of self-expression the satisfaction of narcissistic needs that may be inherently related to such activities. Taken in themselves, however, as objective activities without considering the underlying narcissistic components, it would seem that the borderline personality often enjoys considerable capacity for sublimatory activity.

The synthetic function undergoes severe regression in borderline states, but in the borderline personality maintains a fairly well integrated level of functioning. Most descriptions of the failures of synthesis have to do with this regressed level of functioning (Rosenfeld and Sprince 1963, Kernberg 1967, 1970b, Masterson 1972). The synthetic function is also more characterologically and chronically impaired, however, to the extent that there is a failure to integrate various contradictory components of the introjective alignments around which the organization of the self is constructed (Meissner 1978b). The extent of the failure of snythesis is thus reflected in the splitting of the internal self-organization and self-representations and the tendency to alternate between various introjective configurations and corresponding ego states. Thus the borderline personality's self-cohesiveness is rather tenuously maintained and is constantly jeopardized by the tendency to retreat to and to respond in terms of the respective introjective configurations.

In the same vein, reality testing is generally well maintained in the borderline personality and is placed in jeopardy only in the context of a regressive borderline state (Rosenfeld and Sprince 1963, Kernberg 1967, Frijling-Schreuder 1969, Masterson 1972). It is the maintenance of reality-testing under ordinary circumstances that distinguishes the borderline conditions from the psychoses (Kernberg 1970b, 1971), and, in the borderline personality, this weakening or loss of the capacity to test reality is seen only in regressive crises (Gunderson and Singer 1975). In contrast to the psychotic character, the borderline personality is less susceptible to regressive pulls, and therefore has a more solid footing in reality. By way of contrast, in the psychotic character, reality may be pushed aside and fantasy substituted for it with relative ease, even though these patients retain an intact capacity to test reality so that psychotic reactions remain brief and transient. The borderline personality, however, retains a relatively firm sense of his or her relationship with reality and the feeling of reality along with a maintained capacity to test that reality.

The tendency to primary process thinking in relationship to regressive potential has already been noted. Here also it can be said that the indices for primary process organization and cognition reflect the regressive functioning of the borderline state and are intimately connected with the reactivation of early pathological introjects and primitive defensive operations, as well as the partial refusion of self and object images (Kernberg 1967). Consequently, it can be said that on a general characterological level of functioning, the borderline personality shows little greater inclination to primary process organization than higher order forms of character organization and functioning.

Some degree of primary process is found in even the best functioning and well-adapted personalities. On clinical examination, borderline personality may give no greater indication than that expected of average neurotic patients of thought disorganization or of a formal thought disorder. Similarly, on unstructured projective tests, these patients cannot be expected to provide evidence of disorganization of thinking either. Such evidence would suggest that the patient was functioning in a regressive modality or that the diagnosis should be changed in the direction of a lower order of character pathology. The presence of subtle indicators of less than totally logical or fully consistent thinking or a combination of percepts may be entirely consistent with the borderline personality diagnosis, but similar findings can be found, for example, in the Rorschach protocols of neurotics or higher level forms of character pathology. A higher incidence of these more subtle signs, however, may reflect a primary process tendency, but does not suggest a formal thought disorder or psychotic cognitive organization.

The object relations of borderline personalities require careful delineation. As already observed, the borderline personality shares in the need-gratifying quality of object relationships in general. Object relationships also tend to reflect the influence of relatively intense narcissistic needs. However, the more typical picture in the borderline personality is for these needs to emerge gradually over time as the therapeutic relationship develops and as the more regressive aspects of the relationship mature and emerge. The rapid, precipitous, and intensely ambivalent involvement with objects is not characteristic of the borderline personality as it might be of the psychotic character or the pseudoschizophrenic.

When that form of intensely ambivalent and clingingly dependent involvement with the therapist is observed in the borderline personality, it is usually in the context of at least a partial regression. It is not altogether uncommon for such patients to come to the therapeutic situation propelled by the distress and turmoil associated with a regressive borderline state, so that such behavior may be seen but it cannot serve diagnostic differentiation until the further evolution of the developing therapeutic relationship brings more adequate data for assessment.

In addition, object constancy is relatively well maintained, but remains vulnerable (Rosenfeld and Sprince 1963, Frijling-Schreuder 1969, Kernberg 1970b, 1971). As the intensity of the involvement with a given object increases, the borderline personality's capacity to tolerate and integrate aspects of increasingly intense ambivalence feelings generally becomes more and more tenuous. Thus, even at levels of characterological functioning, there is a certain instability in object relations, a diminished capacity for empathy (Kernberg 1970b), or a peculiar quality of the experience of meaningful relationships in which the subject is considerably more responsive to the instinctually derived aspects of the object rather than the more enduring and consistent character traits or ego qualities (Krohn 1974). The need–fear dilemma in such patients on the level of characterological functioning remains an unexplicit but subtlety pervasive concern that runs as a constant countermelody under the more predominant themes and day-to-day concerns. When there is a significant involvement with objects, the entire tenor of the relationship is pervaded by a subtle and often implicit, but also often relatively conscious and explicit, fear of abandonment.

There is a constant seeking and tendency to cling to available objects as a means of allaying or filling up the sense of inner emptiness, but no object seems to satiate that deep and inner craving, and the patient is left with an unfulfilled sense of need that may reach even desperate proportions and an intensified sense of frustrated and disappointed longing. Under these circumstances, the borderline personality is quite capable of provoking struggles and turmoil in a frantic attempt to gain concern, attention, and caring from objects that are seen as in part frustrating or rejecting. The tenuous capacity to maintain libidinal constancy and the difficulty in integrating aspects of the ambivalence remain a constant source of difficulty. In general, they tend to feel needy and unsatisfied in their relationships (Adler 1975), but these motifs are expressed in a muted and more or less chronic fashion, with occasional exacerbations that tend to be relatively transient and labile and create brief periods of turmoil and conflict in the patient's life, but then quickly return to a more day-to-day level.

The components of this dilemma in relationship to objects may frequently enough be resolved, particularly in women, by a certain clinging dependency and compliant submissiveness. The issue of borderline compliance has been focused on recently by Robbins (1976). If borderline aggression and attempts to control are frequently striking aspects of this syndrome, it is no less true that borderline compliance and victimization are important and frequently observed components (Robbins 1976, Meissner 1978b). This form of object choice has been described by Reich (1953) as a form of narcissistic object choice in women. This form of object involvement and relatedness tends to teeter on the brink between object relationships and introjection, and comes close to the descriptions of "as if" personalities and false-self configurations. However closely the issues may be related among these various expressions of borderline compliance and object need, the patterns are sufficiently diverse to sustain diagnostic differentiation. The compliance in the borderline personality is primarily an expression of the victim-introject and lacks the plasticity and imitativeness of the "as if" personality or the quality of schizoid protectiveness of the false-self organization. Nonetheless, it seems clear that the tendency for such compliance can be a source of difficulty that must be consistently and cautiously sounded out in the therapy of such patients.

The difficulties in object relationships are reflected in the transference dynamics. While the rapid involvement in intense clinging and demanding with the therapist makes a shambles of therapeutic alliance and impairs the utility of transference interpretations (Little 1958, Adler 1975), this transference behavior is not by and large characteristic of the borderline personality in its nonregressive phases. Kernberg (1968, 1976) characterizes the borderline transference by a premature activation of conflict-laden object relationships along with mutually dissociated ego states. This premature activation of regressive ego states is much more characteristic of the psychotic character, or even in a more fragmented way of the pseudo-schizophrenic, but it is exceptional in the borderline personality. Such reactions may be seen in these patients in the early stages of therapy when the patient is seen in a regressive crisis, but cannot be said to be characteristic of the general run of transference reactions characterizing the borderline personality. The descriptions of transference disturbances tend to focus on the regressive manifestations that accompany borderline states (Little 1966, Adler 1970). These patients may show tendencies to transference acting-out, to projective distortions of the therapeutic relationship, and to valuing and devaluing, but these tendencies are often muted, may be quite subtle, and do not have the disruptive, chaotic, or severely disturbed aspects that are associated with more regressed states. In fact, it can be safely said that such transference reactions, if less frequent, are not difficult to identify, even in relatively healthy and nonregressive neurotic patients.

Perhaps the most helpful discrimination in understanding the borderline transference is Modell's (1963, 1968) analysis of the "transitional object relationship." While there is a tendency to read the transitional object relationship as akin to that of the schizophrenic, it must be maintained that the quality of the transitional object relationship found in the borderline personality is distinct from a transference psychosis. As a transitional object, the object is perceived as outside of the subject, as a separately existing individual, but is perceived or interpreted in terms of elements that are contributed to the object from the subject's own self. These transference distortions, while they are based on the operation and interplay of projections and introjections (Meissner 1978b), do not reach delusional proportions and are not marked by the loss of ego boundaries, the sense of fusion and merger that may be found in a frankly psychotic transference.

While such manifestations may be found in regressive states, it is more typical to find that the transference relationship is increasingly contaminated and distorted by the patient's conviction of certain attitudes, judgments, opinions, feelings, or other states of mind that he or she attributes to the analyst and that tend to undermine the precarious alliance and the patient's capacity to engage meaningfully and productively in the work of the treatment. Generally, such distortions are corrigible, however, since the patient's sense of reality and capacity to test reality remains intact. This tendency is one, as has been previously stressed, that can also be found in relatively neurotic or even normal individuals, and it differs in the borderline personality only in the degree to which it reflects the underlying introjective configurations. Thus the predominance of the transitional object relationship within the transference requires that considerably greater attention and greater activity be mobilized in the interest of establishing and sustaining a therapeutic alliance. This remains a valid rule of thumb even when such patients are in an analytic situation.

These factors point to the predominant area of pathology in the borderline personality—the pathogenic organization of introjects. That is to say, the primary defect in the borderline personality is not a defect in the structure of the ego, as might be the case in lower-order borderline forms. Rather, the impediment is in the organization of constituents of the self. The identifiable pathogenic configurations of introjects in borderline personality include the victim-introject, the aggressor-introject, as well as the narcissistically determined and impregnated configurations of grandiosity and inferiority. These pathogenic configurations can be found across a broad range of forms of psychopathology, but what is characteristic about the borderline personality is the manner in which these configurations are organized and maintained relatively available to consciousness without adequate communication between the dissociated ego states or a capacity to integrate elements from the respective introjective organizations. It is this phenomenon in part that has been addressed by Kernberg (1967) in terms of "splitting." Within each configuration, however, the introjective alignment is maintained with relative consistency and often with considerable investment and resistance to change. It is these introjective configurations and their relative availability and variability that underlies the multiplicity of identities often seen in the borderline personality (Fast 1974). The multiplicity of identities is not unlimited, however, but relates rather to different underlying introjective configurations. Moreover, it is this variability and capacity to shift relatively easily from one narcissistic configuration to another, as well as the greater susceptibility to regression, that distinguishes the borderline personality in its narcissistic aspects from the narcissistic personality. By way of contrast, the narcissistic personality tends to develop relatively consistent narcissistic transferences, of either the mirroring or idealizing forms described by Kohut (1971).

To summarize the borderline personality, then, it is a form of character disorder that represents a distinct step up the developmental scale from the psychotic character. The borderline issues are no longer substantially psychotic, the level of anxiety is pervasive but of a signal variety dealing primarily with issues of separation, dependency, and loss or loss of love. The propensity for regression is limited to more or less special circumstances as opposed to the more general, marked, and readily expressed regressive potential of the psychotic character. The particular vulnerability of the borderline personality is on the level of object relations and particularly the characteristic quality of the interplay of projections and introjections that continually color and, to a certain extent, distort the borderline's experience of the interpersonal environment. In general, these patients maintain a consistent relationship to reality, an integral sense of reality, and an intact capacity to test reality. These capacities are diminished only during periods of crisis and in regressive states. The quality of object relations and transference are subject to a characteristic variability, which reflects the internally organized configuration of introjective elements. These patients are able to maintain relatively good ego-functioning in general, and reveal ego weakness only in regressive crises—a characteristic that distinguishes them from lower-order borderline conditions. Thus Kernberg's description of ego weakness is more pertinent to these lower-order disorders (pseudoschizophrenias, psychotic characters) than to the borderline personality as such. Rather, the locus of pathology in the borderline personality seems to reside more in the organization of the self and its correlative introjective configurations.

Primitive (Oral) Hysteric

The primitive hysteric is a form of character pathology that presents with more or less flamboyant hysterical symptomatology, but the character organization tends to be somewhat more infantile. The role of more infantile factors in the hysterical personality was noted by Marmor (1953), particularly in regard to more primitive oral characteristics. The presence of such infantile characteristics in the hysterical personality may reflect the organization of the personality on a more infantile borderline level; it may also suggest that the discrimination between this level of personality organization and the higher level of hysterical personality functioning was not adequately made.

Prominent hysterical characteristics that are included in the description of the hysterical personality might also be included in a list of characteristics of the borderline personality, particularly emotional lability, strong suggestibility, easy disappointment, alternating idealization and devaluation of objects of dependence, compulsive needs for love and admiration, intense feelings of inadequacy, strong dependence on others, approval for maintenance of self-esteem, a tendency to dramatize or act out feelings, etcetera. Reich (1933) noted the tendency of the hysteric to genitalize mouth and anus so that these always come to represent the female genital and may be accompanied by perverse tendencies. He also remarked on the tendency of hysterics to oral regression and that oral fixation is accompanied by a tendency to depressive reactions. Marmor emphasized the predominance of oral elements in the more primitively organized hysterics and raised an important question regarding their susceptibility to regression. This picture of the more regressive aspects of the hysterical personality may be more applicable to the present category of primitive hysteric than to the current understanding of the hysterical character as such.

A discrimination along these same lines is made by Kernberg (1967) in his attempt to distinguish hysterical personality from infantile personality. The infantile personality shares the hysterical features, but these are organized on a lower level of character pathology than in the hysterical personality. Thus emotional lability in infantile personalities is more generalized and diffuse so that there are few conflict-free areas in their life experiences and a higher degree of social inappropriateness. While the hysteric lacks impulse control in specific areas and in periods of intense conflict, the infantile personality lacks impulse control in a much more diffuse way. Hysterical overinvolvement becomes in the infantile personality a much more childlike overidentification and more desperate and inappropriate clinging. The motives and inner experiences of others are often grossly misread, even if there remains a capacity for good social interaction and adaptation.

Long-lasting or significant involvement with objects frequently shows a progressively more regressed childlike, oral, demanding, and frustratedly aggressive quality that is not characteristic of the hysteric. The need to be loved, to be the center of attention and attraction, functions on a less specifically sexualized level and has a quality of greater helplessness, inappropriately demanding and reflecting more primitive narcissistic trends. The hysterical tendency to pseudohypersexuality in combination with sexual inhibition turns into a sexual provocativeness that is often more crude and inappropriate, and reflects more orally determined exhibitionism and demandingness than in the sexualized hysterical approach. When this takes the form of promiscuity, it has a more drifting quality with little stability of object relationships. There may also be a tendency to conscious sexual fantasies of a primitive polymorphous-perverse character in the infantile personality, which is generally missing in the more diffuse repression of the hysteric.

The infantile character is generally less competitive either toward men or women, but there is often a rapid shifting between positive and negative feelings, between submission and childlike imitation and stubborn resentful negativism. Pregenital and specifically oral problems predominate so that there is a reduced capacity for stable object relationships and a weakening of the capacity to maintain object constancy. Involvement with objects tends to have a more childlike dependency that is oral and demanding as well as aggressive. These characteristics seem quite consistent with the primitive hysteric as described here. As Kernberg (1970b) further notes, these patients may present as predominantly hysterical, but careful examination and particularly extended experience, particularly of the development of the transference, may be necessary to reveal the underlying infantile structure.

The careful discrimination of these patients from the more usual neurotic hysteric is important, particularly for the practical implications for therapy. For example, an attractive and intelligent young woman came to therapy with a history of recurrent depressions, repeated episodes of impulsive acting-out sexually, and a strong tendency to eroticize previous therapeutic relationships. The patient presented more or less as a classic, if somewhat flamboyant, hysterical personality. The early phases of the analysis were marked by rapid but conflictual transference involvement. Her tendency was to seek to establish a somewhat clinging and idealizing relationship with the therapist, alternating with angry denunciations and devaluations when the therapist failed to respond or tried to interpret or even examine her need to idealize him.

As the transference evolved, it became more specifically and intensely erotized. The patient became involved in a continuing attempt at seduction, which was never blatant but was intensely felt by her. There was difficulty in keeping the analytic work going; her motivation seemed to shrink to nothing but the wish to get gratification from the therapist. Her fantasies were explicit, erotic to the point of perversion, and were accompanied by powerful impulses to give up the analysis and make the relationship as sexual as she wished. Along with this eroticization of the analytic relationship, there was a continuing tendency to act-out her sexual frustrations in the form of depressive episodes that had a highly labile and intense quality (although never to the point of suicide) and expressed themselves in repeated masochistic interchanges with important male figures, especially her somewhat paranoid and sadistic husband.

It was noteworthy that, in this young woman whose capacity to function and to deal effectively with her environment was in other areas outstanding, her ability to test reality in the therapeutic relation seemed so tenuous. Her wishes were so powerful that she chose to ignore any of the aspects of the reality of the therapeutic relationship that did not fit the requirements of the fantasy. Much of the analytic work concentrated on establishing and maintaining the therapeutic alliance, which remained fragile and uncertain for much of the early period of the analytic work. As it became more stable and consolidated, the analysis settled into a form more consistent with the basically hysterical organization of the patient's personality. During the early phases of working through these more tempestuous transference vicissitudes, however, the issues were to a significant degree borderline in character.

The categorization provided by Zetzel (1968) is particularly useful in discriminating the levels of hysterical pathology. The first group represents the more classically described hysterical character, whose conflicts are essentially genital, who has been able to reach an effective level of Oedipal involvement and is able to tolerate a triangular conflict. Such patients are able to maintain significant object relationships with both parents, even though post-Oedipal relationships are often more ambivalent than the pre-Oedipal. They are easily able to recognize and tolerate internal conflicts and to distinguish between internal reality and external reality. In contrast, the second group of potentially good hysterics usually present a wider range of symptoms, are generally younger and less mature, and are generally less successful and consistent in their work achievement and in the maintenance of relationships. They are less consistent and more passive, and are often fearful of dependent wishes that are closer to the surface than in the good hysteric. Zetzel notes that these patients generally have difficulty in establishing a stable analytic situation (therapeutic alliance) and may react by a flight into health or a plunge into a regressive transference neurosis before an effective alliance can be established. This group of potentially good hysterics belongs to the primitive hysterical group.

The third group that Zetzel described are hysterical women who have an underlying depressive character structure. These women generally reveal an impoverished sense of self-esteem and tend to devalue their own femininity. They may have experienced a genuine triangular conflict, but usually with excessive idealization of the father and accompanying devaluation of the mother. They may have the capacity to tolerate considerable depressive affect, but they fail significantly in the area of positive mastery, so that they tend to see themselves and experience themselves as passive, helpless, and vulnerable. They can easily develop passive and dependent transference reactions that interfere with their capacity to distinguish between transference neurosis and alliance. They present serious problems in the terminal phases of analysis and present a serious risk of drifting into relatively interminable situations. This group also belongs within the primitive hysterical category.

The last group, Zetzel's "so-called good hysterics," present a floridly hysterical symptomatic picture and in treatment prove incapable of tolerating a genuine triangular conflict. They have intensely sexualized transference fantasies and tend to regard such fantasies as areas of potential real gratification. They are incapable of distinguishing between internal and external reality, have considerable difficulty in maintaining a distinction between alliance and transference neurosis, and thus are poor candidates for analysis. These patients reflect a basic developmental failure in ego functioning that results in an impaired capacity for reality testing. This last group would seem to be more primitively organized than the primitive hysterics and would be more consistently categorized with the psychotic characters. The characteristics of the primitive hysteric are quite consistent with the group described in Grinker et al.'s (1968) study as closest to the border with neurosis.

The primitive hysterical personality, then, shares in the basic borderline issues that are common to the rest of the borderline conditions and has some characteristics in common with them. The transient attachment and involvement with objects and the alternation between idealization and disparagement is reminiscent of the as-if personality, but the primitive hysteric maintains a better integrated and more cohesive sense of self without the as-if characteristics that define the as-if personality. At a more primitive level of organization, the primitive hysteric can look like the borderline personality, but here again the borderline personality is distinguished by its inability to maintain a cohesive sense of self and the tendency to alternate between a variety of introjective configurations. The primitive hysteric, even at its lowest level of character organization, tends to articulate itself around the victim-introject, thus assuming some of the qualities of a depressive structure. Moreover, it must be remembered that the primitive hysteric retains the capacity to mobilize hysterical defenses and an hysterical style in the interest of defending against underlying conflict.

This consideration of the primitive hysteric rounds off an important subsegment of the borderline spectrum. The sequence from the pseudo-schizophrenic group through the psychotic characters and the borderline personality to the primitive hysteric represents a progression in levels of pathological disorganization from the more severe to the less severe. The sequence might be envisioned as an extension of basically hysterical features to progressively lower levels of character organization and functioning. The parameters that characterize this sequence are increasing affective lability, diminishing anxiety tolerance, increasing intolerance to frustration, increasing tendencies to externalization and acting-out for the release of tension, increasing signs of ego weakness, increasing signs of the instability or fragmentation of introjective configurations and a corresponding failure in self-cohesion, an increasing titre of primitive pregenital aggression, increasingly primitive organization of defenses, and increasing susceptibility to regressive pulls and the tendency to regressive states. Most importantly, the quality of object relations is marked by an increasing clingingly dependent and ambivalent involvement with significant objects, constantly threatened by fears of abandonment and loss. This sequence may be characterized as the hysterical continuum; it can be contrasted with the schizoid continuum, which follows.

The Schizoid Personality

The schizoid continuum is a rather loosely organized group of character pathologies that represents a variety of resolutions of the basic schizoid dilemma. That dilemma is an expression of the need–fear dilemma in which the intense need for objects is countered by the fear of closeness or intimacy with the same objects. The schizoid defense counters this fear of involvement (which in its more severe manifestations becomes a fear of engulfment) by withdrawal or minimization of the need for objects. For purposes of the present discussion, the schizoid continuum will include the schizoid personality, the "as-if" personality, the false-self organization, and finally the condition of identity diffusion.

The schizoid dilemma and defense are seen most characteristically in the schizoid personality. The schizoid personality has been the object of study of a small group of object relations theorists, particularly Guntrip (1969). The schizoid patient complains of feeling isolated, cut off, shut out, out of touch, apart, strange; or of life seeming futile and meaningless, empty, leading nowhere and accomplishing nothing. External relationships seem to be affectively empty and are characterized by an emotional withdrawal. Vital and effective mental activity has disappeared from sight into a hidden inner world, so that the patient's conscious self is emptied of vital feeling and capacity for action and seems to have become unreal. Glimpses of an intense activity in this inner world can be captured in fragments of dreams or fantasies, but the patient merely reports these as if he or she were a dispassionate and neutral observer not involved in the inner drama and turmoil of which he or she is but the passive spectator. The attitude to the outer world is one of noninvolvement and mere observation, without any feeling, attachment, or sense of participation.

The schizoid's primary defense against anxiety is to keep emotionally isolated, inaccessible, and remote. The schizoid condition, then, consists of a relative cancellation of external object relations and an attempt to live in a detached and withdrawn manner. While the depressive dilemma is that of anger directed toward a love object such that the expression of that anger would destroy the object and the anger must consequently be turned against the self, the schizoid dilemma is that of destructive love, in which the anxiety arises from the fear of destroying and losing the love object through the intensity of devouring, hungry, greedy, and needy dependency. The schizoid personality cannot exist in a relationship with another person, nor can it exist out of it without risking the loss of both the object and himself or herself. Love relationships consequently are seen as mutually devouring and destructive. The dilemma of the need and fear of objects in the schizoid is particularly intense.

Although the position of schizoid withdrawal may be regarded as a regressed posture (Guntrip 1969), it is nonetheless a protective, highly defended position that buffers the ego against disruptive regression at the cost of maladaptive external effects (Giovacchini 1973). In both children and adults, there is a constricted and underdeveloped affective life, a quality of emotional distance, and preoccupation with inner thoughts and fantasy life. Despite this turning inward, there is a maintenance of the integrity of other ego functions without the characteristic shifting ego organization seen in psychotic characters or even in the borderline personality in its shifting back and forth between dissociated ego states. Thus the schizoid personality is able to maintain a position of reasonably good functioning in the real world even while holding himself or herself emotionally aloof. Consequently, the defenses are so rigidly maintained that the character structure is quite stable, and disruptive regressive states are relatively uncharacteristic of this entity (Pine 1974).

The stability of character functioning and the emotional withdrawal and lack of affect distinguishes the schizoid personality effectively from all other borderline conditions, including the as-if personality and the false-self organization. The as-if personality does become attached to objects and does show emotional responsiveness, even if they are of the as-if quality described. The false-self organization is often and regularly involved with objects, even apparently meaningfully involved with objects, but this involvement itself is utilized for defensive purposes.

A young man who started and remained in analysis for a period of several years demonstrated these personality characteristics. He originally complained of no particular inner distress except that he did not feel that his relationship with his wife was particularly satisfying. The reason for seeking treatment was the development of some cardiac irregularity that his physicians had related to stress and for which psychoanalytic treatment was recommended. Psychiatric evaluation suggested that he was so well defended that only analysis would get to the underlying conflicts. The assumption was probably correct, but one might more accurately guess that not even analysis could reach behind the rigid schizoid shell this patient erected around himself.

He was quite successful in a responsible and demanding job, but he had little to do with his fellow workers beyond the bare superficialities related to work tasks. He did not leave his office to socialize with other employees, he would not eat lunch in the company cafeteria, nor would he ever attend any of the frequent office parties. He was a loner—held in respect for his efficiency and ability, but friend or intimate with none. His marriage was little better. It was a marriage of convenience in which there was little affection, rare sex that usually took the form of his wife masturbating him, and little or no sense of giving or sharing. When they would go out to dinner, for example, he would insist that his wife pay for her half of the check. He refused to have children, feeling that the idea of giving or sharing with them was intolerable. It was a marriage, indeed, that was no marriage.

In the analysis the patient's severe obsessionalism became apparent, including keeping of detailed lists, even to the number of times he wore articles of clothing, preoccupations with anal matters and functioning, his penchant for efficiency and punctilliousness, his punctuality (never late for an hour), and his generally obsessional demeanor. In the analysis he would go on at great length relating trivial details, and when the therapist commented on the defensive aspect of this behavior, he would become indignant and pose the classic obsessional dilemma—wasn't he saying what came to his mind? Was that what the therapist wanted or not?

For a long time, the work of the analysis focused on diminishing the level of his obsessional defenses—with some success, but with continuing difficulty. Little by little, the nature of the transference difficulties became clear. He was an only son who had been born nearly a decade after his parents' marriage. He saw his father as a weak, petty, selfish man who was basically a failure in life and who functioned more-or-less as his mother's man-in-waiting. His mother was dedicated to her career and put that before any consideration for him. She had not wanted to have him, and after he was born turned her attention back to her work, putting him in a secondary position. As he was growing up, his parents sent him away to camp in the summers and, from secondary school on, put him in boarding schools—obvious proof to him that they did not want him, did not love or care about him, and were only involved with him to the extent that he could be drawn into the service of their narcissism.

All of these elements came into play in the transference. He saw the therapist as only interested in him as a patient, as a case to study, and only worth the money he paid. He saw the therapist as more interested in what could be learned by studying his case, and only concerned to the degree that he could use the patient as material for writing an article. He wanted the therapist to care about him, to take a deep interest in him and do things for him. He particularly clung to a magical conviction that if the therapist so wished, he could explain all the patient's difficulties to him and do something magical to make things better in his life. Regardless of the therapist's attempts to modify or challenge this conviction, he clung stubbornly to it. The analysis became for him a stubborn effort to get the therapist to do for him what he wished. If the patient did the analysis correctly, if he came, talked (no matter about what!), paid his bills, didn't get angry at the therapist for denying him what he wanted, eventually he would win out and the therapist would work the magic.

There were in addition other preoccupations that suggested that he was functioning on less than a neurotic level. His generally schizoid life style suggested more severe pathology. His narcissism was quite pathological and pervasive, reflecting pathological residues of the grandiose self along with correlative inner feelings of worthlessness and inadequacy, which were usually related to bitter complaints about how his parents had treated him. The analysis turned into a stubborn holdout for the fulfillment of his infantile and highly narcissistic wishes. His rage mounted over the therapist's refusal to comply with those wishes. His effort became an attempt to defeat the therapist, to prove the analysis worthless, to make the therapist admit his inadequacy and defeat in the face of the patient's impervious defenses and impossible demands. The underlying borderline issues remained impervious to analytic influence, and the analysis was finally terminated on the patient's initiative—after long exploration of the motives and reasons behind his need to end the analysis prematurely.

In retrospect, this patient presented with a well-functioning and obsessional facade, but the basic issues were of a borderline order. It was on these issues that the analysis foundered. The threat posed by the analysis was too great, particularly the need to give up his schizoid defense and to allow himself to engage in a meaningful and dependent way with another human being. At no point in the analysis was there ever a meaningful therapeutic alliance. The issues were narcissistic and were caught up in the intense conflicts over the need to be accepted and loved against the fears of dependency and the threatening involvement with the analyst. His realization that he would never have it on his terms and that further progress in the analysis meant exposure of his schizoid vulnerability was more than he could tolerate.

These conditions are all preoccupied with the central problem, namely that of the potential dissolution of nuclear narcissistic structures that is an ever-present potential danger. In these terms the narcissistic vulnerability of the schizoid stands in marked contrast to that of the narcissistic character (Kohut 1971). The schizoid withdrawal results from intense narcissistic vulnerability and the fear that narcissistic injury will initiate an uncontrollable regression. The retreat from real objects, then, does not serve as a protection of what is vital in the self against unappreciative or threatening objects, but occurs because of the danger inherent in the frustration of narcissistic needs. By way of contrast, the narcissistic character seeks out and is involved with objects, or more specifically self-objects, as sources of needed and sought-for narcissistic sustenance.

The quality of emotional withdrawal, in any case, should not mislead one into a belief that the schizoid individual is uninvolved or withdrawn from object relationships. Indeed, his or her contact with objects is intense, highly ambivalent, and subject to the torments of the schizoid dilemma that has been described. Commerce with objects is intensely colored and distorted by projections that turn these objects into threatening, persecuting, engulfing, devouring objects. The basic organization of the schizoid self, then, is formed around an internal victim-introject that provides the core of the personality organization. It is the protection of this vulnerable and victimized core of self-organization that the schizoid withdrawal is intended to effect. The basic defect of the schizoid character, then, lies at an extremely early level of the introjection of primary objects. The schizoid condition is based on the internalization of hostile, destructive introjects. These internalized unconscious objects are locked away within the psyche, where they remain always rejecting, indifferent, or hostile. The result of this negative introject is that it becomes a focus for feelings of inner worthlessness, vileness, inner destructiveness, evil, and malicious power. These introjective configurations are the victim-introject and its correlative aggressor-introject (Meissner 1978b).

To summarize this differential focusing of the schizoid personality, then, it can be said that the schizoid is confronting the same basic issues that underlie the other borderline conditions, particularly the closely related conditions of identity diffusion, the as-if personality, and the false-self organization. The primary differentiating characteristic, however, is the quality of emotional withdrawl and isolation that serves as the characteristic defense against these underlying needs.

The False-Self Organization

The false self is essentially a schizoid condition that is marked by a form of turning away from interpersonal relationships, motivated more by the need to preserve a sense of inner autonomy and individuation than by a specific anxiety from intimate contact with objects. The idea was originally introduced by Winnicott (1960), who described a split between the false self, that part of the personality that is related to and involved with the external environment and real objects, and the true self that inhabits the inner core of the personality and is hidden away from the scrutiny of observers. The self equivalently regards itself as the true self and correspondingly regards that part of the personality related to external objects or to the physical body as false.

The false self is essentially erected to protect and preserve the true self and to guard it against losing its sense of subjectivity, vitality, and inner autonomy. Thus the dilemma is essentially a schizoid dilemma, in that the inner autonomy and authenticity of the true self is threatened by engulfment in its relationships to objects. The reality of these objects and the relatedness to them is an impingement, similar to the infantile impingement of the "not-good-enough-mother" that may threaten to overwhelm or obliterate the self.

The narcissistic vulnerability underlying the false-self organization relates to the persistence of an infantile grandiose ego ideal or grandiose self. The false-self individual feels that his or her early caretakers and later significant objects do not appreciate or accept his or her grandiose attempts to preserve a sense of inner spontaneity and integrity, and thus retreats to an inner world to preserve this sense of vitality and spontaneity. This retreat to a kind of grandiose self-sufficiency is characteristic of schizoid states (Modell 1975). The need to retain spontaneity and vitality is, however, somewhat different from the schizoid dilemma in which the fear of disorganization and engulfment is attached to attempts to relate with any intensity to real objects so that the schizoid retreats primarily to avoid the outcomes of this disastrous object involvement.

The other important component of the false self that Winnicott delineated is the element of compliance. There is a compliant aspect to the true self in any healthy personality that derives from the ability of the infant to comply without fear or danger or the risk of exposure or vulnerability. Thus the socialization of the child involves compliance and adaptability, but even here Winnicott noted the capacity to override this compliance at crucial points or periods, for example in adolescence. The compliance of the false self, however, forms a substitute way of relating to objects and dealing with the external environment that is both fallacious and unreal, and fragile. The operations of the false self seem false, often empty, lacking in vitality or significance, and may serve as a source of inner desperation and hopelessness.

The false self may to all intents and purposes appear quite normal and adaptive. It may even provide the individual with at least a partial sense of "identity." The same observations relevant to identity diffusion regarding the tendency to adhere to causes, groups, leaders, etcetera, may also apply to the false-self organization. Nonetheless, trouble arises where authenticity and real object involvement are called for. When the false self cannot measure up to or sustain itself in the face of such pressures or demands, the outcome may be a severe regression into a borderline state. At its pathological worst, the

false-self organization may cover an underlying schizophrenic process so
that, when the false self begins to fragment, the schizophrenia emerges, often
in the form of acute disorganization and decompensation.

The false-self organization, then, represents another form of adaptation to
or defense against an underlying schizoid dilemma. In this case, rather than
adopting a form of as-if involvement or schizoid withdrawal, there is a split
within the organization of the personality that allows the true self to retreat
to an inner withdrawal colored with narcissistic isolation and self-sufficiency,
while another self-organization is constructed based on compliance and the
need to protectively buffer the true self from the impingements of the outside
world. The false-self organization may thus carry on at a high level of
adjustment and involvement with reality, but the true self remains hidden
and withdrawn. Consequently, the pathology takes the form of the internal
organization of the self that is motivated by underlying narcissistic and
object-related conflicts.

As-If Personality

Deutsch's (1942) original description of the "as if" personality focused on
the patient's impoverishment of emotional relationship. Such patients may
be unaware of their lack of normal affective involvements and responses, in
which case the disturbance may be perceived by others or may be first
detected in treatment; or they may be keenly distressed by their emotional
defect, which may be experienced as transitory and fleeting or recurring in
specific situations, or may persist as an enduring distressing symptom.
Deutsch explains:

. . . that every attempt to understand the way of feeling and manner of
life of this type forces upon the observer the inescapable impression that
the individual's whole relationship to life has something about it which
is lacking in genuineness and yet outwardly runs along "as if" it were
complete. Even the layman sooner or later inquires, after meeting such
an "as if" patient: what *is* wrong with him, or her? Outwardly the person
seems normal. There is nothing to suggest any kind of disorder, behavior is not unusual, intellectual abilities appear unimpaired, emotional expressions are well ordered and appropriate. But despite all this,
something intangible and indefinable obtrudes between the person and
his fellows and invariably gives rise to the question, "What is wrong?"
(p. 263).

The patient's relationships are devoid of warmth, expressions of emotion
are formal, the inner experience is excluded. Deutsch compares it to the
performance of an actor who is well trained to play the role, but who lacks

the necessary spark to make his enactment of the role true to life. She takes pains to distinguish this inner emptiness from the coldness and distance of a more schizoid adjustment: in one there is a flight from reality or defense against forbidden instinctual drives, while the other seeks external reality in order to avoid anxiety-laden fantasies. In the as-if personality, it is loss of object cathexis that is involved rather than repression. The relationship to the world is maintained on a level of childlike imitation that expresses an identification with the environment and results in ostensibly good adaptation to reality despite the absence of object cathexis.

The result is a passivity to the demands of the environment and the highly plastic capacity to mold oneself and one's behavior to such external expectations. Attachment to objects can be adhesive, but there is a lack of real warmth and affection in the relationship that creates such emptiness and dullness that the partner often breaks off the relationship precipitously. When the as-if person is thus abandoned, he or she may display a spurious ("as if") affective reaction or a total absence of affective reaction. The object is soon replaced with a new one and the process is repeated.

Deutsch also comments on the moral character of these patients, which generally seems to be weak or lacking. Their moral standards, ideals, and convictions simply reflect those of the individuals to whom they attach themselves, whether for good or evil. They easily become involved with social, ethical, or religious groups, and thus seek to give content and reality to the experience of inner emptiness that characterizes their sense of self. Their adherence to one point of view after another may be overenthusiastic and easily shifted, even from one contradictory view to another. They are also quite suggestible, as a result of their passivity and automaton-like identification. The failure of superego formation is related to the failure to achieve a strong enough Oedipal involvement and the resulting impairment of a failure of identifications. Thus the superego precursors are not effectively internalized and remain dependent on external objects. The organization of the internal world in these patients is based primarily on the interplay of imitation and introjection, and fails to reach a higher level of more autonomous identifications (Meissner 1974).

Subsequently, Ross (1967) reviewed the literature on as-if phenomena and suggested that although the as-if personality was rare in clinical experience, there also existed a wide spectrum of as-if states that range from the apparently normal to the definitely psychotic. There are also affinities with states of depersonalization. Reich (1953) has described a type of as-if narcissistic object choice in women. Greenson (1958) has described patients with what he has called a "screen identity," who resemble as-if personalities. Like the as-ifs, they constantly seek the company of others, searching for need-satisfying objects, ceaselessly looking for new experiences and objects, but are well-oriented to reality and usually socially successful. They are often sensitive, perceptive, empathic, narcissistic, orally fixated and exhibition-istic, and possess eminently corruptible superegos. Katan (1959) also dis-tinguished between true as-if personalities in which identifications tend to be of the primary type and "pseudo-as-if" states in which the identifications are secondary and in which the personality contains an hysterical core. Similarly, Masud Khan (1960) pointed to the possible connections between as-if states and Winnicott's notion of the false self. Ross (1967) also explores the relationship between as-if characteristics and states and the psycho-pathology of the impostor and the psychology of acting as a profession. Both the as-if personality and the impostor reflect a failure of identity as "doer" insofar as they easily acquire roles without any inherent interest or need for a sense of real accomplishment within them (Deutsch 1955; Fast 1975).

The literature has frequently associated as-if characteristics with border-line conditions. Modell (1963) regards the as-if syndrome as part of the borderline spectrum, and Kernberg (1967) also includes the as-if disorder as described by Deutsch within the borderline psychopathology. Others, how-ever, point to the intensity of affect, particularly destructive hostility and anger in the borderline conditions, and discriminate between these condi-tions and the as-if personality and schizoid personality on these grounds (Gunderson and Singer 1975).

Object relations in the borderline conditions have often been described as superficial and transient. Knight (1953) observed that the borderline's con-ventional, although superficial, adaptation to the environment and the main-tenance of relatively superficial object relationships revealed varying degrees of intactness. It has in fact been thought that the borderline's capacity for adequate social functioning may depend on maintaining such superficial involvement (Gunderson and Singer 1975). It may be, however, that this quality of superficiality and transiency of relationships is related more to the as-if characteristics of borderline conditions, as typified in the as-if per-sonality, and is relatively less applicable to other borderline entities.

It should be noted that in the Grinker (1968) study, one of the defined groups, group III, is more or less congruent with the description of the as-if personality and is empirically distinguished from the more characteristic borderline group (group II)). This "as-if" group is described as having bland and more or less adaptive behavior with little evidence of negative affect or negative behaviors. Affective behavior is generally appropriate, but there is little manifestation of positive affect as well. These patients reveal no evidence of a capability for loving anybody or anything and give no indications of any well-developed sense of identity. Their relationships remain complementary ("as if") and their demeanor is generally isolated and withdrawn. They wait for cues from others in the environment and attempt to relate to them by assuming complementary roles. They are equivalently as-if characters who behave as they are expected to behave and often appear to be involved in the contexts and situations in which they are present, yet their role continually vacillates depending on the important other to whom they must relate and adapt. They have given up the search for identity and have settled for an imitative substitute. They repress all individuality and relate by passive compliance and mimicry as a way of defending against the threatening pain of abandonment. Individuation and individuality for them imply separation and abandonment.

The as-if personality reflects a certain quality of borderline compliance that reflects the underlying dynamics associated with the victim-introject (Robbins 1976, Meissner 1976, 1978b). It represents a resolution of the problems related to the victim-introject, as well as the dilemmas of narcissistic peril and object relations conflicts, through the vehicle of transitory and superficial as-if involvements and their associated internalizations. The issues of compliance are shared with other borderline conditions, particularly cases of identity diffusion, schizoid personality, and false-self organization. The discrimination between them on this level lies in the manner in which these conflicts are dealt with—whether by diffusion of identity, by as-if imitative attachments, by schizoid withdrawal, or by the organization of the false self. Similarly, the as-if involvement with love objects must be differentiated from the hysterical identifications that result from powerful libidinal object cathexes. Hysterical repression is used to alleviate this essentially neurotic anxiety, whereas the inner conflict in the as-if patient is reduced by a defect in the development of affect that leads to an impoverishment of the total personality (Deutsch 1942).

In summary, although as-if states may be found in a variety of pathological conditions, either in conjunction with or as a defense against depersonalization, the as-if personality may also be identifiable as a distinct clinical pattern within the borderline spectrum. The disturbances in narcissism, the capacity for object relations, and the internal organization of the self in the as-if disturbance may function at a number of levels of pathological intensity, and in this range of expression, they are roughly parallel to disturbances in identity diffusion, schizoid character organization, and the false-self organization. The as-if personality resolves these underlying conflicts by a transient, often superficial and imitative and idealizing attachment to an object. This attachment is paralleled by a modification of the self in terms of imitative and introjective mechanisms that, because of their defensive vicissitudes, lead to no further or more meaningful internalizations (Meissner 1974). Thus these patients do not present with a significant deficit in ego functioning as a general rule, but rather the pathology lies in the realm of the organization of the self, which achieves a transient cohesiveness through such as-if mechanisms. Deficits in structural organization, not only of the ego but more particularly of the superego, are thus secondary to this basic dynamic.

Identity Diffusion

We are indebted to Erik Erikson for the notion of identity diffusion, which he described as a problem that presented itself in borderline or adolescent patients, frequently as a life crisis (Erikson 1956). Erikson describes a condition of "acute identity diffusion" that is familiar in the context of borderline regression; the attempt here is to focus the notion of identity diffusion as a chronic enduring modality of personality organization. As Erikson envisions the state of acute identity diffusion, it arises when developmental experiences, particularly in adolescence, demand a commitment to physical intimacy, occupational choice, competition of various sorts, in general to a specific form of psychosocial self-definition. The necessity of choice and commitment gives rise to conflicting identifications, each of which narrows the inventory of further choice; movement in any direction may establish binding precedents for psychosocial self-definition. The result is an avoidance of choice, a lack of inner definition of self, and an external avoidance, isolation, and alienation.

For the adolescent caught in this turmoil, there is a regressive reattachment to old libidinal objects, a re-emergence of primitive introjections, along with their associated more or less archaic conflicts. Engagement, whether it be in terms of friendship, competition, sex or love, becomes a test of self-delineation. Engagement carries with it the constant threat of fusion and loss of identity, which may result in various forms of social isolation, stereotype or formalized interpersonal relationships, or even the frantic seeking of intimacy with improbable or inappropriate partners. Such attachments, whether as friendships or affairs, become simply attempts to delineate identity by a form of mutual narcissistic mirroring. Such patients have a characteristic difficulty in committing themselves to any line of action or career choice. Particularly difficult is a commitment in the areas of work and love: they find themselves unwilling or unable to make a definitive choice of life partner, just as they may find it extremely difficult to decide upon and commit themselves to any line of life's endeavors such as a profession or choice of career. All of the difficulties in work identification that have been noted in other contexts can be found in this group of patients as well (Fast 1975). At times these difficulties in self-definition and commitment are found in one area but not in others. The patient may have a well-defined work life or career, but be unable to make the defining commitment in an intimate love relationship.

Erikson also describes a variety of reactions to this underlying diffusion of identity. There may be a variety of forms of distancing that result in a readiness to repudiate or ignore or even destroy forces that are seen as somehow dangerous to the self. They may result in an intense and devoted attachment to a set of ideas or ideology, a group, a cause, or even a leader— all of which by implication involve repudiation of other causes, groups, leaders, etcetera. Attachment to such causes or groups may take on some of the as-if characteristics or even evolve into a false-self configuration. The attachment to and repudiation of groups, leaders, causes, and ideologies may attain an almost paranoid flavor, even as these processes always involve identifiable paranoid mechanisms, particularly the interplay of projections and more or less primitive introjections (Meissner 1978b). The failure of these devices, however, may lead such individuals in a position of withdrawal to a position of constant self-questioning and introspective uncertainty, a need for constant and doubtful self-testing that can result in an almost paralyzing borderline state in which there is an increasing sense of isolation, a loss of a sense of identity, a deep sense of inner uncertainty and shame, an inability to derive any sense of accomplishment from external activities, or a feeling that one is the victim of circumstances and forces beyond one's control, without any sense of initiative or responsibility for the direction of one's own fate.

There may in fact be a retreat to an identification with the victim-introject as a convenient escape from the uncertainties and emptiness of identity diffusion. Moreover, the narcissistic aspects of this configuration should not be missed. There are protests of potential greatness, missed opportunities, a need to cling omnipotently to a sense of the availability of all possibilities and an unwillingness to sacrifice any possibilities or limit any potentialities in the inevitable determination and self-limitation of specific choice. There is a fear of engagement, a reluctance to compete or assert oneself as separate and individual, a fear of time and its passage, and a constant vacillating doubt and uncertainty, an unwillingness to choose that often looks obsessional but is in fact driven by motivations of a different order.

Such conflicts may also express themselves in the form of adolescent or late adolescent crises; these patients may be willing enough and reasonably successful in playing the role of the student, the one who is only learning and preparing in some tentative and uncommitted way for a possible future career, or that of the diligent apprentice or graduate assistant; yet when the issues of choice and self-direction emerge as they inevitably must, there is considerable difficulty in making that commitment, whether it be to write a thesis, to apply for a job, to marry, to father a child, etcetera. It should be noted that identity diffusion and the accompanying chaos in the sense of self reflects an inability to establish a stable self-concept and, correlatively, a lack of integration of internalized object derivatives (Kernberg 1967, 1970b). The emergence, establishment, and consolidation of a consistent and coherent sense of identity is related to the integrity and cohesiveness of the self and depends upon the capacity for positive and constructive identifications. To the extent that the sense of identity is vulnerable and lacks cohesion, it reflects the internal organization of introjects that are sufficiently embedded in issues of conflict and defense to prevent meaningful or substantial integration. The diffusion of identity is not to be regarded as equivalent to the loss of identity that occurs in psychotic fusions or delusional states of merger with the object. Such severe psychotic regressive states of merger and fusion entail primitive operations of incorporation (Meissner 1971).

An important question is the extent to which identity diffusion is an aspect of all of the borderline conditions, particularly in regard to regressive borderline states. This is undoubtedly a prominent feature of such regressions and must be regarded as correlative to the acute disorganization and loss of cohesion in the organization of the self. However, it is suggested here that identity diffusion can take a more characterologic form and may represent a more or less persistent personality configuration that is capable of separate and differential diagnosis. It should not be left out of consideration, however, that under the impetus of developmental pressures, or external pressures stemming from environmental situations or life conditions, or other possible modifying influences, the configuration may evolve into other forms of borderline adjustment. The availability to the patient afflicted with identity diffusion of resolutions of the as-if or false-self variety are considerably greater than resolutions of the borderline or schizoid type. Although these latter forms of resolution are less available and less frequently observed, they remain nonetheless possible. Similarly, identity diffusion rarely if ever shifts into the configuration of the psychotic character or the pseudoneurotic schizophrenic.

In sum, then, the identity diffusion represents a form of character pathology that involves an impairment of meaningful identifications and an inability in self-definition. The pathology does not reside in the ego or even superego as much as in the organization and delineation of the self. There is a defect in what Federn called "ego feeling" (Krohn 1974). There is a complex interplay with object relations conflicts related to the incapacity to define or commit oneself. On a primitive genetic level, however, the underlying fears have to do with the threat imposed in separation and individuation and the surrender of infantile objects and one's dependence on them. Ultimately, commitment to a life, whether of work or of love, means to accept limitations and change, the surrender of infantile omnipotence and narcissistic entitlement, and the ultimate acceptance of the finitude of human existence and death. Maintaining the self in a posture of persistent uncertainty, lack of definition and commitment, is to maintain a condition of continuing possibility and a denial of the necessity to ultimately come to terms with the demands and expectations of reality.

The four categories of personality disturbance composing the schizoid continuum can be regarded as variant modalities of dealing with the same underlying problem, namely the incapacity to establish and maintain a coherent and individuated sense of self in the face of a powerful need for and dependence on objects that is accompanied by a fear of loss of or dissolution of self posed by attachment to that object. Thus the respective entities, identity diffusion, the as-if personality, the schizoid personality, and the false-self organization are all struggling with a form of need–fear dilemma; all suffer from impediments of libidinal object constancy and represent variant modalities of the attempt to come to terms with this underlying set of object-related conflicts.

The schizoid personality resolves the conflict by affective withdrawal and the preservation of self by defensive avoidance of object involvement. The false-self personality resolves the conflict by a protective withdrawal of the true self in a truly schizoid manner and a compliant compromise with reality through the false-self facade. The as-if personality resolves the conflict by adopting a superficial, transient, imitative involvement with objects that equivalently minimizes real, meaningful, or enduring commitment to an object relationship. The as-if adjustment can be taken as a more fragmentary, transient, and superficial version of the false-self organization. Finally, the resolution of the conflict in identity diffusion is achieved by the maintenance of inner ambiguity and the avoidance of self-definition.

The schizoid continuum therefore shares certain characteristics that offer some differentiation from the hysterical continuum, although considerable overlap, or even shifting, within the continuum is clinically evident. There is generally, besides the sense of withdrawal and isolation, a rigidity of defenses and a resistance to regression that is quite different from the hysterical continuum. This is more true of the schizoid personality and the false-self organization, whose defensive organization is well maintained in the face of regressive pressures. The as-if personality is more likely to show regressive features, but these are easily absorbed in a new as-if configuration. Regression in cases of identity diffusion may be countered by increased schizoid withdrawal or by retreat to a negative or pseudo-identity (as, for example, in fanatic adherence to a "cause"). These patients tend to show a much higher titre of what has been described as borderline compliance (Robbins 1976).

In the treatment of such patients, the relatively rapid mobilization of transference paradigms seen so characteristically in patients from the hysterical continuum is more exceptional in the schizoid continuum. The difficulty with these patients lies much more in the direction of gaining any degree of meaningful object involvement. Although they are dealing with the same borderline issues, these patients tend to respond with varying degrees of withdrawal or lack of involvement, even though this may at times be marked by or mixed with superficial compliance. The analyst is forced to wait a long time before meaningful contact with the patient's inner self becomes possible. Thus, while the problem with patients in the hysterical continuum tends to be that the analytic relationship and the therapeutic alliance are inundated by transference distortions driven by an intense clinging need and dependence, the problem with the schizoid continuum tends to take the opposite form of withdrawal from any meaningful transference involvement. The result is that not only the therapeutic alliance, but the transference as well, are difficult to establish and maintain. Thus it can be inferred that the therapeutic problem and approach will differ considerably for these respective dimensions of borderline pathology.

SUMMARY AND CONCLUSIONS

The present differential diagnosis of the borderline conditions is an attempt to impose a greater degree of order on a sometimes chaotic and confusing picture. The differentiation has its weakness insofar as it is based on a narrow range of experience and primarily on clinical impressions. There is need for systematic study and evaluation of such differentiations on much larger patient populations in order to establish the potential validity of these groupings. The difficulties inherent in finding sufficiently large numbers of patients and of subjecting them to adequate diagnostic scrutiny should not be underestimated. Many of the differentiations involved here require long-term experience with the patient and a reasonably intense setting to allow for the important discriminators to emerge, particularly those having to do with the experience within the transference.

If this differentiation proves supportable, there would seem to be important implications to be drawn for the understanding of borderline pathology. There are certainly theoretical implications, since the nature, degree, and location of the pathology in various categories differ and are subject to a considerable range of variation. Thus the understanding of the pathology involved in the as-if personality must be considerably different from that involved in the understanding of the borderline personality or the psychotic character. Previous theoretical attempts have tried to span too wide a clinical gulf and consequently, to that extent have had only limited success and limited explanatory power (Meissner, 1978c).

There is also the question of levels of psychopathology. Although a rough organization can be described in terms of levels of psychopathology, it must be remembered that these differentiations are within a common grouping of disorders, all of which share certain characteristics and each of which may function at a more or less integrated level of personality functioning. In the differentiation presented here, clearly the pseudoschizophrenic group is the most primitively organized. The primitive hysteric may generally be the best organized and best functioning of all, although even here there is the presence of borderline characteristics that may carry poor prognostic and therapeutic implications nonetheless.

There is also a broad discrimination that can be suggested to be related to forms of pathology. A distinction can be drawn between those conditions marked by affective liability and availability in which the affect becomes more intense, conflicted, and disorganized with increasing pathology, leading toward increasing disorganization and destructuring of personality functions. Opposed to these conditions are those that are marked by affective restraint and control in which affect becomes increasingly withdrawn and isolated with greater pathology, leading in the direction of increasing retreat from object involvement and a rigidity and hyperstructuralization of personality organization. The dichotomy runs between a basically hysterical continuum and an obsessional or schizoid continuum. The former continuum is characterized by affective lability and increasing disorganization, and leads from the hysterical character at the highest level (Zetzel's true hysteric) through the primitive hysteric to the borderline personality, and at even lower levels of character pathology to the psychotic character and the pseudoneurotic schizophrenic. The latter continuum follows the obsessional line from the obsessional character neurosis toward increasing degrees of withdrawal and rigidity of structure in the schizoid grouping, through the as-if personality, the false-self organization, and finally the schizoid personality in which withdrawal and rigidity are most pronounced and pervasive.

A relevant question is whether, in the decompensation or therapeutic progression of the borderline conditions, they may not follow along the lines of these respective continua. Does the primitive hysteric regress in the direction of the borderline personality? Does the psychotic character make therapeutic progress through a phase in which he or she resembles the borderline personality?—and further moves in the direction of a primitive hysterical integration? Does the severely isolated and withdrawn schizoid evolve toward healthier functioning toward a potential false-self configuration? These suggestions must be left as questionable speculations.

In any case, one cannot assume that any progression in levels of organization carries with it direct implications for prognosis without taking other factors into account such as those spelled out in considerable detail by Kernberg (1971). The prognostic indicators are likewise closely related to indications of optimal therapeutic approach, but it must be stressed that such indications require more subtle and detailed diagnostic considerations for each individual patient and cannot rest simply on diagnostic categorization.

REFERENCES

Adler, G. (1970). Valuing and devaluing in the psychotherapeutic process. *Archives of General Psychiatry* 22:454–461.

————. (1975). The usefulness of the "borderline" concept in psychotherapy. In *Borderline States in Psychiatry*, ed. J. E. Mack, pp. 29–40. New York: Grune and Stratton.

Arlow, J. A. (1966). Depersonalization and derealization. In *Psychoanalysis—A General Psychology*, eds. R. M. Loewenstein, L. M. Newman, M. Schur, and A. J. Solnit, pp. 456–478. New York: International Universities Press.

Atkin, S. (1974). A borderline case: ego synthesis and cognition. *International Journal of Psycho-Analysis* 55:13–19.

Blum, H. P. (1972). Psychoanalytic understanding and psychotherapy of borderline regression. *International Journal of Psychoanalytic Psychotherapy* 1:46–60.

Brody, E. B. (1960). Borderline state, character disorder, and psychotic manifestations—some conceptual formulations. *Psychiatry* 23:75–80.

Bychowski, G. (1953). The problem of latent psychosis. *Journal of the American Psychoanalytic Association* 1:484–503.

Chessick, R. D. (1974). Defective ego feeling and the quest for being in the borderline patient. *International Journal of Psychoanalytic Psychotherapy* 3:73–89.

Collum, J. M. (1972). Identity diffusion and the borderline maneuver. *Comprehensive Psychiatry* 13:179–184.

Deniker, P., and Quintart, J. C. (1961). Les signes pseudo-néurotiques dans les formes limites de la schizophrénie. *Encéphale* 50:307–323.

Deutsch, H. (1942). Some forms of emotional disturbances and their relationship to schizophrenia. In *Neuroses and Character Types*, pp. 262–281. New York: International Universities Press, 1965.

————. (1955). The imposter: contribution to ego psychology of a type of psychopath. In *Neuroses and Character Types*, pp. 319–338. New York: International Universities Press, 1965.

Dickes, R. (1974). The concepts of borderline states: an alternative proposal. *International Journal of Psychoanalytic Psychotherapy* 3:1–27.

Ekstein, R., and Wallerstein, J. (1954). Observations on the psychology of borderline and psychotic children. *Psychoanalytic Study of the Child* 9:344–369.

Erikson, E. H. (1956). The problem of ego identity. *Journal of the American Psychoanalytic Association* 4:56–121.

Fast, I. (1974). Multiple identities in the borderline personality organization. *British Journal of Medical Psychology* 47:291–300.

————. (1975). Aspects of work style and work difficulty in borderline personalities. *International Journal of Psycho-Analysis* 56:397–403.

Frijling-Schreuder, E. C. M. (1969). Borderline states in children. *Psychoanalytic Study of the Child* 24:307–327.

Frosch, J. (1964). The psychotic character: Clinical psychiatric considerations. *Psychoanalytic Quarterly* 38:81–96.

———. (1967a). Severe regressive states during analysis: introduction. *Journal of the American Psychoanalytic Association* 15:491–507.

———. (1967b). Severe regressive states during analysis: summary. *Journal of the American Psychoanalytic Association* 15:606–625.

———. (1970). Psychoanalytic considerations of the psychotic character. *Journal of the American Psychoanalytic Association* 18:24–50.

Giovacchini, P. L. (1965). Transference, incorporation and synthesis. *International Journal of Psycho-Analysis* 46:287–296.

———. (1972). Technical difficulties in treating some characterological disorders: countertransference problems. *International Journal of Psychoanalytic Psychotherapy* 1:112–128.

———. (1973). Character disorders; with special reference to the borderline state. *International Journal of Psychoanalytic Psychotherapy* 2:7–36.

Greenson, R. R. (1958). On screen defenses, screen hunger and screen identity. *Journal of the American Psychoanalytic Association* 6:242–262.

Grinker, R. R., Werble, B., and Drye, R. C. (1968). *The Borderline Syndrome: A Behavioral Study of Ego Functions.* New York: Basic Books.

Gunderson, J. G., Carpenter, W. T., and Strauss, J. S. (1975). Borderline and schizophrenic patients: a comparative study. *American Journal of Psychiatry* 132:1257–1264.

Gunderson, J. G., and Singer, M. T. (1975). Defining borderline patients: an overview. *American Journal of Psychiatry* 132:1–10.

Guntrip, H. (1969). *Schizoid Phenomena, Object Relations and the Self.* New York: International Universities Press.

Hoch, P. H., and Cattell, J. P. (1959). The diagnosis of pseudoneurotic schizophrenia. *Psychoanalytic Quarterly* 23:17–43.

Hoch, P. H., Cattell, J. P., Strahl, M. O., and Pennes, H. (1962). The course and outcome of pseudoneurotic schizophrenia. *American Journal of Psychiatry* 119:106–115.

Hoch, P. H., and Polatin, P. (1949). Pseudoneurotic forms of schizophrenia. *Psychoanalytic Quarterly* 23:248–276.

Katan, M. (1959). Comments on "ego distortion." *International Journal of Psycho-Analysis* 40:297–303.

Kernberg, O. F. (1966). Structural derivatives of object-relationships. *International Journal of Psycho-Analysis* 47:236–253.

———. (1967). Borderline personality organization. *Journal of the American Psychoanalytic Association* 40:641–685.

———. (1968). The treatment of patients with borderline personality organization. *International Journal of Psycho-Analysis* 49:600–619.

———. (1970a). Factors in the psychoanalytic treatment of narcissistic personalities. *Journal of the American Psychoanalytic Association* 18:51–85.

———. (1970b). A psychoanalytic classification of character pathology. *Journal of the American Psychoanalytic Association* 18:800–822.

———. (1971). Prognostic considerations regarding borderline personality organization. *Journal of the American Psychoanalytic Association* 19:595–635.

———. (1975). *Borderline Conditions and Pathological Narcissism.* New York: Jason Aronson.

———. (1976). Technical considerations in the treatment of borderline personality organization. *Journal of the American Psychoanalytic Association* 24:795–829.

Khan, M. M. (1960). Clinical aspects of the schizoid personality: affects and technique. *International Journal of Psycho-Analysis* 41:430–437.

Knight, R. P. (1953). Borderline states. In *Psychoanalytic Psychiatry and Psychology*, ed. R. P. Knight, pp. 97–109. New York: International Universities Press, 1954.

Kohut, H. (1971). *The Analysis of the Self*. New York: International Universities Press.

Krohn, A. (1974). Borderline "empathy" and differentiation of object representations: a contribution to the psychology of object relations. *International Journal of Psychoanalytic Psychotherapy* 3:142–165.

Little, M. (1958). On delusional transference (transference psychosis). *International Journal of Psycho-Analysis* 39:134–138.

———. (1966). Transference in borderline states. *International Journal of Psycho-Analysis* 47:476–485.

Maenchen, A. (1968). Object cathexis in a borderline twin. *Psychoanalytic Study of the Child* 23:438–456.

Marmor, J. (1953). Orality in the hysterical personality. *Journal of the American Psychoanalytic Association* 1:656–671.

Masterson, J. F. (1972). *Treatment of the Borderline Adolescent: A Developmental Approach*. New York: John Wiley.

Meissner, W. W. (1971). Notes on identification. II. Clarification of related concepts. *Psychoanalytic Quarterly* 40:277–302.

———. (1974). The role of imitative social learning in identificatory processes. *Journal of the American Psychoanalytic Association* 22:512–536.

———. (1976). Psychotherapeutic schema based on the paranoid process. *International Journal of Psychoanalytic Psychotherapy* 5:87–114.

———. (1978a). Notes on some conceptual aspects of borderline personality organization. *International Review of Psycho-Analysis* 5:297–311.

———. (1978b). *The Paranoid Process*. New York: Jason Aronson.

———. (1978c). Theoretical assumptions of concepts of the borderline personality. *Journal of the American Psychoanalytic Association* 26:559–598.

———. Notes on the levels of differentiation within borderline conditions. *Psychoanalytic Review* (in press).

Modell, A. H. (1963). Primitive object-relationships and the predisposition to schizophrenia. *International Journal of Psycho-Analysis* 44:282–292.

———. (1968). *Object Love and Reality*. New York: International Universities Press.

———. (1975). A narcissistic defense against affects and the illusion of self-sufficiency. *International Journal of Psycho-Analysis* 56:275–282.

Perry, J. C., and Klerman, G. L. (1978). The borderline patient: a comparative analysis of four sets of diagnostic criteria. *Archives of General Psychiatry* 35:141–150.

Pine, F. (1974). On the concept of "borderline" in children: a clinical essay. *The Psychoanalytic Study of the Child* 29:341–368.

Rangell, L. (1955). The borderline case (panel report). *Journal of the American Psychoanalytic Association* 3:285–298.

Reich, A. (1953). Narcissistic object choice in women. *Journal of the American Psychoanalytic Association* 1:22–44.

Reich, W. (1933). *Character Analysis*, 3rd ed. New York: Farrar, Straus and Giroux, 1949.

Robbins, L. L. (1956). The borderline case (panel report). *Journal of the American Psychoanalytic Association* 4:550–562.

Robbins, M. D. (1976). Borderline personality organization: the need for a new theory. *Journal of the American Psychoanalytic Association* 24:831–853.

Rosenfeld, S. K., and Sprince, M. P. (1963). An attempt to formulate the meaning of the concept "borderline." *Psychoanalytic Study of the Child* 18:603–635.

Ross, N. (1967). The "as-if" personality. *Journal of the American Psychoanalytic Association* 15:59–82.

Stone, M. H. (1976). Manic-depression found in subtle symptoms. *Psychiatric News*, December 3, 1976, pp. 28–29.

Weingarten, L. L., and Korn, S. (1967). Pseudoneurotic schizophrenia: psychological test findings. *Archives of General Psychiatry* 17:448–453.

Winnicott, D. (1960). Ego distortion in terms of true and false self. In *The Maturational Processes and the Facilitating Environment*, pp. 140–152. New York: International Universities Press.

Wittels, F. (1930). The hysterical character. *Medical Review of Reviews* 36:186.

Zetzel, E. R. (1968). The so-called good hysteric. *International Journal of Psycho-Analysis* 49:256–260.

———. (1971). A developmental approach to the borderline patient. *American Journal of Psychiatry* 127:867–871.

Zetzel, E. R., and Meissner, W. W. (1973). *Basic Concepts of Psychoanalytic Psychiatry*. New York: Basic Books.

Zilboorg, G. (1941). Ambulatory schizophrenias. *Psychiatry* 4:149–155.

———. (1956). The problem of ambulatory schizophrenia. *American Journal of Psychiatry* 113:519–525.

———. (1957). Further observations on ambulatory schizophrenias. *American Journal of Orthopsychiatry* 27:677–682.

Definitive Treatment
of the Borderline Personality

DAN H. BUIE, M.D.
GERALD ADLER, M.D.

A discussion of "Notes on the Potential Differentiation of Borderline Conditions," by W. W. Meissner, M.D. Through psychotherapy, borderline personalities can develop a mature level of emotional autonomy. Their fundamental psychopathology involves annihilation anxiety consequent on inadequacy and instability of holding-soothing introjects. Psychological corollaries of this deficit render them unable to effect the internalization of real caring relationships that is necessary for development of effective holding introjects. Ideally, psychotherapy proceeds in three phases. Phase I is devoted to amelioration of the pathological impediments to using relationships with the therapist and others as resources for a holding-soothing form of emotional security. The outcome is development of a relatively stable idealized self-object transference in terms of holding-soothing, along with formation of relatively stable idealized holding-soothing introjects. Phase II of treatment involves optimal disillusionment in relation to idealization of the therapist as holding-soother; this results in gradual acceptance of the realistic use of external objects along with modification of holding-soothing introjects to correspond more nearly with reality. Stable autonomy in the area of self-security is fully attained in Phase III, in which the relationship with the therapist provides the context for the patient's developing capacities by means of identification to care for, esteem, love, and trust himself or herself. Psychotherapy of narcissistic issues is also important, but special precautions must be observed.

Clinical experience with patients designated "borderline" (Kernberg 1967, Grinker et al. 1968, Gunderson and Singer 1975) indicates that this diagnostic category comprises a heterogeneous group, portions of which are more effectively treatable than others. Meissner's current paper very usefully describes this heterogeneity and offers tentative groupings of patients who share differentiating characteristics. His work delineates a particular group, the "borderline personality," which corresponds to a series of patients who have captured interest because they are characterized by a developmental defect that is definitively treatable. That is, unlike "borderlines" as seen by Zetzel (1971) and Friedman (1975), patients whose reality-testing and affect tolerance are too tenuous to allow intensive therapeutic work, these patients are able to maintain enough therapeutic alliance and ego stability to evolve in intensive psychotherapy from a chronic state of unfulfillable dependency to a mature level of autonomy.

It would be well to review Meissner's theoretical delineation of the border-line personality, both to provide an overview of the kind of patients that will be discussed here and to provide a clear counterpoint to certain of the present authors' views, which emphasize different elements of psychopathology as more fundamental. His description is in terms of ego psychology, object relations theory, psychology of the self, and the nature of regressive episodes.

Except in regressive episodes, the borderline personality maintains a relatively good level of functioning and adaptation to reality, along with a relatively firm sense of reality, feeling of reality, and testing of reality. There is, however, some degree of ego instability and weakness, often manifested by a nonspecific diminution of impulse control with a tendency to direct expression of impulses. When not regressed, defenses operate at a relatively high level, with use of repression and other higher order defenses as well as lower order defenses in a manner essentially similar to that found in neurosis. Splitting of the type Kernberg (1967) describes is usually not apparent. Capacity for sublimation is considerable. (It should be added to Meissner's description that these patients have established themselves in personally meaningful pursuits, such as education or a profession, that serve as resources for emotional sustenance and reinforcement of ego integrity. They have also developed significant healthy identifications.) Anxiety tends to be free-floating but of a signal type; qualitatively it relates to castration and separation, but not to annihilation. (This point will be questioned later in the present paper.) Inclination to primary process organization, disorganization of thought, or formal thought disorder is no greater than in higher levels of character formation.

The capacity for object constancy is tenuous and, although object constancy is relatively well maintained, it remains vulnerable. Relationships with objects are of a need-gratifying nature and are influenced by often intense narcissistic needs. Objects are constantly sought to allay a sense of inner emptiness; fear of abandonment is conscious and explicit. At the same time, a need–fear dilemma is subtly pervasive, and no object can satisfy these needs. The predominant focus of pathology lies in the organization of introjects and the correlative constituents of the self. The pathogenic alignments of these elements center on one or another of two issues. One issue is expressed in the duality of victim-introject and aggressor-introject (Meissner

1978). The other issue is narcissistic, involving grandiosity and inferiority. These contradictory introjective, ego, and self configurations are relatively conscious, but the capacity to integrate them is inadequate. The failure of integration constitutes a kind of "splitting" that exists between the various alignments of introjective configurations with their correlated ego and self constituents. The interplay of projection and introjection of these introjective and self configurations to some extent continually distorts experience with the interpersonal environment. This becomes especially clear in the developing transference, which evolves in the form of a transitional object relationship (Modell 1968).

Although functioning generally in a fairly well-integrated fashion, cohesiveness of the self remains tenuous because of the failure of integration of contradictory introjective components around which the self is organized. This is reflected in the splitting noted above, along with a tendency to alternate between the various introjective and corresponding self configurations. (It should be added that cohesiveness of the self is also tenuous because of narcissistic vulnerability of the type described by Kohut [1971, 1977].)

Regression emerges gradually as the therapeutic relationship progressively develops. (Regression can also occur precipitously in the context of stress arising out of the visissitudes of involvement with objects outside the therapeutic relationship.) With regression, intensive affects of hostility, destructiveness, and depression are unleashed. These affects derive from the inner organization of victim-introject and corresponding aggressor-introject. It is only under these circumstances that there emerges a full use of primitive defenses, e.g., denial, splitting of the type Kernberg describes, primitive idealization, projection and projective identification, omnipotence, and devaluation. There may be brief psychotic episodes, usually of a paranoid nature, sometimes involving schizophrenic symptoms.

This view of the borderline personality takes note of a tenuousness of object constancy with an attendant sense of emptiness and fear of abandonment; it also notes the pervasiveness of a need–fear dilemma. However, it emphasizes the pathological organization of introjects as the most fundamental psychopathology. It is on this point that the present authors' view differs from Meissner's. Like Meissner, many authors (e.g., Kernberg 1967, Masterson 1976, Volkan 1976) consider the quality and organization of introjects to be most central in borderline psychopathology. They are important; however, more crucial to borderline psychopathology and more significant for treatment is a deficit as well as instability of certain kinds of introjects and identifications that are needed to sustain the psychological self (Adler and Buie 1979). Pathogenic experiences with primary objects are responsible for the relative failure of development of these introjects and identifications, and the need–fear dilemma is responsible for inability to make use of subsequent caring relationships to achieve the development of introjects that life experience had orginally thwarted.

The present paper is concerned with definitive treatment for the borderline personality, a treatment that promotes intrapsychic structural development to redress this developmental failure, correct developmental abnormalities related to maintenance of narcissistic balance, correct pathological organization of introjects, and provide insight and working through of a variety of neurotic issues. It is, however, impossible in this account to cover all the psychopathological elements that must receive therapeutic attention. Neurotic issues require no special comment; they can be approached in standard ways once basic borderline and narcissistic problems have been adequately resolved. The treatment process in regard to pathological organization of introjects can involve many well-known approaches, including one recently advocated by Meissner (1976). Treatment of the narcissistic sector of the borderline personality will be addressed only insofar as it interrelates with the most fundamental problem. Otherwise, the understanding and treatment of narcissistic disorders as elucidated by Kohut (1966, 1971, 1977) is quite applicable. In this paper, then, the focus will be almost entirely on definitive treatment of that sector of the borderline personality that the present authors' believe to be its primary feature. It will be referred to as the primary sector of borderline personality psychopathology. Although the theoretical and clinical accounts will be focused accordingly, they should not be taken as a depiction of the whole patient or the whole treatment process.

DEVELOPMENT OF TRANSITIONAL OBJECTS AND STRUCTURAL COMPONENTS OF THE INNER WORLD

Those theories concerning the ways in which the infant and child gain significant autonomy in maintaining a sense of security are particularly germaine. Two qualities of experience are especially involved. One is narcissistic, having to do with feelings of personal value. The other, more fundamental quality of experience is described by the terms "holding" and "soothing." In infancy the subjective sense of being soothingly held requires the caretaking of a "good enough mother" (Winnicott 1953, 1960). To some extent real interpersonal relationships always remain a resource for psychological holding, but with development certain intrapsychic structures play an increasingly prominent role. The advent of object representations provides a means by which resources of soothing-holding can be recognized and, eventually, sought out in the environment. Transitional objects are "created" (Winnicott 1953) in part from intrapsychic components. Later on, the holding function of external objects (and transitional objects [Tolpin 1971]) is internalized in the form of introjects. Finally, identifications with these functions of external objects and introjects yield structural components of the ego that serve the same purpose. In these ways the infant, child, adolescent, and adult become increasingly able to provide a subjective sense of security to themselves from their own intrapsychic resources, depending less and less on the environment for it.

Object Representations

The conceptualizations of "object representation" and "introject" are important in these formulations. Because they are used differently by different authors, their meaning in the present context is noted here. "Representation" signifies a construction with purely cognitive and memory components, not in itself containing affective, libidinal, or aggressive qualities, and performing no active functions (Sandler and Rosenblatt 1962, Meissner 1971). Such representations correspond to Sandler's (1960) concept of "schemata," i.e., intrapsychic "models" of objects and self (p. 147). He ascribes formation of schemata (object representation and self representations) to the "organizing activity" of the ego (pp. 146–147).

Holding Introjects

Conceptualization of introjection and introjects is drawn especially from the studies of Meissner (1971, 1978). Introjection is a means of internalizing object relationships, especially as they play a part in gratifying instincts and fulfilling survival needs. Introjects are the internal structures thus created for the purpose of carrying on these functional qualities of external objects in relationship to the self. For the purposes of this paper, a simplified view of introjects, likening them to internal presences of external objects, is adopted. Introjects, as such, are experienced as separate from the subjectively sensed self (Schafer 1968), functioning quasi-autonomously in relation to the self, and exercising influence on the self, with the self in a dynamic relationship with them.

Concepts of introjection and introjects are in fact quite complex, especially as they involve projective processes that endow introjects with qualities derived from the self as well as from external objects and as they relate to internal modifications of the self. However, the focus here is on one particular kind of introject, one that promotes in the self a feeling of being soothingly held and that is termed a "holding introject." For greater clarity, this kind of introject is described in a more simplified manner because, in dealing with the borderline personality, the concern is with levels of development at a time in infancy when the inherent capacity for self-soothing is very slight and can provide little resource for a projective contribution to forming holding introjects. Therefore, at this level of development, one can apply a paradigm of the introject as a straightforwardly internalized structure that acts as a resource to the self for holding. (Later on, in normal development and in definitive treatment of borderline personality, introjective processes— and identificatory processes as well—promote modifications of the self such that it takes on attributes of its holding resources. In this way, internal resources are developed for holding, which are more or less integrated with the subjective ego core. These can then serve as contributions via projection to the further formation of holding introjects.)

Incorporation and Fusion

"Incorporation" is viewed as designating the mode by which one person while in the presence of another experiences the other person as if "inside" himself or herself, yielding a sense of that person's qualities, e.g., warmth or inspired thinking, as if they were merging into his or her own self. Meissner writes of incorporation as "the most primitive, least differentiated form of internalization in which the object loses its distinction as object and becomes totally taken in to the inner subject world" (1971, p. 287). Operationally this would be accomplished through volitional suspension of attention to the delimiting contours of the other person's psychological, and perhaps even physical, self. While incorporation can be described as primitive in terms of modes of internalization, in the mature adult it constitutes, along with fusion (see below), a means by which the experience of intimacy is attained.

Incorporation is the means by which the infant, toddler, and adult attain an inner suffusion of soothing warmth from the presence of an external holding object. (Of course, prior to differentiation of self from object this incorporative experience is not under elective control.) When memory capacities develop, these incorporative experiences can be remembered and can have, as Meissner (1971) noted, a structuralizing influence. This structuralizing is conceived here as proceeding from memory schemata that are organized into merged self and object representations and can then be developed further to introject status through introjection of the external object's functional contribution to the incorporative experience. Further structuralization can occur through identification, by means of which the ego develops a pattern of functioning like that of the introject.

Fusion would seem to be the counterpart of incorporation, in which one's self is felt as merging into the emotional, and perhaps physical, being of another person. For persons who developmentally have achieved differentiation of self from objects, fusion would seem to involve volitional decathexis of ego, and even physical body, boundaries. Like incorporation, it is a means of gaining a sense of intermixing with qualities of someone else. As phenomena of object relating, both introjection and fusion are important in experiences of intimacy, and they can occur together. Perhaps the experience of fusion can in itself contribute an influence on structuralizing process.

These comments on incorporation and fusion are particularly relevant in discussion of the borderline personality because of their importance in sustaining the self, in influencing the formation of introjects, and, as will soon be discussed, in posing a seeming threat to survival.

The Inner World

The concept of the inner world as elaborated by Hartmann (1939) and Rapaport (1967) is useful in thinking about psychopathology and therapeutic work with borderline personalities. The concept holds much in common with that of the representational world as described by Sandler and Rosenblatt (1962).

While ideas about the inner world are very complex, it is viewed more simply here as a kind of psychological internal environment that contains, among other things, self and object representations and introjects. The inner world is not included in the subjective sense of self.

Development of Memory, Transitional Objects, and the Inner World

It is reasonable to assume that memory configurations are basic to the means by which the infant and toddler gain some autonomous capacity for providing themselves with a sense of being soothingly held. Piaget (1937) described six stages in the infant's development of an "object concept," two of which bear particularly on this discussion. Stage IV begins at about age eight months. At this point the infant first gains the capacity to recognize an object as familiar even though he or she cannot yet evoke the memory of the object without the aid of visual cues. Fraiberg (1969) terms this capacity "recognition memory." Its development makes possible the beginnings of an inner world of object representations, one that allows the infant to recognize his or her mother as familiar, and on that basis experience a sense of inner soothing. At the same time not-mother is also now recognized as not familiar, resulting in stranger-anxiety (Fraiberg 1969).

The development of recognition memory also coincides chronologically with the beginning use of transitional objects (Winnicott 1953). The creation of transitional objects depends upon recognition-memory capacity. Since the holding function of the mother is especially effected through the medium of touch, it is hypothesized here that the infant is enabled to maintain ongoing awareness of the recognition-memory schema of his or her soothing-touching mother through actually holding and feeling the touch of a familiar object that reminds the infant of mother's touch. Simultaneously this object, the transitional object, serves as an actual resource, by way of the infant's manipulations, of sensory stimulations that, when combined with the sustained memory of the mother, are adequate to induce actual soothing.

Stage VI of object concept development begins at about eighteen months of age. At this time the infant gains the capacity to remember an object without being reminded of its existence by external cues. Fraiberg (1969) terms this achievement "evocative memory." According to Sandler and Rosenblatt (1962), the development of the representational world depends on this degree of memory capacity; it might be said that at this time the formation of continuously available object representations commences. These would be equivalent to Sandler's (1960) schemata, which are derived through the organizing activity of the ego. Object representations are the prerequisite for introject formation and serve as the substrate for introjects. Sandler's concept, originally applied to superego formation, can be utilized here. Accordingly, it may be hypothesized that the object representation is converted to introject status through internalization (introjection) of the influential functions (attitudes, affects, and impulses) of the persons after whom the object representation is patterned. The former schema now takes on a functional capacity. As an introject it can perform for the self certain functions, e.g., holding, that previously were performed by external objects.

The holding introject derived from the relationship with the soothing mother enables the toddler to manage for a while out of the sight of and at some distance from his or her mother without suffering separation anxiety (Mahler et al. 1975). Over time, holding introjects are progressively stablized; to some extent they remain important resources throughout life against depression or anxiety that would result from separations.

The acquisition of enduring holding introjects puts the toddler or child in a position to elect to give up the tangible transitional object. According to Winnicott the transitional object then becomes to some extent diffused into certain areas of experience with the external world, especially the area of culture. Experience with the transitional object can also be internalized in the form of an introject or an identification; according to Tolpin (1971) it is internalized by means of "transmuting internalization."

HOLDING SELF-OBJECTS, TRANSITIONAL OBJECTS, AND THE INNER WORLD OF THE BORDERLINE PERSONALITY

Fundamental Psychopathology of the Borderline Personality

The fundamental psychopathology of the borderline personality is in the nature of developmental failure. It is described in detail elsewhere (Adler and Buie 1979) and will only be summarized here. The developmental defect lies in failure to develop adequate internal resources for holding-soothing to meet the needs of adult life. Specifically, the formation of holding introjects is quantitatively inadequate, and those that have formed are not stable, being subject to regressive loss of function. Similarly, object representations of sources of holding, as well as use of transitional objects, are also vulnerable to regressive loss. The developmental failure appears to result from mothering that is not good enough during the phases of separation-individuation (Mahler 1971). While the toddler would be ready for the neuropsychological development of memory needed to form representations and introjects, the environment does not facilitate it. Just as good-enough mothering is required to form and maintain transitional objects (Winnicott 1953), so is it necessary for formation, maintenance, and finally solid establishment of holding representations and introjects. The inadequacy of mothering can be of many types, of course, ranging from traumatic unavoidable separations, to inconsistency of supportive presence, to the toddler's being subject to the mother's aversive anger and purposeful abandonment. The formation of the holding kind of representation and introject is especially affected; by and large hostile representations and introjects are abundant in the borderline personality's inner world. Perhaps the reason for the divergence is that the toddler's reactive hostility is a plentiful resource via projection for formation of negative representations and introjects. However, since the toddler possesses little innate resource for holding-soothing and must rely on good-enough mothering for it, when mothering is inadequate there is little experience available for formation of positive representations and introjects.

The consequences of inadequate internal resources for holding-soothing is the ever-present threat of separation anxiety. This is the quality of the free-floating anxiety that Meissner describes. It is generally experienced at the level of signal anxiety. However, his exclusion of annihilation as an issue is mistaken. For the borderline personality, as for any pathological condition to which separation anxiety is integral, the basic cause of the anxiety is the threat of loss of the self through psychological disintegration as a consequence of being abandoned. With the serious threat or condition of abandonment, the borderline personality's anxiety intensifies beyond the signal level and is experienced as a threat to the psychological self, i.e., a threat of annihilation. In a similar vein, Little (1966) writes about "annihilation anxiety" in the borderline patient.

Holding Self-Objects

Because their internal resources for holding-soothing are always inadequate, borderline personalities must depend in an ongoing way upon external objects to supplement them enough to keep their muted anxiety at a signal level and to maintain relative psychological stability. The term "self-object," which was first defined in relation to the use of objects by narcissistic personalities (Gedo and Goldberg 1973, Kohut 1977) is used to designate the various persons used for this purpose. The essence of the self-object is that it provides functions for another person that are necessary to maintenance of psychological integrity but cannot be adequately performed by the other person for himself or herself. To the extent that self-objects are internalized, they are represented in the inner world in the ways defined here. For the narcissistic personality the self-object is needed to maintain a sense of self-worth through providing a mirroring function or serving as an object of idealization. Failure of the self-object function threatens not only serious depression but also loss of cohesiveness of the self. For the borderline personality the self-object is required to provide forms of holding-soothing; otherwise the borderline is faced with the ultimate threat of disintegrative annihilation of the self. Here the borderline personality's self-object is referred to as a "holding self-object".

Hate and Regressive Loss of the Sustaining Inner World and Transitional Objects

By virtue of relatively good adaptation to reality and relatively good object-relating, the borderline personality by and large maintains sufficient interaction with holding self-objects to avoid intense separation anxiety. However, crises are precipitated when relating with self-objects becomes disturbed and, as Meissner notes, long-term engagement in psychotherapy induces a progressive and eventually intense emergence of psychopathology. In either case the impetus for regression is the failure of friend or psychotherapist to perform the holding function to the degree needed. This is experienced by the patient as a threat to his or her "entitlement to survive" (Buie and Adler 1972, p. 95), and there is no more assured way to induce murderous rage than this. The result of the rage is the compounding of the perceived external threat of abandonment with a greater or lesser degree of loss of internal resources for holding. This comes about in two ways.

One is purely psychodynamic and quite common. The patient feels the impulse to reject and destroy the offending therapist. In the regressed state he or she is more under the sway of primary process thinking, so that he or she tends to equate impulses and fantasies with fact. The patient feels as though he or she has evicted the felt image of the good therapist (the holding introject) from his or her subjective inner world. Moreover, the urge to destroy the therapist is felt as an accomplished act; this primitive mode of thinking about the external object is also reflected in his or her inner world, where the corresponding introject also seems lost.

The other way in which intense rage diminishes internal resources for holding is more important and is particular to borderline personality psychopathology. The rage induces a regressive loss of functional use of holding introjects, representations, and transitional objects by virtue of a regression of cognitive quality that specifically affects the memory foundations of these resources. The sequence of the regressive loss is the reverse of that of the development of these psychological entities. Thus the regression can extend through two levels. The first level is termed "recognition memory rage" because with enough separation anxiety and rage there is loss of evocative memory for the holding self-object. This is reflected in functional loss of both the holding introject and the sustaining object representation based on the self-object. In this sector of the inner world there seems quite literally to be a regression to Piaget's Stage IV of object-concept formation, with only recognition-memory available. At this point rage is directed at the self-object that is recognized as depriving. Nevertheless, use of the external holding self-object remains possible through direct interpersonal contact, and transitional objects also remain useful as resources for holding-soothing, depending as they do on at least a level of recognition-memory for their functioning. If the threat of separation anxiety and consequent rage are intensified even more, a second stage of regression is precipitated, in which the use of recognition memory is also lost. The external object is then no longer recognizable as a potential source of holding, and resort to transitional objects is no longer possible. This situation is termed "diffuse primitive rage," characterized as it is by the unchanneled, generalized discharge of hate and aggression. At this point separation anxiety becomes annihilation panic.

Loss of Cohesiveness of the Self

Although the borderline personality is subject to feeling vulnerable to annihilatory disintegration, ego strength is sufficiently developed to avoid it. (Less well-organized personalities, such as those Meissner terms pseudo-schizophrenic and psychotic character, are indeed subject to a psychological disintegration under circumstances of self-object loss that is similar to that described by Sacher et al. [1970] as ego disintegration.) The borderline personality is, however, subject to more severe manifestations of loss of self-cohesiveness (Adler 1981) than Kohut (1971) describes for narcissistic personalities. Cohesiveness of the self in borderline personalities is as dependent on an equilibrium of holding-soothing as it is on self-worth (as with narcissistic personalities), so that failures of holding in their relations with external objects can precipitate not only separation anxiety but also loss of cohesiveness of the self. The present authors have observed manifestations of this loss of cohesiveness especially as degrees of incoherency, or disjointedness of thinking, as feelings of loss of integration of body parts, as a subjective sense of losing functional control of the self, and as concerns about "falling apart." Disruption of self-cohesiveness in itself causes anxiety, but never of the intensity of annihilation panic.

INCORPORATION, FUSION, AND THE
NEED–FEAR DILEMMA

As mentioned earlier, incorporation and fusion are modes of intimacy by which a person can experience a feeling (e.g., soothing) as if through psychologically intermingling with a related quality (e.g., holding) of another person. Because of the relative dearth of holding introjects, the borderline personality must seek such intimacy with holding self-objects. When under the influence of intensified separation anxiety and when regressively deprived of the use of holding introjects, the impetus toward incorporation and fusion is urgent and mandatory. However, these modes of gaining soothing are also felt as presenting a threat of destruction to the self and/or the self-object, and the greater the need, the greater the felt threat becomes. When the borderline personality is in relatively good equilibrium, this threat is well controlled by adjusting interpersonal closeness: not too close to be too threatening, not too distant to be too alone. Sometimes the equilibrium is maintained by diffusing the sources among many self-objects, not allowing prolonged intimacy with any one of them. Or it may be possible to maintain a steady regulation of the degree of closeness within one or a few relationships. Or relating may be characterized by rather rapid oscillations back and forth between several relationships, each of which is experienced intensely for a brief time.

One threat that incorporation and fusion seem to pose arises out of the quality inherent in these experiences that involves loss of attention to the separate and defined existence of the self or the other. Under the influence of intense need, the awareness of the defined existence of self or self-object is sacrificed in the interest of maintaining the need-satisfying experience, but the price is bearing increasing anxiety about the destructive dissolution of the self or self-object that seems to be inherent in these modes of relating.

A greater threat resides for the borderline personality in that incorporation and fusion also involve oral-level impulses, and the more intense the need for soothing-holding, the more intensely are oral impulses mobilized. It is the impulse to eat or absorb the self-object concomitant with psychological incorporation that, in the fantasy representation of it, involves literal destructive consumption of the self-object. Similarly, the wish to be eaten or absorbed by the self-object concomitant with psychological fusion involves fantasy representation of literal destruction of the self. The more intense the need, the more intense are the impulses, wishes, and fantasies. The more regressed the patient, the more primary process dominates, to the point that the borderline personality can experience vivid fear because he or she believes that what must be done to avoid annihilation anxiety will only involve him or her in destroying the self-object upon which he or she depends for survival or in being destroyed himself or herself. With progress in psychotherapy these fears gradually emerge into consciousness. Along with fear, the patient must also deal with horror in finding cannibalistic impulses within himself or herself, especially as they are directed at people that he or she loves. While this need–fear dilemma is overtly evident only in a regressive state, especially as it occurs in the progressive course of treatment, at an unconscious level it pervades all relationships of a soothing-holding nature.

It is here that one finds the reason that the borderline personality has not been able to correct the developmental defect that is central to his or her psychopathology, even though he or she may have been involved in many trustworthy, caring relationships subsequent to early childhood. These fears, predominantly at the instinctual, but also at the object-relational, level, prevent the steady, trusting, soothing-holding relationship over time that constitutes the necessary facilitating environment.

ALONENESS: THE SUBJECTIVE EXPERIENCE ASSOCIATED WITH THE PRIMARY SECTOR OF BORDERLINE PSYCHOPATHOLOGY

In our terminology, loneliness is a state of yearning, often mixed with sadness. Like sadness, loneliness always carries with it the felt sense of the presence of the person or milieu longed for. In theoretical terms, a functional holding introject is prerequisite for loneliness, and for sadness as well. The pain arises from the real object not being available, and one must make do with the felt presence within while concomitantly wishing for the company of the real object. In contrast, aloneness is the experience that accompanies the need for a real holding (self-) object under circumstances of not having an adequately functioning holding introject. It is the experience of aloneness that is central to the borderline personality's subjective being. At its most intense it is felt as stark panic that threatens annihilation of the self, and with it the issue of separation is absolutely clear. When holding introjects are to some degree functional and some use can be made of holding self-objects, the feeling of aloneness is diminished. Repression also plays a role in muting it. But still, the unconscious feeling is there in some degree. It may be in the form that Chessick (1974) describes, a feeling of not being really alive, a sort of deadness that he terms, after Federn, a defective ego-feeling. In his observations the role of separateness, of the need for holding contact, is very clear. Masterson (1976) describes another form of what may be termed "attenuated aloneness," a "sense of void," which is a feeling of "terrifying inner emptiness or numbness." It may be added that the sense of void is often felt as pervading the environment too, so that one is surrounded by meaninglessness and emptiness.

These affective experiences could all be subsumed under the term depression, but it is a special quality of depression related to relative inadequacy of holding. One seldom witnesses it in extreme form—only in crises or regressed states. So far as can be determined these lesser degrees of it are not elsewhere in the literature ascribed to an actual developmental deficit of resources for holding. Instead of there being an absence of intrapsychic structure, the general view is that the problem lies in the presence of introjective structures that exert a negative influence. Meissner's understanding of the psychopathology of the borderline personality in terms of the paranoid process is an example. Masterson (1976) expresses views along these lines, but at the same time comes closer to the ideas of the present authors. He ascribes the sense of void in part to "introjection of the mother's negative attitudes that leaves the patient devoid, or empty, of positive supportive introjects" (page 42). Modern literature deals with the subject of aloneness abundantly, but always, it seems, in these attenuated forms, usually in terms of defenses and desperate ways of coping with it. Chessick notes this element in *The Stranger* by Albert Camus. Other examples are Virginia Woolf's *The Waves*, Joyce Carol Oates' *Wonderland*, and Thomas Pynchon's *The Crying of Lot 49*. Many patients also refer to Eduard Munch's painting, *The Scream*, as a depiction of their emotional state of aloneness.

Borderline patients are, of course, to the extent they have use of holding introjects, capable of sadness. But the sadness that depends upon tenuously functional introjects is hard, in that it lacks softness and tenderness, and is desperate in quality, often frightening to the patient because he or she feels the edge of terror in it and fears that he or she will fall into it. Two patients described a photograph that conveyed this particular form of intense, fearful sadness. It was a famous one that appeared in *Life* magazine at the time of the Japanese attack on China. It shows a lone infant sitting with eyes closed, crying, screaming, amidst the rubble of a Shanghai railroad station a few seconds after its mother had been killed by a bomb (Wong 1937).

In "The capacity to be alone," Winnicott (1958) wrote in theoretical and experiential terms that are altogether compatible with the concepts being advanced here. Because of the present authors' debt to Winnicott, and because of confusion that might otherwise arise, we wish to clarify that what we are calling aloneness Winnicott referred to as not being able to be alone or not being able to enjoy solitude. The person whom we would say is capable of being comfortable by himself, without the presence of others, Winnicott referred to as a person capable of being alone by virtue of the presence of "a good object in the psychic reality of the individual" (p. 32). We would say that such a person is subject to loneliness as opposed to aloneness.

TREATMENT OF THE PRIMARY SECTOR OF BORDERLINE PERSONALITY PSYCHOPATHOLOGY

The treatment of any one type of patient is too complex to cover in detail in a paper. Therefore many sectors of treatment that actually are vital but do not pertain to the most central elements of borderline personality psychopathology will not be discussed here. For example, the crucial therapeutic work with the pathological organization of introjects in the form of victim-introjects and aggressor-introjects, to which Meissner (1976) has called attention, will not be described. Nor will issues of primitive guilt be considered, vital as they are. Also, the efforts required with neurotic sectors will be left to one side.

In the experience of the present authors, definitive treatment of the primary sector of borderline psychopathology involves three successive phases. The present paper outlines the work involved in each and illustrates it with aspects of a clinical case. Because the narcissistic sector can bear in a particular way on the primary sector, it is also noted.

Phase I: Inadequate and Unstable Holding Introjects

The primary aim of treatment in the first phase is to establish and maintain a dyadic therapeutic relationship in which the therapist can be steadily used over time by the patient as a holding self-object. Once established, this situation makes it possible for the patient not only to develop insight into the nature and basis for his or her aloneness but also to acquire a solid evocative memory of the therapist as sustaining holder, which in turn serves as a substrate out of which can be formed adequate holding introjects. That is, developmental processes that were at one time arrested are now set in motion to correct the original failure. This process would simply require a period of time for its occurrence were it not for psychodynamic obstacles that block it in therapy just as they block it in life. These obstacles must, therefore, receive intensive therapeutic attention. They are consequences, or corollaries, of aloneness. The inevitability of rage is one such corollary that interferes with the process of forming holding introjects. This rage has three sources for the borderline:

1. Holding is never enough to meet the felt need to assuage aloneness, and the enraged patient is inclined to vengeful destruction of the offending therapist or a fantasied eviction of him or her from the patient's psychic inner world. Under these circumstances, the patient feels as if he or she imminently will, or even has, lost or killed the therapist. In addition, the patient expects to lose the therapist through the therapist's responding to his or her rage by turning from "good" to "bad" in reaction to the patient's hostile assault and rejection.
2. The holding self-object that does not meet the need is not only the target for direct rage but is also distorted by means of projection of hostile introjects; thus the patient carries out what he or she experiences as an exchange of destructiveness in a mutually hostile relationship; subjectively, the inevitable result of this projection is the loss of the good holding object.
3. The object that is so endowed with holding sustenance as to be a resource for it is deeply envied by the needy borderline. This envy necessarily involves hateful destructive impulses.

Any of these sources of rage can lead to the states of recognition-memory rage or diffuse primitive rage, with transient loss of holding introjects or object representations or even loss of use of transitional objects. At such times the patient is subject to the terrifying belief that the therapist has ceased to exist. When that occurs all possible support of the holding-soothing type may be required to maintain his or her psychic integrity and stability.

There is another corollary to aloneness that acts as a serious impediment to the process of forming a holding introject. It is the intensity with which the borderline personality must employ incorporation and fusion as a means of experiencing holding with a self-object, an intensity that involves oral impulses as well as experiences of psychological merging. Belief in the imminence of destruction of the self-object, the self, or both, demands that the borderline distance himself or herself from his or her self-object to such an extent that the subjective experience of holding-soothing is not adequate to promote the needed development of solid holding introjects.

There is yet one more impediment to the use of the therapist as a holding self-object. It is a primitive guilt-related experience that involves the belief by the patient that he or she is undeserving of the therapist's help because of his or her evilness. This patient response is akin to the negative therapeutic reaction (Freud 1923); it can lead to the patient's rejection of all therapeutic efforts, as well as the rejection of the real relationship with the therapist in the service of self-punishment. In extreme situations it can lead to suicide attempts.

Acquiring insight into and working through the impeding corollaries of aloneness—threats posed by rage from various sources, incorporation and fusion, and primitive guilt—are necessary in order for the borderline to be in a position to use his or her self-object relationship with the therapist over time to develop a stable evocative memory for and introject of the therapist as holding sustainer. By far the major focus of treatment in Phase I is, therefore, upon these dynamic impediments to the use of the self-object therapist for attaining the desired intrapsychic development for experiencing stable holding-soothing. Each of these impediments must be worked with in the standard ways as it manifests in transference, through use of the therapeutic maneuvers of clarification, confrontation (Buie and Adler 1972, Adler and Buie 1972), and interpretation. Once insight is gained, each aspect requires working through. This treatment must be conducted in an adequately supportive therapeutic setting, one that attempts insofar as possible to help maintain the tenuous holding introjects and internal objects, hence keeping annihilation anxiety within tolerable levels and maintaining cohesiveness of the self. The amount of support may considerably exceed that involved in most psychotherapies. To some extent the therapist in reality acts as a holding self-object. Transitional objects (e.g., vacation addresses and postcards), extra appointments, and telephone calls reaffirming that the therapist exists are required at various times and, for the more severely borderline personalities, brief hospitalizations, at least once or twice, might well be expected. At times, in the interpersonal setting of the therapy hour, the therapist must vigorously clarify, interpret, and confront the patient with reality, especially around matters of the therapist's continued existence as a caring object, his or her not resembling the hostile introjects or identifications that the patient projects, and the patient's minimization of dangerous situations in which he or she may through acting out place himself or herself when struggling with these issues. When splitting of the type Kernberg describes occurs acutely with the danger of serious acting out, it requires priority attention for correction.

The outcome of this work with the impeding corrollaries of aloneness is this: the patient learns that the therapist is an enduring and reliable holding self-object, that the therapist is indestructible as a "good object" (Winnicott 1969), that holding closeness gained by incorporation and fusion poses no dangers, and that the patient himself or herself is not evil.

Indeed, the initial increments in development of a holding introject take place as the patient gains a bit of credulence about the survivability of the therapist as a good object. Hope is aroused that the relationship and the therapeutic work, involving understanding of object and self-object trans-ferences plus genetic reconstructions, will open the way for psychological development and relief. Once the holding introject gains some stability, a positive cycle is induced, which results in a diminution of the intensity of aloneness and, along with it, a diminution of the corollary impediments; this in turn allows for further development and stabilization of holding introjects.

The healing of splitting of long-standing nature (of the type Kernberg [1967] describes), e.g., in the relationship with mother, must await this formation of stable holding introjects. Efforts to bring together the positive and negative sides of the split can be therapeutic only after development of more stable holding introjects along with correction of distorting projections that have acted to intensify the negative side of the split. Development or recognition of realistically based love on the positive side of the split is also helpful in healing it. With these therapeutic developments, the external and internal resources for love and holding are sufficient to endure acknowledging that the loved and hated object are one and the same and that the loving and hating in one's self toward the object must be reconciled.

Clinical Illustration of Phase I. Mr. A. began treatment in his mid-20s when, as a graduate student, his life-long feelings of depressive emptiness grew more intense and he was progressively enveloped by diffuse anxiety. He was very successful in his field of study and was highly regarded by his professors and peers. But he had no truly close friends. Those who did gain some intimacy with him found themselves repeatedly rebuffed as he time and again withdrew on some pretext into an irritated reserve, oftentimes then drawing closer to someone else. The person who most often occupied his mind was his mother, usually with a sense of rage. He respected his father as a hard-working semi-skilled man with principles. In his own pursuits as a student he was rather like him, but his father was a reserved man who was dominated by his wife and related to the patient mostly at a distance. His mother was often emotionally involved with the patient, but always in terms of her own wishes and needs and rarely, if ever, in terms of him as a separate person with his own identity. Alternately she was either intensively close or preoccupied to such an extent that she appeared to have forgotten him. She involved him in sensuous body closeness, only to repell him in disgust when he responded. When angry she would declare that she had made him and she could kill him, and as a child he believed it. She also had clinical episodes of depression, during which she would take to bed and become literally unresponsive to everyone. Nevertheless, she was a compelling person for the patient. She was beautiful, and the positive times of closeness with her were heavenly. She gloried in his high intelligence and always backed his efforts to achieve academically.

From early childhood, at least from age three, his mother repeatedly sent him to live with her childless sister for periods of weeks, up to a year. At times her motivation seems to have been the need to ease her burdens while having a new baby. The aunt and uncle were kindly and quiet but did not relate well to the boy. He felt desolate, describing these visits away from his mother as like being stranded on a frozen desert. Sometimes he could manage his feelings with blissful fantasies of being harmoniously close to his wonderful mother, but he could not sustain them.

As twice-a-week psychotherapy deepened over a period of months, the patient felt increasingly dependent on the therapist. Looking forward to seeing him began evolving into an increasingly urgent sense of missing and needing him between hours. Longing was mixed with anxiety; by the time a year had passed, he began to express anger that the therapist was not with him enough and did not care enough. The transference evolved into a clear projection of his introjected relationship with his mother, which was clarified and interpreted. Insight was of little value, however, as he began to experience times with the therapist as wonderfully helpful and times away from him as a desert-like isolation where, despite continued good academic performance, all other involvements most of the time seemed meaningless.

As rage with the therapist intensified, the patient stopped looking at him. For the next two years, he never looked directly at the therapist, finally explaining that he was so full of hate toward him that he felt that his gaze would fragment the therapist's head into slivers of glass.

His intense yearning for the presence of the therapist contrasted with his increasing aloofness in the hours. The distancing behavior extended further. On entering and leaving the office, the patient began walking along a path that was as far away from the therapist as the room contours and the size of the doorway would allow. Whenever the therapist moved forward a little in his chair, the patient with a look of fear moved as far back in his chair as he could. Clarification of his apparent fear of closeness led first to emergence of overt fear that on entering and leaving the office he might fall into the chest of the therapist and disappear; similarly, he feared the therapist's leaning forward in his chair because it felt like the therapist could fall into the patient's chest and be totally absorbed. None of these fears were at the level of delusion, but the fantasy was so intense that it dictated behavior. Tentative interpretations of the possibility that his fears involved a wish led to emergence of overt cannibalistic impulses, first discovered in a dream that involved eating meat, which he recognized as the therapist, and later emerging also in a dream of the therapist as a large-billed bird who was going to eat the patient.

As rage with the therapist mounted, the patient began acting out in consciously self-destructive ways. He started drinking straight whiskey in bars noted for perversion and violence, thinking about the therapist and saying to himself, "I'll take what I have coming!" It was in this part of therapy that he experienced nearly intolerable times when he could not summon any memory-image of the therapist beyond a vague inner picture. He could not sense the feeling of being with the therapist; he described these times as very frightening periods of belief that the therapist did not exist. On one such occasion he drank heavily and in a rage of aloneness recklessly crashed his car into the side of a bridge. The therapist responded with added vigor in interpreting the patient's transient incapacities to know that the therapist existed. He insisted that at such times the patient must not act on his fear and his rage but must instead telephone the therapist and, if necessary, make extra appointments. The therapist emphasized that in this way the patient would have a chance to learn that the therapist did continually exist, did continually remember the patient, and really was available to him. The patient did as the therapist urged, contacting him with brief calls and occasionally seeing him extra times as a means of managing these crises.

In these ways the therapist was attempting to help the patient bear and understand his aloneness, rage, regressive memory loss, and frightening belief that closeness meant mutual destruction through incorporation and fusion. The clear transference to the therapist as a seductive and abandoning mother led to genetic interpretations and insight. But it also was essential that the patient repetitively have the opportunity to learn that despite his rageful attacks on the therapist, the therapist remained a caring person who consistently tried to help. For example, the patient spent 40 minutes of one hour verbally assaulting the therapist. He hated him intensely and wanted to kill him. He was certain the therapist did not understand what he was going through, that he couldn't understand how he felt because he did not care—he only collected the fee. He absolutely wanted to kill the therapist, to crash into him, drive his car into his house and smash it, rip it apart as though it were canvas. He hated the patient who preceded him and thought that she was in analysis, getting a higher form of caring than he was. He wanted to run over people in the neighborhood with his car and run over the therapist. He knew the therapist's family was there in the house, and he wanted to kill them too. He expressed all this with great intensity, feeling at the time that he really meant it. But with the therapist's persistent attitude of attentive acceptance, the patient in the last ten minutes grew calmer, saying finally that his problem really was that he wanted to possess his therapist completely, literally to swallow him whole.

With all of these efforts the patient gained a steady capacity to remember the therapist and to feel what contact with him was like at times between hours. He stopped having to make emergency telephone calls. His rage diminished. He began looking at the therapist, and he developed comfort with his wishes for incorporative and fusion closeness.

He told about a fantasy that he had had since childhood and now attached to the therapist. He was quite fond of it. It first developed after he learned about slaughterhouses for cattle. What he yearned for was closeness with the therapist gained through their each having been split down the abdomen so that their intestines could mingle warmly together. It was clear from the way that he told it that this was a loving fantasy.

Phase II: The Idealized Holding Therapist and Introjects

In general, the holding introjects established in Phase I are considerably unrealistic, in that they are patterned in part after qualities of whatever positive introjects were formed in early years. As such they are idealized in a child-like manner. The self-object transference is strongly colored by projection of these idealized introjects, and introjection of this transference experience results in formation of an idealized holding introject that the patient takes to be a homologue of the holding qualities of the therapist. Were treatment to stop here the situation would be quite unstable for two reasons. First, the unrealistic idealization of the holding introjects, along with the projections of them onto persons who serve as holding self-objects, would continually be confronted by reality and would inevitably break down. Second, at this point the patient is still heavily dependent on a continuing relationship with holding self-objects (including the therapist), as well as holding introjects, for an ongoing sense of security; this is not a viable setup for adult life, where self-objects cannot realistically be consistently available and must over the years be lost in considerable number.

The therapeutic work in Phase II parallels that described by Kohut (1971) in treating the idealizing aspects of self-object transferences with narcissistic personalities. (Indeed, the introjects of interest here are idealized not simply in the area of holding but also in terms of worth. For purposes of this discussion, the two qualities that are idealized are artificially separated, and the one concerned with worth is addressed in a later section.) Kohut describes the therapeutic process as "optimal disillusionment," and it is applied, in the present paper, to idealization in the area of holding-soothing as he utilizes it in the area of self worth. No direct interventions are required. The realities of the therapist's interactions with the patient and the basic reality orientation of the patient always leads to the patient's noticing discrepancies between the idealized holding introject, based on the therapist and reflected in the transference, and the actual holding qualities of the therapist. Each episode of awareness of discrepancy occasions disappointment, sadness, and anger. If each disappointment is not too great, i.e., is optimal, a series of episodes will ensue in which insight is developed, and in which working through relinquishing unrealistic idealization is accomplished. (Any disappointments that are greater than optimal precipitate recurrence of aloneness and rage in a transient regression that resembles Phase I.) Ultimately the therapist as holding self-object is accepted as he or she realistically is—an interested, caring person who in the context of a professional relationship does all that he or she appropriately can to help the patient resolve conflicts and achieve mature capacities. Holding introjects come to be modified accordingly.

Clinical Illustration of Phase II. At this point, Mr. A. was preoccupied with interrelated idealized holding introjects based on good childhood times with his mother and unrealistic beliefs about the therapist. Directly and indirectly he declared strongly positive feelings for his therapist. He was not concerned about vacations because he knew the therapist kept him very much in his thoughts. He fantasied their hugging in greeting when the therapist returned (something that he in fact never attempted). At the same time, he reminisced tearfully about the passive bliss of being with his mother at the times she cared for him. He referred to her by her first name, Joanna.

He grieved repeatedly as he recognized, little by little, that the idealized images of Joanna and the therapist were unrealistic. This work required no active stimulus from the therapist. Reality intruded on idealizing illusion enough to keep the work going. The therapist helped the patient bear his grief and put it into perspective by empathically staying with him, by providing clarifications and interpretations about dynamic and genetic bases for his disappointments, and by avoiding any confrontations that would intensify his disappointments. The grief process consisted of sadness, crying, nonmurderous anger, and relinquishment of impossible yearnings.

For example, for several weeks he had talked tearfully about how beautiful life had been with Joanna. She was everything to him and he would do anything for her. He also spoke of the solidity he felt in his relationship with the therapist. It was like the large oak trees that stood outside his office. Then in one hour he related a dream in which he was descending the stairs of an elevated streetcar station. There were several people on the ground waiting for him, including a woman and the therapist. He noticed that the stairs ended several feet above the sidewalk and he was expected to jump. The people could have made it easier by catching him, but it was safe enough; so they simply stood by watching. He was angry, jumped anyhow, and was all right. After telling the dream he said that he had been wishing the therapist would talk to him more. He didn't know much about the therapist personally and really longed to know more. He felt deprived, and he was angry about it. He felt jealous of other patients and the therapist's family. They all got something special from the therapist. He wanted to be like a man in a recent movie who lived to be adored. He wanted all his therapist's adoration. He wanted him to smile affectionately, touch him, clean him all over, touch and clean every crevice of his body, like a mother would her baby. He was jealous of people whom he fantasied the therapist to be close to sexually. The wonderful thing the therapist had to give was like two golden pears in his chest. He yearned for them so much and did not get them. He was furious about it, felt like destroying them. Then he turned sad and tears streamed down his cheeks. He felt badly about his anger because he knew that what he wanted was unreasonable. The therapist said to him that it was like his dream. He wanted to be helped in his jump to the sidewalk though he knew he actually didn't need it. His anger arose not because a need to be saved was ignored, but because he wasn't receiving something he very much yearned for. Mr. A. agreed that this was the meaning of his dream and was the way he felt.

The excerpt that follows is taken from the last portion of Phase II. The patient said, "I feel like I'm missing Joanna, like I'm looking for her everywhere, and she ought to be all around, but she's not." (He looked mildly depressed and sad.) "I miss her. I miss her, and you can't bring her back, and nobody can. It's like she died." (He began to laugh.) "I wonder what the real Joanna is like. The Joanna I yearn for isn't the real one at all. It's some ideal Joanna I'm wanting, someone very wonderful and very exciting. A Joanna like that never really existed." (He grew sad, but retained his humor.) "You know, the trouble is that I don't see people and places for what they really are because I keep looking for Joanna there. There are lots of girls I know but haven't ever appreciated because I haven't really related to them. I've missed out on them. I had a dream. All I remember is that there was a wonderful celebration for me, but I couldn't enjoy it because Joanna wasn't there. It's like part of me has died, but it's not so much that I can't do okay without it. It's really as if she's been everywhere or is everywhere. She's part of me, and its awfully hard to give her up." (With good humor, slightly hypomanic.) "It feels like I can peel Joanna off now, that it's like a layer of skin. And when I do, most of me is still left there very solid."

TREATMENT OF THE NARCISSISTIC SECTOR OF
BORDERLINE PERSONALITY PSYCHOPATHOLOGY

The majority of borderline personalities also exhibit serious pathologies of narcissism of the type Kohut (1971, 1977) and Goldberg (1978) describe, manifested in everyday life by grandiosity and narcissistic idealization of others and in psychotherapy by self-object transferences of the mirroring and idealizing types. By and large the modes of treatment delineated by Kohut are applicable to treatment of the narcissistic sector. However, approaching this therapeutic work is complicated by the interrelationships of pathological narcissism and pathology of holding-soothing the self. There are three concerns here:

1. Narcissistic grandiosity and idealization can substitute for holding-soothing in effecting a subjective sense of security. Some borderline personalities make significant use of this substitution as a regular part of their character functioning; others temporarily resort to it as a means for feeling secure at times when use of holding self-objects is compromised. Perhaps this substitution is effected through the medium of the satisfaction and pleasure inherent in possessing or partaking of perfection, as well as through the assurance and security offered by the sense of invulnerability that accompanies narcissistic grandiosity and idealization.
2. Cohesiveness of the self depends upon maintaining equilibrium in the areas both of narcissism (Kohut 1971) and of holding-soothing.
3. Although dynamically different, undermining of pathologically maintained narcissism can be a life and death matter, as can also be the loss of the borderline personality's means of maintaining holding-soothing of the self. Undermining of grandiosity or idealization can precipitate a subjective experience of worthlessness that is unbearably painful. By itself it does not, as aloneness does, portend danger of annihiliation, but it can prompt serious suicidal impulses as a means of gaining relief and/or punishing whoever is felt to be responsible (Maltsberger and Buie 1980).

The importance of pathological narcissism for maintaining a subjective sense of security and self-cohesiveness and for avoiding unbearable worthlessness bears greatly on the timing of therapeutic approaches to narcissism in the borderline personality. Insofar as possible, pathologically maintained narcissism must not be weakened during Phase I of treatment, when soothing-holding security is so vulnerable and the risk of aloneness, with annihilation anxiety and loss of self-cohesiveness, is so high. In Phase II, narcissistic idealization and grandiosity are often interwoven with idealizations of the holding type. At this time therapeutic disillusionment can often be successful in both areas, provided it remains optimal for both. It may be necessary, however, to delay definitive treatment efforts with the narcissistic sector until after the work of Phase II is accomplished in the primary sector of borderline personality psychopathology. Timing must, of course, vary from patient to patient. The guideline is that narcissistic issues can be approached only insofar as a stable holding self-object transference and adequately functioning holding introjects are firmly enough established to prevent regression into insecurity and loss of self-cohesion.

For Mr. A., narcissistic pathology was not extreme. It was expressed in Phase II especially in the context of the idealized holding self-object transference, e.g., in feeling and wanting to feel adored. Optimal disillusionment in the area of holding proceeded hand in hand with optimal disillusionment in the area of narcissism.

Clinical Illustrations. Ms. B., a 25-year-old social worker, by documented history had since infancy suffered intermittent rejections by her immature and volatile mother, as well as excessive verbal and physical abuse. She exhibited in her history and in therapy a narcissistic developmental arrest of the type Kohut describes, along with the elements of a borderline personality. She was especially fixated at the level of a grandiose self through having been very important to her mother as an idealized self-object. For her mother's sake and her own she needed to be outstandingly bright and popular. In late grade school, the equilibrium between them began to disintegrate under the impact of her real position vis à vis her peers and teachers. The intense urgency and importance of her needs had made her a socially awkward girl, and the tension lest she fail to achieve perfection had immobilized her in academic competition. As her position with teachers and peers deteriorated, she tried to meet her mother's and her own needs by lying to her mother, conveying fantasies of achievements and popularity as if they were facts. Eventually her gullible mother learned the truth, and the narcissistic equilibrium of each was permanently shattered.

Treatment in Phase I was more difficult with Ms. B. than with Mr. A. In addition to problems with aloneness, she also was subject to desperate feelings of worthlessness when her self-object means of maintaining narcissistic equilibrium were jolted. This added extra dimensions of intensity to the therapy, including greater levels of rage and envy, and at times the therapist had to provide vigorous support to her fragile sense of self-worth. In Phase II she worked through her idealizations of the therapist as self-object holder and modified her introjects accordingly. Thereafter some effective work was done with her pathological narcissism, especially as in Phase III it became possible to modify her need for grandiosity by substituting self-worth derived from effective involvement in personally meaningful pursuits and achievements. At termination, narcissistic pathology still persisted significantly. Followup has shown that the process that began in treatment continued, however. Successful life experience made possible further replacement of the grandiose self and idealizing transferences with realistically rewarding career achievements and more realistic involvements with worthwhile people.

Certain patients who are insecure because of relative paucity of holding introjects and relative inability to use holding self-objects may exhibit considerable pathological narcissism yet require little direct therapeutic work with it. These are patients who use pathological means of maintaining narcissism as a substitute form of security that supplements their inadequately available means of maintaining holding security. The case of Mr. C. illustrates this.

He was a successful historian whose background included marked deprivation of security from the time of infancy. He was a brilliant man, however, and he possessed outstanding charm of a mannered sort. He was preoccupied with this image of himself and loved to indulge in fantasies of being Henry VIII and other magnificent men of history, oftentimes in affairs with great women of the past. But all his relationships were emotionally shallow, and his mannered charm obscured the fact that he had no close relationships, including with his wife and children. They often entered into playing out his fantasies of being a king whom they obediently revered. The magnetism of his personality was such that a great many people quite willingly provided the mirroring admiration that he needed to maintain his fantasy life.

Mr. C. was able to live well financially by virtue of an inheritance; this was a most important prop for his grandiosity. When the money ran out, he decompensated into a prolonged phase of severe depressions alternating with mania, at times exhibiting evidence of delusions. On several occasions he attempted suicide. Finally, he began psychotherapy with the aim that it be definitive in nature. He desperately reached for closeness with the therapist, probably for the first time in his adult life, and soon was involved in the therapeutic situation that has been described for Phase I. Concomitantly, he reconstituted his old grandiosity, using the therapist as a transference mirroring self-object. As with Ms. B., this part of his psychopathology was not worked with and was not challenged in Phase I. When he entered Phase II, he was in a well-established self-object transference of the holding idealization type. However, unlike Ms. B., he now altogether discontinued his transference use of the therapist, or other people, to support his pathological narcissism. At the same time, more realistic modes of maintaining self-worth emerged. Prior to his decompensation he managed the primary sector of his borderline psychopathology (1) by maintaining a guarded distance in all relationships and (2) by supplementing the inadequate resources for holding in his inner and external worlds with substitute security derived from maintaining a grandiose self. Once an adequate stable idealizing transference of the holding type was established in Phase II, he was able to and did essentially dispense with his grandiose self (apparently permanently) because he no longer needed it for security.

TREATMENT IN PHASE III FOR THE PRIMARY SECTOR OF BORDERLINE PERSONALITY PSYCHOPATHOLOGY: SUPEREGO MATURATION AND FORMATION OF SUSTAINING IDENTIFICATIONS

Theoretical Considerations

To become optimally autonomous, i.e., self-sufficient, in regard to secure holding and a sense of worth requires two developments: (1) A superego (as an agency comprising both the conscience and the ego ideal) must be established that is not inappropriately harsh and that readily serves as a source of a realistically deserved sense of worth. (2) The ego must develop the capacity for pleasurable confidence in the self (the heir to grandiosity) and for directing love toward itself that is of the affectionate nature of object love. (Object love is differentiated from narcissistic love, in that object love is attached to qualities of the object that do not necessarily serve purposes for oneself and are not vicariously felt as if one's own; the reward of investing with object love is simply the experience of affectionately loving the other person. Narcissistic love, however, centers around qualities of worth and survival that involve qualities of oneself, or qualities or functions of another person that are felt as enhancing personal value and survival. While love feelings may be associated, narcissistic love is rewarding only insofar as self-experiences of worth and security are somehow enhanced.) This development of the capacity to love the self in the manner of object love contributes not only to enjoyment of being one's self but also in the face of losses that involve the self—through accident, disease, aging, approaching death— makes possible a reaction of genuine sadness, a grief that is homologous with that experienced with object loss. Without this ego development the reaction is instead that of depression, fear, and despondency, reactions that typify "narcissistic" loss instead of object loss. These are the hoped for developmental achievements of Phase III of definitive treatment of the primary sector of borderline personality psychopathology.

The therapeutic endeavors in Phase III are based on the principle that capacities to know, esteem, and love oneself can be developed only when there is adequate experience of being known, esteemed, and loved by significant others.

Once the inappropriately harsh elements of the superego (or superego forerunners) have been therapeutically modified, the process by which superego development is initiated in this phase of treatment is introjection, as described by Sandler (1960). Accordingly, early in this sequence of development, one can speak of superego forerunners that have the quality of introjects in the psychological inner world, i.e., of being active presences that exert an influence on the ego. An example might be expressed by a patient as, "I can feel how my therapist would guide me and value me for this work." Such superego forerunner introjects evolve into an agency, one that still functions with the quality of an introject; however, through a process of depersonification, it comes to be experienced as part of the self rather than as part of the inner world. One can now speak of a superego and illustrate this development by altering the example just given into, "My conscience guides me and gives me approval for pursuing this work well." Further development occurs through increasing depersonification and proximity of the superego to the "ego core" (Loewald 1962) along with integration of the superego with the ego. These developments can properly be subsumed in the concept of the process of identification (Meissner 1972), and it is in this way that superego functions are ultimately assumed as ego functions. Now the ego is no longer in the position of being responsive to the influence exerted by an agency external to it, but becomes its own guardian of standards of behavior and its own source of a sense of worth. At this point the example under consideration evolves into, "I feel good about this work of mine which is in line with my values and meets my standards."

Often these patients also require help to gain the capacity to experience subjectively the factualness (validity) of their esteemable qualities as well as to experience feelings of self-esteem. This requires the transient self-object functioning on the part of the therapist that will be described in the clinical section that follows.

In this phase of treatment, the ego evolves as its own resource for pride and holding through development of intrasystemic resources that are experienced as one part providing to another, both parts being felt as the self. These ego functions are developed through identification with the homologous functioning of the therapist as a self-object. That is, the therapist, verbally but largely nonverbally, actually does provide the patient with a holding function, a function of loving in the affectionate mode of object love, a function of validating (enhancing the reality of valence of) the patient's competences, and a function of enjoying the exercise and fruits of the patient's competences. To varying degrees these functions are internalized, first in the form of introjects, but in Phase III they become depersonified and increasingly integrated with the ego, ultimately becoming functions of the ego by means of identification. This is the process that Kohut designates as transmuting internalization (1971). The experiential quality of these newly gained ego functions might be expressed as follows: (1) "I sustain myself with a sense of soothing-holding;" (2) "I love myself in the same way that I love others, that is, affectionately for the qualities inherent in me;" (3) "I trust my competence in managing and using my psychological self and in perceiving and interrelating with the external world; hence I feel secure in my own hands;" and (4) "I enjoy knowing that I am competent and exercising my competence."

The impetus toward effecting the introjections and identifications involved in these superego and ego developments arises out of relinquishing the therapist as an idealized holding self-object, as well as relinquishing whatever use has been made of him or her as a narcissistic transference self-object. Such relinquishment also involves homologous modification of introjects in the inner world that have been patterned after the self-object transferences. Then the patient is forced by his or her needs to develop other resources for maintenance of holding security and narcissistic equilibrium. The introjections and identifications just described provide the necessary means of accomplishing this task. They also establish a stability of self in terms of holding and worth that is far greater than was possible before. The depersonified introjections and identifications are by their nature more stable and less subject to regressive loss under stress than the configurations and arrangements they replace (Loewald 1962).

Total self sufficienty is, of course, impossible. For its healthy functioning the ego requires interaction with the other agencies of the mind as well as with the external world (Rapaport 1957), and no one totally relinquishes use of others as self-object resources for holding and self-worth, nor does anyone relinquish using selected parts of the environment (art, music, etcetera) as transitional objects (Winnicott 1953). These dependencies are the guarantees of much of the ongoing richness of life.

It is only through the developmental acquisitions of Phase III of treatment that the former borderline personality acquires a genuine psychological stability. Of course, the degree to which it is achieved varies from patient to patient.

Clinical Illustrations of Phase III. While superego development cannot be divorced from ego development (Hartmann and Loewenstein 1962), for purposes of clarity a partial and artificial division of the clinical material will be made along this line.

Superego development. In a time when nearly all hostile introjects had been altered and tamed in Mr. A., it became noticeable that one remained of a superego-like quality. It was like a harsh taskmaster that in fact too much dominated the conduct of Mr. A.'s work life. His associations included one of the dicta belonging to this introject: "You must sweep the corners of the room first; then you will be sure to clean center." In fact his thoughts had been intrusively dominated by that maxim while cleaning his apartment the day before, and he hated the driven way he worked in response to it. It derived from his mother, being one with which she often regaled him. Further exploration revealed that nearly the entirety of the harsh taskmaster introject phenomena under study was derived from interactions with this harsh quality of his mother. Although the genesis and present-day inappropriateness of this part of his inner world were clear to the patient, no modifications occurred. In a later hour the therapist, on a hunch, asked whether the patient would miss this harsh mother-like conscience if it were gone. The question stimulated a mild grief reaction as the patient associatively discovered that he would in fact miss the felt presence of her that was the concomitant of the harshness. Indeed it became clear that this introject partook of both negative and positive qualities of the interaction with his mother, and it seems for that reason it was the last significantly negative introject to go.

Thereafter a more mature superego began to develop. He already possessed appropriate guiding standards as well as the internal authority to promote them (Sandler 1960). Therefore, some of the therapeutic work described above was not required. What he did need was a sense of satisfying and pleasurable self-value. Attaining it was a two-step process. To a degree he "knew" about many aspects of himself that were worthy of esteem, but he did not know them solidly and effectively so that his knowledge could carry the full value, or valence, of reality. The full reality of his positive qualities had, therefore, to be established first. This took place in the therapy through the process of "validation," by which it is meant that the therapist reacted, verbally and nonverbally, to accounts of episodes in which esteemable qualities played a part in such a way as to convey simply that these qualities had registered in his mind as realities. Communication of this to the patient enabled the patient, then, to experience these qualities with a sense of realness himself. Validation is a self-object function performed in this way by the therapist; the interaction provides an experience such that the patient can not only feel the realness of his or her qualities but also gain, through identification, the capacity to "validate" his or her qualities himself or herself. The qualities thus covered in therapy by Mr. A. were myriad. His capacities as, by then, a college teacher of sociology, constituted one such area. He was very successful with his students and with other faculty members. There were numerous events that demonstrated their appropriate esteem for him, but he was not in a position to understand and appreciate their expressions of esteem or to develop a similar sense of esteem for himself until he related it to the therapist. He could then gain a sense of the validity of their judgment.

The second step in acquiring a capacity for appreciating his own self-worth was faciliated by another aspect of the therapist's behavior when the patient related such episodes. The therapist responded with appropriate, subtle, but similar expressions of esteem. This directly promoted the patient's feeling an approving esteem for himself. Ultimately, through processes of introjection and identification, he developed a much improved capacity for autonomous self-esteem. He then no longer required it as a self-object function from the therapist.

Ego Development. The patient required ego development that involved all the functions referred to in the brief theoretical considerations for Phase III of treatment: (1) self holding, (2) self-love with "object love," (3) trust and security in one's competence, and (4) prideful enjoyment in one's competence. Examples can be given of each.

1. *Self-holding.* Originally the patient worried fearfully about his health—signs of illness, being overweight, working too hard, etcetera. But there also was a real basis for his concerns. The therapist never responded with a similar worry, but he did show interest and a warm concern that carried with it the implied message that the patient should care for and take care of himself. Eventually this became the patient's attitude, displacing the old fretful, nonproductive worrying. He began to care for himself with a sensible attitude toward himself; at that time the therapist stopped responding with a self-object level of involvement. The patient then went on a diet, losing the weight he needed to lose, and he ordered his life better, e.g., getting more nearly the amount of rest and relaxation he needed. All in all, it could be said that he developed an essentially autonomous caring about himself that effected a self-holding function.

2. *Self-love with "object love."* In Phase III especially, the patient related many stories of his work and personal life—how he managed a difficult committee problem, how he helped a student advisee who was in serious difficulty, or the conversational interchange with an old friend. Increasingly the full quality of his subjective experience in these episodes was regularly expressed in a spontaneous manner. The therapist in fact liked the patient very much, though he never said so. But his mostly nonverbal listening to these stories certainly conveyed his affectionate enjoyment of the companionship involved in his empathic vicarious participation. Eventually a new attitude emerged in the patient toward himself, one that was implied rather than explicitly stated. It was an affectionate attitude toward himself, one that partook of the quality of affection he felt for other people: his friends, students, therapist, etcetera. It was a self-love that mostly differed in quality from the holding form of caring about himself described above (i.e., it did not specifically involve concern for himself or taking care of himself even though it could be combined with them). The therapist surmised that his own love for the patient had been important in the patient's coming to love himself,

probably through the mechanism of identification. A further benefit of this development was that in loving himself he could more readily acknowledge and accept the love others expressed for him.

3. *Trust and security in one's competence.* Prior to Phase III of treatment, the patient was always beset by doubts about his competence to do the task at hand, even though he nearly constantly was called upon, for example, to teach, give speeches, organize meetings. He was never sure that he could express himself effectively despite the fact that he never failed to do so. This doubt of his competence was present from the beginning of therapy and persisted unchanged over a long period of time. The therapist's function of validating seems again to have provided the necessary experience to bring about change. The therapist developed a realistically founded judgment that the patient was indeed solidly competent in a large number of ways, and by his attitude conveyed this judgment repeatedly to the patient, though he rarely put it into words directly. Gradually the patient came to regard his competences as facts about himself; they had been "validated" by the therapist. It seemed that the patient finally assumed the function of validation of his competence himself, probably through identification with the therapist's similar functioning. With this development, his confidence in himself as he conducted day-to-day matters in his life grew more solid; with it he seemed to gain a significant increment in his overall sense of security. It is as though he now could say to himself with authority, "I can handle what life brings me."

4. *Prideful enjoyment in one's competence.* The therapist enjoyed the patient's competence, and this, too, was subtly conveyed. As in the case of establishing value through superego functioning, so it was with taking pleasure or pride in the exercise of his competence. First he had to know securely that it was "real," valid; then he was in a position to enjoy it. This capacity, too, developed over time in Phase III.

PSYCHOTHERAPY OR PSYCHOANALYSIS FOR THE BORDERLINE PERSONALITY

The ideas presented are for the definitive treatment in the setting of two to five times a week psychotherapy. Some analysts report successfully using the psychoanalytic situation for treating patients broadly described as borderline, some of whom would be borderline personalities. Chase and Hire (1966), for example, employ analytic techniques along with some parameters, and Boyer and Giovacchini (1967) restrict technique to classical procedures.

The present authors believe that very important elements of the treatment are analytical—the development of stable transferences, the use of spontaneous free association along with clarification and interpretation for gaining access to unconscious content, and working through in the context of transference and the living of everyday life. However, treatment of the primary sector of borderline psychopathology also requires actual self-object functioning by the therapist in addition to facilitating the use of and resolution of self-object transference. In Phase I, when the patient transiently loses capacity to conduct his life safely, the therapist must set limits and otherwise participate in protecting the patient. As regression deepens there is a need for the therapist to confront the patient with the fact of the therapist's existence and availability (Buie and Adler 1972), as well as to extend his or her availability outside treatment hours in order to provide additional actual psychological self-object holding. Providing transitional objects may at times be necessary, the effectiveness of which may depend on the actual functioning of the therapist as a holding self-object. In Phase III, various kinds of subtle self-object functions are necessary to provide the experience out of which the patient can through introjection and identification gain certain autonomous capacities: to guide and approve of himself or herself according to his or her ideals, to experience the validity (realness) of his or her personal qualities including his or her competences, to enjoy having and exercising his or her competences, to provide himself or herself with a sense of security, and to love himself or herself affectionately. All of these crucial self-object functions of the therapist fall outside the realm of classical psychoanalysis. More important, these self-object functions in large measure are effected nonverbally, especially through facial expression and body gesture. As such, the face-to-face context of psychotherapy is facilitating, and for some aspects of treatment it is essential. Therefore, psychotherapy is advocated for Phase I of treatment of all borderline personalities (as Meissner defines them). The psychoanalytic format can often be instituted sometime thereafter, depending on the psychological qualities of the patient, the therapist-analyst, and their interaction. For borderline patients of higher level integration, whose holding introjects are more nearly stable, psychoanalysis might be used throughout treatment. In some cases it could even be the treatment of choice.

SUMMARY

This paper is concerned with the borderline personality as it has been delineated by Meissner and others, and is a theoretical and clinical account of a psychotherapy that the present authors term definitive. The primary sector of pathology is seen as a relative developmental failure in formation of introjects that provide to the self a function of holding-soothing security. This developmental failure is traced to inadequacies of mothering experience during separation-individuation. Holding introjects are not only functionally insufficient but also subject to regressive loss by virtue of the instability of the memory basis for their formation. Because they are functionally inadequate to meet adult needs for psychological security, the borderline personality is constantly subject to degrees of separation anxiety, felt as aloneness, and is forced to rely on external holding self-objects for enough sense of holding-soothing to keep separation anxiety relatively in check. Incorporation and fusion are the psychological means of gaining a sense of holding security from self-objects. Because of the intensity and primitive level of his or her pathological needs, the borderline personality unconsciously believes that incorporation and fusion also carry with them the threat of destruction of self-object and self. This belief, along with vicissitudes of rage arising out of unmet need, makes it impossible for the borderline personality to maintain the kind of steady closeness with holding self-objects in adult life that is necessary for developing a solid memory base for formation of adequately functioning holding introjects.

Psychotherapy for this primary sector of psychopathology proceeds in three phases. Phase I involves regression, with emergence of marked separation anxiety and rage, transient regressive loss of function of holding introjects and transitional objects, and emergence into consciousness of impulses and fears associated with incorporation and fusion. Clarification and interpretation, limit-setting, actual provision of self-object holding at a psychological level, and proof of indestructibility as a good object are the means by which the therapist enables the patient to understand and work through the impediments to the use of him or her as a holding self-object. This accomplishment frees the patient to develop holding introjects based on experience with the therapist along with other past and present experiences with holding self-objects. These introjects are, however, unrealistically idealized in terms of holding. Phase II is concerned with modification of this idealization through a series of optimal disillusionments with the therapist as holder-soother in the context of a self-object transference. Relinquishing the idealization compels the patient to develop additional internal resources for security, ones that do not necessarily promote a feeling of holding-soothing, but which provide various qualities of experience of self that contribute to a sense of personal security. Through various forms of subtle self-object functioning, the therapist provides the patient with experiences out of which he or she can by introjection and identification develop autonomous capacities not only for feeling soothed and held out of means of his or her own, but also for feeling the reality of his or her personal qualities, sensing his or her own self-worth, enjoying his or her qualities and competences, and affectionately loving himself or herself.

For most borderline personalities treatment must also be concerned with pathological means of maintaining narcissistic equilibrium. Treatment can proceed along lines advocated by Kohut. However, especially because pathological narcissism contributes to a sense of security, it is important that this therapeutic work be delayed until holding security based on stable self-object transference, introjects, and identifications is solidly established.

There are many other essential aspects of treatment for these patients that are not considered in this account because they are well described elsewhere and are not germaine to this contribution.

ACKNOWLEDGMENTS

The authors wish to express their appreciation for the clinical teachings of Louis S. Chase, M.D., especially in the areas of abandonment (aloneness) and the complications attending the fantasies associated with incorporation. We appreciate the help we have obtained from discussions of some of our ideas with members of the Sustaining Fantasy Workshop in the Department of Psychiatry of Tufts-New England Medical Center Hospitals: Paul G. Myerson, M.D., Stephen Bernstein, M.D., Cornelus Heijn, M.D., Robert Jampel, Ph.D., Ana-Maria Rizzuto, M.D., and Martin Zelin, Ph.D. We also thank Sterrett Mayson, M.D., for permission to use clinical material that he has shared with us, and W. W. Meissner, M.D., for his critical assistance in preparing this manuscript.

REFERENCES

Adler, G. (1981). The borderline-narcissistic personality disorder continuum. *American Journal of Psychiatry* 138:46–50.

Adler, G., and Buie, D. H. (1972). The misuses of confrontation with borderline patients. *International Journal of Psychoanalytic Psychotherapy* 1:109–120.

———. (1979). Aloneness and borderline psychopathology: the possible relevance of child development issues. *International Journal of Psycho-Analysis* 60:83–96.

Boyer, L. B., and Giovacchini, P. L. (1967). *Psychoanalytic Treatment of Schizophrenic and Characterological Disorders.* New York: Science House, Inc.

Buie, D. H., and Adler, G. (1972). The uses of confrontation with borderline patients. *International Journal of Psychoanalytic Psychotherapy* 1:90–108.

Camus, A. (1957). *The Stranger.* New York: Alfred Knopf.

Chase, L. S., and Hire, A. W. (1966). Countertransference in the analysis of borderlines. Presented to the Boston Psychoanalytic Society and Institute, March 23, 1966.

Chessick, R. D. (1974). Defective ego feeling and the quest for being in the borderline patient. *International Journal of Psychoanalytic Psychotherapy* 3:73–89.

Fraiberg, S. (1969). Libidinal object constancy and mental representation. *Psychoanalytic Study of the Child* 24:9–47.

Freud, S. (1923). The ego and the id. *Standard Edition* 19:3–66.

Friedman, H. J. (1975). Psychotherapy of borderline patients; the influence of theory on technique. *American Journal of Psychiatry* 132:1048–1052.

Gedo, J. E., and Goldberg, A. (1973). *Models of the Mind.* Chicago: University of Chicago Press.

Goldberg, A., ed. (1978). *The Psychology of the Self.* New York: International Universities Press.

Grinker, R. R., Werble, B., and Drye, R. C. (1968). *The Borderline Syndrome: A Behavioral Study of Ego Functions.* New York: Basic Books.

Gunderson, J. G., and Singer, M. T. (1975). Defining borderline patients: an overview. *American Journal of Psychiatry* 132:1–10.

Hartmann, H. (1939). *Ego Psychology and the Problem of Adaptation.* New York: International Universities Press, 1958.

Hartmann, H., and Loewenstein, R. M. (1962). Notes on the superego. *Psychoanalytic Study of the Child* 17:42–81.

Kernberg, O. (1967). Borderline personality organization. *Journal of the American Psychoanalytic Association* 15:641–685.

Kohut, H. (1966). Forms and transformations of narcissism. *Journal of the American Psychoanalytic Association* 14:243–272.

———. (1971). *The Analysis of the Self.* New York: International Universities Press.

———. (1977). *The Restoration of the Self.* New York: International Universities Press.

Little, M. (1966). Transference in borderline states. *International Journal of Psycho-Analysis* 47:476–485.

Loewald, H. W. (1962). Internalization, separation, mourning, and the superego. *Psychoanalytic Quarterly* 31:483–504.

Mahler, M. S. (1971). A study of the separation-individuation process and its possible application to borderline phenomena in the psychoanalytic situation. *Psychoanalytic Study of the Child* 26:403–424.

Mahler, M. S., Pine, F., and Bergman, A. (1975). *The Psychological Birth of the Human Infant.* New York: Basic Books.

Maltsberger, J. T., and Buie, D. H. (1980). The devices of suicide: revenge, riddance and rebirth. *International Review of Psycho-Analysis* 7:61–72.

Masterson, J. F. (1976). *Psychotherapy of the Borderline Adult.* New York: Brunner/Mazel.

Meissner, W. W. (1971). Notes on identification. II. Clarification of related concepts. *Psychoanalytic Quarterly* 40:277–302.

———. (1972). Notes on identification. III. The concept of identification. *Psychoanalytic Quarterly* 41:224–260.

———. (1976). Psychotherapeutic schema based on the paranoid process. *International Journal of Psychoanalytic Psychotherapy* 5:87–114.

———. (1978). *The Paranoid Process.* New York: Jason Aronson.

Modell, A. H. (1968). *Object Love and Reality.* New York: International Universities Press.

Oates, J. C. (1971). *Wonderland.* New York: Vanguard Press.

Piaget, J. (1937). *The Construction of Reality in the Child.* New York: Basic Books, 1954.

Pynchon, T. (1966). *The Crying of Lot 49.* Philadelphia: J. P. Lippincott.

Rapaport, D. (1957). The theory of ego autonomy: a generalization. In *The Collected Papers of David Rapaport*, ed. Merton M. Gill. New York: Basic Books, 1967.

———. (1967). A theoretical analysis of the superego concept. In *The Collected Papers of David Rapaport*, ed. Merton M. Gill. New York: Basic Books.

Sachar, E. J., Kanter, S. S., Buie, D., Engle, R., and Mehlman, R. (1970). Psychoendocrinology of ego disintegration. *American Journal of Psychiatry* 126:1067–1078.

Sandler, J. (1960). On the concept of the superego. *Psychoanalytic Study of the Child* 15:128–162.

Sandler, J., and Rosenblatt, B. (1962). The concept of the representational world. *Psychoanalytic Study of the Child* 17:128–145.

Schafer, R. (1968). *Aspects of Internalization*. New York: International Universities Press.

Tolpin, M. (1971). On the beginnings of a cohesive self: an application of the concept of transmuting internalization to the study of the transitional object and signal anxiety. *Psychoanalytic Study of the Child* 26:316–352.

Volkan, V. D. (1976). *Primitive Internalized Object Relations*. New York: International Universities Press.

Winnicott, D. W. (1953). Transitional objects and transitional phenomena. In *Collected Papers*, pp. 229–242. London: Tavistock, 1958.

———. (1958). The capacity to be alone. In *The Maturational Process and the Facilitating Environment*, pp. 29–36. New York: International Universities Press, 1965.

———. (1960). Ego distortion in terms of the true and false self. In *The Maturational Process and the Facilitating Environment*, pp. 140–152. New York: International Universities Press, 1965.

———. (1969). The use of an object. *International Journal of Psycho-Analysis* 50:711–716.

Wong, H. S. (1937). Chinese baby. In *Photojournalism*. Alexandria, Virginia: Time-Life Books, Inc., 1971.

Woolf, V. (1931). *The Waves*. New York: Harcourt, Brace and World, Inc.

Zetzel, E. (1971). A developmental approach to the borderline patient. *American Journal of Psychiatry* 127:867–871.

Notes on Countertransference in Borderline Conditions

W. W. MEISSNER, S.J., M.D.

"When dealing with borderline or severely regressed patients, as contrasted to those presenting symptomatic neuroses and many character disorders," Kernberg (1975) observed, "the therapist tends to experience rather soon in the treatment, intensive emotional reactions having more to do with the patient's premature, intense and chaotic transference and with the therapist's capacity to withstand psychological stress and anxiety, than with any specific problem in the therapist's past" (pp. 16–17). The argument in the present paper contends that Kernberg's description of countertransference reactions to borderline patients is a caricature that applies only within a limited range of borderline conditions, specifically the most primitive or poorly organized level of borderline functioning or regressive borderline states. The description does not apply to the full range of borderline psychopathology, and in many cases can be misleading. It has generally been recognized that countertransference vicissitudes play an extremely important role in the therapy of borderline patients at one or another phase of the treatment. At critical points in the development of transference (TR) and countertransference (CT) and their interaction, the therapist's recognition of and capacity to deal with CT issues become crucial to the treatment progression. The present paper explores the dimensions of CT experience and provides a tentative model for the understanding of transference-countertransference (TR/CT) interactions. The central points emphasized are: (1) that borderline disorders form a spectrum of character pathology falling between the psychoses on one side and the narcissistic personality disorders on the other; (2) that these conditions reflect varying degrees of pathological disruption and varying levels of personality integration; (3) that, depending on the form of pathological organization, these conditions manifest a variety of types and degrees of intensity of TR involvement and elicit corresponding CT reactions; and, finally (4) that these forms and degrees of TR/CT call for corresponding modifications in therapeutic response.

The term CT has been used with various connotations, sometimes referring to all of the therapist's responses to the patient, and sometimes referring more restrictively to specific unconscious TR-like reactions on the part of the therapist to the patient. Langs (1976b) has provided a useful description:

Primarily countertransference reactions would therefore be those responses in the analyst evoked by stimuli emanating from the patient, and at times from sources outside the analysis, that distort his relationship with the patient because of their effect on his unresolved intrapsychic conflicts, fantasies, and introjects (p. 276).

The effect of CT would, therefore, always be to introduce some distortion or interference into the therapeutic interaction. CT primarily reflects reactions taking place on an unconscious level deriving from infantile residues in the therapist's own personality. These reactions may also reflect significant interactions with important objects in the therapist's developmental history. Such CT reactions are a form of transference taking place in the therapist. They may take place in response to and in conjunction with the eliciting stimulation of the patient's TR (the TR/CT interaction) or may be motivated solely by the therapist.

A useful distinction in describing these variations has recently been introduced by Chediak (1979). He distinguishes between counter-reactions and CT:

When the analyst's state of mind pertains to the dyadic interaction, it would be necessary to differentiate among: (1) *intellectual understanding* based on information given by the patient and intellectual knowledge possessed by the analyst; (2) *the general response to the patient as a person*, the counterpart of what Strupp (1960) stresses when talking about the patient's reaction to the analyst's personality; (3) *the analyst's transference* to the patient, i.e. reliving of early part object relationships as elicited by certain features in the patient; (4) *the analyst's countertransference*, i.e. the reaction in the analyst to the role he is assigned by the patient's transference; (5) *empathic identification* with the patient (p. 117).

The last four categories are forms of counter-reaction in Chediak's formulation, while CT is given a more restrictive meaning. In the present account, CT would include both the third and fourth categories, rather than simply the fourth. Although primarily unconscious in origin, CT reactions in varying degree can give rise to conscious derivatives, as is the case for all unconscious reactions. The therapist has the task of continually monitoring his or her own behavior and experience, just as he or she continually monitors the patient's behavior and experience, with a view to detecting the manifestations of unconscious transferential processes. At times these manifestations are dramatic and forceful, at other times subtle and implicit.

Clearly, with this understanding of CT, not all reactions of the therapist to the patient are CT. The therapist experiences a wide range of responses to the patient, many of which may reflect his or her current experience with the patient and the interaction with the patient's personality. The tendency to feel assaulted as the result of a patient's angry attack may not, in fact, involve CT elements; it may simply be a normal and immediate defensive response to assault—but it may also tap in on and stimulate CT reaction. The therapist's self-awareness and reflective self-knowledge may help to discriminate.These non-CT aspects may be conscious or unconscious or both, but they tend to provide a more realistic and valid basis for the therapist's interaction with the patient. Non-CT aspects of the therapist's involvement with the patient encompass both the factors that contribute to the therapeutic alliance and the real relationship, which unavoidably plays a part in the interaction between two human beings (Greenson and Wexler, 1969).

CT in relation to borderline conditions is not an univocal phenomenon, but rather a spectrum of levels and intensities of TR/CT interactions that can vary considerably in both quality and quantity. Kernberg takes one form of such interaction as paradigmatic of TR/CT interactions with borderline patients. Nonetheless, a strong case can be made for the inherent heterogeneity of borderline conditions, spanning a range of pathological expressions from the lower-order borderline conditions, as represented by the pseudoneurotic schizophrenic and psychotic characters who live much closer to the border of psychosis, to the higher-order borderline conditions as represented by some forms of borderline and schizoid variants, as well as the more primitive hysterics, who come much closer to the quality of personality organization found at the level of analyzable narcissistic characters or other forms of more treatable character disorder (Meissner 1982).

One of the major points of this paper, and one that will provide a recurrent theme in what follows, is that our understanding of CT reactions in the therapy of borderline patients must take into account the diagnostic heterogeneity of borderline conditions. The analysis of the sometimes bewildering variation in borderline patients remains at this juncture unresolved and confusing, and much clarification remains to be done. An initial attempt has been made to sort out some aspects of the borderline spectrum in terms of currently available diagnostic characterizations (Meissner 1982), each of which seems to describe a segment of borderline pathology but does not apply to other segments of the borderline spectrum. Space does not permit a review of that discussion here, but the diagnostic consideration does provide a backdrop for the present account of TR/CT interactions. The major point that recurs in the following discussion is that the nature of TR/CT interactions varies in relation to the kind of borderline condition with which one is dealing, and that this will in turn determine within limits the nature of appropriate therapeutic interventions.

COUNTERTRANSFERENCE MODEL

The model of TR/CT interactions presented in Meissner (1978b) is based on the operation of the paranoid process and on the interaction between introjective and projective processes that form an important aspect of human interaction in general. It is particularly poignantly displayed in the therapeutic interaction.

In terms of the model, the patient's pathological sense of self is structured around a core set of pathogenic introjects. These introjects are products of the internalization of significant ambivalent and defensively elaborated object relationships that have taken place during the course of development (Meissner 1979b). The introjective configuration, therefore, provides a form of internalized record and recapitulation of the vicissitudes of the individual's developmental history. At the most primitive level, the internalizations are motivated by fundamental fears of abandonment and loss, and represent a defensively motivated internal possession of the object in the face of such primitive fears. Later in development, the internalizations may reflect more differentiated and less defensive forms of motivation, but in general reflect the inherent ambivalence to the object and the need to retain, control, and preserve some form of relationship with a loved, yearned for, feared, and hated object. The potential for CT is based on a similar introjective organization—less defensive, less pathogenic, better integrated and differentiated—that may be found in the therapist as well (Grinberg 1962, Racker 1968, Langs 1978–1979, Searles 1978–1979).

The introjective configuration has a structure that reflects these dynamic vicissitudes. The primary dimensions reflected in the organization and functioning of the introjects are the narcissistic, aggressive, and erotic. These defensive internalizations, particularly at earlier phases of the developmental sequence, have the effect of preserving infantile archaic narcissism. Kohut (1971) describes the organization of the grandiose self as one aspect of this introjective configuration. This narcissistic configuration, however, can be descriptively analysed in polar terms. Corresponding to the residues of the grandiose self, with its attributes of superiority, specialness, privilege, entitlement and grandiosity, there is an opposite configuration in which the attitudes and images of the self are characterized by inferiority, inadequacy, worthlessness, shame, etcetera. These configurations are the superior and inferior narcissistic configurations, respectively.

It must be emphasized that these configurations are intimately linked together such that they never occur in isolation but are always found functioning in reciprocal relationship within the intrapsychic economy of the self-organization. There are dynamic as well as genetic reasons for this. Dynamically, the narcissistic push toward the special and entitled has an absolute character that accepts no compromise or middle ground. Narcissistic grandiosity can accept nothing less than to be first and best. Anything less is worthless and inferior. Reality inevitably frustrates or refutes the narcissistic demand; in the face of this frustration and failure to meet the narcissistic expectation, the individual feels a sense of defeat, deprivation, and failure, and retreats to the inferior narcissistic position in which he or she feels worthless, inferior, and shameful. This position is in turn intolerable and forces the individual to compensate by recourse to the extreme of narcissistic superiority and expectation. Genetically, these configurations are linked as well, since they reflect narcissistically embedded internalizations derived from specific object relations in which these same narcissistic configurations played a prominent role (Meissner 1978b). These narcissistic polarities, therefore, may be regarded as mutually defensive, mutually dependent, linked in a complex and continuing interaction, and always represented together in the psychic organization.

In various clinical settings one or another aspect of this basic polar configuration may be more or less evident. A familiar example of the way in which one aspect of the introjective configuration may remain concealed can be found in depressed patients. Clinically depressed patients usually present themselves and act in terms of a self-image generated from the narcissistically inferior alternative. At the same time, as is amply demonstrated in the therapy of such patients, the narcissistically superior dimension remains a relatively concealed or repressed, but nonetheless dynamically important force motivating the patients' pathology.

One borderline woman, who had managed to maintain a level of quite adequate functioning through most of her 50-odd years in virtue of being able to attach herself to a supportive sustaining object, became disorganized and depressed as a result of the loss of her central sustaining object. Her depression took the form of intense and persistent feelings of helplessness, hopelessness, worthlessness, emptiness, and feeling abandoned and without resource to help herself deal with life and its difficulties. Without the "significant other," life had no meaning. However, behind this depleted, empty, and at times suicidal stance, there was an intense and powerful narcissistic current that took the form of the expectation that life should be on her terms—people should be available to give her what she wanted, to fulfill her expectations, to provide for and care for her, all without any effort or work on her part. Her depressive stance was an adamant refusal to meet the demands of reality and to come to terms with its limits. She would do nothing for herself, but clung to the demand and expectation that others, including her therapist (the present author), would do it for her, would make her life what she expected it to be.

The introjective configuration can also be analyzed in terms of the vicissitudes of aggression. Here the polar opposites consist in dimensions of victimization, passivity, and vulnerability, as opposed to dimensions of power, destructiveness, and aggression. These polarities have been characterized respectively as the victim-introject, in terms of which the patient experiences and expresses himself or herself as weak, vulnerable, victimized and helplessly impotent, and its opposite configuration, the aggressor-introject, in which the self is displayed as powerful, destructive, evil, terrifying, and even murderous. This latter aspect of the aggressive-introjective configuration is equivalent to the classically described "identification with the aggressor" (A. Freud 1936). The "identification" in this case is to be taken as a form of mingled imitation-with-introjection of the aggressive or threatening object (Meissner 1971, 1974).

A comparable reciprocal relationship arises between these polar opposites as between the narcissistic dimensions. The victim-introject is never found without its companion aggressor-introject. This basic configuration is long familiar in terms of sadomasochistic personality organization and its instinctual dynamics and in classically described depressive syndromes in which aggression plays a significant role, often transformed into superego aggression—another form of introjective organization. Similar dynamics can also be defined in paranoid states in which the apparent victimization is ultimately matched by the aggressive, hostile, destructive side of the patient's personality projected as a persecuting object.

In the borderline conditions, these polar configurations remain both relatively easily available to conscious processing and characteristically maintain their polar opposition and independence. The patterns of expression of this tendency may vary from patient to patient and from time to time in a given patient. At one point in the therapeutic work with a patient, the victim-introject may tend to dominate the patient's psychic functioning, but then at another time the aggressor-introject may come to the ascendency. A similar process may take place with the narcissistic configurations as well, so that the patient may be at one time operating, in a sense, in the mode of cold, contemptuous superiority and devaluation of the therapist, while at another time he or she may be functioning in terms of the opposite configuration of feelings of worthlessness and shameful inferiority. Not only are the polar configurations readily available to consciousness, but there is also a tendency for these patients to shift back and forth from one configuration to the other, often with great ease and rapidity—the more so, the more primitive the level of borderline functioning. These introjective configurations are most clearly, and often chaotically, mobilized in regressive borderline states (Meissner 1978a, in press). The mobilization of such segregated self-schemata in borderline patients has also been addressed as an aspect of splitting by Horowitz (1977).

It should be noted in this connection, however, that there are, as has already been suggested, degrees of difference in the patterning and expression of these configurations. The polar tension of this organization in the borderline personality creates a situation in which the capacities for integration of a more harmoniously functioning and cohesive sense of self are continually being undermined. In the more severely disturbed borderlines, where the polar tensions are at a higher degree of intensity and where the opposite dimensions tend to operate at the quantitative extremes, self-cohesion is fragile and easily susceptible to regressive fragmentation. In better organized borderline personalities, however, these polar tensions are considerably muted and allow for significant areas of cohesive and relatively autonomous functioning and self-organization.

This analysis of the introjective organization provides a basis for the understanding of TR/CT interactions. The introjective organization gives rise to projections that color the experience of objects and modify the quality of object relations. This is the basic mechanism of so-called projective or "externalizing" TRs (Berg 1977).

The projections are usually specifically based on and derived from those aspects of the introjective configuration that remain inactive or repressed at any given point in the patient's experience. The patient who is functioning in the terms of the victim-introject, for example, will tend to project the polar opposite aggressor-introject, so that in the interaction with the therapist the aggressive projection will color and influence the patient's perception of and interaction with the therapist. The therapist is then cast in the role of victimizer and aggressive persecutor. Similarly, the patient who is functioning in terms of the narcissistically inferior configuration will tend to project the narcissistic opposite in a form of idealization of the therapist. The projective device is not simply an intrapsychic or subjective phenomenon; it also creates a pressure in the interpersonal interaction to draw the other member of that interaction to fulfill the expectations and the inherent demands of the projection. The therapist in such a situation is not only seen by the patient as, for example, an aggressive persecutor, but the projection has an inherent gradient that tends to elicit an aggressive response from the therapist in his or her interaction with the patient.

Thus the patient's projections can create a counter-response and reaction in the therapist. The patient's projections may elicit an unconscious tendency in the therapist to introject the content of the patient's projection and, insofar as this response takes place, to begin to function in terms of the inherent demands of those introjections. This may set the stage for and mobilize a counterprojective response on the part of the therapist that derives from the amalgamation and combined influence of the introjected content from the patient and the therapist's own introjective configurations, which he or she carries as part of his or her own personality organization. The resulting introjective organization and the derivative counterprojections coming from the therapist to the patient form the core of what has been described as CT.[1]

The interlocking of introjection and projection on the part of both patient and therapist gives rise to the most profound TR/CT interactions that have the potential to be mutually reinforcing. Thus the patient, for example, who projects the aggressive derivatives onto his or her therapist sets up an unconscious process in the therapist that tends to introject the aggressive content, which thus becomes amalgamated with and reinforces aspects of his or her own aggressor-introject configuration. This sets in motion within the therapist the process by which he or she not only begins to act the aggressor toward the patient, but also projects the aspects of victimization and vulnerability back onto his or her patient. This projective content is, in turn, internalized and introjected by the patient as a reinforcement of his or her own victim stance. These mechanisms have been described in some detail by Racker (1953, 1957). Racker (1957) distinguishes concordant identifications, which reflect a recognition of what is experienced in the other as belonging to oneself, from complementary identifications produced as a result of the patient's projection and the corresponding internalization by the therapist. The complementary types are equivalent to the introjections being discussed here. Racker also underscores the potential threat from mutually reinforcing TR/CT interactions, which he describes as a vicious neurotic circle.

It must be remembered that these unconscious TR/CT pressures may be active to some degree in all forms of therapeutic interaction, but are particularly poignant and forceful in work with borderline patients. The easy availability of these configurations for projection creates a particular pressure within the therapeutic interaction for such CT manifestations to arise. This may be seen with particularly dramatic impact in the lower-order and more poorly integrated borderlines in whom the propensity for projection is relatively strong. However, it is also true in lesser degree even in the more highly organized and better functioning forms of borderline organization in which the polar opposites of these configurations may not be so extreme and may not be as readily apparent. In this latter category of patient, considerable therapeutic regression and intensification of the therapeutic relationship often has to take place before these manifestations become operative.

One of the pervasive influences in borderline conditions is the strong need

1. These processes have been described by Grinberg (1962) in terms of projective identifications and projective counteridentifications. This basically Kleinian usage is not followed in this discussion for technical and theoretical reasons that are more fully discussed elsewhere (Meissner 1980).

for and dependency on objects to help the patient stabilize a sense of inner continuity and self-coherence. Kohut (1971) describes something similar in narcissistic terms as dependence on "self-objects." The object for borderline patients is needed as an external prop or stabilizer for the threatening fragmentation or disruption of the patient's sense of self, yet at the same time this dependency is highly ambivalent and feared. Such patients react with varying degrees of withdrawal or isolation in an attempt to deny their basic need or dependency out of the fear of objects.

As Kernberg (1968) points out, insofar as the therapist is drawn into this projective interaction, there is risk of recreating in the external interaction within the therapy the original pathological introjective configuration within the patient. The inner pathological tension between the introjective polar configurations can thus be displaced to a conflict with the external object, with the correlative gain that the pattern of self-organization can be organized, for the time being, around the residual configuration. In this manner the projection of aggressive derivatives onto the therapist eases the inner tension required to defend against such impulses internally and allows for a more consolidated sense of self around the victim configuration. To the extent that the therapist can be drawn into fulfilling the expectations of this projection, the patient gains an inner sense of consistency and self-organization, but at the expense of consolidating a basically pathological situation.

Although the basic dynamics of TR/CT interactions are primarily unconscious, they can have more conscious reverberations and concomitants that can alert the therapist to their operation. Unconscious CT reactions, as long as they remain at that level, are usually disruptive of the therapeutic interaction and interfere with an effective therapeutic alliance. However, when such dynamics can be identified and consciously processed, they provide an opportunity for recognition and resolution of aspects of the patient's pathology that may otherwise remain hidden.

ASPECTS OF BORDERLINE COUNTERTRANSFERENCE

The projection of relatively intense and often primitive affects in the borderline TR can often have a powerful effect on the therapist. These feelings are often disruptive and threatening, and include homicidal anger, intense and clinging dependency, helplessness, incestuous wishes and primitive fears of abandonment, despair, hopelessness, and even suicidal depression. To the extent that they feed into the therapist's unresolved conflicts, his or her own unconscious and unresolved wishes, and the primitive urges and defenses against them, they can often create a difficult impasse or turmoil that tends to frustrate the therapeutic work (Masterson 1972).

CT Variation

The quality of borderline TRs can vary over a wide spectrum of intensity and degrees of pathological expression. The nature of the CT reaction tends to vary accordingly. At the more primitive level of TR interaction with borderline patients, the therapist is often caught up in intense emotional reactions reflecting the patient's primitive emotional struggles with aloneness, abandonment, the primitive hunger for objects, and devouring rage. The therapist, in turn, may then begin to feel drawn into this emotional maelstrom and begin to experience similarly intense and relatively primitive emotional turmoil. Reactions at this level have more to do with the emotional force generated by the patient's projections and TR than with the therapist's own internally derived CT elements.

Clinical experience has repeatedly demonstrated the sensitivity of borderline patients to CT reactions. Particularly in dealing with lower-order forms of borderline psychopathology or with regressive borderline states, it becomes important to the therapeutic work for the therapist not only to be in touch with his or her emotional responsiveness to the patient, but also to be able to freely acknowledge such reactions to himself or herself and, where appropriate, to the patient. The capacity for the therapist to become conscious of, identify, and acknowledge his or her initially unconscious CT reactions is primary and essential to effective therapeutic management. Such internal acknowledgment may alert the therapist to hidden therapeutic issues or to failures in the therapeutic alliance. Self-analysis and monitoring of his or her own responses may be adequate and appropriate. Where the alliance is severely threatened, some more direct interaction with the patient may be called for. At such times, the therapist's capacity to be open and frank about such reactions can be reassuring to the patient, in that it confirms the patient's perceptions of the reality of the therapist and helps to consolidate the discrimination between fantasy and reality. On the other hand, the failure to acknowledge such reactions can be extremely disruptive and may even contribute to a malignant regression in the patient (Giovacchini 1973). As Langs (1976a, 1976b) notes, such regressions may reflect the failure of the alliance. In addition, such misalliances and the push toward regression they precipitate in borderline patients are often caused by unresolved CT difficulties.

A clinical example may help to clarify some of these issues. The patient, a quite primitive borderline woman with many characteristics of a psychotic character, would, at points of severe regressive crisis, look quite psychotic and have a strong propensity for acting-out aggressive impulses in suicidal and self-destructive ways, including repeated overdosing and episodes of self-laceration. After the therapist had been seeing this young woman for about a year in twice-weekly psychotherapy, it happened that a holiday came along and he neglected to remind her that they would not be meeting on that particular day. As it turned out, the patient came to the therapist's office door and found it locked.

The patient went away in a rage, but much to her credit was able to call the therapist the following day, still bitterly angry, and tearfully reproach him for this unkind oversight. He replied with some concern that she had been inconvenienced, apologized, and told her that they would talk about it when he next saw her.

When she subsequently came to his office, the episode was still obviously on her mind, and there was a simmering resentment and bitterness that was not difficult to discern. The therapist asked her about her feelings, and she told him about the fantasies she had had on coming to his locked door. At first, she said, she felt bitterly disappointed and hurt, and then was over-whelmed by a wave of anger in which she imagined herself screaming at the therapist and finally throwing things at him. She was afraid that her anger would destroy him somehow, but was able to acknowledge that she was angry enough at that point to want to kill him. Moreover, quite consistently with her paranoid disposition, she felt that this oversight had been deliberate on the therapist's part and derived from his anger at her and his wish to retaliate against her because of the angry wishes and feelings she had about him. She felt that his behavior had been the result of his own wish to get rid of her, to lock her out in the hopes that in a fit of anger she would leave the treatment.

In the course of the discussion, the therapist told her that he was really not aware of the sorts of feelings that she ascribed to him, but that, in looking at the behavior, both she and he had reason to be suspicious: When she had called him to tell him that she had come to his office on the holiday, he had truly been surprised and somewhat chagrined that he had forgotten to tell her about the holiday. But the fact remained that her perception might in some way be accurate, namely in that his forgetting might have been motivated by some anger at her and some wish to retaliate in ways that he might otherwise not even consider.

The effect of this admission was quite striking. She seemed to be relieved and almost immediately relaxed her tense and worried demeanor. She seemed to be considerably mollified. In fact, the therapist's admission had legitimated and justified her anger. The anger began to look realistic and in some degree reasonable, rather than the product of her distorted thinking and her craziness. The discussion led on to a consideration of the patient's fear of the therapist's anger and of the possibility of his retaliation against her, and moved from there to an extremely useful discussion of her fear of her father's explosive and somewhat paranoid anger. She recounted several episodes in which she had been terrified of his rages and his seemingly capricious, cold, rejecting anger. She was able to talk about her difficulty in dealing with such feelings, as well as her difficulty in expressing her own angry feelings in ways that were appropriate and constructive.

It became clear to her that even though such angry feelings might arise in the context of the therapeutic relationship, they could still be put in perspective and did not necessarily destroy the relationship, nor did they mean that, when such feelings were operating in the therapist, it would wipe out or eliminate the warm feelings he might have toward her or the wishes on his part to be therapeutically useful and helpful to her. The therapist's admission meant that any supposition that he was always right and sane in the therapeutic relationship and that she was always wrong and crazy was decisively undermined. This understanding between them made it considerably easier for her to talk about angry feelings, to express them without fear of destructive retaliation from the therapist, and consequently to be able to explore and understand them.

Sensitivity to CT reactions is characteristic across the borderline spectrum, but it remains especially telling and disruptive in the more primitive range. This reflects the differential tuning of such personalities to a different range of interpersonal exchange than is customary in neurotic or healthier patients. There is often an immediate and intense response to a CT reaction, which is experienced as though it were consciously intended or, in the case of aggressive components, as a deliberately instigated and direct attack (Krohn 1974).

In the more primitive borderline patients, acting-out becomes a major vehicle for relieving the tension arising from conflicting object needs in the therapeutic relationship. It may also serve as an important way of testing how much the therapist can take and how able he or she is to control the situation and protect the patient from the choatic impulses within himself or herself. Insofar as possible, the therapist's interventions should be approached from the perspective of the therapeutic alliance. The emphasis on alliance factors in this connection is particularly important, since the acting-out is almost always a reflection of underlying TR/CT difficulties (Langs 1975a, 1975b, 1976a). The therapist at such points needs to maintain his or her autonomy and to accept the responsibility for his or her interventions and their consequences. This extends even to hospitalization, which may be essential in gaining control of an otherwise destructive situation when the patient is acting-out self-destructively (overdosing, cutting himself or herself, otherwise disorganized) or when suicidal acting-out is in question (Meissner 1977).

The issues of tolerating regression and of maintaining a therapeutic stance are particularly joined in an acute way in the management of the patient's tendencies to act-out. In dealing with lower-order borderline pathology, the difficulties related to acting-out are always a prominent part of the therapy and are particularly crucial in the initial phases of treatment. In the higher-order range of the borderline spectrum, however, the acting-out tendencies are less dramatic, less self-destructive, often more subtle, and often do not appear until significant levels of therapeutic regression have been attained. Acting out at this higher level of borderline organization frequently takes the form of more subtle forms of behavior outside the therapy reflecting transference dynamics. Such behavior may be precipitated particularly at times of interruption or separation in the therapy. This contrasts with the often more dramatic, manipulative, and tension-related acting out of more primitive borderline patients. In both cases, CT problems can interfere with proper management and effective therapeutic response.

The therapist's task in dealing with tendencies to act out is to maintain a firm, consistent, and assertive stance in setting limits on such tendencies without entering into the TR/CT interaction that would recapitulate the patient's victimization and put the analyst in a threatening, prohibiting, accusatory, and chastizing position. The therapist's introduction of limit-setting and controlling parameters can be easily translated in terms of the patient's projection into sadistic images.

In more primitive acting out, direct limit-setting and an active attempt to explore the meaning of such behavior are indicated; unresolved aggressive conflicts or unconscious hostile or destructive wishes toward the patient can inhibit appropriate and effective action. For higher order forms of acting out, interpretation and the exploration of meaning in terms of the therapeutic relationship are more effective.

One discriminable form of borderline pathology is the schizoid variant. These patients present a facade of affective isolation and cold, grandiose self-sufficiency (Modell 1975). The affective block and failure of communication are due to fear of closeness to the therapist. There is a basic object-related conflict, basic to the borderline condition, of both an intense need for and a terrifying fear of objects. They cope with this underlying conflict by a posture of isolation and withdrawal, warding off any affective contact with objects and adopting a rejecting and disdainful attitude in a vain attempt to convince the other and themselves that the vulnerable and helplessly impotent sense of themselves that pervades their inner world does not exist. The patient behaves almost as though the therapist were not in the room. The therapist experiences this attitude as a narcissistic effront and may respond with impatience, anger, boredom, distraction, sleepiness, etcetera.

For example, one such patient presented superficially as a classical obsessional personality. The analytic hours were filled with superficial and largely irrelevant material. As the analytic regression began to take effect, hints of the patient's underlying narcissistic vulnerability and intense rage began to appear. These moments of affective turmoil were quickly covered over and denied. Gradually the hours were increasingly filled with silence. Gentle and occasional attempts to ease the patient's aloof retreat behind a wall of silence were futile. Whole hours would pass without a word. The therapist found himself impatient, frustrated, and bored. His mind would wander and get lost in all sorts of distracting reflections, none of which had to do with his patient. He found himself frequently dozing and falling asleep. Even worse, he began to think that the patient was unanalyzable, that the therapist should have had better sense than to have accepted him for analysis, wishing that he would quit the analysis, etcetera. Clearly, the therapist's narcissism was on the line and was suffering considerable duress.

To make a long story short, the patient did express a wish to stop the analysis. Thus they were able to find out that the patient's magical conviction was that the therapist could alleviate his difficulties if he wanted to. All the patient had to do was come to the hours, be there for the required time, and that was enough. The rest was up to the therapist. The patient would exert no effort, undergo no pain, and take no responsibility for the progress of his analysis. He was simply waiting the therapist out. If the therapist refused to perform the magic, the patient would quit. This reflected powerful transference issues having to do with his infantile expectations of his parents, which had been severely disappointed. He was an only child with no history of real friendships or other meaningful human involvements. He looked to his parents for his human involvements. Even though he was an only child, he cherished bitter resentments that his parents would not make him the center of their lives and that they had not given him more or done more for him. He felt that his mother had not wanted him and that she was more involved and committed to her artistic career than to him. He saw his father as inadequate and impotent, a failure in life who had failed to provide him a model of real manhood. He saw the therapist as more concerned with the scientific study of his "case" than with him as a human being. The therapist was also inadequate and impotent as an analyst because he could not deal effectively with the patient's difficulties. Quitting the analysis would confirm both these transferential convictions.

The patient clung to his posture of blaming his parents for his problems. They had made him the way he was, and he would make no effort to change himself. It was up to them to do for him what they had not done. It was up to the therapist to do for him what they had not done. Any notion that he had to take responsibility for his own life and happiness was rejected out of hand.

When it became clear to him that the therapist could not or would not meet his demands, he stopped coming. Despite the therapist's conscious efforts to the contrary, the hostile CT wish was fulfilled. The patient was able to fulfill and live out his fantasy of becoming the therapist's victim.

The schizoid variant forms a dramatic contrast to the more intensely involved, conflicted, clinging, and hostilely dependent picture found in other forms of borderline pathology. The conflicts in both of these primitive types of patients are similar, but the patterns of defense and behavior organized to cope with these fundamental conflicts differ radically. The desperate reaching out for contact and infantile dependence on a sustaining object in the one contrasts radically with the aloof and isolated withdrawal of the other. Within the borderline spectrum, however, they can both be taken as expressions of relatively primitive conflicts over involvement with objects, representing comparable levels of personality organization and functioning.

In contrast to these more primitive interactions, TR/CT interactions toward the more differentiated and higher order end of the borderline spectrum tend to be less intense, less primitive, and less easily mobilized. Frequently enough in such patients, the borderline characteristics remain concealed or muted for considerable time, and only under significant degrees of therapeutic regression does the borderline quality of the patient's personality organization become more manifest. The TRs of such patients may be pervaded by a subtle but nonetheless detectable form of magical expectation that the therapist's power will somehow solve all of the patient's problems, or a subtle idealization that is reflected in an all-too-willing compliance. Or the therapist discovers only gradually over time that the therapeutic effort has stalemated in the face of a continuing elusiveness and subtle isolation of the patient's real feelings behind a facade of therapeutic compliance.

At this level of borderline pathology, the CT difficulties are of a quite different order. Not only are the TR/CT interactions more subtle and less dramatic, but there is less of the quality of evoked affect in the therapist's relation to the patient. The capacity for differentiating reality from fantasy and the ability to tolerate affective tension is more highly developed in these patients, so that the quality of TR projections and their impingement on the therapist has a different character. The impact of the patient's projections is neither as intense nor acute as in lower order borderlines. The corresponding CT reaction is a more gradual process that evolves more slowly over time as the regressive aspects of the therapy evolve and begin to exercise greater influence over the therapeutic interaction. Such patients may for long periods look no different than neurotic or narcissistic personalities. The borderline aspects may emerge only gradually, or may rapidly intrude on the therapeutic effort as a result of a more acute regressive crisis. At such points, there may occur a "paranoid spike," which seems strikingly at variance with the patient's usual posture. Such regressive moments are transitory for the most part and readily yield to subsequent exploration and interpretation, thanks to the patient's capacity for reality-testing and his or her capacity to distinguish reality from fantasy.

Rather than the interactional struggles that characterize more primitive borderline TR/CT transactions, the TR/CT difficulties in these patients are more frequently found in more subtle distortions of the therapeutic alliance, which tend to be pervasive and persistent. The therapist does not become aware of CT reactions and their derivatives directly, but more frequently finds himself or herself experiencing stalemate or some faltering in the therapeutic work. This may relate to therapist's own aggressive or narcissistic conflicts, which lead him or her to collude with the patient's subtle neurotic stance. Thus appropriate interpretations may be withheld because the patient's inherently victimized stance elicits aggressive elements in the therapist that obtrude on his or her ability to be appropriately assertive or confronting in the therapy. Or similarly, the narcissistic aspects of the interaction may provoke the therapist's narcissistic vulnerability, or conversely draw the therapist into a position of therapeutic omnipotence on the basis of a presumed but unexamined inadequacy in the patient.

In many lower-order borderlines, acute and intense TR/CT interactions may be precipitated quite early in the therapy, even in the first few sessions. The intense, precipitous TR involvement and its related CT turmoil are very nearly classic for more primitive borderline conditions, as represented by the psychotic characters or the pseudoschizophrenics. This is not characteristic of higher-order patients, but even in these patients the potential exists for more subtle deviations in the therapeutic alliance that may begin to manifest themselves in early sessions. These deviations or misalliances (Langs 1975a) are often slow to develop, at least to the point at which the therapist can recognize them, and lack the peremptory quality of lower-order TR/CT influences. Early detection and therapeutic response to initial alliance deviations can help in generating an effective therapeutic relationship.

The difficulties may take the form of persistent resistance that do not seem to yield or modify under the influence of continuing and extensive interpretation and working through. In the analytical situation, for example, such patients can comply with the amenities of analytical work, yet effectively avoid any authentic or meaingful involvement with the therapist over extensive periods of time.

The difficulties with borderline patients in the separation phase are particularly important in view of the classic difficulty of the borderline patient to effectively separate from self-sustaining objects and of accomplishing the difficult task of internalization that would complete the work of separation.

In this final phase of the therapy, the therapist's inability to tolerate the patient's infantile dependency may lead to a precipitous termination and a need to see the patient as more resourceful or autonomous than the patient may in fact be. The opposite difficulty may also obtain, namely that the therapist has difficulty separating and letting go of the patient. Such therapists run the risk of reinforcing the patient's need for symbiotic dependency and recreating in the therapy the kinds of parental interactions that thwarted the patient's striving for autonomy in the first place (Masterson 1972).

These CT difficulties are reactivated with particular force in the termination phase of the therapy. Conflicts over dependency and the therapist's role as helping and sustaining object become central. The CT problems generally have to do with the therapist's need to keep the patient dependent or, conversely, with his or her inability to tolerate the patient's emerging autonomy and separateness. This can provide the basis for a collusive mesh with the patient's own inability to tolerate these aspects. The need to see the patient as needing help can play a role here, buttressed by the therapist's own need to be needed and to see himself or herself as helping and as important to the patient. As is often the case with parents, it is difficult for the therapist to see himself or herself as superfluous.

These CT difficulties must be counterposed to the actuality of the patient's incapacity to effectuate the work of termination. In the face of the separation from the therapist and the inevitable mourning process associated with it, there is a tendency for a regressive retreat to and reactivation of the prior pathogenic introjective configuration. As these formations are reactivated under separation pressures, the tendency for associated projections and negative TR elements to re-emerge is significant, and these dimensions must be reworked in the interest of sustaining and reinforcing a persistent alliance that will allow the patient to undergo the necessary pain of the mourning process. However, one frequently finds that the capacity for internalization, which is required to make this process an effective and therapeutically useful one, is lacking in such patients—particularly in patients at the lower-level of the borderline spectrum. With such patients, a straightforward termination may not be possible, and the alternative course of attenuating the therapy over time may be a necessity (Zetzel 1971). The therapy with such patients may become quite attenuated indeed; patients may ultimately be seen on rare occasions at intervals of over a year, or even maintain therapeutic contact by occasional telephone calls or letters. In fact, the therapeutic contact may never be severed, and the therapy never terminated. The sustaining function of the therapist as an important object in the maintenance of the economy of psychic equilibrium in the patient cannot be underestimated in this context.

In higher-order borderline conditions, the capacity to separate and internalize may be compromised to some degree, but there is nonetheless sufficient capacity to tolerate the necessary mourning and to effect a meaningful separation. With these patients, the separation work should be attempted with as little dilution as possible. The issues are basically issues of separation and individuation, and require both tolerance of separation and continuing support from the therapist. In any case, the work of separation is more problematic in these patients, requires more time, may suffer regression more easily, and often requires occasional reworking and reinforcement, in contrast to the typical separation work with neurotic patients. By the same token, separation work is possible for these patients, while for more primitive borderlines it may not be. Thus CT difficulties will differ accordingly.

Aggressive Aspects

The aggressive aspects of TR/CT interactions express themselves in terms of the interplay between agressor- and victim-introjects in both therapist and patient. The TR regressions that are seen in more primitively organized borderlines are frequently the result of primitive TR reactions of a negative sort as a consequence of aggressive projections onto the therapist. These may be expressed as an intensification of distrust or fear of the therapist, who is seen as hurtful and attacking, and may result in sadistic or destructive defensive efforts on the part of the patient to control the powerful and feared therapist. The borderline patient is caught on the horns of a dilemma created by his or her strong yearning and need for objects along with his or her continuing rage and rejection of others as these deeply affecting narcissistic needs fail to be met. The patient's rejection and demeaning of the therapist and the correlative projection can arouse feelings of worthlessness and impotence in the therapist and correspondingly evoke his or her own restitutive aggression.

In the interest of maintaining the therapeutic alliance, the therapist must pay careful attention to negative TR elements. A consistent element is the patient's efforts to defeat the therapist, to make the therapy into a meaningless and ineffectual game as well as to destroy whatever there is in the experience that may be positive and constructive (Kernberg 1970). Behind this lies the inner necessity on the part of the patient to maintain the introjective configuration which provides the core of his often fragile and unstable self-organization. As we have already suggested, the projective elaboration which underlies the TR/CT interaction has as its underlying motivation the preservation of the pathogenic introjective organization. Thus, a constant attention to focusing, clarifying, and interpreting of the negative TR elements is of particular importance in the interest of establishing and maintaining a therapeutic alliance (Kernberg 1970, Friedman 1975).

The therapist must maintain a consistent, tactful, nonretaliatory, and therapeutically productive attitude toward the patient's rage. It is only by the working-through of these introjective dimensions and their introjective reprocessing that the patient is gradually able to give up the pathogenic introject and is capable of experiencing the therapist as a relatively good object. The patient must learn the difficult if primitive lesson that he or she can feel a sense of intimacy and helpless vulnerability with the therapist without fear of being engulfed or consumed in the process. Similarly, the patient must learn that he or she can experience anger and rage and express it within the therapy without the danger of provoking a retaliation or of destroying the therapist, or of disrupting the relationship. In addition, he or she must learn that it is possible to experience the therapist's anger without being destroyed, abandoned, rejected, or otherwise punished.

These aggressive dynamics can play themselves out, not only in more primitive borderline conditions in which the desperate intense clinging need for objects is considerably more apparent and available, but also in schizoid conditions in which the same powerful dependency needs are operative, but in which the patient mobilizes strong isolating and distancing defenses. The patient's rage at the therapist's disappointing or frustrating of this need can be stimulated particularly in contexts in which, for example, the therapist goes on vacation or is absent for some reason, or even when there is failure in the therapist's empathy, responsiveness, or understanding. The patient's readiness to mobilize feelings of vulnerability and weakness and to project the aggressive and hostile components onto the therapist can easily stimulate CT responses that diminish or interfere with the therapist's capacity for empathic understanding. This can often give rise in severely disturbed borderlines to a paranoid TR distortion in which the therapist is seen as hostile or destructive and must be rejected, defended against, or even devalued and discounted.

In the TR/CT interaction, the borderline patient may adopt a masochistic-depressive posture, accompanied by the projection of aggressive derivatives onto the therapist. The therapist may respond with a variety of aggressive CT manifestations. The therapist may feel that he or she must rescue or somehow alleviate the helpless patient's pain, but is then met with escalated narcissistic demands and intensified regression. This stimulates the therapist's own sense of rage and envy, and may lead to angry or destructive confrontations (Adler and Buie 1972). The patient's anger, helplessness, and despairing impotence when these intensified narcissistic demands are not gratified prompts the therapist to respond by giving more time, wishing to support the patient in various pain-alleviating ways, providing reassurance, etcetera—a kind of corrective emotional experience that may provide temporary relief, but may also contribute to the intensification of regressive wishes and precipitate a malignant regression. Langs (1976b) describes this as a form of misalliance cure.

The therapist in these situations feels helpless, frustrated, and depleted. He or she may respond with an angry assault on the patient's entitlement that merely reinforces the primitive aggressive projection as well as the correlative victimization in the patient. The therapist avoids his or her own inner despair and the related narcissistic threat by an implicit devaluation and confrontation of the patient. In general, the intense demands placed on the therapist are not only a constant assault on his or her own self-esteem, but can leave him or her feeling drained, frustrated, depleted, and impotent. The therapist's own retaliatory impulses are stimulated primarily in the interest of self-preservation. The result can be a form of counteraggression against the patient that makes it difficult to draw the line between the appropriate uses of positive aggression in therapy (confrontations, limit-setting, etcetera) and the expression of hostile and destructive impulses in the CT.

Therapeutic confrontation is particularly useful in regard to the patient's victimization, reflecting the underlying victim-introject. A clear statement of the patient's victimized position, or of the potential victimizing effects of a projected course of acting-out, can serve as a useful way of focusing on the underlying dynamics and the motivations related to them and of bringing into focus their effects on the therapeutic work and particularly the therapeutic alliance. Such clarifications and confrontations with the patient's potential self-destructiveness and need to assume the victimized position carry with them a reassurance that the patient is not on this account abandoned or rejected and undercut the pull in the CT reaction to playing into the patient's victimization, thus reinforcing it. This is especially pertinent and poignant in the confrontational stance required with regressive suicidal impulses or tendencies to suicidal acting-out (Maltsberger and Buie 1974, Meissner 1977).

In fact, the more or less acute manipulative demandingness and provocativeness of the more flamboyant borderline patient is at times easier to deal with than the more chronic oral rage and resentment directed against the therapist because of his or her failure to gratify the patient's wishes for an idealized parent. Such patients have a genius for intuitively sensing the therapist's narcissistic vulnerabilities and for choosing the right moments to exploit them. This may take the form of belittling the therapist's interventions, negating his or her interpretations, or constantly devaluing the treatment and the therapist, making the therapist feel impotent and helpless. Under the continued erosion of such influences, the therapist's largely therapeutic attitudes can be gradually transformed into subtle and pervasive CT manifestations that become increasingly aggressive and even sadistic.

Under such CT pressures, the therapist may be moved to terminate the therapy prematurely, thus relieving himself or herself of a relationship in which he or she feels trapped, defeated, and helpless—obviously an acting-out of the therapist's wishes to be rid of a patient who provokes such uncomfortable feelings (Nadelson 1976). The therapist's aggressive impulse may also take the form of excessive activity or becoming more interactive with the patient, either in the interests of overcoming the sense of frustration and helplessness or as a means of exerting control over an otherwise anxiety-producing situation.

The therapist must be cautious of the tendency to sadomasochistic acting-out in the therapy; it often serves to mask underlying narcissistic trans-ferences (Oremland and Windholz 1971). This is particularly a problem with therapists whose own sadomasochistic conflicts remain to some degree unresolved. As Nadelson (1976) notes, the therapist who believes himself or herself to be invulnerable to such feelings or conflicts may be at significant risk for missing an essential part of the therapy and for falling into CT difficulties. The aggressive CT stance may also express itself in the therapist's need to reassert his or her authority, defensively insisting to the patient on the therapist's own professional competence and value. The patient may then respond, also defensively, with an increased level of anger or anxiety, or may resort to a more compliant stance in which anger is withheld. The need for the patient to protect and buffer such a therapist becomes part of the therapeutic interaction and contributes further to the undermining of the therapeutic alliance.

When the derivatives of the victim-introject are projected onto the thera-pist, this can stimulate the therapist's own conflicts over aggression and defensively reactivate the therapist's own masochism (Racker 1958). The therapist's guilt over counteraggressive impulses may result in a reactive masochistic submission to the patient's aggression by which the therapist begins to doubt his or her own capacities and competence, and begins to assimilate the masochistically tinged victim-introjective elements. The pa-tient's aggressive posture, acting out the aggressor-introject, is accompanied by the projection of the elements of vulnerability and victimization onto the therapist. The masochistic introjection of these elements gradually under-mines the therapist's sense of self-esteem and competence, and gradually erodes his or her sense of professional identity. There is a strong temptation for a masochistic submission to the patient's efforts at control. This ex-presses itself in a sense of guilt, depression, and shame that the therapist is unable to live up to and gratify the patient's magical expectations.

The patient's failure to respond, accompanied by a continual effort to frustrate the aims and objectives of the therapy, creates a sense of helpless-ness and hopelessness in the therapist. The patient may respond not so much with rage as with a sense of sadness and disillusionment reflecting the original disappointment in the incompetent or unresponsive mother. These aspects of the patient's own self-image are projected onto the therapist and produce a therapeutic stalemate in which the therapist feels impotent and frustrated, and finds himself or herself experiencing the urge to do something, anything, even though he or she may feel it to be ultimately unproductive or countertherapeutic, to relieve the sense of helpless frustration. The CT then becomes the vehicle for redeeming the therapist's own injured narcissism and for preserving a sense of competent and effective self and self-esteem.

Narcissistic Aspects

Narcissistic projection also plays an important role in the TR/CT interactions with borderline patients (Giovacchini 1975). When the inferior and devalued side of their own inner narcissistic introjective organization is projected, this frequently takes the form of devaluing or demeaning the therapist (Adler 1970). In particular, lower-order patients essentially refuse to accept what the therapist offers, but maintain the level and the intensity of their demand, often resorting to a form of narcissistic rage when the therapist is unable or unwilling to respond to their demands. In virtue of the projection, the therapist may be seen as angry and rejecting. The therapist may introject the implicit projection in a way that reinforces and plays into his or her own narcissistic vulnerability, or may find himself or herself urged to resort to self-defense in a variety of aggressive manifestations, or may try to redeem his or her tottering narcissism by attempting to prove to the patient that he or she can be the good, loving, and giving parent that the patient so insistently demands (Greenacre 1956, Myerson 1974).

If the inferior aspects of the patient's narcissistic organization can be projected, the superior aspects are equally available for projection in borderline patients. Such patients may approach the therapy with an attitude of submissive compliance to a powerful and all-wise therapist whom they invest with the capacity to fulfill their needs and to transform their lives magically. These expectations of magical rebirth may even become delusional as a manifestation of psychotic tranferences (Giovacchini 1973). The therapist's own unresolved narcissistic needs to assume the omnipotent role and to be the one to provide for all the patient's needs, or to be able to effectively deal with all of the patient's pathological expressions, put him or her in a position of vulnerability in this regard. These pressures may be particularly poignant in the opening phases of therapy with patients in a state of transient regression, as is frequently the case in the initial therapeutic encounter in more primitively organized borderlines. It is particularly important in such settings that the therapist not present himself or herself as an omnipotent figure with inexhaustible resources or capacities to respond to the patient's needs. The need for structuring the therapy effectively and for setting appropriate limits in such contexts is a primary aspect of the therapeutic interaction (Zetzel 1971).

A second form of narcissistic projection is idealization, a mechanism that is described by Kernberg (1967, 1968). In the more primitive or regressed borderline patient, this idealization is unrealistic and archaic, and usually serves to protect the therapist from the patient's negative transference dispositions, i.e., the projection of aggressive introjective derivatives. It may also serve as a defense against the impulse to devalue or depreciate the therapist. The therapist's own narcissistic need to be admired or to defensively counter his or her own feelings of inadequacy in dealing with such patients can easily put him or her into the position of being drawn into this narcissistic bind and entering into an implicit magical contract with the patient or implicitly accepting the patient's idealization (Greenacre 1956). However, such idealizations clearly set up difficult TR/CT distortions that effectively undermine any possibility of an effective therapeutic alliance.

At the same time, the therapist's reaction can be subtle and often quite well disguised, and can give rise to significant CT vicissitudes. Such patients may engage the therapist by an attitude of hopefulness and compliance, attributing a special power and wisdom to the therapist. This has the quality of an attempt to re-experience a kind of symbiotic relationship with a powerful object who will bring about some form of magical rebirth in the patient—something that the inadequate and vulnerable mother was unable to accomplish. The patient's helpless impotence is matched by the projective magical power of the therapist. This may lead to an inevitable disappointment and disillusionment in the patient, and a sense of frustration and impotence in the therapist. Such a patient seeks to draw a therapist into the position of an omnipotent rescuer, to play the companion to his or her own helplessness, sense of weakness, and vulnerability (Giovacchini 1973).

As Kernberg (1968) notes, to undo such idealizations it is necessary to confront the patient continually with the transference distortion while at the same time acknowledging the positive feelings toward the therapist. This task is particularly difficult, since such idealizations often mask paranoid fears or primitive aggressive hostile and aggressive feelings toward the transference object. It should be remembered that such idealizations are accompanied by a feeling of worthlessness and inner shame in the patient. The patient's wish is for the therapist to overcome these painful and self-demeaning feelings. The therapist's failure to respond to these needs may be translated into his or her withholding and rejection—the therapist becomes the idealized figure who refuses to give the patient the good things that the patient so desparately desires and needs (a situation that repeats the original traumatic experience in relationship to parental figures). The therapist's failure to respond to and meet such narcissistic expectations may turn him or her from an idealized figure into a magically powerful persecutor.

The same narcissistic dynamics can be identified in patients at the higher order borderline level. The quality of narcissistic interaction at this level of character organization—as in other aspects touched on in this study—tends to be more subtle and muted, less acute, more pervasive, and has much less tendency to evoke any specific reaction in the therapist. These patients often look much like narcissistic characters clinically, and only the gradual emergence of specifiable borderline features justifies diagnostic differentiation (Meissner 1979a). Narcissistic transferences are identifiable and tend to shift the therapeutic alliance in the direction of a narcissistic alliance. In these patients, however, the narcissistic traumata are not as severe and the degree of narcissistic vulnerability not as profound as in more disturbed borderlines. The preservation of ego strengths and reality-testing make the narcissism of the higher-order patients much more approachable and amenable to interpretation. Correspondingly, confrontation is less frequently required.

Erotic Aspects

Regarding the role of erotized TRs and their correlative CT reactions, as Blum (1973) notes, the original, erotic libidinal sense of Freud's observations on such transference reactions has been broadened to include a diversity of related phenomena, including demands for physical contacts, the more disguised desire for sexual relations manifested as wishes for adult love or as assaultive antagonism, demands for approval and admiration, needs to please, wishes to gain acceptance by compliance, dependent clinging, fears of object loss, etcetera:

> The intensity and tenacity of erotized transference, the resistance to interpretation, and the continuing attempts to seduce the analyst into a joint acting out, as well as the frequenting acting out of such transference with a substitute for the analyst, confirm the complicated infantile reactions of these patients. . . . For the borderline patients manifesting this reaction, transference and reality may be dangerously confused. . . . Patients developing such erotized transference delusions have been predisposed by early ego impairment. The analyst may be "loved" as the single most precious object tie and reality representative (Blum 1973, pp. 63–64).

This quality of erotized TR is more attributable to the lower level of the borderline spectrum, but better organized and better functioning borderline patients are more likely to emphasize the importance of their tie to the analyst and to magnify the sense of clinging dependence on the analyst, without losing the capacity to distinguish between the reality of the therapeutic relationship and the erotized fantasies. Such patients may freely express and indulge themselves with highly erotic and even perverse fantasies about the analyst that have a highly seductive quality, but at the same time experience a sense of frustration and disappointment that the real relationship with the analyst offers something quite different. Fairly erotic dreams involving the analyst are also frequent.

Such erotized TRs in borderline patients tend to arise secondarily to the patients to the underlying but intimately related narcissistic dynamics. In other words, the erotic dynamics in the borderline patients are usually found to be related to and to draw their impact from the underlying narcissistic disequilibrium and need experienced so intensely by the patient. In this respect the erotized transferences of borderline patients differ markedly from the erotized neurotic transferences of healthier patients. The clinging dependence on the therapist as the single most important sustaining object has a sense of totality and urgency that the neurotic TR does not. Moreover, the intensity of this clinging dependence is more often than not found to have powerful narcissistic determinants. The therapist may be attuned to the more explicitly erotic aspects of the TR and fall victim to subtle narcissistic pulls. With more explicit reference to the CT, Blum (1973) notes:

> In the charged analytic situation, the pleasure of love and the love of pleasure can be an all-too-welcome escape from analytic abstinence and the recurrent encounter with disappointment and hostility. The analyst can enjoy the aggrandized glory of the patient's childish attraction and adulation. The analysis can be silently stalemated by an unconscious conspiracy of mutual admiration and endearment. There can be a subtle repetition of the parents' use of the child for their own narcissistic needs (pp. 73–75).

Recapitulation

The above discussion emphasizes the differential aspects of TR, CT, and TR/CT interactions that can arise in borderline conditions, particularly between lower-order and higher-order borderline groups. This rather complex discussion is schematized in Table 1. The attempt has obvious risks and may be premature. Tables tend to separate and overclarify. There are patients who can clearly be placed in one or another category, others for whom this may be difficult or problematic. Moreover, distinctions regarding phenomena that may be more continuous than discrete, and may in addition

TABLE 1. Differential Aspects of TR, CT, and TR/CT Interactions in Borderline Conditions

Borderline Conditions	General TR Qualities	TR Aspects	Possible CT Reactions
Lower-order Schizoid Personality Psychotic Character Pseudoneurotic Schizophrenic	1. Intense, acute, often rapidly mobilized, especially in regressive states, emotionally labile. 2. Reflect failure of reality-fantasy discrimination (experienced as real by patient). 3. Involve clear projective distortion—projective TR → displacement TR. 4. At severe levels, may involve delusional distortion (TR psychosis). 5. Introjective split unstable, vacillating, extreme.	1. *Aggressive.* A/V split, projection, projection experienced as affectively real, acted out → felt, often paranoid. 2. *Narcissistic.* S/I split, projection, idealization/devaluation, unrealistic, disillusion → depression/rage. 3. *Erotic.* Intense, clinging, dependen-, delusional, secondary to narcissistic need.	1. Reaction tends to be experienced emotionally, subjectively, often intensely. 2. Tendency for reaction to be acted out in therapy. 3. Pull toward regressive split—A/V, S/I—of therapist's introjective organization. 4. Activation of counterprojective dynamism. 5. Require more active therapeutic stance—limit-setting/confrontation/clarification → interpretation.
Higher-order Primitive Hysteric Borderline Personality As-if Personality False-Self	1. Muted, develops gradually in proportion to therapeutic regression, prolonged. 2. Reality perspective usually not lost, split between cognitive awareness and emotional reaction. 3. Projective mechanisms more muted, subtle, inferential—displacement TR → projective TR. 4. Rarely becomes delusional; regressive crises less severe, less frequent. 5. Tends to stabilize around one polar introjective organization; split less extreme.	1. *Aggressive.* A/V split less apparent, depressive/masochistic tendency, compliance. 2. *Narcissistic.* S/I split more subtle, rare grandiosity, idealistic, illusions/expectations. 3. *Erotic.* Similar to neurotic; object relation more narcissistic; can be affectively intense, but almost never delusional.	1. Reaction less subjectively/emotionally experienced, but tends to be reflected in disturbance of alliance sector. 2. Reactions generally more subtle, less acute/intense, more pervasive. 3. Less regressive dissociation in therapist; polarization more ambiguous. 4. Less tendency for counterprojective distortion; liability for implicit misalliance. 5. More specifically analytic stance feasible, greater passivity—association/interpretation → limit setting/confrontation/clarification.

overlap to some degree, can be misleading. With these cautions, let the table serve those who can use it with discretion—*caveat lector*!

The categories of borderline conditions are in some degree arbitrary and represent a concession to pre-existing descriptions of segments of the borderline spectrum (Meissner 1982). Psychotic characters and pseudoneurotic schizophrenics clearly belong to the lower-order gorup. Schizoid personalities are more equivocal, but the severity of underlying borderline issues is sufficiently intense to allow inclusion, despite the fact that the defensive organization is quite different. The as-if personalities, the false-self organizations, and the schizoid personalities are schizoid variants in which the former two represent generally less severe forms of personality impairment. The primitive hysterics and borderline personalities—the latter not to be confused with Kernberg's (1967) borderline personality organization, which includes all of these groups—are more definitively higher-order.

The major point of emphasis in the chart is that the quality of TR and the corresponding CT reactions is different and can be discriminated in these respective groupings. The differences can be decisively stated and recognized in some patients. In others the discrimination may be less clear, thus making the diagnostic picture more obscure and calling for greater therapeutic flexibility.

THERAPEUTIC RESPONSE TO CT DIFFICULTIES

As the preceding discussion might suggest, the varieties of borderline TR and the spectrum of possible CT reactions cover a wide-ranging complex of forms and degrees of difficulty. Within this far-reaching arena, the divergent features of CT experience and the quality of TR/CT interactions have been delineated in terms of the varying aspects of the borderline spectrum, casting the distinguishing characteristics in terms of the rather broad categories of lower versus higher-order borderline organization. Within this frame of reference, this diagnostic differentiation and the correlative aspects of TR and CT provide a basis for differing emphases in therapeutic response and in setting priorities for therapeutic intervention. The purpose here is to introduce this perspective into a discussion that all too frequently regards the therapy of borderline patients in relatively univocal terms without sufficient regard for the inherent variability within the borderline spectrum.

As a general principle, one must keep in mind that therapy takes place on more than one level. At a minimum, the influence of the therapist expresses itself not only on the level of verbal exchange, but also on the level of behavior and action. What therapists say to the patients must be placed alongside how they treat their patients, how they behave with their patients, what the affective quality of their interaction with their patients is, and how they react in the various contexts of interaction that arise in any course of therapy. These all communicate significant messages to the patient about the therapist's thoughts and feelings about him or her. Ideally, the therapist's thoughts, verbalizations, and actions should be consistent and directed to therapeutic goals. The potential for CT difficulties to influence the therapist's thoughts, feelings, attitudes, and words to the patient is great enough; the potential for these unconscious processes to find expression in the therapist's behavior and action is even greater. Moreover, while all patients are sensitive to such multiple messages, the borderline patient tends to be extremely sensitive and takes a back seat to none in this regard. There is a pressure in such patients to search out evidence to support the pathogenic introjective organization.

As noted, this pressure is especially intense in the lower-order group. When and to the extent that the pressure affects the TR/CT interaction, the priorities fall not on the more usual technique of interpretation, but on aspects of action and reaction with the patient that often have a much more immediate and often superficial quality. It is only when these aspects of the therapeutic interaction have been adjusted and the regressive strain has eased that further associative exploration and interpretation become feasible (Little 1966). The priorities for the higher-order group are different. Although the importance of verbal-actual consistency remains in force, the capacity to maintain perspective and the somewhat lessened need to assimilate elements of their experience to support the pathogenic configuration (while ignoring contradictory data) allows for a greater availability to reality testing and interpretation. These patients are more capable of accepting the therapist as a person with multiple aspects whose unconscious CT expressions need not interfere with or override his or her basic good will and therapeutic orientation.

Particularly with lower-order patients, in dealing with the projective-introjective interaction, the therapist must carefully discriminate between the patient's projections as such and the potential CT responses. Where such CTs are operative, it can be countertherapeutic to ascribe them simply to the patient's projections, since this would fail to acknowledge the reality component in the patient's perception. This can both undermine the patient's hold on reality and jeopardize the therapeutic alliance, thus contributing to further regression in the patient. Such discounting of the patient's perception in the therapeutic interaction and a reduction to projection can be both hostile and demeaning to the patient, and may represent a form of CT counteraggression. This would certainly have been the case for the patient described earlier whose rage was roused by the therapist's failure to notify her at a holiday. On the other hand, the open and honest focusing on CT reactions and their further exploration in terms of the meaning for the therapeutic interaction can be extremely useful and helpful (Giovacchini 1972).

This does not mean that the therapist will necessarily communicate all thoughts and feelings, even those reflecting CT difficulties, to the patient. This is by no means always indicated or always useful (Little 1957). It is extremely important, however, that the therapist be in touch with such feelings and such attitudes, and that he or she should be ready and able to do so when it becomes therapeutically useful, in terms of the need to work through the TR/CT interaction, particularly in the interest of re-establishing or maintaining the therapeutic alliance. Contrary to the usual situation in the treatment of neurotic patients, the borderline patient has a more intense and primitive need at critical points to reassure himself or herself of the therapist's reality. The need to know what the therapist is feeling, to know details of the therapist's life and personality, or even the need to know where the therapist will be when on vacation can often serve important functions in sustaining the patient's sense of inner equilibrium and cohesion. The intensification of such demands may reflect the patient's need to confirm contact with a desperately needed sustaining object, the therapist, who is experienced as excessively remote, unavailable, or frustrating.

The handling of CT vicissitudes has a powerful impact on the regressive tendencies within the borderline patient. The therapist must continually monitor CT reactions and their impact on the regressive potential of the patient. Particularly devastating is the effect of CT omnipotence. Balint (1968) notes that such omnipotence in the therapist can determine whether the regression in the patient is benign or malignant. Such omnipotence can be reflected in the therapist's attempts to be actively giving or to rescue the patient out of the therapist's own need to be the good, all-caring, all-giving, and all-powerful parent who can solve every need and ease every pain. The CT stance thus reflects the therapist's own needs more than a responsiveness to the patient, and presumably reproduces the parental position. This reenacts and reactivates the earlier infantile trauma and can effectively undermine the patient's attempt to gain a therapeutic foothold.

The anxiety posed by the reactivation of such basic inner conflicts often stimulates defensive reactions, which play themselves out in inhibiting and interfering ways in the therapeutic interaction. As Atkins (1967) notes, the danger is not in the regression itself, but in the therapist's unreadiness or inability to meet the patient's regression and the infantile dependence related to it and to deal with them therapeutically. The more capable and ready the therapist is to meet and accept and deal with the patient's regression, the less need there is for the patient to follow the regressive option.

The necessity for establishing and maintaining a sufficient degree of structure in the therapy of borderline patients has been frequently stressed (Kernberg 1971, Adler 1975). The need to maintain structure, to be able to test the reality of the patient's perceptions, to set effective limits, to continually work within the frame of reference set by the therapeutic alliance, and to maintain respect for and support for the patient's autonomy are all essential aspects of the therapy with these patients—all the more so in the more primitively organized borderlines and in states of transient regression. In many higher-order borderlines, however, there is not the same degree of deficits in ego organization, so that these patients can tolerate a considerably higher degree of regressive strain and do not require the same degree of structure in the therapeutic situation. Such patients may tolerate considerable degrees of therapeutic regression without undue disorganization or disruptive acting-out.

Nonetheless, even in these better organized patients, the therapist must maintain careful attention to the degree of structure maintained in the therapeutic interaction. At times of increased regressive strain, the therapist needs to increase compensatorily the degree of structure in the therapeutic interaction, usually by becoming more active in the therapeutic interaction and by focusing more on current reality situations rather than on past developmental history, or on patterns of current behavioral interaction rather than on primitive affective content. He or she must pay particular attention to maintaining aspects of the therapeutic framework (Langs 1976a). There is a delicate titration that is often required in such periods of regressive strain, since there must be a balancing of the patient's need to regress, along with the therapist's capacity to tolerate regression, with the need to maintain sufficient structure, so that the regressive pull does not undermine the therapeutic alliance and the regressive strain become malignant.

This is, in fact, one of the most difficult aspects of the therapy with borderline patients—again, particularly those in the more primitive range—namely, titrating the degrees of activity and passivity, of structure and lack of structure, of regressive strain and ego support. The failure to maintain adequate structure can lead to excessive regression, acting-out, and the predominance of TR/CT interactions. By the same token, the maintenance of an excessively rigid or controlled therapeutic situation can interfere with the development of TR manifestations, particularly with the expression of negative TR reactions. This can lead to a therapeutic stalemate in which effective therapeutic work is negated, the therapeutic relationship becomes shallow and unproductive, and may be accompanied by acting-out outside the therapy. In higher-order patients, there may evolve an attitude of therapeutic compliance that is accompanied by a noticeable lack of change and lack of therapeutic progression. The therapist consequently is constantly confronted with a therapeutic dilemma: between the need to maintain structure as an essential ingredient in the therapeutic situation and the need to approach the borders of regression as a means of sustaining and activating the potential for therapeutic change.

The setting of limits is a specific instance of the need for establishing and maintaining structure, particularly in the face of acute regressive crises or acting-out (Adler 1975, Friedman 1975). The failure to set such limits may often lead to the undermining of the therapeutic alliance and a consequent stalemating of the therapy. In the more primitive borderlines who suffer from more severe ego defects, this is a particular need. Such patients frequently do not respond to verbal interpretations in areas of regressive functioning, so that a new set of experiences is required. The therapist's activity and actual setting of effective limits can supply this primitive, nonverbal need for "good-enough mothering" (Little 1966). The patient thus finds an appropriate degree of protective and caring intervention, which was presumably lacking in the early developmental interaction with the mother.

In such primitive patients, it is often only after the patient has experienced this kind of caring intervention on the part of the therapist that it becomes possible to explore and interpret some of the meanings of these interactions. In higher-order patients, however, limit-setting need not take an active interventionist form, but is more frequently a matter of sharing concern and exploring consequences of projected courses of action, emphasizing the more realistic aspects of options that may be to the patient's advantage rather than in the service of discharging tension or expressing unconscious and often self-destructive needs. Higher-order patients do not share the same ego-defects that are found in lower-order patients, particularly the lack of anxiety tolerance, the lack of impulse control, and the poverty of sublimating channels described by Kernberg (1967). These ego-weaknesses are more readily found in lower-order patients and contribute to their acting out potential. In higher-order patients, then, the emphasis shifts from limit-setting as such to confrontation, clarification, and interpretation as preferred modalities of intervention. These interventions play a role in the therapy of all patients, but there should be a differential emphasis in their application to various groupings within the borderline spectrum.

In the psychotherapy of borderline patients, confrontation often plays a major role; along with clarification, it is the primary channel for dealing with manifest content in the patient's ongoing behavior. The whole issue of confrontation has been usefully explored in a series of articles by Adler, Buie, and Corwin (Adler and Buie 1972, Buie and Adler 1972, Corwin 1972), although the discussion there is cast in terms of the use of confrontation with lower-order borderlines. Confrontation is a part of the therapy in some degree with all patients, but in borderline patients, particularly in regressed patients or in regressive crises, confrontation is often essential. The important issue is that therapeutic confrontation not become a vehicle of irritation, frustration, or sadism, but that it be offered from a therapeutic perspective and with the therapeutic gain of the patient as an objective.

In the ordinary run of therapy, confrontation is usually offered with regard to resistances as a means of overcoming the resistance, promoting further therapeutic progress, and as leading to interpretation of the patient's defenses and their underlying motivations. In the treatment of character disorders, the confrontations with the patient's patterns of characterologic behavior are frequently a necessary step in arriving at the underlying conflicts and their unconscious motivation. With borderline patients, however, the occasion may easily arise for confrontation concerning TR/CT vicissitudes.

With such patients the confrontation may be heroic. As Corwin (1972) describes it, such an heroic confrontation

> . . . has very specific characteristics and is employed at varying phases of analysis or therapy. A heroic confrontation may be defined as an emotionally charged, parametric, manipulative technical tool, demanded by the development of an actual or potential situation of impasse and designed ultimately to remobilize a workable therapeutic alliance (pp. 71–72).

The confrontation that is offered from a position of consistent caring and respect for the patient's autonomy, and generated from a basic concern for maintenance and reinforcement of the therapeutic alliance, can have a powerful therapeutic effect (Adler 1974). It must be remembered, however, that the confrontation is a vehicle leading in the direction of further therapeutic work and understanding. Confrontation for confrontation's sake inevitably runs the risk of CT contamination. As Myerson (1975) cogently notes, it is more valuable to try to understand where the patients are, and why they are where they are, than to confront them where they are not. Consequently, confrontations that lead in the direction of further exploring the basis for resistances or of examining the roots of TR distortions are therapeutically helpful. Where they do not, they run the risk of simply reinforcing the TR/CT dynamics and may simply lead in the direction of further patient compliance and counterproductive submissiveness.

SUMMARY AND CONCLUSION

The present study has concentrated on formulating a model of the TR/CT interaction derived from analysis of the paranoid process. The model infers that in borderline personalities the organization of the self-system takes place around core pathogenic introjects that are the derivatives of disturbed developmentally significant object relationships. The introjective organization takes the form of polar configurations based primarily on dimensions of narcissism and aggression. Libidinal dimensions probably remain secondary within this configuration.

In lower-order borderline personalities, these introjective configurations remain relatively close to the surface and, separately or in combination, may readily dominate the inner organization of the self and the patient's experience of it. This both introduces an internal instability and lability into the patient's self-organization and functioning, and provides the basis for projections that tend to influence and distort the patient's experience of significant others. In higher-order forms of borderline disorder, these introjective configurations tend to be more stable, better integrated, and less prone to projection. These patients tend to stabilize their personalities around one introjective configuration, even though the others remain relatively available for activation under regressive pressure or crisis. The parts of the introjective configuration that are dissociated or repressed tend to be projected. The patterns of these projections and their TR derivatives are described and discussed.

The operation of these projective derivatives in the therapeutic interaction sets up reciprocal patterns of introjection and counterprojection in the analyst, which serve as the basis of CT reactions. CT reactions involve a partial introjection of the patient's projection and a counterprojection that derives from the interaction of these therapeutically derived introjections with the therapist's own inner introjective configuration.

This model may be applied to the understanding of the therapeutic interaction with borderline patients to determine differences in TR manifestations between lower-order and higher-order forms of borderline pathology and their characteristic patterns of TR/CT interaction. The respective qualities, intensity, timing, and therapeutic response to these various forms of TR/CT interaction across the borderline spectrum are thus suggested. Further study of the diagnostic variations within the borderline spectrum, and their implications for the expression of TR, TR/CT interactions, and appropriate therapeutic intervention, is imperative.

REFERENCES

Adler, G. (1970). Valuing and devaluing in the psychotherapeutic process. *Archives of General Psychiatry* 22:454–461.
———. (1974). Regression in psychotherapy: disruptive or therapeutic? *International Journal of Psychoanalytic Psychotherapy* 3:252–264.
———. (1975). The usefulness of the "borderline" concept in psychotherapy. In *Borderline States in Psychiatry*, ed. J. E. Mack, pp. 29–40. New York: Grune and Stratton.

Adler, G., and Buie, D. H. (1972). The misuses of confrontation with borderline patients. *International Journal of Psychoanalytic Psychotherapy* 1:109-120.

Atkins, N. B. (1967). Comments on severe and psychotic regressions in analysis. *Journal of the American Psychoanalytic Association* 15:606-625.

Balint, M. (1968). *The Basic Fault: Therapeutic Aspects of Regression.* London: Tavistock.

Berg, M. D. (1977). The externalizing transference. *International Journal of Psycho-Analysis* 58:235-244.

Blum, H. P. (1973). The concept of erotized transference. *Journal of the American Psychoanalytic Association* 21:61-76.

Buie, D. H., and Adler, G. (1972). The uses of confrontation with borderline patients. *International Journal of Psychoanalytic Psychotherapy* 1:90-108.

Chediak, C. (1979). Counter-reactions and countertransference. *International Journal of Psycho-Analysis* 60:117-129.

Corwin, H. A. (1972). The scope of therapeutic confrontation from routine to heroic. *International Journal of Psychoanalytic Psychotherapy* 1:68-89.

Freud, A. (1936). *The Ego and the Mechanisms of Defense.* New York: International Universities Press, 1973.

Friedman, H. J. (1975). Psychotherapy of borderline patients: the influence of theory on technique. *American Journal of Psychiatry* 132:1048-1052.

Giovacchini, P. L. (1972). Technical difficulties in treating some characterological disorders: countertransference problems. *International Journal of Psychoanalytic Psychotherapy* 1:112-128.

———. (1973). Character disorders: with special reference to the borderline state. *International Journal of Psychoanalytic Psychotherapy* 2:7-36.

———. (1975). Self-projections in the narcissistic transference. *International Journal of Psychoanalytic Psychotherapy* 4:142-166.

Greenacre, P. (1956). Problems of overidealization of the analyst and of analysis. *Psychoanalytic Study of the Child* 21:193-212.

Greenson, R. R., and Wexler, M. (1969). The non-transference relationship in the psychoanalytic situation. *International Journal of Psycho-Analysis* 50:27-39.

Grinberg, L. (1962). On a specific aspect of countertransference due to the patient's projective identification. *International Journal of Psycho-Analysis* 43:436-440.

Horowitz, M. J. (1977). Cognitive and interactive aspects of splitting. *American Journal of Psychiatry* 134:549-553.

Kernberg, O. (1967). Borderline personality organization. *Journal of the American Psychoanalytic Association* 15:641-685.

———. (1968). The treatment of patients with borderline personality organization. *International Journal of Psycho-Analysis* 49:600-619.

———. (1970). Factors in the psychoanalytic treatment of narcissistic personalities. *Journal of the American Psychoanalytic Association* 18:51-85.

———. (1971). Prognostic considerations regarding borderline personality organization. *Journal of the American Psychoanalytic Association* 19:595-635.

———. (1975). *Transference and Countertransference in the Treatment of Borderline Patients* (Strecker Monograph Series, no. 12). Philadelphia: Institute of the Pennsylvania Hospital.

Kohut, H. (1971). *The Analysis of the Self.* New York: International Universities Press.

Krohn, A. (1974). Borderline "empathy" and differentiation of object representations: a contribution to the psychology of object relations. *International Journal of Psychoanalytic Psychotherapy* 3:142-165.

Langs, R. (1975a). Therapeutic misalliances. *International Journal of Psychoanalytic Psychotherapy* 4:77-105.

————. (1975b). The therapeutic relationship and deviations in technique. *International Journal of Psychoanalytic Psychotherapy* 4:106–141.

————. (1976a). *The Bipersonal Field.* New York: Jason Aronson.

————. (1976b). *The Therapeutic Interaction. II. A Critical Overview and Synthesis.* New York: Jason Aronson.

————. (1978–1979). Responses to creativity in psychoanalysts. *International Journal of Psychoanalytic Psychotherapy* 7:189–207.

Little, M. (1957). "R"—the analyst's total response to his patient's needs. *International Journal of Psycho-Analysis* 38:240–254.

————. (1966). Transference in borderline states. *International Journal of Psycho-Analysis* 47:476–485.

Maltsberger, J. T., and Buie, D. H. (1974). Countertransference hate in the treatment of suicidal patients. *Archives of General Psychiatry* 30:625–633.

Masterson, J. F. (1972). *Treatment of the Borderline Adolescent: A Developmental Approach.* New York: John Wiley.

Meissner, W. W. (1971). Notes on identification. II. Clarification of related concepts. *Psychoanalytic Quarterly* 40:277–302.

————. (1974). The role of imitative social learning in identificatory processes. *Journal of the American Psychoanalytic Association* 22:512–536.

————. (1977). Psychoanalytic notes on suicide. *International Journal of Psychoanalytic Psychotherapy* 6:415–447.

————. (1978a). Notes on some conceptual aspects of the borderline personality. *International Review of Psycho-Analysis* 5:297–311.

————. (1978b). *The Paranoid Process.* New York: Jason Aronson.

————. (1979a). Narcissistic personalities and borderline conditions: a differential diagnosis. *Annual of Psychoanalysis* 7:171–202.

————. (1979b). Internalization and object relations. *Journal of the American Psychoanalytic Association* 27:345–360.

————. (1980). A note on projective identification. *Journal of the American Psychoanalytic Association* 28:43–67.

————. (1982). Notes on the potential differentiation of borderline conditions. (This volume).

————. Notes on the levels of differentiation within borderline conditions. *Psychoanalytic Review* (in press).

Modell, A. H. (1975). A narcissistic defense against affects and the illusion of self-sufficiency. *International Journal of Psycho-Analysis* 56:275–282.

Myerson, P. G. (1974). Two types of demanding regression: discussion of paper by Dr. Adler. *International Journal of Psychoanalytic Psychotherapy* 3:265–272.

Nadelson, T. (1976). Victim, victimizer: interaction in the psychotherapy of borderline patients. *International Journal of Psychoanalytic Psychotherapy* 5:115–129.

Oremland, J. D., and Windholz, E. (1971). Some specific transference, countertransference and supervisory problems in the analysis of a narcissistic personality. *International Journal of Psycho-Analysis* 52:267–275.

Racker, H. (1953). A contribution to the problem of countertransference. *International Journal of Psycho-Analysis* 43:313–324.

————. (1957). The meaning and uses of countertransference. *Psychoanalytic Quarterly* 26:303–357.

————. (1958). Psychoanalytic technique and the analyst's unconscious masochism. *Psychoanalytic Quarterly* 27:555–562.

————. (1968). *Transference and Countertransference.* London: Hogarth.

Searles, H. F. (1978–1979). Concerning transference and countertransference. *International Journal of Psychoanalytic Psychotherapy* 7:165–188.

Strupp, H. (1960). *Psychotherapists in Action*. New York: Grune and Stratton.

Zetzel, E. R. (1971). A developmental approach to the borderline patient. *American Journal of Psychiatry* 127:867–871.

Countertransference in Borderline Conditions: Some Further Notes

JOHN T. MALTSBERGER, M.D.

A discussion of "Notes on Countertransference in Borderline Conditions" by W. W. Meissner, M. D.

Treating a borderline patient is like the enterprise of rescuing a drowning man. The drowner, despairing of his life and in a panic, is likely to seize the lifeguard so aggressively as to imperil both himself and his rescuer. When the lifeguard tries to bring some order to the situation, the drowner may not understand. Not until he has been towed halfway to shore by the hair does he fully realize that cooperation, not attack, is the only way out. To get the necessary grip on the situation, a lifeguard must keep his head, resisting impulses to panic or counterattack that arise in himself, and gradually enlist the cooperation of the weaker swimmer.

Borderline patients resemble poor swimmers in that their defective identifications have ill-prepared them for negotiating the currents of object relationships. Meissner notes that the sense of self in such patients is structured about pathological introjects derived from ambivalent object relationships, formed in the fear of abandonment and colored with the need to retain, control, and preserve some form of relationship with a person yearned for, feared, and hated. Under such circumstances the sense of self is always tenuous. The patient is liable to feel flooded with helplessness when those upon whom he relies to keep afloat seem to behave in the terrifying ways those childhood objects did whose images were introjected into the pathological core.

Before Freud elaborated the theory of narcissism, he referred to the self-preservative instincts of the ego and closely related them to aggression. The difficulties with aggression that borderline patients suffer intimately relate to the need to ward off harrowing affects of terror, aloneness, and dying. These exquisitely painful feelings arise when sustaining relationships with others falter and the patients must rely on an inadequate internal introjective world to provide a sense of peace in solitude. "Preservation of infantile narcissism" in terms of the patient's subjective experience means keeping afloat in life without being flooded with intolerable affects. The sadism borderline patients display illustrates vividly the wedding of the libidinal yearning for closeness to the aggressive drive to dominate and control that Freud has pointed out (Freud 1930, 1933). This emotional attitude arises from the need to relate to others without feeling helpless.

Because of the pathological introjective structure, all borderline individuals, to some degree or another, will be seen to fall prey to the harrowing affects just noted. These derive from the separation-individuation phase of childhood, which such patients have not very successfully negotiated. The less primitive patients, to be sure, defend against such fears more effectively, prove less mercurial, and hold faster to reality and to the therapeutic alliance. Nevertheless, the more muted patients, like their primitive brethren (the psychotic characters, pseudoneurotic schizophrenics, and schizoid characters), convey to the therapist the sense that survival depends on the therapeutic relationship. The therapy takes on a life and death quality, which poses special difficulties for the therapist, who must also deal with an onslaught of unusually complicated and aggressive manifestations. These patients discuss suicide, assault, and murder not as fantasies remote from the possibility of action; it is a rare borderline case who does not threaten aggressive or suicidal acting out at some point in the treatment. The intensity of the aggression, rapid shifts in transference attitudes, the threat of acting out, the burdening of the therapist with the potential for lethal or mutilative outcome, the fluidity of the therapeutic alliance, and the occasional abandonment of reality-testing, all challenge the therapist's capacity to keep his balance in the unusually intense and primitive countertransference flood. So stressful is psychotherapeutic work with these patients that therapists are constantly tempted to rationalize abandonment of the effort or to take measures frequently in the name of limit-setting, that arise from unconscious countertransference hate and predictably may provoke interruption of the treatment.

No therapist can expect to treat a borderline patient without feeling aggressive excitement, an excitement that tends to discharge. There are a variety of responses possible in which the aggression may be discharged against the patient (through repudiation or a variety of sadistic derivatives), and there are others in which the therapist may turn the aggression against himself. Impulse discharge of this sort is likely to be unconscious and tends to perpetuate the difficulties that brought the patient to treatment in the first place (inasmuch as the patient tends to repeat the sadomasochistic pattern dictated by the pathological introjects). It is not easy for therapists to deny themselves the tension relief sadomasochistic activity promises, and to hold fast instead to the goal of promoting growth in a patient who regularly provokes unpleasant affect and who cries out to be rejected as hopeless.

Meissner describes three dimensions of the pathological introjections that lie at the core of the ego disturbance encountered in borderline patients—the narcissistic, the aggressive, and the erotic. He further observes that the psychotherapist has sufficient developmental kinship to his borderline patient so that reciprocal introjective dimensions are to be found in his ego as well, capable of resonance when excited by the patients' stimulus and giving rise to instinctual and defensive responses that would tend to perpetuate and reinforce the patient's pathological structure unless correctly managed. The poles of the narcissistic dimension are formed by the attitudes of superiority and inferiority, those of the aggressive by the aggressor and victim introjects, and those of the erotic by the attitudes of erotic overestimation and degradation. Some further comment on the transference and countertransference importance of these three dimenions is found in their relationship to anxiety and the development of the defensive functions of the ego.

The profound anxiety to which borderline patients fall prey (helplessness, imminent death, and aloneness characterize it) is almost never appropriate to the adult situations in which it appears, most obviously not in the therapeutic relationship. Anxiety and despair of such an order belong in adult life to overwhelming traumatic situations that threaten life and limb, true victim situations. Freud ascribed anxiety of this order to those overwhelming moments when an influx of stimuli too great to be mastered or discharged took place, and referred it not only to disastrous moments in adult life but to moments of perceived danger in childhood. His name for it was *automatic anxiety*. The development of that capacity of the ego to respond to danger situations with signal anxiety instead of automatic anxiety took place, as he saw it, in the context of a lasting object cathexis. When the ego fails to develop a power over anxiety, transforming it to a more muted and expedient signal in situations of danger, it is likely to reproduce itself automatically in situations analogous to original dangers in an inexpedient way (Freud 1926). Later writers have considered in greater detail the development of the ego's capacity for anxiety mastery (Kohut 1966, Tolpin 1971).

While one must assume a reasonable capacity to respond to threats with signal anxiety in the therapist, the capacity is limited in borderline patients. Their anxiety responses to threatened danger are likely to be unrealistic, massive, and maladaptive. They are particularly sensitive to what they perceive to be the aggression of abandonment, not castration. The therapist's signal anxiety responses may structurally be organized more around castration anxiety, but not exclusively so. Is not the dread of abandoment a deep primitive fear in all of us? It is well to remember that the first hurt inflicted on the infant Oedipus was a double one, the piercing of his feet with a nail and abandonment on Mt. Cithaeron (Graves 1955).

These reflections lead naturally to the clinical moments when the patient's fear begins to rise. On many such occasions, his sense of himself is colored by the victim introject. These are the times, experiencing or anticipating what seems to be hateful mistreatment, he will feel helpless. Helplessness is not a state consistent with high self-esteem; in fact, depression has been defined as "the emotional expression (indication) of a state of helplessness and power-lessness of the ego" (Bibring 1953). Perhaps there is a necessary link between the position of narcissistic inferiority and the experience of victimization, forged from the sense that the incapacity to cope with a threat is to be worthless. The gradual development of the capacity for signal anxiety weakens this link, because in mature individuals signal anxiety is usually accompanied by a sense of hopefulness and readiness to cope. This is lacking in borderline cases; automatic anxiety, unlike signal anxiety, is an anxiety of despair.

The posture of the inferior victim is obviously one intolerable for a borderline patient. In such a state, an automatic self-preservative reaction may be called forth in which the therapist may be attacked in an effort to reverse the poles. It is better, at least for the moment, to be attacking, powerful, and narcissistically secure, than victimized, weak, and worthless. The only other alternative for the patient is to surrender to the suffering of the victim posture, an attitude that implies abandonment of hope. The aggressive hypomanic patient familiar in every inpatient ward demonstrates this defensive stance: puffing himself to grandiose proportions, making others feel helpless, he tries to ward off a sense of worthlessness, aloneness, and vulnerability.

When the therapist is attacked, he too will feel some degree of the anxiety that belongs to victimization and, to the extent that a sense of helplessness is aroused, some drop in self esteem. There are differences, however, between his response and the patient's. These arise from his capacity to react less globally to the threat and without the degree of helplessness that triggers inferior narcissistic response.

Meissner reviews the spectrum of introjections that may take place in the therapist when the patient feels close to one pole and projects the other. He discusses the three dimensions of narcissism, aggression, and erotism, stressing the complementary mode of introjection and following the terminology of Racker (1957). Consider the aggressive dimension. In the complementary mode, the patient, feeling himself to be a victim, projects the form of aggressor that the therapist tends to introject. This disposes the therapist to behave in an attacking way. Similarly, the patient, under the sway of the inferior narcissisitc attitude, projects superiority, and the therapist, introjecting, tends to the grandiose.

When one views a possible clinical misinteraction in which the patient, out of the victim posture, provokes the aggressor potential of his therapist in the complementary mode, one may say that the therapist has formed an "identification with the aggressor." It seems, however, that more complete illumination of this common clinical difficulty may be obtained, at least in the aggressive dimension, by taking note of what transpires simultaneously in the concordant mode. Racker's concordant identification takes place when the patient and the therapist are under the sway of the same introjective configuration at the same time. Consider the two configurations of the aggressive dimension. Complementarily, the patient as victim evokes the therapist as aggressor; concordantly, the patient as victim evokes the therapist as victim.

It seems more satisfactory to take the point of view that both the victim and the aggressor introjects are at work in both patient and therapist at the same time when the pressure for sadomasochistic exchange rises. Each party to the interaction, perceiving the other to be potentially harmful or aggressive, experiences an activation of the victim introject. This is accompanied by a sense of greater or lesser anxiety, narcissistic instability, and a readiness for defensive action. Under these circumstances each is disposed to behave aggressively to the other, but not to experience himself subjectively as an aggressor so much as a victim. In fact, the behavior dictated by the aggressor introject is often not experienced as hostile or even aggressive at all by him who displays it. Therein lies the potentiality for many a clinical mistake on the part of the unwary psychotherapist. One may say that, in the aggressive dimension, the concordant mode of introjection mutually intensifies the self-perceptions of victimization; the complementary mode mutually intensifies the disposition to behave aggressively.

There is a position of some dynamic stability highly characteristic of many borderline individuals that merits some scrutiny here. I refer to the patient who feels more or less chronically close to or is even identified with the victim introject (Meissner 1971). Here the sense of victimization is easily activated by the most trivial or imaginary slight. Out of a sense of righteous indignation this patient may attack and devaluate those who give offense. Here is an instance in which the victim position is coupled with a sense of narcissistic superiority, quite probably because the aggressive activity of "self-defense" relieves the sense of helpless inferiority that in other circumstances is the victim's lot. Projected onto the offender is the inferior narcissistic pole (he is seen as insensitive, incompetent, stupid, or what-have-you) and the aggressor pole of the aggressive dimension.

Such patients the reader may recognize as the borderline type of the class Freud (1916) called "the exceptions". Conceiving himself to have been unfairly victimized by some past misfortune, this patient feels special. He feels he may not rightfully be constrained or checked by the limits life places on ordinary people. Such a patient feels entitled to extraordinary considerations and privileges because life owes him compensation for his unjust hurts.

The combination of aggressive demandingness, a narcissistic inflation that gives rise to hauteur, and contemptuous devaluation of those who frustrate comprise a formidable challenge to the clinician's capacity to maintain balance. The reactive pressure to devaluate, punish, and reject such individuals is so intense that in some psychiatric centers the term "narcissistic entitlement" has taken on a contemptuous, pejorative, and most unfortunate meaning never intended by John Murray (1964), who coined it.

Successful management of the hauteur of the patient who sees himself as a victim requires of the therapist the capacity to resist the threatened complementary introjection of degradation-fighting-back and the resolution to show the patient that his attitude is a defense against a sense of wounded defectiveness and helplessness not congruent with the circumstances of the patient's life.

In recent years it has been pointed out that the mild if good humored contempt that once colored many therapeutic interventions with grandiose and narcissistically entitled patients may tend to constrict results and obscure significant pathology. Therapists of all kinds are now alert to the importance of dealing empathically with such phenomena in the service of deeper understanding. For this advance much is owed to Heinz Kohut (1966, 1978). Looking back, it seems obvious that the devaluative attitude stirred up in the therapist by a grandiose, narcissistically superior individual may be the consequence of concordant introjection of the superior attitude and complementary introjection of the inferior attitude that the haughty patient projects. The complementary introjection of the narcissistically inferior position would give rise to sufficient signal anxiety to mobilize a defensive aggressive response in the therapist that may find expression in subtle mockery of a highfalutin patient.

To the extent that the therapist is prone to feel himself inferior and to ward off the concomitant anxieties by narcissistic overinflation, he will be particularly vulnerable to countertransference errors when the patient projects the pole of narcissistic superiority. Vulnerable to flattery, this therapist will find himself pleased by the patient's seeming appreciation of his art and subtlety. Enjoying an unusual sense of well-being, he may be tempted to offer gratuitous advice or to relate anecdotes boastfully that have little to do with the patient's concerns. Chaucer (ca. 1393) suggested how easy it is to lose empathic touch with others when in the grips of such overinflation. The cock Chauntecleer, puffed up by the idealizing words of a fox, closed his eyes in an ecstatic moment of self-importance and was carried away by the throat. Apart from the obvious opportunities for empathic error such a state implies, in some circumstances it can open the door to suicide.

Many borderline individuals with suicidal potential begin therapy with fairly intense idealization of the therapist. Often distorted accounts of previous therapeutic relationships gone awry will be presented, coupled with such statements as, "You are the only person in my whole life who has ever understood me." A warm interplay may evolve in which both parties to the interaction enjoy a sense of closeness, the patient deeply appreciative of what both see as the superb empathic capacities of the therapist. Meissner refers to such a state. What may not be immediately obvious is that the patient's projection of superiority is often predicated upon the confident expectation that sooner or later the magic therapist will provide solutions or confer all the happiness of the Garden of Eden.

Disappointment is of course inevitable, and when it comes, the borderline individual will probably reverse his projection along all three axes. Suddenly the once beloved therapist will find himself barraged with devaluation, hated, accused of treachery, and caught unawares with an acutely suicidal patient. Those experienced in the treatment of such patients are likely to avoid such contretemps, but surprises of this nature can occur in the consulting rooms of the well-seasoned when misdiagnosis has occurred.

The lethal potential lies in the temptation to act out aversively against the patient. Struggling to maintain narcissistic (superior) balance and warding off awareness of reciprocal hateful impulses against the patient, the therapist may tend to rationalize abandonment of the case by some form of subtle devaluation (e.g., "This patient is just not treatable"). Ill-timed transfer to another therapist, hospitalization, or outright discharge can precipitate successful suicide (Maltsberger and Buie, 1974). Such therapeutic disaster clearly depends on the therapist's unconsciously introjecting the aggressor posture in the complementary mode. It also reflects, however, the empathic disturbance that follows narcissistic inflation. It appears that to the extent the therapist must adapt the grandiose mode in order to protect himself from a sense of vulnerable inferiority, he unconsciously renders himself incapable of empathic contact with the patient's sense of inferiority. Thus complementary introjection may be used as a defense against the degree of concordant trial introjection necessary for empathic work. This phenomenon is probably responsible for the mislabelling of many borderline patients as unsuitable for psychotherapy, not only at moments of impasse, but from the hour of first consultation.

To the extent that the therapist is caught up in the matter of preserving his own narcissism and quieting his own anxiety by counterprojecting one introject or another, he will fail to discern that the patient's behavior is defensive. Furthermore, there is a repeated pattern that displays itself when patients attempt to maintain a self-protective stance of narcissistic superiority. Projection and distortion are the two interplaying ego defense mechanisms. To the extent that this configuration is successful, the superior stance may be so stable as to be a mark of character. In borderline patients, the defense configuration is not so successful, and a fairly rapid oscillation between superiority and inferiority of self with projection of the opposite pole will be seen.

In this defensive configuration, the fundamental task is to justify the acting out of hostile-sadistic impulses without loss of self-respect, meanwhile maintaining the illusion that one is a superior individual badly treated by others. As I have suggested, the acting out of the aggression is necessary to ward off a sense of helplessness and depression.

The important part projection plays has already been extensively discussed. The importance of distortion in this narcissism-saving operation lies in achieving enough reality-warping so that the devaluative projection the patient undertakes does not violate his reality sense. The defensive operation cannot succeed if some part of the patient cries out, "This cannot be so!" while another part represents an object as a contemptible aggressor. The work of distortion is to validate the false and debased object representations toward which projection reaches (Murray 1967). Systematic interpretation of this defense constellation will help the patient see how he holds on to the narcissistic entitlements of the pregenital era by justifying his rage at the expense of reality and his objects.

One of the unconscious purposes of the patient's aggressive activity is to provoke in objects some counteraggressive behavior that can be seized upon, amplified, and elaborated through the action of distortion. The patient will often respond with a distinctly paranoid "Aha! I knew it must be true!" remark when his hostile barrage succeeds in arousing something in the therapist that can, with a little distortion, be understood as devaluative and attacking.

Unless the therapist is aware of the patient's defensive need to evoke a hostile response to feed the projection-distortion machinery, he may be puzzled by a frequently observed phenomenon. Let the therapist restrain himself from acting out devaluative or aggressive impulses against a borderline patient and the patient will often intensify the aggressive and devaluative behavior in an attempt to provoke something hostile. In short, such a patient is compelled to play *agent provocateur* to keep his narcissism afloat.

Many therapists can manage provocative behavior as long as the patient is able to confine it to verbal activity within the confines of the therapy hour. Quite often, however, borderline individuals will make aggressive forays around the perimeter of the formal demarcations of the therapeutic relationship. Abuse via telephone, appearances at unscheduled times, demands for extra sessions, missed appointments, and withheld fees can all serve as extraordinarily effective irritants. When caught unawares on the telephone, in the waiting room, or on the street, it is difficult to respond therapeutically in the face of provocative invasions of personal privacy and time.

It is obviously impossible to treat such patients without appropriate limit-setting, and it is very difficult indeed to set limits with them without playing into the hands of the distortion-ready *agent provocateur*. Obviously, limit-setting should be avoided whenever investigation can be substituted; when limit setting is necessary, the therapist should take care that he speaks and acts from a posture of empathy with the patient's helplessness.

A most difficult therapeutic sector is the arena of drug abuse and self-mutilation. Clearly, active preventive intervention, including hospitalization, is necessary from time to time. Experience has shown, however, that self-cutting is often as difficult to prevent inside the hospital as it is outside. The only secure protection from such activity the patient can obtain is from his own insight into the motivation for and self-object confusion implicit in such behavior. Therapists sometimes force such patients into the hospital because they cannot endure the helplessness in themselves the patients engender.

Forced hospitalization often intensifies the patient's sense of victimization and weakens an already tenuous therapeutic alliance. While forced hospitalization may be necessary in some instances, it often represents the successful effort on the patient's part to provoke what can be seen from his point of view as a betrayal and an abuse—it ends the treatment and perpetuates the pathological introjections.

If untimely limit-setting of this sort can be avoided, and acceptable levels of self-destructive activity tolerated for a time (e.g., minor cutting or head-banging), the patient may come to see that he is treating his body as though it were the therapist's possession; injury to it feels like injuring the therapist's property (Laufer 1968). Successful exploration of the question of body ownership can illuminate early difficulties in self-object differentiation and provide substantial therapeutic gain for some individuals. This is most difficult if the patient succeeds in getting the therapist to take charge of his body.

Just as the patient can provoke the therapist to end a treatment by alliance destroying (sometimes necessary) limit setting, the therapist may also provoke the patient to act out in such a way so as to end the treatment, so that the unhappy outcome has the superficial appearance of being primarily the patient's responsibility (e.g., when the therapist informs the patient that in the event of one sort of behavior or another the treatment will be terminated). The patient will usually be destructively driven to do the very thing against which he has been warned. This he does to achieve an unconscious wish—he wants to establish for himself once and for all that the therapist is an abandoning aggressor and the patient is a victim. In at least one instance, such a termination resulted in suicide.

Such forewarnings of termination represent the therapist's effort to ward off intolerable helplessness and to establish for himself a position of power and authority that the patient cannot endure (Adler 1971). In those instances when the therapist concludes that he must give up his attempt to be useful, it is best that he take direct responsibility for the termination and initiate it himself without drawing chalk lines for the patient to step across.

REFERENCES

Adler, G. (1972). Helplessness in the helpers. *British Journal of Medical Psychology* 45:315–326.

Bibring, E. (1953). The mechanism of depression. In *Affective Disorders*, ed. P. Greenacre, pp. 13–48. New York: International Universities Press.

Chaucer, G. (ca. 1393). The nun's priest's tale. In *The Poetical Works of Chaucer*, ed. F. N. Robinson. Boston: Houghton Mifflin Co., 1933.

Freud, S. (1916). Some character types met with in psychoanalytic work. *Standard Edition* 14:311–315.

———. (1926). Inhibitions, symptoms, and anxiety. *Standard Edition* 20:144–149, 161–162.

———. (1930). Civilization and its discontents. *Standard Edition* 21:117–122.

———. (1933). New introductory lectures on psychoanalysis. *Standard Edition* 22:102–111.

Graves, R. (1955). *The Greek Myths*, vol. 2. Harmondsworth, England: Penguin Books.

Kohut, H. (1966). Forms and transformations of narcissism. *Journal of the American Psychoanalytic Association* 14:243–272.

———. (1978). *The Psychology of the Self*. New York: International Universities Press.

Laufer, M. (1968). The body image, the function of masturbation, and adolescence: problems of ownership of the body. *Psychoanalytic Study of the Child* 23:114–137.

Maltsberger, J. T., and Buie, D. H. (1974). Countertransference hate in the treatment of suicidal patients. *Archives of General Psychiatry* 30:625–633.

Meissner, W. W. (1971). Notes on identification. II. Clarification of related concepts. *Psychoanalytic Quarterly* 40:277–302.

Murray, J. M. (1964). Narcissism and the ego ideal. *Journal of the American Psychoanalytic Association* 12:477–528.

———. (1967). Personal communication.

Racker, H. (1957). The meaning and uses of countertransference. *Psychoanalytic Quarterly* 27:557–562.

Toplin, M. (1971). On the beginnings of a cohesive self. *Psychoanalytic Study of the Child* 26:316–352.

Frame Disturbances in No-Fee Psychotherapy

JOEL PARIS, M.D.

The frame of psychotherapy shows both universality and social relativity. Since the intrapsychic world is permeable to social reality, the meaning of insurance in psychotherapy depends on context. Experience with Canadian National Health Insurance suggests that when no-fee psychotherapy in normative, it is absorbed in the frame. There are still trouble spots in the Canadian system, particularly the management of missed sessions. Depending on the needs of the patient, charging for missed sessions can disrupt therapy entirely or be constructive for the treatment.

The frame (Langs 1976a, 1976b) in which psychotherapy is conducted is determined in part by psychological factors, the need for both patient and therapist to have a clear and well protected field for the exploration of unconscious material, and by sociological factors, the norms within the community under which professional relations are conducted. The therapeutic frame is a set of rules that provides what Langs (1976a) calls a "firm hold," important for all patients, but particularly for those who have already been traumatized by inconsistency in significant objects.

Any set of rules provides expectations that, when deviated from, produce a jarring effect. Enlarging on the metaphor of the frame, picture frames in the 19th century were expected to be gilded and ornate; a plain frame would have looked bare. In our own century simple wooden frames have become customary. To seek a work of art without being distracted, its setting must be conventional. In the same way, psychotherapy is normally contained in a frame that remains invisible because it is part of the shared expectations of therapist and patient.

SOCIAL INFLUENCE ON THE INTRAPSYCHIC WORLD

The concept of psychotherapy itself is in part cultural, carrying a heavy load of norms that are so widely taken for granted as to be ignored (Frank 1973, Wittkower and Prince 1974). Most prominent among these is the value of individualism, which underlies an arrangement that focuses on intrapsychic, not external, reality. The same individualism, in many ways the driving force of western society (Weber 1930), is associated with free enterprise in the professions, so that contractual arrangements for a fee are determined by the marketplace. The United States, where these values have always been strongest, remains the only country in the world where medicine is largely free of government insurance and regulation.

Psychoanalytic psychotherapy deals with the unconscious mind, but there has always been controversy about the universality of intrapsychic phenomena. To what extent is the unconscious permeable to and influenced by social reality? Some psychoanalysts who have studied non-western societies have concluded that the structural theory itself may not apply in settings where the individual superego is underdeveloped and dependent on the collectivity, where projective identification is to some extent normative (Ortigues and Ortigues 1966), and where true depressive phenomena are not experienced (Murphy et al. 1967).

If these kinds of radical differences can be observed in a crosscultural context, is it possible that more subtle differences can be observed within western society and its subcultures? Horney (1937), impressed by her experience in immigrating from Europe, thought so, noting the prominence of competitive themes in the dynamics of her American patients. A decline of the strength of the superego and an increase in the frequency of narcissistic characters has been noted both by psychoanalysts (Misterlisch 1969, Kernberg 1975, Kohut 1977, Wheelis 1958) and by social critics influenced by psychoanalysis (Lasch 1979).

INSURANCE AND THE RELATIVITY OF THE FRAME

If the quality of intrapsychic conflict shows evidence of socio-cultural relativity, how can the frame and ground rules of psychotherapy be universal? Langs (1979) has made a very precise definition of the psychoanalytic frame, and his views probably reflect the practice of analytic therapy in private offices located in American cities, but it would take an enormous amount of research to validate these rules point by point or to prove that changes in them interfere with the therapeutic process.

The question of whether insurance and the absence of a fee interfere with psychotherapy depends on the relativity of the frame. For example, Halpert (1972a, 1972b) found clinical material in such situations suggesting that patients felt like charity cases receiving inferior treatment. One could ask, did their analysts feel this way and transmit these attitudes covertly to their patients? Alternatively, were the patients themselves ashamed of not being able to pay for a treatment considered by society to be both prestigious and expensive? Similarly, Nash and Cavenar (1976) thought that clinic patients not charged a fee were "too guilty to improve." Again one wonders, who made them guilty?

In a relevant Canadian example, a qualified psychoanalyst wished to offer psychoanalysis to a few patients at a lower fee prescribed by government insurance schedules. Unfortunately these treatments showed a strong tendency to break up or prematurely terminate. The ambivalence of the analyst about his fee may have been responsible for this. In one case, the analysand was abruptly informed after six months that since he was "difficult," he would have to pay the full fee forthwith. In another case the patient left after two months when told that his complaints about the analyst's lateness indicated his "guilt" about receiving insured treatment. Whether or not patients feel too guilty to improve, therapists may feel too deprived to treat.

Conversely, if the therapist is comfortable with the insurance situation, these problems need not arise at all (Glasser and Duggan 1969, Chodoff 1972). Lorand and Console (1958) found little difference in analysis practiced in a free clinic. One wonders whether the analysts working in this clinic felt comfortable with the situation, which, after all, only continued a tradition established by Freud of treating a certain percentage of patients free of charge.

In a critique of no-fee psychotherapy, Langs (1979) attempts to show how insurance derails treatment by altering the frame, and he certainly succeeds in showing how uncomfortable filling out insurance forms can make a therapist. In focusing on the frame issues, which are real enough, Langs tends to ignore the implications of the dynamics of the individual case. For example, the patient described in this chapter has anxiety symptoms related to marital conflict, and broke off treatment by announcing that he and his wife were getting along so well that it was no longer necessary. Patients who back out of therapy for fear that it may endanger a relationship are common, and it is not clear whether frames by themselves will create a therapeutic alliance when motivation is shaky.

Langs (1976a, 1976b, 1978) has made a creative contribution to the study of psychotherapy by opening up the issue of frames, but it is questionable whether there is any such thing as the "right" frame; every therapist has to some extent an idiosyncratic one. Frame disturbances could therefore be classified as absolute or relative. The first class would include "universal" deviations, such as physical contact with a patient. The second class would include deviations from expectations created by the normal practice of the therapist, such as whether the patients are expected to take the same vacation time as the therapist.

INSURANCE AND THE SOCIAL CONTEXT IN THE U.S.A. AND CANADA

Insurance for psychotherapy is a social phenomenon. Its very existence has made intensive treatment available to many for whom the fee is a hardship or a barrier. In areas such as the District of Columbia, liberal coverage for federal government employees has made insured therapy virtually normative (Sharfstein and Magnus 1975). In most parts of the United States, major medical plans have insured short-term therapies (Marmor et al. 1975), but the expected pattern of the professional relationship in America is still the payment of a fee, and insurance has the potential to be disruptive under certain conditions.

In Canada, as in most other countries, there is comprehensive government insurance of medical care. Psychiatric treatment is covered, and the plan functions smoothly for both doctor and patient (Liptzin 1977, Markson 1977). In most provinces there is unlimited coverage for psychotherapy. In Quebec the plan precludes the setting of any surcharge, and only formal psychoanalysis is normally practiced outside the scheme. Patients seeing psychiatrists in Quebec feel that they have already paid for the service through their tax money and through a special health care premium. Instead of being expected to pay a fee, the patient is required only (1) to be present at a psychotherapy session and (2) to present a card, which is then stamped by the psychiatrist and used to bill the government for the service.

One problem arising from government insurance is the danger of third-party intrusion into the confidentiality of psychotherapy (Applebaum 1978, Uchill 1978). Based on experience with private insurance companies and Medicaid (Shwed et al. 1979), which are constantly auditing in search of savings, American psychiatrists have tended to assume that national health insurance would involve the same level of intrusiveness, with frequent questions about what is going on in therapy and why it is being carried out at all. Thus far in Canada what investigations the government has done have been mostly for such expensive specialities as surgery, and psychiatry has been largely left alone. The only reporting to the government consists of the coded diagnosis. Even this represents information that can be restricted, and many psychiatrists in private practice have coded only the most innocuous diagnostic categories. Patients seem to be aware that government is not threatening confidentiality, and this is reflected in the failure of this issue to come up in psychotherapy.

TROUBLE SPOTS IN THE CANADIAN SYSTEM

Some of the problems that arise include (1) the requirement to present the insurance card, (2) the nature of the therapist's gratification from his or her work, and (3) the handling of the problem of the missed session.

The requirement for presenting the insurance card seems a trivial matter, yet like so many other small issues in psychotherapy it can become a repository for transference and resistance. One example would be the patient who loses his card or consistently forgets to bring the card. This resembles failure to pay a bill, familiar in psychotherapy with a fee. Under previous regulations it represented only a minor annoyance to the psychiatrist, who was allowed to fill out the insurance slip by hand and receive payment with only some delay. Recent legislation passed in Quebec to require the presentation of the card at each visit could make this an important area of struggle and conflict between patient and therapist.

Since patients are aware that psychiatrists make a comfortable income under government insurance, one may wonder if the issue of the therapist's gratification from his work would present a problem. In those centers where there are a large number of psychiatrists, therapists need patients and referrals. In Montreal a peculiar situation has arisen; since the very first week when government-insured psychotherapy was available, there has been a demand for service that far exceeds the supply of psychiatrists (Paris 1973, 1977). Thus, for every patient accepted into psychotherapy, there is an almost endless number of others asking for the service and not getting it. Most patients in psychotherapy know a friend looking for therapy, often less than successfully. Thus every patient is a kind of "V.I.P." This causes some patients to wonder why they were chosen and not someone else.

The most frequent frame disturbance in psychotherapy without a fee is the missed session. In psychotherapy with a fee, a missed session is charged for and that forms part of a monthly bill, but a missed session in a no-fee psychotherapy is the only charge, and therefore stands out of context in a way that tends to focus an intense affect on the fee.

For this reason many therapists have explained this rule as part of the initial contract for psychotherapy. Patients are told that if they come at their scheduled hour, the government will pay, but if they do not, the patients will have to pay. This could then be further explained by pointing out that missed sessions represent a serious threat to the continuity and value of the psychotherapy and that holding the patient responsible for them is for the patient's benefit. (It should also be made clear that the policy is for the therapist's benefit, to protect him or her from a loss of income.)

It is customary to exclude illness and major snowstorms from this rule. Aside from possible abuse, to do otherwise would be protecting the therapist's vested interest at the expense of reality. Some patients find it difficult to understand why a psychiatrist would be so ethical as to refuse to bill the government for services not rendered, but the majority of patients find the arrangement acceptable. Unless the psychiatrist selects his or her practice for high levels of obsessionality, missed sessions are by no means infrequent.

THE MISSED SESSION AND PREMATURE TERMINATION

In some cases the management of payment for missed sessions may determine whether or not the patient stays in therapy. There are patients, as described by Eissler (1975), who require a period in which the therapist must do a maximum of giving and make minimal demands before they are able to bchave in a responsible manner. In one such case, a 22-year-old man was in psychotherapy for characterological problems associated with the effects of having been abandoned by his father at the age of 8. He had grown up in poverty, with an intrusive, depressed mother. He knew that his father, who lived on the other side of the continent, was quite wealthy. He had the fantasy that there would eventually be a reunion and that he would gain both the father's love and his financial support. When he actually did go to meet him, he suffered a profound disillusionment: the father, although ready to receive him, showed little interest in following through on the relationship and made financial promises that he failed to carry out. Thus it was not surprising that after six months of treatment with a male psychiatrist, the patient spoke of wanting the therapist to be his "backer."

This patient had spent several years of his life carrying a gun at all times to protect himself from possible attack. It was predictable that at some point hostile feelings to the therapist would emerge. The patient, who was a musician, asked for a change of hour because of heavy involvements in cutting a record. The therapist agreed to this, but only had available an early morning hour that did not coincide with the habits of the patient. The necessity of payment for any missed sessions had been explained some time before, and he had agreed, pointing out that in his own work, a rented studio has to be paid for whether one uses it at that specific time or not. However, when the patient once overslept and, following that, was presented with a bill for the missed time, he angrily left therapy without paying.

It is possible that changing the hour already disturbed the frame, but it is equally possible that not doing so would have been used by the patient to escape therapy. The manifest content of the preceding sessions centered around the patient's wish to be successful and independent. However he had also spoken of homosexual anxiety, and was overtly afraid of separating from his mother, leaving her alone and unhappy. In this respect his developing relationship to the therapist may have been frightening. Two years later, he made another visit to the therapist. He now owned a recording company but was still having great difficulty leaving his mother. He did not reenter therapy, stating, "I want to do it on my own."

In this kind of case, six months was probably too short a time to expect the patient to act responsibly in spite of his former protestations. The demand for payment for the missed session was just one more betrayal by a person who purported to be helpful to him but only exploited him for his own ends. The therapy was in any case at a crisis point: by becoming self-supporting he identified with the therapist in the work sphere, but had not had time to truly individuate, as shown by the follow-up. The treatment therefore required protection. Given the context of no-fee psychotherapy, it would have been more helpful to have discussed with the patient the meaning of the missed session, but to wait for him to offer payment.

Eissler makes a useful distinction between contracts of "indenture" and the "gentlemen's agreement." The indenture system, where even the patient's vacations must be arranged around those of the therapist, is probably set up as much for the financial security of the therapist as for any real benefit to the patient. As Blanck and Blanck (1974) have pointed out, the autonomy needs of many patients can be nipped in the bud by too strict an adherence to this rule. In fact, indenture may repeat past situations in which a parent demanded the presence of the patient for narcissistic reasons and prevented separation. The therapist must therefore be prepared to accept occasional financial sacrifice in the interest of his or her patient's individuation.

As Eissler points out, the "gentlemen's agreement" is necessary in patients with profound narcissistic deficits who would simply not tolerate therapy under conditions of indenture. It also is a model for a degree of reasonableness and flexibility that may be a new experience for these patients. Even among patients who can tolerate paying for missed sessions, the response will be as if the frame were disturbed.

THE MISSED SESSION AND RESISTANCE: A CLINICAL VIGNETTE

Studying the handling of missed sessions is complicated, in that they already reflect some disruption in the treatment. In neurotic character structures, however, one can more easily use the patient's responsibility for attendance in a constructive way.

A 30-year-old man was in therapy for lack of direction in life. In his career he was an underachiever; with women he would either let himself be exploited or become passive when commitment became an issue. His family constellation involved an overly close and intrusive mother, who used him as a companion, and a father whose own sense of defeat in life led him to treat his son with indifference or hostility. In childhood, he was an overprotected "good boy"; in adolescence, a rebel who became heavily involved in the drug scene. As he grew older he continued to see women as engulfing, and wished for a strong man by his side who could protect him. But his image of other men was of dangerous opponents who were ultimately unavailable to him. His relations to authority figures were passive–aggressive. He saw himself as an eternal child in an adult world, essentially incompetent to handle any serious tasks, and retreating to the use of marijuana whenever reality demanded too much.

In the course of intensive psychotherapy, after an initial "honeymoon," he began to display characterological resistance, wishing to be given power and manhood by the therapist but suspecting the therapist simply did not have it to give. If he could prove the therapist was no better than himself, and defeat him by not changing, he would emerge victorious, after a fashion. He would often come late for his sessions, and once missed a session by mistaking the date of the therapist's return from a holiday. For this he was charged and paid the fee to the therapist.

The following sequence occurred ten months into therapy.

Session 1: Patient came late, on crutches. He had just had a knee cartilage removed. He talked of not knowing how to be a man, or how to handle women. He felt "castrated" by the operation. Time was running out for him. The therapist would be like his father, unable to help. His doctors at the hospital could never agree on treatment. A man in the next bed was flirting with the nurses. He had two dreams in hospital: (1) homosexual relations with a man in the next bed and (2) searching for a missing "cartridge," which his sister had. His sister had received more love from his father. The therapist intervened by pointing out his wish to obtain his lost masculinity from a potent man, even at the cost of playing a female role. This was also coming up in his relation to the therapist. The patient seemed relieved at the implication that he was not really homosexual. He wished that he was more like the therapist, whom he imagined to be successful with women.

Session 2: He slept late and missed the session.

Session 3: He acknowledged missing the previous session and described a dream in which he was studying to be a psychiatrist. He was presenting a case of a woman possessed by the spirit of a dead Indian named "Tepit." He associated that name as an anagram of "petit" (small), and to an earlier anagram dream of throwing a bag of fluid at a doctor, crying "Kaerf" (Freak). He went on to talk of skits satirizing doctors and of his own resentment of authority. The therapist intervened by pointing out how the last session had been about his competition with the therapist, that he had then missed a session, which was a quiet way of attacking the therapist, and now was speaking of his wish to be like the therapist and his resentment of him. The patient replied by saying that he sought treatment because of his failure to get what he needed from women, but was disappointed at not getting the potency he needed from a man. He feels uncomfortable with his anger because he fears retaliation. It was the same with his father, who kept his power to himself and left the patient unable to handle his mother.

Session 4: The therapist reminded the patient that he would be away the next week and presented the bill for the missed session. The patient said, "You really want me to resent you, but what I resent the most is that you are the doctor and I am not." He wants to be a friend or colleague of the therapist, but doesn't think he would support his own ambition to be a musician. He used to feel like killing his father to get what the father had. The knee operation made him feel small and weak (petit). The therapist intervened to point out his wish to overthrow the therapy as well. The patient said that perhaps the therapist should pay *him* for missed sessions when *he* goes on vacation.

Session 5: The patient paid the bill. He was angry at the therapist's impending vacation. He thought of quitting but realized he did that to avoid trying and failing. He dreamt of holding a frying pan and moving it up and down. He associated this to masturbation and his sense of impotence and effeminacy. The therapist pointed out how this reflected the patient's anger and helplessness in therapy. The patient said he could do nothing to assert himself against his father and had to fall back on passive resistance. He could defeat the therapist this way, but would have to defeat himself as well.

The vignette demonstrates how the presentation of a bill outside the ordinary frame can represent the powerful and arbitrary aspect of the therapist. In this case the patient, who had been billed once before in similar circumstances, knew the consequence of sleeping late.

Does the frame disturbance and the missed session have anything to do with insurance? There are no specific associations to suggest this. There clearly are derivatives describing the therapist as impotent and incompetent. An observer who sees all missed sessions as due to errors in technique would find support for the hypothesis of the therapist's incompetence in the multiple critiques of the medical profession in the material.

Langs (1979) has shown how easy it is for therapists to write off their errors as "transferences." Certainly all material in therapy must be heard for reference to the therapeutic interaction before transference is considered, but over-concentration on interactive elements could lead to neglect of transference; one must steer a middle course. Here we have a patient who sees a therapist alternately as he saw his father, hostile and unavailable, and as he sees himself, incompetent and castrated. He sees the two hours a week of therapy as a very far cry from the fathering he craves, yet he fears closeness to the therapist. If anything the therapist did produced a missed session, it was most likely the interpretation of homosexual wishes, which may have been premature and frightening, especially so close to a vacation.

One of the peculiarities of insured therapy is that missed sessions become doubly disturbing because the therapist introduces a fee, which is felt by the patient as a frame disturbance. Sessions 4 and 5 are full of rage about the fee, compounded by the therapist's vacation, and transferentially colored by the patient's perception of the father demanding everything and giving nothing. Nevertheless, this patient had enough ego strength to weather the crisis and did not miss any further sessions. At the end of therapy, he became more assertive at work and with women, while decreasing his use of drugs at home.

In a benign form, frame disturbances do not threaten the therapeutic alliance. If expectations in treatment are generally reasonable and predictable, that is enough to provide the "firm hold" the patient needs. With higher level character pathology, ambivalence can be tolerated, and disruptions are less likely to lead to angry devaluation of the treatment and premature termination.

PSYCHOANALYTIC VALIDATION: A CRITIQUE

Progress in psychodynamic theory has always been held back by the lack of an agreed framework for the proof or disproof of interpretations put upon clinical data. The single case study method, traditionally used in medicine when experimental methods are impractical, suffers in assessing clinical results in psychoanalytic writings from theoretical dogmatism and from "testimonials."

In this respect Langs' (1978, 1979) method of validation through Type Two derivatives offers a refreshing contrast. The accuracy of an intervention can be measured by the material and the therapist need not fall back on "resistance" to explain lack of confirmation. Yet psychoanalytic validation as used by Langs in his many books is less than satisfactory because it lacks the controls with which scientific research attempts to exclude personal bias.

Validation is an art, not a science, and can only be a relative, not an absolute, explanation of clinical material. When a phenomenon as complex as psychotherapy goes awry, any number of factors may be operating, individually or simultaneously, and it is all too easy to pick out what the observer chooses, whether that is a missed interpretation or an altered frame. In particular, if an author has a vested interest in the necessity of a particular kind of frame, there is sufficient material in almost any therapeutic session that can be interpreted in that light.

In appraising Type Two derivative validation as valuable but too open to the subjectivity of interpretation, one is left with the equally subjective clinical method and all its pitfalls. Accumulated clinical experience carries a certain weight, but falls victim to bias and preconceptions. There are no definitive data in psychotherapy, nor can there be until psychoanalytic research becomes integrated with scientific method.

CONCLUSIONS

The intrapsychic world is permeable to social influence. This is amply documented by transcultural psychiatry, but is not obvious when one's patients are culturally homogeneous. The invisibility of social forces is like the cancelled factors on two sides of an equation; they can be ignored if they are the same for everyone.

The frame of psychotherapy is in part a social convention, and the dynamics of fees and insurance are not invariable. In the Quebec context, the dynamics of insurance "cancel out" because they are part of the social frame. There are still pitfalls in the system, especially the handling of missed sessions. In an American context, insurance may or may not be disruptive, depending on the patient's expectations, the therapist's attitudes, and the social prevalence of insurance, but insured therapy is still therapy; a fine picture is still fine in a different frame.

REFERENCES

Applebaum, S. A. (1978). How strictly confidential? *International Journal of Psychoanalytic Psychotherapy* 7:222-224.

Blanck, G., and Blanck, P. (1974). *Ego Psychology: Theory and Practice*. New York: Columbia University Press.

Chodoff, P. (1972). The effect of third party payment on the practice of psychiatry. *American Journal of Psychiatry* 129:540-545.

Eissler, K. R. (1975). On some theoretical and technical problems regarding the payment of fees for psychoanalytic treatment. *International Review of Psychoanalysis* 1:73-101.

Frank, J. (1973). *Persuasion and Healing*, revised ed. Baltimore: John Hopkins Press.

Glasser, M. A., and Duggan, T. (1969). Prepaid psychiatric experience with UAW members. *American Journal of Psychiatry* 126:675-681.

Halpert, E. (1972a). The effect of insurance on psychoanalytic treatment. *Journal of the American Psychoanalytic Association* 20:122–132.

———. (1972b). A meaning of insurance in psychotherapy. *International Journal of Psychoanalytic Psychotherapy* 1:60–68.

Horney, K. (1937). *The Neurotic Personality of Our Time.* New York: Norton.

Kernberg, O. (1975). *Borderline Conditions and Pathological Narcissism.* New York: Jason Aronson.

Kohut, H. (1977). *The Restoration of the Self.* New York: International Universities Press.

Langs, R. (1976a). *The Bipersonal Field.* New York: Jason Aronson.

———. (1976b). *The Therapeutic Interaction.* New York: Jason Aronson.

———. (1978). *The Listening Process.* New York: Jason Aronson.

———. (1979). *The Therapeutic Environment.* New York: Jason Aronson.

Lasch, C. (1979). *The Culture of Narcissism.* New York: Norton.

Liptzin, B. (1977). The effects of national health insurance on Canadian psychiatry: the Ontario experience. *American Journal of Psychiatry* 134:248–252.

Lorand, S., and Console, W. A. (1958). Therapeutic results in psychoanalytic treatment without a fee. *International Journal of Psycho-Analysis* 39:59–64.

Markson, E. (1977). The impact of national health insurance on the practice of psychiatry: the Canadian experience: the clinical practice of psychotherapy. Unpublished paper presented to the American Psychiatric Association, Toronto.

Marmor, J., Scheidermandel, P. L., and Kenno, C. K. (1975). Psychiatrists and Their Patients, A National Study of Private Office Practice. Washington, D.C. Joint Information Service of the American Psychiatric Association and the National Association for Mental Health.

Mitscherlich, A. (1969). *Society without the Father.* New York: Harcourt, Brace & World.

Murphy, H. B. M., Wittkower, E. D., and Chance, N. A. (1967). A cross-cultural inquiry into the symptomatology of depression: a preliminary report. *International Journal of Psychiatry* 3:6–22.

Nash, J. R., and Cavenar, J. O. (1976). Free psychotherapy: an inquiry into resistance. *American Journal of Psychiatry* 133:1066–1069.

Ortigues, M. C., and Ortigues, E. (1966). *Oedipe Africain.* Paris: Librairie Plon.

Paris, J. (1973). Psychiatric practice in Canada pre- and post-medicare. *Canadian Medical Association Journal* 109:469–470.

———. (1977). The dynamics of psychotherapy under medicare. *Canadian Psychiatric Association Journal* 22:137–139.

Sharfstein, S., and Magnus, H. L. (1975). Insuring intensive psychotherapy. *American Journal of Psychiatry* 132:1252–1256.

Shwed, H. J., Kurvin, S. F., and Baliga, K. (1979). Medicaid audit: crisis and confidentiality in the patient–psychiatrist relationship. *American Journal of Psychiatry* 136:447–450.

Uchill, A. B. (1978). Deviation from confidentiality and the therapeutic holding environment. *International Journal of Psychoanalytic Psychotherapy* 7:208–219.

Weber, M. (1930). *The Protestant Ethic and the Spirit of Capitalism.* New York, Scribners, 1930.

Wheelis, A. (1958). *The Quest for Identity.* New York: Norton.

Wittkower, E. D., and Prince, R. (1974). A review of transcultural psychiatry. In *American Handbook of Psychiatry,* vol. 2, ed. S. Arieti, pp. 535–550. New York: Basic Books.

The Payment of Fees for Psychotherapy

JAMES O. RANEY, M.D.

Several specific effects of third party payment of fees for psychoanalysis and psychotherapy are demonstrated. Using some of the criteria for listening that have been set out by Langs (1981, 1982), case illustrations from several sources are reviewed and discussed. Some of the examples have been selected from detailed accounts found in the psychotherapeutic literature, which should permit the reader to turn to the original source for verification and review in greater detail.

Others have considered the effects of third party payment or reduced fees on the course and outcome of psychoanalysis and psychotherapy (Eissler 1974, Gray 1973, Halpert 1972a, Langs 1979, Lorand and Console 1958). With the exception of Langs, none of these has looked at how the therapist's compensation or activity around the fee payment is represented in the derivative material of the patient. In Langs' assessment of the derivatives in a case where insurance was used, the effects appeared detrimental to the therapeutic course.

METHOD OF STUDY

According to Langs (1976), each aspect of the therapist's being and activity (Grotstein 1982) constitutes what is described as the therapeutic frame. This is the reality (i.e., the context) that is perceived by the patient. The reality or context induces intrapsychic thinking and feeling, or the adaptation to the context. Thus, what the patient perceives of the therapist and the therapist's surroundings is termed the *adaptive context* (Langs 1976). The intrapsychic thinking–feeling in turn, stimulated by the adaptive context, generates activity in the form of speech or behavior. The adaptive context stirs unconscious conflicted introjects, fantasies, memories, and feelings. The perception and all it activates remain unconscious and are disguised by the adaptive function or defenses of the ego (Brenner 1981), and are expressed in words or actions that are acceptable to the ego's view of the external world. These ultimate expressions are therefore "derived" from the unconscious perceptions and thoughts, and are termed *derivatives*. Derivatives are equivalent to Brenner's "symptoms," which are the results of the ego's revisions of the unconscious contents (Brenner 1981).

When the therapist, author, or reader listens and interprets with the assumption that derivatives include symbols or are symptomatic of unconscious adaptive contexts, the derivatives are termed *Type Two derivatives* (Langs 1981). When derivatives are considered to refer only to activated unconscious imagoes and processes, and the always present adaptive contexts are not included, therapists are listening and interpreting *Type One derivatives* (Langs 1981). With no consideration of the material as symbolic of unconscious contents, the therapist listens only to *manifest content* (Langs 1981).

In the bipersonal interaction, patient and therapist communicate in one of three distinct modes or styles. These modes are the final expression of varieties and degrees of disguise and defense that depend on earlier adaptation experiences (Billow and Lovett 1982, Erdheim 1982), the adaptive contexts and state of the therapeutic frame, and the intermixture of activated unconscious memories, feelings, and imagoes.

Langs applies alphabetic designations to these three modes. He terms them, respectively, Type A, Type B, and Type C communicative modes or styles (Langs 1978b, 1981). The first mode, characterized by a predominance of symbolic imagery, communicates the most meaning. Adaptive contexts are usually identified in the derivative images and are sometimes explicit. Unconscious genetic and dynamic memories, affects, and processes are disguised and condensed into the symbolic derivatives. In the second mode of communication (Type B), action and words are used to project inner tensions and contents, as though the unconscious thoughts and feelings are actually inside and can be discharged or attributed to an external target. In the third mode of communication (Type C), words or actions destroy and interrupt meaning in the communication between therapist and patient.

To complicate the situation, in each therapeutic interaction, consisting of contributions from each side, one participant may not speak or listen in the same communicative mode as the other, nor does each participant necessarily listen in the same mode as he or she speaks. Finally, during a single therapy session, the participants may shift their styles of listening and speaking a number of times.

The thesis presented through the following examples and discussion is that the method of compensating the therapist and the therapist's activity concerning the method are adaptive contexts. Type Two derivatives in the patient's material will reveal how the patient perceives and unconsciously works over these adaptive contexts. The state of the therapy and of the communicative styles of each participant will either be directly apparent or symbolically represented in the derivatives. From these assessments the value or liability of the method of payment for the therapeutic process will be weighed.

FOUR CATEGORIES OF COMPENSATION

Four general categories of compensation for psychotherapy can be distinguished:

1. Timely payment in full by the patient.
2. Payment by the therapist by discounting the fee or permitting a debt to accumulate.
3. Payment by a relative or other significant person.
4. Payment by an institution; e.g., all or in part by an insurance carrier, government, charitable agency, or the like.

In each case example selected, one or more of the latter three methods of payment was used. Case descriptions that are found in the literature may be quite detailed, but some are not clear about the fee arrangement, and even less so about the therapeutic implication of the fee arrangement. In some of the cases, details of the fee arrangements must be indirectly inferred from other material such as the derivatives, or are found buried in the detail of the text.

Most of the "translations" of the derivatives described in this paper will be written as declarative statements and are the counterparts of the silent hypotheses that a therapist makes in the clinical setting. In a study such as this, however, such statements can only be conjectural and hypothetical. Like clinical silent hypotheses about adaptive contexts, however, they may find validation in how well each statement organizes the material, sheds new light on existing material, and leads to new hypotheses.

First Clinical Example

Sequential hours of a psychoanalytic case were presented in several meetings of a seminar using process notes that were prepared shortly after each analytic hour. When each hour was described to the seminar, the group thought the material to be mildly interesting, but lifeless and static. Some material suggested Oedipal rivalry. There was little progress in the analysis. The analyst's interventions focused on rivalry, competition, and how the patient displaced the object of the rivalry from the therapist onto other people. The interpretations did not seem to have an effect. The group discussed genetic issues and defenses that seemed to be used to avoid the transference. A sense of confusion prevailed among the seminar participants. After a time the group was silent after hearing each hour, even though each seemed rich with material. The hours were repetitive and the discussion seemed as futile as the analyst's interpretations. Something was still amiss.

At one point the analyst mentioned that his patient, although keeping current for several months, had not paid a much earlier bill. The patient's claim of financial troubles may have prevented the therapist from addressing the issue. With this information, the group seemed to take greater notice of the imagery in many of the sessions of people who cheated the patient and were out to get everything he had. He had to constantly guard against them.

The vignettes from three hours are provided. Background for the first vignette includes a recent vacation taken by the analyst. The patient had paid a little more than he owed for the previous month. He owed money to another therapist who treats one of his children. He owed his attorney money. The patient had just described how he missed his daughter and how she seemed threatened by his new woman friend. His ex-wife had taken his daughter somewhere else to live. In the hour excerpted here, the analyst had just suggested that the patient might feel responsible for his ex-wife's leaving:

Patient: I agree (weeps). (Angrily) The child's mother wants revenge and is screwing me by charging on the credit card. I feel like a hurt child. I have trouble feeling close to my present woman friend. My former wife is passive–aggressive but the present woman is similar. I want my present woman-friend to do something but she is not accommodating. I should be more directive. She wouldn't wash her hair but I didn't talk to her about it. I want people to see my needs but I am reticent to ask.

Analyst: Perhaps you felt the same way with me.

Patient: I am aware of that. I try to train people to perform on cue; like the woman I am living with. I am not afraid of her. It is hard to sleep. She awakens when I do. I mix her up with my previous two wives. She expresses her love and does care.

In comparison with the hypothesis of the Oedipal rivalry, the discovery of the debt organized the material much better and therefore became the most likely primary adaptive context. The communicative theory holds that the adaptive context would not so much be the debt as it would be the therapist's actions or inaction in regard to the debt. In this instance the neglect of the debt appeared from the derivatives to be the best hypothesis. With the identification of an adaptive context, the case material can be heard as Type Two derivatives.

The patient's derivatives suggest that he thought the therapist was hurting him, was reticent and passive–aggressive. The therapist was not accommodating, and was reticent in his not addressing the fee owed. The patient feared the analyst and may have believed that the analyst feared him. After the analyst's intervention, the patient's derivatives may be translated as follows:

> I can get you to perform (or) you are trying to get me to perform. You are afraid of me. This is a confusing, disturbing (hard to sleep) communication. I am mixing you up; you are mixing me up. You do seem to care, however.

In the following excerpt, the analyst struggles to decode the meaning of the derivatives. He makes assumptions about the material, based on Type One derivatives (no adaptive context). The patient manifestly denies each intervention and progressively provides more derivatives. The patient had been talking about relatives dying, driving too fast, and worries about dying and leaving his daughter alone with his ex-wife. He didn't want to support the ex-wife:

Analyst: It sounds like you are telling us that you are suicidal.
Patient: No, no. (*He expresses more detail.*)
Analyst: Perhaps you are depressed and denying the depression.
Patient: No, I should feel shitty, but I feel okay.
Analyst: You seem to be indicating that you feel depressed, shitty, and all alone. You are trying to express your anger about this.
Patient: No, I am angry toward my girl friend. She said I would never miss an interview. Of course I wouldn't miss an interview.
Analyst: This anger toward her is anger toward me. The suicidal actions are also equivalent of anger toward me. There is a wish for closeness and a wish to be away from me. You can't control me.
Patient: Perhaps that is true. I would like more time. I have a lot of financial problems. I really worry. I am frightened that as we talked about before, I won't have enough money to come. I can't control the people who are trying to get my money. I am aware that I seem to emphasize the negative and let positive things pass.

The patient was late for the next hour:

Patient: I took my daughter with me to my mother's grave. It was a pleasant experience. I did not want to confuse her with my crying so I controlled myself. . . . I was amazed at how deeply I felt (*weeps*). . . . (*A dream:*) I was about to establish a medical practice. There were two other doctors . . . surgeons . . . handsome. A fourth person. I realized that he was determining whether he should approve of my taking a place. Would the area have enough patients to support another doctor? The second man had a forbidding manner. In real life he had lost his hospital privileges. My daughter then awakened and I tucked her in bed. When I went back to sleep I had this dream: I was going to join a venture that might fail. It would not make enough money to support all of the people (*end of dream*). . . . I feel judged harshly about my lack of patients. Most people seem more ambitious than I am. One doctor who moved out of our group said that we don't take care of sick people. My woman friend got rid of that whiney dog. I hated it. I think of your last remark about anger, that I can't control you. It is like anger toward dogs. Like with my parents; I always lost, no matter what I did. I was angry when I thought my woman friend would keep the dog. If it is similar, I must face the fact of my anger with you. My father and mother. Father was a hard worker but he was insubstantial. He was sensitive to being lied to. He would say that he had no control over comings and goings. I think of Mother's grave. I feel badly that there were no flowers. I am sad to think that both Mother and myself will be forgotten.

Analyst: When you are not seeing me you feel that I have forgotten you.

Patient: (*Crying*) Crying stems from feeling forgotten. Maybe you are right. I had a gray lonely childhood. Time drug (sic) on. I felt neglected and forgotten. There was no challenge or intellectual stimulation. You seem to have a holier than thou attitude. It has to do with our difference in status. I took my family to brunch. Susan told me what a good "mother" I am (*tearful*). I take pleasure in the recognition of what a good "mother" I am. I am angry if not recognized.

Analyst: You are angry at me if I don't recognize you.

Patient: At brunch I saw a lot of drunks. I was infuriated when I was dunned by one. I think, "There for the grace of God go I." But I'll not give them a cent. I feel impermanent, like I am walking on banana skins.

In these derivatives the theme of the unresolved fee issue can be traced from many perspectives. The patient did not feel depressed, in part because he was talking about an introjection of the nonfunctional and "careless" analyst. He referred to the analyst who, like his father, was working hard but, because he had missed a crucial element, was insubstantial. The word "insubstantial" combined the analyst's nonfunctioning aspect as well as his relative poverty because the patient hadn't paid him. The doctor who has few patients, or who doesn't see sick people is a further derivative of the patient's unconscious working over of the reasons that the analyst doesn't engage him on this fee business, i.e., his illness. He was angry; the analyst must have been angry. The analyst was whiney, i.e., ineffective in his interventions, but the patient couldn't get rid of his ineffectiveness. The venture (the analysis) might fail, there wasn't enough money to support. The derivatives here were richly symbolic of the neglected debt. The adaptive contexts of the analyst's missed interpretations were woven into the several derivatives of the sequence.

In desperation, the patient described images of drunks who dun him and who will not get a cent. These are derivatives of the patient's unconscious view of the analyst–patient dyad. To the patient, the analyst appears to be out of control, "drunk," because he has not been overtly "dunning" him, i.e., interpreting the derivatives of the unpaid fee. His anger and unconscious conjectures about why the analyst was reticent about the fee led the patient to feel in a very "slippery" position. The patient's view of the analyst as slippery and dangerous may have appeared in this image as well.

The patient's communication, partly in action (withholding payment) and partly in symbolic imagery, indicated a combined Type B and Type A communicative mode (Langs 1981). The therapist, however, by responding with inaction (omitting reference to the payment) was responding in a combined Type B and C communicative mode. The "B" refers to his action and the "C" to the effect of the action to interfere with the identification of the meaning in the patient's communications. Until the adaptive context was identified, interpreted, and rectified, the net communicative field in the therapy was Type C, because neither participant, following the lead of the therapist, identified the meaning or assumed the existence of an adaptive context. The actions of the patient and therapist and the interpretations of the therapist tended to obscure rather than lead toward uncovering meaning. This Type C field led to the confusion and inanition of the seminar group, who also were listening without an adaptive context—a Type C listening and responsing in the seminar. The discovery of the adaptive context also organized and converted the seminar group into Type A listeners. In the clinical sessions the analyst shifted to a Type A communicative sytle and began to interpret the patient's derivatives with the adaptive context of the unpaid amount of the bill. Shortly afterwards, the patient paid the debt.

There is no data subsequent to the debt payment, but this example illustrates how the discovery of an adaptive context clarified an otherwise confusing sequence and provided a rationale for another approach. In this instance, had the patient not paid the bill, the therapist could have continued his Type A listening and made interventions around the derivatives of the debt. The patient would probably have gradually converted action-discharge and projective mechanisms into a more predominantly Type A communicative mode. The therapist's stance would either address this particular adaptive context, uncover another one, or create a shift in the patient to a Type C mode that might lead to termination. Had the patient not paid, for example, the "cheater" reference might have more clearly referred to himself or changed into other derivatives. The reality that supported the projections on the part of the therapist would have been removed. Interventions still would have been directed first at the interaction and frame disturbance before the transference meaning could be discerned.

Second Clinical Example

In this case the fee was paid for in part by the patient, by insurance through his employment, and by his mother. No detailed hours are described in the account (Gedo 1979). Instead, segments of the four-year analysis were abstracted. Nevertheless, from the descriptive account, principles of the communicative approach can be illustrated and validated.

It is assumed that all descriptions were obtained from the associations that occurred in the analytic hours. Therefore, the descriptions may be considered to have some reference to adaptive contexts, e.g., the analyst's activity regarding the fee and fee sources, as well as to manifest and outside or past history. Thus most of the patient's associations are considered to be Type Two derivatives.

Analysis had been recommended by another therapist. At first the patient expressed reluctance to engage in analytic treatment because of financial problems. A confrontation by the analyst led to the patient changing to a higher paying job that included significant insurance coverage for the analysis. Apparently more money was required for the fee. The analyst tried to clarify the patient's passivity toward his mother by suggesting that he borrow money from her that could be repaid to her estate if necessary (Gedo 1979, p. 41). Gedo acknowledged that the analyst's activity around the fee and establishment of the alliance were not interpretive, but were necessary to establish the holding environment (Gedo 1979, p. 70).

As a Type Two derivative, the patient's passivity in relation to his mother may reflect his relation with the analyst. The description suggests that the analyst's active confrontation was a Type B action-discharge that encouraged the patient to react passively as he apparently had with his mother.

In a later sequence the patient described his sister's "emotional crisis" in which she fell mute, and for which she had been hospitalized. The patient ". . . had tried frantically to make the parents understand that the girl's negativism was a response to their rigid expectations . . ." (Gedo 1979, p. 43). Gedo noted that the patient's concern about the sister's problem was present at the start of the analysis. The patient's willingness to take action regarding his problems was the result of his noticing the apparent result of his sister's therapy: her life course was set and she would no longer need her family's assistance for psychiatric treatment.

The patient seems to have expressed Type Two derivatives of his negativism in response to the analyst's expectations and suggestions regarding finding funds for the analysis. Frantically trying to make the parents understand was a derivative of his unconscious awareness that he had tried and failed to make the analyst understand. Like his sister, he wanted a cure, but did not want the assistance of the analyst, mother or the insurance. The crisis of his mute sister referred, as did the image of the drunk panhandler in the last example, to his unconscious view that he was effectively mute insofar as the analyst had failed to understand him, and/or to the fact that his analyst had been analytically "mute," which had resulted in a therapeutic crisis.

Later, the patient's disorganization, inability to manage tensions, and his consequent failure to accomplish what he had set out to do were contrasted against the superb organization of his mother. The patient's dependence on his mother's organization and guidance in his chaotic life was correlated with his similar need for the structure of the scheduled analytic sessions. The patient then noted that his mother also had a tendency to intrude upon his boundaries and to attempt to organize him according to her needs, not his.

A mixed unconscious perception of the analyst's therapeutic frame appeared in these derivatives. On one hand the patient expressed memories of useful aspects of his relationship with his mother to describe unconscious perceptions of useful aspects of the analytic relationship. The mother was then utilized to express in derivatives the intrusiveness of the analyst and the patient's resultant unconscious rage.

Gedo noted that the patient became enraged and irresolute at the analyst's confrontations, which seemed more in accordance with the analyst's reality than with the patient's. In a long explanation Gedo acknowledged that in one instance the analyst had acted like the patient's mother and had therefore missed a transference issue. The analyst appears to have enacted the transference rather than interpreting it. The explanation does not include a reference to the previous similar involvement with the original fee arrangement.

The specific issue may be seen to have some meaning if considered as Type Two derivatives. The patient expressed an intention to operate the camera in the filming of an underground movie. The analyst confronted him with the impracticality of spending the time and money this project would involve. The project could have been a derivative of the patient's desire to analyze (film) the unconscious implications of his associations (the underground movie), which had not been a major part of the analysis to this point. Upon receiving a confrontation rather than an interpretation, the patient shifted from a Type A communication to a Type B action or dramatization of the derivative and acted upon his unconscious need and determination to function independently of the analyst. The patient's action prevailed and the camera work was a success. The fee adaptive context could not be discerned in the symbolic imagery specifically, but the analyst introduced it in the confrontation in which the patient was told he could not afford the money.

Both patient and analyst seem to have been unconsciously entangled in the fee and finance issue. The boundaries were not clear. The analyst, like his patient, may have been making an effort unconsciously to disentangle the confusion. Thus while the patient did not specifically refer to finances in the sequence about the underground movie, the analyst's introduction of the patient's inability to afford the expenses the project involved signalled the analyst's unconscious awareness of the problem with the fee in the analysis.

The analyst's confrontation may be considered to have been a Type Two derivative of the *analyst's* unconscious awareness of the problem and of the adaptive context. Additionally, the confrontation may have been a derivative of the analyst's unconscious effort to rectify the situation and respond to the patient's effort to establish boundaries of a metaphorical secure therapeutic frame. As the analyst responded to the patient's intention to work as a derivative symbolic cameraman, the analyst's derivative confrontation could be decoded: the analysis should not be continued (afforded) under these conditions. An additional view, then, of the confrontation is that it was incorrect in its level of communication and translation of the unconscious. It represented, in derivative form, an unconsciously perceived real problem in the analysis and an effort to correct it.

Another derivative thread that may be related to the fee was the repeated derivative that Gedo termed a transference distortion: The patient was convinced ". . . that, like his mother, I wanted to see him safely married and furnished with professional qualifications" (Gedo 1979, p. 44). If the range of ego defensive functions is taken into account along with the existence of the reality (adaptive context) of the analyst's acceptance of money from the mother, an unconscious meaning of this repeated image can be conjectured. The patient's ego may have utilized introjection and identification to construct this derivative of the unconscious view that the analyst was safely (or unsafely) "married" to the patient's mother via the fee. In the brutally frank terms of the unconscious, the patient wished the analyst would function as though he were "professionally qualified." An interpretation based on ego defense mechanisms utilizing the adaptive context would include these derivative images.

Such inclusive and complete listening to and decoding of the patient's unconscious perception is extraordinarily difficult (Raney 1981) and requires "the maximum ego integration of which the therapist is capable" (Flarsheim 1972).

Later the patient described unbearable overstimulation and lack of privacy as a child. He had to share a bedroom with no doors which permitted the lights and noises of the "main areas" of the house to intrude upon ". . . the space where the children were put to bed with the injunction to go to sleep" (Gedo 1979, p. 46). The patient's unconscious view of the mother's intrusion into the analysis via the fee and the implied injunction not to speak of it (to go to sleep) are suggested meanings of these derivatives.

The unconscious struggle with the analyst was reflected in a derivative sequence where the patient described himself as independent and needing to get away from his father's prejudices. The unconscious idea that the infusion of money and other nonanalytic influences were present and needed to be disconnected could be seen in a derivative image of the father disconnecting the gas lines in the house.

A reference to the patient's "fervent commitment" that went "beyond any need" and "had the quality of immoderate ambition" (p. 48) suggests an unconscious introjection and identification with the analyst's noninterpretive activity. In a reference to his "general attitude of having to be above mundane matters" (p. 48) the patient may have expressed a derivative of his unconscious perception of the analyst's not having interpreted or analysed the unconscious meanings of the fee situation. This is not to say that the patient did not have the attributes that he mentioned. The existence of the adaptive context and the manifest nature of the descriptions of his characteristics suggest, however, other unconscious meanings and connections.

Another derivative that suggests a connection with someone outside of the analysis is the description of childhood visits to a museum. The museum was similar to the analyst's office. The director of the museum had been a family friend, suggesting a derivative of an unconsciously perceived connection between the analyst and a family member.

The patient connected a fear of learning something discreditable about the analyst with seeing a former therapist with a baby carriage and holding a toddler by the hand. This therapist had left her job for a second marriage. The association with analyst and mother could be seen in this image, but the image also contains the analyst/mother connected to two children, suggesting again the triangle that the patient unconsciously perceives in the analysis. "Discreditable" and "second marriage" could refer not to something that he might have learned, but to the existing unconscious awareness that the analyst's function was incomplete and that there was still another connection in addition to the analyst's connection with the mother. The second marriage may also have referred to the unconscious perception of the analyst's link to the insurance carrier via the fee payment and perhaps the reports and summaries that are ubiquitous to insurance paid therapies.

The patient, in a development very similar to the fourth case example, progressed through several sequences in which he seemed to despair of the analysis. There was then ". . . a period of stubborn unwillingness to associate, which brought into focus his lifelong anal retentiveness" (Gedo 1979, p. 51). The patient apparently stopped his analytic work, i.e., his associating. After some interpretive work about his fecal retention as a child and envy of his mother's ability to create new life, he offered the analyst a present which the analyst admiringly accepted. In a patient with tenuous object relations and a narcissistic organization such as this, rejection is very painful. There may also be more information that was not included which influenced the decision to accept the gift. Nevertheless, if the sequences that followed are considered from the communicative approach and perspective, the patient's Type Two derivatives and other actions seem to suggest that, from this point on, from the patient's perspective, the analytic alliance was functionally disrupted. The patient may have, through the gift, found a way to "pay" the analyst. According to the author, the gifts (woodcuts) were annual Christmas gifts that continued to be sent after the analysis. The gifts may be considered to have dramatized, in an action-discharge, the patient's efforts to correct the unanalyzed and unchanged fee aspects of the frame. The gift giving may also, by continuing after the analysis, have picked up the thread of the analyst's suggestion that the patient could pay the mother back after her death.

In another sequence, the patient mentioned being robbed at gunpoint. This was another concise derivative in which the fee has been condensed as well as his unconscious opinion that he was being "robbed" of analytic interventions that he required.

His salary was increased so he could completely support himself, including the payment of his analytic fees. There were other setbacks described, but the improvement in the frame in regard to the mother and/or the analyst and the fee issue may have appeared in a derivative of his fitting out an attractive apartment with his mother's "welcome assistance" (p. 54).

An image of assistance, however, remained. Perhaps the patient had unconsciously perceived some of the analyst's interventions as helpful assistance. Or was this a derivative of the continued support of the insurance?

As the end of the analysis approached, the patient gave the analyst another gift in the form of his thesis for the analyst to read. The analyst was less enthusiastic about this gift than the first one and returned it, indicating only that it was clear. This response of the analyst, in contrast to his earlier one, may have communicated some discernment of the patient's need to be separate from him.

Following the termination, the patient, as mentioned, continued to send the annual woodcuts. He also mentioned on one occasion enjoying intellectual exchanges with outstanding scholars in his department. Also, after the analysis, the patient became engaged to a woman who may have been one of the women who was described during the analysis as casual and lacking in enthusiasm. If this is the same woman, the possibility of her casual and less than enthusiastic aspect and the description of the enjoyable intellectual interchanges may have represented enacted derivatives of the aspects of the analytic experience that were gratifying, but intellectual and less than analytically meaningful, i.e., "casual." The continued gifts and engagement to the girl may have symbolized both the residual fusion with the analyst and a continued derivative communication of the unanalyzed fee issue and connection via the fee to mother.

The issue here is not that the outcome of this analysis was unfavorable. It seemed a very good result in comparison to the patient's pathology at the outset. Perhaps splits and recombinations are part of normal development (Grotstein 1981) and a part of the outcome of each analysis. The derivatives that appeared during and after this particular analysis suggest that the analyst's noninterpretive interventions around the fee, coupled with further noninterpretive interventions during the analysis, seem to have led ultimately to a split in the patient's unconscious perception of the analyst and analytic experience. The patient seemed to engage in a "cure" that was somewhat independent of the analyst's designated function. The symptomatic improvement may have been accomplished with a beneficial hold characterized by noninterpretive gratifications and misalliances (Langs 1981).

Third Clinical Example

This example is taken from one of the most detailed accounts of a psychoanalysis that can be found (Dewald 1972). Its author risked exposure of technical and personal idiosyncracies to advance the study of psychoanalysis. Despite the extraordinary detail about the events leading up to the beginning of the analysis, specific references to many details of the framework, including the fee, were not made explicit. Much of the pre-analytic information suggested major participation in the relationship by third parties. An unclear fee arrangement, however, appears to have been rectified in the second analytic session.

The first reference to the fee arrangement occurred in the initial evaluation, nine months before the first analytic session. The patient then mentioned her desire to pay for the analysis out of her limited income. This was an ambiguous expression: on the one hand, she desired a nondeviant fee sector of the therapeutic frame but, on the other hand, her "out of her limited income" part of the derivative was an expression of an unconscious contradictory wish (fear, resistance) for some limitation of the analysis.

Reference to the fee appears next in the description of the clinic committee decision that she could not be offered a low-cost analysis, but no reason is given. Dewald, by coincidence, had analytic time at the same time. He relayed through the social worker who had been seeing her in the meanwhile that if she could make the necessary financial arrangements for private analysis, he could begin treatment with her. The patient called to accept this offer.

In the beginning of the first session of the analysis, the schedule and the financial arrangements were made. She would be given a bill on the first session of the month and was to bring a check prior to the tenth of the month. Her method of payment was not mentioned in this description. Her resolution in the second analytic session to pay the entire fee implied that at the time of this first session in the analysis, the fee arrangement had either not been settled or was paid in some part by someone else. In the same early segment of the first session, other aspects of the procedure, including the rule of free association, were explained.

It is assumed that a standard analytic convention of a regular appointment time and place was arranged. Nonstandard details of the office, the waiting area, the decorations, and other details that vary from analyst to analyst were not described. Some aspects of the analyst's activity can be inferred from later descriptions. These minor details are revealing of the analyst and can influence the productions of the patient (Lichtenberg and Slap 1977; Langs 1981, 1982).

In addition to the fee element, other frame issues that acted as adaptive contexts and hindered the identification of the fee issue in the derivatives can be described: the evaluation for the analytic clinic was done by Dewald. The information from his evaluation was most likely transmitted to clinic personnel. Apparently, he answered knocks on his door. Dewald's note-taking may have anticipated confidentiality breaches, such as his later request to use the patient's material for his book. Private analysis was discussed in the evaluation session, but neither the reasons for the discussion nor the details were mentioned. Dewald saw her in an evaluation for one purpose and then invited her into private analysis with him.

What did Dewald and the patient work out that allowed her to afford private analysis after she apparently had declared insufficient means? The details were not presented. A source such as her in-laws seems the most likely. Derivatives with allusions to third parties began with her first question after she moved to the couch and appeared repeatedly in her sequences throughout the analysis.

The first communication after she moved to the couch is noteworthy. This was not the first comment in the session, but was the first comment made within the defined and therefore mutually agreed upon illusional space of the analysis. Her first sentence was: "What will I do if I am pregnant?" The reader will know by now that this question can be considered as a highly condensed derivative that contains one or more adaptive contexts as well as activated unconscious memories, affects, and other elements. Dewald's immediate response also implied that the question had meanings beyond its manifest content: ". . . it is important for us to try to understand what's behind the question and see if it has other meanings than the question itself" (p. 21). His response, however, was made too soon to see if she would have provided more associations and derivatives. He directed the patient to do something that she already seemed to be doing satisfactorily and, by suggesting that meaning was forthcoming when some meaning had already been communicated, set out what she might have perceived as a puzzling contradiction. There may have been other considerations, but from the communicative perspective, his response seems to have initiated a non-interpretive Type C communicative style that was continued throughout the analysis.

If the patient questions with a Type Two derivative bias, which assumes an adaptive context or contexts, several hypotheses about the latent meaning of the question can be immediately made. Dewald referred to one adaptive context when he mentioned later that her material may have had something to do with the beginning of the analysis. The events that preceded the analysis and the ambiguous fee element provided additional adaptive contexts. Pregnancy as a possible interference to the analysis suggested an image of a third-party interference. Third parties had been a consistent part of the relationship with the analyst to this point: the initial evaluation was not confidential—a committee would have been involved; later a counselor was brought in for supportive counselling and then used to convey Dewald's invitation for analysis. An earlier reference to her husband, as a consultant about the type of analysis she should have, may have been the first Type Two derivative of the analyst's collaboration with third parties. The fee source was another third-party element that was not made clear.

In the second session she announced that she had arranged to pay the fee herself and that she appeared to be pregnant. She linked the fee issue, the analysis, and the derivative by describing the difficulties of supporting the analysis and children simultaneously.

Relatively few references to the fee occurred later in the analysis. Nevertheless, communications in two widely separate hours hinted that she had not paid for the analysis herself. In one hour she did not endorse the check properly. Dewald asked for associations about the endorsement. At one point she said: "I had a discussion with Tom about money and it panics him. He's doing extra work and I figure that we will borrow if necessary to pay for this" (p. 117). Later in the same hour: "It's Tom's parents who are helping to pay for this and not mine" (*elaborates*) (p. 118). Here the extra work suggests an effort to rectify the fee element. Tom's panic implies a derivative of her panic about the deviant frame and its implications. Borrowing to pay and the reference to Tom's parents were an explicit representation of the fee arrangement and a derivative of the analyst's third-party communication. Distinguishing Tom's parent's and not hers may have been a derivative of her recognition that it was not all her responsibility in the situation. She disavowed herself and placed the responsibility on her husband's parents, a derivative of the analyst.

Twenty months later she again failed to endorse a check properly. She said: "I am sorry about the check. (*Silence*.) I'm finally coming to the point where this is so hard for me and the answer for me is to get out" (p. 473). She suggested some of the problems with the fee arrangement and a solution to the difficulty. The nature of the difficulty in the frame was expressed in the same hour: "I always felt that my strength comes from somebody else. It always comes from mother or from Tom or Tom's mother or Mrs. Jones or Tom or Jean or you" (p. 475). And:

> It's only when I let go and I'm loving, do I feel good and I am happy. (*Silence*.) I'm sorry about the check. To me . . . that's it when I give you the check. (*Analyst asks for detail of the feeling*.) There's no money in the bank. Oh, we can get more if it's necessary, but also I feel that I'm handing you everything that we ever wanted to hang on to, and it's just like saying goodbye. I know that I will. It's like saying, "I realize everything and I'll not hang on any more." But I *did* hang on, didn't I? Oh shit! (*Silence*.) I realize that it's not going to go on every month. (*Silence*.) I can't wait to get out of here and start over. I feel that only after I leave here will I really start growing (p. 476).

These hours suggested that she had some assistance in paying for the analysis. If so, Type Two derivative inferences can be made. It was not that she was struggling to hold on to the analyst in the context of impending separation entirely; she was instead communicating her unconscious perception that the analyst seemed to be holding on to her. Feeling loving when she gave him the check was a derivative of her appreciation that the boundaries were not clear around the fee and to comply was to fuse with the analyst. She did not endorse the check properly in an unconscious effort to separate herself from the analyst's merger attachment to her and hers with him. These efforts were similar to the images in the last session of Gedo's patient. The rest of this hour contains descriptions of other derivatives of the struggle over this issue.

Derivatives which suggested issues over third parties and privacy were much more a part of her associations (e.g., pp. 80, 82, 135, 221, 318, 344, 443, etcetera) than were references to the fee. The analyst's acceptance of payment from someone else might have explained these, but the earlier breaches of privacy and those that continued, such as notetaking and knocks on the door, may also have accounted for those derivatives. Transference distortions cannot be excluded but, from the communicative perspective, the constant presence of these uninterpreted frame deviations interferes with the separation of the transference and the nontransference.

The outcome of the analysis appeared to have been beneficial. The follow-up interviewer noted, however, a marked contrast between images of the pre-analytic therapist and the analyst. In this instance, the therapist's nontransference activity was not distinguished from the patient's transferences, as she appeared to have created a defensive split that the follow-up interviewer noted in the derivative of the good and the bad therapists. Because the follow-up interview may have been similar to the analytic sessions, she again removed herself and did not appear for a second interview. As with the improper check endorsement, she attempted again to separate herself from the ambiguous and uncertain analytic frame.

Fourth Clinical Example

In this example (Goldberg 1978) an explicit reference is made to the patient's "modest fee" (p. 369). The analytic method in this example included other perspectives and interventions than those used in the communicative approach. The analyst therefore was disposed to interpret other aspects of the patient's material than the patient's reaction to the low fee or to the effect of the fee arrangement on the course of the analysis. The analysis was tumultuous and seemed to have ended prematurely. The portions extracted here are those that appear to be direct or derivative references to the low fee.

The editors of the original description suggest that the case "is hardly an exemplary analysis," but commend the analyst for her extremely effective response to the patient's needs. This contradiction seemed reconciled by their conclusion that the analysis produced dramatic results in a short period of time. The patient's derivatives, however, suggested that the analyst's "supportive" interventions were largely nonempathic and not responsive to the patient's therapeutic needs. The analyst's interventions and behaviors had the effect of a "misalliance cure" (Langs 1981), which is usually a dramatic and short-term outcome. These cures can be beneficial and enduring, but are not the ego restructuring outcomes that are the usual goal of psychoanalysis. The rich derivatives in this example fit an idea of Langs that frame deviations seem to produce Type Two derivatives (Langs 1981). This may have been a move by the patient to notify the therapist of the deviation. If these notifications fail, patients retreat to either depression or self-cure.

With these clearly problematic frame issues unresolved and in the background, it becomes difficult to consider the patient as an entity separate from the active analyst. Because the analyst's provocations and responsive omissions are stimuli *external* to the patient, to discuss the analysis of the patient's *internally* generated narcissistic tensions is at least incomplete.

The first segment is from the first analytic hour:

> At what was planned to be the first couch hour, he appeared obviously uncomfortable and disorganized and indicated his wish to sit up, and of course, I accepted that. He spoke mainly about his current life: the decision regarding the divorce is now final, his teaching is flat and empty, and yet his role as teacher is the only one in which he feels truly comfortable. He asked if I had seen a particular movie, and before I had time to answer, he burst into an emotional statement about the uniqueness and value of each individual's life in society; he then broke into tears. After recovering, he indicated that he is attempting to solve some of the economic problems in his life, to settle his coming teaching contract, and to get on with his Ph.D. problems. I said it sounded as if he had been making plans for the analysis. He is convinced that the essential thing in his life is to know really better what he thinks and feels, but he fears his feelings are almost too chaotic to be described even when he can recognize them. He spoke glowingly of his younger brother and then about his unsuccessful efforts to make contact with his father and share some of the pleasure of fishing with him. He talked bitterly about his mother's complicated combination of controlling him and rejecting him. His feelings in this area are terribly chaotic; he is afraid he is going to weep again because there is so much he has to get out. When I suggested that we had a good deal of time and that he could take things as slowly as he needed to, he was visibly relieved (Goldberg 1978, pp. 368–369).

Here was the first hint of trouble: the patient seemed very uncomfortable and indicated a wish to sit up. What must have been an enormous pressure on very likely an inexperienced analyst is not described. Whether the analyst, when she "accepted that," was silent or made some comment was not made clear. The patient's next comments about his teaching being flat and empty were derivatives that suggested that the analyst did speak and what she said unconsciously appeared to the patient a nonanalytic, i.e., flat and empty, response.

His question about the movie offered the analyst another chance to respond, but he interrupted her answer, perhaps unconsciously guessing that her answer would be like the first, not analytic and thus not empathic. His interruption both dramatized and achieved his aim to be unique and respected. His statement about the individual's uniqueness and value was a derivative of his directive that the analyst treat him accordingly and not for her needs, which he perceived her to be doing. His communication had components of a Type B (action) and Type A (symbolic) communicative mode. The action component seemed not so much to rid himself of inner contents that generated from his own intrapsychic conflicts, but from the disturbance caused by the therapist's inability to contain and respond interpretively to his provocations. He was struggling to get the therapist into a Type A mode from her currently prevailing Type B and C mode. He offered Type Two derivatives to communicate his unconscious thoughts.

The economic problems, the contract, and getting on with the Ph.D. problems were derivatives of the fee, the unsettled analytic frame (contract), and the analytic process.

The patient talked about unsuccessful efforts to make contact with his father, and "He talked bitterly about his mother's complicated combination of controlling him and rejecting him" (p. 368). If adaptive contexts (analyst's interventions) were not considered, these ideas would seem disorganized and lacking focus. The analyst's gratifying responses and overlooking interpretations of the derivatives of the fee and other disturbances of the frame were, in these derivatives, revealed to have evoked negative images. Further derivative images of his manipulative mother, forbidden wife, sore penis, and ceiling filled with breasts and vaginas in the next (second) hour of the analysis suggested similar contradictions.

The gratification of the modest fee as a part of these derivatives was implied in the following reference, which was surprisingly manifest:

He wonders why I am seeing him at such a modest fee, and decides it must be because I am especially concerned about him, and then he asks me for detailed confirmation of this.

The analyst answered: "I agree in general with his concern, but suggest that if I were to answer, it would stop his associations and he would feel intruded upon" (p. 369). The ominous dangers in the analyst's gratifications led the patient to attempt to confront her directly with the manifest fantasy that he must be special to her. This fantasy of a positive concern was meant to reassure himself that his unconscious ideas about the modest fee are incorrect. She agreed with the concern, but did not interpret the derivatives in which were encoded the specifics of his concerns. Her comment about not answering communicated clearly that she had not apprehended the derivative meaning. The patient responded to the manifest content of the intervention with delight but, to his unconscious perception that she had not understood, with tears: "He laughed delightedly. How lucky he feels to have somebody who is this understanding of him. He again broke into tears" (p. 370).

The next several hours were taken up with similar sequences. He produced memories of being accused, controlled, and feeling inadequate. The fee appeared in a derivative, and his unconscious view of the mother-like analyst can be surmised as condensed into this image:

> He had a dream in which he was living at home in a small town and had gone to the post office to mail a package, but the woman clerk deliberately overweighed the package, and, even though the patient accused the clerk of cheating him, he paid what he was asked because some other woman came in and convinced him that he had been wrong to argue (p. 372).

The reference to the fee was now condensed into the concise sequence of the woman clerk and the overcharge for the package, which he paid in deference to the *other* woman. This was a derivative of his perception of the analyst/mother who, by undercharging him, was cheating him. The other woman was a derivative of the analyst who did not listen and implied that the fee, among other things, was a topic not to be discussed.

In another sequence, "Humorously, he wonders if there is any point in his having sexual fantasies about me since I am obviously not going to have an affair with him" (p. 380). This derivative suggests that the patient had given up the prospect of the analysis (sexual fantasies) because of the lack of a secure therapeutic frame. He translated the gratifications into an affair that, unconsciously, she had engaged with him. That she was *obviously* not going to have an affair was an attempt to reassure himself that the frame was more secure than it was. No affair as a derivative of no analysis was confirmed when he asked her where she was taking her vacation and she told him (p. 380).

In the first hour after the vacation, he attempted to reintroduce the fee derivatives. The disappearance of the fee issue prior to the vacation might be explained by the several more pressing adaptive contexts around the vacation. Perhaps he returned with renewed hope for a more secure frame and responsive analyst:

> Typically, when we resumed he was initially quite uncomfortable and disheveled. He had few crises except for the chronic, running battle with his ex-wife. He literally does not have enough money to pay her settlement and to do his Ph.D. at the same time (p. 383).

In this derivative the fee was condensed with other aspects of the analyst's stimulating behavior. The low fee, the patient suggested through the displaced symbols, is incompatible with getting analyzed.

General references to the disturbed frame appear in these derivatives:

> Mr. B. wonders how much I really am like his mother; will I grill him about his behavior, will I insist on knowing what he does every weekend? Will I insist that he make every appointment on time and never ask for a schedule change? He suspects that some of his intense concern over how angry he is with me, even now, is in terms of not being able to manage the fear that his own separate independence may damage me some-how—but he doesn't follow this up (p. 383).

The second sentence refers to his wish for a more secure frame. The others are derivatives of the intrusive analyst whom he symbolizes as "damaged." The patient seems, via his derivatives, to have suggested that the analytic method in use with him, which does not utilize adaptive contexts and Type Two derivatives, is equivalent to no response from the analyst. The hours appeared to have continued with rich derivatives that indicated the patient's increasing despair about the prospects of the analysis. The patient's accounts of increasing activity seem to have led the analyst to think that her interpretive efforts were on the right track. A reference to money came up with an intention to do something about it:

> He informed his ex-wife that he really doesn't intend to continue paying her at the rate he was doing, that his needs are important too. But this decision made him feel terribly anxious, as if something vital was continuously being lost (p. 384).

This appeared to be a warning of the later acting out. The derivatives suggested that he was going to take action to deal with the unproductive analysis. The analyst was missing his needs, and vital interpretations were being lost.

He has found a new girl, much more reliable than the one that he had been going with for the first few months of the analysis. I announced that I would have to cancel two hours at the end of September, and he accepted this without much question. He had a dream about having trouble getting admitted to a hospital because of something being wrong with his stomach, but he isn't particularly afraid of dying. He associated with pleasure to childhood experiences with hospitals because they had always been delightful places where he was the center of a good deal of attentive interest, so much so that on two different occasions as a child he cried when it came time to leave the hospital to go back home (p. 384).

The analyst interrupted again with manifest content and a Type C communicative mode. "More reliable" and "attentive interest" were derivatives of the patient's desire that his analyst would respond to his material interpretively. The fee had disappeared as a distinct element and was condensed into the broader derivatives of the analyst's lack of understanding. She made an untimely intervention and failed to notice that the dream was a rich response to her announcement. In the derivative of the dream, the patient described how he could not get her to treat him for what he needed. (Later she literally provided him with money for food). The analyst must have been very preoccupied during this hour.

Another analyst vacation and self-revelation was followed by this:

He had forgotten his boat keys in school and in order to get into his boat he had had to force the hatch open. This had precipitated a series of "assault" fantasies which culminated in his preparing to initiate a fraudulent insurance claim: i.e., his boat had been broken into by robbers and valuable items had been stolen from the cabin. He stimulated the rather imaginative son (of the marina manager) to support his story about having seen some evil looking fellows sneaking around the dock and actually wrote a letter to the insurance company, but he came to his senses before he mailed it (p. 385).

The therapist's nonanalytic interventions, separations, the revelation of her abdominal surgery, and the reduced fee were possible adaptive contexts that were condensed into this one elaborate sequence. The derivatives decoded may have meant that the analyst had forgotten her analytic "key" and, instead, was making forceful and intrusive interventions. The patient felt "assaulted" or assaultive. The fee seems fraudulent either because the patient is not getting analytic value, or it is discounted because of the analyst's intrusive interventions. He and the analyst are cooperating in the untenable situation. In the last derivative he may have expressed his hope that the analyst would "come to her senses" and secure the frame.

He did not mention a money issue after the separation for the illness, but it came in a very clear derivative that followed the next break in the analysis:

> His more comfortable state comes to an end rather abruptly, as I discover after I return from my brief absence. His cat requires expensive treatment for an illness; he is short of money; he calls home, and his mother suggests that he ought to have the cat put away since it wasn't worth the $100. Mr. B. weeps as he describes how the cat feels like a part of himself (p. 389).

Here the derivatives suggested the idea that he doubted whether paying for his *in*expensive treatment was worthwhile. Inexpensive treatment that doesn't work is expensive. Perhaps he should quit. As derivatives of the previous case examples have implied, the inexpensive treatment had created another problem. He felt merged with the analyst. Separation would be very difficult.

Later he seemed to have worked independently of the analyst, despite having viewed her ". . . as a stable point, like his thesis." He again mentioned a telling derivative of his perception of the analytic set-up:

> A new anxiety began to intrude when he recalled that, without the special postgraduate scholarship, he really didn't have enough money to return to his home university to finish his thesis this coming summer. Might I let the bill ride for a few months so that he could use that money? I did not respond directly. He had an elaborate, complicated dream essentially involving a flood of sexual feelings, perverse and sadistic, about various girls he has known, condensed with anxiety about the rebuilding of his broken-down boat. This is occurring under the benevolent guidance of a reliable marine engineer—clearly me he feels. He wondered if he might return to shoplifting to make up the deficiencies in his budget (p. 396).

In this sequence the fee discount was clearly identified as the adaptive context. Derivatives for the discount appeared in his request and the image of the scholarship. The analyst did not, as she might have otherwise, respond immediately. The patient then validated her nonresponse as correct with derivatives that suggested that he viewed the analyst as split. On the one hand, the perverse, sadistic feelings in the dream represented his unconscious view of the nonempathic analyst toward him ("various girls") that break him and the analysis down. On the other hand, the reliable marine engineer who was helping to rebuild his boat represented a positive introject of the helpful functional analyst who did not respond to the last question. The return to the shoplifting derivative of the fee element remained, despite having been briefly left or secured by the recent correct response (the nonresponse). Her noninterpretive intervention confirmed his fear as she missed the unconscious meaning of the sequence: "I suggested that while he obviously wants me to dissuade him, the real issue is that it would be very hard to continue the analysis if he were jailed." His response was ambiguous: "He is pleased by this humorous rejoinder and indicates that he will be able to pay and go back to school this summer. Sometimes his childish gluttony is uncontrollable" (p. 396). Here he responded manifestly to her noninterpretation. The sentence that followed reflected the unconscious introjection and identification with the uncontrolled (nonanalytic) analyst.

He later described a beginning relationship with a girl:

> He begins an affair with another new girl, who is low key, responsive, relatively undemanding, but ominously, somewhat fragile. He is initially delighted with her because when she starts staying over at his house in the woods on weekends, he is able to work on his thesis very effectively, simply with her being present (p. 399).

This perception seems to describe the patient's split perception of the analyst. She was low key and analytically undemanding, yet conveyed an ominous fragility. He described in a derivative his perception of the analytic work. He was working on the analysis himself, with the analyst simply being present.

The low fee was brought up in a dramatic derivative and action confrontation:

> Suddenly, his complex financial plans, based on a part-time selling job, came to crisis, and in the middle of an hour he asked if he could borrow $10 from me for the weekend because he had not a dime for eating money. He was obviously very anxious about asking me, and, after hesitating a bit, I lent it to him. In response, he had a rather complicated dream about financial concerns, owning two cars at the same time. Then there is a vivid scene in which he goes to visit a friend who turns out to be living on a lovely coast on a South Seas Island. The man is out surfing, and he is left with the man's wife, and she will teach the patient how to surf, but the husband-friend snubs the patient when he returns and the patient feels acutely uncomfortable (p. 399).

The patient's request for a loan was another derivative of the lowered fee. The analyst was unable to contain and interpret the interactional pressure that the sequence must have evoked. The circumstances, some of which were probably not described, led her to loan him money, and effectively block the communication. From the communicative perspective, the analyst responded in a clear Type B and C communicative mode. Although the patient's next sequence was this time correctly recognized as a response, the split, symbolized by two cars and two people was not noticed. As Type Two derivatives, the surfing man represented the absent functional analyst. The wife was a derivative of the nurturing and present Type B-C analyst who promised valid treatment, but with the loan was controlling, seductive, and ineffective instead. His loan request condensed into one derivative the discounted fee and an effort to convert the discount-gift into a loan that, paid back, would free him. The request conveyed his anxiety and the urgency of the issue. The analyst appeared to acknowledge as she hesitated, but then she asked him to associate to the dream related in the previous hour. This request foreclosed the dream as a meaningful response to the dream and suggested that the meaning must be found elsewhere.

Her redundant request was an implied demand to remain in a Type C communicative mode. From the communicative point of view, there was enough information to make at least a hypothesis and perhaps an interpretation. The patient would unconsciously hear her question following the information that he had just provided as a confession of her refusal to see meaning. Paradoxically, her question was not a request to gather more information, but an interference of the meaning that existed in the field already (see Dorpat 1982). The patient exerted his emerging autonomy by refusing to comply with her request. Instead he provided a derivative that is a view of himself in the analysis:

> . . . he told me in great detail about the subject of his thesis, which had to do with an analysis of the writings (i.e., the influence of personality variables on the ideas, style, and professional behavior) of one of the ranking but least well-understood German sociologists (Goldberg 1978, p. 400).

The patient made several connections between himself and the sociologist, but then described memories of his mother's unresponsiveness to him as a child. With his thesis he was doing what his analyst should have been doing with him. The image could also have referred to the self-analysis that he was doing and to his efforts to understand the personality variables of his analyst that influenced her professional behavior.

Next, he interrupted the analysis for several months. The interruption, which had been announced in earlier derivatives, was an effort to "cure" the merged analyst-patient, insecure, and boundaryless analytic frame.

When he resumed, he spoke a little more directly about the analyst's not understanding him. Initially she seemed to respond, but then they both resumed the old pattern. He tried the fee issue derivative again and she made some effort to analyze, but relented and again loaned him some money:

> Suddenly his finances are in a state of disaster again, and can I lend him five dollars so that he can eat over the weekend? I hedge a little bit, and he is very annoyed with this, accusing me quite correctly, not of unwillingness, but of not understanding how humiliating it is for him to ask. I lend him the money, but ask him if he isn't perhaps once again not facing something, i.e., it is two weeks until his next paycheck (p. 404).

He caused many other disruptions and his derivatives were filled with references to deviant relationships, duplicity, and broken trusts.

The patient seemed to make a desperate effort to salvage the analysis:

> He wrote to his parents that, in the light of his realistic financial burdens, he really does not want them to send him the usual meaningless Christmas gift. "Would you believe it, Doctor, my mother called immediately, insisting that she be permitted to send a little, harmless gift, or else she'd feel deprived!" The feeling over the telephone was like the sticky glue falling on him. He acquired a new girlfriend who, in contrast to the last one, is low-key and willing to let him lead, makes fewer demands than his previous girls, and he is delighted to discover that he can in turn be casual with her (p. 406).

The split between the analyst who realistically burdened him, who treated the discounted fee as harmless, and the opposite is implied here. The gratification was like sticky glue. The low-key girl was again apparent. The patient's unsuccessful attempts to tell his analyst of the sticky merger aspects of the low fee were dramatically symbolized in the derivative of his writing and the return call. These hypotheses are somewhat validated by the patient's development of an increasingly separate functional existence. A premature interruption that followed shortly thereafter set up a situation that permitted a permanent interruption. He married and found a job in another city.

Paris' Case Illustrations

Paris (this volume) observes a tendency for treatment to break up or prematurely terminate when there is a complication over the fee. He overlooks the possibility that his examples of complications over the fee are derivatives that imply perceptions of and efforts to rectify deviant therapeutic frames. His case vignettes are similar to those of Dewald and Goldberg in that other major frame interruptions eclipse the fee issues as obvious primary adaptive contexts. Here are two of his examples:

> In a relevant Canadian example, a qualified psychoanalyst wished to offer psychoanalysis to a few patients at a lower fee prescribed by government insurance schedules. Unfortunately these treatments showed a strong tendency to break up or prematurely terminate. The ambivalence of the analyst about his fee may have been responsible for this. In one case, the analysand was abruptly informed after six months that since he was "difficult," he would have to pay the full fee forthwith. In another case the patient left after two months when told that his complaints about the analyst's lateness indicated his "guilt" about receiving insured treatment.

Serious technical errors stand out in these vignettes. Major countertransference interferences were suggested but no derivatives were provided to point to more specific inferences about ambivalence, guilt, deprivation, or issues with the fee.

In another example, derivatives of the complication over the fee may be discerned despite the brief detail of the case. As in Goldberg's case, the split between the manifest promising therapist and his function and the unconscious disillusionment were implied in several derivatives. The wealthy father and his promise of financial backing are linked to the therapist who provides "free" treatment in the derivative of the wish for the therapist to be his backer. The unconscious negative introject appears in derivatives of disillusionment and not carrying out promises. A dramatic crisis is precipitated with a scenario in which the patient forces the therapist to become the disappointing object. The therapist does not interpret the derivatives. The patient's derivatives imply that "free" therapy is unconsciously perceived as very costly. The patient feels disillusioned, let down, and endangered. His final derivative, difficulty leaving his mother yet wanting to do it on his own, expresses his unresolved attachment to the therapist and a model of rectification. He implies that he had to act to resolve the attachment rather than resolve it through interpretations and rectification of the deviant fee sector of the therapeutic frame.

In his major case vignette, Paris does not find evidence that the insurance payment feature played a problematic role in this therapy. His introductory images of engulfing women and hostile disappointing men are similar, however, to images in previous illustrations where fees were paid for by others. These images suggest to a Type Two listener that some adaptive context was unconsciously negatively perceived and worked over. Images of disinterested people and drug use suggest derivatives of Type C communicative resistances (Langs 1981). In the Goldberg example, similar resistances seemed to be the results of incorrect noninterpretive interventions. The fee did not appear specifically in these derivatives.

If the previous case examples—e.g., those of Gedo, Dewald, and Goldberg —were characteristic, Type Two derivatives of the patient's perceptions of the fee set-up would probably have appeared more clearly earlier in this case, rather than ten months along.

In the most detailed sequence, covering several sessions, Paris suggests that a major problem is the frame disturbance caused by the introduction of a fee and a bill when the patient misses a session. Strictly speaking, because the convention had presumably been set up at the outset, these were part of the existing, albeit deviant, framework rather than frame disturbance that came up anew at this time. As suggested in the previous case examples, when activated, a deviant frame element usually does not appear quite so clearly in derivatives as does a current frame disturbance.

A deviation that occurs in an already deviant therapeutic frame is like a moving figure against a moving background. It is less noticeable than a figure that moves against a stationary background.

In the therapy sessions that are described, the fee issue appears first as an action, missing the session. This forces the therapist to bring it up according to the frame that was set out. The patient may have projected the troublesome aspect of the fee issue into the therapist. Then, rather than a split of images that seemed to appear in the associations of the Goldberg patient (the surfing man, the at home woman, etcetera), this patient describes only part of the split—the damaging, intrusive, castrating images. The full derivative of the split in the unconsciously perceived therapist is precluded by the action and the response of the therapist. The patient continues to reflect the problem and his attempt at a solution in his derivative that perhaps the therapist should pay him, the patient, for missed sessions. This is a derivative of the patient as the functional therapist and the therapist as the functional patient.

In contrast to other varieties of fee arrangements, in each of the Paris examples the therapeutic frame is set up so that a patient, by missing a session, could force the therapist to shift from a Type A communicative mode to a Type B mode because of the need to react and present a bill. This creates a difficult resistance because derivatives are enacted rather than being spoken. The therapist, by reacting, precludes his observational and interpretive capacity. (Other insurance programs might similarly encourage shared communicative resistances.)

Another hypothesis can be constructed for the meaning of the missed session. As did Dewald's questioner, this patient may have attempted with his breach of the frame to repair another breach. By missing a session, he escapes from a deviant, destructive, and humiliating situation. At the same time, he sets up a treatment session for which he pays himself, is confidential (no reports), has no incorrect interventions (no material: no misinterpretations), and has no untimely diagnoses or self-revelations by the therapist (no report and no coded diagnosis).

In the session that follows the missed session, the theme continues. Studying to be a psychiatrist could be a thinly disguised derivative of the patient's perception that he has again become the functional therapist. It also could be a message to the therapist that he should rectify the treatment in some way (go back to school?). This is a form of competition, but the Oedipal rivalry component cannot be distinguished from the derivatives of the efforts to rectify the reality of the disrupted frame.

In the remainder of the session and those that follow, the theme continues. The patient becomes increasingly angry and helpless, yet struggles to comply and to convey to the therapist how his needs for therapy are not being met. Despite this development, the latter months of therapy show some symptomatic improvement. The information is not present to determine if this improvement is related to more empathic interpretations or to the patient's independence of the therapist and the process. The course of the Goldberg and the Gedo cases would point to the latter.

A CHANGE FROM A REDUCED FEE TO A FULL FEE

In another example, a young man was seen in analysis by a colleague for several years at an acknowledged reduced fee. His associations were replete with violent images and sexual aggression. Castration and homosexual fantasies, dreams, and images about the analyst were manifold. Hours were also characterized by long initial silences. Modest increases in the fee were geared to increases in his income. Each fee increase was followed by hours of silences, profanity and violent ideas directed to the analyst, and floods of erotic or more commonly, polymorphous perverse fantasies, jokes, and puns. The patient feared that the analyst would never be satisfied. After the second increase he suggested increasing the fee to one hundred dollars. He described masturbating each night, and each morning completely evacuated his bowels with laxatives taken the night before.

The analyst's interpretations attempted to link each fee increase and the actions that the patient demonstrated and described. The fee increase was interpreted as an intrusion and enema-like demand. Derivatives of the discounted fee or of negative aspects thereof were not considered or interpreted. Little change was noted in the general themes of the hours. The fee finally was raised to the analyst's current "regular" fee, with the explanation that this would seem to address the issues that could not be clearly differentiated or analyzed in the context of a discounted fee. The analyst also offered the suggestion that the analytic hours be reduced to two or three times a week rather than the present four times a week so that the patient would be able to afford the higher fee. The patient readily agreed to the increase but, after two weeks of trying the reduced frequency, indicated that he had found some moonlighting that would permit the full four-day schedule. He could not believe that the fee was the regular fee.

He began to speak of his pride in being able to pay and in now being a fully qualified patient. He learned that insurance was available through his work, but after a brief consideration and no response from the analyst, he dropped the idea as a manifest possibility. This man had very early in the analysis established the convention, self-initiated, of paying on the first of the month without being presented a bill. He mentioned frequently, however, fantasies that others in the analyst's practice still paid discounted fees and used insurance. The initial silences in each hour diminished and the pressured flood of perverse and violent images decreased over the next four to five months.

Being a fully qualified patient could have been a derivative of the secured therapeutic frame and of the perception that he was both a designated and functional patient (Langs 1981, 1982). Other patients paying discounted fees or through insurance could have been a derivative of his disbelief that this was a full fee, or it could have been a derivative of a transference distortion that referred to his background, which included several younger siblings and memories of their preferred treatment. Even with the secured fee sector of the frame, these derivatives remained unclear because of the previous deviations that, in a manner similar to the third party interferences of the Dewald frame, may continue to be adaptive contexts.

One of the first of the images to disappear from the patient's descriptions was the recurrent idea that each morning when he bent over to pick up his shoes or some clothing, the analyst would appear behind him and rape him anally. Despite acknowledgment of the unreality of the idea, he would nevertheless bend over with his buttocks to the wall to avoid the assault. This idea was absent about six months after the fee increase. Direct and derivative references to the fee disappeared, but he would occasionally mention that he expected another increase on the anniversary of the last.

The disappearance of the violent rape images after the rectification of the reduced fee implies that these were derivatives of a perception of a forcing seductive aspect of the reduced fee rather than the fee increases. After setting the termination date, the images of violence, the attacks of profanity, perverse ideas, and, briefly, fears of anal rape returned. All were attenuated in comparison to before. The context of the termination seemed now to evoke a clearer reference to fears and wishes regarding images of depressed, ineffective, and dependent parents. For example, he was not convinced that the analyst would keep the date that was set. The patient considered avoiding the ending issue with an attempt to extend the time, or by abruptly walking out on the analysis.

The return of the violent images, profanity, and anal rape fears could now be seen as derivatives of the termination setting of the date, which he might have perceived as having been forced upon him. He also mentioned that, as the anniversary of the last fee increase approached, he anticipated another fee raise. This old adaptive context emerged as a manifest reference, in part because it had been interpretively worked over and rectified, but also as a derivative of something else yet to be analyzed. It now could imply some unconscious perception of the therapist's struggle with the termination, e.g., it was not timely in some respect or, coupled with the derivatives of dependent parents, it might allude to some aspect of the therapist's difficulty with terminating. There is the possibility that, with the secure frame, a derivative of an unconscious internal imago that was subjected to ego modification and projected upon the analyst might have finally appeared with little provocation from the analyst and his struggles with the frame.

In this case, as in the other examples, the derivatives of the reduced fee were not interpreted. The derivatives seemed to disappear with the removal of the deviant fee arrangement. The better technique would have been to interpret the derivatives and their connection to the hypothesized adaptive context. If the patient confirmed the interpretation through derivatives (see Langs 1981 and 1982) then the fee would have been changed and the deviant fee sector of the frame secured. Further derivatives or, as in this instance, disappearance of the derivatives would tend to confirm the accuracy of both the interpretation and the frame rectification.

INSURANCE AS A DERIVATIVE

Halpert (1972b) wrote that a patient in psychoanalytically oriented psychotherapy does not form a transference neurosis, does not free associate and, because of a focus on immediate symptomatic difficulties, does not prominently bring the question of insurance into the therapy. He described an exception where, because of the dynamic and genetic constellation of the patient, payment by insurance became emotionally charged and a focus of resistance. In his case example, however, the patient delayed payment of the fee, so it was instead an example of the second category, in which payment is made in some part by the therapist.

For a four month period, when late paying had been the rule, Halpert explored the patient's customary style of living in debt. Then he discovered that the patient had been unable to protest his wife's outrageous telephone expenditures and:

> . . . as we were working on his inability to be realistic and firm with his wife, particularly in regard to her use of the phone, the patient said that he would be delayed much longer than usual in paying his bill. He spoke further of his financial burdens and of his fear that, if he didn't give his wife all the money she asked for, she would make him leave the house. I asked if he were delaying payment to his wife's psychiatrist as well. He replied that he wasn't and repeated that he was afraid not to take care of her needs first. I said that he was asking me to subsidize both his illness and his wife's and to take care of him (p. 65).

Because he did not refer to an adaptive context, Halpert was working with Type One derivatives. By interpreting the patient's inability to be firm with his wife rather than the interactional aspects of the delayed fee, Halpert tacitly accepted the delay of the fee. The acceptance then became the adaptive context, and the derivatives could have been decoded with a different meaning than Halpert's interpretation.

Instead, the patient's statement of a longer delay could have been a derivative that indicated the unconscious perception that the therapist had not addressed the adaptive context, i.e., a "delay" in interpretion. The delayed fee was also indicated in this derivative. The derivative of the wife asking for money could have been a model of rectification, i.e., the therapist should be asking for his money or interpreting around that issue. That she would leave if he did not pay suggested the patient's unconscious view that the therapist should not have been treating him under the circumstances of his not paying. Finally, the therapist was not taking care of his needs and should be concerned about that, i.e., "afraid not to." Halpert came close with his intervention, but did not pick up the patient's perception and working over of the perception that he had already been subsidizing the patient.

The patient then learned that he was soon to acquire an insurance that would pay for part of his therapy. When he learned that the percentage of the fee covered would not be what he originally expected, he decided to terminate treatment:

> He left treatment at the end of that month despite my interpretation that he was angry at the insurance company (and at me) because he had unconsciously equated the insurance with the all-protecting, all-caring mother he had longed for and because he felt deceived by the lower than anticipated coverage, just as he had been deceived by his mother (p. 66).

Halpert may have made a correct dynamic interpretation, but without a reference to the patient's Type Two derivatives of unconscious working over of the adaptive context, the patient seemed to have had to act to solve the issue. The issue was revealed when he provided a telling derivative. In the last session, he described for the first time that he had seen another therapist several years before:

> He had stopped that (previous) treatment "because I couldn't afford it. She wanted me to continue and offered to see me at a lower fee. I felt that she was trying to seduce me." He wished, and at the same time feared, that I, too, would try to seduce him. He had felt seduced into great expectations by the insurance company and then had been disappointed, (in his mind) rejected by it (p. 66).

The patient's derivative of the other therapist referred to the analyst's uninterpreted, and therefore tacit acceptance of the delayed fee payment. The acceptance of the delay was unconsciously perceived as a seduction. The delay in payment could be rectified and changed; an insurance arrangement, however, would affirm the therapist's complicity in a similar resistance to the delayed fee payment, but would remove the ambiguity. The patient's decision to terminate could therefore be an effort to prevent the seduction by the therapist that was still up in the air. In the Type Two listening schema, the patient's descriptions of the insurance could have been Type Two derivatives of the therapist's participation, i.e., partial payment of his fee. The description of the insurance reducing the planned coverage might have been a result of a valid interpretation that was not described, but the disappointment that he felt as a result and the resolve to terminate would point to an adaptive context that was not therapeutic. He may have been symbolically describing a perceived reduction, for example, in the therapist's interpretive coverage. As in the other examples, this patient decided to take his treatment into his own hands in the context of a mutual resistance that was seductive and blurred the boundaries between them.

CONCLUSIONS

The study of a single variable such as the fee arrangement is made difficult by the complexity of the psychotherapeutic situation. Other frame disturbances obscure derivatives of the fee arrangements. In the examples where the fee was paid for by others, rather than discounted, derivatives implying therapist collaboration with third parties presented a particular problem. Third party payments usually seem to involve direct therapist interaction with the fee source. Issues of the therapist accepting third party money and communicating with the fee source have not been distinguished.

Although usually obscured by other adaptive contexts, a single adaptive context appears most clearly in the derivatives shortly after the variable, frame disruption, or deviation has been introduced or reactivated by the therapist. The effect seems eclipsed or obscured by subsequent events and the passage of time.

Derivatives in these examples suggest that, in therapies with deviant frames, when the therapist does not interpret or rectify, the patient becomes the functional therapist and the therapist, the functional patient. Through derivatives or by their spontaneous changes, the patients that were described in these examples seemed inclined toward self-payment of an adequate fee.

A review of several examples may have brought into focus the effect of a single element of the frame more clearly than a single case study. Although not conclusive, a tendency toward early termination, splitting of the images of the therapist, formation of collaborative resistances (bastions), and failures to adequately separate can be seen in some of the instances where someone other than the patient pays the fee.

The method of compensation of the therapist does not seem to be a benign event in the course of psychoanalysis and psychotherapy. Alterations other than self-payment deserve much more study before and after they have been instituted. Insurance and other programs that pay for part of the fee but also oblige therapists to take actions that are not in harmony with therapeutic requirements deserve much more research.

REFERENCES

Baranger, M., and Baranger, W. (1966). Insight in the psychoanalytic situation. In *Psychoanalysis in the Americas*, ed. R. Litman, pp. 56–72. New York: International Universities Press.
Billow, R. M., and Lovett, J. G. (1982). Psycholinguistic phenomena of the bipersonal field: towards a model of field research. In *The Bipersonal Interaction*, ed. J. Raney (in press). New York: Jason Aronson.

Brenner, C. (1981). Defense and defense mechanisms. *Psychoanalytic Quarterly* 50:557–569.

Dewald, P. A. (1972). *The Psychoanalytic Process.* New York: Basic Books.

Dorpat, T. L. (1982). The technique of questioning. In *The Bipersonal Interaction,* ed. J. Raney (in press). New York: Jason Aronson.

Eissler, K. R. (1974). On some theoretical and technical problems regarding the payment of fees for psychoanalytic treatment. *International Review of Psycho-Analysis* 1:73–101.

Erdheim, J. B. (1982). Communicative field theory: Developmental reconsiderations. In *The Bipersonal Interaction,* ed. J. Raney (in press). New York: Jason Aronson.

Flarsheim, A. (1972). Treatability. In *Tactics and Techniques in Psychoanalytic Psychotherapy,* ed. P. Giovacchini, vol. 1, pp. 113–131. New York: Jason Aronson.

Gedo, J. E. (1979). *Beyond Interpretation.* New York: International Universities Press.

Goldberg, A. (1978). *The Psychology of the Self: A Casebook.* New York: International Universities Press.

Gray, S. H. (1973). Does insurance affect psychoanalytic practice? *Bulletin of the Philadelphia Association for Psychoanalysis* 23:101–110.

Grotstein, J. S. (1981). *Splitting and Projective Identification.* New York: Jason Aronson.

———. (1982). The higher implications of Langs' contributions to psychoanalysis and psychoanalytic psychotherapy. In *The Bipersonal Interaction,* ed. J. Raney (in press). New York: Jason Aronson.

Halpert, E. (1972a). The effect of insurance on psychoanalytic treatment. *Journal of the American Psychoanalytic Association* 20:122–132.

———. (1972b). A meaning of insurance in psychotherapy. *International Journal of Psychoanalytic Psychotherapy* 1:60–68.

Langs, R. (1976). *The Bipersonal Field.* New York: Jason Aronson.

———. (1978a). *The Listening Process.* New York: Jason Aronson.

———. (1978b). Some communicative properties of the bipersonal field. *International Journal of Psychoanalytic Psychotherapy* 7:87–135.

———. (1979). *The Therapeutic Environment.* New York: Jason Aronson.

———. (1981). *Resistances and Interventions.* New York: Jason Aronson.

———. (1982). *Psychotherapy, A Basic Text.* New York: Jason Aronson.

Lichtenberg, J., and Slap, J. (1977). Comments on the general functioning of the analyst in the psychoanalytic setting. *The Annual of Psychoanalysis* 5:295–312.

Lorand, S., and Console, W. A. (1958). Therapeutic results in psychoanalytic treatment without a fee. *International Journal of Psycho-Analysis* 39:59–64.

Raney, J. (1981). Narcissistic defensiveness and the interactional approach. *Society for Psychoanalytic Psychotherapy Newsletter* 1:4–9.

On the Silence of the Therapist and Object Loss

MARTIN GREENE, D.S.W.

The therapist's silence is viewed as a component of the medium within which early self/object experiences may be revived and resolved. After reviewing the literature on silence and on early object loss, the author concludes that the denial of loss accompanied by reunion fantasies interferes with normal processes of internalization and separation-individuation. Clinical material is presented and discussed, emphasizing the role that appropriate analytic silence plays in actualizing and beginning to work through the patient's early loss experience, thus facilitating appropriate internalization. This approach is contrasted with the view that such cases require the use of parameters.

"But in psycho-analytic relations things often happen differently from what the psychology of consciousness might lead us to expect" (Freud 1912, p. 118).

"Creating an empty space may be the only way to discover its meanings" (Fiumara 1977, p. 175).

This paper attempts to clarify several issues concerning the silence of the psychoanalytic psychotherapist.[1] (1) It is concerned with the significance of the therapist's silence in managing a particularly difficult case in which the patient's core problems and resistances represent a reaction to an early object loss. (2) It is intended to add to an understanding of why, contrary to appropriate behavior in social situations, it is often essential that the therapist remain totally silent for long, seemingly unendurable lengths of time. (3) It is an effort to substantiate the view that psychoanalytic psychotherapy is most effective when the therapist remains committed to an unwavering adherance to the basic ground rules and procedures of psychoanalysis exemplified by Langs' (1978c) conceptualization of the "framework" and its management.

---

1. Throughout this paper, the term 'therapist' will be used to refer to both the psychoanalyst and the psychoanalytic psychotherapist.

While puzzling, it is not inexplicable that the literature on silence is primarily concerned with the silence of the patient. It is apparently easier to study our patients than it is to study ourselves. For example, the complexities of transference phenomena were understood prior to those of counter-transference. Knowledge of metapsychology and of development appears to be more advanced than knowledge of psychoanalytic technique. Disturbing as it may be, it is extremely difficult to ascertain what it is that psychotherapists actually do and how they validate their contributions to the therapeutic process (Langs 1978c). Nevertheless, at least one article deals exclusively with the silence of the therapists (Aull and Strean 1967), and a number of others, while primarily concerned with the silence of the patient, also explore aspects of the silence of the therapist. Thus this discussion of the literature on silence will be limited to a review of those contributions that emphasize the silence of the therapist as a means of facilitating patient communications, emphasizing those that are relevant to the theme of object loss.

THE SILENCE OF THE THERAPIST

In a paper written in 1926, Reik made a statement regarding the significance of silence and its therapeutic power, that encompasses much of what others have since repeated:

Speaking is in any case the central point of analysis but . . . it is nevertheless not correct to attribute the effect of analysis entirely to the word. I believe it would be more correct to say that psychoanalysis shows the power of the word and the power of silence. So much has been said about the subject of talking in analysis, that the emotional effect of silence has been almost completely overlooked (p. 181).

He inferred that, " . . . behind a fear of silence stands the unconscious fear of loss of love . . . [and] people often speak because they cannot bear silence" (p. 184). Like Reik, Nacht (1964) also emphasized that the analyst's silence can facilitate the patient's communications. In noting that exchanges between the patient and analyst often occur without speech, he asked, "Are there communications which words allow and even foster, and others which it perhaps prevents? Are some affects born from speech, while others can flourish only in silence?" (p. 299).

Blos (1972) referred to silence as a form of communication on the part of both participants. Silence is an analyzable phenomenon and a powerful therapeutic force that may have both positive and negative effects. Silence can facilitate the communication of feelings, fantasies, affect-laden events, and long-forgotten and repressed material. While the silence of the analyst "at the right time" can be perceived as a great gift of understanding and compassion, it is also a period filled with pitfalls, and to be silent at the wrong time can be a devastating event for the patient. Aull and Strean (1967) emphasized the variability of patients' responses to the silence of the analyst in accordance with their developmental needs and the core problems activated in the transference. They concluded, "prolonged silence of the analyst serves as a form of 'intervention,' and, as such, can have both positive and negative therapeutic effects" (p. 78). The silence of the analyst in some instances fulfills a need for "blissful fusion," while in others it temporarily intensifies fears of desertion and abandonment.

Freud (1912) viewed the analyst's silent, listening attitude as the necessary counterpart to the patient's free-associations. In Langs' view (1978b), silence is one of six basic forms of intervention and an essential aspect of the analytic, listening attitude:

Silence is by far the best way of facilitating the patient's free association, communications of indirect derivative contents and mechanisms, and unconscious interactional thrusts; it is the optimal means through which expressions of the patient's neurosis become available for interpretation (pp. 635–636).

In the articles discussed, the therapist's extended silences, when appropriate, facilitate the patient's communications. While silence is viewed as a form of intervention, the therapist's silence may also be viewed as an essential component of the medium within which the therapeutic process unfolds. While the silence of the therapist may evoke a multiplicity of meanings specific to each patient, it is often associated with object loss.

ON EARLY OBJECT LOSS

There are a few seminal articles primarily concerned with the theme of object loss. The potential impact of early object loss on the developing child, the adult he or she becomes, and on the issues that arise with such patients in psychoanalytic psychotherapy are explored.

Khan (1963), in a paper primarily concerned with the analyst's use of countertransference for understanding the patient's silence as a communication of an internalized experience of early maternal deprivation, makes a contribution that seems directly pertinent to the relationship between the silence of the analyst and object loss. In the case described, that of a depressed and listless adolescent, tolerance of the patient's silence coupled with Khan's judicious withholding of interpretations over the course of six sessions, led to the actualization and reconstruction of the mother/infant cumulative trauma reenacted within the silent space of the therapeutic relationship.

Winnicott (1971) used a spatial metaphor to describe the potential of the analytic situation to provide illusory experiences that serve as a bridge toward creativity and constructive object relationships. In such a space, analagous to "the space between the baby and the mother," early self/object experiences could be actualized.

In discussing the positive value of the silence of the patient, Fiumara (1977) noted, "I believe that creating an empty space in a relationship may be the only way to discover its meanings" (p. 175). Although she does not emphasize the silence of the analyst, it seems reasonable to assume that it is also essential to the creation of an "empty space."

In a discussion of silence viewed as an integrative and adaptive form of communication in the service of the ego, Shafii (1973), in speculating on why there have been so few studies of analytic silence, concluded that it is due to the repression of the fear of silence rooted in early separation anxieties and the terror of abandonment. The following passage conveys the origins of such fears:

> Bedtime and going to sleep usually mean separation from mother, quietness, darkness and silence, so we can understand how children associate silence and quiescence with the fear of separation from mother and loneliness. Fear of silence in childhood and adulthood could be related to the fear of separation from mother during the first few years of life (p. 432).

In silence, discarding space-filling clichés and verbal automatisms, there is the possibility of a gap within which symbolic expression becomes possible. Since the potential symbols may represent experiences of loss, separation, and death, however, there comes the possibility of discovering intolerable feelings of mental pain. Bion (1962) states, "People exist who are so intolerant of pain and frustration (or in whom pain and frustration is so intolerable) that they feel the pain but will not suffer it and so cannot be said to discover it" (p. 9). Thus Fiumara (1977) writes, "To avoid the anxieties of separation and loss which are experienced in the analysis of transference, the patient may attempt to destroy the analytic setting" (p. 177). Among the numerous ways of achieving this are the involvement of the analyst in an affectionate relationship, frightening the analyst out of the analysis, or filling the space with such a profusion of empty material that the analyst is unable to think and the links between associations are broken. Taken together, the works cited lead to the conclusion that a silent analytic space contains the potential for actualizing early loss experiences. But, since this is accompanied by painful and frightening affects and fantasies, it is reasonable to assume that both participants (not only the patient) will resist.

There appears to be a vulnerability to emotional disorders among children who have lost a parent (Barry 1949, Brown 1961). Of course, this is a complex phenomenon since the precise nature of the impact would be affected by such factors as the age when the loss occurred, as well as by pre- and post-loss experiences. The immaturity of the child's ego is undoubtedly a severe impediment to the working through of the mourning process. Bowlby (1961, 1963) developed the thesis that children do go through a mourning process, but because of the enormous demands upon the young child's ego, faulty resolutions are common:

Unfavourable personality development is often to be attributed to one or more of the less satisfactory responses to loss having been provoked during the years of infancy and childhood in such a degree, over such length of time, or with such frequency, that a disposition is established to respond to all subsequent losses in a similar way (1961, pp. 317–318).

Among the less than satisfactory responses, Bowlby (1963) cited a repression of yearning for the lost object, together with an unconscious demand that the object return and a denial that the object is permanently lost, coexisting with some awareness of the loss, and resulting in a splitting of the ego. For Bowlby, the seeds of pathological resolutions lay within the persistent effort to recover the loss object despite the reality of the futility of the quest.

Wolfenstein (1966), in a study of 42 children and adolescents who had experienced the loss of a parent, inquired into the nature of the mourning process in children. In discussing Freud's view of mourning, she gives the following description of the process and its adaptive function:

The lost object is thus gradually decathected by a process of remembering and reality testing, separating memory from hope. The mourner convinces himself of the irrevocable pastness of what he remembers: This will not come again, and this will not come again. . . . Painful as it is to endure, mourning serves an invaluable adaptive function, since by this process the mourner frees major amounts of libido which were bound to the lost object, which he can utilize for other relations and sublimated activities in the world of living (pp. 93–94).

On the basis of her observations, Wolfenstein concluded that the children had been unable to mourn. As Bowlby (1963) has also noted, instead of the necessary decathexis of the lost object, there is an intensified cathexis together with an overt or covert denial of the irrevocability of the loss. Realistic memories are replaced by a glorified view of the parent, perpetuated by a fantasy that the parent continues to live and will some day return. Given the immaturity of children's egos, the loss of a parent is too overwhelming an event to work through. The need for the parent persists and is maintained through the denial of the loss.

However, the view that mourning frees the libido for new investments in external objects doesn't quite capture the significance of faulty mourning in childhood and its impact upon the later adult. Freud (1923) emphasized that, ". . . the ego is a precipitate of abandoned object cathexes. . . ." (p. 36). Thus ego development is, at least in part, a consequence of the mourning that accompanies normative processes of separation-individuation. In relinquishing the investment in the object, the child is freed from the dependence upon an auxiliary ego for the performance of equilibrium-maintenance functions. Via transmuting internalization (Tolpin 1971), the mother's capacity to perform such functions as soothing and anxiety-reduction is gradually relinquished to the child. In the course of this process, the transitional object serves as a way station, an external yet internal soother whose function is taken within. Considering this perspective, when the early loss of a parent is denied and the fantasy that the object will return persists, the consequence will be failures in internalization. Components of equilibrium-maintenance functions will remain undeveloped, still vested in the fantasy of the lost object, or now displaced onto a substitute in real life.

Fleming (1972) and Fleming and Altschul's (1963) observations, drawn from the analyses of 60 adults who had experienced the early loss by death of at least one parent, illuminate the impact of loss on adult functioning, delineate common problems encountered in treating such patients, and offer specific suggestions for their treatment. While the significance of the silence of the analyst is not discussed specifically, their suggestions do touch upon this topic and are most pertinent to the focus of this paper.

The patients studied had not sought help in dealing with a specific loss, but instead, they came for help with some current problem involving a change in their way of life, some situation seeming to represent the threat of separation and loss. Similar to Wolfenstein's observations of children and adolescents, these adults denied the finality of the loss and failed to grieve. The myth that the relationship with the lost object persisted was maintained by fantasy as well as by the acting out of such a fantasy through an actual relationship with a living parental substitute.

Fleming speculated that these adults, due to their childhood loss, had not learned to tolerate separations essential to adequate separation-individuation and normal autonomous development. "They disavowed one sector of reality that was intolerable to them" (p. 28). A segment of their functioning seemed to be arrested in a self/object relationship at the "pre-loss" level. "This encapsulation of one sector of reality allowed other sectors to develop and the ego to function in fairly adaptive ways until something in the immediate reality situation disturbed their make-believe" (p. 28).

In psychoanalytic treatment, these patients lacked an observing ego and had specific difficulties in forming an adequate working alliance. This was observed in two forms: (1) they sought to maintain the fantasy of the persistence of the pre-loss level of relationship with the parent through transforming the analyst into an actual substitutional form of direct gratification; (2) they denied that the analytic relationship had any personal meaning, and thereby perpetuated the denial of loss by denying the losses inherent in the analytic relationship.[2]

Fleming notes, "With each of these patients, the usual initial analytic attitude of expectant waiting was not enough object response to initiate a working alliance" (p. 42). Fleming speculates that these patients require the use of parameters in order to reduce deprivations that recapitulate the earlier loss experience and initiate regressive anxieties that the patient is as yet unable to bear. Thus she emphasizes that the analyst should play a more active role at the beginning of treatment, serving as an empathic, symbiotic, auxiliary ego until further progress in achieving separation-individuation is achieved and the patient can tolerate the mourning process. She mentions the positive value of one analyst's frequent "mmhms" and supportive comments intended to make his presence felt. Such an approach is apparently viewed as preferable to the use of prolonged silence. In addition, to promote the mourning process, Fleming recommends that the patient's denial of loss be actively confronted, its impact on the patient's development be emphasized, and efforts to help the patient recall memories of the dead parent be initiated (pp. 37–45).

Fleming's observations offer a wealth of information concerning the treatment of patients who have experienced early object loss. Her assumption that an attitude of "expectant waiting" proves inadequate due to these patients' needs for an active "auxilliary ego" is not substantiated through any actual clinical data. It is possible to formulate numerous alternative explanations, among them the analyst's failure to discern and interpret relevant themes, and the analyst's own intolerance of silence. Merely saying that "expectant waiting" proves inadequate seems to be based on the assumption

2. In a recent paper, Sandler and Sandler (1978) offer an illuminating conceptualization of the process through which early affective states and associated self/object images are actualized within current relationships. Early wishful strivings and defenses against such strivings, maintained as unconscious fantasies, create wished for interactions that in turn lead to actual efforts to recreate the past or to defend against the past through evoking interactional responses from significant others. Most pertinent to the thesis of this paper, they state, "It could be said that the patient in analysis attempts to *actualize* the particular role relationship inherent in his current dominant unconscious wish or fantasy, and that he will try to do this (usually in a disguised and symbolic way) within the framework of the psychoanalytic situation." Such efforts to actualize specific role relationships create within the analyst a countertransference pressure to respond. The therapist maintains a "free-floating responsiveness" (p. 289) and, to varying degrees, either complies or does not comply to the demand. The Sandlers do not address the issue of the extent to which the therapist should or should not comply, although they emphasize that the therapist can learn from such interactions and utilize them as the content of his interpretations.

that the problem is in the standard technique. The review of the literature leads to the conclusion that a silent analytic space contains the potential for the actualization of early loss experiences not because the analyst manipulates the transference but merely because he or she listens and waits until there is enough material for a meaningful interpretation. Only when there is a gap, does it become possible for the patient to use the analyst as a symbol of the earlier loss. Contrary to this, supportive fillers and confrontations would serve to perpetuate the patient's fantasy that the analyst is an actual parental substitute.

CLINICAL MATERIAL

Mrs. W. is in her forties, married and the mother of three children. A successful pediatric nurse, she sought treatment when she became confused and depressed after her husband suffered a minor heart ailment.

Outstanding in her history, and only barely mentioned in describing herself, was the fact that her father had died when she was still a young child. Her mother remarried when the patient was nine, at which time Mrs. W. developed severe bronchial asthma. Her stepfather was described as a mean and morose man who constantly criticized her mother. Life with him was filled with conflict and turmoil. She and her mother became allied in the battle, colluding to deceive and outwit the stepfather while her mother provided her with illicit, special favors on the sly. Her mother was described as caring and competent on the one hand, while intrusively clinging and masochistically self-sacrificing on the other. At the time Mrs. W. began treatment, mother and daughter were locked in a mutually dependent relationship that was threatened by Mrs. W.'s implicit recognition that her relationship with her mother constituted an intrusion that had an adverse effect upon her marriage.

Mrs. W.'s early marriage to a man who exemplified her ideal of an active, gregarious paternal imago, served as a realistic bridge that enabled her to leave her stepfather and create a family modeled upon her romantic fantasies. Fortunately, reality served her well and her dream appeared to have become an actuality as her relationship with her husband grew and her children thrived. Until the time of his recent illness, conflicts were avoided, although communication between them appears to have been sparse. Mrs. W. perceived herself and her husband through "rose-colored glasses" as a perfect couple, "very special." After her husband became ill, marital conflicts were exacerbated and they almost separated, so such views were no longer possible to maintain and Mrs. W. was thrown into a turmoil as her mode of organizing her world was threatened.

Pertinent to this presentation is the apparent fact that throughout her childhood and adolescence she had been sheltered from experiencing any pain in response to the death of her father. To compensate for his loss, her relatives treated her as a special child, lavishing their attention and affection upon her. Throughout childhood she maintained the fantasy that her father was her imaginary companion, protecting her and using his extraordinary powers on her behalf. Thus, through the denial of loss, she believed she had a far better father than reality could provide, and her subsequent experience as an adolescent confirmed this belief. When the reality of life with her mother and stepfather became overwhelmingly discordant with her fantasy, she married and the marital relationship became the bearer of her fantasy, safely nurtured until her husband's illness.

Seen in twice-weekly psychoanalytic psychotherapy, Mrs. W. wished to initiate a "special," rather chatty, and quasi-social relationship with the therapist. She found his efforts to maintain the proper boundaries of the analytic relationship somewhat "silly," rather strange, and totally discrepant with what she imagined the therapeutic situation would be. With the awareness that, despite her protests, she was experiencing a range of emotions previously unavailable, she came to accept the limits introduced. These included payment for missed sessions without makeup hours and the notion that the therapist would listen to her in silence and make interpretations when appropriate rather than chat. Thus, in time, a working alliance was achieved.

Despite her intelligence and relatively rich life-experiences, she communicated in a style that made it extremely difficult to detect anything beyond the surface. She talked constantly, seeming to fill the analytic space with the details of the discussions she had engaged in with her husband, friends, or relatives prior to her session. There was an absence of direct expression of fantasies, and when she reported an occasional dream, the meaning of the dream, its connection to the session and the therapeutic interaction, and the specific adaptive context (Langs 1978c) that evoked the dream, remained obscure. Despite great effort, it was generally difficult to discern themes expressed via unconscious derivatives, and similarly, vague references to chaos and inner turmoil lacked links to the therapeutic interaction and the adaptive context that would serve to organize her associations and provide a key to meaning. Her form of associating and the denial of any links to the therapist constituted a massive resistance to the emergence and analysis of the transference illusion.

In all respects, Mrs. W. conformed to Langs' (1978a) conceptualization of the Type C narrator. The communicative style of the Type C patient, characterized by endless descriptions of the rather insignificant details of the day, serves as a massive and impenetrable barrier to the discovery of meaning likely to emerge should unconscious fantasies, introjections, and perceptions be discovered. In essence, as Langs (1978a) notes in drawing upon the work of Bion (1965):

> These communications (Type C) are utilized to inhibit thought; they constitute ideas used to deny more accurate, but more frightening, ones that serve as barriers against turbulence and psychological upheaval. At times, in the form of commonsense facts, they are used to deny expressions of fantasy; their manifestations pertain to the patient's defenses and resistances (Langs 1978a, p. 429).

The exception was the persistence with which Type One derivatives (Langs 1978b), those readily available inferences derived from manifest content, began to emerge concerning themes of loss, separation, and death.

To provide material illustrating the therapeutic process that characterized the work with this patient, a series of sessions is presented, constituting one segment of the treatment which lasted approximately four months. The first break in this stalemated therapeutic process occurred a few weeks before the therapist's summer vacation when Mrs. W. requested that the sessions be reduced from two to one session per week after the vacation. When this attempt to modify the therapeutic situation was interpreted as a means of diluting the impending loss of the therapist, she at first denied this, but then, just prior to the last session before the break, she had a terrible feeling and began to cry, leading to a momentary recognition that her pain was evoked by the therapist's impending absence.[3] Of course, since a considerable amount of time passed before she was seen again, this gap served to destroy the vital link between the emotions experienced in the relationship, much of them transference-based and involving the person of the therapist.

Following the summer break, Mrs. W. reported that while away she had experienced a sense of loss, mood swings had increased in intensity, and references to her fear that her husband might not be getting proper treatment for a recent physical problem, seemed to convey some expression of concern that with therapy she might begin to feel worse. Derivatives dealing with deprivation and loss became more insistent. The therapist was convinced

---

3. In this instance, in response to the trauma generated by a specific, identifiable adaptive context, the therapist's vacation, her manifest associations contained Type Two derivatives that the analyst was able to organize around a specific adaptive context. (Adaptive context refers to the specific reality stimulus, usually located within the therapeutic interaction, that evokes the patient's unconscious efforts, conflicts, and fantasies. Type Two derivatives refer to unconscious content related to a specific adaptive context.) When unconscious derivatives are organized around a specific adaptive context, it is then possible to understand the relationships between reality and fantasy, past and present, and interactional and intrapsychic contents (Langs 1978b, pp. 60–105).

that she was responding to the summer break as well as to certain depriva-tions inherent in the analytic process, such as the relative absence of direct forms of gratification. Again, since her associations lacked even the barest of links to the therapist, interpretations emphasizing such a connection proved futile, with such connections being easily dimissed as the products of the therapist's own imagination. Throughout this period, the therapist main-tained a relatively silent, listening attitude, generally not intervening more than once or, at the most, twice per session. On the surface, she professed a sense of satisfaction with the progress of the treatment and constant amaze-ment over how much she was discovering about herself. Searching for deeper meaning not easily denied or dismissed, recognizing that her associa-tions increased in emotional intensity and depth when appropriate silence was maintained, the therapist struggled with himself to remain silent for greater periods of time.

When the therapist had remained silent for two sessions, derivatives related to twin themes of a dread of loss together with a wish for increased autonomy emerged with some intensity through associations concerning friends who had died or who had divorced, a concern about the possible consequences of her husband's poor health, and the potential rewards to be gained through experi-menting with alternative relationships. After talking of her mother, who drove her "crazy by saying one thing and meaning another" (was she driving the analyst crazy or visa versa, or both?), she acknowledged being aware that she was herself communicating in double messages that were difficult to decipher.

In the session that followed, she referred back to the double messages, made numerous references to people she didn't wish to see, talked of going away on vacation, and reported that her asthma was beginning to act up. In the next session, she reported feeling awful, the asthma had gotten worse, and the word, "loss, loss, loss," kept going through her head. She said that she hoped to understand why she was feeling such a sense of loss and mentioned having been impressed by the notion that "the unexamined life is not worth living." Throughout the prior session and this one, the therapist remained silent, actively listening to the associations as they organized about the adaptive context of his silence, making silent hypotheses but refraining, as yet, from intervening. She mentioned how her husband soothed her by rubbing her back; then she spoke of earlier fears of dying and of losing those she loved in accidents, while in the past she had never revealed such fears, but instead had overcome them through counterphobic acts. This was followed by memories of her stepfather, her rage at his indifference, and then by the revelation that she and her mother often colluded so as to make it impossible for the stepfather to speak, preferring those moments of calm silence to the stormy turmoil that ensued when there was open disagreement with him. She then offered the hope that the therapist would have something to say.

At this point, the therapist formulated a silent hypothesis that seemed to organize the derivative network around a specific adaptive context, her response to his silence, which was then communicated to Mrs. W. through the following intervention:

> The terrible sense of loss you feel and the consequent exacerbation of your asthma is in response to the terrible pain you feel when I remain silent. You speak of hoping to understand yourself—"the unexamined life is not worth living"—but, in contradiction to that you wish that, like your husband, I should speak to soothe you and thus alleviate the pain of loss through covering it over.

Her immediate response, the recollection of a recent incident forgotten until then, seemed to validate the intervention. She dwelt on the upset she had felt when a little girl who was seen at the hospital where she worked came to her, crying and relating that her mother had recently married, and that her stepfather and his son had then moved in. Now, the child painfully recounted, her mother was giving all of her attention to his boy, and she felt all alone. Thus, from the insight emerging out of the immediacy of the emotions and fantasies experienced within the therapeutic field, a memory was evoked, though not directly expressed, that provided the vital genetic link essential to accurate and authentic reconstructive work. In this instance, it does not require a leap of the imagination to conclude that the story of the little girl recapitulated the loss that precipitated the onset of her asthma following the arrival of her stepfather and stepbrother when she was nine. The therapist interpreted this just as the session was ending. Mrs. W. responded with silence.

In the next session she reported that she was feeling much better. The asthma was gone, although she wondered what had set it off. She felt closer to her husband, had enjoyed the beauty of the mountain scenery on the weekend, but then referred to "inner chaos" and "conflicts that get pushed under the carpet by my relatives." She wondered if the asthma had been set off "by the weather or by something I ate." She then mentioned the "mixed messages," that she gave to the therapist and her "deceit" in having hidden things from her stepfather. The therapist speculated, to himself, that while his intervention had an impact—the asthma was gone—it had also precipitated further anxiety and a manic defense. The inner choas was gone, covered over. The link to the prior sessions, the memory of the little girl, was lost, masked by a false sense of euphoria. The pain was gone as if it had never been there. In essence, unable as yet to recognize and decathect the loss, but also unable to deny so fully the loss and inner chaos mentioned, she achieved a temporary compromise that momentarily maintained the pre-loss fantasy while revealing both the defense and that which was defended against.

In the session that followed, her report that she continued to feel great was contradicted by references to the death of a friend, talk of funerals, and of her "inclination to lie and be deceitful." Her eyes filled with tears as she expressed a fear that her "cool facade" was breaking down, and then said, "I'm sure you have some purpose in being silent, but right now I don't like it, and I do wish you'd speak." After listening and silently attempting to organize her associations in a manner that would illuminate the meaning of the material, the therapist concluded that as yet nothing new had emerged, and decided to maintain his silence, wait for the next session, and hope that, through waiting, derivatives would coalesce around a specific adaptive context, providing the content for a valid interpretation.

On arriving for the next session, she announced that she had thought of not returning, but reconsidered on recalling that, in the past, the therapist's silences had often led to fruitful discoveries. She recalled how she used to want her husband to put her on a pedestal and worship her, but that she no longer wanted that, and she spoke of a friend who felt so stifled by her husband's clinging attentiveness that she had left him. She expressed admiration for her daughter, who was able to live independently. She told of another child who came to her at the hospital, overwhelmed by her terrible awareness of the truth. Her father had of late been irritable and obsessed with getting his finances into order. He seemed to be concerned only with money, but the little girl knew why. Despite his total denial of the truth and refusal to discuss it, she knew that he had an inoperable form of cancer and was soon to die.

The therapist, at this point, having listened intently to her associations, believed he last had the derivative material essential to a valid interpretation. He said that she was like the little girl who had lost her father but had been unable to bear the truth until now. The therapist could sense her pain, the terrible pain that had emerged within the silent space when he had not spoken. Now, however, in acknowledging a bit of that pain through the story of the little girl who knew the truth, she felt, somehow, more independent and less in need of her husband's, and similarly of the analyst's, paternalistic admiration. She replied that silence was hard for her to bear since it had so many upsetting meanings. Teary-eyed, she again mentioned the child whose father was dying, how that reminded her of her own father, and how hard that was to bear. On the other side, she did feel good about many positive experiences with her husband and at work, particularly the recent sense of being able to function independently.

Discussion and Conclusions

Mrs W. conforms to Fleming's description of adults in treatment who have lost a parent in childhood. She sought help when a threat of loss was precipitated by her husband's illness. She had not grieved but, instead, had denied the impact of the paternal loss and maintained a fantasy that her father remained her idealized companion. Her asthmatic condition followed the trauma of the realization that her fantasy could not be maintained in the face of her destructive relationship with her stepfather, but the equilibrium was restored through a marriage that perpetuated the fantasy through the reality of a husband who conformed to her idealized expectations. The dread of loss found expression through her fear of dying and of losing those whom she loved in accidents. The maintenance of the fantasy required the perpetuation of the myth of narcissistic grandiosity and invulnerability, a myth that had severely strained the marriage and could no longer be supported in light of her husband's illness.

Her pattern of resistance, expressed through a communicative style that emphasized the surface of experience, served to foster the re-creation of the pre-loss daughter–father imagoes through her relationship to the therapist. In lieu of insight to be achieved through maintaining the "frame" and through the analysis of transference, she persisted in ignoring the personal meaning of the therapeutic relationship while wishing to be soothed and gratified directly. The therapeutic task was to actualize the loss experience by resolving the resistances against the sense of catastrophe associated with the grief work. In relinquishing the pre-loss level of relating to primary objects, a more mature, holistic, autonomous experience of self and object relationships could be achieved, thus fostering progress in separating and individuating. Since her childhood and adolescent experiences precluded sufficient decathexis of the lost object, the accrued strength of her adult ego and analysis of pathological defenses, together with normal maturational advances, made it feasible to accomplish the grief work that was incomplete.

Although the above discussion of dynamics substantiates those findings noted in the analytic literature, it is in relation to treatment practices that differences arise. The crucial issue concerns the question of parameters. Given common acceptance of the dynamics of object loss, do such patients require deviations from the "model" technique, which as Eissler (1953) notes "requires interpretation as the exclusive tool"? Are deviations, such as serving as an "auxiliary" ego, or the wide variety of suggestions emphasizing that the therapist must be a "real object" (Roland 1967, Zetzel 1958), essential to promote a therapeutic alliance with patients who have experienced an early object loss? In considering the role of the therapist's silence in the treatment of such patients, does the extended silence of the therapist constitute too great a deprivation, posing an unnecessary threat to the therapeutic alliance? Or, on the contrary, can such silences promote the therapeutic process, and perhaps even be essential to the working-through process with patients who have experienced early object loss?

If the patient's defense against grieving is to deny the personal meaning of the therapeutic relationship while initiating a pre-loss relationship with the therapist, it would seem to follow that noninterpretive comments would only serve to create a reality that would conform to the patient's pathological images and expectations. Given such a reality, together with confrontations intended to activate memories of the lost parent, the actual experience of loss would be circumvented and the use of denial fostered by substituting intellectualizations for the immediacy of experience that is essential to the actualization and working through of the transference constellation. In this view, transference phenomena ought not be constructed from *a priori* knowledge of the past, although such knowledge provides clues, but must first emerge within the therapeutic relationship *in vivo*. Thus what is current may be actively experienced as a repetition of a past that is in the service of reconstructing the past, and it is the reworking of this past within the therapeutic relationship that offers opportunities for structural change.

So long as the material is not ripe for an interpretation, silence would seem to be the only valid activity. As Winnicott (1971), said so eloquently, "Interpretation outside of the ripeness of the material is indoctrination and produces compliance" (p. 51). The appropriate silence of the analyst can give the patient permission to go on, allowing him or her "to be," to communicate as freely as possible without the suggestions, questions, or implicit directions that inevitably influence the flow of associations toward more superficial and conscious content.

Within the medium of the therapist's patient, silent, but empathic, stance, unconscious derivatives related to themes of loss, separation, death, and autonomy, permeated Mrs. W.'s associations with increasing intensity and urgency. "Loss" reverberated within her mind and throughout these sessions. While on one level she sought to discover the truth, on another she resisted the impending pain of the loss already suffered and sought to deny the pain through severing the links between the inner experience of loss and her relationship with the therapist, while striving to maintain the pre-loss relationship. After her contradictory expectations had been interpreted, she recalled the story of the little girl who had lost her mother to her stepbrother, thus re-experiencing and gaining insight into her own loss. But again, the grief work could only be tolerated piecemeal, through the bit-by-bit decathexis of the lost object. Thus the process had to be lost, forgotten, and repeated over and over again, and after feeling better, she expressed the fear that her "cool facade" was breaking down, following this with the story of the little girl whose father denied the truth of his terminal cancer while the child knew he was going to die. The vivid and intense actualization of her inner sense of loss, an experience fostered by the appropriate silence of the therapist, provided the direct emotional experience that was then interpreted, both as a contemporaneous reaction to the loss of the therapist's parental-soothing function and as a repetition of the earlier pain associated with her father's loss. As a consequence she was able to begin to sever her dependence on unconscious fantasies of restitution and a substitutive external object. By refusing to conform to the patient's wish to be soothed like a child and by instead maintaining his empathic-interpretive stance, the therapist promoted her reliance upon her own equilibrium—maintenance functions—thereby furthering the process of internalization and separation-individuation. She felt more independent and less in need of her husband's and the analyst's paternalistic admiration.

It should be emphasized that while this paper focuses on the painful affects associated with object loss, it should not be misconstrued as implying that most patients experience pain during the prolonged silence of the therapist. As has been noted in the literature (Nacht 1964, Blos 1972), silence has a multiplicity of meanings, in part dependent upon the specific unconscious fantasies of each patient that are evoked and fill the empty space with meaning. Contrary to the pain associated with object loss, many patients experience a silent, holding environment as an invitation to a blissful symbiosis. For example, after a number of sessions during which the therapist was silent, a patient recalled the image of her infant daughter lying on her breast, cooing delightfully after both had fallen asleep. For this patient, silence was secure and nurturing, whereas the end of the session brought pain almost too difficult to endure.

In contrast to the oft-emphasized use of deviations to promote the therapeutic alliance, the above approach stresses the maintenance of therapeutic neutrality and the limiting of interventions to accurate and empathic interpretations. By maintaining an analytic stance and hold even in moments of great stress and crises, the therapist creates a truly analytic space, that potential space within which the actual experience, both realistic and distorted, is expressed via unconscious derivatives, providing the live material for analysis. Only through the patient's experience of the actual interaction can the past be relived and the necessary grief work performed. Given such material that is ripe for interpretation, the continued silence of the therapist would be as misplaced as speaking in the absence of adequate material.

For both the psychoanalyst and the psychoanalytic therapist, their ultimate effectiveness is a function of their interpretations, and this is so regardless of how often the patient is seen. The patient's need for accurate and empathic interpretation does not diminish with fewer sessions, although it may take the therapist longer to achieve a therapeutic aim. This position should not be misconstrued as placing undue emphasis on a detached and overly technical stance. The analytic therapist must be able to experience and convey his or her empathic-introspective awareness of the pain to be suffered in actualizing an object loss. It is within his or her interpretation, however, not in his or her deviations, that the appropriate concern is conveyed.[4] As Fiumara (1977) so beautifully said it, "Analytic empathy, in fact, moves along on the razor's edge as the only place where true concern for the patient may advance. And this is the only true love that the analyst can offer. Or, we can behave like benevolent wizards; but wizards, good or bad, do not bring maturity" (p. 174).

REFERENCES

Aull, G., and Strean, H. (1967). The analyst's silence. *The Psychoanalytic Forum* 2:72–80.

Barry, H. (1949). Significance of maternal bereavement before the age of eight in psychiatric patients. *Archives of Neurology and Psychiatry* 62:630–637.

Bion, W. R. (1962). *Seven Servants.* New York: Jason Aronson, 1977.

Blos, P., Jr. (1972). Silence: a clinical exploration. *Psychoanalytic Quarterly* 41:348–363.

Bowlby, J. (1961). Processes of mourning. *International Journal of Psycho-Analysis* 42:317–340.

———. (1963). Pathological mourning and childhood mourning. *Journal of the American Psychoanalytic Association* 11:500–541.

Brown, F. (1961). Depression and childhood bereavement. *Journal of Mental Science* 107:754–777.

Eissler, K. (1953). The effect of the structure of the ego on psychoanalytic technique. *Journal of the American Psychoanalytic Association* 1:104–143.

Fiumara, G. C. (1977). The symbolic function, transference and psychic reality. *International Review of Psycho-Analysis* 4:171–180.

Fleming, J. (1972). Early object deprivation and transference phenomena: the working alliance. *Psychoanalytic Quarterly* 41:23–49.

Fleming, J., and Altschul, S. (1963). Activation of mourning and growth by psycho-analysis. *International Journal of Psycho-Analysis* 44:419–431.

Freud, S. (1912). Recommendations to physicians practicing psycho-analysis. *Standard Edition* 12:111–120.

———. (1923). The ego and the id. *Standard Edition* 19:13–66.

Khan, M. H. (1963). Silence as communication. *Bulletin of the Menninger Clinic* 27:300–310.

Langs, R. (1978a). Some communicative properties of the bipersonal field. In *Technique in Transition*, pp. 413–472. New York: Jason Aronson.

———. (1978b). Interventions in the bipersonal field. In *Technique in Transition*, pp. 627–678. New York: Jason Aronson.

———. (1978c). Validation and the framework of the therapeutic situation. *Contemporary Psychoanalysis* 14:98–124.

Nacht, S. (1964). Silence as an integrative factor. *International Journal of Psycho-Analysis* 45:299–303.

4. It is assumed that the appropriate concern of the therapist subsumes the notions of holding and containing, therapeutic conditions that are a function of the therapist's empathy, compassion, respect, dependability, belief in the analytic process, search for truth, and tolerance of primitive and pathological phenomena.

Reik, T. (1926). The psychological meaning of science. *Psychoanalytic Review* 55:172–186, 1968.

Roland, A. (1967). The reality of the psycho-analytic relationship and situation in the handling of transference resistance. *International Journal of Psycho-Analysis* 48:504–509.

Sandler, J., and Sandler, A.-M. (1978). On the development of object relationships and affects. *International Journal of Psycho-Analysis* 59:285–296.

Shafii, M. (1973). Silence in the service of the ego: psychoanalytic study of meditation. *International Journal of Psycho-Analysis* 53:431–443.

Tolpin, M. (1971). On the beginnings of a cohesive self. *Psychoanalytic Study of the Child* 26:316–352.

Winnicott, D. W. (1971). Playing: a theoretical statement. In *Playing and Reality*. New York: Basic Books.

Wolfenstein, M. (1966). How is mourning possible? *Psychoanalytic Study of the Child* 21:93–123.

———. (1969). Loss, rage, and repetition. *Psychoanalytic Study of the Child* 24:432–462.

Zetzel, E. R. (1958). Theapeutic alliance in the analysis of hysteria. In *Capacity for Emotional Growth*, ed. Elizabeth R. Zetzel, pp. 182–196. New York: International Universities Press, 1970.

An Interactional Approach to the Treatment of Patients with Developmental Arrests

OZZIE SIEGEL, Ph.D.

A discussion of "On the Silence of the Therapist and Object Loss," by Martin Greene, D. S. W. Some of the clinical and technical issues raised by Dr. Greene regarding the treatment of patients who have suffered early loss are examined in relation to the conflict and deficit models. It is concluded from a re-examination of the material presented that terrifying drive wishes play a major role in the patient's communicative style and in the development of resistances. It is further suggested that the therapist's fears of the patient's primitive wishes and fantasies and what they evoke in both therapist and patient may lead to blind spots and incomplete interpretations. The technical modifications that are usually deemed necessary because of the patient's ego deficits may, in this connection, reflect the mutual anxieties generated within the secure frame.

Although Dr. Greene's stated purpose is to explore the effects of the therapist's silence on the treatment of patients who have suffered early loss, his paper nevertheless addresses broader, more basic issues of technique, the therapist's posture, and the conditions necessary for effective psychotherapeutic work and change. What constitutes an optimal therapeutic environment is, of course, controversial and often heatedly debated by therapists of different orientations. Questions regarding adhering to the basic ground rules, invoking parameters, the level of the therapist's activity, and the nature of the therapist's interventions are often addressed polemically in the psychoanalytic literature, but are perhaps best answered on the basis of clinical evidence. In this regard, Dr. Greene's presentation of case material that includes his own interventions as well as the patient's responses affords us an all-too-infrequent opportunity to look closely at the process of a therapist at work and to allow the material to speak for itself. In the place of distant, abstract conclusions preformed on the basis of psychoanalytic doctrine, Dr. Greene emphasizes the organic nature of the therapeutic process, with a focus on the communicative process as clinical data that can be subjected to methodological investigation.

Dr. Greene has placed before us a number of important questions concerning the treatment of patients who have suffered early loss. The answers will ultimately determine the nature of our therapeutic approach. One such question is whether silence, in contributing to the creation of an analytic space (Viderman 1974), thereby creates the potential for facilitating the therapeutic process by allowing the patient to use the therapist as a symbol of the earlier loss, and hence for discovery, growth, and cure. Or, on the other hand, is the therapist's silence merely a recapitulation of loss and, therefore, intolerable and even hurtful for patients who, because of early object loss, have suffered arrests in ego development? A third question concerns the implications of the therapist's activity. Albeit in the name of functioning as an auxiliary ego (i.e., because of the patient's presumed inability to tolerate silence due to his or her developmental arrests in separation-individuation, inability to form a working alliance, and denial of the meaningfulness of the therapeutic relationship), does the therapist's active, supportive role nevertheless serve as a substitutive gratification, and does the analyst thereby participate in the patient's denial of loss? Dr. Greene has addressed himself to each of these questions and has articulated the clinical-evidential, as well as conceptual, basis for his position that the unfolding of the therapeutic process and the elaboration, clarification, and amelioration of the patient's psychopathology is realizable within a "secure frame" (Langs 1976).

However, another dimension of this same issue involves the therapist's own anxieties and fears of functioning within the secure frame. Anxieties generated by silence, for example, do not belong exclusively to the patient in this setting and, in considering anxieties that can be magnified into terrors for patients who have early loss experiences, the therapist's anxieties must be taken into consideration as well. It seems legitimate to ask then, to what extent modifications of the therapeutic environment are in the unwitting service of protecting both participants from the frightening discoveries of their pathology that are made possible by and within the establishment of an analytic space.

The questions and issues raised in Dr. Greene's paper also touch on what has developed in recent years into a major controversy in psychoanalytic circles and has been the subject of books, journal articles, and conferences: the division between what might be referred to as the developmental arrest theorists (e.g., Kohut 1971; Stolorow and Lachman 1975, 1978) and the conflict theorists (e.g., Arlow 1963, Brenner 1976). The former group, represented in Dr. Greene's paper as well by Fleming (1972), argues that, because of arrested areas of ego development and the patient's inability to affirm the reality of a traumatic loss, waiting silently is inadvisable, and parameters and other technical modifications must be a necessary part of the treatment of such patients. In addition to therapists such as Arlow and Brenner, who clearly place conflict at the center of analytic work, many others have called attention to the dangers inherent in ignoring conflict, even in patients with developmental arrests (e.g., Kernberg 1974, Langs 1973, Slap 1977).

Without intending to diminish the importance of the substantive clinical, technical, and theoretical considerations involved in this area of controversy, one cannot help but feel that this dialectic also appeals to and satisfies certain of our personal and professional needs at the same time. Over the last decade, for example, our journals have been filled with debates between Kernberg and Kohut and their respective followers. The lines have been drawn, the camps established, and an air of excitement created. Nevertheless, there exists in all of this the dangers of oversimplification and loss of distance that often accompany entrenched positions. Perhaps the gravest danger is the creation of artificial divisions of development (e.g., pre-Oedipal versus Oedipal), and correspondingly different treatment approaches based on these divisions. It may very well be, as Blum (1981) recently noted, that the quite different problems of conflict, developmental deficit, disharmony, lag, and arrest "often exist side by side and interpenetrate" (p. 50). An empirical approach involving a close examination of the clinical material (i.e., the patient's associations and the therapist's interventions) allows for the possibility of achieving some degree of resolution. After all, on the most practical level (that is, in the consultation room), the therapist's task is to listen and understand the patient. In this connection, as Langs (1973) stated, even in patients whose psychopathology is rooted in an early disturbance in the mother–child relationship, and whose problems include impairment in self-object boundaries, in the therapeutic or analytic situation itself "these basic defects virtually always become crystallized around moments of acute trauma, and the intrapsychic anxiety, conflict and fantasies that such traumas evoke" (p. 249).

Yet it is also true that there is great variability in the ways therapists listen. It may even be that some of the prevailing theoretical disagreements can be traced to listening material in different ways and at different levels. Dr. Greene proposes a model of listening and understanding that can be compared to the reading of a literary text (Auerhahn 1979)—the patient's associations in a given hour can be listened to at the level of the manifest content and/or they can be organized into a number of latent themes and/or the therapist can discover (decode) the major personal and quite specific, although disguised, statements (i.e., unconscious fantasies or perceptions) that are related to the patient's illness or, more accurately, to that aspect of the

illness currently being activated. This approach is based on the most fundamental of psychoanalytic concepts, including those of psychic determinism
(hence the commitment to allowing the patient's thoughts to unfold without
undue influence or interruption) and unconscious processes (e.g., the language of primary process, unconscious fantasies, unconscious derivatives).
Central to this approach as well, however, is the more particular recognition
that patients are attempting something adaptive in their communications:
specifically, to communicate, although in disguised and encoded ways,
something of critical importance about their disturbance that has been
reactivated by a current traumatic event within or outside of the therapeutic situation. Langs (1973, 1976) has, of course, developed and presented a systematic approach to psychoanalytic psychotherapy based upon
the pivotal concepts of the adaptive context and unconscious derivative
communication, placing particular emphasis on the therapist's behaviors
(posture, interventions, management of the treatment situation) as primary
adaptive contexts in eliciting and evoking both neurotic and non-neurotic
reactions.

The patient, then, seeks through disguised, indirect derivative communications to guide the therapist toward answers to such questions as: What are
the optimal conditions of the therapeutic situation (i.e. the ground rules or
framework)? What is optimal in terms of the therapist's stance and the nature
of the interpretative work? Indeed, as DeRacker (1961) has demonstrated, the
patient even attempts to assist the therapist in developing and formulating
the needed interpretation. Beyond this, it is possible to utilize the patient's
associations as data for the validation or, on the other hand, as a nonconfir-
mation of interventions. It is this kind of empirical approach that will now
be applied to the case material at hand.

Hearing and understanding his patient's thoughts as at least in part a
response to his silence, and in this regard, as a commentary on his silence
(i.e., how it was experienced, what it evoked and re-evoked, the derivatives
of pathogenic unconscious conflicts as well as areas of ego dysfunction),
enabled Dr. Greene to organize the patient's derivative comunications and
facilitated his interpretative work, which was aimed at modifying the patient's symptoms and defenses related to loss. However, in focusing on the
pain that the patient experienced in connection with loss, Dr. Greene may
have underestimated the patient's *rage* associated with loss. The patient tried
to initiate a "'special,' rather chatty and quasi-social relationship with the
therapist" and "communicated in a style that made it extremely difficult to
detect anything beyond the surface." She "talked constantly." The therapist
established and maintained a certain set of specified ground rules for the
treatment, which included an adherence to an essentially interpretative

stance. For several sessions he did not intervene and instead remained silent. The patient, Mrs. W., spoke then of friends who had died and of her concerns about her husband's poor health. At one point there was a reappearance of Mrs. W.'s asthma. She spoke of earlier fears of dying and of losing loved ones in accidents. She mentioned her husband soothing her by rubbing her back. She directly mentioned feeling enraged at the analyst's "indifference." For present purposes, however, the patient's revelation that she and her mother colluded so as to make it impossible for the stepfather to speak may prove a more meaningful communication about her rage. It is, after all, what she attempted to do in her sessions.

In this connection, then, the following formulation may be offered: that in addition to activating painful feelings associated with loss, asthmatic symptoms, and wishes to be soothed by the therapist, the therapist's listening attitude and appropriate silence also activated the patient's *rage*, as well as her efforts to protect both herself and the therapist from this rage. This dimension of the material suggests that the patient was communicating something not only about her pain but also about her fury, which she experienced in connection with being left alone. Specifically, the patient's style of talking and her wishes to modify the treatment arrangements and to make the relationship "real" may be viewed as resistances based on a compromise formation that reflects at once Mrs. W's fears of confronting her own rage, as well as indirectly expressing her destructive wishes in talking so as to prevent the therapist from speaking (i.e., in effect reflecting her wish to "silence" the therapist). This particular facet of the therapeutic relationship seems, in turn, to rest upon specific unconscious, pathogenic murderous wishes to "silence" the stepfather. It might be added here that the role of rage in the development and activation of psychosomatic syndromes such as asthma is well known (Karol 1980, Mintz 1980, Wilson 1980) and seems once again confirmed by the present case. It is suggested, then, that a significant element in the treatment of a patient such as Mrs. W. is an appreciation of the interplay of unconscious conflicts and fears of primitive and terrifying instinctual drive wishes that occur in conjunction with the existing ego deficits.

It remains, then, to be asked if there is any evidence in the material following Dr. Greene's interpretation of the patient's sense of loss and pain resulting from the therapist's silence, and to suggest that this interpretation was perhaps incomplete insofar as it neglected to focus on the patient's rage. Several of the patient's associations in the following session seem organizable around and in response to the previous intervention. Specifically, the patient spoke of "conflicts that get pushed under the carpet." She continued to feel unclear about the causes of her asthmatic attacks and wondered if they were perhaps "set off by the weather." She spoke of "mixed messages," "deceit," and having hidden things from her stepfather. Listening to this material as the patient's unconscious commentary on the adaptive context of the previous intervention, and furthermore as the patient's efforts to assist the therapist—to guide and correct him—may sensitize us to other layers and meanings embedded in the patient's communications. Looked at in this way the content of the material, as well as the patient's "euphoric" mood and "manic" denial in this session, would seem to reflect an introjective identification with the therapist; specifically, one based on an unconscious perception of the therapist's own fears of approaching the issues related to the patient's rage. In the next session the patient's thoughts turned to "the death of a friend," "funerals," and her "inclination to lie and be deceitful." She became directly angry with the therapist and his silence. She mentioned in the session following that she had even thought of not returning. What follows is especially fascinating and instructive, for as Mrs. W. went on to talk about truth (referring to a little girl's fear of the truth about her father's illness) and denial of the truth (the same little girl's father refused to discuss his inoperable, terminal cancer), she seemed to be indirectly and via displacement telling the therapist that he as well as she could not afford to be afraid of the truth about her illness. These thoughts, associations, and reactions are examples of "nonvalidating responses" (Langs 1976), most meaningfully understood as mobilized by the therapist's last intervention. It is important to recognize that confirmation is not to be equated with the patient's direct, conscious response to the therapist's intervention. In this instance, Mrs. W. in effect tells the therapist that his intervention evoked images of deceit, hiding, and pushing matters under the carpet. She did not feel that she understood anymore about her illness, and in the next session there is a depressive, angry tone and thoughts of funerals and death, as well as a thought about ending treatment. The interactional basis of such responses (including symptoms and resistances) must be emphasized.

This is, of course, but one of several dimensions of the material. Dr. Greene's appreciation of his patient's exquisite sensitivity to and fears of his silence and his maintenance of the ground rules is amply reflected in the case presentation. In focusing on the validating process, it is with the understanding that it is perhaps the most difficult analytic task of all to hear one's own personal areas of anxiety, neurosis, and conflict represented in the patient's associations. To recognize that, to some extent, one has been hurtful because of one's own shortcomings, blind spots, or other neurotic problems is a still more difficult matter. Yet if we are able to hear the disturbing truths about ourselves as we are alluded to in the patient's associations, we stand to learn and to be guided toward a more empathic understanding of the patient and a fuller and deeper appreciation of the mutual and reciprocal relationship between the patient's psychopathology and the therapeutic environment and interaction.

REFERENCES

Arlow, J. (1963). Conflict, regression and symptom formation. *International Journal of Psycho-Analysis* 44:12–22.

Auerhahn, N. C. (1979). Interpretation in the psychoanalytic narrative: a literary framework for the analytic process. *International Review of Psycho-Analysis* 6:423–436.

Blum, H. P. (1981). Some current and recurrent problems of psychoanalytic technique. *Journal of the American Psychoanalytic Association* 29:47–68.

Brenner, C. (1976). *Psychoanalytic Technique and Psychic Conflict.* New York: International Universities Press.

DeRacker, G. (1961). On the formulation of the interpretation. *International Journal of Psycho-Analysis* 42:49–54.

Fleming, J. (1972). Early object deprivation and transference phenomena: the working alliance. *Psychoanalytic Quarterly* 41:23–49.

Karol, C. (1980). The role of primal scene and masochism in asthma. *International Journal of Psychoanalytic Psychotherapy* 8:577–592.

Kernberg, O. F. (1974). Contrasting viewpoints regarding the nature and psychoanalytic treatment of narcissistic personalities: a preliminary communication. *Journal of the American Psychoanalytic Association* 22:255–267.

Kohut, H. (1971). *The Analysis of the Self.* New York: International Universities Press.

Langs, R. (1973). *The Technique of Psychoanalytic Psychotherapy*, vol. I. New York: Jason Aronson.

———. (1976). *The Therapeutic Interaction*, vol. II. New York: Jason Aronson.

Mintz, J. L. (1980). Multideterminism in asthmatic disease. *International Journal of Psychoanalytic Psychotherapy* 8:593–600.

Slap, J. (1977). The eroding concept of intrapsychic conflict. *International Journal of Psychoanalytic Psychotherapy* 6:469–477.

Stolorow, R., and Lachman, F. (1975). Early object loss and denial: developmental considerations. *Psychoanalytic Quarterly* 44:596–611.

——— & ———. (1978). The developmental prestages of defenses: diagnostic and therapeutic implications. *Psychoanalytic Quarterly* 47:73–102.

Viderman, S. (1974). Interpretation in the analytical space. *International Review of Psycho-Analysis* 1:467–480.

Wilson, C. P. (1980). Parental overstimulation in asthma. *International Journal of Psychoanalytic Psychotherapy* 8:601–621.

The Holding Environment and Family Therapy with Acting Out Adolescents

EDWARD R. SHAPIRO, M.D.

The pathology of the holding environment in families of borderline, schizoid, and narcissistic adolescents is reviewed. A model for family therapy is described in which this pathological family environment can be examined. In this model, the family therapists function to contain displaced, projected, and acted-out affects and impulses. A clinical example illustrates how a therapist's capacity to acknowledge, bear, work through, and redirect these impulses in the family treatment offers family members an opportunity to reestablish previously severed communications, allowing for continued family support at a critical period in the adolescent's development.

In a recent series of related papers, my colleagues and I have presented developmental and clinical observations of acting out adolescents with borderline, narcissistic, and antisocial disorders and their families in interaction (Berkowitz et al 1974a, 1974b; Shapiro 1978a; Shapiro et al 1977; Shapiro et al 1975; Zinner and Shapiro 1972, 1974, 1975). These observations were drawn from a particular combination of treatment situations. The adolescent was in intensive individual therapy with one therapist, the marital couple was in marital therapy with a second therapist, and both therapists treated the entire family in conjoint family therapy.

It was our observation that families of these adolescents undergo a group regression during the adolescence of the index child in which certain characteristics of the adolescent's behavior as well as of parental views of him appear to be repetitious of parent–child interactions during earlier

A version of this paper was presented at the Spring Meeting of the American Society for Adolescent Psychiatry, Chicago, Illinois, May, 1979 and was awarded the Felix and Helene Deutsch Prize, Boston Psychoanalytic Society and Institute, 1980. The author would like to thank Drs. Robert Langs, David Berkowitz, Jonathan Kolb, and Dan Lippman, M. S. W., for their helpful comments on an earlier draft of this paper.

periods of the child's life. Similarly, characteristics of the adolescent's transference view of the individual therapist appeared to match closely the reality of regressive parental responses in the family therapy. In families with borderline adolescents, an understanding of these phenomena and the use of this combination of individual and family therapy was useful in reducing an intense unworkable individual transference and in stabilizing and supporting a working alliance with both patients and family (Shapiro et al 1977).

One assumption of this mode of treatment is that there are important sustaining forces within the family, and that in certain families shared unconscious fantasies and assumptions, and resultant regressive responses between family members, may interfere with their capacity to mobilize these forces. Powerful and dystonic affects and conscious and unconscious meanings are evoked in this interaction between parent and child that make communication difficult. Often, uncomfortable aspects of the self-image of various family members are disavowed and projected onto other family members, with a complex bond of conscious aversion and unconscious identification sustained between them (i.e., projective identification). These unintegrated affects, impulses, and images within the family deprive the adolescent of the opportunity to respond realistically to parental communications and deprive the parents of a clear recognition of the needs of their child. The family therapist is in a unique position to mediate these important communications.

This paper reviews the nature of this pathological communication in families of acting out adolescents and examines the function of the family therapist as container, metabolizer, and eventually interpreter of the unbearable affects and projective identifications involved in these interactions. Clinical material illustrates the combined effect on the therapist of projections onto him from both adolescent and parents. The therapist's clarity about his task as facilitator of family communications and his capacity to contain, metabolize, and feedback intolerable affects that are denied, projected, and acted out by these patients constitute a holding environment within which essential family communication can take place. This containing function is a prerequisite for interpretive work and serves as a basis for positive introjective identifications of the therapist that facilitate change in the family interaction.

DEVELOPMENTAL IMPLICATIONS OF "CONTAINMENT": THE HOLDING ENVIRONMENT

The "holding environment" is a term initially described by Winnicott (1965). It derives from the maternal function of holding the infant, but metaphorically extends to broader caretaking functions of the parents in relation to the older child. In the analytic situation, Winnicott describes the holding environment as accurate empathy, suggesting that it " . . . takes the form of conveying in words at the appropriate moment something that shows that the analyst knows and understands the deepest anxiety that is being experienced or that is waiting to be experienced" (p. 246).

In relation to the empathic containment of rage, the holding environment derives from the parental restraint of the child with a temper tantrum so that his aggressive impulses can hurt neither him nor the caretaker (Modell 1976). In the face of the child's outbursts, parental responses of nonanxious, firm limit-setting in an atmosphere of love and understanding help the toddler to master separation anxiety during the rapprochement subphase of separation-individuation and to internalize the image of a stable, constant object. Such a response is of critical importance in the move from a symbiotic relationship toward the development of an autonomous individual. It demonstrates to the child that the mother is neither created nor changed by the child's impulses, and that she is separate from him and not a creature of his projections. It allows the child to develop a relationship with her as a real and autonomous person, and helps the child to tolerate his own anger and put it in perspective by allowing him to recognize that it cannot destroy his loving mother (by turning her into a bad, angry, or anxious mother). In addition, the mother's stable response will help strengthen the child's conviction in the strength of his good self-image and that of his mother and will decrease his fear of his own aggressive tendencies (Shapiro 1978b).

Modell (1976) notes that "caretaking adults stand between the child and the actual environment and that the child and its caretakers constitute an open system joined by means of the communication of affects" (p. 290). The clarity with which affects and needs are transmitted and understood provides the child with a sense of safety and protection. When there is a loss of this holding environment, either because of illness, absence, or emotional unavailability of the parents, the child feels unsafe and is forced into a premature maturation, developing an "illusion of self-sufficiency" (Modell 1975). In schizoid and narcissistic patients, this illusory self-sufficiency is manifest by an aloof detachment; in the borderline patient it is seen in an overt denial of neediness combined with a chaotic and seemingly unrelated series of instinctual outbursts requiring some kind of containment (Shapiro et al 1977).

These two outcomes appear to relate to difficulties in different aspects of the holding environment. For schizoid and narcissistic patients, analytic and developmental data suggest that there has been a broad parental failure of empathic communication at the symbiotic and separation-individuation stages of development and a resultant lack of protection of the child from the stimulation of his needs (Kohut 1971, Shapiro 1978b). This lack of empathic response contributes to the child's development of a defensive belief in his own omnipotence, which exists side by side with a dissociated, intense, and overwhelming dependency, often expressed in the narcissistic patient as a craving hunger for admiration and approval. For borderline patients, the hypothesis is that the parental environment has been unable to contain the child's rage during rapprochement, resulting in a prolongation of defensive splitting, failure of the development of object constancy, heightened separation anxiety, and a sense of internal emptiness (Shapiro 1978b).

Modell (1976) comments from his analytic data that "for there to be a failure of the holding environment . . . it is necessary that both parents in some way be involved." He suggests that "in the older child, the father's role is significant either in opposing or augmenting the maternal elements" (p. 303).

Our work with families in interaction suggests the presence of a more complex dynamic family interaction than Modell presents. In our studies of families of disturbed adolescents, the failure of the holding environment, as defined by inaccurate or unresponsive parental empathic sensitivity to the adolescent's developmental needs, is determined not by one pathological relationship, but by a *shared* family regression (Zinner and Shapiro 1974). In this regression, a re-creation of the failure of the early holding environment, family members respond to autonomous or dependent needs (in the borderline adolescent) or narcissistic needs (in the narcissistic adolescent) with withdrawal, retaliation, or empathic failure (Berkowitz et al 1974a, 1974b; Shapiro et al 1975). We observe a complementary use of projective identification of dystonic aspects of their self-representations by these parents, which blurs their capacity to experience themselves as separate from the particular child in areas of conflict. Through the use of this shared defense, parents fail to perceive accurately the reality of the child, developing defensive stereotyped delineations of him (Shapiro et al 1977, Shapiro and Zinner 1975). The adolescent's developmental reliance on parental evaluations of who he is (Erikson 1956), and his wish to protect his parents from anxiety (Zinner and Shapiro 1972), interfere with his capacity to react against the constraints imposed by their defensive needs and inhibit his identity formation.

These shared defensive phenomena during the designated child's adolescence are regularly seen to have precursors in his early childhood. The following excerpt from the couples therapy of parents of a hospitalized adolescent reveals characteristic elements of holding environment failure in early childhood as seen retrospectively by the parents.

Excerpt I

Father: Mary was *never* an affectionate child. Never. From the time she was a baby. And it always bothered me. You could never hold her on your lap. You could never kiss her. I used to kiss her every night. I used to go in and kiss her good night when she was a baby until she got to be maybe ten, twelve, something like that. Every night I'd go in faithfully, and every night she'd pull the covers up over her head, and I'd have to fight with her to kiss her good night.

Mother: Now I think she's rejecting us because we put her in the hospital.

Father: She's mad at us.

Mother: She is really mad at us because we did that.

Therapist: What kept you going back night after night if she put up such a fight?

Mother: I was thinking that, too.

Father: Many a night we talked about that, too. We thought, "The hell with it, you know this is ridiculous. I'm making a fool of myself." And I said, "Well, she's only a baby." She was then, and I just happened to think that children need affection, and I figured, "If she doesn't want to give it to *me*, I will show her I love *her*, and how else do you do it?" That's one way, certainly. Be close physically with her. Many a night I figured, "Well, the hell with it."

Mother: We had a tough time there. Something would happen, and we wouldn't for two or three nights, but it would bother us. She could care less that we went in, and you feel like—well, you love her after all—you do like to . . . Then it got to the point where Daddy would go to bed first, and she would come in and kiss him good night.

Father: Under protest.

Mother: She did that—but this was, of course, because we forced it on her I suppose.

Father: Yah . . .

In this excerpt, the parents are associating to their feelings of being rejected by their "unappreciative" adolescent. Parental love is always, in part, supported by a child's capacity to respond. When a child is hypersensitive or otherwise unresponsive to parental attempts at loving interactions, feelings of abandonment and need in the parents may contribute to angry responses or defensive withdrawal. In this example, the parents' defensive delineation of their daughter is that she has *never* been capable of love. The flexibility necessary for accurate perception of the child's changing affects and needs is obscured by their stereotyped delineation. Their anxiety makes it impossible for them to offer a more empathic form of loving and to convey to their daughter that she can be mad at them without losing affective contact and threatening the relationship. In their shared anxiety about being loving, "good" parents (derived in part from their wishes not to repeat their experiences of rejection as children in their families of origin), the parents are hypersensitive to their child's unresponsiveness, rapidly experiencing it as a powerful rejection of them, as though their child were a reincarnation of their own "rejecting" parents. In a dread of this repetition, they are determined to love her even if they have to force it on her.

The controlling elements in this "love" are, however, apparent to the child, who is forced into responding to parental needs with a pretense of a good-night kiss. Her anger and isolation can neither be heard, contained, nor responded to by her parents, since the recognition of these affects would threaten their fragile defensive "loving" self-perceptions and compel them to re-examine their own childhood experiences. In addition, parental anxiety about their capacity to love a needy child cannot be acknowledged and put in perspective by them, since their child cannot fulfill the holding parental function they require for such an acknowledgment. A "holding" response in this situation would convey to the parents that it is possible to be angry at a stubborn and difficult child and still be a loving parent. In this family, neither parent can supply this symbolic holding function for the other. In the face of the continued absence of adequate holding responses for both parents and child, the antagonism and isolation in this family remain untouched.

THE HOLDING ENVIRONMENT AND
THE THERAPEUTIC MILIEU

Several authors have suggested that important aspects of the early empathic holding environment may be duplicated in the treatment environment of psychoanalytic psychotherapy. Based on Bion's (1962) seminal formulation of the therapist–patient interaction as an oscillation between the container and the contained, Langs (1973, 1976, 1977, 1978a, 1978b) and others (Kernberg 1979, Viderman 1974) have described the "bipersonal field," which consists of patient and therapist and is defined by a specific framework with well designed ground rules that delimit the field and contribute to its communicative properties.

These authors limit their description of this field to the one-to-one interaction. They focus on the specific framework or boundaries of the interaction (limited hours, fees, rules about extra therapeutic communications, etcetera), on the psychological capacities of both patient and therapist, and on ways in which the clearly defined framework provides a safe environment for the communication and interpretation of derivatives of the patient's unconscious conflicts.

In his own investigation of this model, Langs (1978a) sees the therapist's inclusion of family members in the treatment as possibly representing an acting out of the therapist's unconscious countertransference-based difficulties. Langs' assumption is that, in relation to the therapist's defined task of containing, metabolizing, feeding back, and interpreting the patient's pathological projective identifications, bringing in other family members may be in the service of protecting the therapist against the vicissitudes and anguish of such containment. In his book on technique, Langs (1973) suggests that the patient in individual treatment must be made aware of his own responsibility to effect change in other family members by "analyzing his own role in evoking the other person's disturbed behavior and his need for that behavior" (p. 183).

Langs focuses on the treatment of adults, assuming similar therapeutic requirements for adolescents. Other investigators, however, draw attention to the stage-specific intensity of the adolescent's family ties in terms of their treatment implications. In her summary article on adolescence, A. Freud (1958) suggests that the adolescent's painful tasks of withdrawing himself from his involvement with his family and giving up his past ties with them occupy much of his energy, leaving little for a transference involvement with a therapist. While some adolescents may eagerly turn to the therapist as a new object, their urgent search to replace their parents may interfere with their capacity to observe and integrate transference phenomena. She suggests that in such circumstances, "neither transference events nor the past (may) become meaningful enough to yield material for interpretation" (p. 262), asserting that "the immediate object has to be given up before analytic therapy can become effective."

In these cases, the intense family struggle may serve as a useful focus for therapeutic work if, in the family therapy, affects and impulses can be sufficiently contained for their origins to be understood. Four factors contribute to the usefulness of family therapy with these families: (1) the stage of adolescence itself and the shared family regression that recapitulates and allows for the reworking of earlier conflicts, (2) the adolescent's continuing need for family support during this period, (3) the powerful effects of new experience with his parents on strengthening the adolescent's still flexible character structure, and (4) the possibility of reintegration of projected and acted out conflicts leading to a modification in parental functioning (Shapiro 1978a).

FAMILY THERAPY MODEL

Our therapeutic format for work with severely disturbed adolescents and their families involves two therapists. The individual therapist has a one-to-one relationship with the adolescent, with the classically defined therapeutic tasks plus an explicit delineation of himself as functioning in two roles: individual therapist and family therapist. He makes no promises to the adolescent about confidentiality and, if the question arises, informs the adolescent that the extent to which the adolescent trusts him will have to be judged on the basis of the therapist's behavior, not on his promises. A significant tension that is sustained in the individual therapy while concurrent family treatment procedes, is the therapist's implicit freedom to bring relevant material into the family session.

In the family session, he functions as a therapist for the whole family, not as the patient's ally against the parents. He brings to this task his intimate knowledge of the adolescent's transference to him and of his own countertransference responses. In addition, he defines his task in the family therapy as a consultant, attempting to rapidly interpret any group transference to him rather than allowing it to deepen, and attempting to help the family marshall its resources to be more helpful to one another. This effort is facilitated by the therapist's attention to shared unconscious processes within the family. The second therapist is a couples' therapist who functions in a parallel manner with the marital couple, with a similar family focus as a co-therapist in the family therapy.

In the family therapy setting, then, the family is encouraged to interact in the presence of two therapists who hold shared information about the internal processes of the family participants. In families with borderline, narcissistic or acting out adolescents, family members' intolerance of painful subjective experience contributes to communication that is dominated by projective identification and action discharge as a defense against experiencing and introspection. In the therapeutic management of these family communications, the therapists' task is to supply the containing element missing within the family, so that these unconscious impulses and instinctual fragments can be processed and cognitively interpreted. In effect, the therapists in their separate and combined interactions with family members function as a "splint"—holding together disconnected communication.

This therapeutic task is congruent with Langs' description of the therapist's "main function" in the bipersonal field: to receive, contain, and metabolize the patient's interactional pressures toward cognitive and affective understanding. This "containing" function represents more than empathy. It includes the demonstration of the therapist's capacity to bear the painful affects that are projected. With individual patients, it is an everyday clinical phenomenon.

For example, when an anxious parent asks the therapist, "What if my daughter runs away from the hospital?," the question contains both a projection of helplessness into the therapist and an anxious implicit request by the parent for the therapist to manage the affect. If he responds, "In that case, we'll have to discharge her," it is a demonstration that the therapist cannot bear the feeling and the underlying unconscious fantasies, and that he must handle it by premature closure and an action response. If he replies,

"That's up to you" or "What do you think?", he demonstrates his surrender to the affect and an attempted counterprojection of helplessness back into the parent. If, however, the therapist's response is to acknowledge the possibility of the adolescent's running away and the staff's relative helplessness, and to interpret the parent's anxiety by pointing out his or her projection of anxiety and helplessness onto the staff and the wish that the staff manage these affects better than the parent was able to, then he will have recognized the problem as a shared one for discussion. In effect, he will have provided a holding environment by demonstrating his capacity to acknowledge, contain, and help put into perspective the projected painful sense of helplessness (Semrad 1969).

In the family setting, this kind of "interactional pressure" comes from *all* family members. Since the primary focus of tension is the relationship between the symptomatic adolescent and his parents, the individual therapist is often in the focal role in the family meeting. His own interaction with the adolescent gives the individual therapist a perspective from which to understand the way in which the adolescent evokes particular parental responses (Shapiro et al 1977). The parents' responses to the therapist's "care" of the adolescent reveal areas of their anxiety about their own parental functioning (Shapiro and Kolb 1979) and about their own experiences with their parents.

Often, in a manner similar to Langs' (1973) observation, a major containing function of the family therapist relates to his management of the framework of the therapy. It is frequently in family members' actions and deviations around the framework that dissociated and acted out affects and impulses occur, requiring some kind of containment.

Clinical Observations

The following description of an ongoing family therapy illustrates the breakdown of family communication and family members' use of both projective identification and action discharge in the service of avoiding painful affects in their relationships with one another. The issues in this case, as are so common in families with borderline adolescents (Masterson 1972, Shapiro and Zinner 1975), are those of abandonment, reactive rage, and depression. These themes, played out in the past between parents and child, are recreated in the family therapy around a deviation in the framework (i.e., altered therapy hours). In this case, the individual therapist's attempts to rectify the framework allowed him to experience and metabolize these affects, facilitating a reintroduction of these themes in a way that allowed the central focus of family discussion to proceed.

The B. Family consists of Mr. and Mrs. B. and their three adolescent boys including Fred B., a 16-year-old schizoid adolescent, hospitalized after a

series of suicide attempts, the most recent by hanging. Their family interaction was characterized by oliqueness, indirectness, a suspicious, detached
stance on the part of the adolescent and a profound sense of helplessness and
incompetence on the part of the parents, with manifest wishes for the
therapists to take over and tell them both how they had failed as parents and
what to do to change the situation. Despite active attempts at interpretation
and clarification, the therapists had great difficulty both in interpreting
adequately the parents' dependency on them and in helping family members
talk directly to one another. Over the course of almost a year's hospitalization, although Fred became less self-destructive, he and his family continued
to have difficulty in establishing a working alliance in which tension-filled
interactions either within the family or between family members and treatment staff could be adequately addressed and understood. In the central
family triangle (mother, father, and Fred), characteristic stereotypic positions were taken: mother was guilt-laden, weepy, and ineffectual; father
was brusk, insensitive, and preoccupied with business details; Fred remained
aloof, detached, unrelated, and sullen. The B.'s responded to Fred with great
delicacy and hesitation, with a clear delineation of him as fragile, incomprehensible, unpredictable, and alien. In part, this defensive parental withdrawal and fear of Fred was determined by how much they had suffered
from his current anger, suicidal withdrawal, and hatred; in part it represented the outcome of chronic difficulties in family members' capacities to
communicate affects in words.

During the latter part of the first year of therapy, after Fred had improved
enough to be transferred to a halfway house, the parents' repeated cancellations and attempts at rescheduling weekly family therapy sessions became increasingly confusing. These plans were brought up at random times
during the hour, and occasionally were phoned in during the week. The
therapists' attempts to rectify the framework (by setting fixed times, charging
for unplanned missed hours, etcetera) seemed to be of no avail. Attempts to
connect these cancellations with events in the sessions themselves were
equally fruitless. Father, whose successful business life required frequent
trips, became instantly suspicious and defensive when his plans were questioned; he seemed to be unaware that these absences would have any impact
on family members. Mother, who joined him for many of these trips, seemed
passive and confused. None of the children had comments about the cancellations and seemed indifferent. Fred remained detached and unconnected,
never seemed to remember when family meetings were held or cancelled, and
participated only in a superficial sarcastic manner, often remaining silent.

In the individual therapy, Fred developed an intensely negative transference to the individual therapist, in which he viewed the therapist as
powerful, controlling, and fearsome. He was unable to accept anything from

the therapist or to let the therapist know verbally when he was in distress; on one occasion he impassively extinguished a live cigarette on the palm of his hand in front of the therapist in a desperate attempt to communicate both his sense of being controlled and his feelings of anxiety, helplessness, and rage. At the same time, he also became increasingly irregular in his attendance at individual therapy sessions. He would come late, "forget" the time, arrange other meetings during the hour, remain silent, and generally indicated his sense of not being held and his inability to develop a predictable relationship with the therapist. The therapist, who had initially been able to engage Fred around a discussion of anger, began to feel disconnected. He sensed that the therapy was in a stalemate. Both therapists felt hopeless, confused, and unable to think clearly about the treatment. They wondered whether rehospitalization was necessary and struggled with the possibility that they were not capable of engaging the family in treatment. There seemed to be some link between the adolescent's behavior and that of the parents, but all relationships seemed disconnected and unfocused. They speculated that their feelings of helplessness and discontinuity of the emotional relationships represented affects that family members could not tolerate, but could find no way to reintroduce them (Kernberg 1979).

After several months of fruitless attempts at interpretation in both therapies, and similarly fruitless attempts at limit-setting by half-way house staff, the individual therapist had an unusual experience. Ordinarily a very sound sleeper, he awoke at 3:00 a.m. one morning in a fury. He had a dream in which he was profoundly identified with Fred and in a rage at the B. parents, who had gone off unpredictably, leaving him alone. The therapist's analysis of this dream over the next several weeks took him through aspects of his own past and his relationship with his own parents. He began to recognize his detachment and despair as a familiar defensive avoidance of his own internal anger, protest, and grief at being abandoned. He increasingly recognized his countertransference rage at Fred for abandoning him in the therapy. The dream provided him with a deeper understanding of the B.'s parental responses, since part of his own anger at and withdrawal from Fred was based on his now feeling unresponded to as a therapist. With this perspective, he began to examine his dual role in the conjoint family therapy. He suspected that Fred might be responding defensively to the therapist's and his parents' abandonment by an identification with the aggressor, manifest in an abandonment of the therapist, with an implicit wish for *him* to manage the affects. The therapist's countertransference identification with Fred in the family meeting intensified his response, since he also felt abandoned by the B.'s. With this perspective, he began to feel like a poorly prepared babysitter left to manage a child who was taking out his anger at the parents on him.

In a family session later that month, when the B.'s announced another absence, the therapist reviewed both their absences and Fred's, stating somewhat sharply that family members were continually leaving and abandoning each other and him and that *he* didn't like it. Mrs. B., quite tentatively, asked the therapist if he were angry at them. Before the therapist could respond, the adolescent, who had been seemingly lost in dissociated thought, broke in with a sudden outburst of anger at the parents and spoke at length in a new and quite connected manner about his longstanding confusion about whether his parents were there or not. He recalled numerous instances from his childhood of sudden unplanned parental trips and bewildering placements with babysitters or other family members. He talked of his sense that he had done something wrong each time they would leave, of his certainty that they'd never return, and of his fantasies of running away to find them.

The parents, astonished at this outburst, said that they'd never known he'd minded their trips. They revealed their fears of upsetting the children by discussing their trips ahead of time and their insistence on talking only to the babysitters when they'd call home "for fear of upsetting the children." Fred commented that he had never known that they had called. Mother talked of her sense that she and her husband could just disappear for trips and that the children would not mind very much. Father, with great sadness, talked of his perception that his children did not like him very much and of his conviction that all he had to offer them was physical comfort and financial support, that his presence was not significant. In the couples therapy, both parents began to recognize that their defensive withdrawal from Fred represented both the consequence of an unconscious projection of their own vulnerabilities onto him and an avoidance (like the therapist's) of their anger and pain that their loving attempts were not responded to by their son.

In the individual therapy, the adolescent reviewed these childhood events in greater detail. The therapist, who had now experienced these sudden abandonments by both adolescent and parents, was able both to communicate his understanding of the patient's bewilderment, confusion, and rage, and to interpret the repetition of these early experiences in the individual transference.

In the following family meeting, the adolescent turned to his parents with tears of rage and sadness and told them that he did not know them at all, that they were strangers to him, and that he had no sense of who he himself was. He revealed his confusion, despair, and loneliness and began to talk of his longstanding feeling that he had to take care of himself and that he could depend on no one. He spoke with sadness and anger of his feeling that he had missed important years during his childhood and that they could not now be made up. In response, both parents recalled similar feelings of isolation from childhood and were able to see the lack of contact in their current family.

The B.'s response to Fred throughout his childhood was characterized by a failure of empathic understanding of his dependent needs. To prepare him adequately for their absences would have required an acknowledgment of their own fears of abandonment and loss. Their conflicts about these issues derived from earlier conflicts with their own parents in which their wishes for nurturance were not acknowledged and not met. The therapist's capacity to confront the implications of separation allowed these memories to surface and be discussed, precipitating a shared sense of grief over what had been lost in past family relationships. Only with this acknowledgment could family members begin to examine the possibilities for future family contact, and Fred begin to realize his need for individual treatment for himself.

Discussion

In reviewing the case material, the reader might wonder at the length of time the individual therapist took to understand and interrupt Fred's developing intense psychotic transference to him. Why was it necessary to have a dream in order to understand the paranoid transference? Could he not have earlier utilized a counterprojective intervention to interpret the patient's anger as displaced from his "abandoning" parents (Havens 1976)? Was he not simply joining the adolescent in an assault on the parents in the family meeting?

In the family meeting described, the therapist's anger is directed at the abandonment by *both* Fred and the parents. He is, in fact, making a statement that differentiates from the family *himself* ("I don't like being abandoned"). The length of time needed to respond to this therapeutic dilemma is directly related to the complex manner in which these therapists have become involved or "enmeshed" (Bowen 1978) in the family process. In a way, they have "become" family members, with the content of the complex family dynamics contained inside of them (Whittaker et al 1965). This is related to the fact that the therapists leave the family after each session and that they return home to their own beds so that the processing and differentiation from the family can occur within them.[1] This differentiation requires a working through of idiosyncratic countertransference responses as well as identifications both with the parents, whose loving attempts are not responded to, and with Fred, who denies his need for loving responses. The therapist's implicit comment, "I now can stand outside this process," is a model for introjective identification for all family members that allows Fred's anger to be expressed and both heard and responded to by his parents.

As evident from the case description, the two therapists in this combined therapy approach are in continual danger of countertransference confusion.

1. I am indebted to Drs. Mona and Michael Bennett for this clarification.

As family therapists, they must remain in empathic contact with all members of the family to sustain their functioning as consultants in the family process. This position requires continual awareness of the possibility of an identification with particular family members. The individual therapist may be pulled into an identification with the adolescent, the couples therapist into an identification with the parents, or vice versa. In addition, family members' transference wishes for omnipotent rescue and the therapists' own rescue fantasies may be manifest by a shift from a position of attempting to understand to a position of wanting to "fix" the family or to take over some aspect of parental functioning in the face of an obvious family regression. The wish to be a better parent can contribute to retaliatory anger in the therapists, which may interfere with their capacity to contain and interpret.

The therapeutic use of countertransference responses is hazardous. It is essential to work through one's own neurotic contributions to these responses. Langs (1978b) warns of the therapist's countertransference attempt to misuse his own subjective experiences by holding the patient solely responsible for them. He suggests that such a move may reflect a lack of effort on the therapist's part to understand the basis in himself for these responses. Such a nonreflective maneuver serves only as a confession of the therapist's own disorganization and as an effort to attack the patient, to engender guilt, and to blame him for the therapist's pathology. In family therapy, because of the opportunities for unconscious identification with parents or child, careful scrutiny must be given to one's subjective reactions. The therapist's goal should include an attempt to validate his subjective experiences in terms of his own internal fantasies, as well as data from the patients, and to deal with the material in terms of its communicative meaning from the patient to the greatest extent feasible.

Despite these cautions, the use of the therapist's subjective experience is an important tool. In the excerpt about the goodnight kiss (Excerpt I), the parents' hurt and angry feelings were defended against in part because of the intimacy and anxiety of their family ties, as well as by their unconscious repetition of earlier conflicts in their relationship with their daughter. In the case of the B. family, the therapist was also upset and angered by family members' repeated abandonment of him. Because of his position outside of the family, however, he was more able to acknowledge, understand, and use his feelings in the service of an empathic response to the family that facilitated the maintenance of a holding environment and helped family members to transform action into subjective experience that could be communicated and understood.

In the B. Family, dissociated affects of guilt, rage, despair, and loneliness were clearly missing in the interaction between family members. Parental guilt, isolation, and feelings of inadequacy were denied, acted out, and projected. The therapist's task in this situation included the need to contain and not be overwhelmed by these feelings so that they could be put into perspective. In containing parental affects, the therapist had to perceive that despite feelings of inadequacy, there was enough potential in these relationships to continue the work. In containing the adolescent's rage, he needed to know that his anger was not destructive, that the parents could survive a confrontation, and that continued contact was essential. In addition, the therapist's clarity about his task as family consultant and his recognition that the major therapeutic work needed to occur within the family, allowed him not to act on his rage and rescue fantasies by offering the adolescent a "better experience" with himself and devaluing the parents. Both parents and child, in their identification with the therapist, utilized his containment of these affects as supports for a new and important family exploration of grief and rage over abandonment.

CONCLUSIONS

An attempt has been made to utilize psychoanalytic developmental concepts about pre-Oedipal psychopathology to define and describe a treatment framework for patients with these problems during their adolescence. This framework is designed to work with both the intrapsychic consequences of these developmental failures and the ongoing interpersonal family conflicts that interfere with development. Initially developed for hospital patients on the verge of death or intrapsychic chaos who had been unreachable within standard treatment approaches, the framework makes unusual demands on therapists whose task requires them to work on the boundary between intrapsychic and interpersonal phenomena.

Langs (1980) feels strongly that a confidential bipersonal framework is essential for treatment, and that the construction of a framework that includes family treatment contains "unrectifiable flaws" that result in a "misalliance cure" that ultimately fails to address the patient's responsibility for his own continuing pain and limitations. If, in fact, such a framework led the adolescent to the conclusion that his parents did something to him that resulted in his difficulties, there would indeed be a significant hazard for ultimate resolution. Winnicott (1960) says that the therapist "(must be) prepared to wait until the patient becomes able to present the environmental factors in terms that allow of their interpretation as projections" (p. 38).

With these chaotically disturbed adolescents, however, the stresses on the therapist are often more than can be managed in an individual treatment alone and often result in unmanageable countertransference repetitions of the patient's familial traumas, as well as the need for environmental stabilization through hospitalization. If, during this period, the capacity for the patient's family members to perceive their own psychological needs is strengthened, and the patient is simultaneously confronted with the reality of his family life and his responsibility for his share of evoking similar difficulties in the individual transference, then his capacity for reality testing may be strengthened (Shapiro et al 1977). Such an approach avoids the dilemma of placing the adolescent in a loyalty bind (Boszormenyi-Nagy 1972) and helps the family to provide more reasonable support for his ultimate separation.

The general course of treatment of such patients is for the intensive family work to lead to greater internalization of conflict on the part of family members, which results in a gradual cessation of family therapy, leaving the adolescent (and occasionally a sibling) more responsibly involved in an individual therapy and the couple in marital therapy. In the case described, the adolescent and his parents were able to acknowledge and mourn their past difficulties and undergo a more coherent differentiation. With the resultant strengthening of the adolescent's reality testing, the individual therapist was able to demonstrate interpretively the way these issues were woven into the individual transference, including a recognition of the adolescent's share of the responsibility for evoking repetitive countertransferential responses from important people in his life.

Semrad (1971) defined individual psychotherapy as "an encounter between a big mess—and a bigger mess." The psychological traumas of therapists constitute a major element in the quality of the holding environment that they can provide their patients. The chaotic, preverbal communications that dominate the interactions within the families described in this paper require therapists to stretch themselves to face and take full responsibility for all of their experiences without projecting them onto various family members who may easily serve as receptacles for the therapists' own family dilemmas. This effort, and the perspective provided by the therapeutic focus on the adolescent's primary relationships with his family, illuminates the need for all participants to pay serious attention to their own needs as a prerequisite for the provision of an adequate holding environment for others.

REFERENCES

Berkowitz, D. A., Shapiro, R. L., Zinner, J., and Shapiro, E. R. (1974a). Family contributions to narcissistic disturbances in adolescents. *International Review of Psychoanalysis* 1:353–362.
———. (1974b). Concurrent family treatment of narcissistic disorders in adolescence. *International Journal of Psychoanalytic Psychotherapy* 3:371–396.
Bion W. (1962). Learning from experience. Reprinted in *Seven Servants*. New York: Jason Aronson, 1977.

Boszormenyi-Nagy, I. (1972). Loyalty implications of the transference model in psychotherapy. *Archives of General Psychiatry* 27:374–380.

Bowen, M. (1978). *Family Therapy in Clinical Practice*. New York: Jason Aronson.

Erikson, E. H. (1956). The problem of ego identity. *Journal of the American Psychoanalytic Association* 4:56–121.

Freud, A. (1958). Adolescence. *Psychoanalytic Study of the Child* 13:255–278.

Havens, L. (1976). *Participant Observation*. New York: Jason Aronson.

Kernberg, O. (1979). Psychoanalytic psychotherapy with borderline adolescents. *Adolescent Psychiatry* 7:294–321.

Kohut, H. (1971). *The Analysis of the Self*. New York: International Universities Press.

Langs, R. (1973). *The Technique of Psychoanalytic Psychotherapy*, vol. 1. New York: Jason Aronson.

———. (1976). *The Bipersonal Field*. New York: Jason Aronson.

———. (1977). Some communicative properties of the bipersonal field. In *Technique in Transition*, pp. 413–472. New York: Jason Aronson, 1978.

———. (1978a). Interventions in the bipersonal field. In *Technique in Transition*, pp. 627–678. New York: Jason Aronson, 1978.

———. (1978b). The adaptational-interactional dimension of countertransference. In *Technique in Transition*, pp. 501–535. New York: Jason Aronson, 1978.

———. (1980). Personal communication.

Masterson, J. R. (1972). *Treatment of the Borderline Adolescent: A Developmental Approach*. New York: John Wiley and Sons.

Modell, A. H. (1975). A narcissistic defense against affects and the illusion of self-sufficiency. *International Journal of Psychoanalysis* 56:275–282.

———. (1976). The "holding environment" and the therapeutic action of psychoanalysis. *Journal of the American Psychoanalytic Association* 24:285–307.

Semrad, E. (1969). *Teaching Psychotherapy of Psychotic Patients*. New York: Grune and Stratton.

———. (1971). Personal communication.

Shapiro, E. R. (1978a). Research on family dynamics: clinical implications for the family of the borderline adolescent. *Adolescent Psychiatry* 6:360–376, 1978.

———. (1978b). The psychodynamics and developmental psychology of the borderline patient: a review of the literature. *American Journal of Psychiatry* 135:1305–1315.

Shapiro, E. R., and Kolb, J. E. (1979) Engaging the family of the hospitalized adolescent: the multiple family meeting. *Adolescent Psychiatry* 7:322–342.

Shapiro, E. R., Shapiro, R. L., Zinner, J., and Berkowitz, D. (1977). The borderline ego and the working alliance: indications for individual and family treatment in adolescence. *International Journal of Psychoanalysis* 58:77–87.

Shapiro, R. L., and Zinner, J. (1975). Family organization and adolescent development. In *Task and Organization*, ed. E. Miller. London: John Wiley.

Shapiro, E. R., Zinner, J., Shapiro, R. L., and Berkowitz, D. (1975). The influence of family experience on borderline personality development. *International Review of Psychoanalysis* 2:399–411.

Viderman, S. (1974). Interpretation in the analytical space. *International Review of Psychoanalysis* 1:467–480.

Whittaker, C. A., Felder, R. E., and Warkentin, J. (1965). Countertransference in the family treatment of schizophrenia. In *Intensive Family Therapy*, eds. I. B. Nagy and J. L. Framo. Hagerstown, Maryland: Hoeber.

Winnicott, D. W. (1960). The theory of the parent–infant relationship. In *The Maturational*

Processes and the Facilitating Environment. New York: International Universities Press, 1965.

———. (1963). Psychiatric disorders in terms of infantile maturational process. In *The Maturational Processes and the Facilitating Environment* (1965). New York: International Universities Press.

Zinner, J., and Shapiro, E. R. (1975). Splitting in the families of borderline adolescents. In *Borderline States in Psychiatry*, ed. J. Mack. New York: Grune and Stratton.

Zinner, J., and Shapiro, R. L. (1972). Projective identification as a mode of perception and behavior in families of adolescents. *International Journal of Psychoanalysis* 53:523–530.

———. (1974). The family as a single psychic entity: implications for acting out in adolescents. *International Review of Psychoanalysis* 1:179–186.

The Abandoned Therapist

DAN H. BUIE, M.D.

A discussion of "The Holding Environment and Family Therapy with Acting Out Adolescents," by E. R. Shapiro, M.D. It is presupposed that the central motivation of psychotherapists is to derive a secure holding environment from the patient. The most fundamental need of human beings is the allaying of separation anxiety. As parents use their children to maintain an inner sense of security, the unresponsive child will cause the parent significant depression and anxiety. The parallel of the therapist's and parent's position with the patient/child is explored.

Psychotherapists become psychotherapists out of a need to be sustained, and they look to patients to provide them with a holding environment that sustains them. Other motivations play a part in becoming a psychotherapist, but this one is central. Specifically, the therapist hopes, consciously or unconsciously, to be relieved of his sense of aloneness; prior to his own therapy or analysis he is unable, however, to conceive of the possibility of achieving for himself a comfortable sense of security as an autonomous human being. Instead he implicitly hopes that in meeting his patient's needs his own need for the kind of sustaining togetherness that mitigates depressive aloneness will be fulfilled. Even when his own treatment is successfully completed, he continues to yearn for comforting closeness with his patients, but his yearning is less a need and more simply a wish. Thus therapists remain vulnerable to using their patients this way, but the more mature they become and the more experienced they are, the less pressing is the need or wish, and the more likely it is that they will observe it in perspective before it grows troublesome.

The sicker spectrum of patients, including schizoid, borderline and some narcissistic personalities, are especially vulnerable to aloneness; they require a holding environment that supplies them with sustaining togetherness, e.g., from their parents and their therapist. When they are able (as much of the time they are not) to accept this caring togetherness, the parent or therapist who is allowed to give it experiences the pleasure of participating in the patient's state of peaceful security. The provider (parent or therapist) and the recipient (patient) both partake of the essential quality of the holding dyad, which is a feeling of close, soothing togetherness that allays separation anxiety. For the therapist this is the relief he has always sought. For the parent it is likewise palliative against the depression that was left unhealed by too much abandonment at the hands of his own parents. Both parent and therapist then share in common a need to gain an inner soothing security against their own separation anxiety through participating in a holding environment, which the patient/child makes possible by accepting, with implicit gratitude, the soothing togetherness that they offer him.

Separation anxiety—aloneness—precipitates states of depression and panic of such quality as to threaten subjectively the survival of the self. The most fundamental psychological need of human beings is, therefore, the allaying of separation anxiety, either through use of other persons or through use of one's own developed autonomous resources. When another person is elected to allay one's separation anxiety, failure or threat of failure by that person to do so elicits remarkable aggression and deep hostility. Mary's father (Excerpt I) needed her to accept his love in order that his aloneness might be soothed, but she was unresponsive and rejecting, fighting off his goodnight kisses and not allowing herself to be held. He was threatened with too much aloneness and responded with aggression and anger. His adaptability must be credited for salvaging something for himself and his daughter. He did not reject her in his rage. Instead he turned his aggression and hostility into years of persistence in kissing her goodnight, thus maintaining, probably to the benefit of both of them, a holding environment of sorts.

Inherent in parenthood is the need to use children for maintaining an inner sense of security (as well as worth and hope) and this need persists, silently in fortunate cases, throughout life to some degree. Quite apart from psychopathology, parents could be expected to react to an unresponsive or rejecting baby and child with significant depression and separation anxiety, along with aggression and hostility. If this child at some point becomes a patient, the psychotherapist would need or wish to use him as a resource for security in a similar way and would be vulnerable to reacting to rejection with similar anxiety and anger. The parallel of the therapist's and parents' positions in relation to the patient/child lends itself to direct empathic understanding of the parent's experience with their child. This was evident in the excerpt involving Fred B. and his parents. Although the therapist responded with anger at the abandoning parents, in empathic accord with the patient's anger with them, he also was aware of being angry with Fred for subjecting him to the same kind of rejection that he inflicted on the parents.

The example invites closer attention, which in turn requires speculation in the service of making a general point.

Despite their pathologies and limitations, Fred's parents loved him; although defended against it, with help they could also acknowledge their yearning and hopelessness about his loving them. They had not been able to prepare him for their absences through the years, because to do so would have meant painfully acknowledging that they yearned to be truly important to their son. This acknowledgment would have threatened them with despair and aloneness to whatever extent they believed he did not need them. To the extent they believed that he did need and love them, it would have threatened to precipitate the grief "over what had been lost in past family relationships" that finally came to light in family therapy. They could not have stood this grief outside a therapeutic holding environment. They loved and needed Fred, then, and even though they could not acknowledge it, they needed Fred to love and need them.

Unlike their other children, Fred rejected his parents overtly, not only in the form of obliqueness, indirectness, suspiciousness, and a detached stance toward them, but also by means of the most hateful possible punishment and rejection—repeatedly threatening to deprive them of their child by suicide, on one occasion violently. In the face of their need for him, they must have responded with separation anxiety and murderous rage. The excerpt does not tell us about these feelings in the parents and how they managed them. Undoubtedly they used various defenses to avoid awareness, especially of hating Fred. To what extent did their struggle with these feelings lead to further guilt, helplessness, and incompetence in relating to him? To what extent was their unpredictable cancelling of appointments, about which the father was very defensive, a means both of expressing and avoiding their rage? To what extent was their cancelling an evidence that an adequate holding environment had not been established for them?

The forces of need (e.g., for a closeness with Fred that would quiet his own residual separation anxiety) were operating in the therapist also. He may not have elected Fred to serve that purpose on first meeting. It probably happened slowly as Fred initially responded to the therapist's efforts to engage him in discussions. As Fred allowed himself to be "held" by the therapist, the therapist came to depend somewhat on holding him in order to feel better held himself. Then came relentless behaviors, now directed at the therapist, of the sort that the parents had suffered. Fred once expressed his angry, assaultive rejectingness by putting out a live cigarette on the palm of his hand in front of the therapist. Open rejection was displayed in silences as well as lateness and nonattendance of therapy. The therapist began to feel disconnected, hopeless, and confused, rather like the parents had come to feel.

In this setting Fred's therapist had a dream, " . . . in which he was profoundly identified with Fred and in a rage at the B. parents who had gone off unpredictably leaving him alone." One can guess the ways this dream deepened understanding of Fred's rage with his parents and the parent's rage with Fred. Self-analysis yielded insight into two countertransferences, both traced to the same genetic roots in the therapist's having been too much abandoned by his own parents. One countertransference was expressed in the manifest content: the therapist was enraged with the B. parents. In part this rage derived from empathy with Fred; in part it was the therapist's rage with his own parents displaced onto Fred's. This insight must have enhanced the therapist's understanding of the intensity and quality of Fred's rage, as well as relieved the therapeutic situation of some inappropriate anger toward the B. parents.

The other countertransference was contained altogether in the latent content of the dream and was the more powerful stimulus for the dream. It consisted of rage with Fred for threatening the therapist's sense of security. Fred's rejecting behavior stirred the therapist's repressed feelings and memories about the abandonment by his own parents, which had formed the basis for his ongoing wish to use Fred and other patients to feel secure. This latent content was disguised in the manifest content by using the B. parents to stand, by displacement, for his own parents and also to stand, by displacement, for Fred himself. Rage at his own parents and at Fred could be focused then on the B. parents. Analysis of the dream allowed recognition of countertransference rage with Fred, which in turn, provided the therapist access to better understanding of the B. parents. It became apparent that they must be enraged with Fred for reasons similar to the therapist's, and their need for Fred and rage with him must similarly be based on childhood experiences that resembled the therapist's.

It is important that the therapist analyzed his dream so completely. He discovered that, in order to preserve hope for secure togetherness with Fred, he had been displacing his anger with Fred onto Fred's parents. Without this insight the crucial parallel between his countertransference experience with Fred and the B. parents' experience with their son would have been missed. The parents would have been deprived of empathic and cognitive understanding of their need and rage, and their acting out through abandoning Fred and the treatment would have continued. The therapist's empathic understanding of them, which he undoubtedly shared with the couple's therapist, enabled provision of a more therapeutic holding environment for the parents. This must have alleviated some of their anger and much of their rejecting behavior, diminished their guilt, and helped them to relate more effectively with their son.

CONCLUSION

This is another in a fine series of papers describing Dr. Shapiro's excellent clinical studies of acting out adolescents and their families. The report of clinical work, countertransference, and self-analysis is a courageous one that allows a discussant to engage freely with the material. It provides a context for expressing some opinions about parents, patients, and psychotherapists:

1. Therapists become therapists partly in search for a holding environment that will allay their own separation anxieties.
2. The holding environment that the therapist provides to patients, when it is accepted by patients, serves to hold the therapist as well.
3. The rejecting patient deprives the therapist of holding, thereby precipitating separation anxiety, depression, and rage.
4. Parents similarly have need for a holding environment provided to them by the patient/child's acceptance of their caring, and rejection by the patient/child similarly brings separation anxiety and rage.
5. A natural parallel exists between the countertransference of the therapist and the reaction of parents, and this countertransference is a resource for the empathic understanding of parents that is necessary in order to provide them with a therapeutic holding environment.
6. The therapist, in order to safeguard his dyadic holding environment with the patient from his own reactive hostility, may unconsciously displace his hostility onto the parents; he may then rationalize this defense by declaring it to be a simple empathic response to the patient's rage with his parents because of the rejection he suffers at their hands.
7. Defensive means of avoiding countertransference rage with the patient threaten to undercut the holding environment the therapist could otherwise offer the parents; they also threaten to interfere with the patient's therapy because, to the extent it is kept unconscious, the therapist's hostility with the patient is likely to be expressed in unseen ways.

The Fear of Being Fat and Anorexia Nervosa

C. PHILIP WILSON, M.D.

It was found in the analysis of patients with anorexia nervosa that when they resumed normal weight and began menstruating again, analysis focused on their complex and pathological body image, which was manifested consciously by an intense fear of being fat. Scrutiny of nonanorexic women in analysis showed them to have a less intensely cathected fear of being fat or body-image disturbance, and observation and questioning of normal women in our culture showed many of them to also have this fear. Unconsciously caused by their feminine identification, many male homosexuals and men with severe latent homosexual conflicts were found to have the fear of being fat, in contrast to other men who do not evidence the fear. The fear of being fat is greatly overdetermined, and clinical material is presented to demonstrate that conflicts from evey level of development—pre-Oedipal, Oedipal, adolescent, and adult—are displaced onto and masked by the fear.

A central hypothesis of this paper is that anorexia nervosa symptoms are caused by the ego's attempt to defend itself against an overwhelming terror of being fat, which has been primarily caused by an identification with a parent or parents who have a similar but less intense fear, and that anorexia is secondarily reinforced by what seems to be a general irrational fear of being fat that can be observed in most women in our culture. "Normal" women readily admit to the fear; no matter how "perfect" a woman's figure may be, if she is told she looks fat, she will have an emotional reaction out of all proportion to reality. On the other hand, if you tell her she looks thin or has lost weight, she will usually be inordinately pleased.

The findings in this paper come from the following sources:

1. Twenty-five years of analysis and psychotherapy of anorexia patients and of the parents of anorexic adolescents who were in therapy with colleagues. As is well known, anorexics strive to be thin, are afraid of being

fat, and unless treated effectively go over to phases of obesity. Many have a childhood history of chubbiness or obesity.

2. Many years of supervising the therapy of anorexic patients in private practice and as a member of hospital liaison staffs.
3. The deliberations of the psychosomatic workshop of the Psychological Association of New York, which in recent years has focused on anorexia nervosa.
4. The American Psychoanalytic Association's discussion group on late adolescent girls, led by Dr. Samuel Ritvo (1976b), where the author of this paper presented aspects of the analysis of an anorexic girl (Wilson 1976).
5. The analysis of obese patients and of one patient with an intense fear of being fat who had an impulse disorder (nail biting that dated from early childhood).
6. The analysis of neurotic women with "normal" figures who had a fear of being fat.
7. The analysis of overt and latent homosexual men who evidenced the fear.
8. The fear of being fat was viewed and analyzed partly as a mannerism of speech (Wilson 1968). In addition, other research on stone and sand symbolism (Wilson 1967b, 1980b) pointed to the developmental vicissitudes of oral incorporative conflicts such as those that were etiologic in determining the fear of being fat.

There has been no in-depth psychoanalytic exploration of the fear of being fat. Bruch (1978) observes that the fear of being fat in anorexic girls has many different meanings, among them sensitivity to criticism, fear of growing up, fear of loss of control, and fear of superconformity. However, Bruch does not use the structural hypothesis or the concept of the unconscious in her formulations. Orbach, a social worker, in a recent book for the lay public, *Fat is a Feminist Issue* (1978) mentions some superficial psychological meanings of the fear without giving their deeper psychodynamic causes. Orbach concludes that compulsive eating is an individual protest against the inequality of the sexes, but again does not substantiate her hypothesis with clinical analytic data, her experience being with group therapy.

Intimately related to the fear of being fat is the wish to be thin, which has been noted in anorexics by many researchers, among them Bruch (1973) and M. Sperling (1978). Bruch (1973) observes that "thin fat people" have the same conflicts as obese patients and that millions of young women in our culture are obsessed with being thin. She also notes (1978) that the mothers of anorexics are often overly preoccupied with weight and diet. M. Sperling (1978) emphasizes the etiologic role that parental attitudes about food and dieting play in predisposing a child for the development of anorexic symptoms. However, Sperling does not explore the psychodynamic and genetic meanings of the-fear-of-being-fat body-image disturbance in normal, neurotic, and anorexic women.

CLINICAL MATERIAL

Anxiety and the affects of shame, guilt, humiliation, and fear associated with the fear of being fat in patients are defended against by the ego with the defense of denial, which in certain anorexics can appear to be psychotic in its intensity. As this primitive defense is analyzed, a large variety of conflicts emerge, only some of which can be described here. To protect the anonymity of patients, identifying data has been changed and for the focus of the paper, case material has been condensed. In no instance did the author ask about (i.e., induce) the fear of being fat. The first five cases were patients in analysis for neurotic conflicts. The last eight suffered from anorexia nervosa.

Neurotic Patients

Case 1. A married woman with a mixed neurosis and intermittent depression was 15 pounds overweight and had fears of being fat. At a stage in her analysis when she had made considerable improvement, she reported a fight with her great aunt. The patient's eleven-year-old daughter, dressed in a leotard, was standing on her head to the amused admiration of everyone except the great aunt, who said that Sue, her great neice, was too thin to do such exercises. Mrs. X., the patient, said that Sue was healthy, that exercise was good for one, and that she herself did similar exercises. The great aunt snapped, "You do *that* in a leotard with your figure! You're *too fat* to do that!" The patient, getting angry, said to the great aunt, "You'd do well to do exercise yourself, it would be good for your arthritis." The great aunt rejoined that she got plenty of exercise doing housework. She then asked what size the patient was. The analysand replied that she was size 9, which she felt was good for a woman with her build. The mother-in-law said, "I don't believe it. You must be size 11 or more." The patient asked, "Are you calling me a liar?" The great aunt then weakly apologized, which was received by a hostile silence.

In her associations, the patient said that she and her daughter had exhibited their genitals by standing on their heads dressed in leotards and that her great aunt expressed moral disapproval, telling her that she was too fat and her daughter too thin. The patient thought her great aunt was jealous; she was always trying on new clothes that the patient bought. Angrily, the patient reflected that the great aunt never did anything pleasurable like calisthenics or tennis. All she ever did was housework, which was tiresome. The patient laughed at how hypocritical women were; all they talked about was dieting, instead of admitting to wishes to be sexy and beautiful. Here one can see that sexual conflicts and moral disapproval are displaced onto the fear-of-being-fat quarrel.

Case 2. Some of the psychodynamic meanings of the fear of being fat are illustrated in the case of a compulsive married man with intense latent homosexual conflicts who sought analysis to help him resolve marital conflicts. Deprived of his father, who was killed in a car accident when the patient was six years old, he had grown up dominated by his mother, a teacher, who was overweight, addicted to cigarettes, and preoccupied with fears of being fat and diets. He was becoming aware in analysis that he was as controlling and disapproving with his wife and children as his Bible-quoting, hypermoral mother had been with him. He was very proud of his "figure," keeping his weight by diet and exercise at exactly 150 pounds.

The day before the following session his wife had burst a seam in her dress and he had told her it was because she was too fat. In his session he said his wife was still angry from his criticism. He felt his concern with her weight was unreasonable, that she was only ten pounds overweight and sexier now than when she was thinner. However, he feared she would not get as many modelling jobs unless she dieted. He realized his fat comment was "bitchy"; that ninety-nine out of a hundred women would be upset if you told them they looked fat. He realized he would have to watch his tongue, which was as mean as his mother's. Displaced onto the fear of being fat were heterosexual and latent homosexual conflicts; this fear of being fat reflected his identification with his mother.

Case 3. Anal components of the fear of being fat are graphically illustrated by the pantaloon dream of a divorced woman in analysis for a compulsive neurosis. It occurred when she was in the process of analyzing her intense, irrational fear of being fat. In her dream she had no fresh clothes for her six-year-old daughter to wear. Hung up to dry on a clothes line were frilly pink pantaloons that her daughter had dirtied. In the dream the patient was confused with her daughter. There was also a classroom she felt lacked a teaching structure. There was an outspoken woman from the Bronx in the dream.

In her associations, the patient said that she was proud of her legs, but was ashamed of her hips and thighs, which she felt were fat. The lumpy flesh on her thighs reminded her of indulgence and of lumps of feces. She knew that Titian and Rubens painted voluptuous women whose figures were like hers. The previous day she had purchased a sexy leotard, cut high on the buttocks, at a lingerie store that sold "beautifully made pants and bikinis." Asked why she said "pants," she said that the word panty was sexy and exciting and she feared being embarrassed. She was afraid the analyst and her husband would be disgusted with her if she wore her leotard. An interpretation was made that she felt it was dirty to exhibit her hips and buttocks, which are hidden in the dream by pink pantaloons, that she had conflicts about asserting herself as a woman and wanted to hide behind a front of being an innocent little girl. The patient confirmed the interpretation in a recollection of being on a beach on her honeymoon wearing a bikini. A man had stared at her and she had been afraid she looked fat. She realized now from the man's behavior that he had been admiring her sexy figure. Further associations were to childhood confusion about her mother's vagina and anus; that the area was dirty and mysterious like a cloaca and that her adult figure was like her mother's, who also had a fear of being fat and anxieties about her "lumpy" thighs. Here displaced onto the fear of being fat are anal conflicts.

Case 4. A married businesswoman came to analysis for sexual conflicts and phobias of airplanes, elevators, and subways. A dietician, she was obsessed with weight and dieting and fantasies of being young and beautiful. She kept her figure zealously on the thin side, ten pounds under normal. Her mother had been chronically 15 pounds overweight, whereas her father was obsessed with dieting and weight control. This patient, in associating to the scales that she weighed herself on daily, referred to them as her conscience and the law of her father. With the analysis of the transference neurosis in the context of a strong therapeutic alliance, her severe phobic symptoms subsided, but she reported that her 12-year-old daughter was amenorrheic and had symptoms of anorexia. The analysis of the mother's fear of being fat revealed many conflicts, a most important one being her inability to tolerate any aggression in her daughter. Associations to fat led to a memory of her father telling her that she had a "fat lip" as a girl, that he used to slap her for "sassing him." By the defense of identification with the aggressor she was repeating the same harsh discipline with her daughter. All roundings of the female body, breasts, buttocks, or a "tummy" in herself or her daughter repelled her. As these and other conflicts that had been displaced onto the fear of being fat were analyzed and the mother could accept her own as well as her daughter's feminity, the latter's anorexic symptoms cleared.

Case 5. A narcissistic 25-year-old female patient in analysis for a severe character disorder complained of obesity and nail biting that dated from the time of weaning. Her mother had developed a progressively more incapacitating mental illness culminating in suicide when the patient was ten years old. The mother was of little use to the patient, who described her as always "moping around the house"; the father, maids, and two aunts brought the child up. As the patient interrupted her intense nail biting during analytic sessions, fantasies of a breast and nipple and affects of depression, anger, and wishes for maternal love and tenderness emerged in the transference. The patient had an intense fear of being fat out of proportion to her weight, which at most was 15 pounds above normal. She often woke up at night in panic states, which she relieved by drinking a mixture she concocted of milk and sugar that she realized was like mother's milk. She was aware that she kept herself overweight to avoid being sexy, which made her anxious. Displaced onto her fear of being fat were her fears of her oral impulses, nail biting and overeating, and her shame at the regressive affects and fantasies masked by these oral habits.

Anorexic Cases

Case 6. An anorexic patient came to her session angry. She was at a stage in analysis when she had gained 20 pounds and was expressing wishes to get her periods again, to master her sexual fears, and to get pregnant. She said that she had gone to a cocktail party wearing a revealing dress to show off her "new" figure. The hostess exclaimed, "Why Jane, you've gained 50 pounds!" In telling this, the patient burst into tears of rage saying, "She is so smug. She has two beautiful children. Her whole life she has been made to feel loved. She has everything. How could she say anything like that!" Actually the changes in the patient were startling. Her figure was beginning to be voluptuous. The hostess' hostile and envious comment triggered a dream of a fluffy puppy. Associating to this dream, the patient thought that she wanted to have a puppy because she was afraid of childbirth. She realized that her feelings about her hostess were like those that she had had about her mother, whom she idealized as a little girl. Mother had everything—a husband, children, a beautiful home and everyone's love. The patient recalled that when she was five years old, their collie had two puppies and a baby was born next door. She recovered repressed memories of being frightened seeing Mother's and Grandmother's genitals in the bathroom and thinking they had been mutilated by childbirth. She knew that she had denied the female genitals down below and by displacement up replaced the fear-provoking birth process with fantasies of oral impregnation and birth.

The patient's Oedipal incestuous rivalry with her mother was repeated by her anger with her hostess. Her anorexic gorging had expressed fantasies of oral impregnation, and her vomiting a giving birth. Her fear of being fat masked fears of being voluptuous and sexy, which could cause her to be impregnated, which to her meant vaginal mutilation. The hostess' comment about her gaining 50 pounds seemed to contain the critical idea that the patient had lost all control of herself and/or that she might be pregnant. The patient did look beautiful, voluptuous, and feminine, which was in sharp contrast to her previous anorexic figure. Sexual conflicts and loss of impulse control are displaced onto the fear of being fat in this material.

Case 7. The wish to be ethereal is routinely hidden by the fear of being fat in anorexics. This is expressed graphically by an anorexic married woman's dream: a doctor gave her a pill, and then she was in a garden with Mrs. St. Clair and a plain-looking girl wearing a sun bonnet. In her associations, the patient thought that she was jealous of Mrs. St. Clair, who is a wealthy, beautiful, divorced, jet-set woman whose teenage daughter is a mess, unorganized, and inhibited. She has large doe-like eyes. In the dream, only the girl's face could be seen, no body. Not having a body reminded the patient of wanting to be a beautiful ethereal child, of having no body, no fat, that she herself in childhood had studied ballet. The bonnet reminded her that she wanted to buy a winter hat. The child made her think that her husband would go "bananas" about a baby, but that she would be jealous of a baby if she had one. The pill made her think of the therapist giving her a magical cure, of an oral impregnation. As a child she used to want a pill that would give her complete knowledge of everything. The night before the patient had avoided intercourse; pregnancy she prevented by her anorexic amenorrhea. She kept her figure at around 90 pounds, although her normal weight was 120 pounds. People often asked her if she was a dancer, as she had a gliding, graceful, lighter-than-air manner of walking. Once when crying silently, she got up from the couch and took a kleenex from a box on a table by the analytic chair and resumed her position on the couch in such a swift, graceful, synchronous silent fashion that if the therapist had not been looking at her, he would not have noticed her and even seeing her, it was as if it did not happen. She was ethereal.

The dream wish was to divorce her husband and become a wealthy, beautiful, pleasure-loving princess who could have a magical oral pregnancy. Among the other meanings of the dream were the wish to be the doe-like innocent child and to have no fleshly desires, no body, no fat—to be ethereal.

Case 8. The opposite of the wish to be ethereal is expressed by the dream of another anorexic woman. In the dream she was looking at her mother-in-law, who was dressed in a brassiere and panties. Someone referred to her as a "fat pig." Her associations were that her mother-in-law was a sensual woman. The looking aspect of the dream reminded her of being fascinated at five years of age watching her mother dress and undress. A new baby had been born next door whom she adored, but it had been unclear to her how pregnancy or birth occurred. She felt that the "fat pig" represented her terror of losing all controls, and particularly her fear of multiple pregnancies, of being blown up fat by pregnancy.

This patient was another anorexic who gorged and vomited, and she had long since realized that she was trying to get a magical pregnancy in her eating, that her full belly was a pregnancy and that her vomiting was a giving-birth fantasy. There were many other meanings to this dream, an important one being the childhood idea that women had periodic seizures of uncontrollable sexual arousal like animals. Here one can observe two conflicts masked by the fear of being fat: a fear of losing all controls and a fear of a disfiguring multiple-birth pregnancy.

Case 9. The mechanism of displacement from below up to the mouth in the fear of being fat is graphically reflected in the following dream of an anorexic: "I started my periods but realized that the red color was not from the vagina but came from a red lollipop I had eaten." The previous night the patient had been depressed and wished she could get her periods back. In her association she recalled at six years of age finding wrapped, stained menstrual pads in the wastebasket and asking her mother about them. She thought they had something to do with her older brother, who had been sick. Her mother replied that she'd have to tell her older sisters to be more careful, but did not explain menstruation. She then thought of having had heavy menstrual flow in adolescence and not seeing a doctor until she was dangerously anemic.

Interpretations were made of her intense denial of fears about menstruation, which to her meant bleeding to death and castration. She noted that she loved to eat cherry candies, which are red. A dream wish was that the periods were caused by something she ate. She was beginning to understand that her denial derived from her mother's denial. At this stage of her analysis, her fear of being fat was less intense, she wanted her menses and was gaining weight. She was beginning to be aware that an aspect of her fear of being fat was her fear of menstruating.

Case 10. Another pre-Oedipal fantasy masked by the fear of being fat is that of the breast penis, which is illustrated by the dream of an anorexic analysand. In the dream, the patient's boyfriend was trying to make love to her. She was turned on, but his penis turned into a celery stalk. It was a long green thing; there were no testicles. He was lying next to her making love, then his penis went down. This dream occurred at a point in her analysis when the patient was trying to spend time on her own without clinging to her boyfriend or to food, which she substituted for him. The previous night she had returned home late from an art class to find that her boyfriend was still at his office working. Although hungry, she waited to eat dinner until he returned, and was playing the piano when he came home. Although she had intended to have intercourse, she picked a fight with him and they went to bed angry. Other associations were to "freezing" when doctors examined her as a child and when her clitoris was touched. The celery stalk reminded her of the penis of a horse, which she had seen mounting a mare when she was 6 years old. She knew it was sexual but was not clear as to what they were doing, what the sexual organs were, or whether the vagina or anus was entered.

The interpretation was made of her fear of mutilation as a child by a tremendous phallus that would enter her *a tergo* as she had witnessed with the horses, and that she covered this fear with the wish that the penis was something to be eaten. Quite literally, as the patient was trying to stop relating to her boyfriend as if he were a female with a phallus, she dreamt of the breast phallus (the penis turning into celery). Parenthetically, the present author has found, as in research with stone (Wilson 1967b) and umbrella symbolism (Wilson 1967a), that when a patient dreams of a penis-like object that does not include testicular-like representations, the regression is to 18-to-30-month-old developmental levels, to a time before the child's ego can conceptualize the functions of the penis and testicles or the vagina, tubes, and uterus. The fantasies are oral and anal. This is the early phallic phase described by Galenson and Roiphe (1976).

Case 11. An anorexic had a nightmare in which a big penis was being thrust down on her face. Her associations were to her father having the money and controlling her mother, that everyone had to go to him for everything, that she hated him and hated to take money from him. Her fantasy had been that her mother did not love her father but was forced to have sex with him to please him and for the sake of the children, i.e., mother had to "suck father off."

This patient avoided intercourse, which was a pleasure (something fat) that her strict conscience forbade her. She had sex to please her husband, often avoiding intercourse by fellating him. However, fellatio disgusted and frightened her, as it revived repressed incestuous fantasies about her father's and brother's genitals, which she had frequently seen as a child, particularly in the bathroom where there was no privacy. The forbidden oral sucking fantasies asssociated to fellatio are repressed into the fear of being fat.

As Grossman and Stewart (1976) point out in discussing penis envy, "the meaning of the discovery of the 'anatomical distinction' will depend upon a complex variety of preparatory experiences. . . . the child's cognitive and libidinal levels will naturally play a part in his interpretation of this new information . . . to narcissistically oriented patients, 'penislessness' can at any time in the psychosexual development become a prime example of deprivation, and they experience this in the same way as when they were 18 months old."

Analysis revealed that this patient, like other anorexics, had a body-phallus equation. She said that she knew she was vain and proud of her thin figure, straight back, and small waist. She did many exercises to keep in perfect shape. Anorexia ablated her breasts, hips, and buttocks. The analysis of dreams in which she beat up her husband uncovered an identification with her father, who frequently exhibited his genitals, walking around the house in boxer shorts and swimming in the nude, in contrast to the mother who had been very modest. Extending M. Sperling's (1978) finding that the anorexic sees father as a rival for mother's love, the present author's research shows that the anorexic envies and desires father's body and magical phallus, which will gain her mother's love. In the female unconscious, fat equals feminine, thin equals male, so the wish to be thin and the fear of being fat mask conflicts about penis envy.

Case 12. Pre-Oedipal and Oedipal fantasies about the penis were condensed in an anorexic's dream of a great serpent slithering down a flight of stairs. The patient had had intercourse the night before, with her husband on top. She preferred the superior position herself, as it gave her control. This woman was at a stage in her analysis where her anorexic symptoms had been resolved but she was still amenorrheic. Her associations were to her husband being a snake in the grass as he went out to play poker; that men, her father, the analyst, had everything and got away with everything; women had to stay in the home. She thought of how proud she had become of her new figure, that she could do all sorts of tricks with her body in intercourse. For example, when she was on top, she could writhe with her body and drive her husband wild. She said it was as if her body could be a snake. She thought of a pet snake she had as a child. The patient had not been orgastic and did not communicate with her husband during intercourse.

The dream was precipitated by her letting her husband be on top in intercourse, which allowed him to be the "writhing snake." This aroused castration fear and provoked pre-Oedipal and Oedipal penis envy and body-phallus fantasies of being the snake herself. This patient had studied and loved ballet as a child, as was the case in many of the anorexics analyzed. One anorexic whose therapy was supervised by the present author was a professional ballerina. All anorexics are very conscious of their figures and constantly exercise, work out at health clubs, and engage in strenuous athletics. These pseudosublimations reflect their body-phallus conflicts. Similar but less intensely cathected preoccupations with the figure, weight, and exercise are the obsessive concern of women in our culture with the fear of being fat.

DISCUSSION

Conflicts Displaced onto the Fear of Being Fat

In the neurotic patients, conflicts that are displaced onto the fear of being fat include: sexual exhibitionism and moral disapproval (case 1); heterosexual and homosexual conflicts, a feminine identification and fears of female sexuality (case 2); anal phase conflicts and a cloacal fantasy confusing the anus with the vagina (case 3); a mother's fear of her own and her daughter's sexuality and fear of the daugther's aggression (case 4); and fears of oral impulses, of nail biting, and of concommitant regressive affects and fantasies, as well as fear of sexual conflicts (case 5).

In the anorexic cases, one sees displacements of sexual conflicts and loss of impulse control (case 6); the fantasy of being ethereal, of having no body, no fat, and of being an innocent child (case 7); fears of total loss of impulse control, of a disfiguring multiple-birth pregnancy (case 8); fears of oral regression, of bleeding to death from menstruating (case 9); fantasies of a breast phallus and castrating fantasies (case 10); and fellatio conflicts and penis envy (cases 11, 12, and 13).

In summary, one can see that in the neurotic cases displaced onto the fear of fat are sexual conflicts, fears of oral and anal impulses, fears of regression, and a superego prohibition against facing these conflicts. Similar but more intense pre-Oedipal and Oedipal conflicts are displaced onto the fear of being fat in the anorexic cases. Conflicts from every developmental phase can be repressed and displaced onto the fear.

Friedman (1978), in discussing this paper, cited a novel, *Final Payments,* by Ruth Gordon (1978), in which a woman has incestuous conflicts about exhibiting her breasts to her father; in self-punishment she destroys the beauty of her breasts by overeating, eventually becoming depressed and bulimic. Friedman's confirmatory case material included a woman who at 9 years fellated a 12-year-old boyfriend who ejaculated in her mouth. She fantasied that the seeds remained inside her and in adolescence awaited every period with the anxiety that she might be pregnant. Her weight shifted radically. Her fear of being fat concealed a wish to become pregnant by her brother, and she made herself sexually unattractive by excess body fat.

Another patient was convinced that a weight of 129 pounds meant being female, while 131 meant being male, the extra fat concealing a fantasied penis. The masturbation fantasy of a woman analysand was that she was in a Nazi brothel where the soldiers only liked fat women so that all sorts of tempting foods were made available. To eat and become fat meant to be sexually out of control, a prostitute. Mintz (1978) noted an anorexic for whom the folds of fatty flesh in the inner aspect of her thighs symbolized a penis. She starved herself to get rid of her conflict. M. Sperling (1978) and Goiten (1942) noted that anorexia nervosa can defend against prostitute fantasies and wishes. One anorexic whose therapy the present author supervised, worked as a prostitute when she was bulimic; when fasting, she withdrew from people (men) in a self-imposed punishment. Likewise, in a nonanorexic woman, sexual fantasies and conflicts can be avoided or gratified depending upon the amount of weight the patient wants to gain.

As the clinical cases show, the fear of being fat masks fears of loss of impulse control. Control is a central symptom in anorexia, as M. Sperling (1978) and Bruch (1978) have also noted. Diagnostically, anorexia nervosa is a symptom complex that is found in patients with a wide variety of pregenitally fixated character disorders (M. Sperling 1978). Associated difficulties with impulse control are frequent: thumbsucking, phases of obesity, head banging, nail biting, nose picking, enuresis, and addictions to cigarettes, marijuana, alcohol, and other drugs. The persistent use of dangerously large amounts of laxatives occurs in certain patients. Other cases give a history of neurotic childhood vomiting, encopresis, anal masturbation and hair-pulling, and eating. In certain cases the abovementioned habits are not present; instead one finds excessive good behavior interrupted by isolated episodes of loss of impulse control. As with other psychosomatic disorders (M. Sperling 1968, Wilson 1968b), when anorexic symptoms subside in treatment, acting out is a problem. Displaced onto the fear of being fat are these fears of acting out.

As illustrated in Case 2, the fear of being fat covers anal phase conflicts. Kaplan (1976) feels that there is a greater tendency toward oral and tactile contact in latency girls than in boys. Ritvo (1976a) attributes the probably universal feminine attitude of concealment, not only the menarche but sexual feelings and fantasies of all kinds, to the more powerful degree of repression of pregenital and particularly of anal strivings in the girl than in the boy. An unconscious purpose of anorexic self-starvation is to repress any manifestation of anal impulses. Sours (1974) noted the analization of the ego (Sandler and Jaffe 1965) in the more seriously disturbed group of anorexia nervosa patients. In the present author's experience, such patients, by their anorexic constipation, try to stop having bowel movements; when they become thin enough, they stop perspiring, which for them means to smell. Their amenorrhea eliminates the menses, which they unconsciously confuse with excretory anal processes.

The fear of being fat in general hides a fear of regression in the female. Anorexics in particular are stoically proud. Although showing by their emaciation an appeal for sympathy, pity, and feeding, they vehemently deny any such emotions and wishes. It is an advance in analysis when they admit to these feelings, in contrast to neurotics, who openly say, "I am guilty, half the time I behave like a baby." The fear of being fat is a denial of neurotic and normal dependency needs.

Superego and Ego Ideal

Blum (1976) concludes that the female ego and superego are different from but not inferior to the male. Analysis of the fear of being fat shows that an important aspect of this difference is caused by the demands of the woman's maternal ego ideal, which confronts the feminine ego with a longer and more complex maturational process than is the case in males. Blum's conclusion that "conflicts between the maternal ego ideal and infanticidal impulses are ubiquitous" may be extended to include conflicts about homicidal impulses toward all objects. Freud's observation that the female has the more difficult task of changing her object choice from mother to father to a lover are also borne out by this research.

In the extreme of the fear of being fat, anorexia nervosa, one sees a harsh, punitive superego. As Ritvo (1976a) and the present author emphasize (Wilson 1976), in anorexia nervosa the rage with the mother initially rooted in repressed oral sadomasochistic conflicts has been externalized and displaced onto food. Because the parents of anorexics are overly conscientious people with strict superegos, they legislate against the expression of emotion in their children (Bruch 1978, Minuchin 1978, M. Sperling 1978, Wilson 1980a). There has been a failure to internalize a good object representation of the mother and of the self. It is the introjected bad mother (Wilson 1978), and by extension other objects, whom anorexics try to starve in their fasting or incorporate in their gorging. One anorexic expressed it graphically in a parapraxis. She intended to say that when she visited her polio-crippled older sister she ate a normal meal; what she said was that "she ate her sister." In her association, she said that when she gorges she gets rid of her sister (and other objects, including the analyst).

The reason that the most frequent time of onset of anorexia is adolescence is because this phase demands final separation and individuation. The anorexic-prone girl develops too strict a superego. As M. Sperling (1978) points out, there is a shift from a positive to a negative Oedipus in the girl along with a regression. This regression is not just to pre-Oedipal levels of functioning as emphasized by M. Sperling, but to preadolescent latency levels of functioning and fantasy. It is in adolescence that one sees the symptoms of anorexia most frequently.

Many years of experience in the analysis of patients suffering from symptoms of anorexia nervosa, as well as in the analysis and psychotherapy of the parents of anorexics, has shown the present author that the predisposition to develop anorexia is established in the mother–child relationship in the earliest years of life (Wilson 1971, 1980; Sperling, 1978). Food is used by the mother to control. A graphic example was an anorexic's mother who cooked dinner for her professor husband at 5:30 because he had an evening lecture, another meal for her anorexic daughter at 6:00, and a third for her son who came home from work at 7:30. The mother, herself a business executive, ate on the run, so to speak. This mother controlled feeding so much that her children had never learned to cook.

BODY IMAGE

The fear of being fat is a conscious manifestation of unconscious body image conflicts. Freud (1923) stated that the ego is first and foremost a body ego and is itself the projection of a surface. In the terror of being fat (anorexia), the basic conflict is rooted in a massive pre-Oedipal repression of sadomasochistic oral-phase conflicts that have been elaborated by the ego with new defensive structures at each subsequent libidinal and maturational phase of development. It is the surface of the mother's breast, and by extension her figure, that has been projected in the anorexic's body image. The fear of being fat reflects the terror of oral sadistic incorporation of the breast, of mother and later of other objects. The analysis of nonanorexic patients showed that less intensely cathected psychodynamics also determine the nonanorexic woman's fear of being fat. The average expectable environment of a female in our culture offers the fear of being fat as a normative value that secondarily reinforces the developing girl's body-image conflicts. The intensity and irrationality of the fear of being fat points to its primitive ontogenetic source, and analysis reveals that the fantasies and repressed impulses that underlie the fear of being fat derive their configuration and impetus from the primary process. A graphic example is the anorexic's ambivalent all-or-nothing fear of being totally fat or totally thin, which can result in psychosomatic suicide by starvation.

As Freud (1923) emphasized, the perception of pain is of importance for the development of a normal body image. Because of the mother's psychopathology, the anorexia-prone child has been overindulged and suffers from an impulse disorder so that the ego does not develop sufficient capacity to delay on impulse gratification. The mother's oral conflicts disturb the important role of the mouth and hand (Hoffer 1950) in differentiating between the self and nonself. Pre-Oedipal and Oedipal primal-scene experiences and other overstimulating parent–child sensory interactions whose significance is completely denied severely distort the significant role of visual perception of the face and genitals (Greenacre 1958) in the development of a normal body image. The strict superego of the mother and/or father limits and warps normal autoerotic and playful body investigations, which build up early self and object representations (Jacobson 1946) and differentiation between self and non-self (Fenichel 1945). The parents' need to retain their child as an infantile object and their need to control prevent normal separation-individuation. The parents' intolerance of aggressive and libidinal drive manifestations also prevents normal separation-individuation in the anal phase. The histories of the present author's cases correlate with and confirm Sours' (1974) observations that details are lacking about Mahler's (1972) 16-to-25-month rapprochement phase.

The pre-Oedipal component of the body-phallus identification is the most important, as one does not frequently observe overt homosexuality in the life histories of anorexics; nor when the anorexic symptom complex is anlayzed do they go over to a phase of overt homosexuality. For nonanorexic women, parallel but less intensely cathected developmental body-image conflicts underlie the fear of being fat. Pre-Oedipal penis envy and pre-Oedipal pregnancy fears, as well as the maternal ego ideal, are particularly important factors in the formation of the fear-of-being-fat body-image disturbance.

The fear of being fat is an aspect of concealment in women because it is related to or part of the defense of denial that is so intense in anorexics, but is also characteristic of females compared to males. In the author's opinion it is caused by the different superego structure in women. As Ritvo (1976b) says, "Concealment particularly of masturbation fantasies and activities is more pronounced in the analysis of women than in the analysis of men" (p. 130). He attributes this to the girl's more powerful repression of pregenital strivings, particularly the anal strivings, starting in the pre-Oedipal period and extending all through childhood. He connects concealment and secretiveness to the narcissistic hurt of penis envy and feels the absence of a penis is a focal point for the greater feelings of inferiority and shame in the female. The technique of analysis of anorexics proceeds from the defense of denial to the fear of being fat and then to concealment and secretiveness.

The female's obsession with being beautiful and young and her conflict about her age is related to concealment: the more stringent biological timetable that the female must face is a contributing factor. The denial of time and aging in anorexia is startling, but there are comparable conflicts in most women and in men with latent or overt homosexual conflicts. Because of her narcissistic investment in looking young and beautiful, a woman executive, for instance, avoided pointing out to subordinates, when necessary, that she had 20 years of business experience.

The female body-image conflicts manifested in the fear of being fat are particularly heightened during adolescence, which recapitulates the conflicts of earlier phases of development with the added libidinal and aggressive manifestations of puberty. Anorexia most frequently develops in this phase because of the parental intolerance of adolescent aggressive and libidinal drive expression. The more complicated physical and emotional changes that the developing female must pass through (Freud 1932, Blum 1976), the stringent pressures exerted on the ego by the maternal ego ideal, greater dependency needs, and pre-Oedipal penis envy are factors that seem to cause the universal fear of being fat.

To the therapist's surprise, one finds that anorexics are often admired and envied by their female friends, who unconsciously have a similar but less intensely cathected body-image conflict. Every female in her development shares aspects of this body image and the fantasy of being thin. Thus at all maturational phases the developing girl has potential secondary identifications with women who have the fear of being fat. The fear of being fat is part of the average expectable female environment.

SOCIAL AND CULTURAL FACTORS

Another factor in the apparent increase in the fear of being fat and anorexia nervosa in our culture is the breakdown of established societal institutions and attitudes that have afforded the female definite paths for identity formation, impulse control, and sublimation. Faced with complete freedom on leaving home or going to college, the anorexia-prone girl has no choice but to regress and starve herself. This social anomie is a precipitating but not a root cause of anorexia. These cultural and societal changes have resulted in much earlier puberty for the female, with ensuing conflict. The fear of being fat in general reflects the fear of loss of impulse control.

In recent decades there have been cultural factors pressuring women to overvalue thinness and weight loss. O. Sperling (1978), in a discussion of this paper, suggested that in Victorian times women, and particularly young pregnant women, were encouraged to eat because of the fear of tuberculosis for which there was no cure, which may have contributed to the cultural acceptance of a full voluptuous female figure. The advance of medical research, which has emphasized the dangers of obesity in relation to disease, particularly hypertension and coronary artery pathology, has resulted in the proliferation of a multitude of diets. The greater participation of women in athletics of all kinds also sets a premium on a thin figure. In its extreme this has even led to attempts to masculinize the female figure by hormone treatment for superior athletic performance.

Female fashion has been another cultural force. *Vogue* and other women's magazines emphasize the thin figure, and careful scrutiny of some models shows them to have anorexic figures. One anorexic seen by the present author was a model; another was in the fashion business, and she commented on the number of anorexics in the field. Still another anorexic woman operated an exercise facility that was predominantly used by anorectic women. A pertinent comment was made by a doctor who resigned his job at what he called "a fat farm" in Florida, i.e., a resort health spa. He said there was no point in his work because the women were in two groups; the obese females who weighed 250 pounds and lost 10 pounds only to put it on again, and a second group who weighed 100 to 110 pounds who came to lose 5 pounds. This latter group were, he said, obsessed with a fear of being fat and actually did not have to lose weight at all.

Another important cultural factor is the changing value that society gives to motherhood. As Ritvo (1976b) points out, "In a time when a woman's fertility and childbearing functions had high economic value her prestige and worth depended very much on her fertility . . . instead children are an economic burden" (pp. 136–137). Ritvo (1976) emphasized that the age of menarche and of beginning sexual relations has been progressively lowered in girls. Jawetz (1976) notes that this change gives girls less time to resolve older conflicts before having to deal with problems of emotional and sexual intimacy, a situation to which she attributes the current increase in bulimic and anorexic eating disturbances. Jawetz (1976) feels that the marked preponderance of eating disturbances in adolescent girls rather than boys points to a difference in their psychosexual development, which for the girl involves a type of incorporation that is now genital (vaginal) but that may revive an earlier unresolved oral conflict. Jawetz (1976) also feels that the female's greater need of mothering, society's encouragement that she compete with men, various environmental changes, such as the loss of objective standards of conduct and the opening up of many different life choices, all confront the adolescent girl with difficult maturational problems from which many retreat by way of eating disorder symptoms. It may be that the fear of being fat in our culture masks a basic conflict in women between their biological drive toward motherhood and its diminished societal value.

Lowenfeld and Lowenfeld (1972) observe that where the environment has become more permissive, the symptoms of hysteria have been replaced by a multitude of character neuroses and psychosomatic manifestations. The increased incidence of anorexia nervosa confirms their hypothesis; as it is most often when the adolescent girl leaves the safety of home for the liberated atmosphere of camp or college that she becomes anorexic.

In the analysis of women it is important that their egos face and integrate the emotions and fantasies that are subsumed under the term 'bitch': this is particularly difficult in anorexic females. Here a double standard still prevails; people refer with admiration to a man being 'a son of a bitch' or a 'bastard'. In reference to a man's aggressive narcissistic achievements one may say with grudging admiration, "what a shit he is." There is a more ambivalent attitude toward comparable behavior in women.

The fear-of-being-fat body-image conflict masks a fear of identifying with the bitch mother, which was reflected in the anorexic's dream of the fat pig. Displaced onto and hidden by the fear of being fat are the female's normal and neurotic fantasies of being spiritually and morally beautiful and of being physically, sexually exciting and beautiful. In anorexics, these fantasies are vehemently denied. This was highlighted by the anorexic's dream of being ethereal. In the post-Oedipal model behavior of anorexia-prone girls, one can see the manifestation of these fantasies. Similar but less intensely cathected fantasies underlie the fear of being fat in women in general.

Successful analysis results in a basic change in the female's fear of being fat and her body image. Bruch (1973), although utilizing a different technique of treatment, emphasizes that "a realistic body image concept is a precondition for recovery in anorexia nervosa" (p. 90). This change is most dramatic in anorexics. Dreams of being fat or thin don't usually appear until the later stages of analysis. The self-observing function of the ego is markedly strengthened in analysis. With nonanorexic women the rigidity and persistence of their need to have a thin figure, even though they may have a husband or lover who likes them just the way they are and with whom they are orgastic, is remarkable. In fact, it appears that the body-image conflict expressed in the fear of being fat cannot be changed in women in our culture except by analysis.

The change in the body image of anorexics in analysis is a gradual process, and the total analytic process brings it about. The crucial factor is the transference neurosis, where the analyst modifies the superego and strengthens the ego with a concomitant development of the self-observing functions of the ego.

PARENTAL CONFLICTS AND FAMILIAL INTERACTIONS THAT DETERMINE SYMPTOM CHOICE

Anorexia nervosa and obesity are abnormal manifestations of certain basic conflicts that every woman and certain men with unresolved identifications encounter in their development. M. Sperling (1978) observes that some of the parents of her anorexic patients were latent anorexics (pp. 161–162), citing as an example a mother who when her anorexic daughter began to eat, went on a diet and became anorexic herself. Moreover Sperling had already amply documented her hypothesis that the mother and/or father, by their attitudes towards food and their unconscious conflicts, predisposed their daughter for the development of anorexia (1970, 1978). The present author's experience with adolescent and adult anorexics and their parents further confirms Sperling's findings, as the case of the beautician (Case 4) who induced her daughter's anorexia exemplifies. However, Case 3, the pantaloon-dream compulsive, demonstrates that nonanorexic women have fears of being fat that defend against similar but less intensely cathected conflicts to those found in anorexics, and that these conflicts are found to be manifestations of an identification with a parent who had the same fear-of-being-fat conflicts. A third observation, that the female friends of anorexics often envied the anorexic's thin figure and shared their preoccupations with food and dieting, leads to the hypothesis that most women in our culture have varying degrees of the fear-of-being-fat symptom complex.

Leaving aside genetic and constitutional research (Freedman et al. 1976), which in eating disorders is not conclusive, the solution to the question of why one child develops anorexia and the other obesity is to be found in the study of the parent–child relationship. The present author gathered together the research of the members of the psychosomatic study group of the Psychoanalytic Association of New York, Inc. (Wilson 1979b), which showed that in 30 families of anorexics, there was a psychological profile that appears to have been etiologic in establishing in early childhood a personality disorder that manifested itself later in the symptoms of anorexia nervosa. Four of the components of this profile—(1) overconcern with dieting and fears of being fat, (2) overconscientious perfectionism, (3) repression of emotions, and (4) infantilizing decision-making for the anorexic child—correlate with attitudes and behavior described by Bruch (1978) and Minuchin (1978) in their descriptions of over 100 anorexic families. The last two features of the profile—5) sexual and toilet exhibitionism whose significance is completely denied, and 6) the unconscious selection of a child to develop anorexia because of parental conflicts—are usually uncovered only be psychoanalysis.

The last five features of the profile have been described by M. Sperling (1978) and the present author (Wilson 1968b, 1971, 1980a) in other psychosomatic cases: parental overconcern with food, diets and the intense fear of being fat are etiologically specific in the choice of the mouth, the digestive system, and the eating process for the development of anorexia nervosa. These findings relate to M. Sperling's (1978) hypothesis that specific fantasies and conflicts of the parents, particularly the mother, determine the choice of the organ system for the development of a psychosomatic symptom. Strictly speaking, anorexia nervosa is not a true psychosomatic symptom complex (M. Sperling 1978), but the mechanism of organ choice for symptom development parallels that seen in true psychosomatic disease such as colitis or asthma. Of course, a psychological profile study unless based on psychoanalytic methods will not explain why one child in a family develops anorexia nervosa and another obesity.

The present author's experience confirms M. Sperling's (1978) concept that one child is "unconsciously chosen" by the parents (pp. 27, 28). There may be:

1. The carry-over of an unresolved emotional conflict from childhood, and acting-out of this conflict with their child (the child may represent an unconsciously hated sibling or parent);
2. The projection of part of the mother's own person onto the child;
3. A need for control over the child, so intense that in some of these cases the child is regarded and treated as if it were a part of the mother's own body (a phenomenon described by O. Sperling [1944] as *appersonation*);
4. The psychic situation of the mother and/or father at the time of the child's birth and early years can also influence "the choice of the child" (e.g., the child may be clung to because it is the last baby or it may be taken as an unconscious libidinal object because of the death of the husband or the loss of the spouse by divorce).

Anorexic patients can be divided into the abstainers and the bulimics (the bulimarexics). Whereas the abstaining anorexic's ego has rigid impulse control, the bulimic anorexic's ego is deficient in impulse control. Periodically the bulimic anorexic's ego is overwhelmed by impulses to gorge, purge, and act out. Smoking and alcohol addictions are frequent, and lying and other antisocial behavior are characteristic. The bulimic anorexic's parents evidence all the components of the anorexic family psychological profile but there is more family discord and instability. Divorce and parental addictions also are more frequent. The parental superego structure, although rigid and controlling, is less perfectionist than is the case in the histories of the abstainers.

In the obese case (Case 5), the attitude of the mother toward food was the opposite of the characteristic dietary overconcern of the anorexic's mother (Case 4). The mother of the patient did not use food to control, but neglected her daughter's development in the oral and subsequent maturational phases. This patient used food and nail biting to try to gain the attentive, loving mother she never had. The anorexic, in her fasting, is protecting herself against a dependence on a too-perfect mother and her too-perfect food. Anorexics strive to be fiercely independent of everyone, including the analyst (M. Sperling 1978). In six analytic cases of obesity, the present author was able to resolve the characterologic conflicts that underlay the obesity, and the patients achieved a normal weight. Further research and validation of this concept of the anorexic family psychological profile is needed—a comparison of it with the family psychodynamics of obese and normal children.

SUMMARY AND CONCLUSIONS

Analytic work with anorexic patients has focused on their intense fear of being fat and body-image disturbance. Comparable but less intensely cathected psychodynamics were found in neurotic patients in analysis. These findings, coupled with nonanalytic experience with women, lead to the conclusion that most women in our culture have a fear of being fat.

This prevalence of the fear of being fat in women in contrast to males is caused by developmental differences in the female superego and maternal ego ideal. The markedly greater incidence of anorexia nervosa in women is caused primarily by the female's unique superego structure.

The body-image disturbance reflected in the fear of being fat in women is greatly overdetermined, and illustrative dreams and clinical material have been presented to show the drives, fantasies, conflicts, and defensive structures that are masked and expressed by the fear. Important determinants are (1) the fear of loss of impulse control; (2) the fear of regression; and (3) the fear of the undoing of the ego's defenses of denial, repression, and displacement, with the danger of the emergence of oral, anal, and Oedipal conflicts. The predisposition to develop anorexia is established in the mother–infant relation, and those anorexic mothers who have an intense fear of being fat use food to control, unlike the mothers of other patients who may grossly neglect their children. A secondary reinforcement of anorexia comes from women in the environment who have a less intensely cathected fear of being fat and associated body-image conflicts.

Various societal and cultural factors promoting thinness, including the medical danger of obesity, increased athletics for women, and the female fashion industry's emphasis on a slender figure, appear to play a significant role in the appearance of the fear of being fat in women in our culture. A psychodynamic understanding of the fear of being fat brings anorexia nervosa into connection with normal and pathological female psychology and is crucial for the analysis of this life-threatening disease.

REFERENCES

Blum, H. P. (1976). Masochism, the ego ideal, and the psychology of women. *Journal of the American Psychoanalytic Association* 24 (supp.): 157–191.

Bruch, H. (1973). *Eating Disorders*. New York: Basic Books.

———. (1978). *The Golden Cage*. Cambridge, Mass: Harvard University Press.

Fenichel, O. (1945). *The Psychoanalytic Theory of Neurosis*. New York: Norton.

Freedman, A. M., Kaplan, H. T., and Sadock, B. J. (1976). *Modern Synopsis of Comprehensive Textbook of Psychiatry 11*. Baltimore: Williams and Wilkins Co.

254   C. PHILIP WILSON

Freud, S. (1923). The ego and the id. *Standard Edition* 19:25-26.
———. (1932). Femininity. *Standard Edition* 22:3-66.
Friedman, S. (1978). Discussion of this paper at the meeting of The New Jersey Psycho-analytic Society, Oct. 13, 1978.
Galenson, E., and Roiphe, H. (1976). Some suggested revisions concerning early female development. *Journal of the American Psychoanalytic Association* 24 (supp.):29-57.
Gordon, R. (1978). *Final Payments*. New York: Ballantine Books.
Goiten, P. L. (1942). Potential prostitute: role of anorexia nervosa in defense against prostitute desires. *Journal of Criminal Psychopathology* 3:359-367.
Greenacre, P. (1958). Early physical determinants of the sense of identity, *Journal of the American Psychoanalytic Association* 6:612-627.
Grossman, W. I., and Stewart, W. A. (1976) Penis envy: from childhood wish to developmental metaphor. *Journal of the American Psychoanalytic Association* 24 (Supp.):193-212.
Hoffer, W. (1950). Development of the body ego. *Psychoanalytic Study of the Child* 5:18-23.
Jacobson, E. (1964). *The Self and the Object World*. London: International University Press.
Jawetz, I. K. (1976). Discussion of S. Ritvo's presentation, Panel on the Psychology of Women: Late Adolescence and Early Adulthood, reported by E. Galenson, *Journal of the American Psychoanalytic Association* 24:631-645.
Kaplan, E. B. (1976). The Psychology of Women Panel Report by Eleanor Galenson, M.D., Latency and early adolescence. *Journal of the American Psychoanalytic Association* 24:141-160.
Lowenfeld, H. and Lowenfeld, Y. (1972). Our permissive society and the superego. In *Moral Values and the Superego Concept*, ed. Seymour C. Post, pp. 375-397. New York: International Universities Press.
Mahler, M. (1972). On the first three subphases of the separation-individuation process. *International Journal of Psychoanalysis* 53:333-338.
Mahler, M., and Furer, M. (1968). *On Human Symbiosis and the Vicissitudes of Individuation*. New York: International University Press.
Mintz, I. (1978). Personal communication.
Minuchin, S., Rosman, B. L., and Baker, L. (1978). *Psychosomatic Families: Anorexia Nervosa in Context*. Cambridge, Mass: Harvard University Press.
Orbach, S. (1978). *Fat is a Feminist Issue*. New York: Berkeley Publishing Corp.
Ritvo, S. (1976a). Adolescent to woman. *Journal of the American Psychoanalytic Association* 24 (supp.):127-137.
———. (1976b). The Psychology of Women Panel Report by Eleanor Galenson, M.D., Late adolescence and early adulthood. *Journal of the American Psychoanalytic Association* 24:631-645.
Sandler, J., and Joffe, W. G., (1975). Notes on *Obsessional Manifestations in Children*. *Psychoanalytic Study of the Child* 20:425-438.
Sours, J. A. (1974). The anorexia nervosa syndrome. *International Journal of Psychoanalysis* 55:567-576.
Sperling, M. (1968). Acting out behavior and psychosomatic symptoms. *International Journal of Psychoanalysis* 49:250-253.
———. (1970). The Clinical Effects of Potential Neurosis on the Child. In *Parenthood*, eds. E. J. Anthony and T. Benedict, pp. 539-569. Boston: Little, Brown and Company.
———. (1978). Anorexia Nervosa. In *Psychosomatic Disorders in Childhood*, ed. O. Sperling. New York: Jason Aronson.
Sperling, O. (1944). On appersonation. *International Journal of Psychoanalysis* 25:128-132.
———. (1978). Discussion of this paper at a meeting of the Psychosomatic Study Group of the Psychoanalytic Association of New York, Inc., March 16, 1978.
Wilson, C. P. (1967a). Symbolism of the umbrella. *Psychoanalytic Quarterly* 36:83-84.

————. (1967b). Stone as a symbol of teeth. *Psychoanalytic Quarterly* 36:418–425.

————. (1968a). The boy friend—the girl friend: the psychoanalytic investigation of a mannerism of speech. *Psychoanalytic Quarterly* 38:519.

————. (1968b). The Relationship between psychosomatic asthma and acting out. *International Journal of Psychoanalysis:* 49:330–333.

————. (1971). On the limits of the effectiveness of psychoanalysis: early ego and somatic disturbances. *Journal of the American Psychoanalytic Association* 19:552–564.

————. (1976). The Psychology of Women Panel Report by Eleanor Galenson, M.D., Late adolescence and early adulthood. *Journal of the American Psychoanalytic Association* 24:631–645.

————. (1978). The psychoanalytic treatment of hospitalized anorexia nervosa patients. Panel discussion Anorexia nervosa. *Bulletin of the Psychoanalytic Association of New York.* 15:5–7.

————. (1980a). The family psychological profile of anorexia nervosa patients. *Journal of the Medical Society of New Jersey* 77:341–344.

————. (1980b). Sand symbolism; the primary dream representation of the Isakower phenomenon and of smoking addictions: its psychodynamic significance and otogenetic dating. *Twenty-fifth Anniversary Volume of the Division of Psychoanalytic Education, State University of New York, College of Medicine at New York City*, pp. 45–55. eds. S. Orgel, B. Fine, and M. Kanzer. New York: Jason Aronson.

Anorexia Nervosa:
A Psychoanalytic Commentary

CECIL MUSHATT, M.D., M.Sc.

A discussion of "The Fear of Being Fat," by C. Philip Wilson, M.D. The view is presented that primary emphasis on sexual conflicts, especially Oedipal, as causative psychological factors in anorexia nervosa is a limiting and narrow view of the problem. The symptomatology and sexual and aggressive conflicts and fantasies, with the accompanying defenses, can best be understood within the framework of the process of separation of self from object and the seemingly insoluble dilemma in regard to the struggle to achieve a sense of separateness and individuality. This has its effects on the development of the body image, with its internalized symbolic representations of the environment, and through the body image on the ego, superego, and instinctual life. Anorexia nervosa is an expression of ego-defective development arising from varying degrees of failure to resolve the process of developing a sense of individuality. There result primitive aggression, archaic guilt, and great difficulties in establishing an integrated sense of sexual identity. Sexualization of all aspects of interpersonal relationships is fostered by intensification of the need for sensory stimulation, e.g., by touch, the fantasy of touch, by vision, and by oral fantasies and activities. This leads to intensification of defenses against overt sexual expression on all levels, as well as against primitive aggressive fantasies and guilt. The symbolic significance of various symptoms in anorexia nervosa is discussed.

Dr. Wilson, in his attempt to show the primitive roots of the concerns of normal women about their body-weight and appearance, has succeeded in providing us with a very important contribution to the psychoanalytic study of anorexia nervosa. The main focus here will be on certain aspects of the psychodynamic understanding of anorexia nervosa that bear on Dr. Wilson's paper. Dr. Wilson has given a very extensive clinical picture of the varied presenting issues in anorexia. His examples in the main, like those given by Sperling (1978), seem to emphasize the part played by sexual conflict in the etiology of the illness. Sperling (1978) takes the position that anorexia nervosa is "a specific pathological outcome of unresolved Oedipal conflicts in a female, who by her pre-Oedipal relationship with her mother is predisposed to this particular reaction under certain precipitating circumstances" (p. 165). Wilson places less emphasis on Oedipal conflict and shows correctly that the illness can be derived from any level of psychosexual development. Earlier contributions (e.g., Waller et al. 1964) link sexual fantasies, especially pregnancy fantasies, with the precipitation of anorexia nervosa. Masserman (1941) and Leonard (1944) describe conflicts over assuming a female role as central.

Primary emphasis on sexual conflicts is a limiting and narrow view of the problem. These conflicts belong within a much broader model. Savitt (1980), in his discussion of Wilson's paper, points out that anorexia nervosa, like obesity, involves separation-individuation conflicts. Wilson refers to this concept, but he does not emphasize it to the extent that it should be as central to the development of illness. Anorexia nervosa is an expression of defective ego development arising from varying degrees of failure to resolve the separation-individuation processes and of failure to develop a sense of individuality. This determines the character of disturbances in object relationships. The more serious the symptoms of the illness, the more intense or primitive is the symbiotic level of functioning; although mild symptoms do not necessarily mean the opposite. Stated in the reverse, the greater the impairment of the sense of separation of self from object, the more severe are the symptoms likely to be. This can be said of all psychosomatic illnesses, but it can be seen in very blatant form in anorexia nervosa.

The more defective the ego is in terms of separation of self from object, the more pronounced are primitive elements in the instinctual life and strivings and the less developed is control over transformation and sublimation of the instincts. Control in these circumstances demands the erection of massive defensive maneuvers. Ego defects result in persistence and intensification of pregenital and aggressive strivings. Such intensification of primitive strivings may in turn aggravate the defects in the ego. From this point of view, it is difficult to accept Sperling's (1978) view that anorexia nervosa is an "impulse disorder." Failure in instinctual maturation is here secondary to failure in ego development. The disruption of the process of separation-individuation also creates difficulties in establishing an integrated sense of sexual identity. In persons with ego defects, sexualization of all aspects of interpersonal relationships is fostered by the intensification of the need for sensory stimulation (e.g., by touch, fantasy of touch, vision, and oral fantasies and activities) to help maintain a sense of contact with the environment. This in turn intensifies the need for defensive formations.

The apparent predominance of sexual and aggressive conflicts and fantasies can best be understood within this framework. For example, focus on sexual and aggressive fantasies as ends in themselves can often lead to interminable analysis and failure of resolution. Understanding and translation of such conflicts into terms of ego strivings, developmental efforts toward resolution of the problems involved in separation-individuation, often will make for significant maturational development and relief of anorexic symptoms.

Wilson's emphasis on the fear of being fat rather than on the reluctance to eat and the desire to be thin in patients with anorexia and in normal women is very significant. This may seem at first sight a relatively unimportant distinction, but it is very valuable for the orientation that it induces towards the patient. It helps to focus on some of the major sources of conflict in anorexics, namely the fear of their voraciousness and insatiability and with this of the intensity of their narcissism; with these are the patients' fear of destructiveness associated with such fantasies and the intolerance of the resulting archaic guilt that bedevils the lives of anorexic patients. These fears and fantasies can be understood as derived from the fear of separation, the fear of the destructive effect of separation on the object (mother and also father and siblings), and the rage over the apparent insoluble dilemma in regard to the struggle to achieve a sense of separateness.

On the more symbiotic level of functioning, there is heightening of ambivalence and, as already mentioned, sexualization of all aspects of interpersonal relationships and difficulty in differentiating unconsciously between concrete and symbolic, between primary and secondary process. The fear of loss of control over impulses, referred to by Wilson, can be understood as a fear of loss of control over sexual appetite and aggression as expressions of the struggle to resolve the separation-individuation impasse, as well as the fear of loss of control over the desire for closeness. The desire for closeness unconsciously is equated with total merging with or total incorporation of the object.

The achievement of separation involves renunciation of old ambivalent identifications and taking in of new ones as a form of restitution for the loss and as a form of reunion. In their primitive thinking, the more impaired patients unconsciously equate incorporation and identification with destruction of the object in part or whole, and renunciation of identifications and separation also with destruction of the object. Here one sees how an intolerable impasse in development can arise with an enormous burden of guilt. Wilson describes in some detail the family climate of patients who develop anorexia. Briefly, the environment is one in which the mother and father are unable to tolerate separation and strivings on the part of the child for growth. They infantilize the child and induce guilt over any effort toward independent behavior, while at the same time expecting perfection in behavior and achievement and control. Thus they create intolerable ambivalence, hostility, and guilt. The growing child unconsciously recognizes and identifies with the parents' fear of separation and unconsciously responds to the strong love-hate conflicts in the parents.

Several papers (Mushatt 1954, 1959, 1972, 1975) describe the manner in which bodily functions can express the separation-individuation process, and the loss-destruction-restitution conflict. One particular example comes from the case of a young man, who, though not anorexic, for a long time ate only frugally on the excuse of lack of finances. He had had a symbiotic attachment to both parents and had found going to school as a child very difficult, and later it was extremely difficult for him to leave home to go to college. He was constantly preoccupied with his bowel functions. To pass even one day without a bowel movement made him very anxious, while he also felt unable to defecate or urinate in public toilets. He would hold back both until he could reach the privacy of his own home. At the same time, he was constantly alarmed by stories of violence and rape, and was afraid he would be attacked and raped anally by men. He was especially afraid that his wife would be attacked and raped. These fears justified for him his own rage toward men and his fantasies of attacking them anally. At the same time he came to recognize his own rage toward his wife for having "lured" him away from his mother. Both sets of fantasies were usually followed by longing to return home to his mother and father for safety. Significant resolution of his projections of his fear of rape of himself and his wife and of his own hostile feelings was achieved by repeated analysis of his longings to return home to his mother and father. There came through the fantasy and his longing to be in bed with his parents, lying between them with his father's penis in his rectum, and his own penis in his mother's rectum—a blissful state of complete union and sole possession of both parents. Threat of disruption of this blissful state aroused intense resentment and hostility in him. This material soon led to his remarking, on discussing his problem about "constipation," that defecating gave him a feeling of independence, a feeling of letting go of both his mother and father. These insights were now related to hitherto unconscious transference fantasies and were quickly followed by marked diminution in his preoccupation with newspaper reports of violence and rape and with his bowel activities. He was freed to pursue his career with much less conflict and to develop a much more peaceful relationship with his wife. This particular example is significant because of the occurrence of constipation in anorectic patients, to which both Wilson and Sperling (1978) make reference. Defecation can not only be expressive of riddance and destruction of the object but of separation, while constipation can express the holding onto introjected objects and retention of attachments.

Preoccupation with violence and rape reappeared much later in this patient and was clearly related to primal scene fantasies. Primal scene fantasies and especially fantasies aroused by exposure to primal scene, reinforce regression to, or fixation in a symbiotic position, and interfere with the process of individuation. Furthermore, this patient's symptom of constipation was directly related to fantasies about violence. On later analysis, the primitive fantasy of the explosive destructive power of feces came through. Constipation to him represented a defense against the fantasy of destroying his parents by defecating on them. At the same time it expressed a desire to hold back his feces until he could possess even greater destructive power. In his adolescence, he lived out this fantasy symbolically by behavior endlessly provocative and troublesome for his parents.

Menstruation and amenorrhea can be approached in the same way in terms of their symbolic representations. In addition to arousing conflicts over pregnancy, castration fears, absence of a penis, and over destructive fantasies, the bleeding can represent loss and separation, loss of a part of oneself, loss of the child in oneself, and separation from a childhood attachment to the mother. It can represent identification with the mother as a mature woman with loss of the image of oneself as a child. Amenorrhea can symbolize the retention of the image of oneself as a child, retention of childhood attachments, and denial of maturation. Menstruation can symbolize a sense of deprivation in human relationships. Depression over menstruation in often described as a reflection of disappointment at not being pregnant. In the more symbiotic type of woman, pregnancy can often internally symbolize, through identification with the fetus, the realization of the fantasy of symbiotic reunion of the child with the mother, and in this sense, menstruation can symbolize the disruption of such a fantasy and the unconscious realization and confrontation of the reality of separation from the mother.

The symbolic equation of food and human objects is seen in its simplest form in an adult female patient's remark when examining her episodes of excessive eating, "I need a mother to take care of me, so I stuff myself with food, to be a mother to myself. I'd like you to take me in your arms, and let's pretend I am a baby and you are my mother." An alcoholic woman discussing the fact that she had innumerable friends throughout the country said, "My father hoarded food during the war [actual World War and "war" at home with his wife]; I hoard people."

The case of a young man with peptic ulcer and severe anorexia is a further example (Mushatt 1959). For him food and individuals in whole or in part became identical. Compulsive searching for companions took the place of meals, and when he did have companions at meal time, he could not eat because of his conscious and preconscious oral incorporative fantasies. Sharing a meal is a normal expression of friendship. It can be seen as an expression of a readiness for mutual identification, to share each other with one another. Fear of overeating and thereby becoming fat can conceal not only hostile feelings but the effort to defend against narcissistic longings, entitlement, and the desire to have everything for oneself, and to restrain oneself against excessive closeness or possessiveness.

A man who complained especially of bouts of nausea, after announcing that he had undertaken a plan to reduce weight, went on to describe frequent dinner scenes with his large family. He told how when he noticed any member of his family eating slowly, he would ask, "Are you going to finish your meal?" On a recent such occasion, one son replied, "I think you want my dinner for yourself." The patient immediately recognized his fantasy of sweeping all the filled plates toward himself with his arms and eating all the food himself. This fantasy was a very vivid reflection of his *narcissistic entitlement* (Murray 1964). He had wanted children, wanted them close to him, but resented giving anything of himself to them, while expecting their complete devotion to him. He was jealous of them and the better circumstances in which they grew up. It is not surprising that all the children were very hostile to him, but at the same time found it hard to live their lives independent of the father.

Food and its symbolic relationship to the task of separation from mother and father and to narcissistic entitlement can be seen again in the sequence of associations of a young married woman who had sought treatment for a variety of problems. For some time she had been feeling depressed over the departure of a close woman friend to a distant city to take a new job. In addition, she had been concerned about her mother, relatively recently widowed. The patient herself was still grieving over the death of her father. Her mother, at this point, lived at a considerable distance from the patient, making it difficult to visit. Her mother was now contemplating moving to the West Coast. The patient feared that she would not be able to see her mother if she moved. At the same time she felt torn between having her mother come to live closer to her and the desire to maintain some distance from her mother for the sake of her marriage. At times she felt tempted to have her mother come to live with her and her husband.

In one session, the patient began by saying that she had decided to go on a diet. She felt that she was too fat (she would by no means be considered "fat"); it made her unattractive and set her apart from her women friends, who were all much thinner. She did not want to diet; she liked to eat, especially between meals. "I am naughty to be eating so much," she said, and then went on to give other examples of her sense of entitlement since childhood, which she called her "naughtiness," adding that she liked to do things like a defiant naughty child. One of the recent "naughty" things she had done was to drive too fast on a trip to a reunion with her friend who had moved. The reunion had been a source of great pleasure to her. Then later in the session, she stated that she had reached a compromise solution about her mother. Her husband had agreed that her mother could come to visit with her in their home and then spend a lengthy vacation within easy driving distance, so that the patient could visit with her mother either on weekdays or on weekends. She felt pleased with the arrangement and abruptly said, "The time is up and I can leave now." She had completed the circle from her concern about being fat and her love of eating to her expected reunion with her mother, and relief from guilt over the separation and over visiting her friend instead of her mother. In her next session, several days later, the patient was depressed, and there came through her profound sense of guilt toward her mother, especially over the fact that she was living in more affluent circumstances than her mother, and over all her naughtiness in relation to her mother. Finally she said, "I feel so guilty. I feel I can't care any more what I do, so I ate a lot today. But then I feel guilty over eating so much."

In the final remarks of this woman, there is the hint of the various physical symptoms seen in anorexia, especially the anorexia itself, that can find symbolic expression in various areas of the personality. Another woman, whose male friend had to move to a distant town because of his job, described how she now did not feel interested in eating since she had been alone. With her boyfriend present she could always eat a hearty meal, but now that she was alone, when she came home from work in the early evening, she would often go to sleep instead of preparing dinner, and on awakening several hours later, she would be content with a meager snack. She now, as rarely occurred, reminded the therapist of her anorexia in adolescence, and told of how her mother would often say, "You can always do without . . ." Then she remarked, "I think of looking for a new apartment, for new furniture, for new clothes, but eh! I can't stand it. I'd rather be outside doing anything but being in a store." This patient was not given to bulimia or extravagance in any form, but in other anorexics, one often sees the expression of bulimia followed by vomiting in terms of what for them is extravagant spending of money on themselves and indulgence in pleasurable activities, both followed by extreme guilt and subsequent self-denial.

The stronger the fixation at or regression to a symbiotic position or partially symbiotic position, the stronger are narcissistic elements. Greater degrees of ambivalence, primitive aggression, pregenital sexual problems, archaic guilt, and magical thinking, and greater difficulty in sustaining new identifications that can undo the loss of older more ambivalent identifications with key family figures, go with such a developmental position. All of this accounts to a great extent for the difficulty in treating such patients. The importance of the degree of narcissistic organization and the extreme sense of guilt enhanced by the unconscious demands of entitlement experienced by anorexics must be emphasized. In the more severe cases, it is easy to recognize the expectations of perfection, omnipotence and omniscience, the desire for complete subservience of the mother and the world—i.e. complete control over key persons, internally represented by desire for control over the self and one's body, and the demand to be the one and only, worshipped by all. The intensity of these narcissistic expectations, and the continuing disappointment in achieving them, arouse a profound sense of inadequacy and helplessness, which promotes further intensification of the desire for infantilization. The resulting depression mobilizes rage and guilt. The degree of reaction to the failure to realize entitlement fantasies can be a measure of the degree of blurring of the boundaries between self and the outside world, a measure of the depth of symbiotic attachment. There are instances when the rejection of food expresses the fantasy of omnipotence and invulnerability because of the unconscious fantasy of complete union with the mother. Because of the symbiotic fantasy, there is no need to eat. To eat food is to acknowledge the fact of separation and of one's mortal being. One patient would fly into a rage at the sight of a funeral. It confronted her with her own mortal nature and the need to eat to live.

Not eating is very frequently regarded as an expression of hostile rejection of the mother and father; and, as Wilson points out, it causes suffering for the parents not only externally through worry and guilt, but by unconscious starvation of the introjected parents. However, the appearance of rejection of the parent can mask the fantasy of relentless attachment to the parent. In the more symbiotic patient, the line between love and hate can be very blurred. The symptom, with its symbolic representations, can express both. Rejection of dependency on the analyst, rejection of identification with him in the analytic task, and, through that, rejection of the analyst's interpretations and help through understanding should not always be interpreted as hostile behavior. There are times when such behavior in anorexics is due to unconscious concern for the welfare of the therapist, determined by the unconscious equation of incorporation and identification with destruction in part or in whole of the therapist (Mushatt 1975, 1980).

As indicated earlier, many of these observations are by no means exclusive or specific only to anorexia nervosa; but in cases of anorexia one sees these elements in an extreme form. As Wilson indicates, anorexia may be precipitated by and expressive of conflicts from all levels of development, but when it occurs in patients with more mature egos a significant measure of failure in earlier levels is requisite. The more integrated the ego organization, the more obscure and circumscribed are the primitive elements, and the more the latter are seen in highly derivative form. In the normal woman, the fear of being fat can be understood as derived from unresolved aspects of the more primitive conflicts outlined above, especially from the eternal struggle to solve the separation-individuation conflicts. Overeating, obesity, or relative overweight can be seen as reflecting unconsciously an individual's dependency and infantile longings for attachment, as well as reflecting narcissistic longings that are accompanied by shame, anger, and guilt. Guilt over narcissistic strivings and hostility can be relieved by fasting or token fasting, that is, by constraint and restriction of diet. To eat or not-to-eat can reflect the eternal conflict between love and hate in relationships, as well as conflict over unconscious desire to control sexual and aggressive appetites, as described by Wilson.

REFERENCES

Leonard, C. E. (1944). An analysis of a case of functional vomiting and bulimia. *Psychoanalytic Review* 31:1–18. Quoted by Sperling, M. (1978).

Masserman, J. H. (1941). Psychodynamisms in anorexia nervosa and neurotic vomiting. *Psychoanalytic Quarterly* 10:211–242. Quoted by Sperling M. (1978).

Murray, J. M. (1964). Narcissism and the ego ideal. *Journal of the American Psychoanalytic Association* 12:477–511.

Mushatt, C. (1954). Psychological aspects of non-specific ulcerative colitis. In *Recent Developments in Psychosomatic Medicine*, eds. E. D. Wittkower and R. A. Cleghorn. Philadelphia: J. B. Lippincott & Co.

——— . (1959). Loss of sensory perception determining choice of symptom. In *On the Mysterious Leap from the Mind to the Body: A Workshop Study on the Theory of Conversion*, ed. F. Deutsch, pp. 201–234. New York: International Universities Press.

——— . (1972). Grief and anniversary reactions in a man of sixty-two. *International Journal of Psychoanalytic Psychotherapy* 1:83–106.

——— . (1975). Mind-body-environment: toward understanding the impact of loss on psyche and soma. *Psychoanalytic Quarterly* 44:81–106.

——— . (1980). Melitta Sperling memorial lecture. Presented at Psychoanalytic Association of New York, February 25, 1980.

Savitt, R. (1980). Discussion of "On the Fear of Being Fat in Female Psychology and Anorexia Nervosa," by C. P. Wilson. *Psychoanalytic Association of New York Bulletin* 17:809.

Sperling, M. (1978). Anorexia nervosa, In *Psychosomatic Disorders in Childhood*, pp. 131–173. New York: Jason Aronson.

Waller, J. V., Kaufman, M. R., and Deutsch, F. (1964). Anorexia nervosa: a psychosomatic entity. In *Evolution of Psychosomatic Concepts: Anorexia Nervosa, A Paradigm*, eds. M. R. Kaufman and M. Heiman, pp. 145–276. New York: International Universities Press.

Anorexia Nervosa and the Psychotherapeutic Hospital

IAN STORY, Ph.D.

This paper illustrates psychoanalytically oriented psychotherapeutic work with persons suffering from severe anorexia nervosa who reside in a psychotherapeutic hospital. Anorexia nervosa in its more drastic forms is here viewed as a circumscribed or "spot" manifestation of borderline and schizophrenic pathology; thus these observations also fall within the framework of the psychotherapeutically committed hospital treatment of a wider range of other severe disorders. An exposition of the following elements is included: (1) individual psychoanalytically informed therapy in a therapeutically conceived milieu; (2) firm encouragement to gain weight and modify vomiting by collaborative and voluntary means, if possible, with emphasis on clarifying the contractual boundaries of responsibility; (3) encouragement of the therapeutic alliance and deemphasis of a static symptom-centered approach; (4) coordinated nursing, medical, laboratory, and dietary staffs in an integrative "holding environment;" (5) limited use of pharmacotherapy, with attention focused consistently on the interactional meanings of prescribed medication; (6) physical separation of patient from family. An integrated framework for addressing and pursuing the multiple issues, dimensions, and layerings inherent in intensive psychotherapy with severely anorexic patients in an open hospital environment is presented and is intended as a paradigm for the treatment of other severe disorders.

Bruch and others have observed a near epidemic increase in the incidence of anorexia nervosa; Bruch goes so far as to call it "a new disease" (Bruch 1978a). Until recently a quite rare condition, anorexia nervosa is now an increasingly encountered form of ascetic subsistence living. It is usually uncomplicated by identifiable organic etiology, but has important, and sometimes irreversible, physiological concomitants. The anorexic patient

An earlier version of this paper was presented at the Symposium on Anorexia Nervosa and Obesity, Royal Victoria Hospital, Montreal, April, 1979.

often boasts in a glorifying way and with exceedingly intense feelings of her self-starving solution. Perhaps predictably, a self-help movement has been promulgated in recent years for those less isolated anorexic persons wishing to explore common difficulties in a group forum. Nevertheless, anorexia nervosa has gained a degree of psychiatric attention that continues to be much greater than is commensurate with its actual incidence because, in part, it captures in a vividly exaggerated and compressed way many of the nuclear upheavals, crises, and challenges of more normal adolescent development.

This paper describes and illustrates a psychoanalytically conceived paradigm for the open hospital treatment of anorexia nervosa; in its extreme form, this condition is viewed as a more focalized and psychosomatically focused manifestation of a diversity of other severe disorders, such as borderline and schizophrenic conditions, to which these observations also apply. No final and ideal answer or proven solution for anorexia nervosa is provided. The main purpose is to define, share, and understand observations from one small psychotherapeutic hospital and to pursue unsettled issues; it is not the author's plan to offer a comprehensive exposition of anorexia nervosa or the other disorders to which it is often closely related, nor to interrelate the data exhaustively with all major analytic points of view or technical approaches. Like any description of a wide-ranging form of treatment that has included positive outcome results, however, it would be false as well to pretend that the paper is simply a collection of notes on cases. It also provides material for a kind of ordered therapeutic statement, an argument, or position, and an effort at integration.

Narrowly defined, eating disorders are frequent and widely distributed symptoms of psychiatric illness. Even when no clear-cut eating symptoms are manifest or complained of, difficulties and oddities of eating and of the patterning of appetite and thirst are remarkably widespread, even ubiquitous. To those engaged in carefully conducted, exploratory psychoanalytic psychotherapy, eating problems are familiar as significant symptoms and may occasionally dominate a clinical picture. What may be called the "thin forever" movement, which currently occupies such a commanding place in the outlook of this diet-conscious culture, is also relevant to the epidemiology of this condition.

More broadly conceived, anorexia nervosa constitutes a drastic miscarriage in personal development, amounting in the most catastrophic cases to nihilistic attacks on growth and the pursuit of life itself. The anorexic Ellen West, for instance, observed, "since I acted only from the point of view of whether things made me thin or fat, all things soon lost their intrinsic meaning" (Binswanger 1944, p. 256), but no therapist today would want to compound this inclination—i.e., no therapist would choose to join with the patient in a narrowly defined symptom and illness approach that so systematically destroys a wider sense of the person.

In fact, it was one of Binswanger's (1944) many original achievements to have demonstrated how a combined orthodox symptom-focused and symbol-centered interpretive effort with Ellen West was gravely misleading and distracting in this hunger-obsessed woman's care. Binswanger then proceeded to show how the developmental reality of Ellen West's world and the meaning of her urges to growth, freedom, and sense of selfhood had been largely omitted from therapeutic consideration and were crucial to the illumination of her ultimately life-claiming anorexic dilemma. Although the patient committed suicide, paradoxically Binswanger was the first to demonstrate the aptness of a psychotherapeutic approach to genuine anorexia nervosa. "The Case of Ellen West" can thus be read as an early and primary test for studying the psychotherapeutic hospital treatment of anorexia nervosa and, by extension, other severe disorders, such as schizophrenia. To read Binswanger's account from the 1930s, however, is happily to appreciate how far most contemporary psychoanalytic approaches have moved from the sterile modes of treatment customarily advised in that earlier period.

The patients in this report can be characterized as "severe" anorexics. All the patients described, with one exception, have required hospitalization at least once. They are significantly older chronologically than the early and mid-teenage anorexics written about and seen in more traditional adolescent units, and are more obviously disturbed as well. Based on the drastically anorexic patients reported on here, the anorexia nervosa syndrome is viewed as a circumscribed or "spot" manifestation of severely borderline and schizophrenic pathology. Delusional disturbances in body image and body boundaries, truly paranoid conceptions of food, with corresponding self–other differentiation and bodily awareness difficulties, are the pervasive anorexic phenomena central to this hypothesis. Another statement of this thesis is by Shainess (1979): "The condition can be considered a somatic delusion, and . . . the patient is more than potentially schizophrenic, but actually so, if properly considered" (p. 229). This observation may be extended: the interplay of themes of poisoning and being poisoned as identified in the patient's associations and recapitulated in the transference are crucial to the resolution of the anorexic person's dread of possessing and deriving pleasure from a normal adult body.

The unconscious and conscious fantasies associated with the body by many anorexic patients are that it is shamefully polluting and poisoning, hence untouchable and unlovable. By extension, virtually any form of physicality, of embodiment, may come to be perceived as shaming and potentially or actually harmful, specifically in a poisonous or contagiously polluting and disgusting sense. This too finds support in the work of Shainess (1979): "The unconscious fantasies connected with food are that it is poison. . . . The efforts not to eat can be seen as a phobic avoidance of poison" (p. 230). The corresponding countertransference feelings to which the therapist is then especially vulnerable, given the paranoid and hysterical projection emphasis in this poisoning theme, is that he feels made to seem like a poisoning foreign body whose life-enhancing treatment efforts are not only unwelcome and unappreciated but are necessarily seen by the patient as potentially lethal. The therapist is thereby likely to feel himself equated with the unempathic fattening/poisoning mother. Starvation conditions tend to emphasize and place in even sharper relief these aspects of the anorexic's delusional thought disorder.

The material reported here is provided by the author's work with young adult women. Prior to hospitalization, a few continued to reside at home; but in such cases the parental home is often administered like a modified hospital or psychosomatic unit, and a hostage or siege atmosphere exists, with reciprocal intimidation on the part of patient and family alike underlying a surface picture of seeming mutual goodwill. Mostly, however, the patients attained before hospitalization, a degree of pseudo-emancipation or pseudo-separation from family, never true autonomy, away at college, for example. Most are in their early twenties, some reaching into the early thirties. These women display the usual vicissitudes of self-starvation, gorging, and self-induced vomiting (or "bulimarexia"), attended in some by a range of related symptom chains and clusters that include cutting and scratching, burning, head-banging, hair-pulling, body-rocking, self-biting and self-flogging, stealing, food-hoarding, excessive drinking, and mutism, the latter designed to control the use of the mouth. Laxative abuse, hyperexercising, and compulsive restless pacing also tend to be routinely encountered with these patients as further aspects of the anorexic syndrome of omnipotent caretaking of self.

The treatment and setting characteristics of the work with the severely anorexic patients reported here are psychoanalytically conceived. The meaning of "psychoanalytically conceived" here is not that severely anorexic patients are engaged in formal psychoanalysis without modifications in technique, conceptualization, or, using Langs' term, in the "fixed frame" of the psychoanalytic environment (Langs 1979); rather, the therapeutic work with these patients in this setting originates in a theory of complex human intentionality, including manifest and latent meanings and processes, and in the interpersonal investigation of transference, countertransference, and resistance phenomena (Klein 1976). Additionally, the psychotherapeutic hospital embodies a dynamic treatment philosophy in which other modalities of clinical intervention are used adjunctively and collaterally rather than as substitutes for learning, growth, adaptive inner change, or furthering a mutual understanding of the therapeutic interaction. Thus this milieu is constitutive not of "the psychoanalytic situation" in Stone's (1961) sense, nor of a more traditional psychiatric hospital context in which "psychotherapy" tends to be available optionally or secondarily, briefly, and directed toward symptom removal. Nor does it offer the "eclectic" compromise that Novotny (1973) has called "the pseudopsychoanalytic hospital." Rather, the milieu described represents a particular psychotherapeutic environment (or framework) that is organized around long-term, residential, intensive, psychoanalytically oriented psychotherapy. Since this latter is a cumbersome designation, the treatment program is referred to here simply as psychotherapeutic.

The care and treatment program includes the following elements, each of which is further described below. Enumerated in this way, the fundamentals of such an approach may be readily compared with many alternate formulations and programs devoted to the treatment of anorexic persons (Meltzer 1975, p. 124).

1. Individual, psychoanalytically oriented psychotherapy in a therapeutically conceived and committed milieu.
2. Firm encouragement to gain weight and modify vomiting by voluntary means, if possible, with emphasis on clarifying the contractual boundaries of responsibility
3. Encouragement of the therapeutic alliance and of attachment, with corresponding de-emphasis of a behavioral, symptom-centered approach.
4. Treatment in an integrative "holding environment" with coordinated nursing, internal medicine, and laboratory and dietary staffs.
5. Limited use of pharmacotherapy, with corresponding vigilance as well to the interactional meanings of prescribed medication.
6. Physical separation of patient from family on a long-term basis, usually for the duration of treatment, and thereafter as well.

PSYCHOANALYTIC PSYCHOTHERAPY AND THE COMMITTED MILIEU

The premise is that anorexia nervosa can be successfully treated in the long-term treatment framework of a psychotherapeutic hospital. The pertinent questions to be raised, therefore, are not *whether* anorexic persons can be validly treated but *how*; under what basic conditions, in what kinds of treatment settings, and in accordance with which formulations of the etiology of the illness and of its treatment. Anorexia nervosa and schizophrenia are allied in this way; it is a further postulate that the psychotherapeutic hospital treatment of both anorexia nervosa and schizophrenia may be conceived of in fundamentally similar terms. The author's experience suggests that a minimum of four weekly individual psychotherapy hours is the necessary framework for treating severely anorexic patients. The guiding philosophy and basic concepts of treatment in this milieu are diversely psychoanalytic in the sense already described.

It emerges as a common finding in the author's work with hospitalized anorexic patients who have tried to engage in more formal psychoanalysis before hospitalization that they have found even flexible adherence to the so-called classical analytic procedure to be largely without benefit. For them, formal analysis has turned out to be too threateningly lonely, unreciprocal, and disorganizing in light of their precarious defensive and nutritional, or psyche-soma, equilibrium. For example, having slipped into a borderline state of pervasive confusion and dread during the opening months of her analysis, which was marked also by the analyst's vacation, one hospitalized anorexic woman described this earlier treatment effort as "ghostly." The office atmosphere was "like stainless steel," but she felt "seduced" into becoming overwhelmingly dependent on the analyst "to feed (her)."

The locus of treatment itself is a small, completely open, psychoanalytically conceived hospital accommodating some 46 voluntary patients. "Open" refers to the maintenance of unlocked facilities with free access at all times by all patients; there are no seclusion or quiet rooms nor any means of restricting patients to hospital grounds for precautionary reasons. The patients are youthful (ages 17 and upwards, mostly in their twenties), of above average intelligence and talents, often from privileged backgrounds, with little or no personal experience of physical hardship or deprivation, and representing a range of psychiatric disturbances, mostly in the borderline and schizophrenic domains, as well as severe character disorders. The hospital is located in the middle of a New England village in which patients move freely and mingle without restriction.

Much is omitted in the above precis of this particular setting or "good-enough holding environment"—to use Winnicott's (1960) concept, extended by Modell (1978), and originally applied to the preverbal parent–child context and to the individual psychoanalytic situation. Here, the holding/containing conception is extended to a broader modality of treatment—the psychotherapeutic hospital framework. The dominant working treatment values are upholding awareness, voluntarism, personal learning and the resumption of growth, communal cooperation and mutual accommodation, and an increasingly particularized approach to the psychotherapy of anorexia nervosa and other serious disorders in which the therapist and patient are *both* affirmatively conceived of as basic perceiving and motivated agents. Neither is the sole valid arbiter of reality and meaning. However unreachable, a corollary goal is adaptively treating patients in highly individualized ways rather than preemptively enforcing a blueprint of collective rules and prohibitions. By extension, the prevailing philosophy for this psychotherapeutically committed milieu has been interestingly described elsewhere as striving to be, at the least, anti-antitherapeutic (Talbot et al. 1964).

An initial goal of the hospital admission and early treatment sequence is to convey in a welcoming way to the anorexic patient that her difficulties are incontestably human and can be forthrightly identified, talked out, and understood. The therapist is apt to intervene with the prospective patient with the observation, albeit in an undefined way and without more detailed elaboration or discussion at this early juncture, that she is in the hospital not only to be cared for by the staff but also, and perhaps for the first time, to learn or relearn as much as possible about caring for herself. The first order organizing formulation, in other words, is that the patient has come to the hospital mainly to attempt to *get* better, and not solely to *feel* better or "comfortable" or to obtain peace of mind or simply put on weight (Langs 1978). The core point is not that the therapist favors "pain"; rather, the patient has come to be afraid of engaging in the complexities of growing up into adult womanhood. Without in any way disparaging the patient or her compelling point of view, nor aiming for unrealistic or impossible goals, the therapist suggests that the patient is afraid to get better, fearful of abandoning her rituals and of change, while at the same time recognizing that this is what she is now seeking.

Observations of this type are also exploratory in intent, with a trial-outing quality, especially in light of the obvious initial strategy followed here, which is predominantly noninterpretive, even shielding and protective in approach (Khan 1964), given the often nearly traumatized condition of these patients. This stance is in interplay with what Langs (1979) has established as the "need for an essentially secure treatment environment" (p. xi), which here is actualized as the responsibility of the therapist to be a background coordinating agent for building a secure boundary and framework for the total therapeutic enterprise. Major attention is thus given to manifest and explicit content, while the patient and therapist work to achieve, as necessary, a weight and nutritional status consistent with the patient's being able to engage in more layered and searching therapeutic work. The overall treatment program, including the initial psychotherapeutic processes of listening and formulating interventions, is thus designed to provide the starving patient with barriers against intolerably disturbing unconscious material, especially introjects and transference fantasy themes, until she is relatively more prepared to engage in the heretofore chaotic or unformed cognitive-associative-perceptual tasks and stresses of more interactional and potentially regressive interpretive work (Langs 1978).

Many anorexic patients find completely unrealistic the possibility of unlearning, modifying, or correcting their distorted, larger-than-life, and exaggeratedly destructive and dangerous (yet also ambivalently wished for) ideas. "I can't believe, I don't feel that eating doesn't kill, won't kill me" was voiced by a 19-year-old anorexic patient with a forced, smiling facade even though she had regained 20 pounds, felt less false, was less suicidally depressed, and even aided another anorexic woman to eat enough to live and remain in the open hospital setting. The treatment context suggested to the therapist that the most fruitful response throughout this phase of the patient's learning about and sharing such terrifying feelings was to assist in the identification, clarification, and acceptance of this exaggeratedly violent material and to provide a noninterpretive, holding, and communicative empathic context in which awareness could be deepened and corrected.

Carol, a depressed, fastidious and enigmatic 30-year-old musician, found most of life disgusting and barbaric. She presented a self-starving and gorging–purging syndrome of several years' standing and complained bitterly and tearfully of feeling "like a worm" in comparison to the therapist, whom she perceived as unloving and hopelessly indifferent to her. In fact, she insisted that the therapist wished she would disappear unless she got well (i.e., separated from him) in the innocuous and essentially empty sense that she felt her mother had urged upon her all her life. In this context, she once reported, "I want to get well—or maybe I'm supposed to think getting well would be better than this [vomiting]. Being healthy usually sounds like the most boring and mechanical life, so killing, but now I think vomiting is." Another pertinent comment—"I guess I want to talk to you more than anything about getting better, if only I didn't have to speak in words"—suggested a wish for a preverbal form of relation to the therapist (not interpreted as such, nevertheless), with her ambivalence expressed in a characteristically elliptical and convoluted form.

For many such women, their family lives have been shaped within such fundamentally restricted and sheltered realms that they have never made important contact with others who embody alternate and more flexible ways of thinking and perceiving and who simultaneously matter to them in a deeply emotional way. Either relief through death or an eventually successful treatment outcome then come to be the only remaining hopes for lasting freedom from the chronically disordered context of deliberateness and pathologically extended will characteristic of these patients.

The theme of unwitting mockery and mimicry, a recurrent one in the psychotherapy of severe anorexics, was deeply embedded throughout the lengthy treatment of Louisa, a 29-year-old anorexic woman. In her treatment, caricature was seen to cover an intensely sadistic and cruel superego, which she felt powerless to address or unlearn, and which she believed no human tie could interfere with or be a barrier against.

Louisa's patronizing relations on the unit with more openly disturbed patients led her to generate the painful recognition of her caricaturing impersonation of womanhood (Story 1976). She concluded, "I make a joke of womanhood, I spit on it. It is a sick joke." Growing up in a family of extreme, even bizarre, gentility, refinement, and restraint, where everything seemed to have its own place and fittingness, the patient learned that only the most indirect forms of self-expression, if indeed she even had a "self" that she could identify, were all she could safely display:

> I wanted so badly to be wanted by my parents, but they made me feel that wanting them, wanting to be held and touched by them, that what I needed would crush them. I felt that whenever I wanted to be close it would crush them and make them so afraid of me that I wouldn't even be allowed to be brought in and to sit with them for a few moments during their damned cocktail hour. What is in me will crush another person is what I thought, so I tried to crush my feelings by myself, to overpower the power of my feelings, and so gradually I just felt dead. I knew my parents were just formal and empty, but I couldn't help trying to get them to want me. What I see now was so crazy is that this was all so painful and misguided of me for so many years. And yet when I listen to an opera, like *Madama Butterfly* or *Tosca*, all my feelings, everything I wanted with my father comes up in me still and I don't want to atone anymore.

The therapist noted that she had earlier feared the loss of her tie to him around identical issues (which was mutually apparent, given the larger context of this vignette), and responded to the effect, "You still hope that you can unlearn all your dangerous ideas about your feelings and find some new ways to express yourself that won't be just what I am expecting from you."

As though to validate this observation and in the wider context of the termination of therapy, the patient next proceeded to wonder about the therapist's death and whether he might be angry for realizing how deeply he mattered to her and how much she felt he had given her in a way that she had not had to undo through a familiar "thoughtful" or "grateful" deed in return. Closing this segment of the session, Louisa then recalled her initial experience of treatment in this setting, articulated its meaning for her, and described the conditions of learning to listen, dating from eight years earlier, long before its emergence in the therapy and from a period when she had been living outside the hospital for several years:

Right from the start of my therapy, I found that I could go back to the front hall [a congregating spot in the residence unit] and just sit on the stairs and be with people. Before each session here, I was probably out walking a set number of miles all by myself or practicing my rituals, but you [the therapist] listened to me. So I didn't owe you anything, and afterwards I didn't have to cancel out what had happened between us. I could see that I didn't have to not listen to what somebody was saying anymore, so I learned to listen, too. Something just happened inside and I could be around others when you weren't afraid and didn't make me feel you didn't want me to have any feelings for you.

By the time of her hospital admission, this friendless woman, weighing 71 pounds and at a life-or-death crossroads, had become a functioning, if also grotesque, facsimile of her parents. She had developed, despite a facade of saintliness, a kind of visceral certainty about the ultimately farcical and ridiculous essence of living. Exposed as a child to symbolically unintelligible, conflicting, and contradictory information from her parents, and with a confused underlying mass of unintegratable perceptions, she had been obliged to attempt "integrating the impossible," in Barchilon's (1973) phrase, ending predictably in feelings of mockery and disorganization. Accompanying the softening of her sadistically unaccepting and self-punishing superego attacks, and in ways clearly illustrative of Kernberg's (1975) thesis regarding the sadistic "all bad/all good" object images and superego makeup in borderline pathology, there gradually developed the parallel emergence of unwilled, hence novel and useable abilities to listen and to speak about herself somewhat without superimposed and imitative rules. With a minimum of interpretive intervention by the therapist, which can all too readily be perceived by the severely anorexic patient as invasive and thwarting her perceptual autonomy, the patient relearned self-caring needs and means, developed further in her subsequent pursuit of medical training, her eventual career.

VOLUNTARISTIC APPROACH TO WEIGHT GAIN AND THE BOUNDARIES OF RESPONSIBILITY

Running as a thread through the very complex and imperative matter of weight gain and the cessation of vomiting is the staff's commitment to firm encouragement to eat in individually sensible ways, to put on weight, and to end vomiting, through voluntary and responsible means.[1] Correspondingly, the patient shares the contractual responsibility for maintaining the bound-

1. In this setting, all admissions, including anorexics, are voluntary. Therapists also work voluntarily, in the sense that no therapist is obligated to meet with a patient whom he feels he cannot treat.

ary of at least a minimally adequate weight and nutritional status. An indefinite period of failure or open refusal to do so is understood as a threatening communication by the patient that treatment in a less open hospital may be indicated.[2] Undue therapist and staff attentiveness or hovering with regard to the minutiae of weight and diet is discouraged. Joining with patients to excess in their eating preoccupations and rituals can too easily detour all concerned into mistakenly treating symptoms in isolation and seeing patient behavior in static terms or as only "hostile." In turn, this risks omitting the consideration of less obvious meanings involved in the anorexic resolution, of the adaptive and independent hopes embedded in the seemingly single-minded pursuit of thinness, and of deflecting attention from significant family patterns.

It is equally true that with some anorexics this contractual approach has countervailing limitations. Unremitting weight loss and uninterrupted vomiting cannot continue indefinitely in responsible and prudently conceived treatment. Therapist and staff anxiety levels are pivotal and ultimately involve an adherence to the reality principle. The most useful guideline is that if a patient persists in starving herself and losing weight over a time span that comes to be experienced by the treatment group as intolerably indefinite and uninterrupted, maintains a dangerously marginal nutritional and physical condition, or persists in the antitherapeutic solution of truly chronic vomiting so that the therapist and nursing staff become anxiously preoccupied with these matters to the neglect of the anorexic as a total person, then the patient is told to take fuller and more realistic responsibility for remaining in this hospital. An unrelieved period of failure in upholding this contract or open refusal to do so is understood as a defeating maneuver, i.e., as a communication by the patient that she is seeking to work with another therapist or even a less voluntaristic form of treatment, including the possibility of discharging herself to a closed hospital and consequent termination of treatment with the present therapist. As an overall psychotherapeutic strategy, this plan—clearly a threatening one and in no meaningful sense analytic—has worked, and no anorexic patient has had to be discharged to a more supervised psychiatric hospital. However, the staff does work closely with a nearby general hospital for short-term emergency situations so that the patient does not have to end or seriously interrupt her psychotherapy.[3] This voluntaristic framework and its realistic boundaries contribute to establishing a bond with the patient, who is thereby placed at the core of the

2. The involuntary treatment of anorexia nervosa with an "unwanted psychotherapist"—on the basis of court-ordered retention, for example—has an almost uniformly negative outcome, according to this author's experience (Will 1968).

3. Procedures such as tube-feeding and hyperalimentation are not feasible in this setting, but are available in the neighboring medical-surgical hospital.

therapeutic work, and also clarify the anorexic's role in the maintenance of treatment, including her part in possible defeating processes (Cooperman 1979).

Besides having established that adopting a value position of voluntarism seems best suited in the psychotherapeutic hospital to patient and therapist survival and a lower casualty picture among staff in this exceedingly strenuous work, we have also learned to be sanguinely mistrustful of any prematurely catalyzed prescription for the treatment of every patient or behavior labeled anorexic. Anorexia nervosa is a smokescreen or camouflage for many things: it functions as a facade concealing multiple difficulties, with a highly loaded interactional pull and exceedingly powerful countertransference potential, frequently along rescuing lines. The grandiose fantasy of personal indispensability to a patient is an especially readily triggered countertransference liability when working with anorexics. The patients' feelings of radical powerlessness and inadequacy, and the often early encountered capacity for a delusional transference, may stimulate responses by the therapist based on a contradictory approach to the patient; for instance, the patient may be seen as insatiable and defective, on the one hand, while the therapist may see himself as the only one who understands and can help or rescue, on the other.

For example, one anorexic woman consulted with the author after working for some years without benefit with three different psychotherapists, one of whom taught her how to lose weight by vomiting. In her first session, she recalled the particularly unhappy and destructive experience of a therapist parodying the role of voluntarism and alleged patient freedom, bitterly reporting the doctor's instructions: "It's your body, after all, you can do as you please. Vomiting will help you keep down your weight." She and her family were now worried, even desperate, but were united on the need for an all-knowing "expert" who would "prescribe" a comprehensive treatment program that the patient would "fit into," seemingly at no matter what cost to her prerogatives and judgment. It was hoped, in other words, that one consummately correct and guided path, with related prohibitions, would be laid down as a means of rescue, subordinating all else in the patient, but thereby also structuring a probable therapeutic misalliance (Langs 1979). As another severely anorexic and confused woman put it, "Show me a single way, *the* way." This fruitless, narrowed-down search for a kind of omnipotent deity often characterizes the pseudo-solutions sought by many of the most dutiful and caricaturing anorexics and their families (Story 1976). This represents, of course, the antithesis of what works psychotherapeutically, because such patients have little realistic conception of professional competence, much less of expertness. Mystified patients and families such as this have little sense that what "the expert" does derives from the in-some-ways chance conditions of his experience alone, given his personality, resources, values, and biases, as well as the profiles of the particular anorexic patients he has worked with and the various institutions and environments where this work has developed. When the therapeutic work proceeds favorably, the insight acquired by the patient is that "*the* way" can be safely abandoned and discredited; "the way" turns out to be a kind of involuntary, idealized intruder, which in the past has robbed the patient and engulfed self and body.

The need for tangible signs of "progress in treatment," usually in the form of pounds put back on and in the shortest span of time, is inherent in this work. Characteristically, the focus comes to be on numbers, on some quantity of life rather than on the quality of life. This emphasis may be required in order to calm the therapist and family. There can be serious danger, however, in the premature insistence on weight gain, as advised in some behavioral approaches. As well as trivializing the nature of anorexia nervosa, this approach may lead to a highly refractory pseudo-closure and mutual withdrawal, and unwittingly replicate a family pattern of surface well-being and conformity, which is the hallmark of the families of anorexics (Bruch 1978a). Not only does this lead to collusion with the patient in the illusion that pounds regained is the crux of progress in treatment; the premature resolution of underweight runs the still more serious risk of unwittingly pushing the patient into vomiting or some other potentially addictive practice, often in secret, or into an even more ashamed retreat from the therapeutic interaction, or to suicide.

Malignant Autonomy of Symptoms, Impasse, and the Therapeutic Ultimatum

As a precursor of living according to a more total anorexic style, what may be called a *malignant autonomy of symptoms* sometimes evolves. Because such a vast range of experience is excluded in the anorexic patterning of living, these patients bring a concentrated and compensatory fury to their few gripping but essential concerns. To witness true anorexic desperation is virtually to observe an adolescent or young adult reengage wholly around all the preverbal interactions and presymbolic communication patterns of a distorted infant–mother feeding relationship. For some anorexics, dieting, vomiting, exercising, and laxative rituals gradually undergo a crucial subjectively felt change. Thus these symptoms come to be felt passively as totally automatic, unmotivated and unthinking acts; having a separate life of their own, yet at the same time sanctuaries of ritual that include feelings of near-holiness. Malignant autonomy is observable when the anorexic's violently wasteful symptoms come to operate as attenuated, stabilized, and stereotyped forms of repetitive behavior that the patient feels are functioning impersonally beyond herself and may be mocking her. With the recent increase in the use of various hyperalimentation procedures, it is not unusual for such patients to have been frequently hyperalimentated prior to the emergence of the malignant autonomy picture.

A treatment crisis is ushered in when chronic vomiting, for example, becomes so walled off, disengaged, or dissociated from its original field of meaning and intention that the symptom comes to be experienced by the patient, as well as by the therapist in some instances—and usually with anxious foreboding—as increasingly separated from the conscious goals and purposes of the earlier symptom formation. One patient reported, with alarming indifference, during such a phase, "I started this to try to get people to like me for once, but this is different. I don't know who that was. Now it [the patient] can't get anywhere, it doesn't eat. This disgusting, smelly thing just vomits all the time and wants to stay in bed under a blanket all day." When this sense of illness as an independent system overtakes the patient's sense of herself, feelings of habituation, meaninglessness, and futility worsen, and the now controlled patient feels no longer in control. This led sequentially in the patient just described to the fantasy, and then the conviction that, "I must get rid of food," and then to "I must get rid of myself" and/or "I must finally make the body invisible." This sequence is characteristic for many anorexics.

Chronic anorexia nervosa is frequently irreversible and often characterized by these profoundly established conditions; it has a generally unfavorable prognosis. With less chronic patients who are able to be engaged in psychotherapeutic work, there may nevertheless be times when the malignant autonomy syndrome is ascendant. If this state of affairs becomes unrelieved and entrenched, an interactional impasse or deadlock is a serious likelihood. This therapeutic arrest may then foreshadow a power struggle over the control of symptoms, and the symptom picture may well intensify. Only too often, and especially if there is a bullying countertransference response, a therapeutic ultimatum born of the spiralling economy of stored up feelings of helplessness and tactics of unconscious retaliation is ripe to be delivered from above, as it were. In the process, and as comparably described by Cooperman (1979) in the psychotherapy of schizophrenia, the anorexic person may quietly and irreversibly fall out of the focus of therapeutic attention. In short, nutritional politics may replace the therapeutic frame.

This is a complex state of affairs and, at least in this author's experience, not usefully interpreted from a resistance perspective as a defense against further self-disclosure. On the one hand, the starving patient who has regressed nutritionally to this degree is faced with major cognitive and perceptual restrictions and distortions attributable to the frank starvation effects. For example, the dulling of bodily awareness and sense of ownership, underlying or manifest feelings of weakness, depletion, and fatigue (whether denied or not), perseverativeness, associative and imaginative impoverishment, and retardation in thinking are variably prevalent in starvation states. Such conditions are partly the direct result of lowered caloric intake by the starving organism and readily exacerbate existing feelings of helplessness and powerlessness, which anorexic patients find it difficult to describe effectively in any case (Bruch 1978b). On the other hand, and as Winnicott (1966) has observed, anorexia nervosa represents in some patients an attempted defensive solution in which the patient finds it imperative to dissociate psyche and soma, hence the hyphenated "psycho-somatic" dilemma. Thus, in addition to the restricting effects of starvation *per se*, there may be the anorexic's supervalent requirement of maintaining a persistent split in ego-organization with "a denial of mind content" (Winnicott 1966, p. 512) in consequence of this delusional form of psyche-soma dissociation-fragmentation.

To issue a restrictive ultimatum in this context requiring the patient to sacrifice a working and long negotiated symptom for an unknown therapeutic advantage in the uncertain future is a leap that risks losing everything achieved in treatment to date. If the therapist mistakenly responds only to the patient's provocative but unconscious lead and its derivatives, as elucidated by Langs (1978, 1979), he may unwisely choose to score a point but thereby also lose the match. Yet there may still be a place and time for a carefully conceived, even mutually agreed upon prohibition, depending on conditions. It is particularly fortunate when this can be understood by both participants as drastically reducing key options for the patient rather than simply as a proscription or decree. No attempt is made by the therapist to falsify basic terms and ground rules, however. Given the compelling background of falsification, naiveté, and mistaken superimposition of parental needs characteristic of anorexic patients (Bruch 1973), it is especially critical not to pretend that such a decision is other than an ultimatum. If the therapist can safely trust his countertransference feelings about a patient and pay special vigilance to unconscious issues of rescuing, wishes to intimidate and bully, or to shame the patient and extricate himself from a treatment impasse by abandoning the patient, thus freeing himself of feelings of guilt and failure, there is then a time for him to say, "It's me or starving yourself," or "it's me or vomiting," or whatever. As critical as any issue in such a statement is that it must derive from the therapist in his containing, holding, and securing function for the patient. There must be awareness of how openly threatening this is to the patient and recognition that any subsequent alleviation of symptoms, as in a maladaptive "framework cure" (Langs 1978), is not a cure, but rather is a means to restore basic interactional conditions between patient and therapist. As part of resecuring these conditions, it is important for the patient to know that, while she may well continue in her symptomatic pattern, the therapist also is free to decide about his continued participation in their work; that this too is a choice and not a foregone conclusion.

The aim of such an ultimatum is to establish in an active way those conditions in which it will prove possible "to reach the patient where he needs to be reached" (Bird 1972, p. 280). Bird's context, in this succinct remark, is the need of addressing directly the task of enabling a patient "to include the analyst in his neurosis . . . to share his neurosis with the analyst" (p. 279). So too when anorexic symptoms have become walled off in the independent institution described here as malignant autonomy, it is this transference sharing that is effectively removed from the therapeutic interaction. Both patient and therapist then experience the treatment as surrounded by "an encapsulated structure" or regressive symptom barrier, which nullifies interpretation, disengages interaction, and stalemates the treatment. The therapist is thereby sealed off into a passive spectator role, excluded from "active involvement . . . in the central crunch" of the bedrock problem of the transference (Bird 1972, p. 278). The corresponding countertransference feelings stimulated by being made an overtly ineffectual and passive spectator to this block of nonrelatedness include an angry sense of being rendered invisible, impotent and, in a sense, dead or "missing in action." This is precisely when the therapist is best advised to work actively and closely with these often abrasive and retaliatory countertransference feelings and developmental and family replication patterns, both within himself and as they emerge within other staff members, in order to maintain an engaged and cohesive approach.

The ultimatum to reach a tolerable minimum weight or to stop vomiting, when judiciously conceived and timed, is thus a good deal more than a simple suppressive maneuver by the therapist. It is a strenuous and, not infrequently, an almost despairing effort finally to get beneath the anorexic smokescreen and to bring into the therapeutic interaction the derivatives of what has been excluded or watered-down by the patient through the fixed symptomatic behavior or expressed in secret elsewhere within the hospital. Whatever this hitherto latent and disconnected material turns out to be may then be more directly examined. In this sense, the patient is confronted with having to sacrifice a potent adaptive weapon—and no patient, with or without a grave eating disorder, can be expected to give up something useful, if costly, such as an anorexic symptom, without the reciprocal prospect of eventually gaining something at least as advantageous in return.

Carol, described earlier, made a swift response to a mutually agreed upon prohibition against further ritualized vomiting. She clamored that she felt abandoned by the therapist. No such agreement was possible, however, until the patient could trust that the therapist "meant it," that he could tolerate discontinuing their work, although he would also regret it. Very infrequent lapses in observing this prohibition were also able to be discussed in light of the therapist's assessment of the patient's trustworthiness and ability to speak truthfully about her behavior. Her immediate formulation was that she had had little enough from the therapist during her two years of vomiting, but without it she faced "nothingness" and stood to lose everything. As she had felt with her grandmother and sister, who died under what she perceived as deceptive circumstances, the patient felt she was being "tricked" into losing the therapist. Sacrificing vomiting represented "another insidious step" toward a cold and unpeopled world to which the therapist, in turn and like her parents, was sacrificing her. Echoing Winnicott (1966), it was inconceivable that the therapist might intervene with such an ultimatum until he grasped in a paradoxical way the many compelling reasons why it was heretofore impossible, i.e., why the patient could not comply, why she needed to remain ill.

Introducing this marked deviation or gamble is not an intervention that can be at all strongly advocated or unambivalently advised. Nor does this constitute the writer's naively rationalized disclaimer or glib self-contradiction. If invoked as a usual procedure, the therapeutic prohibition makes voluntarism and choice meaningless, and there must be full appreciation, as illustrated throughout this paper, that such an approach is exactly how not to treat anorexia nervosa within a psychotherapeutic frame. "Or else" provides a therapeutic rationale with anorexic persons only in the restricted context of genuine malignant autonomy of symptoms. It is proposed, however, and with as full an awareness as possible of the unconscious contributions to such a state of affairs by both participants, that the therapist need not always dismiss the ultimatum intervention as unthinkable in the therapeutic engagement. A potential major benefit, providing the patient is not made to feel blamed or ashamed of herself, is the eventual opportunity afforded to demonstrate how an ultimatum response arises out of the context of the patient's own activity and of the therapeutic relationship. There is then an opening for the therapist to clarify that this is not simply an authoritarian response to a passively victimized patient, but a more complex occurrence determined in large measure by the patient's intense negativism, distorted psychological state attributable to starvation and vomiting effects and preoccupations, and latent defeating and splitting operations and aggression. Such a turning point also focuses the necessity for the patient to set limits cn her own behavior—i.e., for regression to proceed no further—and to make significant changes in order for the therapy to become unlocked.

ON THERAPEUTIC ALLIANCE AND ATTACHMENT

The attitude regarding the formation and understanding of a patient's attachment to the therapist and the institution is as critical as any of the divisions among treatment philosophies concerning anorexia nervosa and schizophrenia. Encouraging a patient to succumb to undue dependence and to surrender to illness-thinking are two of the many negative ways in which the psychoanalytically oriented treatment of anorexics is questioned, even ridiculed, whether in or out of a residential treatment setting.

The greatest initial leverage and long-range promise and momentum in treatment are afforded when there is no discouragement of a highly personal alliance, attachment, and dependence between patient and therapist, and when the therapist has a highly personal awareness and self-scrutiny of the mutuality and reciprocal nature of these developing interactional processes. This is out of step with the currently ascendant approach of short-term psychiatric hospitalization and the corresponding advocacy of relatively uncomplicated, symptom-focused treatment for this and other severe disorders including schizophrenia. Nevertheless, this author believes that anorexic persons find the most realistic opportunity to learn that they can be understood and their treatment needs met within the relational framework of the universal phenomena of attachment, separation, and loss as these experiences are then recapitulated in the therapeutic interaction.

Ascetic and "self-sacrificing" anorexics, in particular, may see psychotherapy or voluntary admission to a psychotherapeutic hospital as a futile and indefensible frivolity—a variety of costly, even immoral, foolishness. Parents, doctors, and peers often concur, especially when they fear the likelihood of a therapeutic attachment by the patient that is beyond their sphere of control. On their way to the hospital admission interview, for example, the parents of one saintly anorexic begged her, "Promise us you won't fall in love with your doctor there, we just want you back all better." To this kind of young person, treatment is self-indulgent and at the expense of more deserving others; those less privileged and more genuinely troubled who are entitled to the help that, as "gutless" or as "a weakling," she neither needs nor can justify. All too many will not hear of any such treatment. At a deeper level, however, it emerges that some of the more borderline and schizophrenic-like anorexics have already, and in secret, come to view suicide in the form of death through starving the partitioned-off body as if suicide was an almost palpable transitional object designed to negate separation and to deny feelings of abandonment. It may be death to which they become virtually inseparably tied (Spiro and Spiro 1980). The patient pairs off with her body, with food rituals, or with "suicide," then treated as inanimate and under her domination, and may render the formation of a true pairing relationship to the therapist and the hospital problematical, if not impossible (Aronson 1975).

By way of illustration, let us return to Carol. Among the most distressing of Carol's sessions were those that regularly culminated in the patient's sobbing, with body-rocking and head-banging, that her body ("it" or "this," as she referred to her physical being), vomiting, and dying "are all the same." Her grandmother and sister had both died by suicide, and she made plain that this was her unrelenting goal also. This patient was extraordinarily vigilant to all manner of food-, body-, and death-related issues in her meetings with the therapist, with a frantic, addictive and ritualized quality to this attention. Clearly, the patient had particular difficulty with forming, taking in, and holding a stable mental representation of the therapist. Thoughts of death, in particular, were used in the consoling, comforting manner of a would-be transitional object, but brought only momentary relief from feeling utterly separate from and unacceptable to the therapist. As she relinquished slightly her dual preoccupations with dying and with self-starving as a despairing way to render herself "special" to the therapist, she was correspondingly able to correct and master some of her fears of abandonment, "of dissolving into a puddle that just spreads out all over." She then observed, "Maybe when I say I want to be special, a special person to you, what I mean is specific, a person with specific details, but definite to you also. I'm afraid my body is polluting so you wouldn't want to touch me." The self-soothing and tension-reducing preoccupations with body, food, vomiting, and death were thus exposed as unsuccessful and irreconcilable ways to define and bolster her sense of self and paradoxically both to convey and overcome self-loathing feelings of "vileness," "pollution," and "cruelty."

Most anorexics, however, are admitted for hospital care less gripped by suicide than with an innermost debate whether to reduce further, to overeat and vomit, self-mutilate by cutting, or overexercise, etcetera, or engage in productive work. Others are more simply locked into eating the least possible according to a variety of brittle, exhausting, and boring installment plans. These women have recoiled from every imposed or coercive stratagem designed to fatten them up and are gripped by the feeling of having to defy any authority that provides no room for their own opinions or predictable control over their bodies.

The saintly Louisa, mentioned earlier, devoted her life to atoning for having been born a girl and for once weighing 180 pounds. Her atonement was characterized by sadistic self-flogging and immensely willful attempts to differentiate and elevate self and bodily controls to a level of near-saintly detachment and perfection. Her body was then for her more like a fetishistic object, as described by Barkin (1978). Like a kind of vengeful holy dictator, this radically emaciated woman self-imposed a code where possibilities for change, growth, and intimate human attachments and related separations were systematically obliterated. Her exaggerated efforts to find forgiveness and self-mastery routinely ended in stagnation, thereby mastering and enslaving her. The body then became a kind of magical fetish, and the conditions for workable therapeutic attachment were only marginally present in the sense that the patient valued her negative relationship to her body and to starvation rituals more than a relationship to the therapist as a separate and reliable figure.

The case of Roberta may have a déjà vu character to those who work with anorexic persons in so-called hospitals of last resort. Much of Roberta's seemingly quixotic, snappish, and moody presentation conveyed to her frustrated therapist, in the latter's words, "almost a need on her part not to make an alliance with anyone," least of all with him. She gradually revealed having slipped into anorexic routines marked by secretive vomiting and dieting, eccentric nutritional preferences, laxative abuse, and pronounced weight loss following 11 previous robot-like psychiatric hospitalizations between ages 20 and 27. Her attempted anorexic resolution to periodically florid schizophrenic fragmentation emerged after repeated brief hospital treatments consisting of electroshock therapy, antipsychotic and antidepressant medication, and megavitamins, but without sustained human intervention. Unmistakably, it could be inferred that the guiding purpose in all her treatment had been the fundamentally punitive one of "correcting" her nutrition and obliterating all manifestations of her intense negativism, defiance, sadism, and "anger."

No less clear was the patient's struggle with how confused and frozen she had come to feel. But she was insistent on one point: she and her body were victims of coercion by her family, who seemed to have much more at stake than anyone else in her hospital admissions. Yet she was admitted to this hospital voluntarily, if warily, and met erratically with her therapist, wishing appointments precisely when none were scheduled. In her mistrust and puzzling day-to-day shifts, it was easy to ignore the offhand, subtly phrased, but near-confessional statements of this brutalized anorexic woman that she still sought and hoped for therapeutic contact and understanding. What had earlier looked to the despairing therapist like a need not to make a treatment alliance then came to be evidence to him of the impossibility of making a workable therapeutic contract between a hired hospital and concerned family alone. With anorexics even more than most, it is crucial that whom treatment is for be identified as a means of learning where the patient can be joined. Intensive psychotherapy cannot be successfully conducted or sustained if the anorexic patient persists indefinitely in the unchallenged or uninterpreted assertion that "I'm here only because my mother sent me." Condensing much subsequent data, the therapist gradually learned that

Roberta's need was to create an interconnection or pair formation with a therapist that was not imposed in the sense that it was not "expected" of her, nor was it something she was falsely bribed or coerced into or then smothered by in a one-way operation.

Of Roberta's several deprivations, including being deprived of useable treatment, there was no more striking form of starvation in her life than having missed out on any known experience of mutually established connectedness and positive attachment. Instead, she had been sealed into a despairing and at least partially iatrogenic and adversarial struggle over what nourishment and what feelings were deemed "suitable," then to be grafted on or forced into her.

The treatment needs and planning for such patients, including the conceptualization of attachment and the structuring of the therapeutic environment, are inherently long range. The therapist needs to develop a corresponding internal set that will equip him for the particular cadences and slow tempo of working with such patients and help him keep pace in a way that adheres to the therapeutic values of patience and modest hopefulness—admittedly, a tall order. There are no developmental shortcuts or artificial abbreviations with anorexics to the relearning of more adaptive cognitive foundations or the resumption of expectable attachments and unashamed growth processes.

Dinnage (1979) errs in proposing that anorexics are "peculiarly hard to nourish therapeutically"—they differ little from other seriously disturbed patients in this respect. (She attributes this to their being "dedicated to refusal," but this also is a pessimistic and unempathic view.) Nevertheless, she is on the mark in concluding that for anorexics, "a little psychotherapy may be a dangerous thing; for them, drink deep or not at all" (p. 9). There is, however, the related complication that certain "professional" or "atypical" anorexics harbor unusually strong addictive yearnings and liabilities that may get mobilized through exchanging their addiction to an anorexic style for an addiction to self-preoccupation or for a form of religious conversion via an overdose of psychoanalytic psychotherapy. It is obvious that the "good-enough holding environment" of intensive psychotherapy should not become a holding down or holding back environment by unwittingly becoming a new addictive agent for the patient, as best this can be prevented.

Starving the body and self-induced vomiting take on, for many anorexics, qualities of dependable fetishes that are more reliable than any other tie, animate or otherwise. In treating their bodies and anorexic rituals fetishistically rather than as useful transitional objects or experiences, those with severe anorexia nervosa find that there can be immensely self-soothing and anxiety-regulating results, however short-lived, from their particular approach. All too clearly, the body lends itself to this impeccable kind of mechanical control. But built into this style is the anorexic's private certainty that no end-point is possible to her endless tinkering with this or that aspect of her body, with which an anorexic can never be comfortably or simply alone.

One of the most serious difficulties met with in interpretive psychotherapy with anorexics, therefore, is just that anorexia nervosa unhappily works all too well in terms of attaining total control and predictability. The anorexic discovers that she can depend on her body, on this possession that is all hers (although many complain that they don't feel their bodies or know where they begin and end). She can more or less predict how her body will act, and bring it under her powers of control and defensive dissociation. This is compellingly seductive and, to some, irresistible. Similarly, intervening therapeutically at this manifest level can prove irresistible to therapists who may attempt to sell the patient on something better still. Failing this, the therapist may prematurely and impatiently interpret the patient's "hostility," with the implication that only the therapist speaks with authority about such matters. But, because it is just another manipulation, this tactic is experienced by the patient as trying to bring her under the therapist's control and rob her of her illness, which is more abhorrent even than the isolation and sterility of her anorexic style. This fear of manipulation and of having her own confusing experiences ignored by the therapist is well captured in a kind of brief signature statement by a patient about her retreat from the persecuting world: "My starting point, my premise is that no one will really be there for me. Or that the monsters out there will take over, like my mother who was always doing good for others. And so being alone is what I do. My teddy bear is still here with my food, though. I hate people who try to force their self-respect on me." The patient reported this in the context, described earlier, of revealing how she had been advised by a previous therapist to vomit as a means of weight control.

This author's experience has been that prolonged engagement or intervention exclusively around the minutiae of "reality" about anorexics' symptom life insures that the therapist will get shut out from their dread of separation, loss, and loneliness. A crucial countertransference pitfall created by such patients is their diversionary ability to get therapists to deal endlessly and solely with their quite monotonous symptom pictures, in which it is hard for a careful therapeutic listener to sustain real interest anyway. This is one of the chief ways that anorexics unhappily devise to alienate those on whom they may desperately want to depend. In this way, the therapist unwittingly conspires to shy away from interpreting or tangling with the anorexic's wish/fear of separation and dread of intimacy. There may then be reconfirmation for the patient that "my body is all I have," robbing her of the opportunity to learn with the therapist a path to a transitional experience or bridgework that will make the ambivalently feared and longed for connectedness possible and real.

Evidence of the kinds of cognitive and relational disturbances that may underlie a cluster of anorexic symptoms is glimpsed in an example provided by Carol, a woman who kept elaborate records for many years of every morsel or drop of nourishment she took in daily as an aspect of her pattern of self-starvation, vomiting, gorging, and self-biting. When she had resolved and managed for a period to stop her dieting and vomiting, Carol made a panicky telephone call to the therapist at night:

As I have kept up with my eating schedule, I mean not vomiting too, and I weigh over 100 pounds now, I feel very scared. But something is coming back to me. My perception of time changes as the day goes on into night. I can't seem to change in myself from one experience to another, from being with my aunt when she visits, even though I don't get on well with her, to when she leaves and it is so different. As if I can find no bridge for this, to being so still, alone now. Now my body feels different too, and everything comes together at night, and I want to cry or scream and break this up [relationship to therapist], so that is why I needed to talk to you. Because I know this: I want this [treatment] to work, but I just dread whatever is worse than vomiting, behind the vomiting. I am terrified of having to quit my therapy, but what is in store for me if I stop vomiting I dread even more, and I don't even know what I mean when I say that. It is just like *there is no bridge for me in me* [author's italics].

Also illustrative is the first trip taken after a year and a half of productive treatment by another anorexic woman in her twenties who considered leaving behind her portable scales, or "secret weapon" as she called them, on a trip to Europe. This woman was allegedly "arthritic," but privately her "arthritis" did not convincingly explain to her what was actually very diffuse pain and achiness throughout much of her body, or persuade her regarding the restriction against athletics and ballet. She also lacked clear knowledge of what worked well about her body, relied on mirrors almost exclusively for a pseudo-awareness of her shape and boundaries, and could not eat in public. These difficulties suddenly fused with the tremendous fear and hatred aroused in her during her first meeting, at age 17, with an analyst (also her mother's analyst, as it happened) who inquired "almost before (she) sat down, in the first ten minutes," not about her eating problems, but about the patient's sex life, specifically about whether she achieved orgasm. In this context of empathic failure, she initially experienced psychotherapy with the author as a form of "penetration" prescribed by the referring psychiatrist; she felt numbly opposed.

Carrying her scales represented to her a method of attachment and pairing with a fixed and reliable "friend" (her term), an alliance that could magically help to tell her about herself. Although she had come to feel securely attached with the therapist and self-aware enough to leave her scales at home, she once strayed from an assigned meeting place in a new city, became lost, and felt panicky. Her first thought was to buy new scales and fly home, all the while hearing her mother's warning voice that "it served you [her] right for leaving home." Not for wandering off or for leaving her scales at home, but for leaving home at all, was what she imagined her mother was saying, which she later recognized as "so I see why I thought carrying scales was better than carrying that voice around."

A comparable dread was expressed by another patient who could not safely travel where she might not always have a full-length mirror available. Reports of travelling by anorexic patients routinely reveal their long-standing problems of self-anchoring, the paucity of realistic transitional objects and experiences beyond their own bodies, and their corresponding dread of human alliance and loss issues as these become more clearly focused interpretively.

THE INTEGRATIVE "HOLDING ENVIRONMENT"

There is a very sizeable literature, dating at least to the work of Simmel (1929) in his "sanatorium," the Tegel Clinic, about the enormously complex interplay of psychotherapy and sociotherapy in the therapeutically committed social system. However, in regard to the particular psychotherapeutic hospital as a specially created organization, actual "holding environment," or containing frame, that provides real as well as symbolic gratifications, only a few observations must suffice. With patients caught up in a wearying anorexic marathon, it is crucial that the therapist, nursing, medical, laboratory, dietary, activities, and housekeeping staffs have the ability to recognize and to work patiently, without undue anxiety, in the midst of people who are dependent on self-starving, food-hoarding, vomiting, hyperexercising, etcetera. Relatively few professionals in these fields choose or are attracted to this kind of work, but among those who are, staff feelings about patients and their care run deep, and covert disagreements and confusion are readily created, especially when working with patients in genuine life and death crises, as severe anorexics often are. Each patient's care is led and coordinated by the psychotherapist-in-charge. In treating anorexics, this demands the close collaboration of all hospital departments in a facilitating climate designed to open communication, to reduce oppositional alliances, to clarify boundaries among the hospital's various therapeutic modalities

(Kernberg 1976), and to monitor and mitigate against honest differences of opinion being misinterpreted as, or then escalating into, staff splitting.

The patient is not and cannot usefully be seen as "belonging to" the therapist. The patient is a patient of the particular hospital, not of the therapist alone; the latter also being a hospital staff member, with particular responsibilities simultaneously to the institution, the patient, and to some degree the patient's family as well. Exceedingly prickly countertransference issues can be generated if the therapist sees his two sets of responsibilities, to patient and hospital, as antithetical or as undermining the patient's personal therapeutic relationship. When the therapist is seduced, either by himself or the patient, into believing that the patient is "his" alone, staff integration is threatened, and perhaps impossible.

The issue of the "double agency" position of the therapist (Searles 1978) and the need for coordinated staff participation may be critical in treating those anorexics who are strongly attracted, even addicted, to the kind of brinkmanship that inexorably challenges the continuation of the patient's psychotherapy, especially in an open setting. All the resources of the empathic holding environment may be severely tried and tested by such patients who appear totally involved in the Russian roulette game of false self-sufficiency and self-destructiveness, and who simultaneously appear ignorant of or magically deny any ill effects, while covertly feeling deeply dependent on the milieu and the therapist.

The following illustration captures many of the stormy problems of retributive regressive assault by a chronic anorexic patient being kept alive seemingly against her will. Baptized with an explicitly male first name, Henry, a woman in her thirties, had been anorexic for 12 years before coming to this hospital. She had been in an apparently fruitless treatment for some years with a noted psychoanalyst and eventually conferred for several weeks with a leading consultant. Throughout, Henry was keenly aware of the eminence of her various doctors. On admission, it was as though she wore a sign that proclaimed, "Henry is still an anorexic; the famous doctors have failed." Since this latest hospital also came highly touted, the staff were vaguely prepared for experiencing a similar failure.

The patient could be described as slowly creating a full-fledged, albeit carefully modulated, murderous struggle with the entire hospital. This struggle emerged as her predominant mode of living and proved to be almost the only focus that this woman could actively connect to in her care, a focus familiar to those who have worked with terminal cases of anorexia nervosa. Even to a relatively uninvolved observer of this woman, who came to resemble in her appearance a cadaverous cancer patient, the fantasy was unavoidable that she might "pull the plug" at a moment's notice and bring her life and treatment to a quick end. Instead, she tended to leave both her life and therapy in suspension. In ways not very different from those of some young religious schizophrenics involved in cults, whose schizophrenia is both their illness and their therapy or hoped-for salvation, Henry became consolidated around the identity "anorexic," and engaging in a kind of professional anorexia nervosa became her basic therapy, with its own kind of adaptiveness. Establishing even the simplest forms of collaborative access and leverage with such a patient requires initially and repeatedly conveying in some unmistakable way that she can count on the therapist to respect this simultaneously self-destructive but adaptive stance, to forego intellectual collusion, and to free the treatment atmosphere of any residue of advice to "cooperate," "try harder," etcetera, which may linger from previous attempts in treatment but which disregard the anorexic's long and intensely needed and long worked out defensive dissociation of self and body.

Staff reviews of this kind of treatment challenge are invariably frequent, anxiety-arousing, and chronically inconclusive, while also imperative; in Henry's case, these often included her participation. After several emergency admissions to a medical-surgical hospital because of seriously lowered blood protein and electrolyte levels and weight loss, she made it clear that she had become bent on a course of brinkmanship with death, a course that took on the unrelieved, irreversible tone of a fight to the finish. She was enraged that the staff would not finally concede that she was hopeless and "worthy of death" and battled especially with her therapist to change his mind about her. Yet not killing herself also reinforced staff respect for her integrity. If a more straightforward suicide than by self-starvation was her goal, it was clear that she could carry this out rather simply. Instead, she became drawn to a contest of wills in which the process dynamics involving issues of power monopoly and personal autonomy, including her freedom to die, were far more vital than the specific and predictable content of the day-to-day fights with the staff.

It was also gradually clear that even in this alternately death-seeking and death-defying arrangement there were elements of a paradoxical form of attachment to the environment that included openly stated positive and respectful feelings for the therapist and certain nurses, as well as considerable, but hated, reliance on the entire milieu staff and patient community. Throughout, and with all staff resisting as consciously as possible in all their interactions with Henry the impulse to rob the patient of her own prerogatives and to "be everything" for her, which much of her behavior unconsciously invited, staff integration centered around valuing the staff's own survival, the need of not being overwhelmed, refusing to collude knowingly in the patient's death, and recognizing the voluntarist value structure of the psychotherapeutic hospital. What then? The otherwise predictable confusion and power struggles evoked in a staff could to some extent be headed off, a minimally cohesive treatment contract was sustained, and the holding environment remained open to the care of other anorexic patients, which Henry's monopolistic and aristocratic ways threatened retributively to assault.

The approach by the internal medicine consultant taken in Henry's care was of critical importance. The cohesive hospital-wide treatment enterprise, which may at critical times become quite fragile but is imperative from the point of view of the psychotherapist and hospital staff in treating patient's like Henry, is vitally assisted by an internist's nonalarmist and quiet consultative approach. One is reminded of the controversial recommendation of Winnicott (1966) that "what the psychotherapist needs is the cooperation of a *not too scientific* physical doctor . . . *a scientist on holiday from science*" (p. 512). After observing and working with several different internal medicine and gastroenterology consultants in connection with the anorexics reported in this paper, one becomes partial to the spirit of this claim, although it tends to "break the rules." The collaboration required when working with these patients has been described here as anxiety-arousing and threatening to staff integration. What tends to worsen such divisions is the rigidly pristine application of objective findings in ways that bully the patient in her delusional approach to her body and undermine the collective psychotherapeutic attitude. More useful over the long term is a less compulsive, less scientistic attitude in which the internist or laboratory nurse can be perceived by the anorexic patient as "the understanding one," a relaxed ally who is able not to enter the fray during negative phases of the transference as it develops. Ideally, the internist possesses a well-developed tolerance for uncertainty and ambiguity, and can even be free to engage in a certain kind of adaptive and lenient illogic in the face of the bizarre, stubbornly irrational, and shame-laden nutritional practices and theories that preoccupy these patients as they struggle toward health.

LIMITED USE OF PHARMACOTHERAPY

Anorexia nervosa lends itself to understanding and treatment in ways that are paradigmatic for other severe disorders, such as schizophrenia. But whereas a welter of clashing opinions, judgments, findings, and practices contend for serious consideration in the spectrum of treatments of schizophrenia, especially as regards the use of pharmacotherapy, this is somewhat less the case for anorexia nervosa. Anorexia nervosa appears to be a more clear-cut, more highly differentiated and focalized condition than schizophrenia—a kind of circumscribed "spot" schizophrenia—although often no less disabling. On first contact most anorexic persons are not immediately "crazy," even though possessed by an often bizarre-appearing and alarming symptom that may represent a more clearly delineated form of turmoil and rebellion against expectations of conformity and accommodation than seen in certain more fully schizophrenic patients. It is the case, nevertheless, that the most desperate and brittle anorexics are able, in truly delusional fashion, to take only one position regarding their condition: they live in constant fear of a disorganizing madness that will overwhelm them if they deviate from their ritualized and uncompromising patterns of behavior. In all-or-none fashion, such anorexics come to believe that, "If I am not perfect, I am nobody, and vulnerable to total chaos."

The psychotherapeutic hospital treatment of anorexia nervosa approaches the use of pharmacotherapy as, in the main, diversionary. This is not to stigmatize psychotropic medication, but rather to maintain that such medication can unwittingly provide a screen or disguising context that may further falsify the anorexic's awareness and turn the therapy away from the free pursuit of the correcting of awareness and as a barrier to the analysis and interpretation of the transference and resistance. Recourse to psychotropic medication is thus usually an emergency or exceptional measure in the psychoanalytically informed treatment of anorexics, rather than having a regular adjunctive role, except for allaying truly disorganizing states of anxiety.

It is unusual, except with hypochondriacally preoccupied and excited anorexic patients, for such patients to independently request much in the way of regular prescribed medication. This frequent antimedication bias by anorexics does not simply or obediently parrot therapist preferences for drug-free treatment. The patients tend to perceive the introduction of pharmacotherapy into psychoanalytically oriented psychotherapy as a form of oral coercion identified as originating outside themselves, hence latently disturbing or even poisonous. When medication is requested by anorexic patients, the family background usually discloses marked and uncritical reliance on drugs and/or alcohol for the relief of a wide range of symptoms and a related quasi-magical, family-wide conviction that the hand placing a substance in the mouth is the most trustworthy avenue of tension reduction.

A broader constraint is to avoid the use of medication as a substitute for understanding the anorexic patient and the often gruesome process of clarifying her awareness and experience. The therapist is charged with remaining vigilant to the possibilities for introducing psychotropic medication as an unwitting flight or withdrawal from the anorexic person, as an inconsistent or contradictory shunning of relation, and as an avenue for losing sight of these isolated, lonely, routine-obsessed, and painfully anonymous, invisibility-seeking patients.

It is also important, however, that the frustration by the patient of the staff's sometimes overvalued wishes "to help" not lead to the unwitting use of medication as a countertransference rationalization in the face of the intense rage and the need to "disidentify" with the bizarre perspectives of anorexic and schizophrenic patients that such frustration readily provokes (Kartus and Schlesinger 1957, Deikman 1971). There is, in short, an occasional adjunctive role for pharmacotherapy here, the meanings of which to anorexic patients and to staff need not be disruptive, despairing, or punitive, and medication can be inappropriately withheld (Levy 1977). Thus, when tranquilizing medication is appropriately introduced, it can occupy a role at the level of assisting in basic survival maintenance and for achieving intended antidisorganization and anti-self-mutilation effects otherwise unattainable in treatment to date. These latter circumstances tend to be infrequent, however, and may reveal that the psychotherapist is unknowingly confused, seriously overloaded, and either impatient for or paradoxically intolerant of change in his patient from the conditions of extreme, persistent, and imprisoning stasis that characterize the anorexic syndrome.

SEPARATION OF PATIENT FROM FAMILY

Admission to a psychotherapeutic hospital entails that the anorexic patient resituate herself in a residential treatment center for one, two, or more years. For the patient, this is often a radical and initially resisted disruption from the familiar. It involves a very significant change in and loss of contact for all family members, and is not lightly or casually recommended. The patient is encouraged to think of this living arrangement as a kind of personal "new address," albeit temporary. Correspondingly, the treatment is conceived of as primarily focused on, requested by, and undertaken by the identified or index patient.[4]

Conceived in this way, treatment is not aimed primarily at reuniting patient and family, at least in a physical sense, but rather toward the anorexic's disengagement from family, separation and reindividuation, individual initiative-taking, autonomy, and the resumption of an interrupted developmental progression as a going concern in her own right. It is inseparable from the psychoanalytic attitude that there exist no inspired shortcuts or passwords to human growth and, as noted above, patient and family are encouraged to move in their thinking away from the sterile, palliative, and arithmetic fallacy that simple symptom removal is a meaningful psychotherapeutic goal.

The patient's family, often living at a great distance from the hospital, is not ignored but is worked with as indicated, especially in the opening phases, from

4. This strategy does not devalue the patient's family per se or belittle the family approach to treatment. Instead, the kinds of anorexic patients and families reported on here are considerably older than, say, those described by Minuchin et al. (1978) and Palazzoli (1974), and are confronting rather different developmental difficulties.

an educative perspective. The support and cooperation of most families are best promoted by building in only intermittent direct treatment contact with parents. While these patients initially fear separating from family and the family's eating patterns and rituals before they have been able to find reassurance through the therapist's commitment, strength, and knowledge, virtually all of the anorexic persons treated have felt fundamentally relieved by this disengagement from the vestiges of their enmeshed family life. This separation can then provide "time out" for these young women to learn about themselves with lessened interference from parents.

The parents of many anorexics come across as secret experts on what ails their anorexic daughters, dogmatically prescribing what they perceive as the only acceptable modalities of treatment based on their often extensive reading of the scientific and popularized literature on this recently much publicized illness. Thus, when a patient in this setting profits significantly from treatment, she rarely chooses to return to her original home, which is often associated with a lifelong sense of failure, captivity, intrusiveness, and defensive collusion in illness.

Annette, a schizoid Southern woman, had pursued a driven course of excellence—in fact, perfection—in riding and showing horses, but also came near to death through self-starvation. Realizing how cynical, envious, and boring she had felt within her family, she observed soon after leaving home for admission to the hospital how similar her feelings of personal deficiency experienced in a patient community meeting were to her family life:

> I never know what I feel and they [the other patients] always say I'm misinterpreting, so I can't really say what anything is; it's just something I never get right. . . . So now I get letters from my mother telling me how I feel, how well I'm doing in therapy, even what I'm doing here [in the hospital]. Other people seem to know, too, and I even have to write thank-you notes [for being here]. But I don't trust anything I feel, so how does she know what is going on with me?

Separated from her family, Annette's gross ignorance of her own perceptual life and her resentful adroitness in soliciting or sensing, often incorrectly, the perceptions of others became painfully clear to her. The patient's parents were impressively stimulating and accomplished people, and once apart from them she began to recognize, with a sense of grievance, that she had not developed into a colorful or interesting person herself, but instead was a socially conforming, concealing, and rather tediously ingratiating parrot (her favorite bird, in fact). In corroborating Bruch's (1973) observations, this patient was able, when removed from the pathogenic home environment, to reformulate her previously devotional view of her mother. Her mother was then seen as someone whom she had permitted to mastermind her life and thereby to impose her reality on her at the cost of falsifying her own cognitive development and self-differentiation.

FURTHER IMPLICATIONS AND CONCLUSIONS

One of the most critical issues in the treatment of anorexia nervosa is the cornerstone need for the psychotherapist and hospital staff to clarify what they believe to be the basic nature of this syndrome and to show how their theoretical conceptions relate to how they then go about the treatment. If, for example, the guiding conceptualization of anorexia nervosa is of a weight disturbance, an endocrine disorder, a developmental disaster in body-image formation, a distorted body-phallus metaphor, a perceptual-cognitive impairment, a target symptom in a family neurosis, or an oral perversion, quite divergent treatment methods necessarily follow. Many anorexics come to treatment only too grimly ready to submit to confirmation from the therapist that their difficulties are beyond human comprehension or clarification and, by implication, are lesser, different, more repugnant than or inferior to those of more deserving others; or, conversely, greater, more virtuous, and slyly superior. Failure by the therapist to formulate a coherent picture of the etiology of anorexia nervosa (which requires some depth of therapeutic experience with anorexic patients) and/or adopting a therapeutic attitude that conveys to the patient that her anorexic difficulties are fundamentally "different" and unique or illness-specific are inherent hazards. Both risk having our empathic capacity for access to and understanding of where the anorexic patient subjectively *is* significantly lessened or completely erased (Searles 1975).

The formulations of the etiology of anorexia nervosa that bear out most closely the collaborative work with severely anorexic women reported here are those of Bruch (1973, 1978a, 1978b) and Winnicott (1966). The momentum and focus of Bruch's contributions, in particular, demonstrate multiple ways in which eating disturbances—previously misdiagnosed, misconceived, or mismanaged—may now be reconsidered, and her work marks a new beginning in the enigmatic field of anorexia nervosa.

The psychoanalytically informed treatment of anorexia nervosa, as outlined in this paper, draws us compellingly to the systematic investigation of late childhood and early adolescence, when actual or future anorexic symptoms often appear in manifest form for the first time, but about which so much mystery and ignorance remain. Anorexia nervosa is understood here within a developmental and adaptive framework as a camouflage symptom disguising and circumscribing, in the most disturbed persons, profound underlying early difficulties of a kind encountered in more overt borderline, schizoid, and schizophrenic pathology to which the observations in this paper also apply. Although usually feeling helpless to change, and often unaware of or denying any connection between self (psyche) and body or symptom (soma), the severely anorexic patient actively maintains her self-starving approach within the context of an outwardly disorganized eating pattern and underlying primitive developmental arrest. It is the period *before* the appearance of the manifest but disguising anorexic resolution that is the eventual focus of long-term investigative and corrective psychotherapy. Thus this paper has included extensive clinical material illustrating how it cannot be overemphasized that collusion by the therapist with patient and family into treating weight and eating symptoms alone and in isolation trivializes the treatment of anorexia nervosa.

Many severe anorexics, full of unhappy knowingness about the scientific name of their disorder, now identify themselves as such and as if they might thereby be secondarily envied. Anorexia nervosa is often a hoped-for way to be loved, and for such persons it can become a kind of creed. They then live according to the tenets of an encompassing anorexic style. Covert interest in public display of the starving and skinny body (i.e., a paradoxical exhibitionistic element) is often associated. A high-status disorder of late in some circles, anorexia nervosa has been rendered even more refractory to effective treatment intervention by recent glamorized views of this smokescreen kind of disorder; views that complicate in harmful, cruel, and often silly ways what is shown here and throughout the clinical literature to be an immensely confining illness. Suggestive of this dimension of anorexia nervosa as a facade or a display form of camouflage is the dream-image reported by one emaciated anorexic: in her dream, another young woman in the hospital, also anorexic, is performing cartwheels on a theater stage, wearing a black and white Halloween skeleton costume and counting the number of ribs. The patient's father is in the audience applauding. With sadness, but also pleased to be able to understand this image as a disguise, the patient then said, "that sounds like me and my anorexia."

Admitted as a "last resort" to a long-term psychotherapeutic hospital, many anorexic persons have already suffered previous humiliating treatment failures. Much time is required for those anorexics, who feel brutalized, bitterly forced to eat against their will and ignored as human persons during other hospitalizations, to develop any other perspective or participate in a mutual treatment compact and to feel held in a secure and nonthreatening environment (Bruch 1978b). Such cynical convictions all too easily overshadow embarking on any further treatment initiatives. In part as an attempt to allow the patient to come out gradually from under this overshadowing pessimistic preconception of hospital treatment, and in part as a psychotherapeutic ground plan of making intervention relevant to the investigation of the latent meaning of the symptom, rather than make the palliative effort to remove the symptom, the therapist needs to be able to leave the patient alone about the so-called "realistic" problems of eating matters, except in a true nutritional crisis where a failure to intervene at that level is obviously irresponsible. The critical issue is that, optimally, the patient should be able to perceive this stance as representing the therapist's awareness of and respect for her adaptive and economic need of this symptom for an indefinite period of time. Using whatever means, the therapist is assigned the empathic task of participating in the therapeutic interaction so as to convey that this position does not reveal indifference about or withdrawal from the patient as a total person or demand an expected premature integration in order for her to remain cared for at all levels.

This paper has presented the favorable or facilitating circumstances, or an actual form of "good-enough holding environment," with related symbolic meanings, in which the patient can gradually integrate for the first time in her life, can correct and broaden her awareness, including awareness of the interior life and of hunger sensations, and can abandon the long necessary dissociative and splitting defenses embodied in the anorexic impasse. This waiting and empathic approach appears necessary for an anorexic patient to be able to accept that eating and other rituals, especially vomiting, can provide her only momentary relief, that these practices do not promote the integrative mastery of her dread, or negation, of abandonment, and in true fetishistic style can be neither integrated nor immediately relinquished.

It is painfully and recurrently plain to any therapist attempting to treat an anorexic patient that the latter starts with a considerably greater belief in the controlled life of dieting, starvation, and body management than in the interactional human process of psychotherapy. Some of these patients have recourse to a peculiar form of relentless proselytizing for their rigidly and primitively fixated convictions, both with the therapist and with other hospitalized patients, especially kindred anorexics. It can prove difficult indeed to challenge the anorexic patient's insistence on assuming independent control over her body and destiny, of which many anorexics have long felt deprived. Yet this too may have defensive and splitting functions, with the patient's underlying delusional system hidden beneath a seemingly well-reasoned facade. The therapist may then be faced with the countertransference urge to argue the patient out of her beliefs, as futile and ill-conceived with anorexic convictions as with more blatantly psychotic phenomena. Moreover, since the attempt to argue and debate is experienced by the therapist as a retreat from the usual psychotherapeutic framework of an open, listening attitude, he is led to the disconcerting recognition of his abandonment of his own scientific and therapeutic ego-ideals, which readily threatens the roots of his sense of personal integrity.

Conversely, when an anorexic patient has progressed sufficiently to be able to sacrifice splitting defenses and to progress in terms of the correction of bodily awareness and previous body-image distortions, the therapist's corresponding satisfaction, even complacency, may trigger the countertransference urge to overidentify with the patient's success in gaining weight and in her developing views that are more congruent with his own ideas about the normal body. This overidentification is experienced by the patient as the therapist's desertion of her, as a loss of the mental representation of the therapist that anorexics have such problems in forming, holding, and integrating. A return of symptoms, including a return to the more accustomed body image and self-representation entailed, may be necessary for the patient to reacquire her sense of being held in the therapeutic interaction (Giovacchini 1980).

Anorexic patients share with other kinds of borderline and schizophrenic patients an uncanny ability to evoke a version of their own self-representations in the therapist's own sense of self. In this evocation, the therapist absorbs a projected self-representation deposited by the patient. This may include an absorption of important stylistic aspects of the anorexic mentality, especially the severely arithmetical, equilibrating, and fastidious frame of mind in anorexia nervosa, as well as the anorexic's pervasive feelings of hopelessness, inadequacy, and personal ineffectiveness, which are readily taken in as countertransference images in the therapist's self-representation.

One of the endlessly challenging problems for which anorexic patients become notorious, especially on hospital wards, is their dissociative inclination to separate or split "psyche-care from soma-care" Winnicott (1966). This constitutes a psychosomatic manifestation of the "scatter of responsible agents," another of Winnicott's evocative terms. The natural divisions in a program of patient care are readily exploited by anorexic patients and their families in such a way that the agents of patient care are fragmented and scattered. Fearful of and at the same time seeking a unified personality, anorexic patients incline to "need(ing) us to be split up (yet essentially united in the far background that they cannot allow themselves to know about)" (Winnicott 1966, p. 514). To work psychotherapeutically with such patients risks evoking intolerable feelings of discord, inadequacy, disorganization, and frustration in the therapist and associated staff as the cohesive and integrative functions that hospital agencies aim to promote are routinely undone; such work is accompanied by the array of interlocking countertransference and noncountertransference feelings documented earlier, as in the case of Henry. The therapist's ability to recognize and contend with his own turmoil and counteraggressive feelings in the face of a disavowed relationship, and the patient's need to dictate and split the treatment, are shown here to be critical in developing full recognition that the anorexic patient's need to fragment her care does not have to threaten the treatment but is, instead, its requirement. There appears to be the further requirement that the therapist, as part of his holding/containing capacity, be able to convey to the anorexic patient that her intense criticalness and sadism do not control or destroy him and that these feelings do not need to be medicated out of awareness. The therapist's presumably more accepting and benign superego can thereby be gradually and safely incorporated by the patient. This climate appears to be further facilitated by the long-term separation of patient and family.

Finally, this paper presents and illustrates a point of view about the minimal use of pharmacotherapy and describes a particular kind of therapeutic prohibition technique. With the latter, an ultimatum is invoked which places a limit on the role of sustained empathy in favor of a forceful confrontation, but which is to be used only at the point where the patient's symptoms are characterized by the walled off condition of malignant autonomy. The dangers and unexamined pitfalls of intervening with a poorly conceived or timed therapeutic ultimatum are described in detail.

REFERENCES

Aronson, G. (1975). Crucial aspects of therapeutic interaction. In *Psychotherapy of Schizophrenia*, eds. J. Gunderson and L. Mosher, pp. 43–51. New York: Jason Aronson.

Barchilon, J. (1973). Pleasure, mockery and creative integrations: their relationship to childhood knowledge, a learning defect and the literature of the absurd. *International Journal of Psycho-Analysis* 54:19–34.

Barkin, L. (1978). The concept of the transitional object. In *Between Reality and Fantasy*, ed. S. Grolnick and L. Barkin, pp. 513–537. New York: Jason Aronson.

Binswanger, L. (1944). Der Fall Ellen West. In *Existence*, eds. R. May, E. Angel, and H. Ellenberger, pp. 237–364. New York: Basic Books, 1958.

Bird, B. (1972). Notes on transference: universal phenomenon and hardest part of analysis. *Journal of the American Psychoanalytic Association* 20:267–301.

Bruch, H. (1973). *Eating Disorders: Obesity, Anorexia Nerovsa, and the Person Within*. New York: Basic Books.

——. (1978a). *The Golden Cage: The Enigma of Anorexia Nervosa*. Cambridge, Mass. Harvard University Press.

——. (1978b). Dangers of behavior modification in treatment of anorexia nervosa. In *Controversy in Psychiatry*, eds. J. P. Brady and H. K. H. Brodie, pp. 645–654. Philadelphia: W. B. Saunders.

Cooperman, M. (1979). Some comments on psychoanalytic psychotherapy with schizophrenic people, a possible development, and some caveats. *National Association of Private Psychiatric Hospitals Journal* 10:16–21.

Deikman, A. J. (1971). Phenothiazines and the therapist's fear of identification. *Humanistic Psychology* 11:196–200.

Dinnage, R. (1979). The starved self. *The New York Review* 26:6–9.

Giovacchini, P. L. (1980). Countertransference and therapeutic turmoil. Paper presented at the Austen Riggs Center, Inc., Stockbridge, Massachusetts, March 14.

Kartus, I., and Schlesinger, H. J. (1957). The psychiatric hospital-physician and his patient. In *The Patient and the Mental Hospital,* ed. M. Greenblatt, pp. 286–299. Glencoe, Illinois: The Free Press.

Kernberg, O. (1975). *Borderline Conditions and Pathological Narcissism.* New York: Jason Aronson.

———. (1976). *Object Relations Theory and Clinical Psychoanalysis.* New York: Jason Aronson.

Khan, M. M. (1964). Ego distortion, cumulative trauma, and the role of reconstruction in the analytic situation. *International Journal of Psycho-Analysis* 45:272–278.

Klein, G. S. (1976). *Psychoanalytic Theory.* New York: International Universities Press.

Langs, R. (1976). *The Bipersonal Field.* New York: Jason Aronson.

———. (1978). *The Listening Process.* New York: Jason Aronson.

———. (1979). *The Therapeutic Environment.* New York: Jason Aronson.

Levy, S. T. (1977). Countertransference aspects of pharmacotherapy in the treatment of schizophrenia. *International Journal of Psychoanalytic Psychotherapy* 6:15–30.

Meltzer, H. (1975). Regression is unnecessary. In *Psychotherapy of Schizophrenia,* eds. J. Gunderson and L. Mosher, pp. 123–135. New York: Jason Aronson.

Minuchin, S., Rosman, B., and Baker, L. (1978). *Psychosomatic Families: Anorexia Nervosa in Context.* Cambridge, Mass.: Harvard University Press.

Modell, A. H. (1978). The conceptualization of the therapeutic action of psychoanalysis: the action of the holding environment. *Bulletin of the Menninger Clinic* 42:493–504.

Novotny, P. (1973). The pseudopsychoanalytic hospital. *Bulletin of the Menninger Clinic* 37: 193–210.

Palazzoli, M. S. (1974). *Self-starvation.* London: Chaucer.

Searles, H. (1975). Countertransference and theoretical model. In *Psychotherapy of Schizophrenia,* eds. J. Gunderson and L. Mosher, pp. 223–228. New York: Jason Aronson.

———. (1978). A dialogue on psychoanalysis. *Modern Psychoanalysis* 3:3–11.

Shainess, N. (1979). The swing of the pendulum—from anorexia to obesity. *American Journal of Psychoanalysis* 39:225–234.

Simmel, E. (1929). Psycho-analytic treatment in a sanatorium. *International Journal of Psycho-Analysis* 10:70–89.

Spiro, R., and Spiro, T. (1980). Transitional phenomena and developmental issues in borderline Rorschachs. In *Borderline Phenomena and the Rorschach Test,* eds. P. Lerner and J. Kwawer. New York: International Universities Press.

Stone, L. (1961). *The Psychoanalytic Situation.* New York: International Universities Press.

Story, I. (1976). Caricature and impersonating the other: observations from the psychotherapy of anorexia nervosa. *Psychiatry* 39:176–188.

Talbot, E., Miller, S., and White, R. (1964). Some antitherapeutic side effects of hospitalization and psychotherapy. *Psychiatry* 27:170–176.

Will, O. (1968). The reluctant patient, the unwanted psychotherapist—and coercion. *Contemporary Psychoanalysis* 5:1–31.

Winnicott, D. (1960). The theory of the parent–infant relationship. In *The Maturational Processes and the Facilitating Environment,* pp. 37–55. New York: International Universities Press, 1965.

———. (1966). Psycho-somatic illness in its positive and negative aspects. *International Journal of Psycho-Analysis* 47:510–516.

Treatment in Anorexia Nervosa

HILDE BRUCH, M.D.

A discussion of "Anorexia Nervosa and the Psychotherapeutic Hospital," by Ian Story Ph.D. "Anorexia Nervosa" is a misnomer. "Anorexic" patients do not suffer from loss of appetite but actively pursue self-starvation and are frantically preoccupied with food, and even more with their size and shape. It is not an illness of weight and nutrition but a desperate effort to establish a sense of control to counteract deficits in the sense of effectiveness and the self-concept. After a childhood of overconformity, these patients are ill prepared to meet the demands for independence and self-assertion that growing up implies. Traditional treatment has emphasized the restitution of weight, which, however, is insufficient for cure. For effective treatment, reparation of the underlying personality deficits is essential. Story's paper on the therapeutic hospital describes the desperate plight of chronic anorexic patients in whose early treatment this important factor had been neglected.

Anorexia nervosa has been alive in medical thinking as a distinct clinical entity since the independent reports by Gull (1874) and Lasègue (1873) a little more than 100 years ago. Since then, there has been continuous debate about the nature, diagnosis, and treatment of the condition. Several stages can be recognized in these efforts. Concepts of some nervous or psychological factor bringing about the assumed loss of appetite alternated with an organic orientation, and for a time the field was dominated by the assumption that a deficiency of the pituitary gland was responsible for the weight loss. Even authors concerned with psychological aspects thought of the illness as an endocrine disorder that could be influenced through psychotherapy (Meng 1944). During the 1930s the syndrome was redefined as a psychological entity, distinct from the very rare pituitary cachexia, though the search for some organic cause has persisted. Psychoanalysts were leading in this endeavor. Their efforts to find a specific psychoanalytic formulation led to a diffusion of the diagnosis applied to all kinds of disorders with weight loss and "oral" symptoms. Anorexia nervosa was conceived of as representing symbolically a repudiation of sexuality or of fantasies of "oral impregnation." The underlying psychiatric condition was conceived of as a neurosis (Waller et al. 1940).

The early reports were based on small samples, not infrequently on a single case study. Authors would draw generalized conclusions as if their limited observations applied to all cases of weight loss for psychological reasons. Toward the end of the 1950s the illness began to occur with increasing frequency, and recent reports are based on large numbers of cases (Bruch 1973, 1978, Dally 1969, Selvini 1963, Thomae 1961). It was recognized that a specific anorexia nervosa syndrome (primary anorexia nervosa) needed to be differentiated from a variety of atypical pictures with disturbed eating patterns and weight loss associated with other psychiatric illnesses, such as depression, hysteria, or schizophrenia. Re-examination of the early psychoanalytic reports reveals that the observations were made mainly on atypical cases suffering from conversion hysteria (Kaufman and Heiman 1964).

PRIMARY ANOREXIA NERVOSA

In the genuine picture, and this is the condition that is on the increase, the leading symptom of anorexia nervosa is severe weight loss due to self-inflicted starvation, occurring chiefly in young women and much less often in males. It is associated with an intense fear of becoming obese, which does not diminish as the weight loss progresses. The disturbance of body image is characteristic for the illness and differentiates it from other forms of weight loss incidental to an organic illness or to other psychiatric disorders. The relentless pursuit of thinness represents an effort to compensate for underlying deficiencies in personality and self-concept. After a childhood of robot-like obedience, these young people are ill prepared to meet the demands of adolescence for independence and self-assertion. In their inefficient helplessness, they attempt to establish a sense of control through rigid discipline over the body, and weight loss is experienced as a great achievement that gives them a feeling of well-being. They accomplish it through excessive exercising and restriction of food intake to minimal amounts or, when this is too painful and hard, by removal of food from the body through vomiting or laxatives.

Although concern with weight and food are its most conspicuous features, anorexia nervosa is a much more complex illness than dieting gone wild. The core problem lies in a deficient sense of self and involves a wide range of deficits in body awareness, individuation, and conceptual maturation. This maldevelopment results from disturbances in the early interpersonal experiences and the interaction of psychological, sociological, and biological factors. The underlying psychiatric picture is more akin to narcissistic personality, borderline state, and schizoid reaction than to neurosis.

These patients come from seemingly well functioning, successful homes. They were well cared for in every detail, physically, educationally and culturally, but everything was done according to the parents' decisions without sensitive regard for the child's initiative and expression of his or her needs. This slant in interactional patterns underlies much of the symptomatology, including the unreliable control over the food intake. The starving anorexic lives in constant fear of helplessly gaining weight if he or she relaxes a rigid control. The longer the illness lasts, the more isolated the victim becomes, the greater the danger of becoming completely self-absorbed and overpowered by bizarre and abnormal ruminations. The picture is further complicated by the fact that the state of starvation itself creates psychological disturbances that are physiologically, not psychologically, determined, such as a narrowing of interests, rigidity of thinking, irritability, depression, and even psychotic disorganization.

There is a great variability in the course of the illness, ranging from a single episode to repeated recurrences, chronic anorexic invalidism, or an unremitting course until death. These wide differences appear to be related not only to differences in the psychological picture, and to the rigidity with which a patient clings to the anorexic stance, but also to the adequacy and pertinence of the medical intervention.

Certain common features can be recognized in the psychological picture and manifestations, though with great individual differences. Anorexics do not feel in control of their bodily functions, often lack awareness of living their own lives, and are convinced of the ineffectiveness of all efforts and strivings. With this basic psychic orientation, every anorexic dreads that he or she is basically inadequate, low, mediocre, inferior, and despised by others. All efforts are directed toward hiding the fatal flaw of his or her fundamental inadequacy. The anorexic is convinced that people around him or her—her family, friends, and the world at large—look on with disapproving eyes, ready to pounce and to criticize.

Anorexics seem to be arrested at an early level in conceptual development. The ability to perform new abstract thinking and evaluation—what Piaget calls formal operations—is characteristic for adolescents. This developmental step seems to be deficient or completely absent in anorexics (Bruch 1977). They cling rigidly to early childhood concepts and notions in the way they interpret human relationships. Frequently, they become socially isolated during the year preceding the manifest illness. The new ways of acting and thinking that are characteristic of normal adolescents are strange and frightening to them, and they withdraw or feel excluded. They interpret society's demand for slenderness in an over-rigid way and embark on a weight-losing program in the expectation that this will earn them respect.

TREATMENT

Although there is the beginning of a consensus on the definition of anorexia nervosa as intentional restriction of food intake with the goal of achieving the ultimate in thinness, controversy persists about the cause of the illness and even more about appropriate treatment. Several divergent trends can be recognized. The dominant theme has been the effort to remove the leading symptom, the cachexia, and to effect an increase in weight, and the search has been for a regimen applicable to all. Sometimes this is combined with efforts to correct an assumed organic abnormality, such as so-called replacement therapy for pituitary deficiency. In contrast to this, a psychotherapeutic approach attempts to effect a change in the patient so that he or she no longer needs to use such bizarre means to experience a sense of self-value, and this implies emphasis on the individual needs of each patient.

Psychiatric services also offer widely different programs, depending on the theoretical concept of the nature of the illness. Those who conceive of it as having resulted from abnormal brain function will prescribe psychotropic drugs or use electroshock or even lobectomy. Behaviorists who assume that the noneating is "learned behavior" will attempt to modify it. Behavior modification, introduced only ten years ago, is at this time probably the most widely used method to enforce weight gain (Blinder et al. 1970). Its effectiveness rests on rewarding, "positively reinforcing," any gain in weight, or punishing, "negatively reinforcing," failure to do so. The program varies from one hospital to another, but the principle is always the same: isolate the patient and make it as disagreeable as possible, and give relief only in exchange for eating a prescribed amount of food or gaining weight as "contracted" (Agras et al. 1974). In this way, the patient is forced to act against her inner conviction and goals or suffer the punishment of complete isolation. The anorexic's sense of worthlessness and of being unrelated is dangerously reinforced by the "nonpampering" procedure of making social contacts dependent on weight gain. The great increase in the number of patients with binge eating and vomiting seems to be directly related to having been exposed to such a coercive program.

On the other hand, a wait-and-see attitude—an unrealistic expectation that the weight will correct itself after the psychological problems have been solved—may be harmful, even fatal overoptimism. This error is often committed by psychotherapists who are not aware of the profoundly disturbing effects that starvation has on psychic functioning, which severely interfere with the ability to integrate new understanding.

The psychotherapeutic approach is derived from psychoanalysis, but its application to primary anorexia nervosa demands marked modification of the classical model. The traditional psychoanalytic setting represents in a way a painful repetition of the significant interaction between patient and parents, that "mother always knew how I felt," with the implication that the patients themselves do not know how they feel. "Interpretation" to such patients may mean the devastating re-experience of being told what to feel and think, confirming their sense of inadequacy and thus interfering with the development of true self-awareness and trust in their own psychological faculties. By the time such patients come to a psychiatrist with pertinent understanding of the condition, many years of unsuccessful treatment may have passed, and the patient and family may be desperate about ever finding meaningful help.

Anorexia nervosa has always had the reputation of offering unusually difficult treatment problems. On principle, these patients resist treatment; they feel that in their extreme thinness they have found the perfect solution, that it makes them feel better. They do not complain about their condition; on the contrary, they glory in it. They are reluctant to let go of the security of their cadaverous existence.

For effective treatment, changes and correction must be accomplished in several areas. The abnormal nutrition must be improved, but without depriving the patient of his or her sense of autonomy. (Nevertheless, a certain nutritional restitution is a prerequisite for effective therapy.) The stagnating patterns of family interaction must be clarified and unlocked, but this alone is not enough: Regardless of what the family contribution to the illness has been in the past, the patient has integrated the abnormal patterns and misconceptions, and only individual intensive psychotherapy can correct the underlying erroneous assumptions that are the precondition for the self-deceptive pseudosolution.

The therapeutic task is to help anorexic patients in their search for autonomy and self-directed identity in the setting of a new, intimate, interpersonal relationship where what they have to say is listened to and made the object of exploration. Focus needs to be on the patients' failures in self-experience, on the defective tools and concepts for organizing and expressing needs. Therapy aims at liberating patients from the distorting influences of early experiences and from the errors of their convictions so that they can discover that they have substance and worth and do not need the strains and stressful superstructures of artificial perfection. For true resolution of the underlying problems, the patients need to become aware of their own role in the development of their illness. Patients will cling to their distorted concepts and will let go of them only slowly and reluctantly.

If the therapeutic focus is on a patient's self-doubts, lack of self-confidence, and fear of losing control, instead of on the symbolic meaning of the food refusal or cannibalistic impulses, etcetera, he or she is more apt to accept responsibility for eating voluntarily as a personal decision. Severe and long-standing degrees of emaciation, with weights below 60 or 70 pounds, rarely, if ever, can be handled in ambulatory treatment while the patient lives in the home where the condition has developed. Such patients need the efforts of a well integrated hospital, with an attitude of medical responsibility and a program of individualistic psychotherapy which leads to clarification of the underlying problems.

THE PSYCHOTHERAPEUTIC HOSPITAL

Story's paper illustrates dramatically the complexity of the clinical picture of anorexia nervosa and the many interacting forces in the treatment process. His patients are older than the usual anorexic, more severely disturbed, and have been sick for many years. They have been exposed to various treatment efforts, repeated mechanical hospitalizations, or stereotyped psychotherapies, which have been without benefit or even proved antitherapeutic. They came to the hospital as a place of last resort, though some patients and their families expected to find "the expert" who would prescribe a comprehensive treatment program that the patient would "fit into" and thus be retransformed into the person he or she was before starting this futile search for identity through manipulation of the body.

An important aspect of the therapeutic hospital is that it functions in an individualistic way, supportive and at the same time encouraging voluntary decisions. The whole environment is designed to encourage growth and individual development. Nursing care, activities, and nutrition are integrated with psychotherapy in a comprehensive but flexible treatment program. Psychotherapy, psychoanalytically oriented but deviating considerably from the classical model, is voluntary, so that the patient has the choice whether to attend sessions or not. Psychotherapy proceeds in a highly individualized way, but it is conveyed to each patient initially that his or her difficulties are incontestably human and can be forthrightly identified, talked out, and understood. It is inherently long-range, since it deals with developmental deviations, and the staff must clarify for each patient "whom treatment is for," that the therapy is for the patient's own development and not something to satisfy the parents. The goal is for patients to learn or relearn about themselves so that they can *get* better, not just be made to *feel* better or comfortable. Many patients by that time have been so traumatized by past experiences that they find it completely unrealistic to expect or even to consider the possibility of unlearning and modifying their distorted ideas.

The goal of the hospital experience is to help the patients develop new ways of caring for themselves. Patients are actively encouraged to assume responsibility for regaining weight, but this is not enforced. If a patient's weight reaches a dangerously low level, he or she is admitted to a nearby medical hospital to improve their nutrition. This arrangement permits an active working out of the expectations and the anxieties that are tied up with the feeding situation.

If repeated refeeding efforts without psychological understanding have been made in the past, then there is danger of the emergence of what Story calls a *malignant autonomy* picture, whereby the symptoms that the anorexic has violently defended through the years come to be experienced as totally automatic, no longer the active expression of control over his or her body but so dissociated from their original meaning and intention that the patient now feels controlled by the illness. This automatization may be irreversible, and once chronic anorexia nervosa has reached this stage the outlook becomes rather unfavorable. Even less chronic patients who are still able to engage in psychotherapeutic work are in danger that the malignant autonomy syndrome will take over, especially when the therapist permits nutritional politics (i.e., concern with weight and figures) to replace the therapeutic frame.

Story describes in detail the involvement of the therapist and the strong countertransference reactions that are aroused by the feelings of helplessness and concern about a patient who stubbornly refuses to gain weight or who persists in vomiting. The therapist may feel compelled to render an ultimatum about whether or not treatment can continue. Such an ultimatum is to be used only in exceptional cases, to express that the therapist too has the freedom to decide whether to engage in treatment with a particular patient. It brings home to the patient that there is a decision to be made, that only active involvement will make a successful resolution possible.

When working out such a problem, it is important that both the therapist and patient adhere to basic terms and ground rules. In view of the background of falsification and mistaken superimposition of parental needs characteristic for the anorexic's development, it is critical not to pretend that such a decision is other than an ultimatum. If the therapist can safely trust his or her countertransference feelings about a patient, there is then a time to say, "It's me or starving yourself" or "It's me or vomiting" or whatever. Such an ultimatum is a strenuous but at times unavoidable effort to get behind the smoke screen of the stereotyped anorexic symptoms and to thereby get a chance to explore with the patient the latent and excluded material that has been outside of awareness and never before faced.

The formulation of the etiology and treatment needs in anorexia nervosa on which Story's report is based closely resembles the complex psychodynamics outlined in this discussion. He understands anorexia nervosa in a developmental and adaptive framework as a camouflage symptom disguising and circumscribing profound underlying early difficulties of a kind encountered in more overt borderline, schizoid, or schizophrenic pathology. Although usually feeling helpless to change things, and often unaware of or denying any connection between self and body, the severely anorexic patient actively maintains self-starvation within the context of an outwardly disorganized eating pattern and underlying primitive developmental arrest. Story emphasizes that the period *before* the appearance of the manifest symptoms needs to be the focus of long-term investigation and corrective psychotherapy. For those anorexics who have felt brutalized, bitterly forced to eat against their will, and ignored as human persons during other hospitalizations, much time is required to develop any other perspective or to participate in a mutual treatment compact. To many patients, the psychotherapeutic hospital experience means that for the first time in their lives they can correct and broaden their awareness, including awareness of their inner life and of hunger sensations, and can abandon their long-necessary dissociative and splitting defenses embodied in the anorexic impasse.

Admission to a hospital also means separation from the family. The whole early anorexia nervosa literature stresses that treatment is best carried out away from the family, whose emotional reactions, it was felt, would interfere with refeeding. The present-day trend is to work with the family and to make a disengagement possible while living together (Minuchin et al. 1978). This seems to work successfully for younger patients with a mild illness of recent origin. However, once an anorexic has been exposed to unsuccessful treatment for any length of time and an intense hostile interaction with the parents has developed, all family members are so caught up in the struggle that no true progress is possible. During intensive psychotherapy with ambulatory severely disturbed anorexic patients, those who live away from home (e.g., in a college dormitory) do decidedly better than those who live at home and are enmeshed in paralyzing negative fighting. Family therapy appears to be ineffective with such older and long-standing patients. They are usually in need of the opportunities of a residential treatment center. Such a supportive setting makes it possible even for a severely ill and developmentally arrested patient to work toward true inner self-reliance and independence. Treatment is not aimed at reuniting patient and family, but toward the anorexic's disengagement from the family through the development of her own resources.

COMMENT

The question may be raised whether these seriously disturbed patients at the therapeutic hospital suffer from the same disease as those with more favorable outcome is, or whether they represent an exceptional course of illness. Such a disastrous course is unfortunately not uncommon for anorexic patients who are exposed to treatment procedures that neglect to deal with their basic human needs. In consultation work on treatment-resistant anorexics, this author has seen many who are as seriously disturbed as the ones described by Story. But the early picture was in no way different from those who with appropriate treatment made a good recovery, except that they were somewhat older, even at onset of the illness, than the patients about whom optimistic reports about treatment results are published.

There is increasing evidence that anorexia nervosa in very young patients, with onset below the age of 15, is associated with less severe psychological illness and has a better prognosis than in those with later onset. Minuchin's optimistic report on family therapy (Minuchin et al. 1978) is based on 53 patients, of whom 55 percent were 9–14 years of age, 36 percent 15–16 years, and only 9 percent above age 17. In the group (150 cases) the present author has seen in consultation in recent years, 57 percent were 17–25 years old, only 20 percent were below the age of 17, and in 23 percent the age range was 25–40 years. Several patients were referred to the psychotherapeutic treatment center and are included in Story's report. Unfortunately, few are accessible to the recommendation of long-term residential treatment. Some are capable of working in psychotherapy as ambulatory patients if the living conditions are favorable, but most limp along in an anguished state of chronic ill health with a narrow social life, pushing themselves to top performance in their professional or vocational lives, without ever having the satisfaction of true fulfillment.

The positive conclusion from this work is that even damaged survivors of stereotyped, symptomatic treatment efforts are still capable of constructive change with pertinent therapeutic understanding. Much ill health, anguish, and suffering could have been avoided if their problems had found proper attention when the illness first became manifest.

REFERENCES

Agras, W. S., Barlow, D. H., Chapin, H. N., Abel, G. G., and Leitenberg, H. (1974). Behavior modification of anorexia nervosa. *Archives of General Psychiatry* 30:279–286.

Blinder, B. J., Freeman, D. M. A., and Stunkard, A. J. (1970). Behavior therapy of anorexia nervosa: effectiveness of activity as a reinforcer of weight gain. *American Journal of Psychiatry* 126:77–82.

Bruch, H. (1973). *Eating Disorders: Obesity, Anorexia Nervosa, and the Person Within.* New York: Basic Books.

———. (1977). Psychological antecedents of anorexia nervosa. In *Anorexia Nervosa,* ed. R. Vigersky, pp. 1-10. New York: Raven Press.

———. (1978). *The Golden Cage: The Egnima of Anorexia Nervosa.* Cambridge, Mass.: Harvard University Press.

Dally, P. (1969). *Anorexia Nervosa.* New York: Grune and Stratton.

Gull, W. W. (1874). Anorexia nervosa. *Transactions Clinical Society (London)* 7:22-28.

Kaufman, R. M., and Heiman, M., eds. (1964). *Evolution of Psychosomatic Concepts. Anorexia Nervosa: A Pardigm.* New York: International Universities Press.

Lasègue, C. (1873). On hysterical anorexia. *Medical Times & Gazette* 2:265-266; 367-369.

Meng, H. (1944). *Psyche und Hormon.* Bern: Hans Huber.

Minuchin, S., Rosman, L. R., and Baker, L. (1978). *Psychosomatic Families: Anorexia Nervosa in Context.* Cambridge, Mass.: Harvard University Press.

Selvini, M. P. (1963). *L'Anoressia Mentale.* London: Chaucer Publishing Co., 1972.

Thomae, H. (1961). *Anorexia Nervosa.* New York: International Universities Press, 1967.

Waller, J. V., Kaufman, R. M., and Deutsch, F. (1940). Anorexia nervosa: a psychosomatic entity. *Psychosomatic Medicine* 2:3-16.

Premature Termination:
A Therapist Leaving

JAMES BEATRICE, M.S.

A decision by a therapist to relocate introduced significant disruptions to the bipersonal field. Langs' adaptional-interactional perspective proved valuable in understanding the complexities of this difficult form of termination. The therapist's relocating is discussed as a structuralized interactional effort that compromised the therapeutic frame, induced interactional symptoms in the patient, and heightened countertransference.

There are reports in the literature discussing the termination phase of successful psychoanalysis (Klein 1950, Levenson 1976, Payne 1950, Szalita 1976, Witenberg 1976). For a majority, shared criteria are utilized as indicators for termination to begin. These include successful resolution of the transference neurosis (Hurn 1971), attainment of treatment goals (Robbins 1975), reduction of symptomatology (Firestein 1974), and structural changes commensurate with reported changes in external life (Robbins 1975). Subtle changes in the countertransference are also indicators for termination (Buxbaum 1950). Some authors note a marked increase in the therapeutic alliance, suggesting the patient was ready to assume the role of his or her own therapist (Hoffer 1950).

A review of the termination process itself reveals two distinct viewpoints regarding therapeutic technique. The first advocates strict adherence to the stance of maintaining neutrality and continuing interpretations (Robbins 1975). Primarily, these authors caution against the therapist sharing his or her real feelings, since this would render the therapist less effective in his or her use of transference interpretations (Kubie 1968). It was stated that such interventions might obscure or dilute the transference, defined in its classical sense, burden the patient, and thus impede the mourning process by contributing to the patient's defenses. This mourning process concerned a neurotic attachment projected onto the therapist and therefore related to the loss of transference fantasies, and not to the therapist as a real object (Robbins 1975).

The second viewpoint regards the therapist's leaving as a very real loss to the patient. Alterations in technique are suggested if the patient's personality structure requires it (Firestein 1969). This includes answering questions or allowing the patient to face the analyst. Weigert (1952) states that it is the lack of realism and spontaneity in the therapeutic encounter that prevents the resolution of the transference, and only when strict objectivity and detachment are loosened will the patient really feel accepted as an equal. Kestenberg (1964) states that the analyst interprets in order to differentiate himself or herself from the patient and to suggest to the patient that the therapist is not only the "bad, archaic mother" but can also be a good object. Buxbaum (1950) feels that action is more important than interpretation and recommends that the patient decide when to leave the therapist. This is proposed to allow mastery over early traumas of rejection. The patient is also permitted to write, call, or visit after termination to alleviate the effects of active termination by the therapist. Reich (1950) states that residues of transference always continue and commented that she had never seen an easy relinquishment of the analyst by the patient.

This brief review indicates the debate concerning dividing the therapeutic interaction into transference and nontransference without considering their overlap. There is the implication that patients' comments and responses are to the realistic aspects of the relationship versus the implication that all communications from the patient are transference distortions. Apparently, the transference and nontransference components of the total therapeutic relationships are technically isolated from each other. If these questions are raised concerning termination after successful analytic treatment, it is of interest to see how this issue is addressed when termination is forced or premature.

Regarding premature or forced termination, specifically the therapist leaving the patient for personal reasons of his or her own, reports in the literature are scarce. Pumpian-Mindlin (1958) reports on time-limited therapy in a training hospital, with countertransference cited as the most important contributing factor in technical difficulties. He intervened by having the patient talk about the premature termination. Unfortunately, how this was introduced is not disclosed. Interventions change from interpreting conflicts to reassuring and encouraging the patient's capacity to adapt in order to decrease separation anxiety. The patient's responses to these interventions are not reported, making assessment of the techniques difficult.

Dewald (1965, 1966) states that patients react to the therapist leaving prematurely by reproducing their original response to early parental separation and loss. He feels that by leaving, the therapist introduces a traumatic reality event for the patient. Consequently, he views the patient's reactions as similar to those of any type of termination. Some patients were unable to make use of the therapeutic relationship as they had prior to learning of the therapist's pending departure. For example, one patient felt continued frustration at not being told where the therapist was going. When therapy ended, the patient left and never paid his bill. Another patient became increasingly remote, inaccessible, lonely, and depressed. Other patients experienced increasing symptomatology with reported spontaneous symptom reduction. A rather dramatic vignette was reported where a patient refused to leave the office, fainted outside the office door, and threatened suicide. Countertransference issues of guilt, aggression, grief, and relief were noted, and a personal comment was offered regarding the "difficulty in maintaining analytic composure and freedom from personal tension." His comments point to the disruptive effects on both therapist and patient, yet do not illustrate that these interact and unfold within the therapeutic situation.

Weiss (1972) reports on the loss of the "as if" quality in the transference and attributes this to the therapist being split into a real as well as a transference object. He utilized his leaving as a "special event" to dramatize the transference and thus continue the progression of the analysis. He found patients used the reality aspects of his leaving to ward off and dilute the transference. When the transference was understood and interpreted, the reality of his move became a minor part of the total therapeutic situation. Despite his stance of continued interpretations, he described a patient jumping up from the couch, looking at the therapist's family picture on the desk and reading his diploma on the wall. He notes that the patient actively incorporated aspects of his reality in order to concretely overcome the loss of the analyst. This opportunity was described as working through the feeling of being abandoned. He concludes that patients experienced an increased sense of object loss, mourning, abandonment, rage, and depression. This form of termination, if properly handled, could affect progress in ego mastery. Explicitly, Weiss advocates strict use of interpretation and neutrality, yet implicitly, as the vignette indicates, he also recognizes the need for the patient to focus on the realistic aspects of the situation.

Schwarz (1974) discusses his experience with premature termination and notes the failure of the patients to differentiate past trauma from the present trauma of the therapist leaving. He comments on the loss of the "as if" quality in the transference and states that forced termination had its developmental prototypes. The latter were forced by biological and environmental realities, with the child being aided in adapting to the loss by the "good enough" parent. If an adequate environment was not available, a successful integration of a forced closure of a developmental stage was not possible. Even though he states the need for a facilitating environment for forced realities, he does not extend this to the therapeutic situation he is discussing. By not rectifying the therapeutic alliance and maintaining strict interpretation as his technical approach, the patients could not differentiate past trauma from present trauma.

All the premature literature cited define transference in its classical sense; that is, the patient's responses toward the analyst in the present are viewed as distorted and inappropriate and based on repetitions of past developmental conflicts. The patient's reactions to the current reality of the therapist's leaving are neglected. By neglecting this reality precipitant, the nontransference, that is, the relatively undistorted aspects of the patient's relationship to the therapist are not acknowledged. Therefore the therapists do not realize the patients' needs to rectify the realistic aspects of the therapeutic interaction. The therapists place these needs back on the patients and term them transference distortions. The patients are burdened by their needs not being recognized in the present but remanded to the past. The continuous reference in the premature termination literature to the loss of the "as if" quality in the transference and the patients' inability to make use of the therapeutic relationship indicates disruptions in the therapeutic alliance. The failure to heed the patients' valid and realistic concerns and to rectify the therapeutic alliance are technical errors that further aggravate the patients' struggle to comprehend the impending departure and create confusion between reality and fantasy.

The nontransference aspects of the therapeutic situation also comprise an area of considerable discussion. For Menaker (1942), the real relationship is a direct human relationship between the patient and therapist. This relationship has an existence independent of transference and provides the medium in which transference reactions take place. She advocates that the therapist may reveal his or her personality and behave in a direct and friendly manner, thereby gratifying the patient. For Anna Freud (1954), it is the analyst who avoids or neglects the real relationship who can prompt hostile responses in the patient that are not entirely based on transference. Benedek (1953) states that the analyst's failure to come to terms with the truth of the patient's perceptions can lead to an impasse and to interventions that do not recognize and acknowledge the analyst as a real person. For Fairbairn (1957), the real relationship is more important than details of technique as the therapist's personality and intentions make a contribution to the therapeutic process. Reich (1960) views the analyst as in part a reality object for the patient. Avoiding or treating this reality as if it were transference denies the reality of the patient's observations and reflects the therapist's countertransference difficulties. Stone (1961) writes that the analyst must recognize and at times gratify the patient's adult needs. He advocates modifications in technique in order to have the patient's ego join in the actual nontransference relationship so that the analytic interaction can be understood.

Greenson (1967) defines the real relationship as realistic, reality oriented, authentic, and genuine. This is in contrast to transference, which is unrealistic, distorted, and inappropriate. The real relationship forms the rational core of the working alliance that enables the patient to work in analysis despite the intensity of the transference (Greenson 1969). The recognition of the real relationship requires noninterpretive interventions. These are not anti-analytic, as they promote a productive analytic atmosphere. Greenson urges the necessity to monitor this aspect of the therapeutic relationship in order for the patient to perceive the analyst as being in contact with and sensitive to the patient's feelings. The failure to do so could lead to intractable transference reactions. The real relationship is in the foreground during termination and it should be permitted leeway.

These authors advocate a distinction between transference, real relationship, and the therapeutic alliance. Greenson (1971) comments on overlap among these elements. This work promotes the use of noninterpretive techniques in order to differentiate the analyst as a real object from the patient's transference distortions. Other authors critize these distinctions for unnecessarily shifting away from a balanced approach of the realistic issues and then the intrapsychic elaborations that follow (Arlow 1975, Arlow and Brenner 1966, Kanzer 1975, Langs 1976b). Langs (1976) states that these noninterpretive interventions induce therapeutic misalliances, misunderstand the integrative effects of interpretations in distinguishing fantasy from reality, unduly dichotomize the patients conscious material from unconscious processes, and are initiated by countertransference difficulties. Langs (1976b) defines only one relationship between the patient and therapist, which is a mixture of transference and nontransference as well as countertransference and noncountertransference. It is then untenable to attempt to isolate these components, for they interact with one another. Interventions should begin with the realities and then move outward toward the unconscious derivatives.

Langs (1976b) proposes that the terms 'real relationship', 'working alliance', and 'therapeutic alliance' are best put under the rubric of the nontransference dimensions of the total therapeutic relationship. This avoids the schism of conscious from unconscious processes. The main nontransference aspects include: (1) realities related to the patient's perception of the therapist's personality, management of the frame, use of interventions, the ability to be helpful, and the ways the therapist is harmful; (2) actualities that gratify the patient's neurotic needs and thus repeat past pathogenic interactions; and (3) realities that influence the process of cure, including management of the frame, interventions, and the positive introjects these entail that foster the alliance. The therapeutic alliance is the area of cooperation between the patient and the analyst toward the resolution of symptoms and received input from both the conscious and unconscious spheres.

Langs' (1976a) studies of the therapeutic interaction demonstrate the importance of maintaining the therapeutic framework. This maintenance requires adherence to the rules of therapy, including the therapist's posture of anonymity, neutrality, privacy and confidentiality, the management of fees and the time, and the place and duration of the sessions. It is the management of the framework that makes the transference possible. Transference unfolds in part through interactions with the therapist and is initially based as an adaptive response to specific realities of the therapist–patient interaction and is then elaborated by the patient's pathological memories, fantasies, and introjects. Deviations from the framework and their implications are unconsciously perceived by the patient. The patient's responses following the deviations are primarily in the form of valid perceptions and commentaries regarding such interventions. These interventions then become the adaptive context, the stimulus that evokes a psychological response, around which the patient's associations are meaningfully clustered. These interventions are to be corrected or rectified by implicit acknowledgement of the patient's perceptions, as communicated through derivative material, followed by analysis, interpretation, and working through of the resulting transference elements.

The resolution of a disrupted therapeutic alliance takes precedence over all other areas of work. Langs (1976a) stresses that there is no reason to further damage the frame by using noninterpretive interventions and that only rectifying the frame and offering valid interpretations are certain means of strengthening the patient's ego, distinguishing fantasy from reality, and re-establishing trust.

Langs' (1976a) conception of the bipersonal field underlines that both the therapist and the patient contribute to the therapeutic interaction, though in varying proportions. Projective identification and introjective identification are among the major elements in the field. These processes are utilized in a context of relatively fluid self-object boundaries and more mature and secure self-object differentiation (Langs 1977). They therefore range from the more primitive to the more structuralized forms. Thus, not only does the patient project into the therapist, but the therapist may projectively identify into the patient and use the patient as an inappropriate container. These projections consist of the therapist's pathological inner contents, fantasies, memories, and introjects. The patient's perception and introjection of this material leads to a response. The forms this response can take include misappropriation of the therapist's contents to reinforce the patient's pathology or the evocation of efforts to cure the therapist (Langs 1977).

The therapeutic interaction is constituted by intrapsychic and interactional elements that are responded to in both their real and fantasied modalities. The identification of the adaptive context enables the therapist to distinguish the transference from the nontransference components of the therapeutic interaction. Interventions are formulated around both components.

The decision of the present author to relocate in order to obtain a doctorate disrupted the bipersonal field with patients. Significant alterations in the therapeutic interaction resulted as the frame was compromised. The stance of neutrality, anonymity, and the maintainence of a secure, holding environment, with its offer of a healthy, therapeutic symbiosis, were ruptured. This placed intense distress into the patient. The decision to relocate can be viewed as a structuralized interactional effort that places the therapist's personal needs into the patient. The patient's introjection of these conscious expressions and their conscious and unconscious elaborations induce the patient to shift his or her emphasis to concerns about the nontransference aspects of the therapeutic relationship.

Concurrently, a general ascendancy of countertransference difficulties was experienced by the present therapist. Issues of guilt, anger, loss, and attempts to defend against these conscious and unconscious affects and memories became potential organizers that impinged upon therapeutic interventions. Countertransference is defined in its totalistic perspective wherein the therapist experiences intrapsychic and interactional responses as a consequence of containing the patient's transference and nontransference material. These responses unfold within the therapeutic relationship in a variety of conscious and unconscious manifestations. This working definition enabled me to emphasize the interpersonal connection between myself as therapist and my patients. The pending premature termination became the adaptive context for both participants.

The patients shift to concerns about the realistic aspects of the relationship and my heightened countertransference were indices highlighting the inability to secure and rectify the frame. The shift to primarily nontransference concerns underlined the realistic and genuine trauma of the therapist leaving. The shift in the patients' material occurred on both a conscious and manifest level, as well as on an unconscious and latent level expressed in derivative form. The patients were attempting to evoke adaptive responses from the therapist to attend to the realistic loss and thus facilitate the patients' struggle to introject, work over, understand, and resolve the meaning of the therapist's leaving.

This paper presents detailed clinical material of premature termination. The patients' associations shifted to nontransference expressions, particularly their realistic and alliance aspects. Interventions had to acknowledge the patients' conscious and unconscious perceptions of the therapist before attempting interpretations of the existing distortions based on pathological memories, fantasies, and introjects. The nontransference material and the inability to fully restore the frame increased countertransference difficulties, rendering recognition of the patients' unconscious perceptions incomplete. The question of deviations in technique under these conditions to repair the therapeutic alliance is also discussed.

The following clinical vignettes illustrate the points mentioned. The patients were seen in psychoanalytically oriented psychotherapy of two to three sessions weekly. All patients were in therapy for more than a year. They were informed of the present author's decision to relocate three months prior to the planned departure. The vignettes were taken from detailed notes made after each session.

BREAK OF THE HOLDING ENVIRONMENT AND LOSS OF HEALTHY THERAPEUTIC SYMBIOSIS

Patient I, who suffered a psychotic character disturbance, had achieved a high level of integration via the maintainence of a satellite transference after two years in treatment. Volkan (1976) describes this transference as a compromise situation wherein an individual solves conflicts surrounding separation-individuation by orbiting about another, maintaining distance, and neither moving toward nor away from the object. This position permits certain ego functions to evolve. The patient was repeatedly experienced by the present therapist as literally orbiting, intermittently initiating aspects of personal contact.

Upon being informed that the therapist had made a decision to relocate, she responded that things were coming together for her and the therapeutic work was nearing completion anyway. She spoke of recently signing a new contract at her employment and how she looked forward to the future. She spoke of her children being well-adjusted, making family life very pleasant for her. She talked of errands that she had to do such as going to the bank, shopping, and meeting the children after school. I organized her associations in terms of distancing and denying my initial remark about leaving. I told her that she seemed to be emphasizing things that were pleasant and in relation to others, and perhaps this insulated her from the fact of my leaving. She responded that she would have the opportunity to say good-bye.

During the following session she spoke of fellow employees being angry at her, against her, and threatening to fire her. She began talking rapidly and again about errands. She continually looked at her watch. She spoke of an employee's hateful look and how this devastated her. She stated that she confronted this person by saying that his actions proved, despite his words, that he did not want her in the office. She then stated that she had spoken to her brother and he advised her not to see a psychiatrist but to join EST. She was against this as it was too confronting. She spoke again of the employee and stated that he was "passing the buck," for he refused to take responsibility. I stated that when I announced I would be leaving and then suggested that she was avoiding this, she had perceived me as too confronting and had felt devastated and angry. Further, she was saying that if I was confrontive she viewed this as hateful and if this continued she would consider leaving therapy. She simply replied that this was not true. She then associated to her ex-husband being in town, though not visiting her, and his appearance occurring at the time of a break-in of her home (this was an actual event reported in the local paper). She felt the ex-husband had done this or had hired someone. She then stated that she must be strong to survive work and added, "If only I could unite my splits, though you see my mind isn't in gear." I interpreted that when I was too confrontive about my leaving, she had become disengaged from me and had felt that I was hateful as I broke-up her relationship with me. I stated that this reminded her of the painful feelings surrounding her divorce and the break-up of her family life, that she could not tolerate these feelings so she protected herself with splitting to avoid my loss and to protect herself from in insistence that she face it. I added that when she spoke of the break-in, she was telling me that I was too intrusive yet she was also saying that, just like the divorce, the ending of our relationship broke her up and I would leave her just as her husband had left her. She began to cry and said that since she had learned that I was leaving, she had not been able to focus, concentrate, or see clearly. "My vision is blurring again; my brain is splitting; I can feel the blood channels burning my cells." She said that she was "cut off" from me. Her social life, which had been going fairly well, was now described as a desperate attempt to find and establish a symbiotic relationship. She felt that she could no longer continue therapy in light of my imminent departure.

This description indicates the consequence of the break in the frame and the impossibility of restoring the therapeutic hold. Although I attempted to rectify my countertransference of insisting, the reality of my upcoming departure was too similar to past traumas of loss and rejection for her to tolerate. No longer having the safety and security of my availability, the patient experienced panic at being rejected from the healthy symbiosis of the therapeutic framework. Searles (1973) notes the therapist's need to recognize the intense dependency needs of patients and the creation of a therapeutic symbiosis that is essential in the patients' attempts at individuation. Removal of this symbiosis forced Patient I into the beginnings of a psychotic state, which she was attempting to defend by establishing a displaced symbiosis.

322

Patient II, a schizoid character with borderline personality organization, was verbalizing feeling deeply understood that her ardous and slow manner of relating was accepted. This suggested the beginnings of healthy symbiosis, which was to be met by the announcement of my departure.

After this announcement, she shared having nothing to talk about. She felt that it was best to leave therapy, for, "There's no sense in hurting so much. You know me—feelings belonged tangled in a closet buried under lots of old clothes." She felt that she was not angry with me: "You've already done some good and it won't go away; I'm not angry at you because you didn't do it to intentionally hurt me." She emphasized feeling more "sadness, hurt, and frustration." She described how anger would not make a difference: "Logically, I should be angry but I'm not; I'm in the ozone." This was defined as "spacy, floating, and observing." I asked how she felt about feeling so understood a few sessions ago and now stating that she preferred to leave therapy. She began to cry, yet restrained herself, feeling the need to protect and survive. She felt that she would remember the positive things of our relationship and added, "It was nice to be understood." She chose not to continue with another therapist: "I don't like changes, any changes; I can't risk it." She felt that I wanted her to be angry; yet to her anger meant calling someone a motherfucker: "But it goes away. I know my foul mouth could say anything and you wouldn't bat an eyelash." I stated that she could only risk anger at me indirectly, perhaps because she feared her anger would destroy the parts of our relationship that were good before I had said that I was leaving, that she probably was also angered at herself for risking closeness with me, being understood, and then finding that I will leave, which made her feel that she was foul for trusting a "motherfucker." She responded, "We always did understand each other." The hour ended and I asked if she would return. She asked how long it would be until I left, and I replied that it would be two months. She asked if I would be angry if she did not return. I responded that she was very fearful of me due to my leaving and to her seeing me as a "motherfucker," that I hoped she would choose to explore the meaning of this, but that I recognized the anger, fear, and guilt that prevented her from doing so. She answered that it was important that I understood. I never saw her again.

This patient's associations centered exclusively on the realistic aspects of the therapeutic relationship. The discrepancy between her perception of me before and after the announcement that I was leaving were too difficult to integrate. As a result, she too felt rejected from the symbiosis and therefore could no longer produce unconscious derivative forms of communication. When this did occur, she chose not to explore their meaning. She had to keep her associations solely on a manifest level. This was precisely her intent and a sign of intense resistance. I was moved by her decision and determination not to resume work.

These two vignettes demonstrate the possible effects of a permanently disrupted frame and the impossibility of restoring the therapeutic symbiosis. The patients were no longer able to use the therapist as a safe container to store pathological contents, creating psychic and interactional disequilibrium. This resulted in increased symptomatology. The patients either sought symbiosis elsewhere or fled from the threatening perception of the therapist. These exacerbations were induced by the therapist's decision to relocate, and thus could not be remediated. They represented an interactional syndrome within a damaged therapeutic environment (Langs 1977).

USE OF NONINTERPRETIVE INTERVENTIONS

Patient III initially presented as a borderline personality disorder and had made significant progress during four years of treatment. The therapist's departure was extremely painful for her. She stated, "You're sadistic if you are aloof and I don't know if you are dealing with leaving me; I need to make sense of who you are, to give you shape and form, separate from what I put on you. I want to sort out who you are as a real person, not what I wanted you to be."

She worried about grieving alone, of my being aloof and unavailable to her. The pervasive feeling was that I was leaving to get away from her. She felt like an "abused child." She experienced me as withdrawing, not feeling or sharing myself with her. She reiterated needing to see me as a real person, seeing this as "more real, honest, and not deceiving, not one-sided." She viewed my silence as "unfair and a lie, after all, you brought up leaving first; don't leave it all on me." She stated emphatically, "When you said you were leaving, you lost your right to remain a therapist."

My personal reaction to this material focussed on the patient's appropriate question: where did I stand? I felt that she was indicating her need to distinguish me in a realistic sense from what she would project onto me. Her comments were not demanding, pleading, or intrusive. At this point, I viewed her responses as realistic and without distortion except for the "abused child" image. This comment made me listen for material concerning interactions with her mother.

She was saddened and conflicted over whether my commitment to her over the years had been genuine or contrived. She began voicing her anger at me, wishing to hurt me, and finally wishing to kill me. She commented on how different her anger was now than her earlier rages, which needed some curbing (for example, not to throw furniture at me). She reflected, "My love and hate for you are mingled." Her associations depicted themes of hurting and losing friends, of feeling a need to touch and approach and be close to someone. I reflected that perhaps she had a need to be close to me but was fearful of this. She acknowledged this and spoke of her mother being "cold, like wood; to touch her was to feel awkward and stiffness, and I knew I wasn't wanted." She saw her mother as abandoning and rejecting, leaving her convinced of being flawed and ugly. I stated that her struggle was to be close to me but that she feared doing this because my immenent departure made her feel that I found her unacceptable and therefore rejected her as she felt her mother had. With these rejections, she perceived herself as worthless. She cried freely, not wanting to let go of me, fearful of the emptiness, fearful of not growing and of losing herself: "I don't want you to be like dead."

She said that she knew that she would miss me and implored me to tell her if I would miss her and if she had had an impact on me. I acknowledged her distress and my feeling that I would miss her. She cried and felt relief, and laughed between her tears, saying that she knew my feelings were genuine because I had suspended one of my rules, neutrality. She then spoke of a friend who had recently moved away and from whom she felt estranged. I asked if my comments made her feel estranged from me. She was fearful that she would not contact me and spoke of fears of "going backwards and being again what others" wanted her to be. I stated that perhaps my comment placed an undue demand on her to contact me and that she feared doing something for my needs at the expense of hers.

The material following this intervention indicated that my self-revelation led to a negative introjective identification. Although she consciously expressed relief and satisfaction to hear that I would miss her, unconsciously this burdened her and she feared regressing. The intervention needed rectification. I acknowledged the unnecessary demand I had placed upon her, which I believe removed the intrusive quality of my self-revelation and preserved its genuine concern.

She responded to my rectification by saying that she was "throwing a smokescreen." She wanted to know if I would be happy if she did contact me. I responed affirmatively, yet wondered about the need for the smokescreen. She cried and expressed fears that she had burdened me; she felt she was intruding on me. I gently asked her about this perception of burden. She associated to a childhood experience of a transient psychotic episode. She related this experience to her mother, yet was anguished at being dismissed. She spoke of her sense of being lost, sad, and empty, as her plea for assistance and comfort did not make any difference. She rapidly changed, stating that her mother was all-loving. She berated herself for "smearing" her mother. She then wished that she could tell her mother that she was not fine; yet knew it would not matter, for mother would answer, "You'll get through it." She began to "lose" herself and feel "unreal." Her tone was drained, helpless, and futile.

I interpreted that when she was frightened and confused she wished me, as well as her mother, to comfort her. When mother could not, she felt herself as a burden and unacceptable, yet still left with her feelings. This placed a burden on her because she felt hate at feeling unrecognized, yet needed to defend this hate by idealizing mother to conceal her faults. This created more confusion because, by splitting love and hate, she could no longer distinguish what was real from imagined; what she genuinely felt, from what mother needed to deny. I inferred that she was feeling exactly the same toward me as I was leaving. This duplicated her feeling of mother abandoning her and she now struggled to integrate loving and hating me.

She answered angrily that her mother never recognized and named what she felt, for mother distorted her feelings. She then described something stirring within her. She appeared frightened, then this gradually subsided. "Mother never really beat me. I always believed she abused me. I really felt beaten and defeated because my feelings were left unheard." She began to grieve and mourn the loss of her mother. I waited and then stated that when she saw me as burdened, she was fearful of my rejecting or ignoring her needs, and that she defended herself by devaluation and splitting. This also defended the need to attack me and her mother. I felt that she was mourning a significant loss and thus was able to tolerate depression.

After rectifying my first self-revelation, I repeated this intervention when I said that I would be happy if she contacted me. I felt that to maintain a neutral posture, contain her remark, and interpret, would leave her feeling tormented. I felt a need to concretely demonstrate my feelings by breaking neutrality. I did not subject this to self-analysis. I later realized that I could not contain her anger. My self-revelation was an attempt to demonstrate my concern, which would isolate me from her anger.

I did not organize her material following my second deviation as unconscious commentary on the intervention. The material of the transient psychotic episode can be seen as her unconscious view of my difficulty working in the disruptive frame and my anxiety about it, which she introjectively identified. My interpretation therefore did not utilize my intervention as the adaptive context. Her comments following my interpretation regarding mother "not recognizing and naming" what she felt can be viewed as her unconscious commentary on the incompleteness of my interpretation. She needed a definite statement about my second self-disclosure, which had left her consciously accepting of it while unconsciously angered at being placed in a position that fended anger away from me and onto her mother. She further commented on this by stating that her feelings had been left unheard.

Despite the flawed technique, I experienced her material as contrasting how I had not named and responded to her feelings and how mother was not available to her. Her realization that mother had not abused her, a constellation that she had held for years, was in fact a definite insight. What was clear during the session was her awareness that I genuinely was attempting to be sensitive to her plight despite my countertransference, which interfered with fully understanding her. Her awareness of my attempt to respond to her offered a reparative relationship that defused the destructiveness of the hate that she previously projected onto mother, thus making her the abuser. This partial neutralization of her hate allowed her to realize that the maternal abuse was a fantasy distortion. I felt this to be a meaningful insight as well as a recollection in the service of an unconscious attempt to have me listen closer to the negative aspects of my self-disclosure. She apparently perceived the beneficial aspects of my intentions, which facilitated the memory and my need to rectify the pathological aspects of my self-disclosure. She then was not only grieving the loss of mother but also my inability to hear her adequately.

COUNTERTRANSFERENCE AND TRANSFERRING THE PATIENT

Patient IV had previously sought therapy on three occasions. During an initial screening evaluation, he described these past therapists: "They each had such intensity to help me, offering advice, homework, guidelines, that I became certain it was terribly important that I get better for their sake. I went along and played out my part; they felt pleased and therapy ended. They never knew I was acting." After he found our relationship meaningful, and given the patient's therapeutic history, I struggled with leaving, feeling angry at myself and wanting the patient to continue with a colleague. This formed the background for the following interaction.

The patient described his hope of being "normal" without treatment. He realized that it was a "death sentence" to believe this was possible, yet was conflicted about seeing a new therapist: "Seeing somebody means risking being dealt with differently. A new person brings new variables and maybe they'll see things differently than you. It took such a long time for me to trust and to feel that you are helpful and to hear you. I won't forget it and it will be on my mind with a new person." He recognized his ability to "shut down" and protect if someone intruded, yet felt this to be a burden. "What's the sense in being honest? I'd be too pessimistic—convinced they'll leave, comparing them with you, finding differences and being devastated." I was irritated and said, "How they deal with your fear could indicate if they could be helpful or not!"

As soon as I spoke, I realized that I had blundered and felt miserable. My comment illustrated that I could not deal with his fears and could not be helpful. The patient responded immediately: "I feel slayed; you're changing. You're like all the rest—pushing me away and off to another." He was terribly upset and in tears. This was the end of the hour. The patient phoned me a half-hour later as he could not integrate what happened. I attempted to rectify my error by stating that the abruptness of my comment had upset him greatly, leaving him feeling that I desired to push him onto another without hearing his fears regarding the transfer. My intervention was futile.

Next session, he was distraught. He had purchased razor blades as part of a plan to kill himself. He did not know who his friends or enemies were. He called his parents and argued that his father never listened to his needs. He told his mother of his suicide plan, yet she felt that she had more reason to kill herself than he did. He felt "crazy—real, real crazy." He felt nowhere was safe and desired hospitalization: "I have to have a place to close myself off, be protected so I can pull myself together." He couldn't recall the previous session, but something about my attitude brought on the suicidal panic. He stated, "I need to keep my feelings in because if I project them, like on a screen, no one would come to the movie, they'd be horrified."

I interpreted that my comment from the last session had made him feel rejected and abandoned as I pushed him away and he lost trust and felt that I was not safe. He could not share his feelings for fear that I would be horrified. The suicide plan was the only way to get me to listen. He said that he instigated my anger and therefore was "basically worthless, incurable, and untreatable. Its no use saying otherwise even though I know you believe it." I stated that my anger was a result of my conflict over leaving him, knowing he needed therapy, knowing I could not continue, yet when I did offer an alternative my anger blinded me to his feeling pushed away. When he heard my anger, it made him feel worthless and untreatable. He yelled, "You're supposed to be perfect. That means listening to my signals, that's what I pay you for. I was telling you I felt pushed away and you by leaving were only walking away; then you turned it around and became like them and I lost all balance and hope." He reflected, "Here is a place to relax; not a hospital, too many people take over offering no choices." He then asked where I was going. Previously he had admonished me not to say: "If I don't know where you are, you're gone, oblivion, over; if I do know then there's a connection and you have meaning and substance to me." As the session ended, he said, "Christ, I'm glad you worked that out."

The aspect of this interaction that deserves notice is my error in further damaging the therapeutic interaction. The patient introjectively identified with my anger, which colluded with prior pathological introjects that he kill himself, resulting in suicidal ideation. This incurred an interactional syndrome that needed rectification. The primary emphasis was on the nontransference relationship. The following sessions unfolded material relating to his phone call to his parents.

His request concerning my new residence could be understood as his need for more pathological gratification via my self-revelations. I did not conceptualize his request in this way. Instead, it appeared that the rectification of my error gave me a reality that concretely convinced him that our relationship was meaningful. Consequently, his receptiveness to know my whereabouts is a validation of my intervention and my importance to him. I believe he needed my location to establish in reality what he had difficulty establishing intrapsychically. He functioned at a level of object relations that required concrete awareness of the external object to substantiate its existence. He could not conceptualize me as existing, and therefore as a part of his psyche, if he did not know where I was. I viewed his knowledge of my new residence as a transitional object that would enable him to remember our relationship, would aid in separation from me, and would assist his attempt to establish stable and secure memory traces and introjects of our relationship. I informed him of my new residence at our last session.

INCREASED INSIGHT AS A DEFENSE AGAINST LOSS

A phenomenon frequently reported in the premature termination literature is the patient's increased depth of insight. This is attributed to the departing therapist intensifying previously worked-on traumas with renewed awareness. A neglected aspect of this occurrence is the defense against the realistic loss of the therapist.

Patient V accepted my leaving with calmness and objectivity. She began to focus on her early childhood with uncanny recollections and insights. She interpreted complex family interactions and her reactions to them. When I attempted a clarification, she seized my query and expanded it. I continually felt that I was no longer part of an interaction, but rather a spectator to a monologue. Her material actually consisted of false insights and was defensive in nature. I shared this impression with her and she described herself as a "little professor." She stated, "You can ask me anything you want, I'll answer with the facts." I wondered if feelings were included and she responded negatively. I asked if her "little professor" helped defend against the feelings evoked by my leaving. She answered, "I need to therapize myself; I need this excuse to deaden all these feelings. When I analyze myself and attempt to pull it all together, I feel I'm only a figurehead, while she's running the country." I interpreted that she was defending against feelings of passively experiencing her perception of me as being in control over her, feelings that remined her of her mother's dominance, so that she defended by presuming to be all together.

Next session she was intent on discovering her past. She described only having "memories of feelings." Nothing was "experientially available," so she was perusing childhood photographs where she perceived herself as a "robot," while her parents saw her as healthy. She spoke of always feeling her mind splitting from her body and was uncertain if her mind and body were hers or belonged to others. She experienced sadness and pain, yet suppressed these feelings, preferring to keep them private. I asked if she was fearful that I would take her feelings from her. She associated to her father, his listening to her, yet "not leaving my feelings but changing them to happy." She then felt that she was a burden and lamented, "A child comes into the world and has feelings; if it cries, something is wrong and it needs outside help for balance." I interpreted the lack of verification and acceptance of her feelings and their being transformed by her father, which she endured by keeping her real feelings private, led to her behaving in ways that took care of others' feelings and not hers. Because she took in what others told her she should feel, this developed fears that her body and mind belonged to others, not to her. When she felt something, particularly about my leaving, she was fearful of talking about her feelings because she felt this would burden me. If I was burdened, she was fearful that I would alter her feelings for my benefit, like her father, so she protected by pretending to be all together while suffering silently.

The following session she felt sick and was in pain. She decided not to visit a physician, feeling it would pass. She declined to discuss her feeling, preferring to change the subject; yet she sat silent. I stated that if she changed the subject she would be avoiding her pain, denying its existence and in doing so she perhaps hoped to spare me her distress as she had spared her father. I said that I preferred to hear her distress. She felt a need to lie down and cry, yet restrained herself, stating: "It doesn't matter, what is crying, no one understands, they look away from the tears." She viewed crying as a "mental and physical expression." This comment surprised her and she wanted to stop as she began to cry. I stated that when she was in pain, her feelings were ignored, denied, avoided, or changed by father. Feeling her mind and body now uniting in crying frightened her because it meant that I accepted her pain and she could experience it. Concurrently, she was vulnerable and could not risk this painful sadness because I was leaving and she felt a need to care for me but at the price of her feelings. She stated that if she avoided the pain, it would not affect her, that she did not want to hurt me by sharing her pain. I interpreted her similar reaction to caring for her parents because she felt that her feelings would inflict harm. Although I was pained at leaving her, I had no need to alter or reject her feelings of pain, anger, sadness, and loss for my benefit. She then acknowledged her distress and felt comfortable with my awareness of it. She experienced her helplessness, anger, loss, and aloneness without defense. When the session ended, she described herself as "feeling real," and her pain from the beginning of the hour subsided.

This vignette illustrates the defensive aspect of increased insight to avoid the realistic loss of the therapist and the interpretations of the object relationship that structured the defense. Interventions had to address the interrelationship of the nontransference with the transference aspects of the therapeutic relationship. If I had accepted her persuasive display of psychological acumen without considering the realistic aspects of my leaving, this would have engendered a misalliance of colluding with the patient to avoid the realistic loss of myself as therapist.

The patient appeared to be requiring and defending against a specific object relationship that demonstrated my awareness of her feelings without alterations to accommodate my needs. Her associations regarding "nothing being experientially available," initially could have been viewed as a commentary on my preceding interventions as being unreal. Instead, I conjectured what was unreal for her was an object relation that permitted her expression of feelings without fear of impingement. Thus I felt that she was realistically commenting on an actual deprivation, and her further material indicated to me the motivations that instituted her defensive splitting. Her material brought to mind Giovacchini's (1979) conception of borderline personality organization as being attributable to the relative lack of available, pleasurable memory traces of interactions with significant others. I therefore experienced her as testing my ability not to intrude or distort her affective expressions in the hopes of ascertaining if I could tolerate her expressing herself. I felt my self-revelation offered a reparative relationship of directly experiencing her feelings without intrusion, threat, or distortion. The vignette showed movement from a defensive posture to the interpretation of this defense and the motivations that structured it, culminating in the release of affect to mourn and grieve my impending loss. The use of this noninterpretive intervention introduced a pleasurable interaction previously unavailable, permitting the patient to experience her feelings without defense.

DISCUSSION

The foremost consequence of the therapist's announcement of impending departure for personal reasons is the permanent disruption of the therapeutic frame, resulting in interactional syndromes (Langs 1977). The therapist's behavior is traumatic and similar to the patient's perceptions of past traumas with significant others. The perception of the therapist as rejecting and abandoning fosters intense interactional resistances. These resistances take the form of consciously withholding fantasies, memories and introjects by some patients, leaving communication exclusively on the manifest level with little or no derivative forms of communication to be in evidence.

Patients I and II focused on the realistic aspects of the nontransference relationship. Their reactions were adaptive responses to my decision to leave, coupled with their realization that the therapeutic frame could not be corrected or rectified. Without the certainty and security of the frame and its healthy therapeutic symbiosis, I was perceived as dangerous and uncontrollable. Given this perception, these patients could no longer remain in treatment. Both patients presented with severe psychopathology, with dysfunctional development occurring in the symbiotic and rapproachment stages of individuation. Therapy had not progressed to the point where intense ambivalence and guilt could be tolerated. Thus the contrast between myself before and after announcing my decision to leave was too conflicting to bear. I therefore epitomized being both good and bad, which was the very constellation the patients could not integrate. Flight from therapy was the only recourse for these patients to preserve the minimally established potential for a good object relationship from being overwhelmed by the painful, rejecting aspects of the therapist. My decision to relocate fostered pathological defenses that could not be examined but only respected.

Additionally, my decision to relocate shifted the patients' material to predominately realistic aspects of the nontransference relationship. The patients' associations were conscious and unconscious commentary and perceptions of my inner reality, and aspects of the therapeutic relationship. It became essential to view the patients' associations not only as clustered around earlier traumas of loss and abandonment, but also as underlining the interpersonal conflict with the therapist. The material from patients I, III, and IV indicated their sensitivity to the therapist's avoidance of the realistic aspects of the relationship as an attempt to be rid of painful and disturbing contents instead of understanding them. Patient III alluded to my potential to avoid the realistic components by calling it "unfair and a lie."

The realistic aspect of the nontransference relationship had to be acknowledged, explored, and rectified before intervention could be effected around distortions involving memories, fantasies, and introjects. Rectification was accomplished by implicit recognition of accuracy of the patients unconscious perceptions. Not to give implicit, and at times, explicit recognition of the patients perceptions would distort their reality, deny their ability to contribute meaningfully to this painful experience, and create an imbalance regarding optimal frustration, more tormenting than ameliorating.

Concurrently, countertransference difficulties unfolded within the therapeutic interaction coloring my interventions in response to the patients' nontransference material and the difficulty of working in a permanently disrupted framework. The latter was particularly burdensome, for I was the source of the disruption and this conflicted with my image as healer. This conflict was aggravated by the occurrence of interactional syndromes to which I personally reacted with feelings of guilt for being cruel and harmful, and then felt further anguish that some patients, after achieving a modicum of adequate functioning, grew worse and left treatment. The recognition of the interactional syndromes, my personal conflicts over being hurtful, and my recollections of personal experiences of loss were contributors to erroneous interventions. Patient IV demonstrated the unfolding of these conflicts within the interaction and the need to recognize and rectify the resultant negative introjective identifications. In working in this type of disrupted frame, countertransference cannot be viewed in isolation from the patient, but is intertwined with the patient's material and affect interventions.

The condition of working in a permanently disrupted therapeutic frame, where the patients shift to primarily nontransference concerns and there is an ascendency of countertransference difficulties, raises the question of utilizing noninterpretive interventions to facilitate the therapeutic alliance. The clinical material was presented here in a detailed manner to respond to the need for empirical data, subject to psychoanalytic study, regarding the efficacy of such interventions. This is particularly needed, for these interventions have been criticized for being more hypothetical than empirically demonstrated and not indicated in the patients associations or best interests (Langs 1976b). The necessity of validating these interventions by the patient's responses is extremely useful and pertinent.

The material from Patient III demonstrated the influence of countertransference difficulties to my self-revelation. The intervention of stating that I would miss her contained a defensive component that protected me from the patient's anger at my leaving and displaced it onto the mother. Hence, I could be viewed as all-good while the mother could be the ogre for abandoning the patient and not myself. Fortunately, such a posture was not completely accepted. If it had been, the patient would have maintained her perception of maternal physical abuse. Instead, what occurred was a recognition that my self-revelation contained positive as well as negative elements. The patient perceived the beneficial aspect of my intention, which portrayed that I certainly was aware of experiencing her loss, and by relating this I was in fact not "dead" and unmoved by her distress. This affective response facilitated her introduction of a steadfastly held screen memory and the recognition that her mother did not physically abuse her. Thus my self-revelation defused her hate and permitted material to unfold that was previously well defended. The intervention certainly was incomplete, yet it did offer a reparative relationship that promoted integration of previously defended and distorted memories and fantasies. In addition, her material also indicated the negative aspects of not fully understanding her.

With Patient V, my self-revelation was a more directive attempt to contrast and state definitely my awareness of personal sadness, which did not mean that I would alter her feelings. During the session, I felt that she was aware that I could be feeling sadness due to my leaving her. My subjective evaluation of her material suggested that I state my feeling and thereby demonstrate that I could feel sadness while acknowledging and accepting her distress and not be impelled to manipulate and distort her feelings, which is what damaged her early development.

Both patients utilized my self-revelations in a constructive way because they represented my attempt not to present myself as omnipotent and beyond the strains of their distress. This belied my struggle to understand them, which established pleasurable and meaningful interactions around the trauma of loss and abandonment in contrast to the absence of such interactions in childhood. The material that followed these self-revelations deepened the patients' associations and brought new understanding to the themes being examined. In this sense, the interventions fostered analytic work and cannot be viewed solely as leading to misalliances and pathological introjects. In both situations, the patients were experiencing a re-creation of an earlier trauma that had remained unresolved and in need of a different emotional experience to differentiate the past trauma from the present one. The patients' associations were genuine recollections and reflections on past deprivations followed by recognition and repair of present deprivation.

My adherence to this position stems from my subjective evaluation of Patients III's and V's total responses. The difficulty in fully substantiating this position resides in the transformation from the actual therapeutic interaction to the written description of it. What is lost in this transfer is the affective ambience, specifically the affective modulation of voice patterns and inflections that are of utmost importance in understanding the import of the patients' responses to interventions. In each situation, the patients were very aware and receptive to my attempts to empathize, understand, and interpret their reactions. They felt understood and responded to in ways that contrasted our interaction with past interactions around similar themes. The affective tone of Patient III's comment that "mother never named" what she felt was one of stating that mother had not done what I as therapist had. The patient's affective response was one of differentiating my intention to promote reciprocity from a past interaction where such was not the case. The written description of the session divorces the verbal responses from their affective underpinnings. In subjecting the sessions to the validating process, the affective component of the patients' responses to my interventions is not fully accounted for. During the sessions, the verbal material, in conjunction with its affective inflections, was viewed as genuine reflections upon past deprivations after having obtained a pleasurable interaction around this deprivation and relation to the therapist.

The use of noninterpretive interventions, such as self-revelations regarding my personal sense of loss and sadness, can promote analytic work. Concurrently, these interventions contain negative and burdensome introjects as well as positive and beneficial introjects. They are incomplete and require rectification of their pathological and countertransference-based contents in order to preserve and render less toxic their potentially positive aspects. Patient III showed the incompleteness of rectification due to countertransference difficulties, while Patient V suggested the usefulness of my self-revelation for the patient's expression of grief and loss. It remains an interesting question if noninterpretive interventions contain "good" and "bad" components and if the patient consciously accepts these while unconsciously feeling burdened, does rectification of their negative and burdensome aspects offer the possibility of extracting the pathological introject from the genuinely intended healthy offer of assistance, leading to positive introjection. These interventions may have their place in the establishment of ego structure in the severely disturbed patient, especially under the conditions of a permanently disrupted frame.

CONCLUSION

This form of premature termination disrupts the bipersonal field, making rectification of the framework impossible. Interactional syndromes are induced into the patients. In addition, the patient's emphasis on the nontransference aspects of the total analytic relationship and the need to be cognizant of this in formulating interventions places this form of termination as best understood via Langs' adaptional-interactional approach. The predominant shift by the patient to nontransference concerns and the need to distinguish the unconscious perceptions and commentary about the therapeutic interaction from transference distortions affirmed that it is not valid, as the previous literature had done, to view the patients reactions solely as classical transference.

Although not entirely satisfactory, the use of noninterpretive interventions, such as self-revelations, are not to be dismissed as totally erroneous, but rather as incomplete and in need of rectification to extract their pathological components from their beneficial aspects. It appears they are worthy of further study utilizing detailed clinical material subjected to the validating process.

The question is also raised concerning validating interventions by accounting for both the patients verbal responses and the affective contents that they convey. The issue is the perennial problem of exactly replicating both the verbal and the nonverbal modes of communication within the therapeutic interaction in order to provide empirical data to affirm, alter, or refute technical interventions.

Finally, it is my impression that this form of premature termination occurs far more frequently then is reported. It is hoped that this paper will stimulate clinicians to examine this area and perhaps acknowledge the motivations to avoid doing so.

REFERENCES

Arlow, J. (1975). Discussion of Dr. Kanzer's paper. *International Journal of Psychoanalytic Psychotherapy* 4:69–73.

Arlow, J., and Brenner, C. (1966). Discussion: the psychoanalytic situation. In *Psychoanalysis in the Americas*, ed. R. E. Litman, pp. 133–138. New York: International Universities Press.

Benedek, T. (1953). Dynamics of the countertransference. *Bulletin of the Menninger Clinic* 17:201–208.

Buxbaum, E. (1950). Technique of terminating analysis. *International Journal of Psycho-Analysis* 31:184–190.

Dewald, P. (1965). Reactions to the forced termination of therapy. *Psychiatric Quarterly* 39:102–126.

———. (1966). Forced termination of psychoanalysis. *Bulletin of the Menninger Clinic* 30:98–110.

Fairbairn, W. R. D. (1957). On the nature and aims of psychoanalytic treatment. *International Journal of Psycho-Analysis* 39:374–385.

Firestein, S. K. (1969). Problems of termination in the analysis of adults. *Journal of the American Psychoanalytic Association* 17:222–237.

———. (1974). Termination of psychoanalysis with adults: a review of the literature. *Journal of the American Psychoanalytic Association* 22:873–894.

Freud, A. (1954). Problems of technique in adult analysis. *Bulletin of the Philadelphia Association for Psychoanalysis* 4:44–70.

Giovacchini, P. L. (1979). *Treatment of Primitive Mental States*. New York: Jason Aronson.

Greenson, R. R. (1967). *The Technique And Practice of Psychoanalysis*, vol. 1. New York: International Universities Press.

———. (1969). The non-transference relationship in the psychoanalytic situation. In *Explorations in Psychoanalysis*. New York: International Universities Press, 1978.

———. (1971). The "real" relationship between the patient and the psychoanalyst. In *Explorations in Psychoanalysis*. New York: International Universities Press, 1978.

Hoffer, W. (1950). Three psychological criteria for the termination of treatment. *International Journal of Psychoanalysis* 31:194–195.

Hurn, H. T. (1971). Toward a paradigm of the terminal phase. *Journal of the American Psychoanalytic Association* 19:332–348.

Kanzer, M. (1975). The therapeutic and working alliances: an assessment. *International Journal of Psychoanalytic Psychotherapy* 4:48–68.

Kestenberg, E. (1964). Problems regarding the termination of analysis in character neuroses. *International Journal of Psycho-Analysis* 45:350–357.

Klein, M. (1950). On the criteria for the termination of analysis. *International Journal of Psycho-Analysis* 31:204.

Kubie, L. (1968). Unresolved problems in the resolution of the transference. *Psychoanalytic Quarterly* 37:331–352.

Langs, R. (1976a). *The Bipersonal Field*. New York: Jason Aronson.

———. (1976b). *The Therapeutic Interaction*, vols. 1 and 2. New York: Jason Aronson.

———. (1977). *The Therapeutic Interaction: A Synthesis*. New York: Jason Aronson.

Levenson, E. A. (1976). Problems in terminating psychoanalysis: the aesthetics of termination. *Contemporary Psychoanalysis* 12:338–342.

Menaker, E. (1942). The masochistic factor in the psychoanalytic situation. *Psychoanalytic Quarterly* 9:171–186.

Payne, S. (1950). Short communication on criteria for terminating analysis. *International Journal of Psycho-Analysis* 31:205.

Pumpian-Mindlin, E. (1958). Comments on techniques of termination and transfer in a clinic setting. *American Journal of Psychotherapy* 12:455–464.

Reich, A. (1950). On the termination of analysis. *International Journal of Psycho-Analysis* 31:179–183.

———. (1960). Further remarks on countertransference. *International Journal of Psycho-Analysis* 41:389–395.

Robbins, W. S. (1975). Termination: problems and techniques. *Journal of the American Psychoanalytic Association* 23:166–176.

Schwarz, G. (1974). Forced termination of analysis revisited. *International Review of Psycho-analysis* 1:283–290.

Searles, H. F. (1973). Concerning therapeutic symbiosis. In *Countertransference and Related Subjects*. New York: International Universities Press, 1979.

Stone, L. (1961). *The Psychoanalytic Situation*. New York: International Universities Press.

Szalita, A. B. (1976). On termination. *Contemporary Psychoanalysis* 12:342–347.

Volkan, V. (1976). *Primitive Internalized Object Relations*. New York: International Universities Press.

Weigert, E. (1952). Contributions to the problems of terminating psychoanalysis. *Psychiatric Quarterly* 21:465–480.

Weiss, S. (1972). Some thoughts and clinical vignettes on translocation of an analytic practice. *International Journal of Psychoanalysis* 53:505–513.

Witenberg, E. (1976). Termination is no end. *Contemporary Psychoanalysis* 12:335–338.

Interrupted Treatment and Forced Terminations

SYDNEY SMITH, PhD.

A discussion of "Premature Termination: A Therapist Leaving," by James Beatrice, M.S. The treatment literature offers a plethora of information regarding the beginnings of psychotherapy, but the process of termination is given relatively little attention. The issue of forced terminations, which bring about premature endings, interrupting the treatment in ways often harmful to patients and adding to the negative side of the ambivalence about seeking further help, is even more neglected. This paper examines the nature of forced terminations when they are invoked by the therapist and spells out the variety of circumstances and motivations sparking such endings. Finally, it addresses the nature of forced terminations initiated by patients, and details the conscious and unconscious factors likely to be at work.

The expectation in psychotherapy, as in psychoanalysis, is that the beginning and the closing moves, as in the game of chess, are both predictable and describable in a systematic fashion (Freud 1913). But while the literature on treatment is replete with suggested formulas on opening gambits, and textbooks in psychotherapy give inordinate space on how to begin treatment, relatively little attention has been devoted to the complex issues surrounding termination. Even less has been written about forced terminations—i.e., treatment endings dictated by forces outside of the treatment setting—even though it is likely that only a small fraction of terminations brings about a resolution of the transference neurosis or of the distressing issues surrounding separation. For example, Beatrice's paper in the present volume, "Premature Termination: A Therapist Leaving," lists only three specific references to this topic in its lengthy bibliography.

The relative neglect of the study of the termination process is all the more surprising when one realizes that the greatest difficulties in treatment can appear in the termination phase. If a transference neurosis has developed—

that organization of transference manifestations built around the relationship with the analyst—one can virtually predict that the patient will not have a painless termination. In the absence of a transference neurosis, the treatment may simply reach an end and not in any way arrive at a definable termination phase. In the real work of termination, however, all the infantile longings for the loved object will appear or reappear, and all the difficulties around separation, all the turmoil issuing from the loss of gratification, can be expected to flare up again as they did earlier, but often in a manner not previously seen. In fact, in some patients issues surrounding infantile omnipotence may make their appearance in force for the first time during the termination phase.

Glover (1955) describes those processes that characterize the termination phase. He writes of the resolution of the transference neurosis, but more vividly addresses the process of "libido-weaning," during which the ego is expected to assume relative control of the patient's instinctual life. Before that accomplishment can be effected, however, the ego reengages in a regression in part set off by the renewed danger, posed in the termination, of the loss of the mother or mother surrogate. This ego-regression is in the service of attempting to avoid the threat of separation. One may add that the patient's exposure of his or her deepest infantile fantasies in the termination period is the only way for the patient to work through these fantasies by coming to grips in a more realistic fashion with the pathological aspects of infantile narcissism.

Given the importance of the termination process, one can begin to appreciate how disruptive an interrupted treatment can be. Just how disruptive, of course, depends upon the nature of the relationship between therapist and patient, on how long the treatment has continued and with what intensity, and on the particular nature of the therapeutic work at the time the interruption occurs. It also depends on how the forced termination is presented and how much time is left to deal with the problems raised by a sudden intrusion of a premature ending. Finally, the impact of this kind of ending will differ depending on whether it is introduced by the patient or by the therapist.

FORCED TERMINATION INVOKED BY THE THERAPIST

On the therapist's side, a number of factors may bring about the necessity of a forced termination. First is the issue raised in the Beatrice paper: for whatever reason, the therapist is making a move far enough away from the locus of the treatment that the relationship cannot continue. Under such circumstances, a patient deeply engaged in a treatment process, with every reason to believe that it will continue to a satisfactory ending, receives such news like a lightning bolt, responding to what is felt as abandonment with anger, sadness, loneliness, confusion, depression, and at times with a certain detachment from the therapist, as if suddenly the treater had been unmasked as a thoroughly unreliable, faithless person. On some occasions the news of the therapist's leaving is met initially with the patient's sense of relief—a situation that may be more common in cases where the news of the therapist's imminent departure comes at a time when the negative transference is in the ascendency. A beginning process of mourning, combined with dealing with the reality of the therapist's loss, is the more common response.

Whether, as Beatrice suggests from his critique of the literature and from his description of his own cases, a forced termination needs to result in the patient shifting away from working within the transference to dealing primarily with the realistic aspects of the therapeutic relationship and with the therapist as a real person, having his or her own life and needs and involving decisions in self-interest, is a question that cannot be answered easily. One may wonder if it is not the therapist's countertransference reactions to guilt or to the defensiveness required to justify a move likely to be antitherapeutic that makes the therapist appear more real.

One question always on the patient's mind and often verbalized is why the therapist chose to make his or her move knowing its disruptive effect on the patient and the set back it is likely to create in the patient's progress. The question is a legitimate one. If the therapist takes the patient into treatment, then the patient has the right to believe that the treater has agreed to a process and to work within the "frame" (Langs 1976). Because of the nature of psychotherapy, this commitment must be a serious one, not to be abandoned lightly.

It calls for a certain renunciation on the part of the therapist to postpone or delay personal plans or ambitions until the patient is in a satisfactory place. The psychotherapist must be as much of an adherent to the principle of *primum non nocere* as is the surgeon, and in this sense does not have as much freedom to come and go as other working people, in the same sense that the therapist does not have the freedom to be late for the appointment, to speak thoughtlessly, to talk about other patients, or to divulge to others what happens in the treatment hour.

All of these constrictions have their own well-grounded rationale, and the matter of electively interrupting a patient's treatment represents a serious and usually antitherapeutic change. As with some disturbed character disorders, the tolerance for separation and abandonment and for what is felt as an intolerable rejection is minimal. And yet, despite these professional issues—which speak both to the therapist's sense of values and to his or her adherence to a sound practice of treatment knowledge—interruptions of treatment and forced terminations have become institutionalized in virtually every training program.

Psychiatric residents are moved from training site to training site—usually at yearly intervals, sometimes on six-month rotations—with little consideration given to the repercussions on the patient, or for that matter to important factors in the resident's training. Few residents have the opportunity to carry a psychotherapy case to completion and residents are thereby deprived of a vital learning experience. Similarly, hardly any supervisor has the experience of teaching the resident the intricacies of bringing psychotherapy to a satisfactory conclusion, and indeed, if the supervisor's own training has been typical, the knowledge the supervisor has about the termination process may be as limited as the student's. The situation with the clinical training of psychologists is not much better, unless they avail themselves of a long-term postdoctoral training appointment.

Another unfortunate aspect of this system is that those patients most in need of continuing treatment are least able psychologically to tolerate the annual or semi-annual shift in therapist and are usually passed on from year to year with little accomplished therapeutically. Since their problems so often involve ineffectualities in forming enduring relationships, the very fact of knowing that the same therapist will not be available in a few months leads the patients to hold back in forming the kind of relationship with the therapist that could involve them in the real work of the therapy. Instead they insulate themselves against being hurt by the coming separation. It is not unusual for patients at the beginning of treatment to ask how they can be expected to put their trust in a process where the end result will be abandonment; for ultimately, if they improve, if the symptoms are relieved, the therapist will end the relationship. This belief with its implicit fantasied wish for exactly the opposite to occur—i.e., for the therapist forever to take care of, comfort, and meet every need of the patient—is never worked through, because in the training setting the fear of separation becomes a disturbing reality (Smith 1977). This situation is further complicated by the therapist's tendency to overidentify with the patient's plight, with how difficult the news of the therapist's departure is going to be for the patient, and this factor then leads the therapist to overlook the transference implications of the patient's response to the news of the therapist's departure. One reason for the therapist's nontherapeutic response to the situation of forced terminations is that, for certain therapists, it may fly in the face of the therapist's own unconscious needs.

For example, a young therapist was leaving his residency training and thus terminating with his two remaining psychotherapy patients. One of these patients was an attractive woman in her thirties who had throughout her life depended on her allure and her seductive, childlike qualities to protect herself against being abandoned. The therapist on his part had suffered his own early struggles with being left alone, feeling forlorn and neglected as a child. Although other complicated issues were involved in the lives of both therapist and patient, what occurred following his announcement of his departure was an effort on the side of this partially improved patient to relapse into her old patterns of enticement through expressions of her "littleness" and her dependence. On his side, the therapist identified in the patient his own needs, and through this identification with the patient saw himself as the bad parent, a painful and uncomfortable self-image, quickly replaced by the conscious wish to rescue the patient. This wish was suppressed too, however, and what he presented to the patient was a rigid insistence that the patient could now care for herself and was an independent person, entirely responsible for her own life. It was this rigidity that allowed the supervisor to reveal to the therapist that his own fantasies were producing an uncharacteristic response and leading to a problematic countertransference reaction, which in turn made it impossible for the therapist to deal realistically with the patient's issues around the forced termination.

Forced termination can also develop out of another set of circumstances. The therapist may decide for whatever reason not to treat a particular patient. Such a decision could emerge out of conscious design or could be an unscious reaction based on troubling countertransference feelings, although it is more likely that a subtle blending of these different levels of motivation will be involved. A therapist who brings an ongoing treatment to an abrupt end commonly holds the emotional conviction that the patient in some way is becoming overwhelming. The therapist senses danger in continuing the relationship because of the felt strength of the patient's aggression or individual demands (whether explicit or implicit), or the therapist reacts to the relationship with chronic anxiety or frustration or guilt, until finally a point is reached when the therapist becomes concerned that the therapeutic fit is not a good one.

At such times the therapist might reasonably seek supervision, or in certain cases engage in a return to treatment, but often the pain of the countertransference reactions is severe enough for the therapist to be able to think of nothing but escape. The first hints of such a reaction may come in the therapist's forgetting an appointment with the patient or of arriving at that point in the day when the patient is to be seen but not being able to remember who is in the waiting room. For example, a young woman psychotherapist whom I was supervising complained frequently that her male patient bored her, that he seemed never to speak of anything of importance, and that she felt unable to find a means of grasping the material. She decided that the patient was incapable of entering into a dynamic psychotherapy and suggested bringing the treatment to a close. It was not until her motives for such a precipitous move were explored in supervisory sessions that it was discovered that each time the patient expressed his anger or revealed his aggressive feelings, the therapist became sleepy and unable to concentrate on what the patient was communicating. Her self-described boredom was actually a means of defending herself against what she felt unconsciously was the patient's power to destroy her, and on some level of awareness this threat was so real that she wished to end all contact with the patient.

The sicker the patient, the greater the ability of that patient to reach inside of the therapist to inflame the bad parts of the therapist's self. In this manner the therapist can be put in touch with his or her own rage, destructiveness, envy, or jealousy in ways that cause the therapist to become anxious in the presence of the patient. As Searles (1979) points out, the therapist may decide, in response to this countertransference reaction, that this patient is not a suitable candidate for dynamic psychotherapy but is more appropriately a case for pharmacology. The well-trained and experienced therapist knows the inner countertransference rumblings can be important messages for telling the therapist what is going on with the patient, what transference role is being imposed on the therapist, and what important pieces of information about the self the patient is conveying.

Sometimes the therapist's response to inner feelings is to attempt to expunge them. The result is often that the therapist then responds to the patient affectlessly as a way of punishing the patient or as a way of conveying to the patient—in response to the therapist's anxiety—that "my heart is not with you." Generally therapists have a knack for blaming the patient for whatever goes wrong in the treatment. Patients can be seriously abused by this attitude. The personal difficulties of the therapist are presented as if they were the illness of the patient. Patients can, of course, set traps for therapists or engage in resistances that make the therapist uncomfortable, but the question is, what is that behavior in the service of and what has made the patient so frightened? At such points, patients are likely to regress, to become more infantile as a way of communicating a neediness that they are convinced the therapist is not seeing or hearing. At such times the psychotherapy supervisor should explore the fantasies, premises, or assumptions that the therapist brings to treatment with particular patients. It is not difficult to bring these fantasies to the forefront of the therapist's consciousness because they have not been repressed; it is only the connection between the fantasies and their role in the treatment that has become repressed.

Some years ago a resident psychiatrist noted for his brilliance and subtlety of understanding was having serious difficulty with a particularly demanding woman patient who was several years older than he. In the supervisory

session it was thought at first that he may have developed a countertransference response to this woman as a representation of his own mother, but
without confronting him with such speculations, he was encouraged to talk
during one of the supervisory hours about his own early life. This session
occurred following one in which he had suggested transferring the patient
because he seemed to be making no progress with her. What emerged was a
picture of a bright and sensitive child who clearly had discovered that he
had to meet his mother's powerful needs for accomplishment. She carried in
her purse all of his perfect grade cards in school, which she would proudly
display to relatives and friends, but this narcissistic mother would withdraw
from him whenever he allowed her to see a real need of his own. Even as a
small child he felt exploited by his mother and felt that if he failed to please
her with his accomplishments he would lose her forever. It was this relationship and his fantasies about it that were being displayed in the treatment
with the demanding older female patient, a woman who kept reminding him
that she expected his highly touted education to produce concrete results for
her, and with that message, he was back in the coils of his childhood pain of
feeling pressured to meet the narcissistic needs of a patient who would
otherwise not respect or accept him. His countertransference wish to separate
from the patient was complicatedly related to his identifying with his mother's
role and imitating her response to him of making herself unavailable in times
of his own personal needs.

A third factor that can lead to interrupted treatment or an unconscious
forcing of termination on the part of the therapist is the therapeutic impasse.
This term refers to a condition in which both therapist and patient recognize
that no progress is being made, that the ongoing work together is at a stand-
still, and that the therapist's efforts to move the patient off dead-center have
come to nothing. After a protracted effort in which the therapist experiences
a mounting frustration over the patient's intransigence, the therapist is likely
to suggest termination.

The therapeutic impasse can develop out of a number of circumstances,
but the focus here is on why this impasse leads to what is obviously a
premature termination. A therapeutic stalemate may be looked upon as a
failure of the treater, to use Freud's apt metaphor, to melt down the patient's
resistance in the heat of the transference. In some impasses the dug-in
resistance of the patient engenders a response of dug-in counterresistance on
the part of the treater, but just as the patient's resistance may be unconscious,
so also is the treater's counterresistance. Especially in those cases where a
patient is particularly paranoid, projecting aspects of the bad self, the
therapist becomes the target of such projections, leading to feelings within
the treater of anxiety or anger or possibly fear. If the counterresistance to

SYDNEY SMITH

such projections remains unconscious, the first conscious correlate of such an interaction for the therapist is usually a feeling of dread as the therapy hour approaches. Indeed the therapist can begin identifying with the paranoid projections of the patient, which can then result in distressing tensions in the therapist, from which a forced termination seems the only means of escape.

An example of this phenomenon occurred in the treatment of a middle-aged widow whose social demeanor was warm, charming, friendly, and approachable, but once in the consulting room she would quickly regress into the angry child who would accuse the therapist of secretly recording the hours, which could then be used to destroy her tenuous relationship with her dead husband's family. With such meager evidence, she would jump to major interpretations of the therapist's attitude or intentions toward her. These accusations were abrupt and unexpectedly interspersed with those occasions when she seemed able to handle herself more maturely. It appeared that once she had entered treatment, she attempted to defend herself against the arousal of early disturbing recollections of an uncle who had served during her early life as a father-surrogate. In the therapy she clearly distrusted the present therapist as she had this uncle from long ago, and at times attempted to treat the therapist in the same sadistic and overpowering manner in which this man had treated her. She threatened to visit the therapist's home to tell his wife about the bad things that he intended to do to her and indicated that she knew ways of stealing his patient records, which she could then use to discredit him. She was aware of her anger and her hostility, but was convinced it emerged only as a reaction to his anger toward her. Such a projective identification on the part of a patient is indeed likely to provoke counteraggression and, during the first months of treatment, when her projective potential was at its height, finding a suitable way to terminate the relationship was considered on several occasions. However, this case was clearly an instance in which the patient was putting the aggressive part of herself into the therapist, and the countertransference was largely a representation of the patient's bad self appearing through the therapist's own negative reaction to her. She saw herself at such moments as the frightened, abused child; although her actions and threats seemed so ominous that it was easy to think of ridding one's life of such distressing provocations. The crucial issue of control of the treatment was ultimately resolved with a judicious and resolute interpretation of these negative manifestations of the transference.

If the patient attempts to split himself or herself off from intense guilt-feelings by putting such feelings into the treater, and the therapist remains unaware of the patient's maneuvers in this respect, the therapist then begins to find the imposed guilt an unbearable burden. The key to such problems lies in the therapist's capacity to recognize what is happening within the patient that triggers his or her own sense of stress. The therapist cannot make the resistance conscious for the patient until it becomes conscious for the therapist. Generally the stalemate can be circumvented by a timely interpretation of the negative transference projected onto the therapist, and the therapist's failure to carry this technical effort into action is likely to lead eventually to a therapist-induced interruption or termination of the treatment.

FORCED TERMINATION INVOKED BY THE PATIENT

One can say with assurance that, on the surface at least, patient-induced interruptions of treatment appear to be based more on extraneous events than terminations initiated by therapists. Patients can use almost any event for bringing treatment to a premature end, and on occasion leave the therapist bewildered by offering no reason at all for suddenly closing out treatment.

Just as with the treater, a patient may also bring about a termination based on the necessity of moving. Patients are sometimes transferred to a different job location or have the chance for considerable financial advancement by moving to another section of the country. If the lead time on such a forced termination is a matter of several months, the effect of such a change does not necessarily have to be antitherapeutic. Time pressures can lead to an intensification of the work, a dropping away of old resistances, and an increase in the motivation to bring about resolution of the major problems. The shortened time for treatment may not lead to the same level of resolution as a much more planned termination process can, but it may often lead to some satisfactory symptom alleviation. A sufficient warning of the approaching forced termination allows the therapist to explore with the patient the specific meanings of separations in the patient's life, leading then into the fertile issues of the patient's identity and the specific interactional factors that have occurred in other phases of the patient's life.

A special permutation of this form of patient-induced termination is the situation in which the patient's spouse has decided to make the job move and the patient is caught between the need to adjust to what seems best for the family and the wish to complete treatment. Not only must the therapist deal with the usual separation issues and the consequent mourning of the loss, but also with the anger that the patient feels toward the spouse for forcing the termination. The elation that the spouse may feel in making an important career change may be misinterpreted by the patient as a selfish and unfeeling response to the patient's plight and may even be distorted into a belief that the spouse has deliberately set about to destroy the patient's therapy. Without help in dealing with such feelings before the move, a patient may sustain serious harm not only to the marriage, but also to his or her entire future happiness.

A parallel problem occurs when the child-patient is forced to terminate psychotherapy because the parents cannot tolerate confidentiality as a condition of treatment. The fact that the child seems to have a close, secretive, entirely private relationship with the therapist implies an exclusivity that may bring the parents to feel like neglected outsiders. If, in addition, the patient's behavior toward the parents becomes rejecting, then the stage is set for a parental intervention to bring a quick end to a threatening situation. Often, such circumstances can be mitigated by arranging for the parents to have regular contact with a social worker or by occasionally having joint family sessions including the child-patient, the parents, and possibly other significant members of the household. Providing some opportunity for the parents to raise questions or discuss their own concerns or observations is often enough to keep the family invested in the child's individual treatment.

For example, a resident was treating a 15-year-old boy who had been referred by his parents for abusing marijuana. The boy was angry—refusing to go to school, where he had been making near-failing grades—and was alienated from both parents and siblings. As is typical in these cases, the boy had found acceptance with a peer group. These boys were also family and school drop-outs and heavily into drugs. The drugs served as a way of legitimizing regression and supporting escape from all the psychological pressures involved in school and at home. This patient was essentially suffering from a developmental arrest around the issues of sexual intimacy and the frightening notion of having to choose a form of work. This particular patient was depressed and had begun to see daily marijuana use as a way of life. What brought about the referral for treatment was not the drug abuse, however, but his renunciation of parental influence and authority.

In this instance the family was eager to find a therapist with whom the boy was willing to work. When he was still using marijuana and was still not responsive to social or family influence after several weeks of treatment, there was a spate of anxious inquiries from the family. At first the parents agreed to meet with a social worker, but then complained about the additional expense and insisted on talking to the treating doctor. Not only did they feel left out of the process, a factor in part of their own making, but began to believe that the therapist was colluding with their son's drug problem as well as with the boy's insistence on privacy. Then a misunderstood communication from the social worker regarding the patient's inability to master his sexual drives was interpreted by the parents to mean that the therapist was attempting to encourage his sexual activity. Another comment from the social worker indicating that the boy's preoccupation with pin-ball machines was a "masturbatory equivalent" was too much for this family to hear. This comment only confirmed their worst fears. At this point I advised the therapist to have a meeting with both parents and child in order to head off any jeopardy to the treatment and defuse the parents' anxiety and anger. Unfortunately, the intervention did not come soon enough to save the treatment, for the combination of the ineptness of the communications with the family, the distress of the family at being replaced by a "good parent" whom the boy was willing to see, and their need to see the boy caught up in a process of sexual indoctrination that flew in the face of their own values made them unable to listen to what either the treater or the son had to say.

Perhaps the most common reason patients foreshorten treatment is a financial one. They complain of running out of money or are beset by such heavy obligations on their income that they can no longer afford to pay the therapy bill. No doubt in many cases the concern is a legitimate one, but it is also a resistance that the therapist has trouble confronting, since concerns about money always have an element of reality about them. It is also true, however, that interrupting treatment on grounds of lack of funds is a frequent method patients use to mask other forms of resistance that in reality may have a great deal more to do with the patient's decision to stop treatment than money. The more precipitous such a decision is, the more likely it is that factors having nothing to do with money underlie the wish to terminate. Money, of course, has different meanings for different patients, but in some instances the patient who is feeling that the therapy is not providing the expected fulfillment will wish to withhold the money as a way of punishing the therapist. In addition, while feeling guilty about not meeting the bill, the patient sees termination as a way of resolving this dilemma.

In the case of obsessional patients, money can take on a specially cathected significance. Paying the fee may be experienced by the patient as being drained or emptied out, and since obsessional pathology is almost always colored by manifestations of sadism, the patient may find retention or withholding an important source of satisfaction. In such instances the unwillingness to pay for the treatment (and incidentally, in this way to put oneself in control of the relationship) may bring the treatment to a precipitous end. Unfortunately, because such obsessional issues are rarely treated successfully over a short period of time and since the patient may come down abruptly on the negative side of the ever present ambivalence, the therapist may not be given much opportunity to work with these issues before the termination becomes an accomplished fact. In this instance one can see how the financial issue once again serves to curtain off the real psychological motivations.

These problems can be initiated and often exacerbated by a compulsive inflexibility on the part of the therapist. Since the therapist in the treatment of the obsessional patient becomes quickly aware of the centrality of control issues, he or she may attempt to nail down some hard and fast rules regarding such therapeutic issues as the payment of fees and the missing of hours. In this countertransferential way, the therapist may be adding to his or her therapeutic woes, since the obsessional is likely to fit such rules into his or her own propensity for rituals. The more rigid the therapist makes the rules, the more rigidly the patient adheres to them and thus undermines the therapist's efforts in helping undo the patient's ritualistic tendencies.

In supervisory work with therapists, the present author has attempted to point out how, in obsessional pathology, premature terminations seemingly brought on by the patient almost always result from missing out on the opportunity of bringing feelings into the treatment hour. Often, this aim must be accomplished by the therapist's introducing comments about his or her own feelings in reaction to whatever the patient is saying or doing. The patient will comment on a fact in his or her own life or manifest a particular behavior, and these opportunities are not to be cast aside because they can become ways for the therapist to demonstrate how such communications lead to certain feelings, but without emphasizing that to arouse such feelings in the therapist was precisely the patient's intent. In this manner one can often foresee and avoid those issues that may lead the patient to bring the treatment to an early end.

A third factor that may lead the patient to consider termination prematurely is what the patient experiences as a bad personality fit with the treater. Although it is customary to chalk up such reactions to the patient's resistance, it seems reasonable to assume that in treatment, as in other walks of life, one can discover in another person serious stumbling blocks to forming a working relationship.

This unfortunate experience can occur even to a seasoned therapist. It appears to hinge on an interchange of unconscious messages between patient and therapist that arouse destructive transference and countertransference reactions. Certain forms of psychopathology in a patient may press on sensitive psychological points in the therapist of which he or she is not aware. What the therapist senses is a discomfort in himself or herself, a tension state that may emanate from an internal effort to repress an impulse, or on a more conscious level the arousal of an inappropriate anger that tells the therapist that he or she is in danger of having his or her seasoned judgment intruded upon by too much affect. Or for some mysterious reason, the therapist discovers that his or her neutrality is giving way to a strong desire to gratify a need to punish or damage the patient.

A young psychoanalyst treating a control case—who was himself a physician, but in another specialty—found himself becoming at first uncomfortable, then anxious, and finally angry as the patient would periodically introduce into the hour derogative comments about the analytic community. The patient spoke initially of the professional incest and the elitism in the local analytic institute, but then his derogation took a more inflammatory, slanderous direction by implying a lack of ethical behavior and possibly the existence even of criminal activity on the part of the local analysts. He pointed to their lack of justice and fair play in choosing candidates and their cruelty and abuse in relating to their patients, prolonging the treatment as a way of exploiting the insurance companies. The candidate became increasingly defensive and angrily wished to protect the institute and its teachers from the patient's view of their treachery. He was afraid to respond because he might explode in anger, but this tactic of remaining silent was hiding the fact that he was actually punishing the patient by his withdrawal. The patient took the silence as an indication that the analyst was not easily aroused by such material and only increased the intensity of his attack. The candidate then spoke to his supervisor about a serious misalliance that led the candidate to believe a transfer of the patient would be the best solution for both patient and treater. For his own reasons the candidate was unable to deal with the transference meanings of the patient's communications, but became instead caught up in his own wrath about betrayal of the parents and the need to see the father and mother figures as good and giving and above reproach. His idealizations became more rigid as the patient's derogation became more destructive, an instance where neither participant in this interaction could appreciate how each was playing in each other's fantasies and introjects.

In this example, the difficulty is relatively transparent, in that it is clear that the patient was engaging in transference projections and the treater, because of his own internal issues, had become blind to the fact that the patient was talking about the treatment. In other circumstances, however, the intertwining of such reality distortions on the part of both patient and therapist may be more subtle, more hidden, but nevertheless sufficiently primitive and destructive to bring about a painful misalliance. If the tilt in the relationship created by this distortion is not righted, the patient is likely to abandon the whole enterprise.

From a misguided sense of professional commitment, the therapist in this situation often allows the treatment to continue, feeling guilt in bringing it to an end, or believing that the key to unlocking the relationship will eventually be found, or even wishing not to face the failure of the treatment effort. Thus it is often the patient who finally interrupts the relationship.

Physical illness, or the complaint of physical illness that the patient feels makes the treatment impossible, is another reason that patients offer for termination. The illness, of course, may be a real one, even a serious one, which renders a psychotherapy regimen impossible, and then the relationship with the therapist must be halted. This problem can cause complications for the patient who may feel that not only does the illness itself have to be endured but that it cuts the patient off from needed and useful contacts with the treater. Sometimes these interruptions are temporary, but in some cases they can be sufficiently prolonged to represent a serious disruption and lead to termination.

In other cases, however, the development of a physical illness may be a way of terminating psychotherapy, a somatization of problems or the eruption of physical symptoms that convince the patient that his or her troubles are not emotional or psychological but organic. It is one of the paradoxes of this work that patients often give clear indications that they would prefer to be diagnosed as having a severe physical or organic disorder than to discover that something "mental" is wrong, even though the physical disorder may be less treatable than the psychiatric problem. Despite all the educational efforts, the onus for the ordinary person of a psychiatric disorder is so great as to be avoided at any cost.

Occasionally one sees a patient who has come for psychotherapy because of certain internal issues with which the patient has been struggling and which appear to be legitimate concerns for treatment. Early in the course of treatment, however, the patient either begins to talk about a fixed physical symptom, possibly present for some time, or the patient develops such a symptom during the open phases of treatment. This symptom increasingly becomes the focus of the discussion, often with the patient ruminating over the question of whether the psychological problems that originally brought the patient for treatment are in reality organic in nature. The patient will then decide—rightfully—to seek a complete physical examination. Nothing is found. Instead of being relieved by this result, the patient will decide to see another physician and go through the entire process again. The result is the same: negative findings. The psychotherapist, who has been patient with this preoccupation about the physical symptom, now decides it is time to move the patient back to the therapeutic work. About this time, however, the patient develops a new physical symptom to add to the first and now becomes more troubled and more incapacitated. This process can continue until the patient develops a full-blown "syndrome," which by this time has convinced the patient that he or she is suffering from some dread undiagnosed disease. The patient feels it is now impossible to concentrate on the earlier reasons for seeking psychotherapy. At this point the patient breaks off the treatment and is bent on discovering a doctor who will at last say what is "really" wrong.

Given the difficulty of diagnosing the early signs of such disorders as multiple sclerosis or muscular dystrophy, the psychotherapist is hardly in the position of treating the patient's fears with anything less than serious concern and must certainly support a careful medical evaluation. However, given the level of the patient's anxiety and his or her conviction of being the victim of an as yet undiagnosed dread disease, the therapist finds it impossible to deal with the patient's resistance to the very psychological treatment that the patient initiated in the first place. The interruption of the psychotherapy is carried off by the patient with the same conviction, and the effort on the part of the therapist to interpret the possible meanings of the patient's behavior is brushed aside as no longer relevant. The patient is totally absorbed by the stress and worry created by the physical symptoms and their possibly lethal consequences.

CONCLUSION

Glover (1955), in speaking about such cases in his discussion of the difficulties of treatment, indicates that the course of treatment is more often broken off than carried to a completed termination. Many of the factors mentioned in this review have probably contributed to Glover's impression. It would seem, however, that if the therapist is working with the concept of transference, then that therapist would feel an obligation to bring the transference to some degree of resolution before allowing the treatment to end. Also, one must remember that, in contrast to most of the clinical examples discussed here, most patients are reluctant to end therapy. To paraphrase Menninger (1958), where else will a patient find somebody to listen as attentively, to find every word important, to offer an understanding, empathic, caring concern without intruding one's own ego into the process, and to do it all with a reliability rarely found in any other relationship. It is not surprising that the patient may be in no hurry to bring an end to this uniquely satisfying relationship.

The emphasis in this paper has been on the variety of reasons and causes that bring about interruptions in the treatment and the factors that precipitate forced endings to the therapeutic work. Given these facts, together with Glover's comments about most treatment being broken off rather than properly terminated, one is left with the question of what is involved in a "proper termination." The ideal is probably never reached, but nonetheless if the process of termination can be engaged in fully, it offers a much improved chance that the outcome of treatment will be effective. The termination process brings about a sense of loss and mourning, and the activation of these feelings returns the patient to an idealization of the treater. Since the treater has often served the function no parent has ever served, there are realistic elements in this mourning.

The depressive state so common in termination should be worked through while the treater is still available. The process then allows for deeper levels of the mourning to surface; for example, the guilt that the patient experiences in leaving the therapist or the idea that the therapist is leaving because the patient is bad. One may also observe during the termination period a regression to paranoid ideas as a defense against the depression. Such ideas may come up, for example, in the thought, "I'm not really any good, and I'm fooling the therapist into being willing to let me go."

A good beginning in treatment will generally assure a good ending, and a proper initial evaluation of the patient—not only through collecting historical data, but from a battery of psychological tests—will provide the basis for this good beginning and help predict, even before formal treatment begins, what the ending will likely involve. Neglecting this process of the initial evaluation of the patient may lead to just these identifiable troubles that bring about premature terminations.

REFERENCES

Freud, S. (1913). On beginning the treatment (Further recommendations on the technique of psychoanalysis I). *Standard Edition* 12:121-144.

Glover, E. (1955). *The Technique of Psycho-Analysis*. New York: International Universities Press.

Langs, R. (1976). *The Bipersonal Field*. New York: Jason Aronson.

Menninger, K. (1958). *Theory of Psychoanalytic Technique*. New York: Basic Books.

Searles, H. (1979). *Countertransference and Related Subjects*. New York: International Universities Press.

Smith, S. (1977). The golden fantasy: a regressive reaction to separation anxiety. *International Journal of Psycho-Analysis* 58:311-325.

Alexithymia and the Effectiveness of Psychoanalytic Treatment

HENRY KRYSTAL, M.D.

A subgroup of those patients who are not responsive to analytic treatment, despite meeting the usual criteria of analyzability, is considered. These patients typically have significant addictive, psychosomatic, and post-traumatic problems. They show a characteristic picture, now called "alexithymia." This involves an impairment of the ability to recognize, name, or verbalize emotions. The affects manifest themselves mainly in mixed physiological responses, which call attention to themselves rather than to their meaning or story. These emotions, which are less useable as signals, are dedifferentiated and resomatized. There is also a type of "operative thinking" with marked limitations in wish-fulfillment and drive-related fantasy. There is a diminution of symbolization, and with it an impairment in the capacity to elaborate the kind of fantasies that underly neuroses and the related transferences. They also have a seriously diminished emotional involvement with their objects and a lowered capacity for empathy. Lastly, there are frequently associated problems such as anhedonia, impairments in the capacities for self-care, and affect tolerance. The impediments to psychoanalytic treatment resulting from this picture are considered, and some theories of its causation and therapeutic modifications calculated to enable these patients to benefit from psychotherapy are offered.

The assumption that other people's emotional responses are like our own is the basis of empathy and as such is basic to all human intercourse. The uncritical acceptance of this assumption, however, has led us to the false expectation that all patients have available to them the affective functions necessary for the utilization of psychotherapy. This paper examines some variations of affective function, affect forms, and those factors that make emotions available as signals to one's self. In particular, a major disturbance in affective and symbolic function, which Sifneos (1967) has named "alexithymia" (no words for emotions), is reviewed. This syndrome is of special interest to therapists, since it represents a very common and serious obstacle in the patient's capacity to utilize psychoanalytic or, in general, "anxiety-producing" psychotherapy.

DESCRIPTION AND DEFINITION

Alexithymia overlaps diagnostic categories. Marty and de M'Uzan (1963) and Marty et al. (1963) described the cognitive and affective disturbances found in psychoanalytic studies of psychosomatic patients. Their work was advanced by Sifneos (1967) and Nemiah (1970). About the same time, and unaware of the work of the others, the present author found a lack of differentiation of affects in drug withdrawal states (Krystal 1962) and was describing the same characteristic problems in severe post-traumatic states (Krystal 1968, 1971), and in a study reported with Raskin, in patients with drug dependence (Krystal and Raskin 1970).

Since that time a number of authors have contributed observations on alexithymia. (For a survey see the report of the Proceedings of the 11th European Conference of Psychosomatic Research, Braeutigan 1977). Generally, there is excellent agreement on the affective and cognitive disturbances found in this condition. There are, in addition, problems that are frequently associated: an impairment in the capacity for self-care and an anhedonia (Krystal 1978a). These are discussed separately, following the section on the commonly accepted affective and cognitive problems.

The Affective Disturbance

These patient's impaired capacity in utilizing emotions as signals to themselves is based in the *form* that their emotional responses take. Their reactions are basically somatic, consisting of the "expressive" or physiological aspects of affects, with minimal verbalization. In addition, their emotions are often undifferentiated; i.e., they are vague and unspecific, as if they represented an undifferentiated form of common affect precursors, so that separate responses of such feelings as depression and anxiety do not seem to appear (Krystal 1962). Because of the concomitant diminution in the verbalization of affects, these patients experience somatic, often distressing reactions rather than complete emotions. Only when one experiences the cognitive aspect of an emotion, i.e., the meaning of the affect and some indication of the "story behind it," and simultaneously has the "expressive" reaction and is possessed of adequate capacity for reflective self-awareness, does one have a chance to observe that one is experiencing a "feeling" and to identify it.

Alexithymics often cannot tell whether they are sad, tired, hungry, or ill. Hence they are not accustomed to recognizing their feeling states and to discovering their reactions to events in their lives. Sometimes they display remarkable stoicism and even a lack of awareness of these physical responses, which respresent affect components. The diminished ability to recognize, name, describe, or even use their emotions as guides to self-understanding results in an overdependence on and overutilization of reasoning.

Case 1. Patient I had been severely addicted to barbiturates in the past, but had not used any in several months. On the occasion of this excerpt he was complaining of general distress. His malaise was quite general, and practically every part of his body was in some pain or discomfort. His head hurt, it felt full, heavy, and the skin of his scalp felt tight. There was something wrong with his eyes and at times vision was blurred. His jaw was tight. His mouth was dry and his tongue seemed slightly swollen or awkward. His chest also felt tight. His skin felt "creepy." His stomach felt badly, perhaps he was hungry but the distress was not relieved by food, although coffee did make him feel a little better. His muscles were taut and stiff, and joints not quite sore but "heavy" and "stiff." He felt somewhat "jumpy" as if he was on the verge of hypoglycemia.

Whenever individuals with a history of substance abuse and many addictive problems are under stress from physical or emotional sources, they may develop a syndrome resembling their past withdrawal reaction. When this patient was questioned, he realized that this was the case and was very surprised and impressed with this discovery. (The significance of this reaction is discussed later, as it leads to the very heart of the affective disturbance involved in alexithymia.)

When a survey was made of the patient's complaints, and even when it was recognized that the symptoms were very similar to his drug withdrawal pattern, he did not link his state with his life situation. There were, in fact, many things of a profoundly disturbing and distressing nature in his self-evaluation. He had left his wife and children and had moved to a rented room. When he considered his situation in life, his isolation, his terrible financial and occupational position, he "figured" out that he probably felt very lonely and afraid. He had thoughts of resenting that at his age he was all alone; that he had to give up his house. He thought he should be angry with himself and with his fate, as well as with a number of people. However, neither these, nor a variety of other emotions were identified by him. Nor did he recognize in his distress state either anxiety or depression. Instead, he was experiencing the gamut of physical or expressive aspects of these emotions, which in the past he would have prevented by the use of massive doses of barbiturates. He did not have a cold nor was he hungry out of a lack of food.

This pattern of lacking the capacity for reflective self-awareness (which would enable one to identify one's *"feeling"* as being an appropriate response to one's self-evaluation) is typical of alexithymia. Since such a defect makes it virtually impossible for a patient to utilize psychoanalytic psychotherapy, a preparatory phase of treatment is necessary in which the affective problem is attended to (Krystal and Raskin 1970, Krystal 1979). Hence the work on this and many other occasions proceeded from identifying his physiological responses as parts of an affect the cognitive part of which was either absent or appeared isolated and which, after bringing the elements together, he could start to "feel." Up to this time he frequently named emotions when he thought the situation warranted it. For instance, he would say that he felt angry when someone did not fulfill his wishes. Coincidently, he was also color blind. On one occasion when it was pointed out to him that he neither felt nor believed in the existence of love he said, "I believe you. But it's like you tell me the grass is green—but I only see it as sort of brownish."

Many alexithymics learn to use the common expressions denoting affective responses when they figure they should experience them or in situations in which they have observed others reacting emotionally. Therefore they frequently behave like the color blind patient who has learned to cover up his deficiency in perception by utilizing a variety of clues by which he inferred what he could not discern. However, they are missing a quality in their self-perception that would enliven their self-view and give it a sense of conviction and vigor.

Although the patient in the above vignette had some inkling that the distress he experienced had something to do with his well-being as a person, some patients frequently experience such episodes as "illness." Flanery (1975) reported that alexithymic patients suffering from "unexplained physical distress" were "not an uncommon diagnostic and therapeutic problem for the liaison psychiatrist in the general medical setting" (p. 193). Patients suffering from chronic pain syndrome, "pain prone personalities," turn out to have a very high rate of alexithymia as well.

There is some variation from person to person, and sometimes within a given individual, but these patients share a broad area within which emotions are not differentiated and are unverbalized. Sifneos (1967) was the first one to emphasize that these patients demonstrate a unique and identifiable disturbance. Nemiah (1975) has summarized this contribution: "Many psychosomatic patients, although they use words like 'sad,' 'angry' and 'nervous' are unable to describe their feelings further, appear to be at a loss for language to convey their experiences of them to others, and frequently when pressed by the interviewer for a response, assert that they 'just can't put it into words'" (p. 143). With some sympathetic attention the patients finally realize, and may admit to themselves for the first time, that they cannot describe what they feel because what they experience is a vague and generalized response, often involving every system of their bodies (Freyberger 1977, Nemiah et al. 1976). The emotions are not experienced as distinct, separate, specific responses of a varied and identifiable nature. Rather, a common distress pattern develops, so that the patients refer to a state of tension or unease, which they experience generally with a few areas highlighted as the seat of discomfort. Hence they will say "it's all in one ball," or "in one pot" (Nemiah et al. 1976). These patients commonly experience a general diminution in the ability to "localize affect in their bodies and they appear unaware of any of the common automatic somatic sensations that accompany the experience of a variety of feelings. If there is a somatic component, it is identical with the symptoms of their bodily illness" (p. 431).

This last comment refers to patients with psychosomatic diseases, as does the above-mentioned tendency to stoicism and diminution in proprioception. As McDougall (1974) put it, "Many psychosomatic patients continue on their unwavering tight-rope ignoring the body's signs and the mind's distress signals" (p. 458). This tendency to be like "a rock or an island" (McDougall 1974) is possibly related to a trait of alexithymia that may alert the examiner to the rest of the picture. These patients show a stiffness of posture and a stoney expressionless facies: "They sit rigidly, move their bodies sparingly, use few gestures when they talk and maintain a near expressionless face" (Freyberger 1977, p. 433). But the alexithymics who are prone to addictive behavior show a virtually hypochondriacal preoccupation with the affect-related distressful sensations in their bodies and a driven need to block them.

Related to this tendency is an overemphasis of sensory perceptions in the place of reflective self-awareness, best illustrated by a case vignette of McDougall's (1974): "The patient was aware of *sensations* rather than sentiments in her mother's presence. Encouraged to put these into words she was finally able to say 'I can't bear to *touch* her. As though her body was covered with filth. Almost as though she might poison me'" (p. 456). The importance of this substitution of sensory preoccupation is that it constitutes a predisposition to an *insistence on the concrete* and *externalization*, a major problem in addictive individuals (Wurmser 1978).

Another characteristic finding is that alexithymic patients are subject to sudden affective responses of considerable intensity. Nemiah et al. (1976) have referred to the "brief but violent" outbursts: "Patients will, for instance, suddenly fill up with tears; when questioned, however, they are unaware of feeling sad and cannot explain why they are crying. Or though they felt no anger in the face of aggravating circumstances, they may exhibit explosive flashes of destructive rage" (p. 432). Although the patient shows this intense affectlike behavior, he may realize that there is a disparity between his feelings and violent behavior. Such individuals sometimes resolve to use it "for show" (Krystal 1979) and at other times experience the outbursts as a "crazy intrusion into the mind" (Nemiah et al. 1976, p. 458). These sudden outbursts, which stop as abruptly as they start, have led some to say that addicts behave as if they suddenly switched to another personality (Wurmser 1978).

Pensée Opératoire: The Cognitive Disturbance

It may be noted that the sudden changes in affective behavior so characteristic of the emotions of alexithymics are present in the cognitive area as well. While the major characteristic of these individuals is that they present a dull, mundane, unimaginative, utilitarian, and chronologically dominated recitation of concrete "facts" (de M'Uzan 1974a), occasionally they spring a surprize. De M'Uzan, who is a co-author of the now classical study on Pensée Opératoire (Marty and de M'Uzan 1963) pondered this phenomenon: "The symbolization, almost always poor, becomes dazzling at times, but remains isolated and incapable of entering into a syntax" (p. 462).

The usual situation is that these patients relate the details of their everyday life, and particularly their complaints, in a repetitive fashion. Soon one realizes that they are oriented to "facts" and that there is a striking lack of wish-fulfillment fantasties:

> One cannot elicit such fantasies when they are asked for, and frequently one may observe that when the alexithymic individual is asked to describe how he feels, he responds instead with a description of external events. The operative thinking, in other words, is characterized by thoughts that are more stimulus-bound than drive-oriented (Nemiah and Sifneos 1970a, p. 30).

What is deceptive to those unfamiliar with this disturbance is that these patients, who often function very successfully in their work, appear "super-adjusted" to reality and lead one to expect excellent intellectual function. However, getting past the superficial impression of superb functioning, one discoveres a sterility and monotony of ideas, and a severe impoverishment of the imagination. The tendency to externalization is reflected in a cognitive style focused on external processes and activities (Nemiah 1975). At first glance, objects seem to be of interest to these individuals, especially since sometimes they can "tune in" with great precision on people around them for manipulative or exploitative purposes. However, there is no *personal* investment in these objects as unique individuals to whom there is a sentimental attachment. Instead one sees that the objects are replaceable, albeit necessary. One such patient announced one day without a trace of emotion, "I fired Max." The therapist mistakenly concluded that the patient referred to his employee, but it turned out that he was talking about his mistress by the same nickname, who at other times had seemed so indispensable to him.

The problem here, however, was different from that seen in the narcissistic or borderline personality, wherein a devalued object is discarded as useless and worthless. In this patient, as in the cases described by McDougall (1974), the object was experienced as one on whom he was very dependent. However, just as in McDougall's cases, "their love objects are highly *interchangeable*, the central demand being that someone must be there" (p. 451). When such individuals stay with one object, that is because they think it would be too much trouble to find another one; there being no essential difference. De M'Uzan (1974b) has termed this phenomenon "reduplication": "This concerns a perception of other people strongly marked by a sort of global translation of a rough image of one's self, stripped of truly personal traits and indefinitely reproducible according to a stereotyped form" (p. 106).

The absence of the "human" quality contributes to making these patients' thoughts "operative" or thing-oriented. They are often described as "dull, colorless and boring" (Krystal 1979, p. 159), even when they are intellectual and clever. In psychotherapy one finds, as de M'Uzan (1974a) did, "The patient's language is poor, flat and banal, glued to the present and only producing facts stated chronologically" (p. 462).

The associations of these patients are characterized by (1) the almost complete absence of thoughts relating to inner attitudes, feelings, wishes, or drives; and (2) a recounting "in great and often boring detail, of the events in their external environment and their own actions in this setting" (Krystal 1979, p. 158).

Case 2. Patient II was a middle-aged professional who was an alcoholic and had severe alexithymia and anhedonia. While very bright and successful, both in high school and college, she discovered that she was not able to write on any but the simplest themes. In a class in creative writing in college, she was "passed on" because the teacher recognized that she had an "organic inability to make up any imaginative story". When given a Rorschach, she saw "mainly inkspots—a few looking like vertebrae or a pelvis." When shown TAT cards, she gave concrete, descriptive responses, and despite repeated efforts had only the simplest fantasy responses. For instance, on Card One she said, "This is a boy with a violin. He is supposed to practice, but he doesn't like to." When encouraged to make up a story about the boy, his past and future, she finally said, "Well, he is not going to become a violinist, but he'll find something else to do and will be okay."

Because of her anhedonia, she was questioned about what might give her pleasure. She answered that she might like to take a vacation. Upon another inquiry she added that she would like to go to certain European cities and go to museums. No other fantasies could be obtained. She did recall that as a child she had a favorite fantasy game; she would sit in an overstuffed chair, sometimes draped in some curtains, and imagine that she was a queen. The fantasizing disappeared abruptly and irretrievably during latency years.

Yet, despite this seemingly total inhibition of fantasy, she did enjoy watching television. However, she insisted that when she turned off the set she never continued to think about the story that she had just seen, nor to elaborate on it. Once the television was turned off the story "disappeared." She also enjoyed reading spy mysteries.

All of this patient's productions in therapy were factual, relating events and concerns that took place since the previous session. No associations to her material were available as formal activity.

Another example of the impairment of these patients' capacity for fantasy and association is their difficulty in utilizing dreams. Most of them dream rarely, and then only very simple "one sentence" dreams. When asked to associate to the dreams, they are unable to do so. When pressed, they finally produce more *details* of the dream, but rarely can learn to associate to them (Krystal 1979). This difficulty illustrates what some authors mean when they say that the psychosomatic process is the opposite from the psychoanalytic one (McDougall 1974, de M'Uzan 1974a, 1974b). McDougall (1974) describes these patients as "antineurotic," in the sense of being unable to create neurotic defenses, but also "antipsychotic" in the sense of being "overadapted" to reality and the difficulties of existence. De M'Uzan (1974b) expresses a similar view: "Operatory thinking has no appreciable relationship with unconscious fantasies" (p. 106).

The capacity for fantasy-making and symbolization permits creativity and the formation of neuroses. Symbolization of a conflict makes possible dealing with the cognitive aspect of an affect such as anxiety. In the absence of such capabilities, the patients have to contend with the "expressive," i.e., physiological aspects of their affective responses, and thus are prone to psychosomatic illnesses. Alternatively, they may try to block these responses by the use of drugs, thus resorting to the pattern underlying the addictions.

The Nature of Self- and Object-Representation and the Problem of Self-care

A number of authors have reported separately that addicts, alcoholics, and patients with a tendency to substance dependence have a serious impairment in their ability to take care of themselves (Krystal and Raskin 1970,

Krystal 1978b, Khantzian 1978, Zinberg 1975, Wurmser 1978). McDougall (1974) pointed out that psychosomatic patients are also very poor in taking care of their physical needs, particularly in regard to their illnesses. She stressed that the psychosomatic illness progresses silently:

> When once the symptoms break the bounds of silence they still fail to receive much attention in the analytic discourse. Either they are ignored or are referred to in ways which appear to attach little importance to them. This is frequently accompanied by an attitude of blithe disregard for one's physical welfare as though the body were a decathected object even in the face of evident dysfunction and physical pain. Reported one patient, "I have been having these pains for two years. I didn't know what caused them but I contrived a way of walking which made them bearable. This went on up until the ulcer perforated" (p. 458).

In addition, both psychosomatic and substance-dependent patients, who have the problem of alexithymia in common, are particularly limited in their capacity for self-soothing, self-comforting and providing self-gratification. In some cases this impairment in self-care extends to a global inability to take care of all of one's affairs, so that all welfare functions are greatly impaired (Zinberg 1975, Krystal 1978b, Khantzian 1978).

In an earlier study (Krystal 1978b), the view was presented that this problem was associated with, and allegedly caused by, a distortion of self-representation. *All vital and affect functions are experienced as part of the object representation.* Carrying out any "mothering," life-preserving, or soothing activities is reserved for the "external" mother or her substitute and proscribed for the subject. Their self-representation is one of a child for whom "taking-over" of these maternal functions is forbidden and very dangerous. Since the focus here is on caring and soothing tasks that are provided for the infant by the mothering parent, psychoanalysts are inclined to assume that the individual who in later life cannot provide these for himself or herself has failed to "introject" or "internalize" these maternal functions (Krystal 1978b). In point of fact, what is being described is "externalization," projection or failure of integration of part of one's self by attributing it to the object representation. In regard to the self-caring and self-soothing functions, we were dealing with an *inhibition* in regard to assuming the care for one's own self. Along with it, there is a universal need to deny our "ownership" of all the organs involved in vital and affective functions, and to attribute these to the maternal object representation. That is the reason why we commonly function in a state analogous to a conversion hysteria in regard to the autonomically innervated parts of the body. (For a more detailed discussion, see Krystal 1978b.)

While these functions are "walled-off" within the maternal object-representation, and because the idea of consciously acknowledged self-care is experienced as a prohibited act, the patients must guard against taking over self-care at all cost. Consequently, not only is self-care impaired in the sense of self-soothing and welfare activities, but all those parts of the body related to affective functions are similarly proscribed and alienated from the self-representation (Krystal 1978b). The result is parallel to an hysterical paralysis and anesthesia, only in this case it affects the vital and affect-related areas of the body.

Case 3. Patient III, whose problems had certain elements of an addictive and psychosomatic nature, also had moderately severe alexithymia. He opened the session to be summarized here by commenting that after the previous day's session he felt very relaxed and had slept for a very long time, as if he had "been drugged." This morning he attended his biofeedback training session, which he had skipped twice before.[1] At the time, some of his feelings about going to the biofeedback training were explored, including some transference resistance related to feelings of rejection and oral deprivation.

During the previous session, comments had been made about the nature of his feelings and experiences, but these failed to deal with his "conflicts" as well as other elements of a perfect interpretation. It became clear that since no interpretation was truly complete, he always did and always would feel deprived. The patient responded by describing that when he feels that the therapist does not respond to him "*adequately*," then he has *physical* sensations of emptiness and hunger, and when he feels that the therapist has been mistreating him (i.e., rejecting him), then the predominant reaction is one of tension, particularly in the muscles of his upper extremities. The flexor muscles in his shoulders and arms become tense and sore. This was identified as the physical component that he experienced at times *instead* of becoming aware of anger or fear.

He then observed that when he gets in these states of distress, he is completely helpless. It is not possible for him to help or relieve this distress, except with the use of some external agent such as food or drugs. It is up to the therapist to do something about it; the therapist must first realize his distress, and understand and explain to him what is the matter and then relieve it.[2]

1. In this case, the biofeedback training was utilized for two separate purposes: (1) a modification of his eating pattern, and (2) learning to utilize a relaxation procedure to be used instead of food or drugs to counteract the anxiety and tension states. The difficulty in utilization of such a technique is typical and supplies the clinical material for the points made above (See Krystal 1978b).

2. This kind of self-representation and transference experience has been described and studied in a most insightful and helpful way by MacDougall (1978).

In the course of explaining to the patient the nature of his affective experience—how he could not even ask for help, and how he felt that certain types of physical distress were beyond his province—was also reviewed. It was pointed out that one reason he was having difficulties attending the biofeedback training, was because of the information he was now supplying—notably that not only was he unable to sooth or comfort himself, but that such activities were prohibited for him, as was the acquisition of any such skill.

The patient supplied additional information about his feeling of prohibition about any self-soothing, vital, or affective function. He described a number of rituals designed to ward off his physical distress (involving precursors of anxiety and guilt). The patient had the kind of feeling that is institutionalized in religion—namely that he was not capable of assuring his comfort, just as he could not *assure* his salvation. Not only could he not help himself to the Holy Sacrament, but until recently one wasn't even permitted to touch it with one's hand! These proscriptions represent an incorporation within religion of the process of disowning these parts of functions and attributing them to the maternal object representation.

Alexithymia and Anhedonia

Another observation that derives from work with states following catastrophic trauma is that alexithymia and anhedonia are separate but concommitant aftereffects of massive traumatization. This coincidence makes anhedonia a very useful "marker" for those cases in which the alexithymia is post-traumatic. Since this subject has been discussed elsewhere (Krystal 1978a, 1978c, 1979), it will not be elaborated further here. Probably related to anhedonia, and representing a bridge linking this problem with some aspects of the "operative" life style, is Wolff's (1977) observation that alexithymics have also "lost their ability to play" (p. 63).

ALEXITHYMIA AND PSYCHOTHERAPY

Alexithymia presents a number of problems in regard to uncovering dynamic, psychoanalytic, or "anxiety-producing" psychotherapy. Patients with active psychosomatic diseases may, instead of experiencing strong emotion, develop a serious or even life-endangering exacerbation of their illness. Under these circumstances, one must be mindful of Sifneos's (1974) admonition that psychotherapy should be counterindicated. In the addictive patients, the increase in intensity of their difuse distress may drive them to drink, or whatever their usual form of drug abuse involves (Krystal 1979).

Most of all, the conclusion has been reached by many who have tried it that these patients simply do not respond to insights derived from psychotherapy (Nemiah 1970, 1972, 1978; Sifneos 1972–73, 1974), or to any "form of treatment which emphasized verbal expression and requires a capacity for emotional interaction" (Sifneos 1973, p. 261). Their peculiar rigidity and unresponsiveness to therapeutic intervention made Sifneos (1974) conclude that the defect was organic. Studies in Norway supplied the statistical evidence of an inherited trait involved in alexithymia (Heiberg and Heiberg 1977). The problem was not laid to rest there, however.

Alexithymia varies in intensity from one case to another, and sometimes within the same individual. While there are neither adequate instruments to test large populations nor enough experience to determine the overall incidence, it is quite clear that not all psychosomatic patients show clinically diagnosed alexithymia. One study of peptic ulcer patients reported a 15 to 20 percent incidence of alexithymia (Overbeck 1977). There was evidence of alexithymia developing in several illness and life-threatening situations in intensive care units, and in dialysis and transplant patients (Freyberger 1977). Observations on concentration camp survivors indicated a very high rate of both psychosomatic diseases and alexithymia (Krystal 1968, Krystal and Niederland 1968); but whereas the general rate of psychosomatic disorders was 30 percent, the rate among those survivors who were in their teens during incarceration was 70 percent (Krystal 1979). The difference in rate seems to suggest that the same stresses in adolescence produce almost three times as much regression and fixation on the alexithymia affect pattern. Most of all, however, McDougall (1974) pointed out that despite the aversion that psychoanalysts and other psychotherapists may have to the treating of psychosomatic or addictive patients, and despite careful selection, patients who are primarily neurotic will show addictive or psychosomatic mechanisms and, it may be added, varying degrees of alexithymia. Alexithymia is possibly the most important single factor diminishing the success of psychoanalysis and psychodynamic psychotherapy (Krystal 1979).

Although some organic defects have been inferred (Nemiah 1975, 1978; Hoppe and Bogen 1977), each one could be caused and removed by mental mechanisms. For this reason, this paper emphasizes the views of the problem that provide some openings for therapeutic intervention or preparatory steps for later psychotherapy.

The Genetic View of Affect and Psychic Trauma

Since Schur's (1955) classic paper on the development and regression in affect function, there has been a systematic elaboration of the developmental lines and regressive responses in emotions (Schmale 1964; Krystal 1974,

1977). This framework permits an understanding of those findings in which alexithymia is definitely reactive and where a regression is also apparent in other spheres, as has been reported in severe and life-threatening illness (Freyberger 1977) and post-traumatic states (Krystal 1968, 1978a, 1978c; Krystal and Raskin 1970). This approach also permits an understanding of why alexithymia varies in severity and how the regression from verbalized, desomatized, and differentiated affects toward the resomatized and undifferentiated form represents a predisposition to psychosomatic diseases (Krystal 1979).

The aftereffects of trauma are many and complex. Those disturbances of affectivity that can be understood to represent a regression in the nature of affective responses are highlighted here. The affects in the post-traumatic state are characterized by a vagueness and loss of specificity of responses and poor verbalization. There is very high incidence of certain psychosomatic diseases, especially dermatosis, peptic ulcer, and arthritis (Krystal 1971). All these disturbances can be explained as consequences of regression in affective expression consisting of affect dedifferentiation, deverbalization, and resomatization (Krystal 1968, 1971; Krystal and Raskin 1970). Consequently, it is assumed that developmental lines of affect are differentiation, verbalization, and desomatization (Krystal 1974, 1977).

The affective responses of the infant represent two basic patterns: a state of contentment and tranquility and a state of distress. These two states represent affect precursors out of which evolve pleasurable and painful affects respectively. In the normal course of maturation the mixed affect precursor pattern separates out into specific entities. The several emotions of anger, shame, guilt, envy, jealousy, anxiety, depression, and so on identifiably evolve out of the general distress response. The process continues into a progressive refinement of emotional experiences, so that in the adult these major groupings differentiate into finer nuances of meaning. Clinically one recognizes that the depression is an affective syndrome composed of a number of specific emotions that have to be identified in a given patient. It is essential to establish whether the actual feeling is despair, grief, sadness, guilt, rage turned against one's self, or some other specific affect. To use another example, the feelings of shame can be observed to be further differentiated into affects of dishonor, ridicule, humiliation, mortification, chagrin, embarrassment, or disgust. The same process of differentiation takes place in regard to the evolvement of the state of contentment and tranquility; the affect precursors of pleasure into such affects as security, contentment, joy, pride, love, tenderness, and affection.

The other developmental line of affect involves the gradual verbalization and desomatization of the emotional responses. This process makes possible the use of affects as signals, for affective responses that are primarily somatic are too dangerous and overwhelming and call attention to themselves rather than to the states that they signal. While some factors in the process of verbalization and desomatization may have maturational aspects subject to hereditary influences, this process is intimately related to the early object relations. The mothering parent provides the first object for identification in regard to affective responses. Later the family as a whole influences the establishing of norms for affective expression. However, the mother's role in fostering harmonious and uninterrupted progress in affect verbalization and desomatization lies predominantly in protecting the child from psychic traumatization.

Possibly the most crucial and difficult aspect of mothering consists of permitting the child to bear increasing intensity of affective tension, but stepping in and comforting the child before emotions overwhelm him or her. In this process, the mother's empathy with the child is her only guide. If the mothering parent fails to prevent the infant's affect from reaching an unbearable intensity and overwhelming him or her, a state of psychic trauma may develop. Our conceptions of the nature of the psychic experience in early childhood psychic trauma miss the point without the full appreciation of the nature of infantile affect precursors. To be overwhelmed with an adult type of affect, whether anxiety, rage, or another may be most painful, and even terrifying, but as a model for the early childhood experience, it fails to give us a feeling for the global distress occasioned by the total, unregulated flooding with the undifferentiated, somatic, preverbal, timeless, ur-affects of a young child (Krystal 1978a).

The *direct* aftereffects of infantile and adult catastrophic trauma have certain common features: there is a dread expectation of the return of the traumatic state and an anhedonia. There is commonly a disturbance in affectivity; an arrest in the genetic development of affect in the infantile form, compared to regression (dedifferentiation, deverbalization and resomatization) after the adult trauma. There is also an impairment in affect tolerance.

Pensee Operatoire and the Problems of Transference

The above discussion of cognitive disturbance in alexithymia pointed out how it affects these patients' object representations. Naturally, this problem manifests itself in the type of transference these patients form. It is characterized by being modeled on the medical relationship and its coolness, detachment, distance, and lack of concern (Nemiah and Sifneos 1970b). De M'Uzan (1974a) warned,

What is striking is the very slight interest that the patient shows in the analyst. The relationship is courteous and correct but libidinally very poor. The organization of this relationship seems to be conventional and personalized to such a small degree that the neurotic mechanism seems to be lacking. A sort of inertia, noticed during the preliminary interview, persists and results in a stagnant situation (p. 462).

This kind of transference behavior sometimes results in countertransference responses of boredom and a feeling of despair and helplessness, which may be warded off by withdrawal, with a possible retreat into sadistic or erotic fantasies (Taylor 1977). McDougall (1974) has expressed the concern that as the elusiveness of the patient's psychosomatic mechanism may be experienced by the analyst as a "narcissistic affront to his interpretive powers," the countertransference may "lead many an analyst to a lack of interest in his patient's psychosoma" (p. 444). This astute observation goes a long way to explain our professional reserve toward the psychosomatic, addictive, and other alexithymic patients. Inasmuch as these patients' capacity for fantasy is diminished, the psychotherapeutic process is stifled by their need to continue certain types of object relations. For instance, it may be said that the "doctor" transference is, in fact, a representation of the oral receptive attitude and that behind it lies a variety of fantasies of oral gratification, theories of the illness as a deficiency, and behind that a problem of ambivalence, envy, splitting, and idealization (Krystal 1978b, 1979). Interpretations of the manifestations of these transferences, however, are going to be accepted by the patient with polite indifference, generally with an effort to consider what is said, but rarely will stimulate fantasy or recognizable affective responses. While these patients do not experience "feelings" that they can utilize for the effective psychotherapeutic work, it is most likely that they respond to interpretation with physiological affective responses that could be demonstrated only by the use of appropriate apparatus.

This reaction is an illustration of the "psychosomatic process" which, as McDougall (1974) said, is "the antithesis of the psychoanalytic process" (p. 437). What is most conspicuous in the pensée opératoire is the lack of certain fantasies and types of object representations. Whether there is a true deficiency, however, is of some question. For, while the patients do not produce these fantasies spontaneously, they can "share" or "borrow" them, or form them when presented with them in things that they read or see. The above-mentioned alexithymic patient, for instance, who tried in vain to imagine what she would like to do for fun on a vacation, was certainly able to understand what *other people* would do and imagine doing and enjoying. This patient illustrated that there is no intellectual deficit. The "missing symbolic structures" represent an impoverishment of self-representation, as well as blocking by inhibition of wish-fulfillment fantasies pertaining to one's self.

McDougall (1974) was trying to provide a theoretical framework for this void. She assumed that object representations were formed by experiencing them "externally" and even in a persecutory way, and only secondarily could they be experienced as one's own mental products. However, these patients seemed to have given up their early attempts to form object constancy to reliably available memories and recollections. McDougall felt that psychosomatic patients "simply lost them." She explained, "I would suggest that there are deeply buried archaic fantasy elements incapsulated somewhere in the unconscious, but these are unarticulated linguistically and thus have no access to preconscious or conscious thought" (p. 449). Thus McDougall sees the primary problem as a disturbance in the nature of object representations that are so greatly impoverished, as well as in the block of the process of symbolic representation and "symbolic structures" (p. 449). She summarizes the psychotherapeutic challenge as pertaining to psychosomatic symptoms: "Because of their non-symbolic quality such manifestations are totally silent before their somatic realization and it is therefore necessary to listen to something which is not there, a psychic gap in which a somatic creation might appear instead of a psychological one" (p. 451).

An alternate view presents itself from the study of "catastrophic trauma" (Krystal 1979). In the traumatic process, there is constriction of cognition in which memory, fantasy, problem-solving, and all other functions become gradually blocked. Frequently, the cognition remains severely limited, and from a theoretical point of view this constriction may be considered a form of "primal repression." The point is that it is different in nature and does not appear directly "defensive" nor does it respond to the interpretation of defenses. At least in the post-traumatic alexithymia, this process may be a significant reason for the retention of operative thinking. Either way it becomes an enormous challenge to promote the patient's developing a greater scope of fantasy. After the inhibition in this sphere is dealt with, we find ourselves in totally alien territory, with no techniques available for the purpose of helping the patients to cultivate underdeveloped or deficient functions. The same challenge involves the problem of anhedonia and self-caring. Some therapists have maintained that in the analytic work when the patients develop the self-analyzing function, they also "seem to develop a self-soothing function . . ." (Nash and Cavenar 1978, p. 119).

The issue of helping these patients to attain a normal level of fantasy-making is of great interest from a theoretical point of view, for in doing it we may discover the cause and nature of the problem. Among the most intriguing experiments in this direction has been the use of "directed fantasy" by Brachfeld and Stokvis (1963), in which the patients are shown a picture and encouraged to form fantasies with the active collaboration of the therapist, who leads the patients by his questions. Leuner (1969) has elaborated a similar technique in his "Guided Affective Imagery." Tentative explorations by the present author with the use of TAT cards have not produced either significant material or any noticeable increase in the patient's fantasy-making. Requesting Patient II to write a "spy mystery story" (her favorite reading material) did not result in any imaginative tale. Still, since these patients "borrow" fantasies continually and behave like musicians who need a composer, this problem must be capable of a solution or approach that yet eludes us.

Robert Langs has studied extensively a kind of patient who behaves in therapy just like the alexithymics, and like the "anti-analysands" described by McDougall (1980). In addressing himself to the patient's behavior in the "bipersonal field" and focusing upon the *unconscious fantasy* (or "type two") *derivatives*, Langs (1978–1979) finds that patients can be classified in three groups. The adaptive context determines that a particular type of " *bipersonal and communicative field*" is established. In the Type A field, patients are able to utilize symbolic expression, have a tolerance for regression and anxiety, and one may add, have access and use of their fantasies and affects. The Type B communicative field is characterized by a "discharge orientation" (p. 102): "The patient or the analyst makes extensive use of projective identification designed to rid the psyche of disturbing excretions of inner stimuli, to make use of the other member of the dyad as a container for disruptive projective identifications, and to evoke a proxy response" (p. 105). Thus the patients are inclined to seek pathological need-fulfillment by demanding noninterpretive gratification.

Finally, in the Type C field, which corresponds to the alexithymic, the trend is to "non-communication, for the destruction of meaning, and the absence of derivative expression" (p. 106). So "the field" is described as "static" and "characterized by impenetrable barriers, falsifications, destruction of meaning, and rupture of the link between patient and therapist or analyst" (p. 87).[3] Like the authors who have commented on the sterility and unproductivity of psychotherapy with alexithymics, Langs described the Type C field as a static and distant one, devoid of analyzable derivatives—there is little offered by the patient that the (analyst) therapist can "contain and metabolize" (p. 109).

Obviously the noncommunicative attitude of alexithymic patients corresponds to the "Type C" field of Langs. The question posed is whether the patients who show this characteristic maintain the same cognitive style at all

3. Lang's view of the problem alerts us to the most startling and relevant observation: that the analyst, rather than the patient, may be the alexithymic, or anticommunicative, party in the Type C field.

times. The patients who have been seen by the present author—not for psychotherapy or psychoanalysis, but for evaluation and 25-year follow-up (a population of over 2000 survivors of the Nazi Holocaust)—have shown a very high incidence of alexithymia on the first and follow-up interviews. A questionnaire, which was a modification of the Beth Israel instrument (Apfel-Savitz and Sifneos 1979), was administered prior to the first interview. From these observations, it was concluded that alexithymia and operative thinking are constant characteristics of these patient's cognitive and affective function. It has also been found (Krystal 1978a) that in surveying the autobiographical writings of post-traumatic individuals, the "fact" orientation—the inability to observe, describe, and utilize one's own feelings and fantasies—is quite conspicuous. *The Painted Bird* (Kosinski 1965) is probably the best illustration of this phenomenon.

A useful point of view related to these deliberations is offered by Gedo (1979), who feels that patients capable of establishing a working relationship corresponding to Lang's Type A field represent a relatively small group of neurotic individuals. In Gedo's opinion, their conflicts can be best understood through the model of the topographic theory; they are capable of renunciation and creativity, and can be treated by interpretation as the peremptory type of intervention.

Further, we are still unable to explain just when the operative thinking develops, whether it may be an arrest, a regression, or an inhibition in the sense of a blockage of an established and available function. In the study of the artist Giorgio De Chirico, it was found that during a period when he was creative, albeit suffering from hypochondriasis and intestinal symptoms, he was able to present a spectacularly communicative and symbolic array of paintings. However, after suffering a regressive episode, his art lost its symbolic and communicative nature (Krystal 1966). According to Sarnoff (1978), the capacity for symbolization develops during latency. He feels that two steps are involved in the acquisition of the capacity for symbolic representation. First, there is the question of the use of symbols and, second, the capacity to utilize the kind of symbols that are suitable for communication on the basis of their universality. Thus, in De Chirico, there was a regression to the autistic, poorly stimulating "mannequin" style, whereby affective communication was lost. Perhaps the pensée opératoire represents a similar process.

Some investigators seemed to sense the breakdown in social contacts to be an essential part, and that may have been the reason why they tried to treat those patients in groups. They soon discovered that the alexithymic patients did not "understand groups" (Apfel-Savitz et al. 1977, p. 313), and found it necessary to place neurotic "shills" in the group to promote more symbolic thinking and reflective self-awareness.

Considerations of Technical Modifications

In contrast to those exploratory and tentative approaches, a few simple principles of technical modifications have already proven their value:

1. The nature of the patient's affect and cognitive problems should be carefully explained to the patient, including the methods of covering up their deficiencies in their perceptions and object- and self-representations.
2. Affect tolerance must be improved: before these patients can deal with the emotions themselves, one has to first attend to their "having" them. Handling one's emotions is a challenge in many situations in all affective disorders. However, for these patients, because of the relatively intense physiological responses, the emotions represent a special burden. What affective responses are and how one uses them to one's advantage need to be taken up in great detail by the therapist and practiced by the patients. The acquisition and practicing of the skill of "managing" one's emotions is a necessary prerequisite to utilization of affects as signals. (For a fuller discussion, see Krystal 1975).
3. Dealing with the inhibition in self-care is another early task. The idea of affects being signals to one's self to be used and regulated to one's best advantage is not at all self-evident for these patients. Many of them use their emotions to control their love-object (Krystal 1974) and/or experience their emotions as emanating from their object representations, and their regulation and utilization is reserved for the maternal object representation (Krystal 1978b). Before some of the alexithymic individuals dare to extend their selfhood to include their emotions and proceed to activate their verbalization and utilization of their emotions, their inhibitions in this regard have to be interpreted.
4. Affect-naming and verbalization must be encouraged: supplying to the alexithymic the words and names for emotions is a slow task, because verbalization represents just one half of the task. The other half consists in desomatization. That is why certain things must be repeated and reexperienced many times and require time and practice. No statement of the patient's about how he or she felt can be taken for granted as one goes through a review of his or her reactions. Since the use of dreams and utilization of the transference is limited, it is necessary to start by pointing out the impairment in empathy and sensitivity that these patients show in their object relations. Because they do not have signal affects available to them, they also lack empathy. In particular, they have no feeling or conviction of loving anyone or of anyone loving them.

If a broad view is taken, it is discovered that the same cognitive and affective problems that interfere with these patient's performance in analysis also wreak havoc with their current object relations. Partly out of the necessity to help patients discern the nuances of their interaction of which they are oblivious (they don't even know what they are missing), and partly due to the need to demonstrate to them the primitive forerunner of affective responses, one has to make observations, comments, elucidations, and confrontations regarding the patients' "outside" object experiences. Gradually, it may become possible to shift emphasis and begin to make direct transference interpretations. Even in these patients' current object relations one must not presume that they are aware of even the most basic, common "human" feelings and perceptions. There is a great deal of variation in this respect, with unpredictable lacunae coming into view.

These technical modifications do not represent such *radical* departures that would preclude later psychoanalytic psychotherapy by the same person. These methods may be most useful in mild to moderate alexithymia.

Experiments in Technical Modifications

European workers who deal with hospitalized psychosomatic patients, often with very severe affective disturbances, have been inclined to experiment with more radical departures. Wolff (1977) reported applying Winnicott's (1971) recommendation that patients who cannot play need to acquire that capacity before they can utilize psychotherapy. Wolff felt that the therapist had to serve as a model for his or her patients in "communicating more openly than is the rule in classical analysis how he feels and by using the sessions for creative play in terms of shared fantasies and exploration of feelings, desires and bodily sensations" (p. 62). Incidentally, this intervention also addresses itself to the inhibition in the capacity for pleasure, which was mentioned above. In applying play techniques, one is actually extending to these adults behaviors that were quite usual for the child therapist. The same principle applies to the recommendation presented in this paper for the supplying to the patient words for emotions, as well as helping them with the self-observation regarding their emotions, and their responses to *having the affect*—that the therapist carry out belatedly a function that the mothering parent did originally, and that child therapists expect to perform as a matter of everyday practice. Wolff (1977) also suggested that the therapist address himself or herself directly to the alexithymic patient's physical state and posture: "sometimes by touching him or asking him to modify his posture and breathing pattern" for the purpose of giving the patient an opportunity to become aware of his feelings (p. 63).

Some European psychosomaticists recommended relaxation techniques, decreasing "situational or environmental stresses and demands," and "the use of psychopharmacology" (Bastiaans 1977, p. 292). In addition to various relaxation techniques such as meditation and hypnosis, there was experimentation with the use of groups in which there were "planted neurotic group members" who served as "affect translators," and the use of videotape playbacks (Apfel-Savitz et al. 1977, p. 329).

Hospitalized alexithymic psychosomatic patients in the Heidelberg University Hospital were treated by group psychotherapy, "sensual awareness therapy" ("Konzentrative Bewegungstherapie"), as well as "ergotherapy" ("Gestaltangstherapie"), intended to give them an affective experience (Schellschopp-Rueppell 1977). Braeutigam's (1977) comments on these experiments may serve to sum up the spirit of exploration of these efforts. In regard to the "sensual awareness therapy," he said, "We foster (body) awareness deliberately and encourage the patient to perceive and express bodily feelings in a differentiated manner" (p. 362). In regard to "ergotherapy" he explained, "We encourage patients to deal with emotionally charged material by way of creative expression, e.g. drawing pictures or modeling clay or other materials. Thus, anxieties, desires, memories, but also significant persons from the patient's life become accessible in an elementary fashion" (p. 362). Thus in addition to psychotherapy with alexithymic patients, treatment may be supplemented for severely ill individuals in whom nonverbal techniques are explored (Becker 1977).

These studies may also have an implication for the problems of anhedonia. Psychotherapists are accustomed to removing inhibitions, whereupon the patient's needs and ambitions are expected to rise up and motivate him or her to assume all previously blocked functions. In regard to anhedonia resulting from early or catastrophic traumatization (Krystal 1978a), even after the removal of masochistic problems, there seems to be an inability to experience pleasure, joy, or gratification, so that the question is, "how can we help these patients to *cultivate* these underdeveloped or severely supressed capacities"? (Krystal 1968, 1978a, 1979, 1981; Nemiah 1978).

It is the present author's preliminary impression that in some cases of anhedonia it is possible to encourage and help the patients to cultivate their capacity for pleasure. In those cases the therapist has to step out of the "neutral" role and declare himself or herself in favor of the patient's efforts in the direction of attaining some gratification in life. Admitting that the therapist does not have the "answers" and offering to explore and look out for possibilities establish a partnership of a type somewhat different than the usual psychoanalytic model of the relationship.

Favorable results have been obtained with these approaches with a few patients who were encouraged to keep doing certain things that they thought they may eventually get to enjoy. This technique was derived from working with depressive patients who had temporary anhedonia. In these cases, if the patients resumed their recreational activities, the return of their capacity for pleasure seemed to be speeded. One cannot help speculating that soon drugs may be available that influence the hedonic state—e.g., opioid endogenous peptides, as well as cannabis which, it has been suggested, directly stimulates the pleasure centers of the brain (Heath 1973).

DISCUSSION

In fashioning "alexithymia" as a useful clinical concept, one has to be especially aware of the mercurial quality of that syndrome. It is a characteristic derived through a complex epigenetic process; one intimately related to early object relations and involving the key elements of the self- and object representation. It also involves such complex elements of cognition and reflective self-awareness that it becomes subject to fluctuations and regressions. Recently, at a staff conference, the present author was reemphasizing how some of the alexithymics can not tell, at the end of the day especially, whether they are hungry, tired, angry, or ill. One of the people in the group, who is as "well-functioning as the next guy," spoke up: "Oh, but that's nothing—I sometimes feel that way." "Yes, I have noticed that," his colleague and live-in friend joined in, "and I have noticed your restlessness and constant 'taking-in' all evening, particularly since your ulcer healed!" Thus the occurance of alexithymia among psychoanalysts and other psychotherapists makes these people particularly prone to miss these problems in their patients.

There is another paradox: The degree of differentiation and verbalization (and desomatization) is influenced strongly by social and cultural elements (Leff 1973), but also is subject to individual variation. Sharp contrasts have been found in the attitudes and styles of upbringing in regard to the handling of emotions (Krystal 1975). Families of blue collar workers tend to be authoritarian and shame the children, particularly boys, if they register fear. With the subsequent impairment of affect tolerance, the atmosphere is not favorable to the harmonious maturation of affects and their reaching a form that makes them most useful as signals to one's self.

A new area of observation now available deals with the fate of the children of alexithymic parents. In dealing with the children of survivors of the Nazi Holocaust, it has been found that the parents who have an exceedingly high rate of alexithymia are unable to assist their children in the process of affect maturation. One son of survivors observed, "The only word that was ever heard in my parent's home referring to emotions was 'upset'." Yet, preliminary observations indicate that the children of survivors do not have a rate of alexithymia higher than comparable groups in the community. A tentative explanation of this observation is that the early responsiveness and attentiveness of the mothering parent is a more powerful factor in stimulating the process of affect vocalization and differentiation, and later verbalization, than is the countervailing effect of the parents' own alexithymia. Also, the fact that the "second generation" resembled more their peers than their parents in regard to the nature of their affective maturation, fantasy formation, and affect tolerance suggests that the social element and identification with peers during latency and adolescence may account for the demonstrated cultural variation in affect differentiation (Leff 1973).

The fact that there are fluctuations and variations in alexithymia should not be surprising—after all, so also are the other aspects that are correlated—psychosomatic and addictive disturbances are notably conditions characterized by relapses and remissions. Beyond that, however, there need not be a single cause of alexithymia any more than one would search for a single reason why some people can't play the flute. Naturally, hereditary and anatomic, as well as physiological, factors enter into this equation, as do many others. Just as with memory, or any other highly complex function, when an impairment or regression is present, it is useful to identify some "tags" that lead to the recognition of the type of problem involved.

In regard to alexithymia, anhedonia is one such tag, pointing toward the *post-traumatic* alexithymics. The next step is to determine by history whether one is dealing with the aftereffects of infantile or adult psychic trauma (for a discussion, see Krystal 1978a). The conditions following adult catastrophic trauma have a better prognosis concerning their potential for improvement in regard to affective function and operative thinking. However, the considerations of alexithymia, impairment in affect tolerance, and frequently associated disturbances such as anhedonia and the impairment in the capacity for self-care are essential points to look for in considering a patient for psychotherapy.

A basic question returns: "Isn't alexithymia just a massive defense against anxiety?" The present author's experiences indicate that it is a defense in the teleogical sense only. We are dealing here with a regression in affective and cognitive development or an arrest in it. We are dealing with severe distortions resulting from the aftereffects of infantile trauma or catastrophic adult trauma. We have to consider certain associated disturbances resulting from traumatization at "*critical times*" of epigenetic development, such as an inhibition of self-care, play, fantasy, and symbolization. Although all of these are utilized in various defensive ways, they will not disappear with interpretation. Countless therapists have discovered the utter futility of saying to an alexithymic patient, "You do not permit yourself to experience anger (or love) toward me." They might as well have reproached a color-blind patient for not seeing them in technicolor.

These problems have a much wider distribution than one would suspect. Their presence constitutes a most serious handicap in regard to the patients benefitting from psychoanalytic psychotherapy. With the present state of the art, only patients with mild and reactive types of alexithymia may be "prepared" for utilizing "uncovering" or "insight" psychotherapy. With some of these, it is necessary to have a preliminary phase of psychotherapy in which their alexithymic problems are given special attention (Krystal 1979, Krystal and Raskin 1970). However, whether or not there is an especially designated preliminary phase, once a psychotherapist can identify alexithymic traits, he or she will find himself or herself raising these issues with many patients who enter the treatment for primary neurotic or characterological problems. Most of all, because of the lack of empathy evidenced by these patients, resulting from their not having affects available as signals, one cannot assume the ideal psychoanalytic stance of limiting one's intervention to transference interpretation. First, one has to attend to a quasi-didactic task of helping the patient to discover the bizzarness of their mechanistic, "inhuman" relations with their objects. Similarly, these patients assume that their treatment of themselves as robots or machines is the norm. They have to be disabused of this attitude. Thus the concept of alexithymia opens up a number of psychodynamic and psychotherapeutic challenges.

REFERENCES

Apfel-Savitz, R., and Sifneos, P. E. (1979). Alexithymia: concept and measurement. *Psychotherapy Psychosomatics* 32:180–190.

Apfel-Savitz, R., Silverman, D., and Bennett, J. J. (1977). Group psychotherapy of patients with somatic illnesses and alexithymia. *Psychotherapy Psychosomatics* 28:323–329.

Bastiaans, J. (1977). The implications of the specificity concept for the treatment of psychosomatic patients. *Psychotherapy Psychosomatics* 28:285–293.

Becker, H. (1977). A non-verbal therapeutic approach to psychosomatic disorders. *Psychotherapy Psychosomatics* 28:330–336.

Brachfeld, O., and Stokvis, B. (1963). Aus der Praxis der gelenkten Tag Traeume (anhand eines beispieles). *Psychotherapie und Medicinische Psychologie* 13:73–81.

Braeutigam, W. (1977). Panel—and plenum—discussion: psychotherapeutic problems with psychosomatic patients. In *Toward a Theory of Psychosomatic Disorders*, eds. W. Braeutigam and M. Von Rad, pp. 361–375. New York: S. Karger.

de M'Uzan, M. (1974a). Analytical process and the notion of the past. *International Review of Psycho-Analysis* 1:461–480.

———. (1974b). Psychodynamic mechanisms in psychosomatic symptom formation. *Psychotherapy Psychosomatics* 23:103–110.

Flannery, J. G. (1975). Alexithymia: the association with unexplained physical distress. *Psychotherapy Psychosomatics* 3:193–197.

Freyberger, H. (1977). Supportive psychotherapeutic techniques in primary and secondary alexithymia. *Psychotherapy Psychosomatics* 28:337–342.

Gedo, J. E. (1979). *Beyond Interpretation: Toward a Revised Theory of Psychoanalysis.* New York: International Universities Press.

Heath, R. G. (1973). Marijuana effect on deep and surface EGG on rhesus monkey. *Neuropharmacology* 12:1–4.

Heiberg, A., and Heiberg, A. (1977). Alexithymia: an inherited trait? A study of twins. *Psychotherapy Psychosomatics* 28:221–225.

Hoppe, K. D., and Bogen, J. E. (1977). Alexithymia in twelve commisurotomized patients. *Psychotherapy Psychosomatics* 28:148–155.

Khantzian, E. J. (1978). The ego, the self and opiate addiction: theoretical and treatment considerations. *International Review of Psycho-Analysis* 5:189–198.

Kosinski, J. (1965). *The Painted Bird*. New York: Houghton Mifflin.

Krystal, H. (1962). The opiate withdrawal syndrome as a state of stress. *Psychoanalytic Quarterly* 36 (suppl.): 54–65.

———. (1966). Giorgio de Chirico. Ego states and artistic production. *American Images* 23:210–226.

———. (1968). Studies of concentration camp survivors. In *Massive Psychic Trauma*, ed. H. Krystal, pp. 23–30. New York: International Universities Press.

———. (1971). Trauma: consideration of its intensity and chronicity. In *Psychic Traumatization*, eds. H. Krystal and W. G. Niederland, pp. 11–28. Boston: Little, Brown & Co.

———. (1974). The genetic development of affects and affect regression. *The Annual of Psychoanalysis* 2:98–126.

———. (1975). Affect tolerance. *The Annual of Psychoanalysis* 3:179–219.

———. (1977). Aspects of affect theory. *The Bulletin of the Menninger Clinic* 41:1–26.

———. (1978a). Trauma and affect. *Psychoanalytic Study of the Child* 36:81–116.

———. (1978b). Self-representation and the capacity for self-care. *The Annual of Psychoanalysis* 6:206–246.

———. (1978c). Catastrophic psychic trauma and psychogenic death. In *Psychiatric Problems in Medical Practice*, eds. G. U. Bales, L. Wurmser, and E. McDaniels, pp. 79–97. Boston: Butterworth.

———. (1979). Alexithymia and psychotherapy. *American Journal of Psychotherapy* 33:17–31.

———. (1981). The hedonic element in affectivity. *The Annual of Psychoanalysis* 9:93–114.

Krystal, H., and Niederland, W. G. (1968). Clinical observations of the survivor syndrome. In *Massive Psychic Trauma*, ed. H. Krystal, pp. 327–348. New York: International Universities Press.

Krystal, H., and Raskin, H. (1970). *Drug Dependence*. Detroit: Wayne State University Press.

Langs, R. (1978–1979). Some communicative properties of the bipersonal field. *International Journal of Psychoanalytic Psychiatry* 7:87–135.

Leff, J. P. (1973). Culture and differentiation of emotional states. *British Journal of Psychology* 23:209–306.

Leuner, H. (1969). Guided affective imagry. *American Journal of Psychotherapy* 23:4–22.

McDougall, J. (1974). The psychosoma and the psychoanalytic process. *International Review of Psycho-Analysis* 1:437–459.

———. (1978). Primitive communication and the use of countertransference: reflections on early psychic trauma and its transference effects. In *Countertransference*, eds. A. H. Feiner and L. Epstein. New York: Jason Aronson.

———. (1980). *Plea for a Measure of Abnormality*. New York: International Universities Press.

Marty, P., and David, C. (1963). L'Investigation psychosomatique. Paris: Presses Universitaires Paris.

Marty, P., and de M'Uzan, M. (1963). Le pensee operatorie. *Review France Psychanalytique.* 27 (suppl.):345–456.

Nash, J. L., and Cavenar, Jr., J. O. (1978). The self-soothing function: its appearance in dreams. *The Bulletin of the Menninger Clinic* 42:119–132.

Nemiah, J. C. (1970). The psychological management and treatment of patients with peptic ulcer. *Advances in Psychosomatic Medicine* 6:169–173.

———. (1972). The psychosomatic nature of anorexia nervosa. *Advances in Psychosomatic Medicine* 7:316–321.

———. (1975). Denial revisited: reflections on psychosomatic theory. *Psychotherapy Psychosomatics* 26:140–147.

———. (1978). Alexithymia and psychosomatic illness. *Journal of Continuing Education in Psychiatry* :25–37.

Nemiah, J. C., and Sifneos, P. E. (1970a). Affect and fantasy in patients with psychosomatic disorders. In *Modern trends in psychosomatic medicine*, vol. 2, ed. O. W. Hill, pp. 26–34. London:Butterworth.

———. (1970b). Psychosomatic illnesses: a problem of communication. *Psychotherapy Psychosomatics* 18:154–160.

Nemiah, J. C., Freyberger, H., and Sifneos, P. E. (1976). Alexithymia: a view of the psychosomatic process. In *Modern Trends in Psychosomatic Medicine*, vol. 3, ed. O. W. Hill. pp. 430–439. London:Butterworth.

Overbeck, G. (1977). How to operationalize alexithymic phenomena: some findings from speech analysis and the Giesen test (GT). *Psychotherapy Psychosomatics* 28:106–117.

Sarnoff, C. A., (1978). The shifting symbolic forms of latency and early adolescence—their relation to the observing object in the mind's eye (unpublished).

Schellschopp-Rueppell, A. (1977). Behavioral characteristics in inpatient group psychotherapy with psychosomatic patients. *Psychotherapy and Psychosomatics* 28:316–322.

Schmale Jr., A. H. (1964). A genetic view of affects: with special reference to the genesis of helplessness and hopelessness. *Psychoanalytic Study of the Child* 27:411–436.

Schur, M. (1955). Comments on the metapsychology of somatization. *Psychoanalytic Study of the Child* 10:119–164.

Sifneos, P. E. (1967). Clinical observations on some patients suffering from a variety of psychosomatic diseases. In *Proceedings of the Seventh European Conference on Psychosomatic Research*. Basel: S. Karger.

———. (1972–73). Is dynamic psychotherapy contraindicated for a large number of patients with psychosomatic disease? *Psychotherapy Psychosomatics* 21:133–136.

———. (1973). The prevalence of "alexithymic" characteristics in psychosomatic patients. *Psychotherapy Psychomatics* 22:257–262.

———. (1974). A reconsideration of psychodynamic mechanisms in psychosomatic symptom formation in view of recent clinical observations. *Psychotherapy Psychosomatics* 24:151–155.

———. (1975). Problems of psychotherapy of patients with alexithymic characteristics and physical disease. *Psychotherapy Psychosomatics* 26:65–70.

Taylor, G. J. (1977). Alexithymia and the countertransference. *Psychotherapy Psychosomatics* 28:141–147.

Winnicott, D. W. (1971). *Playing and Reality*. Hammondsworth: Penguin Books.

Wolff, H. H. (1977). The contribution of the interview situation to the restriction in fantasy and emotional experience in psychosomatic patients. *Psychotherapy Psychosomatics* 28: 58–67.

Wurmser, L. (1978). *The Hidden Dimension: Psychodynamics in Drug Use*. New York: Jason Aronson.

Zinberg, N. E. (1975). Addiction and ego formation. *Psychoanalytic Study of the Child* 30:567–588.

Alexithymia, Psychosomatosis, and Psychosis

JOYCE McDOUGALL, M.A., D.Ed.

A discussion of "Alexithymia and the Effectiveness of Psychoanalytic Treatment" by Henry Krystal, M.D. Following a critical appraisal of Krystal's work on alexithymia, the author proposes that alexithymic symptoms may also reveal themselves to be a massive defense against psychotic anxieties. In both psychotic and alexithymic-psychosomatic states there is an attack on mental functioning and perception. However, while the psychotic creates a neo-reality to protect himself from psychic pain, the grave alexithymic drains external reality and relationships of their meaning, leaving a devitalized relationship of a "pseudo-normal" kind with the world.

> "Sticks and stones'll break my bones
> But words'll never hurt me!"
> —Children's rhyme

> "Sticks and stones'll break your bones
> But words'll damn near kill you!"
> —Ogden Nash

It was through the analyses of patients from whom the psychoanalytic process would, from time to time, come to a paralyzing halt, that the present author first became interested in severe perturbations in the psychic economy of affect. These analysands, due to a certain internal fragility, were unable to contain and elaborate strong affective reactions stirred up by external events in their lives; they tended instead to plunge into some form of action. Some would try to drown their painful feelings and mental conflicts by the use of addictive substances; some would engage in frenetic sexual exploits of a perverse or compulsive kind; others would create havoc around them by unconsciously manipulating those closest to them, to live out their own unacknowledged affective crises. Finally, many of these patients showed a strong inclination to somatize when under the pressure of instinctual or external stress. Events such as the death of a parent, the birth of a baby, the loss of a love object or an important job, and other such libidinal and narcissistic wounds were frequent mobilizing causes. Their potential threat to the psychic equilibrium was met with alexithymic calm, apt to precipitate psychosomatic disturbance.

In his ongoing research into alexithymic defects and their accessibility to analytical therapy, Krystal has introduced, among others, two important concepts that are at the same time prognostic tools in the service of such assessment: the concept of *anhedonia* (Krystal 1980) and that of *impairment in the capacity for self-care* (Krystal 1978b). The first underscores the fact that alexithymic symptoms are not confined to the disavowal of painful affects but apply equally, in many cases, to the pleasurable, "welfare" affects; these are also to be proscribed. The second, the incapacity to be a good parent to oneself, has been observed by a number of analysts, including the present author, but Krystal has introduced into this clinical concept the original reflection that "the usual state of Man in regard to the autonomously controlled part of his body is analogous to a hysterical paralysis. . . . [This inhibition] of the exercise of volition over the autonomic or affective aspect of ourselves is, like any conversion paralysis, the symbolic representation of a fantasy . . . [but one which pertains] to the vital functions." He goes on to say that it may be a transgression for certain individuals to take in the maternal object "for the purpose of acquiring the walled-off, self-soothing and comforting function [experienced as] forbidden and punishable" (Krystal 1978b, pp. 221–222). This important insight illuminates the phenomenon that one might term the "drug" mother, an object to be ceaselessly sought in the outer world (addictive substance, addictive use of others, etcetera) in an attempt to repair a gap in the inner object world, rather as though the mother had never been introjected into the child's psychic structure as an object of identification. This has been linked to a pathological development in the maturation of transitional-object phenomena, in the Winnicottian sense (McDougall 1980a).

Anhedonia and deleterious self-care both derive from Krystal's key theoretical concept, which proposes a genetic view of affects: that the developmental lines of affect consist in desomatization, followed by verbalization, and finally, differentiation. This genetic development leads directly onto Freud's (1926) theory of the need for affects to become available as signals to the psyche, thus allowing the individual to take necessary action to prevent affective flooding while preparing him or her to deal with the events responsible for mobilizing the affects in question.

Pursuing his genetic theory, Krystal goes on to distinguish between the infantile and adult types of traumatic experience that may be at the origin of affect pathology. The infantile form consists of an *arrest* in affective development, while the adult form witnesses a *regression*—"dedifferentiation, deverbalization and resomatization." While it is undoubtedly true that severely traumatized adults are subsequently more vulnerable to alexithymic and psychosomatic disorders, the question of the role of early psychic trauma as a predisposing factor for fortitude or fragility in the face of catastrophic adult events is left in abeyance. Krystal's statement that "if the mothering parent fails to prevent the infant's affect from reaching an unbearable intensity and overwhelming him, a state of psychic trauma may develop" is indisputable, but the notion of an ensuing arrest in the organization of affective experience and its representational links seems incomplete. What appears phenomenologically as an arrest may at the same time cloak a precocious but massive defense against affective vitality.

An infant (Latin "infans": "one unable to speak") is by definition alexithymic ("having no words for emotions"), and thus the alexithymic part of an adult personality may be considered as an extremely infantile dimension of the individual's psychic reality. Yet an adult has complete access to language. We might therefore presume that some vigorous mental process is at work, a process that enables the subject to split word-representations from their literal thing-representations, insofar as affect-laden ideas are concerned. On a wide scale such mental functioning is the hallmark of psychotic thought, but the suggestion here is that we are dealing with a nonpsychotic adult who in some respects functions like a helpless, nonverbal child. Perhaps something more active than an arrested development is occurring. An infant's earliest external reality is its mother's unconscious. This includes not only her own inner world created from her personal past, but also her sexual and narcissistic investment of her marital partner. The latter is crucial in determining the nature of the narcissistic and libidinal roles that her baby will unconsciously be called upon to fulfill. Accordingly, there are specific ways in which a mother will relate to, and attempt to control her child's body, its functions, vitality, and affective reactions. Krystal's observations on the autonomic nervous system are pertinent to this latter point. In this connection many alexithymic-psychosomatic patients talk of their bodies as though they are a foreign object, or as though they did not possess certain of their zones or functions, as though, in fact, these were unconsciously represented as still belonging to the mother. As the infant becomes verbal and direct bodily communication gives way to symbolic communication with the parents, the family discourse continues to convey to the growing child the way in which affects are to be named, those that are to be regarded as legitimate, and those that must be despised or denied access to consciousness. A family milieu that claims it is weak, foolish, or dangerous to express strong emotion or to be interested in either the psychological or the physical aspects of feeling states may readily lay the groundwork for a pathological ego ideal with regard to affective experience.

The lack of libidinal investment in the somatic self, coupled with parentally instilled alexithymia, allows bodily pain as well as mental pain to be totally foreclosed from conscious awareness. This again approaches one of the fundamental mechanisms that contributes to the maintenance of certain psychotic states and ways of thought. Affective vitality, whether stimulated by instinctual promptings or by external solicitations, is immediately paralyzed, and such perceptions as are likely to evoke overwhelming affective reactions are rapidly evacuated from consciousness. In the analyses of severely alexithymic patients this process may sometimes be observed in reverse: affective flooding will temporarily produce symptoms of depersonalization or moments of pseudoperception. This creates stormy passages in the analytic voyage, until such time as affect tolerance has been increased and verbal representations are found that are capable of binding the free circulation of primitive affectivity (McDougall 1981). Until such a breach is healed, a radical split between psyche and soma is maintained, laying the subject open to psychosomatic disorganization. When the individuals concerned dispose of no other mental mechanisms in the face of inner conflict or outer stress, this merits the name of a state of *psychosomatosis*, its major signs, other than psychosomatic manifestations, being alexithymia, operational or pragmatic modes of thought, and operational ways of relating to other people. The gap between affective links and their representations destroys meaning, and thus devitalizes the world and the people in it.

All psychological symptoms are attempts at self-cure, and alexithymia is no exception. We might well ask ourselves against what fantasied dangers the alexithymic sufferer is protecting himself or herself, in the defensive maintenance of such devitalized relationships with the world. Krystal (1978a) has proposed that such symptoms prevent the return of a traumatic state. In addition, it is suggested here that the unconscious fears are more akin to psychotic than to neurotic anxieties. Deep uncertainty about one's right to exist and one's right to a separate identity leads to the terror of being in close contact with others: fear of implosion or of explosion, i.e., of losing one's body limits, one's feeling of identity or the control of one's acts. It is further proposed that the similarity between psychosomatosis and psychosis is not limited to the dynamic force of the above-mentioned unconscious anxieties. In addition, the psychic mechanisms employed to keep primitive terror at bay also reveal certain similarities. These comparisons may seem incongruous, in that few individuals appear more bizarre in public than those dominated by psychotic thought, and few seem as well adapted to external reality as the patients suffering from alexithymic and psychosomatic symptoms. Such patients might be described as "normopaths"; it has been suggested that they have created a wall of "pseudo-normality" around them in order to be able to face the world in spite of grave inner distress in their contact with others (McDougall 1980a). In psychosis, thought functions in a delusional way, whereas in psychosomatosis only the body functions delusionally; psychosomatic manifestations make neither biological nor psychological (i.e., psychoneurotic) sense.

In a stimulating article on the fundamental elements of schizophrenic conflict, Ogden (1980) states that in schizophrenia, "there is an attack on the psychological capacities by which meanings are created and thought about . . . the schizophrenic unconsciously attacks his thoughts, feelings, and perceptions, which are felt to be an endless source of pain." Something similar is occurring in alexithymic psychosomatosis. In both states, analysis will frequently reveal that early psychic experience has led to confusion about one's body and one's mind, about their limits, as well as the right to possess an individual body and an individual psychic existence. The latter includes affective vitality, in that affects and affectively charged fantasies both permit children to have a private world that need not be shared with the important adults around them. But the right to this (that includes having the words with which to think the thoughts) may be communicated to the child as totally forbidden. There may be no secrets, no separateness, nor even full possession of one's corporeal self. The psychotic, overwhelmed by affective pain, seeks protection by creating a neo-reality in order to make existence tolerable. With the same aim, the grave alexithymic sufferer also attacks the psychological capacity to capture affect and use it for thought, but instead of a neo-reality, he or she simply drains external reality and object relationships of their meaning. Other than the alexithymic and psychosomatic symptoms, the only visible remains of the internal struggle are perhaps the often-noted "stiffness of posture" and "stony" or "wooden" expression of many such patients. Many somatizing analysands frequently refer to their attempts to "keep things in place" by tightening up their bodies and musculature and generally attempting to use the body in a "stiff" or "stony" way, as though to master the upsurge of strong and frightening affect. An example comes to mind: the patient suffered from peptic ulcer, asthma, tetany, and a variety of cardiac symptoms. In the third year of analysis, he discovered that homosexuals made him feel extremely anxious. The discovery came about when he recognized that sudden tachycardia and asmatiform breathing occurred in conjunction with homosexually linked excitement. He had reached a point in his analysis where his alexithymia was giving way to affect awareness. He would now say that he was suffering from an *attack of anxiety* where once he would have referred to heart-attacks and asthma attacks. Having believed for some forty years that he was open-minded and utterly unaffected by the company of homosexual acquaintances, he now came to discover that his mind was full of sadistic and terrifying fantasies in their presence, including ideas of jumping at their mouths and biting their sexual organs. He summed up these findings by saying, "I close up everything against such ideas—my throat, my lungs, my arteries" (McDougall 1980b).

These magical attempts to make the body impose order so as to deal with the threat of inner disorder and affective outbursts is clearly ineffectual beyond a certain point. Such "somatic" defense measures have to be reinforced by vigorous psychological means. This is best achieved by violent expulsion from the psyche of the somatic pole of affects along with their mental representation. This type of mental functioning contributes to the factors noted by Krystal—insistence on the concrete, and externalization of inner dramas and addictions. These are all ways of ejecting the representation of mental pain from consciousness. With regard to the sudden affective outburst, such as crying or flashes of destructive rage, it may be added to Krystal's supposition that these patients may be using such expressions "for show", that this is a preformed pattern from childhood—the child within the adult is using the only means that, in the past, would draw some attention from the family environment, with the hope therefore of communicating something of his or her psychic reality, in spite of the alexithymic ideal that was promulgated. The expression of affect remains fixated at a childhood level—in Krystal's terms, "undifferentiated."

The continual effort to cut affective links, whether these links are attached to instinctual promptings, emotionally loaded ideas and fantasies, or relationships with other people, is a major psychic activity in alexithymic and psychosomatic conditions. This supposition offers some explanation of other associated phenomena, such as the paucity of dreams so often remarked by different research workers in this field. In normal-neurotic mental functioning the perceptual phenomena or "day residues" that touch off instinctual impulses and significant ties to objects in the inner psychic world are first repressed, and thereby stored to become the nodal points around which dream thoughts will crystalize and seek representation in the dream scene and its theme. This is an everyday observation in any analytic practice. However, in patients whose mental functioning attacks, and rapidly ejects from psychic awareness, both the affect and its representation, these potential dream elements are not stored for further use, but rendered meaningless and foreclosed. There is nothing left with which to make dreams.

This same form of psychic functioning also throws light on the highly specific way of relating to others that is displayed by many alexithymic sufferers. Here, the emotional links to other people are attacked and destroyed, so that the relationship is rendered meaningless. This kind of relationship corresponds, as Krystal points out, to the Type C field described by Langs (1978–1979), but also includes many of the characteristics of the

Type B field, as delineated by the same author. It is possible that the first inklings of this kind of relationship can only be captured initially by the countertransference reactions of therapists. The latter have been well documented, in the first instance by the psychosomaticists of the Paris psychoanalytic school, and more recently by Nemiah (1978) and Sifneos (1974). The effects of frustration and boredom, accompanied by a feeling of inner paralysis, are well-known to all who have worked with alexithymic and psychosomatic patients. The curious upshot of this kind of therapeutic relationship is that, in many instances, the therapist also runs the risk of becoming alexithymic, and avoids phrases and questions that might mobilize some sparks of affect in the patient. What exactly is happening in this kind of relationship?

The psychoanalytic concepts of *splitting* and *projective identification* are pertinent to research into this phenomenon. Taylor (1977) expresses ideas that are very similar to the present author's in this respect. Splitting is an intrapersonal psychic mechanism, whereas projective identification potentially involves two persons. In analysis, we discover through the patients' projective identifications the nature of the relationships to people in their inner worlds, and the extent to which they split off much of what is experienced affectively and seek to control it by experiencing it as an attribute of the other. This also includes, in many instances, reactions in the other who has been chosen unconsciously to represent a personage from the subject's own inner theater. Thus one can observe the extent to which an individual's unconscious fantasies and mental conflicts may be used to bring psychological pressure and induce affects and actions in others. Unavailable affect has to go somewhere; yet severe alexithymics often are quite unaware of the destinies of their foreclosed experiences. These patients remain totally unaware of the fact that they have split off from consciousness large segments of their inner reality, and that a whole series of fantasies and feelings are expelled from their psyche, so that they will not feel them. At the same time, however, they manage, by their particular way of communicating with others, to stir up considerable affect in them. Thus such patients' own inner need to maintain a sterile space between themselves and others actually induces others to join them in keeping this distance.

In a certain manner, alexithymic symptoms may be equated with schizoid withdrawal from others and to the maintenance of a state of inner deadness that no tempestuous affective experience may invade. Certain severe alexithymic patients also keep a prudent distance from others and will admit that they feel ill at ease in most human encounters. Others have developed a "false-self" adaptation to what they feel is expected of them, and this is frequently accompanied by hyperactive involvement in exterior events. These patients tend to use projective identification to a larger degree, or in certain privileged circumstances. It is this latter way of relating that joins Langs's concept of the Type B field, so that the other becomes, willy-nilly, a container for what is too heavy or too affectively disturbing for the subjects to experience and elaborate mentally for themselves. Might we not say that in the interview and/or treatment situation, these patients, cut off from one dimension of their own psychic reality, frequently manage *to evoke in us* their unacknowledged feelings of helplessness and inner paralysis? Nemiah (1978) considers countertransference affect that consists of heaviness, frustration, and boredom when listening to such interviews as one of the diagnostic criteria for alexithymia. With such patients we sometimes discover that we are to experience what they once had to learn, namely, that their psychic survival depended upon their ability to paralyze inner liveliness. No baby is born without the capacity to experience affective reactions, and in fact from birth onward each infant is avidly seeking to control the sources of pleasurable affect and to eject awareness of painful states. A mother who is disturbed by her baby's liveliness or overwhelmed by her infant's affective storms of rage or extreme distress will certainly communicate to her baby that these states meet with no adequate response. One adaptation that is open to the infant is to cease moving toward the mothering parent in states of excitedness and pleasure, and to fall into exhausted sleep in states of unassuaged rage or fright. If, in addition, the ensuing parental discourse continues to condemn affectivity, the child has little option but to destroy the capacity to capture emotion and to think about it. Only by maintaining a state of inner deadness of this kind can the infant avoid the danger of abandonment or the risk of re-experiencing a traumatic state of helplessness and hopelessness in which psychic existence, and perhaps life itself, were felt to be threatened.

Alexithymia is thus an uncommonly strong defense against primitive terrors. It is evident also that the more fragile the subject, the stronger will the defensive walls need to be. The creation of such structures is a lifetime's work, and even though the maintenance of such a fortress may be costly to the patients in terms of physical or psychical disorganisations, they may not be able to face any incursion into their solid personality structure. At such times we also must treat this massive defense with extreme caution.

Krystal feels that alexithymia is not a defensive creation but a severe regression or severe arrest in affective and cognitive development. The two theories—defense and/or arrest—are not mutually exclusive. There is always the question of what precipitates regression or arrested development. Are not all arrested fixations, and regression to earlier fixation points, attempts to deal, by psychological means, with psychic pain and the fear of being overwhelmed? In an earlier paper, Krystal (1978a) himself suggested that the alexithymic defect was an attempt to prevent the return of a traumatizing situation. With regard to infantile arrest, this would suggest that such infants were already learning to protect themselves against physical and mental pain, and to avoid as best they could overwhelming affective storms or excited liveliness. If these have met no containing function in the other, small children, due to their immature psychic functioning, can not deal otherwise with massive states of distress or pain. Just as the potential psychotic is already learning to take the meaning out of perceptions and relationships, so the future alexithymic may already be learning to take the meaning out of affective mobilization.

The crucial matter of prognosis and the effectiveness of psychoanalytical therapy remain to be discussed. The thrust of Krystal's paper leads up to these basic questions. Although he regards alexithymia as a "serious obstacle" to therapy, he clearly believes that there is some hope in therapy for certain severely alexithymic people. The present author is in agreement with this point of view. That therapeutic rewards with many such patients may be obtained does not of course invalidate the opinion of Sifneos (1974) that psychoanalytic therapy is countraindicated in many cases. It might be added that it is also countraindicated for many other categories of patients who are in no way alexithymic! In all circumstances, psychoanalysis or even psychoanalytically oriented therapy should not be engaged with a patient who has not demonstrated a clear realization that he or she has a symptom and a strong desire to know more about his or her individual way of mental functioning with the aim of gaining self-knowledge. Alexithymic patients, like certain psychotic and borderline patients, are likely to remain inaccessible to therapy so long as they are unaware of suffering from any psychological symptoms. Henry Krystal reveals his own creative psychoanalytic approach to these patients. He states that it is essential to lead patients to recognize their symptoms, and from there on to aid them in acquiring a greater tolerance of affective experience, so that they may begin to use affects as signals to themselves. This will lead naturally to dealing with problems created by the impairment in the capacity for self-care that derives from the inability to capture affective representations and make use of them as warning signals. In addition, Krystal stresses the importance of realizing that alexithymic patients, while they may use many affect-laden words, may nevertheless have denuded these words and phrases of their intrinsic emotional meaning. The therapist must not be fooled by the devitalized use of vital words. He further emphasizes the need for helping such patients realize the extent to which they attribute to their objects the emotional experiences that are basically their own (i.e., their extensive use of projective identification). This, he claims, will aid them in recognizing their lack of empathy and their ensuing conviction that they are not capable of being loved or of loving. Krystal's experience had led him to realize that in many cases, this modified therapeutic approach enables patients to better grasp their relationships to external objects and thus perhaps to use the therapeutic relationship and transference interpretations to further their quest for inner truth about themselves and their psychic reality.

In conclusion, the immense importance of language in human psychic existence must be emphasized. Not only does this element distinguish man from animal, but words alone can join affect and representation—and words alone can bind emotion, thus preventing its free and dangerous circulation in the soma, and rendering affective experience and fantasies containable and available for thought (true thought, not operational thinking and "false-self" adaptation to the world of others). Our subjective, sexual, and social identities are all made of words, but it is what we have done with the words that will determine what kind of human beings we shall become. To have denuded words of their affective charge, and thus of the nature of affective links to other people, is an amazing, if near fatal achievement. It is for this reason that the lines of Ogden Nash are quoted at the beginning of this paper. As with all great humorists, he shows an intuitive insight into human foibles, and thus his statement echoes what all alexithymic patients no doubt "know" in the deepest recesses of their minds: "Sticks and stones'll break your bones, but *words* will damn near kill you!"

REFERENCES

Freud, S. (1926). Inhibitions, symptoms and anxiety. *Standard Edition* 20:77–128.
Krystal, H. (1978a). Trauma and affects. *Psychoanalytic Study of the Child* 36:81–116.
———. (1978b). Self-representation and the capacity for self-care. *Annual of Psychoanalysis* 6:206–246.
———. (1980). The hedonic aspects of affects. (In preparation).
Langs, R. (1978–1979). Some communicative properties of the bipersonal field. *International Journal of Psychoanalytic Psychotherapy* 7:87–135.
McDougall, J. (1980a). *Plea for a Measure of Abnormality*. New York: International Universities Press.
———. (1980b). A child is being eaten. *Contemporary Psychoanalysis* 16:417–459.
———. (1981). Corps et métaphore. *Nouvelle Revue de Psychanalyse* 23:57–81.
Nemiah, J. (1978). Alexithymia and psychosomatic illness. *Journal of Continuing Education in Psychiatry* 3:25–37.
Ogden, T. (1980). On the nature of schizophrenic conflict. *International Journal of Psycho-Analysis* 61:513–533.
Sifneos, P. (1974). Reconsideration of psychodynamic mechanisms in psychosomatic symptom formation in view of recent clinical observations. *Psychotherapy Psychosomatics* 24:151–155.
Taylor, G. (1977). Alexithymia and the countertransference. *Psychotherapy Psychosomatics* 28:141–147.

The Opening Phase of Psychotherapy of Hypochondriacal States

R. M. GALATZER-LEVY, M.D.

The Opening Phase of Psychotherapy of Hypochondriacal States

R. M. GALATZER-LEVY, M.D.

People presenting with hypochondriacal complaints are commonly regarded as difficult to engage in psychotherapy. The clinical experiences described here indicate that when therapists communicate their empathic understanding of the patient's distress, the patient's suffering is decreased and it is possible to engage him or her in treatment. These results are demonstrated with regard to eight patients. Treatment failures using this method are demonstrated in a case where its application was delayed and in cases of hysteria and schizophrenia, where the method is not applicable. These clinical results can be conceptualized using ideas of self-psychology.

Hypochondriasis, an undue concern or belief that one is suffering from serious illness, may vary in intensity from a transient worry to a delusional state. Medical reassurance and evidence of lack of organic pathology does not relieve the patient. In contrast to the hysteric, there are no signs and symptoms (except for occasional nonspecific complaints and reports of ordinary bodily sensations, which the patient regards as indications of illness). The patient is intensely worried by his illness, demonstrating no hysterical "belle indifference." Hypochondriacal symptoms lack specific symbolic meaning; hysterical symptoms have highly elaborated and specific meaning. Hypochondriasis appears as an aspect of many illnesses and is only rarely seen as an isolated entity.

Hypochondriacal states (Nemiah 1975, Kenyon 1976) are observed in depression, obsessional neurosis and other neurosis, schizophrenia, affective disorders, personality disorders, situational reactions, organic psychosis and even as part of normal development in adolescence (A. Freud 1969). They are common transient occurrences. Much primary medical practice is concerned with hypochondriacal states (Burnum 1973, Garfield 1970). It has even been recommended (Garfield 1970) that an effective way of reducing medical costs would be to eliminate these "worried well" from the care of physicians.

Physicians, including psychiatrists, are pessimistic about helping such patients. When hypochondriasis is the presenting difficulty, psychiatric texts (Nemal 1975, Redlich and Freedman 1966, Castelnuovo-Tedesco, 1975) give a gloomy picture of treatment. Treatment of the underlying illness is often recommended (Kenyon 1976). When this involves psychotherapy, patients who regard themselves as physically ill are unlikely to cooperate. Indeed, therapists usually complain that such patients are "difficult," unpsychological, and hard to engage in a psychotherapy. Despite their commonness, hypochondriacal patients present a puzzle to the primary care physician (Balint 1957, 1970). Typical responses include anger, nonspecific medication, and elaborate "work-ups." Occasionally, hypochondriacs establish a chronic, stable relationship with their doctors in which the hypochondriac finds some relief and is at least spared the mistreatment that he is likely to receive as he searches from physician to physician (Balint 1957).

Offenkrantz and Tobin (1975) recommend a specific psychotherapeutic technique in the treatment of hypochondriacs. They believe that the therapist should legitimize and dignify the patient's suffering by taking it extremely seriously. The patient is not told that his suffering is imaginary or the result of psychic conflict. The therapist explicitly states that he understands the patient's fears and concerns, as well as the great difficulty posed for the patient by those worries. They further state that "the price for this is our demand that they continue to function." Without providing data to support this contention, they state that the technique is useful in the treatment of "true hypochondriasis."

During the past six years, I have treated or supervised the treatment of fifteen patients whose presenting and principal difficulty was a hypochondriacal state. The clinical experience with twelve of these patients is described here. Three patients are excluded because of confidentiality. None of the patients suffered from severe organic pathology, nor was there evidence of an organic etiology for their psychiatric difficulty. These cases are used to examine (1) the efficacy of a modified form of Offenkrantz and Tobin's (1975) method for relief of symptoms; (2) the process of such treatment (including the therapist's response); (3) the effects of such interventions on subsequent treatment; and (4) possible understandings of hypochondriacal states suggested by these experiences. I have modified Offenkrantz and Tobin's (1975) method in that no demand was made that the patient continue to function.

Because of the confusion in terminology regarding both psychopathology and psychotherapeutic technique, I have tried to give sufficient information in the case reports so that the reader may form his own judgment, at least about the diagnosis and the initial intervention. Obviously, in reporting twelve cases, a detailed description of treatments that lasted on many occasions for several hundred hours, is not possible.

An unfortunate consequence of this abbreviation of clinical material is that it can only be used to illustrate the contentions described in the discussion. In the case reports, theoretical understandings of the interactions with patients are avoided so that the reader may have an opportunity to come to his own conclusions regarding the psychodynamics of the patient and the interaction with the therapist. The final section of the paper is devoted to a discussion of possible understandings of these therapeutic transactions.

TYPICAL CASES

The following cases illustrate the successful use of the technique in a wide variety of syndromes in which the initial presentation was dominated by hypochondriacal concerns.

Case 1

A 26-year-old man in his final semester of business school came for treatment because of intense anxiety over his physical health. For the past eight years he had been preoccupied with various bodily ills and was the object of much medical attention. Aside from a single positive test for occult blood in his stool, the examinations failed to provide findings of physical illness. He had many complaints of his physician, who became bored and then angry with him. For two weeks he had had various, difficult to describe, pains in the muscles of his arms and legs, which he attributed to periarteritis nodosa, a disease that combined all his greatest fears: it was fatal, its symptoms were vague, and in his view it could never be ruled out (since even multiple biopsies might give false negatives). He had increased his attendance at various clinics from approximately once every two weeks to two or three times per week. He was disturbed by an impulsive act in which he had stolen a book on his illness from the university book store. He was convinced that if he were discovered in this crime he would be expelled from the university and banned from his profession.

The patient led an isolated existence, having almost no contact with people aside from his parents and physicians. He fantasized about women but never dated. School work had been accomplished with the greatest difficulty. Hypochondriacal concerns had served as a rationalization for interruption of his studies, as they did at the time he entered treatment.

The patient's father was a depressed, quiet man, who avoided his wife and son by spending most of his time at a successful business. The patient's

mother was anxiously ambitious for her son and experienced by him as
spending her life in a state of worried interest over his well-being.

After getting an outline of the patient's history, the therapist said to him
that it must be extremely frightening to believe that he was suffering from a
fatal, untreatable, and undiagnosable illness. When the therapist said this, he
felt like he was "putting him on," experienced an urge to laugh, and felt
that he was doing something dishonest. A moment later, however, the therapist was struck by how poignant such a situation indeed was. The patient was
surprised by the remark. Was the therapist teasing him? Despite repeated
examinations, physicians had discovered no organic difficulties. Wasn't the
psychiatrist's job to point out to him the irrationality of his concerns or to
reassure him that everything was all right? That was what all his previous
physicians had done. The therapist persisted, saying that regardless of any of
this, the patient believed himself to have a dreadful illness and that this must
be very frightening. The patient concurred.

In the next hour the patient listed many more symptoms, complaints, self-
diagnoses, and fears. He repeatedly invited the therapist to indicate that his
distress was exaggerated or had no "real" basis. As the therapist persisted in
his view that the patient's experiences must be extremely distressing, the
patient became notably less anxious and his interest gradually shifted away
from his hypochondriacal complaints. He began to reflect on his fear that
completing his studies and finding a job would result in his finally leaving
home and attempting to function independently of his mother for the first
time. During the next four sessions, which occurred over a two-week period,
the patient's interests and activities rapidly shifted. Each session began with
a reference to his medical complaints. However, these became more brief,
less elaborated, and clearly of less interest to the patient. In each instance the
therapist indicated a knowledge of the distress that the patient experienced.
The patient dealt more directly with his concerns about leaving home,
finding work, and dating. He stopped attending the medical clinic, returned
to his academic work, and between the fifth and sixth hour had the first date
of his life. He recognized his lack of understanding of his illness and that the
therapist's consistent recognition of his subjective distress had been important in his putting aside his symptoms. He thought he would seek therapy if
his symptoms recurred.

Case 2

A 19-year-old unemployed man who was seeking a career as a photo-
graphic model was referred by a dermatologist he had consulted because he
was "going bald." The dermatologist informed him that he had normal
frontal balding and little of that. The patient became acutely distressed and

was convinced that some severe underlying disease had been missed. The patient was an overt homosexual who spent much of his time picking up men or arranging for them to approach him so that he might feel the pleasure evoked in them. Preoccupation with his appearance almost excluded other interests. Both the overt homosexuality and this preoccupation began at age 16, following by two months the death of his mother from injuries that she had suffered in an automobile accident a year earlier. As the therapist learned later, prior to this time he had had wide cultural interests and an inhibited but intense interest in girls. The patient resented the psychiatric referral, but rationalized that the therapist would tell the dermatologist that he was not "crazy."

After the therapist had some idea of how the patient was proceeding in his current life, he told him that the loss of the enthusiastic attention of his admirers, which he feared would follow his balding, was as distressing to him as a dreadful illness would be and evoked the same kinds of fears. He was concerned that, despite what the therapist said, he didn't "mean" it, that he regarded the patient's attitudes as unreasonable, that the therapist was trying to "talk him out" of regarding his illness as serious. When the therapist persisted in indicating that he knew the seriousness and depth of the patient's distress, concern about his balding essentially disappeared. He became concerned instead about his inhibition in following any career and the emptiness and triviality of his current life.

He became deeply committed to therapy. Following these initial interventions, the therapist's remarks to the patient consisted almost exclusively of clarifications of the situation that the patient found himself in with regard to the therapist, interpretations of the resistance to knowing of that situation, and genetic reconstructions based upon the phenomena observed in his interaction with the therapist. The initial intervention was understood and discussed explicitly as an invitation on the therapist's part for the patient to use him to recognize and thereby provide soothing for the extremely distressing internal state that the patient was unable to manage on his own. A transference formed with a sense of feeling good and alive in the therapist's real or imagined presence and feelings of intense discomfort in his absence, which the patient would at first relieve through homosexual activity but which he grew later to tolerate without recourse to action.

The history emerged of his disrupted idealization of his father, who had become progressively depressed and alcoholic as the boy grew up. The patient became more serious and effective in pursuing his career as a model and then shifted his vocational goals to teaching (his mother's profession) and arranged to return to college to pursue that aim. He became both more competitive and friendly toward other men, and developed an interest in women but did not become sexually active with them. Interestingly, with this development

394 R. M. GALATZER-LEVY

his presenting concern of balding briefly reemerged. At this time, however, its predominant significance had changed. He now feared it as a visible indication of his masculinity, which put him into dangerous competition with the therapist, who was noticeably balding at the time.

He decided to return to his home state where college tuition would be cheaper than in Illinois. The anticipated separation precipitated further work on the loss of his mother. The therapy lasted three years. A letter from the patient two years after the end of treatment indicates that he has continued to pursue his studies with enthusiasm, that his cultural and social interests have become both broader and deeper. He did not return to overt homosexual activity, but his relations with women have not progressed beyond friendship.

Case 3

A 33-year-old historian sought treatment because of his preoccupation with a difficult to define illness whose symptoms included back pains, extreme lethargy, and a concern that he suffered from an undiagnosed lethal ailment. This condition began following an episode of prostatitis two years previously, which had been treated with an injection of a drug into the buttock. He reluctantly accepted psychiatric referral following four independent work-ups for organic illness, only after he was assured that the referring physician would continue to see him as long as necessary. He said his problems were purely somatic, although naturally his life threatening illness depressed him. Aside from his illness he described an idyllic life in which he sensed no difficulty. However, his report of his life left the therapist feeling that the patient's existence was dull, lifeless, and lacking valued ideals. For example, religion, which had played an important role in his earlier life, now seemed only a formal exercise.

In the second hour, the therapist said that it must be frightening to believe himself near death and to be reminded of such fear by various pains. He doubted the therapist's sincerity and told him of his doctor's angry response to his illness. Subsequently, he complained that such remarks made him feel childish, "like a little boy whose mommy kisses it and makes it better." At the same time, the somatic complaints diminished in intensity to the point that after two months they only occurred specifically in relation to the therapist's vacations or empathic failures.

Sessions focused on the chronic and profound sense of meaninglessness pervading the patient's life. The patient formed a relationship with the therapist in which he greatly admired the therapist and felt good about himself because he was involved with a therapist whom he regarded so highly. In examining the vicissitudes of this relationship, we discovered the source of the patient's lack of enthusiasm for his ideals in his incapacity to idealize his severely disturbed and erratic father. However, for the first three years of treatment it remained a mystery why the patient became manifestly ill when he did. It became clear that his illness had begun as his wife completed graduate studies in a highly technical field. However, contrary to plans, his wife failed either to seek employment or to agree to have a baby. The patient was enraged at her and feared the rage was so great that he would disintegrate or would turn the rage against himself. Indeed, his father had failed to control his own rage and the patient believed he needed to control his rage through rigid characterological defenses. However, there later emerged a second explanation more compatible with the patient's transference manifest in treatment. The patient had idealized his wife, regarding her as a perfect combination of intellect, good character, and physical beauty. The patient had felt himself good by virtue of his relationship to this perfect being. On completing her graduate studies, the patient's wife began to manifest all sorts of pathology (various phobias and an intense, almost psychotic fear of childbearing). The patient fell ill as he had lost this idealized object, and his rage and hypochondriasis were a response to that loss.

Case 4

A 27-year-old accountant sought treatment because of anxiety about work, depressed feelings, and a need "to ask a lot of questions." The questions, directed principally to his wife and occasionally to his physician, consisted in inquiries about the appearance of various skin lesions that he feared were cancerous. He feared that he was balding and that all his hair would fall out. Whenever his wife asked, "What's that?" or, "Look at that," he became terrified, thinking she had seen some new lesion on his face. He demanded that she describe what she was referring to and repeatedly reassure him that various pimples had not changed. This questioning went on for extended periods and was experienced as "torture" by both parties. Visits to doctors were dreaded but felt to be essential for reassurance. The patient was terrified that a serious illness would be discovered, that he would fail to mention some symptom so that the doctor would fail to diagnose some grave illness. At the same time, he feared appearing foolish to his doctor or that the doctor would tire of him and grow angry (as several, in fact, had). Afterward he would worry that he had failed to mention some problems and feel impelled to return. The obsessional nature of his pathology should not obscure the hypochondriacal nature of his complaints. He suffered from the belief that he had a grave illness.

His symptoms were relieved for six months when another psychiatrist recommended that he set a time limit on his worrying and then put it aside. However, this technique ultimately failed and he sought treatment elsewhere.

The patient's first preoccupation was his skin lesions. He was amazed when the present therapist responded to his concerns by talking about how frightened he must feel. He was incredulous. He expected an angry response or a recommendation, like his previous psychiatrist's, to put the thought out of his mind.

Two sessions spent in this way initiated a long and successful therapy that will not be described here. The patient's central pathology was in fact an obsessional neurosis with predominantly Oedipal issues at its core. The complaints about skin lesions were highly overdetermined and included, in addition to their hypochondriacal component, elements of aggression against himself and others, a representation of his guilt over masturbation, a mode of interference and inhibition in his relationship with his wife, and an identification with his father. The complaints about skin lesions became less severe and shifted from a predominantly hypochondriacal quality to a predominantly symbolic neurotic symptom. The therapist's commiseration was limited to the first six months of treatment and its function was ultimately understood by the patient. He recognized that the therapist had commiserated with him and eventually discussed how such an action made it possible for him to feel sufficiently calm to both continue with the treatment and examine the meaning of his symptomatology and his interactions with the therapist. Far from using the therapist's remarks as a resistance to the uncovering of the many meanings of the patient's symptoms described above, the sense that the therapist would assist him if his distress threatened to produce over-whelming anxiety allowed him to explore a variety of frightening, previously repressed aspects of himself. Thus, while this was not an analysis, the technique described here is a "satisfactory" parameter in Eissler's (1953) sense (i.e., it was the minimum parameter that could be introduced, it could be analyzed, and it was ultimately eliminated).

The patient had first become symptomatic during the final quarter of his accountancy program. The onset of symptoms could clearly be linked to his first job interview and his entering into an adult position. The episode that brought him into treatment with the present therapist was temporally associated with his wife's increasing demand that the couple have a baby. In the course of treatment it became clear that the patient feared the child's arrival would disrupt the current situation in which he was the center of interest and attention. The patient's need for a primitive relationship to his wife in which she exclusively attended to him diminished sufficiently so that he, too, wished to have a child, and the couple did have a baby. However, the patient's preoccupation with adequate care was displaced from himself to the infant, and he was demandingly insistent that his wife take care of the baby with particular attention to any physical distress in the child.

Case 5

A 44-year-old woman was referred by a gastroenterologist because of "vomicking (sic) so much that she was losing weight." Her physician, who had followed her for six months, found no physiological difficulty and the patient's weight was stable during that time. The patient believed that she had a potentially fatal disease and thought herself unable to retain food except chocolates. Only near the end of the treatment did it become clear that "vomicking" referred not to regurgitation but distaste for food, eruction, and abdominal discomfort. She was distressed and angered by the psychiatric referral. It meant to her that the doctor thought her "problem was in the head" and not "real." When the therapist discussed with her the fears and terror that she must experience on anticipating dying, she first believed that the therapist was attempting to placate her about the referral, but later felt calmed and reassured by his remarks. Only then was she able to discuss aspects of her life that she claimed were without difficulty. Her adolescent daughter, who was "just like me, but she's going to amount to something," was planning to leave home. The very idea of it had made her feel "empty inside." "There would be all this space in the house and nothing there. I wouldn't even feel like I was there." The patient's symptom remitted at this point.

Subsequently additional symbolic meanings of the patient's symptom were discovered. She had been forced to perform fellatio and had gagged and felt like vomiting; her mother had vomited immediately prior to her death. The patient was seen only twelve times, so the therapist remained uncertain about the role these events played in the symptom, and even their meaning to the patient. The phenomenology of the illness indicated a combination of hypochondriacal and hysterical determinants for the symptom and a shift from a nonsymbolic to a symbolic significance in the course of treatment.

Two years later the patient returned with similar complaints, only this time accompanied by a weight-loss of 25 pounds. The valued daughter had actually left. A colleague who treated her diagnosed depression.

Case 6

A colleague referred a 20-year-old undergraduate student; he thought the patient might be schizophrenic. The patient was intensely anxious and greatly concerned about his mental health. He complained of states of "primary process ideation," a phrase that he said with great rapidity and with a grimace. He demanded to know whether he was schizophrenic.

He stated his complaint and question with ever more urgency whenever a suggestion was made that more information was necessary before the therapist could answer his question. Interpretations to the effect that the patient defensively used his urgent request against the clarification of the content or meaning of his symptoms were met with ever increasingly urgent demands for a response to his questions. The confusion aroused in the therapist by the patient's discussions, as well as a sense of helplessness with regard to his situation, led the therapist to try to convince the patient to tell him in ordinary language what he was talking about. With great difficulty, the therapist learned that the patient was performing well academically, had many friends, held down a responsible part-time job, and had a consistent, if complex relationship with his girlfriend. There was no evidence of thought disorder. The patient had a highly sophisticated understanding of psychoanalysis and had learned the phrase "primary process ideation" in his reading.

Interpretation of his style of communication as defensive, however tactfully made, or urgings that he clarify what he was saying invariably led to his repeating the phrase with increased urgency, telling the therapist that, being a psychiatrist, he must know what it means, and his asking in a repeated, urgent, and increasingly anxious way if he was schizophrenic.

Unaccustomed to thinking of psychological complaints as hypochondriacal, it took several weeks before the therapist recognized these as such. At that point, the therapist talked to him about how terrifying it must be to believe he suffered from a disease as severe as schizophrenia. He doubted the therapist's empathy for his distress and skeptically requested repetition of the therapist's interest in and feeling for his symptoms. Failures to respond with an appreciation of his difficulties were met with a renewed barrage of repetitious questions about the therapist's evaluation of him, often extending beyond the therapeutic hours to urgent telephoned appeals for reassurance.

For about a year the therapist's suggestions that patient and therapist attempt together to understand these phenomena were taken as an affront and threat, precipitating both rage and anxiety. At the same time the patient noisily protested that he was uninvolved with the therapy, doubted its usefulness, felt the fees and billing practices were unreasonable, and in general assumed a provocative and obnoxious stance toward the therapist. This made it difficult to reflect to him the intensity of his fear and how desperately he needed the therapist in order to understand it. As it became increasingly obvious to the therapist through repeated experience that the patient's unpleasant manner was a response to the therapist's lack of empathy, it became easier to take a more sympathetic position toward him. By the end of 18 months a firm working relationship had been established with the patient's anxiety reduced to workable levels.

The treatment followed many roads, but at no point was there any indication of severe psychopathology. The patient had picked up with the therapist where he had left off his development at age 13 when his mother had died of carcinoma. He was intensely and ambivalently bound to her. When he was a child she had seemed preoccupied and indifferent. She never responded enthusiastically to his many accomplishments, but seemed only to attend to him at times of illness. He had felt simultaneously tied to her and unloved by her. The prerequisite for her attention was his illness. Her death was experienced both with relief at his new freedom (which he allowed himself to enjoy for a time), and guilt fostered by her dying at the height of his angry attempts to achieve some independence from her. Yet another determinant of his hypochondriacal preoccupation was the sense that he was a "monster" for feeling relieved as his mother's death: someone incapable of fully human feelings and emotions. The therapy, which lasted three-and-a-half years, ended with his symptom entirely relieved, an age-appropriate vigorous pursuit of his career, and a far less ambivalent attitude toward women than at the beginning of therapy.

During his treatment, it was discovered that his acute illness began when he broke off relations with a girl whom he regarded as "too sick." He recognized that sexual pleasure was only a peripheral element in the relationship and that their very active sex life centered around gaining the girl's enthusiastic admiration of him and his genitals in particular. He only felt good when he got such a response, and feared the addictive quality of the relationship.

Case 7

A 25-year-old artist sought treatment to consider whether to have a variety of cosmetic surgical procedures. He believed himself to be very homely and was convinced that his penis was extremely small. He was preoccupied with these defects in his appearance and regarded them as "basically dreadful" and in need of correction. Sometimes he attributed interpersonal difficulties to the imagined ugliness, but these difficulties were of secondary importance. Except for his slovenly dress the patient was not unattractive in appearance. Two urologists whom he consulted told him that his genitalia were normal in size. He was not reassured by these opinions. He believed that the statements of the urologists and acquaintances were designed to placate him and hide the horrible truth. He was reluctant to engage in treatment, since "talking can't change your body," but was willing to come because he was unable to afford surgery and found that his preoccupation disturbed his work. For the first four sessions he angrily discussed the worthlessness of the procedure and threatened to leave. When the therapist began to comment on how terrifying it must be to imagine oneself as profoundly and visibly flawed, the patient concurred, and within a brief time the symptoms remitted.

Only then did the patient's work inhibition become apparent. A year previous to coming for treatment his work was given a prominent place in an exhibition at a distinguished gallery. Although he was initially pleased, his pleasure faded when none of his work sold. How devastating this was, later became apparent when it was realized in the therapy that his work was in a sense entirely self-portraiture and that it was essentially himself that he offered for sale. His work was extremely ugly by conventional standards and had other features that made it unappealing to potential purchasers (unfortunately these cannot be described here). In effect, his ugly and defective self had been rejected. He was chronically enraged at art collectors who rejected him.

The patient formed a relationship with the therapist in which the therapist's enthusiastic interest in him seemed essential to his well-being. As long as he experienced the therapist as interested, he functioned well, pursuing his career, forming some relationships with other people, and remaining unconcerned about bodily deformities. However, any interference with his grandiose feelings precipitated great difficulties. Once he complained about the bad taste of his supervisor at the museum where he was employed and his wish to confront him. The therapist was concerned that he would lose the job and discussed the realistic results of his intended action. On leaving the session, the patient had realized that his ears were intensely ugly and that he should cut them off. He had intended to do this but, fearing the pain, went home and got drunk in an attempt to anesthesize himself. He passed out from the alcohol. On waking he decided not to mutilate himself, but found himself unable to work or sustain interest in anything until his next session. On a subsequent occasion he complained that the same supervisor was insisting that he arrange an exhibit in an unaesthetic way. The therapist concurred that the patient's own high standards made carrying out the order both distasteful and a sort of corruption reflecting to him his own valued ideals. Following this session he worked hard at his creative work and succeeded in a complex realistic arrangement for more satisfying work at the museum.

The work for his second show was neither so grotesque nor as unsaleable as before. The show was critically and financially successful. The patient was far calmer about the acceptance of his work and had achieved some degree of differentiation between himself and his artistic productions. Even when empathic breaks occured, his ideas did not turn to self-mutilation or surgery. He decided to end treatment at this time, saying that it was essential to his career that he move to another city. Therapist and patient were unable to come to any satisfactory understanding of the patient's motives for ending therapy at this time.

Case 8

A depressed 56-year-old woman was psychiatrically hospitalized two years after her husband's death, with delusions that she was gravely ill, had cancer, and her skin and various body fluids had "dried up." For a year following the death of her husband from carcinoma, the patient seemed not to react. She then became increasingly preoccupied with her own medical problems and sought treatment from several physicians. She believed that her veins were empty, that the blood had dried up in her veins, that she had no saliva, that she could not sweat, that her kidneys did not function, etcetera. These complaints varied from day to day in a way that the therapist was unable to comprehend. She was delusional about these matters, fully believing them to be the case, and often insistently demanding that they be medically evaluated and that she be medically treated for her condition. She was initially courteous to her therapist but rather contemptuous in her manner, seeing her psychological distress as secondary to her physical conditions. She complained that ther problems were not being attended to properly.

When her therapist began to make explicit remarks about how disturbing it must be to be preoccupied by ideas of drying up and dying, the patient became more calm and the nature of the complaints became more stable and specific. The patient began also to complain of various psychological problems such as a "lack of support" from her children. Over the course of a month, the symptoms shifted to highly specific complaints of lack of internal sensations in various bodily orifices, which eventually, with the help of her therapist inquiring about sexual frustration, led to a discussion of that topic and her relationship to her husband. At this point the focus of the patient's interest and treatment shifted from hypochondriacal complaints to a complex process of mourning. Hypochondriacal complaints reappeared briefly during this latter part of the treatment in response to three types of stimuli: (1) recollection of negative feelings toward the husband, (2) various separations from her children, and (3) empathic failures on the part of the therapist.

TREATMENT FAILURES

The following cases involve patients whose treatment failed. In one case the therapist did not explicitly communicate his empathic comprehension of their hypochondriasis sufficiently early; in the second, the symptoms were not hypochondriacal.

Case 9

A 43-year-old man was referred by an organically oriented colleague for psychotherapy because "all else had failed." The patient had never functioned independently and supported himself on funds provided by his parents and homosexual lover of fifteen years. He had intermittently attended university classes until three years before the referral. At that time he developed difficulties in studying and a "seizure disorder." The symptoms of the "seizure disorder" were difficult to discover and varied from interview to interview. They generally occurred several times each day, more often in the morning, and were characterized by various difficult-to-describe feelings, a lack of awareness of the environment, and were not detectable by an outside observer.

When numerous elaborate neurological work-ups failed to reveal an etiology or suggest a diagnosis, the patient was referred to the organically oriented colleague mentioned above who diagnosed depression and began trials with antidepression medication. The psychiatrist paid close attention to the patient's response to the medication as well as pursuing the details of the "seizures" at great length. The patient was also given trials of various seizure medications. He often described new symptoms that reminded the psychiatrist of various seizure disorders and led to further investigation and considerations. The psychiatrist reported liking the patient, and although the seizures continued and the patient's social functioning only improved minimally, the patient reported considerable subjective relief. However, after a year of this procedure, the psychiatrist informed the patient that he felt that his therapeutic armamentarium was exhausted and that there was no point in continuing. The patient became suicidally depressed, his "seizures" became much more frequent, and he was hospitalized both because of the severity of the depression and for yet another "work-up." At the end of this hospitalization he was referred to the present therapist.

The patient compliantly accepted the referral. The therapist failed to recognize both the extreme tentativeness of his presence and the essentially hypochondriacal nature of his complaints, and so occupied several sessions learning his history. The patient felt that he had benefited greatly from the previous treatment. He never anticipated, believed, or experienced that the medication would help him, but he felt far better for the sustained interest of the psychiatrist in his suffering and the obvious seriousness with which the psychiatrist attended to his many complaints. The patient spent almost all his waking hours in the library reading about epilepsy. He never mentioned this to the psychiatrist. He did notice the surprising frequency with which he would "become aware" of some aspect of his disorder that corresponded to the articles that he had recently read.

Unfortunately, the foregoing history only emerged clearly in the final hour of the patient's eight visits. The therapist failed to make the diagnosis of hypochondriasis until this time, being engaged in an attempt to differentiate between conversion symptoms, various psychotic manifestations, and epilepsy. While the therapist's manner with the patient always involved attentive and interested listening, he made no explicit statement that he understood the patient's distress, nor did he discuss his attitude toward the patient's difficulties. In fact, he felt reluctant to take such a stance with this patient and rationalized this reluctance, thinking such a position interfered with supposedly scientific curiosity regarding the patient's diagnosis, the effects of the interventions of the therapist's organically oriented colleague, and the nature of the patient's sustained homosexual relationship. It would be more accurate to say that the interruption in empathy was manifested in the therapist's silence, but reflected the deeper failure in such a position with regard to this patient.

After several visits, the patient consulted a neurologist who was famous for diagnosing obscure forms of epilepsy. The patient knew from reading his papers that the neurologist paid the greatest attention to his patients' complaints and often continued various attempts at drug treatment for years. In addition, the neurologist was not deterred by the absence of physical or electroencephalographic findings. The patient consciously anticipated that he would re-establish a relationship like the one with the organic psychiatrist by seeing this neurologist.

This vignette illustrates how this patient could be engaged in treatment and how a failure to commiserate with him drove him from therapy in the search for such commiseration. Whether the patient could have eventually become involved in useful psychotherapy obviously remains unclear.

Case 10

A 29-year-old man consulted the present therapist at the insistence of his ophthalmologist, who had treated him for a period of 18 months for a "spastic accommodation reflex" that caused objects to go out of focus when he looked at them. This symptom failed to respond to the ophthalmologist's suggestion that it would disappear (a treatment the ophthalmologist had found almost universally effective), and the patient had refused to comply with various pharmacologic regimens that would have paralyzed the pupillary reflex. The patient consulted many physicians in several cities. He carefully ensured that they would not communicate directly with each other and represented each physician's view to the others as indicative of organic disease. In fact, the accommodation reflex was disturbed. Despite having graduated from a professional school, the patient lived at home with his parents. He consciously enjoyed his father's distress, but was not aware of the way in which his illness bound his mother to him.

It may be worth commenting on the difference between the ophthalmologist's suggestion that the patient's symptom would be relieved and the entirely different procedure described in this paper. No suggestion is made, but rather only the explicit statement of the therapist's empathic comprehension is given. In fact, it would be antithetical to such a statement to suggest that the symptom would pass, for a major aspect of the patient's beliefs is that the symptoms are grave and will not be relieved in time.

The patient was peculiarly unconcerned about his symptom, although it kept him from working and dominated his relations with other people. In particular, it allowed him to avoid competition with a brother who is a physician, and at the same time put him into a passive position with regard to his doctors, whom he saw as abusing him.

The therapist mistakenly understood this symptom as an instance of hypochondriasis and said how distressing it must be to suffer from such a symptom. The patient responded with increased anxiety and contempt. In fact, in contrast to the true hypochondriac, the patient suffered from a condition characterized by a sign (an objective physical finding), exhibited a *belle indifference* to his symptom, and suffered from a highly specific symptom with symbolic meaning. In other words, this was conversion hysteria. He feared that the therapist would interrupt his relationship to his internist and quickly fled the therapy on the pretext that it was too expensive.

The therapist's misunderstanding of the patient's pathology (motivated in part by the therapist's research interests) resulted in an inappropriate intervention that caused the patient to interrupt treatment. In the discussion of this material I will attempt to show why this intervention was unhelpful in the work with such a hysteric as opposed to a hypochondriac.

SCHIZOPHRENIA

During the course of long psychotherapies of two schizophrenic men, episodes of severe hypochondriasis occurred. These patients differ from those described above both in their pathology and in that hypochondriasis was not a presenting complaint. However, in both instances commiseration was attempted. Instead of resulting in improvement, the symptoms worsened or the beginning of a transference psychosis was precipitated.

Case 11

The therapist had seen a 31-year-old chronic schizophrenic on a weekly basis for three years when the patient developed a variety of hypochondriacal complaints about his abdomen and the conviction that he had cancer of the liver. These difficulties were precipitated by his mother's announcement that her paramour was to live with her and that the patient must move out of the house. Discussion with the patient of his symptoms and comments on their terrifying nature led to an increased preoccupation with the bodily complaints. This approach was a change in therapeutic style with this patient, and such a shift may have been disruptive. The therapist recognized that he was making matters worse and told the patient that his belief was a delusion and that it was a response to the anticipated arrival of his mother's paramour. Although the patient was angered by this remark, his anxiety and hypochondriasis both decreased. The hypochondriacal complaints disappeared only when his living situation was again stabilized.

Case 12

A 28-year-old postman came for treatment because of extreme anxiety and intermittent delusions that other men accused him of homosexuality. There were also auditory hallucinations with similar content. The patient suffered from a continuing unpleasant anal sensation that often intensified simultaneously with his delusions. He often believed this sensation was a symptom of a rectal cancer that might soon spread and kill him. He avoided medical examinations for fear that the doctor would think him homosexual and discover some physical evidence of an episode of anal intercourse that had occurred during his childhood. Commiseration was experienced as very threatening by this patient, who quickly became fearful of a homosexual advance of the therapist's part. A shift to attending to a detailed discussion of the situation in which symptoms became manifest, accompanied by the clarification that the therapist believed his anal complaints to be psychological in origin, proved far more successful.

DISCUSSION

Clinical Generalizations

True hypochondriasis is a state in which the patient believes or is deeply concerned that he suffers from grave illness, is accompanied by the search for therapeutic relief, and lacks the specific symbolic meaning of hysterical conversion symptoms. In such cases, when the patient is not schizophrenic, commiseration is an effective initial treatment, resulting in rapid symptom remission and the forming of a relationship with the therapist. This can serve as a beginning for satisfactory psychotherapy. In no instance did the patient experience the therapist's remarks as a collusion with his or her own unrealistic ideas. In view of the extreme pessimism in the literature regarding the treatment of these patients and the long history of suffering followed by prompt relief experienced in treatment, it seems reasonable to conclude, even in the absence of a control group, that commiseration is an effective treatment. In one instance reported here where the therapist failed to employ this method, the patient's condition worsened and he sought treatment elsewhere with a more sympathetic physician.

In contrast to the true hypochondriacs, the two schizophrenic patients clearly worsened in response to commiseration. Both became intensely anxious and elaborated more bizarre hypochonrdiacal delusions. In both instances this worsening condition was promptly relieved by the therapist's statement that he regarded their beliefs as delusional and the explicit examination with the patient of the precipitating cause of the difficulties. The significance of the explicit statement of the delusional nature of the symptoms was useful because it counteracted the iatrogenic intensification of the symptoms caused by the invitation to a psychotic transference by the therapist's commiseration with their symptoms.

Two possibilities suggest themselves to explain this response. First, in the concrete thinking of the schizophrenic, it may be impossible to distinguish commiseration with a distressing feeling state experienced hypochondriacally from concurrence in the opinion that the patient suffers from organic disease. Second, if, as is posited below, commiseration is experienced as an invitation to an intense narcissistic transference, the schizophrenic patient experiences the situation as tremendously dangerous.

Therapists, either when contemplating using or while using this technique, complain of a variety of difficulties. Often they feel inclined to laugh, and will often do so in reporting such work. Although they are only putting into words the patient's distressing feelings, they often feel dishonest or as if they were "putting something over" on the patient. They worry that the patient will believe them to share the patient's beliefs or fear that they are introducing an irreducible parameter into the treatment. The concerns of the therapist correspond to the anxieties of the general practitioner and internist who often wishes to be rid of these "problem" patients, whom they fear will become "demanding" or otherwise very unpleasant, and whom they label with a variety of pejorative terms.

Theoretical Implications

Based on the above clinical generalizations, it must be discovered whether and to what extent the various theories of hypochondriacal symptomatology are consistent with these findings, and to discover, if possible, how the therapeutic results can be explained. Clinical data cannot prove or disprove psychological theories in the same sense in which a crucial experiment might be used to demonstrate the correctness or incorrectness of a proposition in physics. Rather, it must be left to the reader and his experience to determine to what extent the data presented here is consistent with the various hypotheses mentioned. It may perhaps be regarded as a general weakness of psychoanalytic theorizing that almost any data may be explained. Through sufficiently vigorous manipulation of the various premises of the theory, for example, the notion that all symptomatology reflects the outcome of unconscious libidinal or structural conflicts can lead to a situation in which almost any phenomenology can be "explained." Another criterion that may be useful is the parsimony of the explanation achieved. In any case, it seems worthwhile to examine to what extent this data can be explained by the various psychoanalytic theories applicable to the patients described.

Freud (1914) viewed hypochondriasis as an actual neurosis in which libidinal suffusion of bodily organs produced the states complained of by hypochondriacs. Schilder (1953) extended this idea to the purely mental realm to include the idea that hypochondriasis reflected an increased intensity of cathexis of ideas concerning bodily organs. Fenichel (1945) proposed that a variety of changes in the distribution of psychic energy could result in hypochondriacal states, including increases and decreases in the cathexis of the organ itself or the idea of the organ. Hypochondriacal states were believed by him frequently to represent a transformation of castration anxiety—as in the case of the Wolf Man (Mack-Brunswick, 1928)—and the hostility directed toward ambivalently cathected introjects. Glover (1939) in addition emphasized the use of disturbed bodily states to communicate painful and otherwise unverbalizable experiences. Sullivan (1956) emphasized the interpersonal nature of the hypochondriacal state, indicating that it was the result of a system of communication in which the child could only express subjective distress in terms of such bodily complaints.

Arlow and Brenner (1964) view hypochondriacal complaints from a point of view that avoids psychoeconomics and see it instead as a condition whose dynamics are identical to those of hysteria (the expression in bodily language of a compromise between the wish and the defense against that wish), but which occur in the presence of an ego more disturbed than that of the hysteric.

They emphasize that in this view the manifest anxiety of the hypochondriac reflects a failure of defense.

Klein (in Siegel 1964) emphasizes the role of introjected dangerous objects in the etiology of hypochondriasis. In the paranoid-schizoid position, dangerous, annihilative objects, onto which aggression has been projected, may be reintrojected in an attempt to control them, resulting in the hypochondriacal state (Siegel 1964). Rosenfeld (1958) follows Klein in emphasizing the role of hostilely cathected introjects but goes further in positing a need for such introjection on the basis of a highly disorganizing fragmented state.

Kohut (Kohut 1971, Kohut and Wolf 1978) has formulated hypochondriacal states as a reflection of fragmentation of the self. Stolorow (1977), returning to Freud's initial formulation, observes that the paper *On Narcissism* (1914) was written prior to formulation of the second theory of anxiety and it might be useful to reformulate Freud's observations and thoughts on hypochondriasis in view of this theory—that is, that the individual experienced hypochondriasis when there was a danger of the decathexis of the entire self and recathexis of separate bodily parts, a regression to autoeroticism following fragmentation of the self. On more empirical grounds, Gedo (1979) proposes that the hypochondriacal states are a symptom of impending self-fragmentation:

> Hypochondriasis might be regarded as a regressive phenomenon, one in which the signal function of the memories of former gratifications has been lost and the capacity to distinguish between memory and perception has been impaired in parallel fashion. In the context of such an explanation, it becomes easier to understand that hypochondriasis is generally the mark of a successful adaptive response to a threatened disintegration of the cohesive self through the reliving of a specific infantile experience (p. 221).

The therapeutic approach to hypochondriasis obviously would seem to depend strongly upon which of these etiologies one understood to be primary. I say "would seem to depend" because of an interesting sequence of events having to do with this research. The method described herein was initially described to the author by William Offenkrantz and seemed, at that time, to be based on Kohut's understanding of hypochondriacal symptoms and, in addition, seemed to be a particularly neat application of Kohut's ideas to a *psychotherapeutic* situation. It was only many years later, when Offenkrantz and Tobin read a draft of this paper, that the author learned that their ideas of hypochondriasis were much closer to those of Arlow and Brenner and that they viewed hypochondriacal symptoms as a result of conflict. They understood the mode of action in the therapy as the therapist's lowering his own ego ideal and thereby allowing the patient to identify with the therapist and evolve a less punitive attitude toward himself. This is markedly different from the understanding of the mode of action of the interventions discussed here in self-psychological terms. This episode should serve as a warning that it is extremely difficult, certainly on the basis of the efficacy of a single therapeutic technique, to distinguish the dynamics of a psychopathological state. The fact that the technique proposed here was effective cannot be taken as evidence that will distinguish the various hypotheses listed above as etiologies of hypochondria.

However, it remains important to attempt to discover the mode of action of this therapy. The main features of these therapeutic endeavors that have been demonstrated repeatedly in the above material are (1) that the therapist's deliberate commiseration with the patient's distress results in the prompt relief of the nonschizophrenic, true hypochondriac's hypochondriacal concerns; (2) that the patient is initially highly skeptical of the therapist's authenticity in offering such commiseration; and (3) that therapists experience a sense of acting inauthentically or sadistically often followed by (4) an experience of acute awareness of the degree of the hypochondriac's distress when they put into words what the patient has told them and state explicitly their understanding of the patient's distress. Therapists are also often concerned that they have produced an unmanageable and irrational situation between themselves and the patient. With relief of the initial hypochondriacal complaint, a wide variety of underlying psychopathologies come into focus and may or may not be pursued in depth in the therapy. In those instances where the hypochondriacal symptomatology is pursued in depth, it is invariably found to be highly overdetermined in its specific meaning but seems to recur most commonly in responses to interruptions either actual or empathic in the relationship between therapist and patient. Although it is impossible to fully document this statement, it has not been this author's impression that this initial therapeutic intervention has constituted an interference with the examination of conflictual determinants of the hypochondriacal symptomatology, nor has it interfered with an examination of the function of the therapist's initial activity, but rather has served as a vivid example to the patient of the importance of the therapist's empathic comprehension of the patient's position.

It is my view that when the therapist explicitly commiserates with the patient, he is inviting the individual who is threatened with impending fragmentation to form a self–object transference to the therapist and use the therapist in place of the missing soothing structure. The patient and therapist both initially respond to such an invitation with conscious discomfort and *conscious* concern about the therapist's failure to live up to a physicianly ego ideal. The anxiety arises from the extremely rapid development motivated (on the patient's part) by the extreme danger of an archaic transference. The therapist's discomfort arises by the same mechanisms that Kohut (1971) discusses in detail with regard to the counter-transferences to narcissistic transferences, except that the acuteness of the transference formation intensifies the therapist's discomfort and leads to grosser and more emergency-like defenses, typically the evocation of an ego ideal that would not permit such a regressive mode of relating. The avail-ability of the therapist as a self–object to the patient results in the rapid re-establishment of narcissistic equilibrium, i.e., the removal of the threat of fragmentation of the self, and consequently the relief of hypochondriacal symptoms.

There are alternative hypotheses for the mode of action of this therapy. One, mentioned above, is that the therapist's subjective experience of failing to live up to his analytic ego ideal is precisely accurate, and that his sense of guilt and disappointment in himself results from this. However, when the therapist lowers his own standards and makes himself available for the patient's identification, the patient can decrease demands of the patient's superego, and consequently be relieved of symptoms arising from conflict.

Another group of ideas that would explain efficacy of these therapeutic measures has to do with Glover's (1955) notion of an inexact interpretation and a group of ideas developed by Langs having to do with what he called misalliance cures, type C therapy, and lie therapy (Langs 1978, 1980). All these therapeutic modalities are based on the unconscious or conscious collaboration of the patient and therapist to avoid the full truth of the meaning of the patient's symptomatology. Rather, some statement or position designed to disguise this truth and at the same time sufficiently close to it to constitute a good disguise is used instead. The therapist's discomfort and the patient's initial skepticism regarding the therapist's statement then could be understood as reflecting both their unconscious (or possibly preconscious) awareness of their collaboration to hide the truth of the patient's situation. While it is difficult to demonstrate that a given therapeutic intervention is not an example of lie therapy, certain observations seem to argue against these interventions as properly falling under that rubric. The first is Glover's (1955) observation that the difference between an inexact and an incomplete interpretation is often only the question of whether or not the interpreta-tion is completed or is intended to be completed. For example, an interpretation that emphasizes only the patient's attempt to adapt to a current reality may have the therapeutic effect of an inexact interpretation but is not an instance of lie therapy, unless it is explicitly or implicitly indicated that it constitutes a total explanation of the situation. The state-ment that the patient is suffering greatly, if meant to indicate that all the patient needs is the therapist's appreciation of his suffering, or that this constitutes a complete understanding of the situation, would be an example of lie therapy. However, if it is the beginning of a further exploration of the situation, its patently true character certainly should not form an interference with such examination. In fact, to fail to observe the fact of the patient's suffering would in fact be untruthful. An additional point is that once engaged in lie therapy, it is extremely difficult for the patient and therapist to give up such an approach (Langs 1978). In the subsequent work with many of these patients, not detailed here, this author has not found that this initial intervention was used by the patients as a particularly vigorous defense against the exploration of other aspects of their psychopathology. Furthermore, therapists were not particularly reluctant to examine with their patients the function of these initial interventions.

Since the postulated mechanism of hypochondriasis and the mode of treatment advocated here did not involve psychological conflict, any reader who is committed to the idea that psychopathology invariably has such conflict as its underlying etiology may argue that this mechanism is a falsification of psychological reality. Furthermore, the view that psychopathology results only from conflict will inevitably result in the position that these initial interventions are a form of what Langs has called "lie therapy." Such a view, of course, does not follow in a model of psychopathology that includes the notion of absent structure and developmental arrest as important aspects of psychopathology. This paper is obviously not the place to argue the correctness of one model or the other, but it is useful to make explicit that the view of what constitutes an appropriate and "truthful" intervention, as well as an attempt to assess such an intervention, will depend, to some extent, on the beliefs regarding possible appropriate models of the mind (see Gedo 1979). It may also be observed that the operational criteria proposed by Langs for truth therapy reflect the expectations of the operation of an interpretation in the case of conflict pathology and not the expectation of what will occur when fully accurate statements are made in the presence of deficit pathology.

The description given here of the dynamics of hypochondriasis does not include an etiological role for aggression. Yet the unpleasant fate decreed by the individual for himself, as well as the therapist's response (anger or an urge to laugh), suggests a prominent role for aggression in this condition. The disappearance of aggression with the establishment of a narcissistic transference suggests that this aggression is not a primary phenomenon of the disturbance but rather the expression of the vicissitudes of "narcissistic rage," which Kohut (1972) has described as a fragmentation product and defensive measure in disturbances of the self. Interpretation of the masochistic aspects of hypochondriasis are thus not directed at the patient's central difficulty. The anger experienced by the therapist is a response to the patient's unconscious demand that the therapist function not as an independent center of initiative, but rather as an aspect of the patient's self.

In several of the cases, initially hypochondriacal (nonsymbolic) concerns were replaced by hysterical (symbolic) symptoms. Freud (1905) observed how the same symptoms could change in meaning during the course of an analysis. Kohut (1971) observed a similar transition from dream elements of narcissistic personalities corresponding to feeling states to symbolic elements in dreams. Such a shift emphasizes the shift in the individual's major concerns with the restoration of narcissistic equilibrium. The defenses against understanding these symbolic elements are enhanced by the shift in meaning of the symptom. The therapist must be alert to such shifts and not mechanically assume that his patient's complaints about bodily distress are hypochondriacal. For example, the depressed woman patient, as her treatment proceeded, produced increasingly clear symptoms representing a fear and wish for inner sexual experience.

The relief experienced by hypochondriacal patients when they establish narcissistic transferences to their therapists, as well as a method that aids them to form such a transference, have been described. However, the fate of these transferences following its initial period has only been cited. To the extent that the function of the therapist is recognized and worked through by the patient, alteration may occur in the patient's personality, making the individual less vulnerable to the threat of fragmentation that is experienced as a hypochondriacal state. To the extent that this does not occur, the individual remains vulnerable but, because of the temporarily restored sense of self in the treatment, he is better able to function and establish sources for self-coherence outside of treatment.

REFERENCES

Arlow, J., and Brenner, C. (1964). *Psychoanalytic Concepts and the Structural Theory.* New York: International Universities Press.

Balint, M. (1957). *Problems of Human Pleasure and Behavior.* London: Hogarth Press.

Balint, M., et al. (1970). *Treatment or Diagnosis.* London: Tavistock.

Burnum, V. F. (1973). What one internist does in his practice. *Annals of Internal Medicine* 78:437–444.

Castelnuovo-Tedesco, P. (1975). Brief psychotherapy. In *American Handbook of Psychiatry,* eds. D. X. Freedman and J. E. Dyrud 2nd ed., vol. 5, pp. 254–268 New York: Basic Books.

Eissler, K. R. (1953). The effect of the structure of the ego on psychoanalytic technique. *Journal of the American Psychoanalytic Association* 1:104–143.

Fenichel, O. (1945). *The Psychoanalytic Theory of the Neuroses.* New York: International Universities Press.

Freud, A. (1965). *Normality and Pathology in Childhood.* New York: International Universities Press.

————. (1969). Adolescence. In *The Writings of Anna Freud,* vol. 5. New York: International Universities Press.

Freud, S. (1905). Fragment of an analysis of a case of hysteria. *Standard Edition* 7:3–122.

————. (1914). On narcissism: an introduction. *Standard Edition* 14:67–102.

Garfield, S. R. (1970). The delivery of medical care. *Scientific American* 222:15–23.

Gedo, J. (1979). *Beyond Interpretation.* New York: International Universities Press.

Glover, E. (1939). *Psycho-Analysis.* London: Staples Press.

————. (1955). *The Technique of Psychoanalysis.* New York: International Universities Press.

Kenyon, F. F. (1976). Hypochondriacal states. *British Journal of Psychiatry* 129:1–14.

Kohut, H. (1971). *The Analysis of the Self.* New York: International Universities Press.

————. (1972). Thoughts on narcissism and narcissistic rage. *Psychoanalytic Study of the Child* 27:334–359.

Kohut, H., and Wolf, E. (1978). The disorders of the self and their treatment: an outline. *International Journal of Psycho-Analysis* 59:413.

Langs, R. (1978). *Technique in Transition.* New York: Jason Aronson.

————. (1980). Truth therapy, lie therapy. *International Journal of Psychoanalytic Psychotherapy* 8:3–34.

Mack-Brunswick, R. (1928). A supplement to Freud's "History of an infantile neurosis." *International Journal of Psycho-Analysis* 9:439–469.

Nemiah, J. (1975). Hypochondriacal neurosis. In *Comprehensive Textbook of Psychiatry*, vol. 1, ed. D. X. Freedman et al., pp. 1273–1278. Baltimore: Williams and Wilkins.

Offenkrantz, W., and Tobin, A. (1975). Psychoanalytic psychotherapy. In *American Handbook of Psychiatry*, 2nd ed., vol. 5, ed. D. X. Freedman and J. E. Dyrud, pp. 183–205. New York: Basic Books.

Redlich, F., and Freedman D. (1966). *The Theory and Practice of Psychiatry.* New York: McGraw-Hill.

Rosenfeld, H. (1958). Some observations on the psychopathology of hypochondriacal states. *International Journal of Psycho-Analysis* 39:121–124.

Schilder, P. (1953). *Medical Psychology.* New York: International Universities Press.

Siegel, H. (1964). *Introduction to the Work of Melanie Klein.* New York: Basic Books.

Stolorow, R. (1977). Notes on the signal function of hypochondriacal anxiety. *International Journal of Psycho-Analysis* 58:245–246.

Sullivan, H. S. (1956). *Clinical Studies in Psychiatry.* New York: Norton.

On Feeling Understood

ROBERT D. STOLOROW, Ph.D.

A discussion of "The Opening Phase of Psychotherapy of Hypochondriacal States," by R. M. Galatzer-Levy, M.D. When the therapist communicates an accurate comprehension of a patient's hypochondriacal anxiety, the patient may feel that his or her deepest dreads of self-disintegration and self-loss, represented symbolically in the hypochondriacal concerns, have been empathically understood. This feeling of being deeply understood tends to revive early mergers, whereby the therapist becomes established as an archaic self-object. Working through the self-object tie consolidates the structural prerequisites for a therapeutic alliance.

Dr. Galatzer-Levy has presented several cases of hypochondriacal anxiety in which the therapist's communication of an empathic comprehension of the patient's terror and anguish in the initial phase of treatment resulted in rapid alleviation of the hypochondriacal worries and contributed to the eventual establishment of a working therapeutic relationship. In these cases, hypochondriacal spells both signaled and concretized a disturbance in the sense of self-cohesion (see Stolorow and Lachmann 1980, pp. 120–128), for the most part triggered by the disruption of a relationship with someone on whom the patient had relied as a "self-object" (an archaic object experienced as incompletely separated from the self and serving to maintain the sense of self, substituting for missing or precarious self-structure; Kohut 1971, 1977). Dr. Galatzer-Levy theorizes that a patient who is threatened with self-fragmentation experiences the therapist's early empathic communications as an invitation to form a new self-object tie, which leads to restoration of the sense of self-cohesion. Consequently, the hypochondriacal symptoms recede so long as the self-object bond to the therapist remains intact, and the patient becomes able to engage in joint explorations of his or her psychological problems.

These clinical observations and theoretical formulations seem to be essentially sound and valid, not only for hypochondriacal states, but for the treatment of a wide variety of psychological conditions arising from deficiencies in the structuralization of the sense of self. Dr. Galatzer-Levy has thus contributed a useful application of the psychoanalytic psychology of the self to the initial phase of psychotherapy with developmentally arrested, self-disordered patients.

He does not do justice to his contribution, however, when he refers to his technique as "commiserating" with the patient. What is commiseration for the therapist may constitute a profoundly important experience for the patient of feeling that his or her deepest dreads of self-disintegration and self-loss, represented symbolically in the hypochondriacal concerns, have been empathically understood. It is not commiseration but the feeling of being deeply understood that enables the patient to become immersed with the therapist in the archaic self-object tie to which Dr. Galatzer-Levy rightfully attributes the early symptomatic improvement that he has observed. When the "commiserating" therapist experiences a momentary sense of inauthenticity or a transitory urge to laugh, these in part arise because he or she has not yet fully grasped the significance of his or her empathic communications from within the perspective of the patient's archaic frame of reference. While commiseration may constitute a "parameter," communication of a correct empathic comprehension of the nature and meaning of a patient's subjective states does not. As is shown especially clearly in Dr. Galatzer-Levy's experiences with psychotic patients, such comprehension must include an understanding of the patient's need *not* to be understood and of the specific subjective dangers posed by the self-object bond for which the patient yearns—for example, the threat of self-extinction through merger with the self-object, or of reexperiencing the shattering, traumatogenic disappointments of his or her past.

Dr. Galatzer-Levy's paper alludes to the important problem of establishing a therapeutic alliance with developmentally arrested, self-disordered patients (see Stolorow and Lachmann 1980, pp. 180–184). A prerequisite for the establishment and maintenance of a therapeutic alliance is that self and object representations have in large part become differentiated and integrated. Not until the therapist is recognized and accepted as a more or less separate and whole object can a reciprocally collaborative relationship be formed. To the extent that self and object representations are vulnerable and the therapist is needed as a self-object for the maintenance of the patient's self-cohesion and self-continuity, a therapeutic alliance will be unavailable in the therapeutic situation. In such cases, the inability to form a therapeutic alliance is rooted in the same developmental interferences that produced the patient's psychopathology. Hence the treatment of structural deficiencies and developmental arrests and the establishment of a therapeutic alliance are identical processes. The successful treatment of developmental arrests, through the formation and working through of archaic self-object ties, consolidates the structural prerequisites for a therapeutic alliance.

As Dr. Galatzer-Levy's cases illustrate, in the treatment of developmental arrests, and thus in the establishment of a therapeutic alliance, the therapist's empathy plays a crucial role, compensating for developmental voids in the patient. The patient's experience of the therapist's empathic communications may be viewed as a precursor or *prestage* of a therapeutic alliance (Stolorow and Lachmann 1980, pp. 180–184). Joint explorations of various aspects of the patient's life and difficulties may at times be undertaken, but the patient will tend to experience the therapist's empathic understanding as a revival of early mergers, whereby the therapist becomes established as an archaic self-object.

Empathic communication is to be distinguished from a therapeutic "misalliance" (Langs 1975), in that in the former the therapist's understanding of the patient's subjective states does not constitute an agreement with the patient as to their actuality, but rather a comprehension of their psychological meaning and impact. Empathic communications are those that elucidate aspects of the patient's subjective world, including its affective nuances. The therapist speaks, thereby, not as an outside observer but from the vantage point of the patient's psychic reality. Furthermore, when treating developmental arrests, the therapist accepts the psychic reality of the patient that the therapist must serve as a self-object. The therapist does not demand of the patient that he or she be accepted as a separate and whole object, although as this developmental milestone is achieved, the therapist will recognize and acknowledge it. By accepting the role of self-object, as Dr. Galatzer-Levy was able to do with his hypochondriacal patients, the therapist is in a position to make a contribution to the patient's capacity for self-observation through the eventual internalization of the empathic bond that becomes established (Atwood and Stolorow 1980).

REFERENCES

Atwood, G., and Stolorow, R. (1980). Psychoanalytic concepts and the representational world. *Psychoanalysis and Contemporary Thought* 3:267–290.

Kohut, H. (1971). *The Analysis of the Self.* New York: International Universities Press.

———. (1977). *The Restoration of the Self.* New York: International Universities Press.

Langs, R. (1975). Therapeutic misalliances. *International Journal of Psychoanalytic Psychotherapy* 4:77–105.

Stolorow, R., and Lachmann, F. (1980). *Psychoanalysis of Developmental Arrests: Theory and Treatment.* New York: International Universities Press.

Thoughts on Countertransference (with Reference to Some Aspects of the Therapy of Colleagues)

SUSANNA ISAACS ELMHIRST, F.R.C.P.

This paper describes some countertransference problems revealed by psychoanalytic work with professional colleagues. Guilt can be provoked, consciously or unconsciously, by such patients if they are experienced as parents damaged by being turned in fantasy into babies. This can lead to omnipotent defensive maneuvers in the analyst. What then follows is idealization of self and/or object and abnormal identifications instead of normal, reparative responses.

A PERSONAL NOTE

This paper has been developed from one delivered at a National Conference on Countertransference, organized by the Advanced Institute for Analytic Psychotherapy in April, 1978. The ideas put forward in it were stimulated by the colleagues (from medical and nonmedical branches of the professions) who, during the seven years in which I worked as a psychoanalyst in the United States, have worked with me in analysis and supervision. Since the clinical material was obtained from people who might readily be identifiable in their professional circles, I have been presented with special problems of confidentiality. However, it has seemed to me that additional understandings of countertransference reactions justified publishing my views, even though the clinical examples may seem to the reader to be inadequately detailed and convincing.

In the 36 years since I qualified in medicine, I have been increasingly impressed by the difficulty many doctors have in caring professionally for their colleagues. It is a wry, even generally accepted, "joke" that to be a doctor, or a member of a medical family, is an additional hazard when illness

occurs. I have often wondered why this should be so, about what unconscious anxieties were so commonly aroused that proved unmanageable
to many normally reliable doctors and nurses. When the clientele of my
psychoanalytic practice was changed by my move to this country, I found
some answers which seemed to me to throw light on the above mentioned
problem, as well as on a particular aspect of psychoanalytic work. In
substance, my original contribution lies in an extension of Money-Kyrle's
(1956) discovery that countertransference difficulties, even problems interfering with clinical effectiveness, can be aroused when patients are experienced as the analyst's own damaged internal objects. The aspect of this
problem that I have observed is that the colleague-patient can be experienced
as a parent who, in the analyst's own infant and childhood fantasies, has been
damaged by being transformed into a helpless child.

HISTORICAL SURVEY

When Freud started to develop the psychoanalytic method of study, he
discovered that his patients brought very intense, and often irrational,
emotional experiences into the consulting room and that he became the focus
of these feelings. Freud called this phenomenon transference. At first he
thought of transference as a barrier to insight. In 1912, he wrote of transference as "the most powerful resistance," seeing it as a force working against,
rather than for, his aim of relieving people who were in trouble because
their unconscious minds disturbed their mental and physical functioning.
    In the following five years, he developed his understanding to the point of
the following description:

> Thus the transference becomes the battlefield on which all the mutually
> struggling forces should meet one another. All the libido, as well as
> everything opposing it, is made to converge solely on the relation with
> the Doctor—since a fresh repression is avoided, the alienation between
> ego and libido is brought to an end and the subject's mental unity is
> restored" (Freud 1917, p. 454).

His statement that the alienation between ego and libido will be brought to
an end has been taken by some to mean that Freud believed that the normal
mind does not have to struggle continually with forces that interfere with the
free-functioning of the life instinct. However, this is a misunderstanding of
Freud's awareness of the life-long nature of mental conflict. He made it
clear, particularly in *The Interpretation of Dreams* (1900), that he was well
aware that dreams, and the varying emotional states that they represent, are
a natural, normal phenomenon throughout life. He also discovered that

transference is the way in which internal, mental attitudes influence relationships with all the people in a human being's world, be that person child or adult, healthy or emotionally disturbed.

What the psychoanalytic setting does is concentrate the transference in such a way that the analyst has evidence with which to formulate interpretations. I see interpretation as the essential, distinguishing tool of the psychoanalyst, and thus of the psychoanalytic psychotherapist. As defined by Strachey (1934), a mutative interpretation verbalizes, for the patient, the link between the existing emotional situation in the session with previous unconscious experiences of what Strachey called "archaic fantasy objects." Such interpretations further concentrate the emotional forces of the transference on the analyst.

Freud did not think that psychotic patients could develop a transference but I can find no record indicating that he thought healthy people would not do so if they found themselves in a psychoanalytic situation. This is evidence of Freud's view that unconscious mental processes are real, life-long, and vitally necessary. Living people, however normal, are constantly confronted with situations stimulating affect and thus presenting opportunities for mental growth, or failure. Such a view is incompatible with the notion recently expressed by a senior colleague, who said of a would-be analyst that he should change to a training analyst soon "so that there is something left to analyze." Only in physical death is there no unconscious life, nothing left to analyze. By this statement I do not mean to imply that every patient can respond with growth to psychoanalysis. Not all that the psychoanalyst can see of a patient's mental world is acceptable to, or usable by, all patients. And, of course, what the psychoanalyst can see in a patient's transference offerings depends on the individual capabilities of the psychoanalyst.

Many factors determine the quality of a psychoanalyst's professional work. One factor of fundamental importance is the psychoanalyst's handling of his or her countertransference. The history of Freud's attitude to countertransference was similar to that of his attitude to transference. At first he saw countertransference as a barrier to the analytic aim of helping patients in their struggles for what Freud called "Mental Unity" and what we might be more likely to call integration. His recognition that the countertransference need not necessarily interfere with a psychoanalyst's perceptiveness led him to the realization that his own self-analysis was a unique feat. Freud therefore saw that a basic essential of the psychoanalytic training was for all psychoanalysts to have a personal psychoanalysis. He came to this conclusion in the early 1900s, though he was then still writing of transference as a barrier to a successful psychoanalysis. But he wrote little or nothing about the countertransference thereafter, except to recommend that analysts should return for "refresher courses" of psychoanalysis every five years.

Racker (1968) suggests that Freud did not write much about the counter-transference because of his wish to protect his patients from reading accounts of his personal responses, since he knew that one important defense against understanding the importance of fantasy is to concentrate undue attention on external, objective facts. This view is compatible with Freud's character and professional probity, as portrayed in particular by Jones (1953) and Schur (1972). The temptation to use facts to avoid seeing fantasies can be seen to be greater for patients who are members of our profession than for those who are not. Analytic trainees are bound, through seminars and the associated reading, to know more *reality* details about their psychoanalysts than patients whose relative ignorance does not offer the same opportunity to turn away from the task in hand. The same sort of situation also confronts a psychoanalyst who returns for further analysis after completing formal training. Whatever the reasons for Freud's relative silence on the subject of countertransference, his professional offspring have continued the study of all aspects of psychoanalysis, as he hoped and planned that they should do. It was not until the late 1940s, however, that there was a burgeoning of papers on the importance of countertransference as one of the tools of the psychoanalyst's craft.

It does not seem to me to be chance that the majority of these early papers describing the importance of countertransference as a normal, essential phenomenon, came from psychoanalysts who had been impressed by Melanie Klein's (1932) discovery of the importance and variety of transference responses in all patients, including two-year-old children. Klein's understanding of the relationship between child and analyst, including the child's response to interpretation, opened the way to further study of the psychoanalyst's responses; for she found that interpretation of the negative transference could release the positive transference and free even very young children from fears that were interfering with their use of the nurturing aspects of their environment. But, of course, this discovery led to the realization that it is very difficult to perceive and interpret the infantile negative transference. As would be expected from the early history of psychoanalysis, Klein's discoveries also led to the realization that it was unconscious forces within the psychoanalyst that constituted an important barrier to perceiving what the patient was presenting.

Klein's discoveries about the content and the continuous importance in adults of infantile mental life were greeted by some psychoanalysts with as much shock and horror as that with which the medical profession reacted to Freud's original findings about childhood sexuality. One basic reason for this similar reaction was that their idealizations of themselves as the good children, and their parents as the good adults, were questioned. An un-fortunate response to Klein's attack, as it was experienced, was that a body of psychoanalysts turned against object relations and became convinced that

Freud agreed with them because he wrote once of the psychoanalyst as a mirror, for example, and did not write much about countertransference. In order to maintain their view of Freud as an impersonal, emotionally-uninvolved sounding-board, these analysts had to ignore or deny the evidence of Freud's active involvement in the emotional exploration his patients were undergoing, as vividly revealed in the case histories.

Paula Heimann's (1950) classic paper on countertransference is beautifully succinct. In it she writes, ". . . the analyst's emotional response to his patient within the analytic situation represents one of the most important tools for his work. The analyst's counter transference is an instrument of research into the patient's unconscious" (p. 81). In other words, she looks on countertransference as a normal phenomenon, as an exact counterpart of the patient's transference. For Heimann, the term countertransference covers "all the feelings which the analyst experiences toward his patient" (p. 81). Since thought does not occur without an emotional response I would include all the ideas a psychoanalyst has about the patient, and thus link it with Freud's "free-floating attention." If countertransference is normal, as I, like Heimann, believe it to be, then there can also be abnormal, neurotic, or psychotic countertransference reactions in a way exactly comparable to those of the transference. Psychoanalysts cannot do their work if they are uncontrollably involved in what Strachey (1934) called the patient's "neurotic vicious circle," and in which I would include their "psychotic vicious circle." But we cannot be uninvolved, emotionally or intellectually, if we are going to work successfully as psychoanalysts. So we must search for some way of sorting out our own abnormal from our normal countertransference reactions. Our personal psychoanalysis will be the first, long-drawn-out step, which will have to give way to life-long self-analysis or at least self-analysis throughout one's professional life as a psychoanalyst. If this development in professional independence and awareness is to be achieved, I think it is essential for there to be a considerable period of time in which the analyst-in-training is having supervision of a clinical case while also working, concurrently but of course with a different training analyst, in personal analysis. Failure to arrange this seems to me to deny the initial impact of the transference on the inexperienced and to exaggerate what can be achieved in a training analysis. It is easy enough to read about the transference, but when it first swirls in, over and round one, the impact is very different. Many of the resulting, self-defensive blind spots in the student cannot be perceived, nor their unconscious meanings understood, without the help and discipline of analyst, supervisor, and trainee-analysand cooperating on behalf of the suffering patient.

Racker (1968) wrote, "the direct relationship with the patient lends itself to counter-transference, for the psycho-analyst's choice of profession, like all such choices, is itself based on the object relations of infancy" (p. 106). By this I think that he meant all choices of profession for anyone—not just for psychoanalysts. He was expressing agreement with the concept, first developed by Melanie Klein, of the basic importance for later development of early, internal object relations. So too was Money-Kyrle when, in 1956, he wrote of "normal counter-transference and some of its deviations." He was also developing his own ideas, from a basic agreement with Paula Heimann, that countertransference is a normal phenomenon, use of which is incumbent upon any psychoanalyst who hopes to succeed in his or her chosen aims.

But what are, or should be, the aims of a psychoanalyst? Freud counselled us to beware of "therapeutic zeal." Yet ultimately our aim is to relieve people, if we can, of undue mental pain or undue lack of it, if either is interfering with their mental life and emotional growth. Money-Kyrle's thesis is that our endeavors are in part an expression of a wish to repair our damaged internal objects. It is an essential tenet of the Kleinian theory of mental development that every infant, even in "good enough" external circumstances, sometimes inflicts fantasy damage on its loved objects.

This view is often erroneously taken to mean that Klein believed infants *only* inflicted damage on their objects, or that babies were held by her to be constantly in states of persecutory or depressive anxiety. Actually, she was very concerned with the complexity of concomitant fantasies and their impact on the developing personality. A recent clinical example of simultaneous appreciative and aggressive fantasies comes from the analysis of a colleague who was distressed by my impending absence for ten days. The colleague-patient listened intently to my interpretations which, on this occasion, seemed to be making sense. He described that simultaneously he was having images of a childhood experience in which he remembered reaching out to touch, perhaps to turn on or grasp, perhaps to hit in anger at its coldness, a light bulb over the crib; this bulb was often used to warm and comfort him in an asthmatic attack but was not alight on this occasion. The light bulb shattered and the pieces of broken glass got embedded in the patient's right hand. On this particular occasion, the memory, and the manner of its return, both seemed to me to illustrate fantasies accompanying a good feeding experience (the interpretations he was drinking in) in which the comforting light bulb, representing the mother and my enlightening head, became an object of concrete attack. It was attacked not only when it was coldly absent but also because it had the capacity to be separate, and thus was sometimes out of reach. In this patient such frightening experiences were split off and revealed in childhood as asthma, later in other psychosomatic problems as well as in sexual and work inhibitions.

Acknowledgment of the personally inflicted fantasy damage is an emotionally painful necessity if the internal objects are to be restored to healthy, benign, growth-promoting activity. This acknowledgment is, in normal development, usually achieved largely unconsciously, as is, for example, the resolution of the Oedipus complex. It is this stage of emotional development that Melanie Klein named the depressive position. Repair of the damaged internal objects can follow acknowledgment of damage done and is an extremely important aspect of what Freud called sublimation, which really encompasses all genuinely creative, constructive, and therapeutic activity in childhood and adult daily life.

Agreeing, as I do, with Melanie Klein's idea of the depressive position and its fundamental importance in the growth of the human capacity for constructive and imaginative concern, I also find myself in agreement with Money-Kyrle. And it is his thesis that I want to develop a little further now.

DEVELOPMENT OF PARTICULAR THESES AND ILLUSTRATIVE CLINICAL MATERIAL

In his discussion of the analyst's motivations and possible countertransference abnormalities, Money-Kyrle distinguished the reparative aspects of the analyst's work from the parental aspects, meaning by reparative the healing and caring for his or her own damaged internal objects whom the patient represents for the analyst.

It is necessary to differentiate between reparation and cure. Cure is a medical, not a psychoanalytic, concept. The reparation of an internal object means bringing it to, or bringing it back to, a state of human functioning: alive and benign in the unconscious mind. The process of achieving this inner state is indeed hard, but identifications with such objects are of vital importance in modifying the primitive, harsh, superego and strengthening the ego. Two classic papers that offer fundamental understanding of the affective task involved are Freud's (1915) "Mourning and Melancholia" and Melanie Klein's (1940) "Mourning and its Relation to Manic-Depressive States."

Among the internal objects who were damaged in the infant analyst's fantasies were the parents' imaginary babies, as well as the parents themselves. Thus it is often these damaged babies who are being repaired in fantasy when the analyst's "parental" attitudes are in play. But it is also my experience that all babies and small children damage their parents in fantasy, at times, by reversing the roles of parent and child, using a mixture of projective and introjective identification. This type of fantasy, with the child becoming the idealized, all-powerful parent (or part-object) and the parent turned into the helpless denigrated infant, lies at the root of manic responses and the depressive and persecutory fears resulting from them.

An illustrative example comes from the psychotherapy of a young asthmatic child. In one session, she put me to bed, and kept me there in full view of her preparations (from water and cleaning powder, which represented urine and feces) of a delicious meal for herself, in Mummy's place with Daddy. I was the "silly baby" who was forced to suffer the torments of frustrated greed, envy, and jealousy. I was not allowed to speak. When I inquired what would become of me if I couldn't speak she said "You'll get ill, of course."

Convincing evidence that our adult colleagues are not somehow immune from such responses came to me from a professionally successful patient, not an analyst, with whom I was working on a split-off aspect of the personality manifesting itself as a psychosomatic symptom. He had a dream in which he responded with rage at being given two watches on his birthday. In his rage, he scorned the donor (representing me, as his Mother at a part-object level) and implied that it was babyishly insulting and humiliating to offer *him* anything at all. He was, in the dream, in the fantasied adult position of having no needs, of being above the demands of reality or, indeed, actually the controlling source of it.

Such fantasies, and identifications with parents turned into babies, are commonly found in adults. Assisting the adult patient with growth toward more adult integration is a normal, reparative response to such an internal situation. Countertransference responses that can be responded to usefully are part of this process. But it has been my experience, as an analyst and a supervisor of analysts, that countertransference problems relating to the wish to repair the damaged family are particularly difficult to perceive and control when the patient is a medical or psychotherapy colleague, a term in which I include trainees. Under such conditions the patient *is* an adult member of the family and as such is liable to be the object of any unresolved confusions the analyst may have between fantasy and reality views of his or her own childhood family. Keeping in touch with personal delusional experiences of that nature is no easy task, even if the analyst has previously worked on them in his or her own analysis.

Bion (1962) has been in the forefront of recent investigations into the use and misuse of the patient's projective identifications by the psychoanalyst. In so doing he has provided convincing evidence of how, in very early development, both projective and introjective identifications are experienced concretely. A basic function of the mother, which he calls reverie, is receiving concretely experienced mental states from the infant and acting upon them in such a way as to return manageable, thinkable, feelable, dreamable, rememberable states of mind. The analyst's role is exactly comparable and whatever within the analyst interferes with that function must come under the heading of abnormal countertransference.

Bion, then, sees projective identification as a normal preverbal and non-verbal method of communication. But when it is used with excessive force, either because of great suffering or undue envy of the object, it may be experienced by the recipient as an attack that renders reverie, and interpretative response, very hard. Under such circumstances, interpretations will also be experienced by the patient as attacks, even if not consciously or unconsciously delivered as such.

I think there are indications that therapists nowadays resort too readily to explaining a feeling of assault in themselves as due to the patient's projections into them. The impact of a patient's communications does not always wholly, or even mainly, depend on the patient's unconscious intentions. The psychoanalyst often has personal areas of undue sensitivity in which unbearable suffering can be aroused.

Langs (1976) vividly demonstrates the relevance of Bion's work to analytic psychotherapy. My only worry about Langs' application of Bion's theories is that he seems to me to underestimate the difficulty of reaching a point where normal and abnormal countertransference reactions can be distinguished so that the normal reactions can be used to help the patient. Another way of looking at that problem could be to suggest that Langs overestimates the capacity for self-analysis possessed by his pupils. In my experience, over estimation of the patient's ability to perform self-analysis is not an infrequent problem when the patient is a colleague. Whether or not this is true in his case, as I feared after reading his book, the possibility exists for others.

Dependence, or at least partial dependence, on someone else is inevitable for any patient in analysis, be it called a therapeutic or a training analysis. (I do not agree that the distinction is meaningful.) Therefore, anyone analyzing a colleague will at times be confronted with the experience of an adult member of the family responding as an infant. In other words, the analyst is confronted with his or her own infant fantasies of role reversal come true, and abnormal responses to that guilt-provoking inner situation will be aroused, as well as normal reparative ones. One colleague-patient struggling with such a problem became, unbeknown to me for quite a while, delusionally convinced that I had said he would be finished with his analysis in a few weeks. In identification with this image of me, able to do the impossible, he terminated a patient's analysis prematurely, which led to a very distressing response in the colleague-patient's "baby." One function of this complex phenomenon was intended to be the projection into me of guilt for not being magically curative.

I have a male patient, a nonmedical colleague, who has difficulty in maintaining reliable contact with the affective responses of his patients. Gradually this problem is yielding to our analytic work on his identifications with a mother who has been seen as either a dangerously greedy and envious infant or an idealized, all-powerful, object who could do no wrong. Struggling with a difficulty in experiencing his own feelings about neediness and dependence on me, he had a sequence of dreams in which I, as the Mother, appeared as one or another of his female patients. In these dreams, he was always in the grown-up, leading, dependable, maternal role, so that I was his sick baby.

The detailed associations that made each link between me as the mother and the particular patient in any one dream cannot be revealed for reasons of confidentiality, but they included such matters as linkages of names, eye color, foreign accent, real or imagined foreign or gentile origin, and so on.

Another professional patient, whose associations revealed me as father, dreamt of a little boy asking him, the patient, for help with his unmanageable undergarments, which he called Dr. Brown's. These garments were, by association, revealed as expressing fantasies about me as a mother also, turned into a shitty, confusing mess. So, in this fantasy the patient had no adult parent to identify with normally and was in special difficulty with his own professional patients. With them he had often to confront fear, rage, guilt, and depression about those reactions, from which he tried to escape by omnipotent identifications. In my opinion, this sort of problem is an aspect of the early Oedipal triangle, with one or both parents turned into helpless infants instead of dead adults. Indeed Oedipus' ultimate dependence on his daughter, Antigone, appears to me to represent that aspect of the type of fantasy I am considering.

One patient often reacted to the ringing of the telephone, placed near me, by experiencing the sound as coming from a far corner of the room. Analysis revealed that he projected his intrusive infant self into the phone, usually representing a father but sometimes a mother or baby, and hurled it mentally across the room. When I moved to a new office with the phone in the patient's field of vision, he said it was no longer possible to move it around aurally because it would have seemed "too crazy." This is an example of the increased difficulty people have in accepting their fantasies when they conflict with external reality. Some knowledge of objective fact may help some people differentiate fantasy from delusion; but often a clash between inner and outer reality can lead to repression or splitting off of fantasy, with an idealization of so-called objectivity.

Analysis of this particular problem was certainly made harder by my helplessness in a rented office, with a telephone that would not unplug or be silenced and by the difficulty in getting cooperation from the phone company. However, that intrusion, the ringing phone, is no longer a problem, except that sometimes now its silence evokes anxiety about what has been done to the rivals it has represented.

It has been my repeated experience that real external disasters, such as parental separation or parental death in early childhood, add greatly to the young child's struggles to distinguish external from internal reality, to recognize fantasy from omnipotence. True reparation is interfered with until the internal objects, damaged in fantasy, can be repaired, and this cannot be achieved until fantasy is recognized for what it is. When true reparation is impossible, omnipotent solutions are often sought. This results in neglect of the internal world and increasing persecutory anxiety.

During the course of analytic work with me, an analyst-patient discussed the fact that throughout his career none of his patients had ever got divorced, at least not while they were in therapy with him. He began to be able to consider that this was not necessarily a sign of his success in helping people resolve their marital problems. His confusion between such patients and the divorcing parents of his early life was gradually delineated. It also became clearer that delusional self-idealization had been playing a part, manic (magical) reparation being used to avoid feeling in the countertransference, when, at one year of age, his parents had separated. This added delusional guilt to his struggles with his internal early Oedipal anxieties. What is not at all easy to understand is just *how* such self-idealization is manifest in analytic work unless it leads to actually giving advice to a patient who is idealizing the analyst and thus is prepared to hand over autonomy to him or her. More subtle maneuvers seem to have been in operation with the particular patient I have mentioned and presumably fall in the area of incomplete interpretation, moralistic overemphasis of certain possibilities, implication by tone of voice and choice of word or phrase. I would expect this analyst to continue to have special difficulty with patients with marital problems if they are also colleagues.

A few years ago I had a colleague-patient who often came to his sessions dressed casually, "as he would at home," though he "never did" dress like that with patients. He unthinkingly went to a patient's session in casual clothes, which predictably perturbed his patient. My patient, in turn, was concerned about why he should have behaved in such a way. He consciously accepted my suggestion that he was treating the patient as though he were me, representing some member of the family turned into a sick child. It was a theme we had been working on for some time. Furthermore, his next association was to an occasion when he felt his father to be uncouth and socially inappropriate in dress and speech. This, in turn, led us to a discussion of his identification with a child-like father and how that countertransference response interfered with his reparative function.

On another occasion I was, unusually, ten minutes late for a colleague-patient. I apologized and arranged to make up the lost time. The following day, my patient over-slept and kept a medical patient waiting ten minutes. Following this, my colleague-patient had a dream associated with an appalling sense of guilt, a dream of a room with a stain on the floor for which she felt somehow responsible. It appeared that my lateness was perceived by my patient as evidence that I was a hopelessly damaged mother turned into an infant, able only to make messes or abort babies. Furthermore, this fate was felt to have befallen me because of the projection into the father (the other patients) of a destructive infantile aspect of my patient. The result was a hopelessly irreparable situation, with the colleague-patient's chosen "solution" being confused and complex identifications that did not relieve her guilt. However, she was also working in personal analysis to repair the internal damaged family.

Even had I known at the time what countertransference problems led to my lateness, I would not have thought it helpful to tell the patient. The setting and timing of sessions, our apologies for our mistakes, and our sometimes successful efforts to correct them, seem to be sufficient evidence of our existence as "real" people.

A female patient, a lay psychotherapist, whose father had had a prolonged illness during her childhood, became delusionally confused at times by a very depressed male patient (a medical psychoanalyst) who attempted to project guilt into her. The confusion between a bad internal father, her male patient, and a split-off aspect of the colleague-patient's transference view of me presented a difficult problem. The problem was experienced as intractible, permanent and insoluble by my patient and was projected as such into me. At times, conscious self-analysis on my part was required to prevent or resolve abnormal countertransference reactions to the projections of excessive guilt, despair, and confusional terror. At other times the countertransference worked spontaneously and my mind responded with memories of the patient's previous communications, thoughts of other patients in similar plights, and apparently random notions that turned out to be relevant. In other words my free-floating attention was directed inward as well as outward. I describe this because it seems to me that there is a tendency nowadays to believe that a patient's projections will lead to conscious emotional experience in the countertransference, with some apparent implication that one is in trouble if one responds unconsciously in a way that leads to conscious imagery and thought. Yet unconscious use of knowledge and experience is what we call intuition, which Bion repeatedly reminds us is an essential tool for the psychoanalyst. His much misunderstood recipe of consciously attempting "to inhibit dwelling on memories and desires" (1970), is aimed at freeing one's mind before each session so that the patient can be approached expectantly, waiting to see what experiences he or she brings and arouses from the analyst's own living unconscious depths. Such an approach involves tolerating ignorance, not-knowing, which is an aspect of helplessness that plays an important part in the development of the mind from infancy onward. Avoiding such helplessness by idealizing memory and "facts" interferes with learning from each new experience.

Similarly, idealization of the self and the object, attributing magically curative powers to one or both, works against the internal tasks of mourning and reparation. It is often deeply unconscious and often shows itself in countertransference anger at the slowness or the incompleteness of the patient's recovery. If this anger is aroused consciously, it may be possible for the analyst to work on it. If it shows as cutting phrasing or timing of interpretations, the analyst may recognize his or her own tendencies, including the wish to project guilt and helplessness back into the patient. I think this is an unconscious intention of self-righteous, idealizing identifications. The situation can be like that with which an aggressive child was struggling. In her efforts to avoid a sense of guilt, with its expectations of punishment and demands for internal reparation, she said of a fight: "He hit me back first." The angry or assaultive analyst may unconsciously be offering the patient apparently rational justification for anger or fear. In order to understand why he or she should be reacting in this way, the response must be perceived by the analyst. The degree of self-awareness needed is difficult to attain without loss of spontaneity.

The use of words like "only," "just," or "always" to describe partial, temporary responses may be noticed by the analyst and controlled until self-analysis reveals the underlying reasons. Changes in the analyst's tone of voice may be similarly perceived and dealt with. But if they are not, the analyst who is no longer in supervision must rely on his or her patient's observations, a not very helpful source when the patient is in either a state of idealizing his or her analyst or in a state of persecutory anxiety, searching for evidence that his or her fears are justified and not irrational. The difficulty of confronting primitive internal attacks is always great. Psychoanalysis is a profession that inevitably entails periods of mental pain for both patient and psychoanalyst. This is a fact that is relevant to a social situation where there exist hugh demands for relief of emotional problems and great reality difficulties in finding trainees who can afford to train, patients who can afford to be treated, and personnel who have time to work analytically. Shortcuts are very tempting; those offered by physical remedies are probably not such a problem to readers of this journal as is the shortcut offered by unconscious idealization. Ten years ago, Milton Senn came to visit my hospital department of child psychiatry in London. He said that he was very worried about psychoanalysis in America, as indeed Freud had been before him. Senn said that people were very disillusioned with psychoanalysis in America. My reply was that one good thing to be said for psychoanalysis in England was that nobody had ever been illusioned with it. Of course, that was not uniformly true, but overall it was a valid comparison. I think that one important reason for this difference was Melanie Klein's presence, working in our midst on the problems of idealization in infancy and the persecutory fears that are its inevitable corollary. That she, and Anna Freud, were there at all was because the medical model was not retained in British psychoanalysis and so nonmedical people, including women, were welcomed to enrich us with their work. By their very active presence, they undermined the common tendency to idealize themselves, which doctors share with the many patients who idealize doctors as all-powerful parents in control of matters of life and death.

Understanding the way in which our analytic patients can be seen by us as our own parents, turned in fantasy into children, can also help us as psychiatrists of adults or children understand the way in which parents unconsciously experience their own children as the damaged and dangerous parents turned into children. Working as a psychiatrist with parents and children, I found that one disadvantage of having psychotic parents may not become apparent until the children in turn become parents: then their normal babies, using normal nonverbal methods of communication, can be equated with the psychotic parents and reacted to accordingly. The aim of training programs, and of our self-analyses, must be to avoid similar situations in analytic work or to comprehend them when they do occur, so that we can transform our abnormal countertransference reactions into normal, usable responses.

REFERENCES

Bion, W. (1962). *Learning from Experience*. London: Heinemann.
————. (1970). Attention and interpretation. In *Seven Servants*. New York: Jason Aronson, 1977.
Freud, S. (1900). The interpretation of dreams. *Standard Edition* 4, 5.
————. (1912). The dynamics of transference. *Standard Edition* 12:104.
————. (1915). Mourning and melancholia. *Standard Edition* 14:239–258.
————. (1917). Introductory lectures on psycho-analysis. *Standard Edition* 16.
Heimann, P. (1950). On counter-transference. *International Journal of Psycho-Analysis* 31:81–84.

Jones, E. (1953). *Sigmund Freud: Life and Work*. London: Hogarth Press.

Klein, M. (1932). The psycho-analysis of children. In *The Writings of Melanie Klein*, vol. 2. London: Hogarth Press, 1975.

———. (1940). Mourning and its relation to manic-depressive states. In *The Writings of Melanie Klein*, vol. 1, pp. 344–368. London: Hogarth Press, 1975.

Langs, R. (1976). *The Bipersonal Field*. New York: Jason Aronson.

Money-Kyrle, R. (1956). Normal counter-transference and some of its deviations. *International Journal of Psycho-Analysis* 37:360–366.

Racker, H. (1968). *Transference and Counter-Transference*. London: Hogarth Press.

Schur, M. (1972). *Freud: Living and Dying*. New York: International Universities Press.

Strachey, J. (1934). The nature of the therapeutic action of psycho-analysis. *International Journal of Psycho-Analysis* 50:277–292.

Psychoanalysis of the Impulsive Character: A Linguistic-Communicative Study

DAVID ROSENFELD, M.D.

The importance of the mode of communication, the dreams, and the linguistic study of impulsive patients is examined. The significance of the use of the imperative mood, with a rapid evacuation rhythm and good synchronization between the verbal and paraverbal levels is explicated. The obvious linguistic differences between sessions show, together with thematic clues, that it would be possible to predict impulsive discharges, that is, to formulate a predictive theory. The concept is defined, and clinical material is provided to illustrate the concept. A linguistic analysis of the patient's dreams is presented, as well as a thematic approach to the dreams. The ultilization of linguistics in psychoanalysis is systematized, and the verbs used by the patient are listed.

Psychoanalysis started with the investigation of neurotic symptoms, that is, with phenomena that are ego-alien, ego-dystonic, and that do not syntonically fit the character. Character is the ordinary, habitual ways of behavior, and Freud's insight concerning anal character made it possible to study the habitual behavior modes as motivated by unconscious tendencies.

In his work on Dostoyevsky, Freud (1928) wrote of the compromises of the superego's morality as an organized mode that is used not to purify guilt, but to permit new murders. Freud presented the example of Ivan the Terrible. In Dostoyevsky there coincide contradictory and opposing features: selfishness, violence, gambling, raping, epilepsy, on the one hand, and on the other, his immense capacity for love and manifestations of exaggerated kindness. However, a large part of this conflict could be sublimated, enabling him to live in society. "Dostoyevsky's very strong destructive instinct, which might easily have made him a criminal, was in his actual life directed mainly against his own person (inward instead of outward) and thus found expression as masochism and a sense of guilt" (p. 178).

Here an attempt will be made to correlate the characteristics of Dostoyev-sky within the present author's approach to the impulsive character. It is particularly significant that Freud should speak of the relationship in Dos-toyevsky between "his instinctual demands and the inhibitions opposing them (plus the available methods of sublimation)," classifying Dostoyevsky as an "*instinctual character*" (p. 179, emphasis added). In summary, Freud describes Dostoyevsky's general character traits, his masochism, his guilt feelings, his epilepsy, and his twofold attitude concerning the Oedipus com-plex, and then discusses his passion for gambling and his addiction to alcohol. All these features, so strikingly described and explained by Freud, are to be found in almost all the patients that can come under the label of impulsive characters. The clinical case presented in the present paper can be said to include all the features and feelings attributed by Freud to Dostoyevsky. In this respect, the coincidence is sometimes striking. Both cases include addiction to gambling (the gambler is very attached to masturbation and to the mother's sexual nearness). The murder of the father is witnessed by Dostoyevsky and, in our patient, is carried out in Oedipal fantasy with his mother's help (she castrated and murdered the father's moral standards). Regarding transference, Dostoyevsky's dream of the prison corresponds to the patient's dream of being tied up, afraid of the therapist's revenge. (In Dostoyevsky's case prison also appears as a triggering factor of his epilepsy). Dostoyevsky identifies himself with a woman, adopts feminine attitudes, for example with his first wife's lover, as a reaction-formation against his hostility toward his father. Our patient also makes a feminine identification and tries on female clothes. The criminal component that leads to a search for punishment or masochism in Dostoyevsky appears in our patient's dream, in which there is a search for punishment and masochism is eroticized: it is a dream where the patient is searched by a policeman and receives "blows he finds beautiful." Dostoyevsky behaved impulsively toward women; on many occasions, our patient's intercourse with his wife implied raping her, or else he could have pleasure only if a rape were fantasied. Thus, Freud's work is perhaps the most important starting point for the study of this type of patient.

DYNAMIC THEORY

At one pole the impulsive character acts through impulsive discharges, and then the weakening of a stable organization becomes obvious; at the other pole the same patient may resort to the repertoire of behaviors that are nearer the obsessive type. A psychoanalytic treatment, by modifying certain traits, gives rise to states where the patient fears that every change will lead to a dissolution of the personality to the point of psychotic fragmentation, and in that situation the most impulsive traits may emerge as a last defensive link against treatment, in order to expel or control the fear of mental confusion, the unbearable mental pain, or a psychotic transference.

At the pole of impulsive discharges, patients face the present with past experiences that never became historical, and thus they repeat similar acts. They display their inner world through their associations in transference, which take the form of acting out. With these characters there is an alo-plastic tendency. Impulsive neuroses in patients who are accident-prone are rather similar, insofar as they find it hard to tolerate tension, and do not distinguish between acting and thinking and, as the clinical example illustrates, they sometimes try to avoid displeasure rather than look for pleasure.

Some fragments from the analysis of a patient, Horace, are presented in order to point out some of the motivations behind impulsive behavior and to stress that impulsive acts are the result of the coincidence of the inner infantile world with the psychotic transference. The patient's inner world experiences object relationships as blows, violence, and torture, and therefore, genuine dependence is experienced as being tied up and diabolically possessed. If this inner world coincides with an intense transference experience concerning the therapist, the patient finds a way out of that prison through an impulsive discharge that becomes the vehicle of his or her unconscious fantasies. The strength of dissociation is so pathological that the acting out takes place far away from the consulting room.

CLINICAL MATERIAL

Horace is about 30 years of age, newly married, and has an older brother. He remembers having tried on, as a child, women's hats in the shop his mother ran, and having spied on the customers when his mother helped them to try on clothes. There is reason to believe that he engaged in some sexual play with his brother. He has managed to acquire a considerable fortune by means of behaviors at least partially motivated by his frantic madness for possessing. On weekends he regularly drove at very high speed toward gambling establishments or to a racetrack far away from the city; he places where there was gambling or a racetrack far away from the city; he then participated in a perverse sexual activity with a married couple, in which he and the other man tied up the woman with her arms and legs stretched apart, Tupac-Amarú style, and then punished her and did things that aroused her to the point of "madness." The purpose was to make the woman reach orgasm. The patient described the situation, saying that the whole thing ended up amidst disagreeable smells, feces, sweat and semen, and that he felt a prisoner of it all. In the third step of this sequence, his alcoholic addiction was exhibited when, in a state of semi-consciousness, he came back for his Monday sessions. Sometimes he started drinking alcohol before his sexual activity. In the course of his analysis there was a period during which he recounted many of his dreams, which were very difficult to work on due to their overabundance and to the absence of associations. The great number of dreams is a proof of the strength of his dissociation and the power of his impulses. However, their careful consideration after the sessions led to an understanding of the motivating dynamism in his impulses in connection with his transference and, therefore, to an ability to predict, especially toward the weekend, the occurrence of impulsive discharges.

In order to show some aspects of his transference state on a Monday, the beginning of the session is described. The patient said:

> I disappeared from home on Friday and never saw my wife again until yesterday, that is, Monday. On Friday I went out for dinner with some people, then I had my "little party" with the married couple, then I drove very fast to the racetrack in X (another city), then I returned, went back to this couple's house, and had another "party" between the three of us. Then I think I drank a lot and I think I met a girl. What I do remember is that when I was leaving the house, the husband was fucking with the woman and asked me what I was going to do afterwards.

Then he added something worth taking into account: "Why is it that I do all this on weekends, when I have no session? I told my wife, 'On the weekends I disappear, I have orgies, disasters.'"

He is thus showing his omnipotent defense: on the weekends, he excludes and abandons somebody else, the analyst, and acts this out by abandoning his wife. He offered very detailed descriptions of his sexual activities with the tied up woman which "drove her mad." In transference, this was aimed at reversing the abandonment situation of the weekend. He believed that in this way he encouraged the therapist's voyeurism, arousing the therapist with his descriptions and also excluding the therapist from the primary scene, which he also did with the woman's husband during the acting out. On another occasion the therapist pointed out to him that he was projecting a part of himself on to the humiliated, violated woman, and that he made her feel the way he thinks the therapist wants him to feel, which in turn, represents his conception of having to depend on the therapist as a patient.

His response to this interpretation consisted in returning home and breaking an enormous mirror in which he was himself reflected while he was drinking alcohol. This was interpreted as his desire to break the therapist up into hundreds of pieces, to which he responded with intense anxiety and then with a second attack on the interpretation, recalling fantasies of perverse and sadistic sexuality: "I have just remembered the last orgy and I feel very aroused." These words were interpreted as announcing a new impulsive

discharge that would allow him to evacuate what he thought was to introject an interpretation. For him, to receive an interpretation meant being
a woman ("I've just remembered that I told my wife I wanted to have
intercourse with her as if she had a penis and I, a vagina").

Additional sessions are excerpted in order to illustrate the dynamics of the
way in which transference feelings that coincide with the inner world are the
cause of discharges in these impulsive characters. For example, one Thursday
he dreamt that he ended up in jail, tied up with ropes, while the therapist
enjoyed himself until Horace was driven mad. This is, besides, a projection
onto the therapist of the jail in the patient's inner world. Only when transference (as the dream so clearly shows) coincides with the jail in his inner world
(the prison of his continual reenactment of early object relationships),
does an impulsive act occur. On the next Monday following this dream
he described an acting out: he undressed a girl, lay alone on the bed,
and masturbated saying, "I can manage by myself, I don't need you."
Obviously, he was thus attacking dependency by means of perverse sexuality.
After this type of murder of the analytic dependency by means of food,
alcohol, and orgies, he turned up for his session feeling exhausted; sometimes he looked actually destroyed, that is to say, melancholically identified
with the analyst he thought he had destroyed.

On Mondays he described episodes indicating a certain possibility of
having a dialogue with the therapist (for example, "I spoke with a friend
until six o'clock in the morning; I told him about myself, about the analysis;
I told him a lot about myself"). On the other occasions, after the weekend
orgies, he spoke about having met a very old and sad person with whom
he talked about his orgies. In this case, it was interpreted that he saw the
therapist as an old and destroyed person, and that he was trying to arouse
the therapist so as not to see him depressed and destroyed after the attacks
implicit in his orgies. The patient answered, "Just now, when you sighed, I
thought you were tired, fed up with my stories about the old man," thus
confirming the previous interpretation. Consequently he thought that the
therapist was revengeful, violent, and murderous. That was the prison in
which he lived. He had no symbolic possibility of establishing a certain
distance, and, as usually happens in the psychotic levels of the personality, his
terrifying image of the therapist, which coincided with his inner objects
(attacked and destroyed parents who persecuted him in revenge), had become
utterly concrete.

LINGUISTIC ANALYSIS OF THE DREAM CONTENT

The characteristics of Horace's way of communicating become evident
when one compares some dreams he recounted on pre-weekend sessions to

other dreams corresponding to sessions at the beginning of the week, some time later. The Friday dreams reveal motivations and triggering factors, and the dreams after the weekend reveal the effects caused by the patient's acting out.

Description of Dreams

Dreams previous to the weekend (Friday)

(I) I'm away from the city, in the Delta Islands. The houses are built on pillars and there were two drunken boys. There was a bakery, and a wooden cabin, a bar. They were fighting, but they didn't hit each other. A couple of yards from my room there was a demonstration. It was a series of familiar faces. They were below, saying something. The room had only one door. There were neither walls nor roof: I could see the sky.

(II) I was in jail. I ran away to a hotel in Mar del Plata. I went to gamble at the roulette. Suddenly I am at the race track and I am being persecuted. There is a guy standing on the subway stairs who says, "Examine the liver, examine it with apparati." I have run away from jail and they arrest me. I don't know what's going on.

(III) A car stops in the middle of a tunnel. I got lost when coming out of the stairs. There were doors to go into the subway. I got lost in the labyrinth.

For the patient, depending on the therapist meant being in prison, immobilized, tied to the couch on which he was subjected to humiliations, to sadistic investigating behavior that he could only suffer passively. The therapist was tyrannical and Horace had to submit, although all this saved him from becoming de-structured. When the end came he felt helpless, without any support. In dream III, which shows his uncertainty, there is an indication that during the weekend he would try to find himself again and overcome his confusion by means of acting out.

In general terms, these interpretations were offered, as was the prediction that he was likely to resort during the weekend to a reversal, that is, that he would inflict upon somebody else what he suffered during the sessions.

Dreams following the weekend (Monday)
In one of the sessions, Horace unfolded a piece of paper in which he had written down his dreams. The therapist told him that he was trying to order and keep his dreams on a piece of paper so as not to become a victim of his suicidal and self-destructive part. He nodded.

(IV) I was on board a very beautiful modern yacht on my way to Europe. There was a violent windstorm. Owing to the windstorm there were many fallen trees. I told the steersman to be careful, for the trees driven by the wind made it very dangerous. Suddenly there were violent, enormous waves. They were saying that the difficult thing was to cross the Gulf of Saint Catherine, which was the stormiest area, full of waves and where storms were more frequent than in any other part of the world. Suddenly I thought we were coming out of the Paraná river, but then I looked behind and saw that I was in the Riachuelo and didn't understand anything. Suddenly it seemed that the ship had fallen into the Riachuelo or was there. I was terrified of drowning.

The interpretation of this dream, together with those corresponding to the other dreams, was given to the patient at the end of his description. He was told that being on the yacht represented the vicissitudes of the weekend and the analytic journey in the consulting-room where he lay on a comfortable couch in expectation of an experience that he knew would be very long. It also represented his fear of windstorms, of being alone during the weekend, that is, his fear of what was mad, aggressive, and uncontrolled in him, which could only be overcome if the therapist remained a coherent, strong, and orderly steersman, which is what he was asking the therapist to be in the dream. There was the fear that everything that was chaotic in his mind would force him back into the mud (the Riachuelo).

(V) In a street downtown a guy is running. He is wearing a white beret and they are running after him. A friend who is with me says, "That guy is always making trouble." They get him and they hit him terrible blows, beautiful, violent blows.

The patient had a lot of trouble associating in relation to this dream. He thought it had to do with his homosexuality and his fear of fights. He said that, in general, in other dreams he always disguised blows and turned them into caresses. The dream shows his fear of being persecuted. His head (beret) is the target against which aggression is directed, since it is in his head that the identification with the mother took place (he used to try on women's hats in childhood), his homosexual disposition. He felt possessed by a maddening mother, like the ship in the Saint Catherine Gulf. Likewise, he attributed to the therapist the ambition to control his mind.

(VI) I'm at the bar with a friend. Then the police arrive, just when I was planning to leave. I think I was staying only to drink some glasses of water. They tell me to undress because they are searching for drugs and they take me to the bathroom to undress me. They wanted me to confess quickly. I was afraid they might knee me in the testicles. I was afraid they might hurry me and hit me. Finally I shouted that I was the president of the company L., and one of them told me, "We can fix everything for a million pesos," and then added, "All right, half of it now and the rest afterwards, when the trial is over."

After the dream he said:

Last night I got home very late to see my wife. That was because I had been with the married couple in the "little party." We were driving and I told them I had mixed feelings, that I had felt terribly confused about my feelings that week, that I was very mixed-up* about them. We went to have a drink and suddenly, I don't know whether because I was afraid of speaking up or if I became confused, the thing is I said goodbye and left (*he tried to find a word, but in vain**—the word he could not find might have been "abruptly"*) almost running, and arrived in time to be with my wife at the house of my partner's fiancée. Then I told my partner he should start his analysis because if he wasn't well, what was going to happen to the firm?

This was the first time in which he had abruptly left the couple with which he shared his sexual orgies in order to be with his wife.

Thematic Study of the Dreams

Several elements are common to several of the dreams. Only a few aspects are considered here, though the analysis can be extended to many others. The patient feels himself the object of different actions performed by individuals of superior strength: the object of imprisonment, persecution and searching (II), natural forces (IV), searching and blows (V), and at the mercy of others.

The helplessness inherent to this situation becomes manifest in the absence of walls and a roof in the room, in the fact that the house is built on pillars (I), as well as in his nakedness (VI), in his ignorance of what is going on (II), and in his feeling lost (III). The illegal nature of certain activities is suggested in some scenes (I), or more or less openly expressed in other dreams (II and VI). Another important aspect is the hypochondriacal anxiety (II), which has to do with his confusional anxieties and his alcoholic addiction (I).†

---

*Confusion at a linguistic level.

**Syntactic disturbance during the Monday session.

†In the acting out of many alcoholics, the objective is not a splitting or dissociation of a state of confusional anxiety. Rather, the acting out aims at recovering a confusional state, that is, a state of confusion-defense in the face of intolerable paranoid anxieties and persecutory objects.

The hypochondriacal anxiety as a way of self-expression on the bodily level, confusional and persecutory anxieties, and castration anxiety, are experienced by the patient as a consequence of having carried out the fantasy of a homosexual, oral, primary scene: to drink with other men (I). However, apparently this patient is not a manifest homosexual; rather he shows another type of perversion that is the transformation of the previous one. This is one of the ways in which he defends himself from the risk of an ever greater de-structuralization: to use his economic resources to appease men and see to it that his belongings (especially his penis) may be used by a woman for a narcissistic type of gratification by possessing him.

What meaning did the bond with the therapist have for the patient? The therapist was someone who coveted his fortune and treated him out of selfishness and not altruism. The therapist's cognitive and interpretive activity amounted to a penetration that transgressed the patient's limits, thus evoking hypochondriacal anxieties as a result of the therapist's "revengeful persecution" (II).

The same happened whenever Horace had to recognize his own wish and establish a dependent relationship with somebody else. This was impossible for him, particularly when his need was experienced as a humiliation, a submission (VI). He resorted then to the acting out already mentioned, in which he identified himself with a sadistic, tyrannical object, or else with its counterpart, a submissive masochistic object (i.e., he was a prisoner of his sadistic fantasies, which he compulsively displayed over and over again in the Euclidian outer space in the presence of other people who were also involved).

In the dreams before the weekend, where his language is of a more imperative nature, one can detect transference fantasies of attacks, hatred, blows, revenge, the omnipotent wish to be self-sufficient, getting lost in the emptiness of labyrinths. In the dreams after the weekend, one can detect the disastrous aftermath of his orgies: forcing somebody else to feel humiliated and dependent; experiencing the chaos, the confusion, and the storms; and houses that cannot contain him.

MICROLINGUISTIC ANALYSIS

The microlinguistic analysis suggested here has as its clinical objective in this case the prediction of impulsive behaviors brought about by the loss of the equilibrium in the patient's psychic apparatus, on the basis of a systematization of the clues the patient may offer at a verbal and paraverbal level in the course of the session. In this patient's psychic apparatus there was a tendency to corrupt and bribe his father-superego-ego ideal in order to make it ego-syntonic, as is quite common in the impulsive characters.

The type of verbs used by the patient is significant, since this grammatical category expresses the characteristics of the impulse and the conjugation may indicate the end of the impulse (active, passive, reflexive). Likewise, verbs may give some clues as to the qualities of the actions that the patient regards as specific for the fulfillment of a wish. These types of verbs are addressed to different characters in the patient's inner world, characters or psychic places to which one can give proper names or attribute more general characteristics within the Freudian theory. Some verbs have to do with moving through space and habitually indicate the use of mobility as a means of attaining a specific action through contact with an object in a favorable position.

A higher degree of passivity is found in the Monday dreams. Sometimes the first Monday dream is the continuation of the last dream on Friday as regards its content—in both of them there is loss of orientation, for instance—but in the Monday dream the content and the verbs indicate confusion and loss of orientation. These thematic and linguistic clues allow one to predict whether the acting out during the weekends goes on within the patient's mind or if he can reorganize himself within the setting of the session—for instance, when a Monday dream indicates he has overcome his confusion or found a way out of it. In the Friday dreams, verbs are in general more imperative, and this observation may be useful in detecting the impulsive acting out. In this respect, it should be remembered that in the Friday sessions the words and the verbs were: "they were fighting . . . I want to go . . . they persecute me . . . search him."

On the other hand, on Mondays verbs are in general less imperative and sometimes show linguistic elements that may indicate confusional anxiety and relationships with the superego, or the internalized model of Horace's father and his therapist before whom he tries to show off, and whom at the same time he tries to appease through his acting out during the weekend. This is equated to criminal action when the patient becomes aware of certain values in the infantile inner world, as experienced in transference.

The Friday dreams, characterized by a high percentage of imperative verbs, are the way in which his attempt to dominate or to give orders to take possession of another person becomes manifest at the linguistic level. Within the pathology of the impulsive character is the desire to take possession of the other person's mind and body—i.e., as if his arm extended into the therapist's mind or his accompanying objects, and other people's minds become the extension of his own arm. The imperative verb also announces a quantitative amount of instinctual impulsive charge that is on the verge of uncontrolled discharge due to its increase as regards quantity and quality.

The types of verbs the patient used on Fridays are listed and compared with those used on Mondays; in both cases we categorize four items: (1) action having motor effects on the other, (2) punishment or avoidance of punishment, (3) actions aiming at possessing an object, and (4) space displacement.

Fridays

1. *Action having motor effects on the other*, who then becomes an extension of the subject's activity or motor pole. This is related to the pragmatic distortions that appear with an epic style in those patients known as psychopaths. Sometimes there is a hidden delirious belief. Verbs implying depriving the other of a material good or its equivalent: to fight, to ask, to order, to steal.
2. *Punishment or avoidance of punishment* through action (relationship established with the ego ideal or the superego as a *model* of justice): to run away, to persecute, to arrest, to imprison, to search.
3. *Actions aiming at possessing an object.* Bond with the *object* of the wish (mother): to have a drink, to gamble. Gambling and having a drink imply a search through the addiction for an idealized object (the mother's breast) and, at the same time, this action is put to destructive uses in the acting out.
4. *Space displacement* (verbs that are a means to an end): to go, to get lost (a failure in orientation due to lack of an objective).

Friday verbs are presented in the clinical material mainly in the imperative tense.

Mondays

1. *Verbs of action*: to hit, to order, to confess.
2. *Verbs in connection with punishment*: to bribe, to undress.
3. *Verbs in connection with the object of desire*: to get hold of, to drink, to take.
4. *Verbs of displacement*: to run, to get lost (dream of the windstorm), to find himself.

Monday verbs are presented in the clinical material mainly in the passive tense.

CONCLUSION

The systematization of the verbs presented in the sessions leads to the conclusion that they are addressed to different characters in the patient's inner world, characters or psychic places to which one can give proper names or attribute more general characteristics within the Freudian theory. Some verbs have to do with moving through space and habitually indicate the use of mobility as a means to attain the specific action through contact with an object in a favorable position.

REFERENCES

Freud, S. (1928). Dostoyevsky and parricide. *Standard Edition* 21:175-196.

Speech, The Psychoanalytic Method, and Madness: A "Case History"

M. MASUD R. KHAN

The "case-history" precedes the theoretical discussion. "Case-history" is in inverted commas, because it is not a case history in the accepted analytic sense of that word, in so far as it eschews the use of metapsychological concepts. A theoretical introduction would preempt the reader's freedom to experience and evaluate the clinical narrative.

JUDY, AGE 15

This young patient had been compelled upon me by her physician, with whom I had worked for years, for urgent consultation, because she had attempted suicide a few days earlier. The patient was a plain but wholesome looking, buxom, puppy-fat girl. She was wearing the tightest jeans she could possibly have squeezed herself into. Her blouse was unbuttoned to an indecent point. She sat down and was very silent and sullen at the start. She had evidently tried committing suicide by cutting both her wrists, which were heavily bandaged, and which she flaunted by constantly shifting her arms. I concluded that at this visit she was certainly not going to "speak" to me, but merely establish her presence by exhibiting herself. I decided to go along with her antics.

After some 20 minutes of mutually provocative silence, she asked in an aggressive way, "You know what has led to all this?" I replied, "No."—"Don't you read the papers?" I replied, "No." " Then, what do you read?" "Books," I said. "Well, I can tell you it was headline in all the evening papers four days ago: the scandal, and it will be on the nine o'clock TV news again tonight." I simply said, "I don't see TV either," and that even if I did, I would not see it tonight. Instead, I would wait until she was less shamed and could trust to tell me the whole scandal herself. She sank into a raging silence for another ten minutes or so. I waited. Then, with a strange authority in her voice, she demanded, "If you really want to help me, then get me out of school. I cannot go back. I am too shamed, and I shall really kill myself next time." I asked her how I could get her out of the school. She said, "Are you a fool. Ring the headmistress and tell her you are advising me not to return to school. And ring my father and tell him you have done it." I told her that I would do it the other way around. I asked her to ring her father and ask him to speak to me. She did. When her father came on the phone, I introduced myself and said that I had now *seen* his daughter. She feels too shamed to return to school, I told him, and I am sure she means it when she says that if she returns, she will succeed in killing herself this time. So if I could have his agreement, I would ring the headmistress and inform her of "our" decision. He requested me to do so.

Judy rang her school and the headmistress came to the phone. Evidently an elderly, wise lady, in so far as one could tell by her voice and speech. I introduced myself and told her that I was with Judy at the time and had *seen* her condition. It is her decision not to return to school, I said, and I agree with that. I have talked with her father, and he has requested me to ask you not to put any sort of pressure on Judy to return to school. The headmistress was silent for a while, and then said, "Please write all this to me, and we shall not expect Judy to attend school any more."

I scrutinized Judy's face carefully. There was no sly sense of triumph in her expression; only now she put her hands and wrists under her shirt. I had spent nearly two hours with her and was exhausted. I also felt that there was nothing more left to do in this consultation. I deliberately gave her the next appointment after the weekend. I took that risk—I was seeing her on a Thursday afternoon.

When she left, I rang her physician, who had referred her to me, and briefly told him what had expired. I further arranged with him that on Monday (the next consultation) he should come with Judy and with Judy's father. I told him that what was necessary at this stage was *management* (a la Winnicott) and not psychotherapy, and this I wanted to program together with them.

On Sunday, Judy rang me and, since she was on the list of "critical" patients, the housemaid put her through. Judy said that she felt well, so I instantly knew that she was going to make a demand. She paused, and then in the gentlest voice asked, "Can I bring my girl friend with me on Monday, when I come?" I said, "Certainly." This gave me the opportunity to inform her that her physician and father were also coming. She said that she knew. They had told her. That ended the conversation.

An hour before the consultation on Monday, I began to feel extremely anxious, apprehensive and full of paranoid misgivings, and totally lacking in self-confidence with regard to being able to make a clinically positive encounter with the expected "mob." I have always been a one-to-one clinician, and here I felt that I had been bullied by my physician friend into "group therapy." I also felt acutely self-critical about not bothering to find out what the "scandal" referred to. I could have asked the physician, even Judy, or seen the TV news, or the Sunday papers, particularly those that specialize in retailing scandal. Yet I felt that I was right not to have pried. It was not my style of clinical work, and instead of helping me, it would have further incapacitated me. Clinically, I have never found information as such of the slightest use. Alongside, I had such a vivid afterimage of my consultation with Judy, from which I had inferred three things:

1. That the girl I had *seen* was mad, behind all the antics of hysteria she had learnt to manipulate her environment with.
2. That behind the madness there was an ungraspable psychic pain in Judy, which she could neither experience as such nor speak about.
3. For all her bossing me around to do this, say that, she was an utterly resourceless girl and desperately needy of help.

I felt that it had been sheer madness and arrogance on my part to go any further after the consultation and that I should have advised the physician to refer Judy to a medically qualified analyst.

Whilst I was still sweltering in this subjective and private confusion, the bell rang. Thank God, it was the physician. He had come early and was apologetic about it, but I was relieved. I casually asked him what the "scandal" referred to. He told me briefly what it was, and it was really degrading and humiliating. I felt very sad for Judy, because she would have to live with it socially for at least six months.

The bell rang, and this time it was Judy and her friend. Judy introduced me to her friend, whom I shall call Linda. Linda was a young woman, about 25 years old: tall, gauntly handsome, impeccably dressed in a rather eccentric style, with a pleasant voice, and easy to relate to. To start somewhere, I casually asked Judy if she had slept well. She said "I had a weird dream, and said to myself, I must tell this to Khan. But by the time I got out of bed and found a pencil and a piece of paper, I had lost the dream. So I can't tell you anything." I noted her use of the word "lost." Then I chatted with Linda. She ran a small shop, running it successfully for three years now. Waiting for the father to arrive, and to keep the climate alive, I asked her what made her choose that particular task, because it is very hard work. She told me with a casual and rather self-mocking candor that, after a disastrous love-affair at college at 20 years of age, she had had a breakdown and her parents had sent her with an aunt on a world tour for a year. She had been particularly impressed by South American and Arab cultures. When she returned, she was at a loss as to what to do. She didn't want to return to college. One day she suggested to her father that he might be willing to finance her to open a small shop, and he had said, "Of course." So it had all started. I felt deeply relieved by her story, because if I agreed to take Judy into psychotherapeutic care, at least one third of the management side was settled. I would persuade Judy to work half a day with and for Linda.

The bell rang, and at last the father arrived: very polite and shrewd. So now we settled down to the real business. I told him and the physician that unless I could arrange adequate management for Judy, now that she would be idle all day, there would be no question of my taking her into therapeutic care. I deliberately avoided using the concept treatment, because I knew that it would be a long time before we would achieve that mutuality where treatment becomes feasible. First I turned to Linda and bluntly asked her what she felt about Judy working half a day (10:00 to 1:00) with and for her. She was a bit taken aback, paused, and then said, "Certainly. We get on very well together and I need help." Judy looked both pleased and relieved. The next issue, I told the father, was that of Judy's education. She must have a private teacher and study for at least three hours a day. He, with a bland cooperativeness, asked me if I knew of someone who could be asked to coach Judy. I told him that some ten years ago I knew a young man whom I used a lot to teach and coach boys and girls for O and A level examinations. I had his address, but didn't know whether he was still living there and doing freelance teaching, or if he had taken a full-time teaching post. The father requested me to try to get in touch with him. I called my secretary and asked her to ring him and, if he was not at that address, to find him. Fortunately, he was at the same address, and at home with the flu.

She said that he was on the phone and asked if I would like to talk to him. I said that I would, but before I took the phone, I asked both Judy and her father whether I could name the girl I was going to ask him to coach. I was thinking of the "scandal." They agreed. So I talked with Peter, and briefly told him that I had a young girl in my care whom I wanted him to coach, and gave him the name. I could hear him gasp at the other end. I told him that she needed minimally three hours each day, from 3:00 to 6:00. He asked if he could think it over and ring me back in some 15 minutes. He did, and agreed to coach, but said that he had only two hours, from 3:00 to 5:00, and could not start before next Monday. So that was settled. At this point, I agreed to see Judy five times a week at 6:20 P.M. Then suddenly Judy said that she could go to work for Linda and come to me only if Daddy would send his car to take her everywhere. She was not going to travel by bus, tube, or taxi. The father agreed all too readily to make a car available to Judy. At this point, I abruptly ended the consultation, and we all parted, giving Judy an appointment for the next day.

It was now clear to me that it would be a miracle if I could make Judy come in her person and speak herself. She was most vulnerable, and so she would for a long time arrive as a *collage*, and not just herself.

Judy arrived punctually for her next session. When she took off her poncho, I noticed her arm was in a sling. As she saw me looking at it, she gaily remarked that, going to bed last night, she had tripped on the stairs and hurt her elbow, but it was nothing serious. From this I inferred that Judy's self-inflicted body injuries were her way of coping with her ungraspable psychic pain, physically localizing it. It was also her way of not sinking into totally depersonalized states. In the next three months, I was to hear a long history of such body injuries from the age of five onward.

Judy squatted down into the chair. It is important clinically for me to see how a patient uses my clinical space and the furniture available. It tells me more at the start than the patient can possibly speak. Also, the way a patient dresses his/her nudity is very telling for me. The mink coat that she had arrived in for her first consultation was in fact inflicted upon her, as I learnt later, to make her look a little respectable. Judy's normal dress was track boots, tight jeans, a shirt or floppy sweater, and her favorite football club's long socks. From this it was clear that as yet Judy had not differentiated herself into an adolescent girl. She was still a boy-girl being. Her clothes could be worn just as reasonably by a boy of her age.

As I had expected, Judy chitter-chattered about this and that. She had a really witty way of describing people and events, but she talked about and around herself, and not from and of herself. She said that she had enjoyed working with Linda in the morning, but had felt very down (her phrase) all afternoon. There was nobody at home except the staff, and it was her favorite maid's day off. She asked me whether her teacher could not come in for an hour at least this week. I told her that I had been in touch with him and he really couldn't start before next Monday. I suggested that she should ask Linda to let her work full days this week. She said that she would. Then she told me that since the "scandal" had become public, she had stayed at home and seen no friends, except Linda. She added, with a sly look in her eyes, "I cannot eat either, unless Daddy is there. He makes me eat. I just nibble food all day." Here I returned my first interpretative question: "How often do you steal?" I really had no clue as to why I asked that. She blatantly answered, "Not often, and only from one shop. But they earn a lot from us, and I steal only small things, like pencils, rubbers, envelopes, fake jewelry, beads, etcetera." I dropped the subject, but noted that her present symptoms were anorexia, stealing, and phobia.

Fortunately, Linda was only too glad to have Judy work full time that week because she had her "sale" next week and all the objects had to be repriced. Otherwise nothing of importance was said or learnt that week. That weekend, Judy was going with her father to their country house, and she felt very happy about that because she could ride there. She loved horses.

As I thought about the sessions in the first week, what struck me most was that Judy in fact was a very alert, sensitive, healthy person, with a madness inside her, which circumstances over the past years had dislocated into hysterical antics and manipulativeness. She was basically honest, but had been taught to lie by both the parents, and now she herself could no longer tell when she was lying and when she was telling the truth. I felt disappointed with my own contributions during the week, but I had decided to be reticent and watch.

From the first month of her treatment, Judy worked with Linda regularly and had made a very good relationship with her teacher. He found her a very sensitive, attentive, and cooperative student. So all that was well. The problems needing urgent management were eating and sleeping. I got around the eating problem by asking Linda to take Judy out to lunch and make sure that she had a good meal each day. I had her father's word that he would pay for both of them. The problem of sleep was more difficult to manage, since Judy herself never, as yet, had said to me that she didn't sleep well. Instead of asking her, I decided to discuss this with her physician, since he had taken care of her since she was a baby. He told me Judy had great trouble going to sleep, but he could not give her any sleeping tablets because he feared that she might take an overdose. She had three years ago stolen all the tablets from her parents' medicine cupboard, swallowed them, and had to be taken to the hospital and be cleaned out. But he promised he would try and arrange with one of the ladies in the house to give her a tablet each night. In fact, I knew that Judy's inability to sleep had a deeper and other cause and that she would not take the tablets, and she actually did refuse. This convinced me that she was afraid of having a bad dream and I let the matter drop.

The only other important item was that Judy stole twice during this month. Each time it was when something about the "scandal" appeared in the papers. This gave me insight into one function of stealing for Judy. It was that the stolen object was a private unknowable secret that she could live with. Shortly she was to tell me when stealing had started. Otherwise Judy came, Judy chattered, Judy left. I was quite content that she at least was working in the shop and studying with intense diligence. The subjects she had chosen were English Literature, Spanish, and Geography. Linda spoke Spanish fluently.

It was in the second month that things began to happen. One Tuesday Judy arrived, sat up in the chair, and said to me, "I didn't know I was coming here because I am ill. I have just been gossiping, and it is costing Dad a mint." I asked her who had said that she was ill. She replied, "My doctor, my father, and even Linda. I come here so that you can get me well. But I don't know what to speak about. And you don't help. Why don't you ask me questions?" I responded, "All right, tell me when your sleeping problem started." A sudden fury flashed in her eyes and she asked me defiantly, "Who told you that. I sleep very well. Only these days I have to wake up at 8:00 and I can never go to sleep till nearly six. So I don't get enough sleep." And she sank into a raging sullen silence for the rest of the session. I didn't try to fob off her rage. At the end, she got up and left. Next day, when I was expecting her, I was rung and told that Judy was not well and wouldn't be coming tonight, but would come tomorrow. In the evening her teacher rang to say Judy had sent him away, saying that she was ill and would work tomorrow. When Judy returned on Thursday, she squatted in the chair, without taking off her poncho, but her sullenness was not raging but sad. She did not speak a word, nor did I. The same happened the next session, which was Friday. But as she was leaving she said, "I am going to the country house for the weekend for the last time." And she went.

As I thought about the week's happenings, I didn't feel any regret that I might have made a gaff in asking about her sleeping problem. Instead, I felt relieved. I was sure that the period of chitter-chatter had ended and now I would be encountering the ill Judy, and not the one who had come with the alibi of the "scandal." I had no notion as to what form her illness would take or how it would express itself. I felt fearful all the same, and again had that feeling of apprehension and inadequacy that I had after the first consultation. One thing I had learnt about Judy from this episode was that she was acutely paranoid behind her jolly facade. Her acute touchiness was one ruse to evade a flagrantly paranoid response.

There were other clues to her psychopathology and her ruses (I deliberately use this word rather than the concept of defense mechanism) for coping with it that I had gathered from the chitter-chatter period. I had little doubt that her insomnia was a way of avoiding dreaming, especially a dream that could vividly project some event of the past that she had dissociated and/or repressed from her conscious day-to-day identity of being Judy. The most palpable and yet unspeakable psychic pain in her was masked by a myriad of little demands and stealing. This derived, I had surmised, from the traumatic and tantalizing deprivation of maternal love and care. Her father's over-indulgence later had helped her to screen this psychic pain. But all her injuries, accidental or self-inflicted, were the physical "objective conclatives" (to borrow a phrase from T. S. Eliot 1918) for this psychic pain, as was soon to become all too awesomely clear. I knew little about the actual events of her early familial life. I had only vague clues as to why and how Judy was what she had become as the Judy she was exhibiting at present. She had a vociferously intrusive relative who kept ringing me to tell "all," but I had militantly refused to see her. I didn't want to know anything that Judy couldn't tell or speak.

When Judy returned from her weekend in the country (the last visit to her country house), she arrived punctually and was neither depressed nor sullen and rejective, but just sat very still and sad. After a while she began to cry, and managed somehow to say, "Now I have lost everything except Dad. Tim is dead, and the country house has been sold." I could feel her loss and its pain. But what was more frightening was that I had no clue as to which route Judy would take for self-sustenance. She loved riding and wouldn't be able to ride now. She disliked living in London and the school she had been attending in London, because she felt physically lubberly, in manners gauche and in speech uncouth even though, as I have said earlier, Judy had a real feeling for language. But it was part of her protest to go on strike about moving out of her bucolic environment into the sophisticated London set, where the girls of her class were mannered and full of social connivances. In spite of all her rules, lying, and other ways of masking her psychic pain and madness, Judy was an authentic person with a will of her own. For example, she had refused to wear the fancy school uniform, and stayed in her jeans and a jumper or shirt.

I had noted that, when she had said, "I have lost everything," she had not included her mother. Once her mood had settled to quietude, Judy volunteered to *tell* me about herself. She started by talking about Tim, her pony. Her father had given Tim to her for her fifth birthday. During the rest of the week I heard all about her relation to Tim. How the butler once caught her sneaking out of the country house with pillow and blanket to sleep in Tim's stable. She had been sleeping in the stable for a week or so. Her father got to hear of it and, such was his indulgent generosity of affection for his daughter, he had a stable made as an extension of the house itself. He already knew how lonely and traumatized Judy was. In Winnicottian metaphor, one could say that Tim was Judy's transitional object. She wrote stories *for* him and drew pictures of him with verses, as she grew more capable maturationally. Tim died from a gastric ailment when Judy was twelve. Gradually, I got to know Tim as a person in Judy's life, and it showed me what a profound capacity this girl had for compassion and care. The surprising thing was that the more she talked about Tim, the less phobic she became, and she started to go out with her father and Linda, to theaters and restaurants. She was also eating and sleeping more.

Then one night, she had a dream that frightened her so much that she rang me at 2:00 A.M. to tell it. As she recounted it on the phone,

She is walking in the street. Suddenly she hears a voice shouting, "Look out or you will fall in the pit." She looks up and sees her mother with her typical sardonic smile, standing in front of her.

On the phone, I simply said to her that now that she had been able to dream this awful dream, she would be able to sleep fearlessly and we would discuss the dream when she came to her session. She felt satisfied with that. I myself wasn't sure whether she had seen a dream, had a hypnogogic image, or pure hallucination. When she came to her session, she didn't mention the dream, and I found her chitter-chattering again. I suspended drawing her attention to the dream all that week. Then one accident happened. Over the weekend, she had what she stated as a "flaming row with my bloody nosey relative," whom I have mentioned before. It was over dressing to go out. This relative wanted her to dress up, to be worthy of the guests and host, and she wanted to stay in her jeans and poncho. It ended by her throwing a glass of red wine, in front of her father, and the relative retired, screaming that her best evening dress had been ruined. Her father had passively and quietly watched the whole drama. Now the relative refused to go, and the father went happily with his daughter, dressed in jeans and poncho. He couldn't care a damn, so long as she felt at ease and was happy with life.

During Monday's session, after recounting the episode with her relative, she suddenly stopped and said, "I want to talk about me and my mum." Personally, I felt it was a bit premature for her to start telling me about her relationship with her mother. We had covered a lot of ground talking about Tim, and I would have liked to have had at least another week of that, to stabilize her mood and trust in me. I felt the episode with her relative had somehow distracted her into a triumphant manic mood. But I had no option but to let her talk about what she wished. It is my clinical experience that a patient can give very significant material to us, but in the wrong mood, and often it stays as inert information, and we, the patient and analyst, fail to transmute it into new affective psychic experience.

The most frustrating thing about recounting clinical work is that the small details that in fact make the destiny of the patient as a person and also dictate the destiny of the clinical process, cannot often be told for reasons of professional privacy. This is more true in Judy's case than in any other that I have ever written. She talked a lot about her relationship with her mother, and I shall abstract the crucial themes, but not retail actual events, except a few. I trust that the reader will use his or her own good will and imagination to reconstruct what is left unwritten.

As I have indicated already, Judy had shifted into a manic mood when she started to tell her "story," because it was told without affect or any communicative quality. The essential facts were that her mother was an outrageously hysterical woman and Judy had never seen the parents mutual or happy, even in a formal way. The essence of her mother's affective relating with her was neither rejection nor caring, nor even ambivalence, but *tantalization*. In her sober good moods, when her husband was away, which was often, she would indulge Judy without bothering to find out in the slightest what Judy liked or wished. For example, Judy told me that from all the stuff that was her's, toys, dresses, etcetera, she had brought only Tim's gear (saddle, blanket, etcetera, and her riding boots). The rest she had given to the village people around their country house. She knew her mother's gifts were a way of bribing her for the episodes when she would be quite wildly physically violent and beat her daughter in a rage, which rarely had anything to do with Judy's behavior, but was the overflow of some row with her husband. She once hit Judy so hard with a stick that it fractured her arm. She was eight at the time. Over the weekends when her father was present, the house was always cluttered. I use this word instead of crowded, because Judy related to no one but Tim, Dad, and the butler. She had very precociously begun to realize that her nanny was an accomplice to her mother. It was at nine years of age that, in a drunken state, the mother began to tell Judy secrets. Judy knew of them already. She told all this and other events in a rather manic, impersonal manner, as if they had happened to someone else. Listening to her narrative, which was mixed with gossip from her daily life, I felt that very early on, Judy had been driven mad by her mother and had learnt to live with her madness in her country life. Only the demands of a sophisticated school in London and her father's social life put a strain on her, which was incompatible with her stance of madness and, gradually during the past three years, she had learnt all the manipulative ruses of a true hysteric and hid herself behind them. In fact, she had succeeded so well that she was no longer in touch with her mad self, which was truly Judy. She exploited her environment negatively to her disadvantage as a person. It was very much like a caricature of her mother's character. And her father's indulgent affection was now no longer nourishing to her, because she exploited it to be a nuisance with a cunning devious vengefulness to her relatives, who tried to tame her into a groomed, sophisticated girl in the style of her social status.

It was in this ambiance that a girl friend of hers from childhood returned to London after five years abroad. She had been Judy's chum (her phrase) since she was three. The girl who returned was a very jet-set type now, and Judy took to her with manic passion. She worked at Linda's, studied with her teacher, and then would disappear with her friend, who was in town only for a month, to some discoteque or elsewhere, and stay away all night sometimes, returning just to change to go to work.

Unfortunately, her father was away on business for two weeks and her "nosey relative" kept a very exact record of Judy's goings-on. The nosey relative rang me one evening and bullied my butler to put her through to me. With an arrogant malicious note of triumph in her voice, she told me how Judy had been staying out very late all night and was not taking her "pills" regularly. So she had arranged with her gynecologist to insert an I.U.D. as a preventive, and Judy was going to see the gynecologist tomorrow. I warned her that sometimes the body of a girl does not accept the I.U.D. and, in Judy's case, there was a real danger that all her illness could express itself through somatic symptoms. But she wouldn't listen. I asked to speak to Judy, but she said that Judy had already gone somewhere, and put the phone down. I immediately got in touch with the physician, who even called at their house and was sent off with the information that everyone had gone out to dinner and would not return until very late. He rang me, and we sent the relative a telegram, jointly signed, stating that we were against her plan, and advising her to postpone it until the father returned, which would be on Friday night. We added that if Judy was pregnant, or was going to get pregnant, that couldn't be stopped tonight. And once her father returned, we could take the necessary medical measures to protect her from any accidents.

It was all to no avail. Judy had gone to the gynecologist and the insertion of the I.U.D. had been physically traumatic for her. When she came to her session, she was white as a sheet and in considerable pain. She asked for tea and I got it for her. I asked her why she had not refused and rung me, and she was mute. I noted the similarity of passivity with which this willful girl as a child had impersonally suffered and obeyed her mother, and now her bossy relative. Since her pain grew worse, I sent her home and phoned the doctor to ask him to call on her at his earliest free moment, which he did. I had absolutely no doubt that now Judy's madness would find a somatic idiom and might even lead to a psychotic breakdown. The first thing next morning, the physician rang me and said that Judy's father had rung him at 3:00 A.M., that she had been taken in an ambulance to the hospital, and another gynecologist had been called in to remove the I.U.D.

From here onward, a nightmare started, the like of which I had not experienced in thirty or so years of clinical work. To helplessly watch Judy's hidden madness, which was compatible with living, turn first into the most agonizing physical pain and symptoms, and later into psychotic states of paranoid delusions, hallucinations, and utter delapidation of her person, was most painful for me. Not having been hardened to human suffering, physical and psychic, due to lack of medical education, this phase of her illness was as traumatic for me as it was destructive of Judy the person.

Briefly, the events took this course: The I.U.D. was removed, but the gynecologist had made a real mess of her uterus. Judy was in the hospital, and nothing cured the infection or alleviated her pain except pathedrine, which, being an addictive drug, had to be administered carefully. So Judy lived in relentless physical pain. Then she started to have paranoid delusions about the matron, and one night ran out of the hospital. Fortunately, a police car was passing by and she was brought back. The father asked for consultation with me, the new gynecologist, and the physician. It was mutually agreed that Judy should be nursed at home. So Judy returned home very ill and was nursed at home. Judy's physical condition oscillated, but her mental condition changed to a patently schizophrenic paranoid state. She would not eat or talk. I called on her every evening after dinner for an hour, and so did the physician. We often found her either in a comatose state and mute, or in a state of hallucinosis. In the latter state, she would mutter in a garbled language. I shall recount one such hallucination: I had been sitting quietly by her bedside for half an hour, when I saw Judy stretch out her arm and embrace an "object," muttering, "Darling Tim, Mum has hit and cut your lip. Poor Tim. I am going to make it all right." And she sank back into her comatose muteness. I recalled seeing a scar on Judy's lower lip the very first time I had seen her.

After a month of this, and with progressive deterioration and hallucinations, in one of which she set fire to her night-dress, shouting, "The house (naming the country house in fact) is on fire." The physician and I had a consultation with her father and advised him to let us call in a psychiatrist who specialized in physical methods of treatment of schizophrenic hallucinatory states. He agreed and Judy was taken to a hospital. She was treated by physical psychiatric methods, and her mental condition improved miraculously, in so far as she had no more hallucinations or paranoid delusions. The father was very relieved. I had not seen Judy during this hospitalization, my reason being not to interfere with the possibility of transference to her psychiatrist.

On her return home, Judy immediately asked to see me. Her father rang me, and I cancelled my patients and immediately went over. The girl I saw was now quietly herself and mad. I had no doubt of that, but it made me have some hope again for her. She asked to talk to me alone, so the father and the nurse left the room. Very gently, she asked me to arrange with her father to allow her to leave home and to go and live elsewhere, in the countryside. I promised her that I would do my best to arrange that for her. She was strangely, passively alert and awake, and said that the three weeks in the hospital had not been very bad. She made a faint complaint about the food. Otherwise she recalled little.

I talked with the father and the physician, as well as the psychiatrist, and put forward a very strong case for Judy to be sent to some country house where the family atmosphere was congenial and acceptable to Judy. The father agreed instantly. The question was, which family, and how far from London.

In the two weeks following, Judy gradually became able to walk around and eat with the family. She even asked to have lessons again. The teacher reported that although she was utterly cooperative, she took in nothing. At this point, an event happened that resolved all our management problems.

An aunt of hers, who had a horse ranch in Argentina arrived out of the blue. Judy was fascinated by her aunt's account of the ranch and the people that she employed. Thus it was decided that Judy should go with her aunt to the ranch in Argentina, and July left in a week.

That was some three years ago. She wrote to me regularly, short letters every six weeks or so, with a photograph of a pony, a foal, or a horse. I always promptly answered. Then, some four months ago, I heard nothing from her. I tried to get in touch with her father, but he was abroad. So I sent a telegram to her aunt, asking news of Judy. She rang me and said that while training a horse, Judy had fallen and broken her arm. But it had healed well, and she was writing to me. This made me immediately fearful that Judy was again sinking into a psychotic state. I received a letter from Judy a week later, telling me of the accident and assuring me that she had suffered little pain and was riding again. At the end of the letter she wrote, and I quote her, "A young foal has been talking to me, but I can't understand him. If there are any books on horse language, please send them air mail. Dad will pay."

I knew for sure now that Judy had moved out of her mad state and was getting deluded and hallucinated. I sent a letter, saying I was glad to hear her news and was searching hard to find some books about horse language. In a few days her father returned, and I rang him and asked him to call me. I also called the physician and the psychiatrist. When we met, I read them Judy's letter and told them of my apprehensions about Judy relapsing into psychotic states again. The father volunteered to ring this aunt and tell her that if she should find Judy behaving oddly in any way, she must immediately ring him and he would fly over and fetch her.

Some six weeks have passed since then. I have not heard from Judy, but I ask myself as I prepare to receive her in whatever condition she arrives, what I shall do this time. Would I succeed with the help of her physician and psychiatrist to re-establish her in the privacy of her madness, which is compatible with living, or will the encrustations of mental derangement be irreversible now? But of one thing I am sure: I cannot expect her to free associate or speak her madness, because she would not know how to speak—what, how, to whom!

JUDY CHOOSES A VOCATION: AN ODYSSEY!

Some two months later, one Saturday afternoon, the phone rang. I answered it: it was Judy! She said, "I am in London, can I please see you today. I have a major decision to make and I need your help." I told her that

I could see her at 1:30 that afternoon. As I awaited Judy's arrival, three things kept tugging at my mind:

1. Judy's voice was so reticently articulate, unlike the Judy who used to blurt out things or who was mute.
2. I had never heard Judy use the word "please" before. All her demands were expressed through symptoms, hence she never felt responsible for what was provided for her.
3. She had never admitted her "need for help," which is quite different from a "demand." To accept "need for help" implies that one is not autonomously omnipotent, and acknowledges both the separateness and the resourcefulness of the *Other* to be able to help one.

Of course, by now she had lived some three years and more abroad in a culture and setting that could not be more different from her environment of childhood and puberty. She also had to learn a new language. But I, in fact, knew nothing about her life during these three years, even though she had written laconic cards or notes regularly.

About one thing I had made up my mind: no matter in what psychic condition I found her, I would not initiate or insinuate, from my side, her asking for a book about "horse-language." I would try and meet her on her terms, as she would choose to present herself. Furthermore, I was determined not to refer to her grave illnesses in the past, should she now decide to obviate them from her present identity as a person. I knew all this would entail an enormous discipline of deliberate *un*knowing on my part, but I was convinced that if I was to help Judy, I had to accept her as an as-if person in her own right, different from the *sick* girl. I was a little disconcerted by the precipitate way that she had left Argentina and arrived in London. I had known this type of impulsiveness in her before, but I decided to give her the benefit of the doubt in this respect as well.

Judy arrived punctually and greeted me with affection. One thing I had not thought of, that the girl of 18-plus, working hard on a ranch, would be different in physique from the puppy-fat girl with cropped hair and tight jeans who had left three years earlier. So it took me a little while to get used to her new physicality: she was slim, with long hair, and was discreetly dressed—almost pretty, certainly with a touch of the exotic. Her eyes were strikingly different: she did not have that wild stare or opaque and absent hazed look. Instead her eyes were quietly vigilant and alert. Her voice had also changed. She spoke in a quiet, pleasant, and lively way. When she had taken off her coat and placed it neatly with her bag by her side, along with a portfolio she had brought, she was no longer the "Judy, age 15" who would arrive and scatter herself all over the room. Her total *presence* had a different quality to it: she was discreetly trusting and relating. Her gestures also were consistent with her voice and her words. Of course, she noticed me "watching" her and remarked with a wry smirk, "I have changed, as you can see. And I have not been ill in any way in three years, except for fracturing my arm." I accepted her comment without reacting to it or commenting about the change.

I know it is not usual for analysts to describe the physicality of a patient in such detail. But clinically, to me, the sight of a person—the tone of voice, gestures, and general deportment—speak more at the start than their "prepared" telling and verbal narrative would for a long while. Judy launched straight off with the issue that she had come to discuss. It had all begun a year or so before, when a girl called Luciana had come to their ranch to buy horses. Luciana was a young woman of 27 years or so. She and Judy made an instant rapport with each other, and she invited Judy to dinner the following week. Judy went, and found that Luciana ran a sort of commune in a large house. She had some 20 persons from fifteen to thirty years of age living in her "care." They were all drop-outs, from colleges or jobs, of mixed nationalities and breeds. Some had been drug addicts. All this had deeply impressed Judy. She made up her mind to befriend Luciana. But during her first visit, she had asked no questions and had stayed a shade muted and left early. Then she invited Luciana to lunch and found out about her.

Luciana had lost her mother when she was five years old. She had been brought up by foster parents, who were friends of her father. The father had moved to Europe and did not keep in touch with his daughter. Luciana had a typically turbulent, chaotic, and drugged puberty and adolescence. Then, when she was 21, Luciana was told that she had inherited a huge fortune and was now quite independent. Fortunately, around this time, she met a man much older than herself, who became very interested in her welfare. He had lived in Nepal for five years when young and learnt a lot about Zen Buddhism and its practices. He visited Nepal and India every year and asked Luciana to visit with him. There were no intimate relations between them. Luciana, who had been thrown out of three universities and was in a mess, suddenly decided to go with him. She stayed five years in various Ashrams (like monasteries) and learnt Hindi, Nepali, and Sanskrit. When she returned, she decided to open this "commune," and she explained to Judy how the commune was run. Everybody had a task of their choosing, responsibility toward others, and none could stay for more than three years. She fed them, but they took care of the house, the garden, and they cooked. She also instructed them in "meditation."

According to Judy, she was absolutely fascinated by Luciana's life-story, especially its authenticity, both of the chaos and then the discipline and the dedication. She asked Luciana to teach her Hindi and started to attend some of her "meditation" sessions on Fridays. Gradually, a plan and a purpose began to crystalize itself in Judy. But what decided her was the foal who "talked to her" and whom she could not understand.

The trouble with the foal was that, at the age of eight months, he still only drank milk and refused fodder and bran, so he was not growing up very well. One day Judy mentioned it to Luciana, who agreed to "meet" the foal. According to Judy, Luciana was able to "understand" the "horse language" and to talk it also. In three months, the foal was eating normally. It was this event that decided Judy to leave Argentina and go to India or Nepal for Zen cum yoga apprenticeship. Luciana had given her quite a lot of information about Ashrams and their methods of "apprenticing," and Judy had brought some of the literature with her to show me. She had, in fact, already chosen an Ashram in India to go to, if she was accepted.

Of course, whilst I had listened to her, my mind was buzzing with reverberations from endless facets of her ill states, as well as when she had her healthy patches, but I said nothing. After some two hours she paused, looked at me intently, and asked, "What do you think of my plan, as I have told it to you so far?" I told her, candidly, that it sounded like a splendid program, but I could not advise her without consulting her father, and asked her how much she had shared her intensions with him. "Very little," she answered, "but I knew you would like to discuss it together with us. So he is waiting for me to ring him, and he will come over."

Judy rang her father, and waiting for his arrival gave us both a pause. Judy had been speaking, almost nonstop for nearly two hours now. She asked if she could look around the consultation room, and I said, "Of course!"

I was only too relieved for this respite, before the father arrived, to think things over, before I talked with him and gave my advice. I was gravely concerned and uncertain on many counts. Primarily: was Judy looking for an Ashram, or an asylum in India where her psychotic states could be private to her? Although I have said that "Judy, age 15" was totally unaware of how demanding a person she was and disavowed her *need* of care and others, she was also a profoundly sensitive and precociously overperceptive person, and "knew" what a terrible strain her illness had been on her father. I further wondered whether her father's over-readiness to agree to whatever I advised wasn't his way of avoiding a long bout of "sick-psychotic" Judy at home, completely disrupting and paralyzing his private life, and in a certain measure his professional life as well. Judy in India was safely out of the way, and the burden of that decision and responsibility lay on me.

There were other bits and pieces, casually recounted by Judy, that I had noted mentally. For example, the foal not eating reminded me of Judy's anorectic states during her illness, when she would only take liquids in small doses. Was she fearing another attack of anorexia and hoping to find a mystical cure for it in India? Also, I could not forget that, when I had first seen Judy, she had attempted suicide by cutting both her wrists. So, was she going to India to perish anonymously? Also, from her account of her relationships, except for the year of friendship with Luciana, I could not make out any stable object-relationship with anyone. She merely lived with her aunt and busied herself with work with the horses, cleaning saddlery, etcetera. The folk in the employment of her aunt found her very sympathetic and unsnooty, but largely she lived by herself—I could not say even with herself.

Yet when I weighed all the negatives I still felt, as I had when she was ill before, that Judy was not dreading a psychotic-breakdown and escaping to India. I felt deeply that, in Argentina, not having to play the sophisticated girl, and working and mixing with humble folk, had given Judy a sense of herself and her *difference* from others. By *difference*, I am implying not social status, but psychic states of being. I felt equally sure that she had outlived the creative usefulness of her aunt's ranch and now wanted to truly find herself and a way to speak and actualize it. Thus I was decided as to what I would advise her father.

The father arrived within half a hour. One look at him and I felt reassured that he was both relieved and delighted to find Judy in good physical health and psychically present in her person and being. We three sat and chattered for a while. Then Judy asked me, "Please tell Daddy what I want and why!" I told her that she could do it better, but if she wished me to, I certainly would, but in my own style, and she must correct me where she felt that I was misrepresenting her.

I started back to front, as it were. I told the father that, like him, I was delighted to find Judy in such good health, physically and psychically; that in my opinion, Judy had exhausted, for herself, the creative potential of life at her aunt's ranch. Now she needed to be autonomous and not "in-care," to try her own ways of finding how to be herself in her future and live it both purposefully and creatively with others; that her wish was to go to an Ashram in India and do a complete "apprenticeship" in Zen cum yoga styles of meditation, achieving self-awareness and learning some crafts. I emphasized that to try and get Judy to take examinations in London and to go to some university would not only be futile, but I greatly feared that she could collapse back into her illnesses. I further added that the social life of London would make Judy ill—or that, at least, this was my opinion. I told him that he could ask for a second opinion and that would not offend me in any way.

The father had listened to me very carefully and sympathetically. He asked me whether he could as equally express openly his misgivings in front of Judy. I asked Judy, and she said, "Yes!" The father told me what I already knew, that he had been to India on business many times and had some good friends there; that out of curiosity he had visited a few Ashrams, and they varied from the true and serious and apprenticing ones to mere charlatanism for druggists. So how does one know, sitting in London, where Judy should go? I answered him that I was aware of this hazard, as Judy was herself; that she had known and befriended a girl in Argentina who had spent five years in India in various Ashrams. But Judy does not want to drift from Ashram to Ashram, but to undertake vigorous apprenticeship at one particular Ashram, of which she had the name and address; that I knew of this Ashram, and some very good friends of mine finance its maintenance, but it has a seven-year apprenticeship and it is not easy to get into. I could use my influence, if he agreed, and ring my friends and find out more. It was too late to ring India that day, so I would be in touch with him and Judy the following day when I got through. I gave him their name, address, and telephone number, and asked him to try also to mention my name and find out what was possible.

The second concern that the father had he found difficult to tell in front of Judy. So, after a lot of hesitation, he asked me, "What happens if Judy has a serious *relapse* in the Ashram in India?" I was ready for this question. First I made a mental note that he had not used the phrase, "relapse into her previous illnesses." I respected that! I told him that Judy's type of ailments, and even that word, I added, misrepresents what I wished to say, are really growing pains of the self and the soul, which take an individual time to personalize and speak; that Judy, in my opinion, had never been psychiatrically ill *herself*, as I had said at the time to him, the physician, and the psychiatrist. She had "learnt" the usage of symptomatology, however, and we were all compelled to *act* on that and we had. Today Judy had come through, by her own efforts and, to grow further, she needed a new, different, and disciplined environment, where she could both be apprenticed and be private. She had chosen her route and we all, including Judy, had to take the risk and sponsor her. I asked him whether he had seen or read T. S. Eliot's play, *The Cocktail Party* (1950). He said, "Both." So I got out a copy of the play and quoted him what Reilly (the "psychiatrist") says to Celia (the "patient"):

> There *is* another way, if you have the courage.
> The first I could describe in familiar terms
> Because you have seen it, as we all have seen it,
> Illustrated, more or less, in lives of those about us.
> The second is unknown, and so requires faith—
> The kind of faith that issues from despair.
> The destination cannot be described;
> You will know very little until you get there;
> You will journey blind. But the way leads towards possession
> Of what you have sought for in the wrong place.

He was really moved by this, and what he called my "candor, and taking the risk." I had not minced my words. The father got up at this point and said, "I am sure Judy has more to say to you, that is, if you have time." I said, "Yes, I have!" And he left, thanking me for being always so available.

After he left, Judy was silent for a while. Then she remarked, "Thank God this room has not changed much except for a few new objects and more books!" I realized how Judy's life had been traumatized at every critical stage by change either of environment or familial personages. This assured me further about her *rightness* in choosing an Ashram with the longest training. Seven years would be the longest period Judy would be spending in a consistent, ongoing human ambiance and a "holding" structure.

Judy continued her narrative. "Do you know what was the most important discovery I made at the ranch?" "Tell me," I said.

"After I had been at the ranch for three months or so and got to know all the ranch-hands (*her phrase*), I one day suddenly realized I could tell the 'soulful' persons from the 'minded' people (*her phrases*). And it was by watching the difference between the horses who were looked after by the 'soulful' persons and those by the 'minded' ones. When presented to my aunt for regular inspection, the horses and the saddlery of the 'minded' ranch-hands were always cleaner, smarter, and the horses looked better trained than those by the 'soulful' ones. Gradually I realized the horses of the 'minded' people were more restive and unrelating than those of the 'soulful' ones. So I began to watch carefully how each one behaved. The 'minded' ranch-hands were quick with their grooming, harsh in training the horses, and smarted up the saddlery without really working at it. The 'soulful' people seemed lazy and absent-minded, but in fact they cared about the animals, groomed them thoroughly, and were proud of them. The 'minded' ones were good at putting up a show, but cut corners, whereas the 'soulful' persons were often clumsy, and though more proud inside, felt intimidated by the 'minded' people. By this time I was getting to know their families also, and I could tell 'soulful' children from the 'minded' ones. The latter did well at school and were ambitious and eager to please us. Whereas the 'soulful' children lagged behind at school, were often bullied by the 'minded' ones, and made to do all sorts of chores for them. I asked my aunt if I could give lessons on Sundays for two hours to the 'soulful' children. The difficulty was that the majority of the 'soulful' children were colored or of mixed blood and spoke no English, and my Spanish was not good enough yet. But there was a bright young colored ranch-hand who spoke both Spanish and English and could write them too. My aunt was only too pleased with this plan, because I would not go to any house on Sundays for lunch or dinner, nor join in if others came to my aunt's house. The venture was such a success that, when I left, the aunt agreed that the youth should take on the job of being full-time teacher at her school for children, and give up being a ranch-hand."

I was utterly exhausted by now, yet I felt that the consultation hadn't reached its "critical point." So I waited, with my face in my hands, as is my style when listening, facing a patient. First, I don't like watching a patient with a pretend-blankness of neutrality, nor being stared at myself. Second, I can peep through the chinks of my fingers when I *need* to *look* at the patient. Now Judy volunteered to tell me her real intention and secret. She said, "You know that at 27 I am going to inherit a mint. So when I return from the Ashram I am going to buy a country house with large grounds where I can build many outhouses. I won't have one large house, like Luciana's, because I would have no privacy then. And I will have a sort of Ashram, where I will take 10 or 12 children who do poorly at school from the age of five to ten, and some 20 adolescents from the ages of 15 to 20 who lose jobs or drop out of school, and apprentice them. I shall learn to make pottery and to weave at the Ashram so that I can teach skills."

Suddenly she stopped and I looked full-face at her. Yes, there was the same look of ungraspable anxiety in her eyes that I has seen during her illnesses. So I said, "What is the matter, Judy?" She burst into tears and asked, "Do you really think I will make it at the Ashram?" I paused, and then answered, "If you have made it at the ranch, you will at the Ashram. Only remember that you have chosen a vocation, which is an odyssey. Judy, there is no substitute for time. Don't ask too much of yourself, and let them help you learn slowly and you will make it. You have both the will and the necessary assets." She smiled. I knew that she had no doubt that she would make it, yet she *needed* my *affirmation,* but not any reassurance from me. (There is a difference.)

It took a few days before I could contact my friends in India. They also were phoned by her father, and they assured that she would be welcome to stay with them pending her admittance to the Ashram. They had heard of her father. There were only a few days left to Christmas (1980), and Judy wanted to leave before Christmas. Her father consulted me, and I said that he should let her leave.

At the end of the consultation, which had lasted some five hours, as she got up to leave, Judy bashfully pulled out a wrapped packet from her portfolio and gave it to me as a gift. I opened it. It was a leather-bound cahier of drawings by her "soulful" children. I asked her what would she like to have from me. She said that she would like some verses from a poem of my liking, which she could take to the Ashram. "But please write in your own hand," she added. I chose to write the following verses for her, from Cavafy's "Ithaka" (1911):

As you set out for Ithaka
hope your road is a long one,
full of adventure, full of discovery.
Laistrygonians, Cyclops,
angry Poseidon—don't be afraid of them:
you'll never find things like that on your way
as long as you keep your thoughts raised high,
as long as a rare excitement
stirs your spirit and your body.
Laistrygonians, Cyclops,
wild Poseidon—you won't encounter them
unless you bring them along inside your soul,
unless your soul sets them up in front of you.

SPEECH, THE PSYCHOANALYTIC METHOD, AND MADNESS

Homo sapiens, according to *Encyclopedia Britannica* (1974), "is distin-
ʒuished from other animals and from earlier hominid species by . . . his
ːonstruction and use of tools, and his ability to make use of symbols such as
ɑnguage and writing (p. 107)." Under the caption "Language," it states:

For an adequate understanding of human language it is necessary to
keep in mind the absolute primacy of speech. In societies in which
literacy is all but universal and language teaching at school begins with
reading and writing in the mother tongue, one is apt to think of
language as a writing system that may be pronounced. In point of fact,
language is a system of spoken communication that may be represented
in various ways in writing. Man has almost certainly been in some
sense a speaking animal from early in the emergence of Homo sapiens
as a recognizably distinct species. . . . As far as the production of
speech sounds is concerned, all human beings are physiologically alike.
People have differently shaped faces, as much as they differ in other
aspects of bodily build, but it has been shown time and again that a child
learns to speak the language of those who bring him up from infancy. In
most cases these are his biological parents, especially his mother, but
one's first language is acquired from environment and learning, not from
physiological inheritance. Adopted infants, whatever their race or physical type and whatever the language of their actual parents, acquire the
language of the adoptive parents who raise them just as if they had been
their own children. (Compare Burke 1966, Ducrot and Todorov 1972,
and Smith 1978.)

From these quotations, two things become quite clear. One, that speech is very intimately connected with growth, nurture, and object-relating from infancy onward. Two, that language is a specialized and sophisticated development of speech, especially when written. In fact, no more than ten percent of the living homo sapiens, if that, can write or read language. Be that as it may, for the purposes of this article I shall restrict myself to three usages of speech in the clinical analytic situation: (1) talking, (2) telling, and (3) speaking.

How an hysteric, Anna O., with a touch of genius, compelled her physician, Joseph Breuer, to listen to her "talking cure" in the early eighties of the nineteenth century, has been recorded as it happened clinically, by Breuer (1895) himself, and its traumatic vicissitudes afterward for the patient have been discussed by Jones (1953), Lucy Freeman (1972), and, with greater accuracy, by Clark (1980). Jones (1953) attributes Freud's interest in hysteria and psychopathology to his "experience with Charcot" (p. 75; cf. Freud 1925). This certainly is a shade misleading, because when Breuer, in November 1882 (cf. Clark, pp. 80, 101), had unburdened himself of the story of his treatment of Anna O. to Freud, it deeply impressed Freud. He even tried to get Charcot interested in it, but to no avail. Later on, in a moment of overgenerosity, during his Clark lectures in the United States, Freud (1910) was to attribute to Breuer the origin of psychoanalysis:

> If it is a merit to have brought psychoanalysis into being, that merit is not mine. I had no share in its earliest beginnings. I was a student and working for my final examinations at the time when another Viennese physician, Dr. Josef Breuer, first [in 1880–1882] made use of this procedure on a girl who was suffering from hysteria.

It was Anna O. who had invented the phrases "talking cure" and "chimney sweeping," and made him a devoted accomplice to her "self-catharsis" (if I may use that phrase). Breuer, in fact, had contributed little to the therapeutic process except his availability and presence (cf. Ellenberger 1970).

It was left to Freud's genius to transform "talking" into "telling" in the clinical situation. And it is this that constitutes the essence of Freud's analytic method. Nor did Freud achieve it in a sudden flash of insight—he labored hard with all the current methods of psychotherapeutics and suffered all the agonies of his self-analysis before he could claim, in retrospect, "From the date of *The Interpretation of Dreams* [1900], psychoanalysis had a twofold significance. It was not only a new method of treating the neuroses but it was also a new psychology; it claimed the attention not only of nerve-specialists but also of all those who were students of a mental science." For an exhaustive account of Freud's travails before he established his psychoanalytic method one has to read the Freud–Fliess correspondance (1954)—a complete edition of which is being prepared at present by Professor Jeff Masson-Jones (1953), Robert (1964), Grinstein (1968), Anzieu's monumental study, *L'Autonanalyse de Freud et la decouverte de la psychanalyse* (1975), and Clark (1980).

In 1904, Freud was to give his first definitive statement of psychoanalysis as a method of treatment. For some strange reason, James Strachey changed the title from "Freud's Psychoanalytic Method" to "Freud's Psycho-Analytic Procedure" without explaining why.

If Anna O. had initiated the "talking cure" with Breuer in 1882, some seven years later another hysteric, Frau Emmy Von N., whom Freud took into treatment in 1889, one day changed "talking" to "telling." In Freud's (1895) own words:

> I requested her to remember tomorrow. She then said in a definitely grumbling tone that I was not to keep on asking her where this and that came from, but to let her tell me what she had to say. I fell in with this . . .

This is certainly the first incident of what Freud later was to turn into the method of "free association," but there was a long route to travel yet. It was with Fraulein Elisabeth von R., whose treatment he started in 1892, that Freud gave up the use of hypnosis, and he himself called it "the first full-length analysis of hysteria."

Yet it was only through his self-analysis, conducted largely through interpretation of his own dreams, that Freud arrived at his analytic method (Freud 1904). What was novel to the new method ws "an art of interpretation which takes on the task of, as it were, excavating the pure metal of the repressed thoughts from the ore of the unintentional ideas." And here Freud emphasizes how "the task of treatment is to remove amnesia . . . all repressions must be undone . . . the task consists in making the unconscious accessible to consciousness, which is done by overcoming the resistances." And Freud adds,". . . the aim of the treatment will never be anything else but the *practical* recovery of the patient, the restoration of his ability to lead an active life and his capacity for enjoyment." This indeed is a very different therapeutic undertaking from the one Freud (1895) had stated at the end of "Psychotherapy of Hysteria," where he wrote, "No doubt fate would find it easier than I do to relieve you of your illness. But you will be able to convince yourself that much will be gained if we succeed in transforming your hysterical misery into common unhappiness."

It is interesting to note what for Freud were "various qualifications."

. . . required of anyone who is to be beneficially affected by psycho-analysis. To begin with, he must be capable of a psychically normal condition; during periods of confusion or melancholic depression nothing can be accomplished even in cases of hysteria. Furthermore, a certain measure of natural intelligence and ethical development are to be required of him; if the physician has to deal with a worthless character, he soon loses the interest which makes it possible for him to enter profoundly into the patient's mental life.

He concludes by stating, "Freud requires long periods, six months to three years, for an effective treatment." It is rather strange that Freud does not discuss the role of transference in the analytic process and method in this article. But in the postscript to "Fragment of an analysis of a case of Hysteria" (1901–1905) Freud gives a very lucid and detailed definition and account of transference and its role in the therapeutic work. This theme and that of countertransference are further discussed in his later papers on psychoanalytic technique. It was one of Freud's singular assets that he did not wander away from his chosen task: "My life has been aimed at one goal only: to infer or to guess how the mental apparatus is constructed and what forces interplay and counteract in it" (quoted by Jones, 1953). Freud himself stated his lack of passion for saving suffering humanity and as Jones (1953) rightly states, " . . . from the beginning of his life to the end Freud was never satisfied with emotional solutions only. He had a veritable passion to *understand*."

In the four decades since Freud's death, the whole climate of analytic research and clinical work has radically changed. Freud had invented a setting and a method where a person could tell his or her problems and be understood. Today *telling* doesn't seem to be enough. The patients that come to us are as amorphous in their symptomatology as they are unknowing of what they need or want to tell. Hence the emphasis has shifted from knowing how the mental apparatus is "constructed" to trying to comprehend the patient as a person. Holland (1977) gives a very concise account of the changes that have taken place in psychoanalytic theorizing and practices, as well as the factional proliferation of the basic Freudian psychoanalytic method.

This leads to my last point. How do we assess madness and clinically enable a person to contain it, to live from it and with it? And by madness I do not mean psychoses or psychotic states—the *need* of the mad is not so much to know as to *be* and *speak*! I run into a conceptual difficulty here. Although a lot has been written about madness in the past two decades, Foucault (1961) and Szasz (1971)—to mention only two books—one is hard put to find a definition of madness that clearly demarcates it as being *different* from other psychic and psychiatric states such as the neuroses, perversions, and psychoses. According to Foucault (1961), madness in the middle ages in Europe was treated quite differently, to the point of being almost a privileged state. Then, Foucault states categorically, "Indeed, from the fifteenth century on, the face of madness has haunted the imagination of Western man." After giving a very extensive account of how the mad were gradually driven out of their familial and social settings into vagabondage, then into leproriums, and eventually were "imprisoned" in the nosological medical/psychiatric categories of insanity, psychoses, melancholia, etcetera, Foucault concludes, "Psychoanalysis can unravel some of the forms of madness; it remains a stranger to the sovereign enterprise of unreason. It can neither liberate nor transcribe, nor most certainly explain what is essential in this enterprise." In his later book (revised edition 1966), Foucault argues that, "About the middle of the seventeenth century, a sudden change took place: the world of madness was to become the world of exclusion."

The reason Foucault gives for this "exclusion" is a socioeconomic one:

> In the bourgeois world then being constituted, the major vice, the cardinal sin in that world of trade, had been defined; it was no longer, as in the Middle Ages, pride or greed, but sloth. The common category that grouped together all those interned in these institutions was their inability to participate in the production, circulation, or accumulation of wealth (whether or not through any fault of their own). The exclusion to which they were subjected goes hand in hand with that inability to work, and it indicates the appearance in the modern world of a caesura that had not previously existed. Internment, therefore, was linked, in its origin and in its fundamental meaning, with this restructuring of social space.
>
> This phenomenon was doubly important for the constitution of the contemporary experience of madness. Firstly, because madness, which had for so long been overt and unrestricted, which had for so long been present on the horizon, disappeared. It entered a phase of silence from which it was not to emerge for a long time; it was deprived of its language; and although one continued to speak of it, it became impossible for it to speak of itself. Impossible at least until Freud, who was the first to open up once again the possibility for reason and unreason to communicate in the danger of a common language, ever ready to break down and disintegrate into the inaccessible. On the other hand, madness, in internment, had forged strange new kinships. This space of exclusion, which had grouped together, with the mad, sufferers from venereal diseases, libertines, and innumerable major or petty criminals, brought about a sort of obscure assimilation; and madness forged a relationship with moral and social guilt that it is still perhaps not ready to break. We should not be surprised that, since the eighteenth century, a

link should have been discovered between madness and all *crimes passionels;* that, since the nineteenth century, madness should have become the heir of crimes that find it in their reason for being and their reason for not being crimes; that, in the twentieth century, madness should have discovered at the center of itself a primitive nucleus of guilt and aggression. All this is not the gradual discovery of the true nature of madness, but simply the sedimentation of what the history of the West has made of it for the last three hundred years. Madness is much more *historical* than is usually believed, and much *younger* too.

I have quoted this extensively, because it is precisely the need to "speak" itself that constitutes the essence of the mad person's self-experience, as I have tried to show in the "case-history" of Judy. How we are going to provide "holding structures" for the potentially mad for them not to take on the *given* languages of psychoses or drug addictions is perhaps the most urgent psychotherapeutic task facing us today. Levi-Strauss (1962), discussing his concept of the "savage mind," states his aim as:

> . . . in this book it is neither the mind of savages nor that of primitive or archaic humanity, but rather mind in its *untamed states* as distinct from the mind cultivated or domesticated for the purposes of yielding a return. . . . The exceptional features of this mind which we call savage and which Comte described as spontaneous, relate principally to the extensive nature of the ends it assigns itself. It claims at once to analyze and to synthesize, to go to its furthest limits in both directions, while at the same time remaining capable of mediating between the two poles. (*Italics added.*)

For how some "primitive" societies deal with this problem, see Pouillon (1970).

David Cooper (1978) states that, "We have, I believe, to distinguish between Reason and Knowledge. Reason and Unreason are both ways of knowing. Madness is a way of knowing, another mode of empirical exploration of both the 'inner' and 'outer' worlds." It was precisely such needs that first brought on the illnesses of Judy, because her environment could not *provide* her with the idiom with which she could *speak* herself, and later, through *placement* (Winnicott 1956) in a new environment, which did not make the counter-demands to her own needs, and through her personal efforts, she was able to find what her *difference* was from others and ask for the possibilities, socially and through apprenticeship, to cultivate her own style of being and living with and amongst others, purposefully, but also privately and creatively.

REFERENCES

Anzieu, D. (1975). *L'Autoanalyse de Freud et la decouverte de la psychanalyse.* Paris: Presses Universitaires de France.

Breuer, J. (1895). Fraulein Anna O. In *Studies on hysteria. Standard Edition,* 2:21–47.

Burke, K. (1966). *Language as Symbolic Action.* Los Angeles: University of California Press.

Cavafy, C. P. (1911). "Ithaka." In *Collected Poems,* trans. E. Keeley and P. Sherrard; ed. G. Savidis. London: The Hogarth Press, 1975.

Clark, R. W. (1980). *Freud: The Man and the Cause.* London: Jonathan Cape and Weidenfeld and Nicholson.

Cooper, D. (1978). *The Language of Madness.* London: Allen Lane.

Ducrot, O., and Todorov, T. (1972). *Dictionnaire Encyclopedique des Sciences.* Paris: Editions du Seiul.

Eliot, T. S. (1950). The cocktail party. In *The Complete Poems and Plays of T. S. Eliot.* London: Faber and Faber, 1969.

Ellenberger, H. F. (1970). *The Discovery of the Unconscious.* London: Allen Lane/The Penguin Press.

Encyclopedia Britannica, 15th ed. (1974).

Foucault, M. (1961). *Madness and Civilisation: A History of Insanity in the Age of Reason.* New York: Random House, 1965.

———. (1966). *Mental Illness and Psychology.* New York: Harper and Row, 1976.

Freeman, L. (1972). *Story of Anna O.: The Woman Who Led Freud to Psychoanalysis.* New York: Walker and Company.

Freud, S. (1895). The Case of Fraulein Elisabeth von R. *Standard Edition* 2:135–181.

———. (1900). The interpretation of dreams. *Standard Edition* 4–5.

———. (1901–1905). Fragment of an analysis of a case of hysteria. *Standard Edition* 7:1–123.

———. (1904). Freud's psycho-analytic procedure. *Standard Edition* 7.

———. (1910). Five lectures on psycho-analysis. *Standard Edition* 11:3–55.

———. (1925). An autobiographical study. *Standard Edition* 20:3–70.

———. (1954). *Origins of Psycho-Analysis: Letters to Wilhelm Fliess, Drafts and Notes: 1887–1902.* London: Imago Publishing Co. Ltd.

Grinstein, A. (1968). *On Sigmund Freud's Dreams.* Detroit: Wayne State University Press.

Holland, R. (1977). *Self and Social Context.* London: The Macmillan Press.

Jones, E. (1953). *The Life and Work of Sigmund Freud, vol I. 1856–1900.* New York: Basic Books Ltd.

Laplanche, J., and Pontalis, J. B. (1968). *Vocabulaire de la Psychanalyse.* Paris: P.U.F. English Version: *The Language of Psychoanalysis.* London: Hogarth Press, 1973.

Levi-Strauss, C. (1962). *The Savage Mind.* London: Weidenfeld and Nicholson Ltd, 1966.

Pouillon, J. (1970). Doctor and patient: same and/or other. In *The Psychoanalytic Study of Society.* New York: International Universities Press, 1972.

Robert, M. (1964). *The Psycho-analytic Revolution: Sigmund Freud's Life and Achievement.* London: George Allen and Unwin, 1966.

Rycroft, C. (1968). *A Critical Dictionary of Psycho-analysis.* London: Nelson.

Smith, J. H., ed. (1978). *Psychoanalysis and Language. Psychiatry and the Humanities, vol. 3.* New Haven: Yale University Press.

Szasz, T. (1971). *The Manufacture of Madness.* London: Routledge and Kegan Paul.

Winnicott, D. W. (1956). The antisocial tendency. In *Through Pediatrics to Psycho-analysis.* London: Hogarth Press, 1978.

The Analyst as Manager of the Patient's Daily Life: Transference and Countertransference Dimensions of this Relationship

HAROLD F. SEARLES, M.D.

A discussion of "Speech, the Psychoanalytic Method, and Madness: a 'Case History,'" by M. Masud Khan, M.D. The author expresses admiration of Khan's technique and theoretical conceptions concerning the one-to-one aspects in the psychoanalytic-therapy of the severely borderline young woman whose treatment Khan's paper details. However, regarding those aspects of the treatment wherein Khan found it necessary to intervene as manager of the patient's daily life, it is suggested that the presumably ever-present transference and countertransference dimensions of the work are insufficiently emphasized by Khan. Analyst as well as patient tend, inevitably and powerfully, to use the former's management function for unconsciously defensive purposes.

As a psychoanalytic clinician and theoretician, Masud Khan is unique. He possesses a most rare creativity of thought and of analytic technique, coupled with an encyclopedic knowledge of the contributions of his predecessors and contemporaries. In addition, he writes with lucidity and absorbing narrative skill concerning his work with his patients. His account here, for example, of his work with Judy reads like a gripping detective novel. I have admired, and never failed to learn from, Khan's writings for many years. The present splendid paper evoked in me many thoughts which I have found difficult to organize. I present them as they occurred to me in my reading of the paper from beginning to end.

Khan's nontechnical presentation of the case-history as vividly personal narrative, free from psychiatric jargon, is among this paper's major strengths. Psychoanalysts have a tendency to feel guilty in relation to the professional-psychoanalytic-observer dimension—clearly indispensable though that dimension is—of our participant-observer (in Harry Stack Sullivan's phrase) relationship with the patient. In other words, the analyst tends to feel guilty in the knowledge that his or her relationship with the patient, a deeply personal relationship, is at the same time always professional, always being maintained under the analyst's own psychoanalytic scrutiny. This leads, in turn, into what one might think of as the collage of subjectively genuine and subjectively false components in the analyst's functioning over the course of treating any one patient, comparable with the areas of genuine self and false self in the patient's own ego-functioning. It is clear that Khan, following Winnicott, places much emphasis upon helping the patient to identify false-self areas in the patient's identity-functioning and upon helping him or her to experience and express increasingly genuine selfhood.

Over the course of any one relatively successful treatment endeavor, the analyst's own identity-functioning becomes increasingly genuine, less artificial or otherwise spurious, as he or she becomes relatively free from being intimidated by the patient's early idealizations or diabolizations and increasingly comfortable in being himself or herself with the patient. Thus, as the patient becomes increasingly able to rework false-self personality-ingredients into more genuine self-functioning, he or she does so partly on the basis of identifications with his or her analyst's increasing ability to function in a genuine way.

Judy "had been compelled upon me by her physician." This must have had profound effects upon Khan's countertransference to her, and more shall be said of this later.

Khan describes a "mutually provocative silence" in the initial interview. I have long been interested in the *kinds of* silence, on the part of the patient or analyst or both, that occur during sessions, as regards the feeling-tones that are being nonverbally communicated, and I admire Khan's empathic attentiveness to this realm of the work with the patient. He is similarly astute as regards other areas of nonverbal communication. He says, "It is important clinically for me to see how a patient uses my clinical space and the furniture available. . . . Also the way a patient dresses . . ." Khan has no need of the kind of reminders I often give to analytic candidates—even advanced candidates—in supervision, who tend to assume that verbal communications from patient and analyst comprise essentially all the significant analytic data, unaware that oftentimes the far more significant data are being expressed nonverbally by one means or another. Khan later writes, "I know it is not usual for analysts to describe in such detail the physicality of a patient. But clinically, to me, the sight of a person, the tone of their voice, their gestures and general deportment, speak more at the start than their 'prepared' telling and verbal narrative would for a long while."

During the initial interview, Khan manifests a moving faith in the validity of Judy's plea for him to get her out of the school, and promptly responds in a managerial way to her plea. This kind of response on his part, typical of his subsequent work with her also, *seems* very far removed from psychoanalysis; but I am sure it is not nearly as far removed as many readers might believe. I am confident that the succession of Khan's management-responses, over the course of his work with Judy, are informed in each instance by his wealth of experience in more typical psychoanalytic work, and that his decisions are made in light of his attunement to her transference reactions, as well as to his countertransference-responses and -attitudes. I am sure that he could have provided us, had he chosen to do so in this paper, with a very illuminating contrast between his work with Judy on the one hand and his work with more nearly typical psychoanalytic patients on the other hand. In the absence of such a discussion of his own, I shall attempt briefly to set down my impressions about this aspect of the treatment, as I go along. For the moment, I shall mention merely my distinct impression that this kind of managerial, rescuing response, on his part, is to a significant degree responsible for the non-emergence, in any full flower, of such negative transference and countertransference reactions as are inherent in more typical psychoanalytic treatment.

One of the aspects of his work that is particularly admirable is found in the passage after he acted in compliance with Judy's request to be taken out of the school: "I scrutinized Judy's face carefully. There was no sly sense of triumph in her expression. . . ." For a year or so now, I have been collecting material for a paper concerning the role of facial expressions, on the part of either patient or analyst, and I find that Khan is in the vanguard of those few, to my present knowledge, who have shown an interest in this topic. Much later in the paper, he reports that,

> . . . I waited, with my face in my hands, as is my style when listening, facing a patient. First, I don't like watching a patient with a pretend-blankness of neutrality, nor being stared at myself. Second, I can peep through the chinks of my fingers when I *need* to *look* at the patient. . . . Suddenly she stopped, and I looked full-face at her. Yes, there was the same look of ungraspable anxiety in her eyes that I had seen during her illnesses.

His description of his work with Judy conveys far more of the living reality of psychoanalytic therapy (and of psychoanalysis) than do nearly all the descriptions of interviews that one ordinarily encounters, with their exclusive reliance upon the words that are spoken.

At the end of the initial interview, Khan telephoned Judy's physician and arranged for him to come with Judy and Judy's father for the next consultation: "I told him that what was necessary at this stage was *management* (à la Winnicott) and not psychotherapy. . . ."

To refresh my memory of what Winnicott had written concerning management, I looked through his book of collected papers for such references. Particularly apropos are some of his comments, from his paper of 1954 entitled, "Metapsychological and Clinical Aspects of Regression within the Psycho-Analytic Set-Up" (1954).

> . . . I divide cases into the following three categories. *First* there are those patients who operate as whole persons and whose difficulties are in the realm of interpersonal relationships. The technique for the treatment of these patients belongs to psycho-analysis as it developed in the hands of Freud at the beginning of the century.
>
> Then *secondly* there come the patients in whom the wholeness of the personality only just begins to be something that can be taken for granted. . . . The technique for this work is not different from that needed by patients in the first category; nevertheless some new management problems do arise on account of the increased range of clinical material tackled. Important from our point of view here is the idea of the *survival of the analyst* as a dynamic factor.
>
> In the *third* grouping I place all those patients whose analyses must deal with the early stages of emotional development before and up to the establishment of the personality as an entity, before the achievement of space-time unit status. The personal structure is not yet securely founded. In regard to this third grouping, the accent is more surely on management, and sometimes over long periods with these patients ordinary analytic work has to be in abeyance, management being the whole thing (pp. 278–279).

It appears that Judy belonged, for the most part, in the second of the above two groupings, but that her behavior at the outset, and on occasion later, was so primitive as to require a degree of management more characteristic for patients in the third grouping. Chestnut Lodge, where I worked for nearly fifteen years, is a sanitarium specializing in the psychoanalytic therapy of patients the majority of whom are far more ill than Judy was at the outset. There, such managerial aspects of the treatment are in the hands of one or another of the several administrative psychiatrists on the staff, leaving the therapist free to focus upon his or her more traditional psychotherapeutic realm of responsibility. Thus each patient is assigned a therapist and an administrative psychiatrist who, of course, need to develop a good working relationship with one another. Half my own time, during my first two years there, was devoted to working as an administrative psychiatrist. Nonetheless, since I left there nearly eighteen years ago and increased my private practice from part-time to full-time, I largely have avoided taking on, in treatment, patients who require a high degree of management of their daily lives, for it is not a kind of work for which I feel well suited by interest or personal temperament. Certainly it is enormously difficult work, and I salute Khan for taking it upon himself.

I am troubled, however, lest the relatively inexperienced reader, if not Khan himself, believe that during the phase of management, intensely negative transference and countertransference response are in abeyance, for that view is quite illusory.

It is typical of Khan's personal honesty, and of his rigorously scientific scrutinizing of his countertransference reactions, to report that, "An hour before the consultation on Monday, I began to feel extremely anxious, apprehensive and full of paranoid misgivings, and totally lacking in self-confidence with regard to being able to make a clinically positive encounter with the expected 'mob'. I have always been a one-to-one clinician, and here I felt that I had been bullied by my physician friend into 'group therapy'." Such refreshing honesty is rare, indeed, in our professional literature. But subsequently in the paper, at times when Khan is functioning as a superlatively masterful manager of crucial events in Judy's life, it is unclear whether he is equally ready to scrutinize these personal experiences of his, experiences of presumably unusually great feelings of competence and effectiveness, to see wherein these too may be, in part, responses in keeping with the patient's transference-attitudes toward him. One must learn to try to be as objective toward one's own experiences of superlative mastery, as toward one's experiences of uncharacteristic helplessness, in one's work with a patient. Too often, when the therapist emerges as the hero of the treatment, he or she does so at the cost of strength unconsciously borrowed, and perhaps permanently borrowed, from the idealizing patient. This comment, taken alone, would be quite unfair to Masud Khan, whose humility at many junctures is as clearly evident as is his managerial mastery at a few points. But again, although he himself needs no such reminders, these observations may be pertinent for some of the less experienced readers.

Tantalizingly, Khan does not tell us upon what data he based his conviction, after the initial consultation, "That the girl I had *seen* was mad, behind all the antics of hysteria she had learnt to manipulate her environment with." Perhaps the data consisted in intuitive impressions which, however reliable, simply could not be set down in words. Similarly tantalizing is his discussion, in the closing pages of the paper, of "madness" which, he emphasizes, he does not regard as synonymous with "psychosis." That discussion was the only abstruse part in an otherwise admirably lucid paper.

Early in the treatment, "She said, 'I had a weird dream, and said to myself, I must tell this to Khan. But by the time I got out of bed and found a pencil and a piece of paper, I had lost the dream. So I can't tell you anything'." This sort of comment, heard so often from patients, conveys the implied, unconscious reproach, "If only you had been there in bed with me when I awakened, I could have told you the dream." It is to be noted that the romantic-erotic aspects of Judy's transference to Khan never became clearly delineated as such in the subsequent treatment; but one must wonder whether her decision, finally, to go into something like a nunnery for a seven-year course of study may have involved important elements of reaction-formation against her unconscious erotic feelings toward her therapist, toward whom she showed so much admiration and gratitude.

Although it may by no means be assumed that any such erotic feelings would have to do specifically with father-transference rather than mother-transference. Khan's paper reveals a couple of glimpses of father-transference which are relevant here. He writes, early in the paper, " . . . it would be a miracle if I could *make* Judy come in her person and speak herself. She was most vulnerable . . ." (emphasis added). This links up with her telling him, "I cannot eat . . . unless Daddy is there. He *makes* me eat." (emphasis added). Later, in Khan's description of the patient's rebelling against and throwing a glass of wine upon her intrusive female relative, he writes, "Her father had passively and quietly watched the whole drama." This links up with his reporting, a bit later in the paper, "To *helplessly watch* Judy's hidden madness, which was compatible with living, turn first into the most agonizing physical pain and symptoms, and later into psychotic states of paranoid delusions, hallucinations, and utter dilapidation of her person, was most painful for me. Not having been hardened to human suffering, physical and psychic, due to lack of medical education, this phase of her illness was as traumatic for me as it was destructive of Judy the person" (emphasis added). The link, if there is one, would infer at least two likely possibilities: (1) the father was suffering far more than his passive-observer demeanor would indicate; and (2) both Khan and the father were each having an intense struggle with his own unconscious, passive sadism. I may be attributing, here, to Khan and the father something which is true of myself but not of either of them. Surely it is true of me; more than once, in the depth of my agony at feeling helpless to relieve the suffering of a patient, I have had to face the important role of my own sadism toward the patient, sadism that gave me good reason to feel guiltily responsible for a patient's suffering. Analysts tend to identify with their patients' vulnerability (as Khan apparently identified with the so-vulnerable Judy) as an unconscious defense against violently sadistic feelings toward the patient.

Khan's impression that "Judy had been driven mad by her mother" is an oversimplification that underestimates the role here of her father. Time and time again, in work with schizophrenic or borderline patients, it has emerged only after years of treatment that the patently so-destructive relationship between mother and patient was at work with the father not really off the scene; rather, both mother and patient come to be revealed as mutually helpless to cope in a situation dominated by a *seemingly* tangential, but omnipotently controlling, sadistic father.

"I suggested she should ask Linda to let her work full days this week." This kind of managerial action may strike one as naive on Khan's part, and it may be assumed that it was a reaction not only to Judy's apparent needs; but a reaction, also, to his own guilt at not spending more time with her and, even more likely, a reaction to unfulfilled wishes on his own part to be working with her a greater share of the time as an *analyst*. This last-mentioned impression is supported by his comment concerning his appraisal of the first week of their work together: ". . . I felt disappointed with my own contributions during the week. . . ."

When Khan writes that, "Fortunately, Linda was only too glad to have Judy work full-time that week, because she had her 'Sale' next week and all the objects had to be repriced," he appears, again, far more naive than the present author knows him to be. Surely, as an extraordinarily competent analyst, he must have had ideas about the deeper reasons for Linda's being so cooperative. Of course, he could not tell all these things in a brief paper; but it is jarring that he writes about this phase of management much as though all concerned were not, as always, being influenced powerfully by unconscious passions. Likewise, when he reports that, "It was in the second month that things began to happen," surely he does not need to be reminded that, during the management phase, deeply significant, unconscious as well as conscious, and importantly psychotherapeutic things have been happening all along.

Khan writes, "I knew little about the actual events of her familial life. . . . She had a vociferously intrusive relative, who kept ringing me to tell 'all,' but I had militantly refused to see her. I didn't want to know anything that Judy couldn't tell or speak." The wisdom and courage of his stand here is admirable. Many times at Chestnut Lodge I found more burdensome than helpful the relatively detailed histories that had been provided by relatives—no matter how well-meaning—at the time of the patient's admission to the hospital. Too often, such information was more a barrier than a bond between the patient and myself. Of course, it is not feasible to dispense entirely with the acquisition of such information as regards hospitalizable, or near-hospitalizable, patients generally; but in teaching interviews, for example, at various hospitals, whereas I used routinely to request the patient's therapist (usually one of the psychiatric residents) to give a brief history of the patient and of the psychotherapy thus far, during the past few years I have preferred to interview the patient without having been told, ahead of time, anything about him or her. This way, one has to rely more heavily upon intuitive impressions of the patient, and one misses hearing from the patient many of the most important things that have happened to him or her.

Nevertheless, I feel more genuinely available to the patient, therapeutically, than I used to feel in interviewing a patient about whom I possessed, at the outset, a head full of information that he himself or she herself had not told me.

Perhaps there is a psychodynamic connection between Khan's refusal to speak with the intrusive relative and Judy's refusal to speak to him in some of the sessions. Perhaps she was identifying during the session with his behavior toward her relative; perhaps she was unconsciously showing him the way she wanted him to be toward that relative of hers: refusing, that is, to speak to the other person. Very likely, Khan was enabled to dispose of some of his rage at Judy for her refusal to speak to him by identifying with her in his behaving similarly toward her intrusive relative. Even more likely, still, is Khan's (1) remaining largely unconscious of his rage at Judy, who at the outset had been compelled upon him by her physician, and whose treatment not only intruded severely into his accustomed work-schedule, but invaded, often very disturbingly, his deepest feeling-capacities; and (2) displacing upon her intrusive relative this rage that would be inordinately difficult for any therapist to integrate with his images of Judy as being so vulnerable, so compassionate herself, and so desperately in need of therapeutic help from him.

Here is the kind of omnipotent stance, on Khan's part, that is tenable only on the basis of strength borrowed from the idealizing patient: "On the phone, I simply said to her that now she had been able to dream this awful dream, she would be able to sleep fearlessly . . ." Similarly, he reports later that, "I noted the similarity of passivity with which this willful girl as a child had impersonally suffered and obeyed her mother, and now her bossy relative." One may add, as true for some stretches of the treatment "—and Khan." Further, when he writes later that, "I had absolutely no doubt that now Judy's madness would find a somatic idiom and might even lead to a psychotic break," both his omniscient certainty and his self-righteous ensconcement in the observer role are nettling,—as though he were not causing, in the slightest degree, the terrible changes he saw to be at work in her.

On the other hand, when he reports that, "Gradually I got to know Tim [the pony] as a person in Judy's life, and it showed me what a profound capacity this girl had for compassion and care," one sees Khan at his best, not involved in any heroic or dramatically masterful behavior, but immersed in an appreciation of Judy's own human strengths. Similarly, when he reports, regarding the treatment during the week following her call to him at 2:00 A.M. to tell him the dreams that had frightened her, that "I suspended drawing her attention to the dream all that week," one sees an undramatic and careful psychoanalyst at his most skillful. When he is not feeling required by circumstances to run nearly the whole show, there is little to question and much to admire in his way of working.

He writes, a bit later, that,

> . . . The nosey relative rang me one evening and bullied my butler to put her through to me. With an arrogant malicious note of triumph in her voice, she told me how Judy had been staying out very late all night, and was not taking her "pills" regularly. So she had arranged with her gynecologist to insert an I.U.D. as a preventive, and Judy was going to see the gynecologist tomorrow. I warned her that sometimes the body of a girl does not accept the I.U.D. and that in Judy's case there was a real danger that all her illness could express itself through somatic symptoms. But she wouldn't listen. . . .

The narrative casts the nosey relative as the Bad Manager, as a foil for Khan, the Good Manager. The present author's impression is that Khan is not nearly so aware in this management-context, as he would be in his usual one-to-one analytic milieu, of Judy's proclivity for negative-transference attitudes toward him—as being, from her unconscious point of view, fully as bad-intentioned a manager (or mother) as the nosey relative was being in actuality.

Powerful increments of negative transference, and of negative countertransference, were being displaced out of awareness onto one or another person, portrayed as a villain, outside the relationship between Khan and Judy. In the following passages, for instance, it appears that Khan remains largely unaware of his most negative countertransference reactions to Judy and displaces these, instead, upon the gynecologist:

> . . . The I.U.D. was removed, but the gynecologist had made a real mess of her uterus. . . . The father asked for consultation with me, new gynecologist, and the physician. It was mutually agreed that Judy should be nursed at home. . . . her mental condition changed to a patently schizophrenic paranoid state. She would not eat or talk. I called on her every evening after dinner for an hour, and so did the physician. We often found her either in a comatose state and mute, or in a state of hallucinosis. . . .

Of course, Khan himself did not single-handedly or in any very large part actually cause this worsening of Judy's condition but, through finding a villain in the first gynecologist, he is able to keep largely out of consciousness his *fear* that he himself has caused this. Similarly, as regards his outrage at the mess the first gynecologist made of Judy's uterus, this outrage would help to keep repressed any comparable feelings of outrage at Judy who, for all her youthfulness and puppy fat, was tending to cause vicious damage to Khan's cherished self-images as a loving human being and a constructive psychoanalytic therapist.

Soon after this in the narrative, he describes that, "On her return home [from the hospital], Judy immediately asked to see me. . . . I cancelled my patients and immediately went over." It is striking—"I cancelled my patients" —as if *she* were not one of his patients. It could be simply that, so long as she was in the hospital, she was indeed not a current patient of his, but I believe there is more to it than that. The reader is left to wonder what are some of the deeper meanings of Judy, seemingly so special to Khan by contrast to his other patients, to him. One of the large possibilities is that he was responding here, to a greater extent that he was realizing, in terms of her positive father-transference to him. We are given a picture of the father himself as ready, time and again, to put aside instantly all his other responsibilities in deference to Judy's need of him.

Concerning Khan's arranging for Judy to be sent to live in the country, there are two ingredients worthy of note. First, it is another of many examples of his intuitively acting upon a request by her, trusting the request as valid and constructive. Khan's ability to respond in this spirit is one of his many admirable qualities. Second, his response *may* be seen as attributing omniscience, if not omnipotence, to Judy's own expressed view of what she herself needs. Thus one can say that such a request appeals to something deeply dependent, as well as grandiose-managerial, in the therapist.

Concerning his thoughts and feelings in prospect of meeting with Judy after an interval of more than three years, he tells us that,

> About one thing I had made up my mind: no matter in what psychic condition I found her, I would not initiate or insinuate, from my side, her asking for a book about "horse-language." I would try and meet her on her terms, as she would choose to present herself. Furthermore, I was determined not to refer to her grave illnesses in the past, should she now decide to obviate them from her present identity as a person. I knew all this would entail an enormous discipline of deliberate *un-*knowing on my part, but I was convinced if I was to help Judy, I had to accept her as an as-if person in her own right, different from the *sick* girl. . . .

In the above passage, Khan shows that he has learned well, long since, the patient's absolute need for the therapist to meet her (or him) on the patient's own terms. The present author has been struggling with this issue with a chronically schizophrenic woman—struggling with it during the past year or so and, especially, during recent months. The work has gone on for many years, but her myriad identity-components, each of which holds sway in her ego-functioning for no more than a few sessions, state with absolute certainty that she has met with me for only—variously—two or five or twenty (or whatever *relatively* tiny number, by contrast to the actual number) sessions.

I have found it next to impossible, month after month, to keep from inundating her precariously based and subjectively very young (baby or young-child) identity with my reminiscences about events from years before in our long work together. As recently as two months ago she was finally able to tell me, simply and directly, "I don't see why you don't accept me as I am," without—from her point of view—incessantly misidentifying her as being one or another of those much older persons with whom I had sessions "long before *my* time." If there is anything which, in my envy of Masud Khan, I cannot forgive him, it is my deep suspicion that, had he been my chronically schizophrenic patient's therapist, he might have enabled her to become *relatively* (totally, I cannot believe) nonpsychotic years ago.

The following clearly was a major, if not the major, turning point in Judy's career over those years in her life which this paper describes:

> . . . According to Judy, Luciana [who had stayed for five years in Ashrams in Nepal and India] was able to "understand" the "horse-language" and to talk it also. In three months, the foal was eating normally. It was this event that decided Judy to leave Argentina and to go to India or Nepal for Zen cum yoga apprenticeship. . . . She had, in fact, already chosen an Ashram in India . . .

Judy's identifying here with Luciana is obvious. Hardly less obvious is her identifying, in the same process, with Khan, whose origins had clearly enough been in the Indian subcontinent, and who understands so well the nonverbal language of the unconscious. The evidence of Judy's father-transference, in the identificational process, toward both Luciana and Khan, is of particular interest:

> . . . The father . . . had been to India on business many times, and had some good friends there. . . . out of curiosity he had visited a few Ashrams . . .

In other words, Judy's decision to enter the Ashram in India, for a seven-year course of study, was expressive of her identifying with the good-mother aspects of her father, as personified by Khan in the treatment-relationship.

For colleagues of Khan, the wish to identify with him presents some awesome challenges. It is not easy to gain access to identifying with a colleague whose listing in the roster of the International Psychoanalytical Association shows him to be a prince (raja); whom this paper reveals to have such mastery not only in one-to-one psychoanalytic therapy, but also in the management of this very ill young woman's daily life; and whose far-flung personal influence is such that he can say of the particular Ashram that Judy had selected to spend the next seven years of her life, ". . . I knew of this Ashram, and some very good friends of mine finance its maintenance."

These aspects of Khan's personality are, however, offset by a basic humility, a deep respect for his fellow human beings, including those who are mad. What Jones said was true of Freud, one can see to be equally true of Khan: he has "a veritable passion to *understand*." These dimensions of Khan's self provide wide avenues for our identifying with this remarkably creative and capable psychoanalyst.

REFERENCES

Winnicott, D. W. (1954). Metapsychological and clinical aspects of regression within the psycho-analytic set up. *International Journal of Psycho-Analysis* 36:16–26. Reprinted in *D. W. Winnicott—Collected Papers—Through Paediatrics to Psycho-Analysis*, pp. 278–294. New York: Basic Books, 1958.

The Significance of Kleinian Contributions to Psychoanalysis III. The Kleinian Theory of Ego Psychology and Object Relations

JAMES S. GROTSTEIN, M.D.

The Kleinian theory of ego psychology rests largely on the theory of internal object relations formed through projective identification and re-introjection, and how they undergo transformations from the paranoid-schizoid to the depressive positions via the capacity of the maternal container to transform her infant's "paranoid" content into sobering awareness of truth. It differs from the classical theory in terms of the initial emphasis on projective identification and the only gradually developing importance of introjection of the external world of reality. This contribution develops the Kleinian metapsychology of ego formation from the succession of the paranoid-schizoid and depressive positions, which are the phenomenological-experiential equivalents of Mahler's autistic, symbiotic, and separation-individuation phases of development. It seeks also to develop the Kleinian conception of narcissism and compare it to the classical one.

In this section the Kleinian conception of ego psychology, object relations, and narcissism is elucidated through the examination of splitting and projective identification as they are elaborated in the paranoid-schizoid position, and of introjection as it is elaborated in the depressive position. Klein accounts for a very early ego based upon projective identification and splitting that is capable of internalizing objects, which constitute the scaffolding for ego development. Kleinian ego psychology is based upon the assumption that the infant identifies with the objects that he or she internalizes, and that the more permanent of these phantasied identifications become ego structures. Further, Kleinians believe that ego psychology emerges as a series of transformations from the paranoid-schizoid position to the depressive position, where internal objects evolve into whole object representations and the instinctual "load" contained within these internal objects (e.g., good libidinal object, bad persecuting object) become psychical structures after the instinctual "load" has been rectified through reparations. In many ways it is similar to the classical theory of ego psychology, but it is more phenomenological than mechanistic. This transformation is made possible and is orchestrated by what Bion (1970) calls the container and the contained phenomenon. The container is the mother's capacity to intercept the infant's inchoate screams, withstand them, understand them, translate them into a virtual color spectrum of differentiated meaning, and then "return" them to the infant as "translations" of need-awarenesses, thereby constituting the precursor of thinking. Since it is based almost exclusively on the formation of internal objects and their transformations into whole object representations, this aspect of Kleinian theory is discussed at some length.

AN INFANTILE MENTAL ORGANIZATION BASED ON PHANTASY

The employment of splitting and projective identification led Klein not only to the threshold of understanding universal myth formation but to an understanding of the development of archaic mental life and its inchoate organization. Infantile nightmares, infantile colic, and cannibalistic phantasies now had a sound psychodynamic basis in her psychology. Infantile perceptual chaos could now be brought under the organization of phantasy, which ordered and arranged it narratively in order for it to be mastered.

Phantasy at first was a body language insofar as it dealt with the zones of the self and the geography of the mother's body in phantasized linkages. For instance, the infant's mouth is linked with the mother's breast, his or her body skin to the touch of the mother's body skin, and so on. Klein was able to account for a very early primitive conflictual world in a way that differed quite significantly from Freud's. Since Freud (1900) had always remained wedded to the notion that instinctual drives, which instigated phantasy formation, were nonconflictual in the id but became conflictual only as they erupted into the ego, he was at a loss to understand an infantile conceptual organization that was able to experience conflict prior to the differentiation of the ego from the id. Without actually stating so, Klein (1952a, 1957, 1960) implies what Fairbairn (1952) explicated, that the ego and the id are different aspects of the same agency of mind and are therefore capable of experience, and therefore of conflict, from the very beginning.

No classical writer has developed a satisfactory ground plan for an infantile mental organization that encompasses a psychology coherent enough to have the capacity for infantile psychic conflict. One needs a conception of psychic structure in order to comprehend conflict. Klein's conception of (1) initial separation, (2) instincts being phantasies from the beginning, and (3) the creation of an "autistic" internal world via splitting and projective identification allowed her to posit an inchoate infantile mental organization where there was an epigenesis from the paranoid-schizoid to the depressive position. Freud, on the other hand, was stuck with instincts divorced from the ego and its objects, and therefore had to struggle in Stygian darkness with phantasies on a higher ontogenetic level. Mahler's (1968) conception of normal autism does not allow for sufficient mental organization to warrant the discrimination requisite for psychic conflict, and her stage of symbiosis does little better. Only when she gets to the stage of separation-individuation is a conflict possible. Despite the enormous importance of Mahler's (1971) contributions about early infantile development, they are largely descriptive and lack phenomenological completion. Mahler's concept of autism beautifully coincides with the concept of adhesive identification (Bick 1968, Meltzer et al. 1975—Klein's students) as stated earlier. Mahler's three stages of separation-individuation are easily congruent with Klein's conception of the depressive position. Erikson's (1959) stages of epigenetic development in the life cycle are easily reconcilable with both theories, to give them even greater dimension.

INTERNAL OBJECTS AND OBJECT REPRESENTATIONS RECONSIDERED

An internal object is the object that is first *presented* to the senses, and is therefore an object *presentation* (without re-). At the same time, the term "senses" is understood by Klein to be a projective entity that projectively identifies the infant's sensuous experience onto the image of the external object whose own behavior modifies the reintrojection of this image. Thus an object presentation is created by the projective identification of the infant's sensuous experience as an image that is modified by the external object but is not the external object per se. An object *re-presentation*, on the other hand, is the expression of a re-created image of an object in the mental space left vacant by the object and patrolled by the infant's cooperating protectiveness; i.e., it is the symbol that the infant has been able to reconstruct in the absence of the concrete object of the senses. The relationship between a concrete object presentation and an object re-presentation is paralleled in Scripture by Abraham's rejection of the idols (objects of the senses) for the ultra-sensual spirit of the one God. Autoerotism is the classical shorthand for a primitive relationship between the ego (self)[1] and the self as its first object, where this "object-self" is felt to be indistinguishable from the caretaking external object, i.e., a self–object. Thus the excitement at the autoerotic zones re-establishes a sense of at-one-ment between subjective "I" and objective self–object. In the classical literature it is called a self–object representation, although erroneously, as has been detailed earlier. Hartmann (1964), Jacobson (1964), and Kernberg (1975), and most other classical analysts appear either quite confused about this distinction between a concrete object of the senses (object presentation) and an ultrasensual representation of an object.

The classical picture of object relationships does not distinguish between internal objects and object representations. It merely distinguishes between object and part-object representations. A part-object cannot be a representation, but only a presentation, because it is confused with the infant.[2] This is a subtle but exceedingly important point: A presentation is the perception of an object that is sensual; i.e., the infant's senses "sense" and therefore possess the object and he or she therefore does not experience separation from it at the moment of sensing. Because of the omnipotent capacity of his or her senses to possess the object, the infant develops the notion of a "sense" of oneness, albeit transitionally, with the object. Separation from an object— i.e., the state of *re*-presentation—can be achieved only by hallucinatory or imaginative conjury of the object in its absence. This re-presentation is now a nonsensual object and therefore does not lend itself to a state of projective identificatory confusion with the senses.

The term self–object representation seems first to have been coined by Giovacchini (1967) but has been used differently by him than by the before-mentioned writers and also by its greatest popularizer, Kohut (1971, 1977). It seems that Giovacchini conceived of the self–object representation as the conception of secondary narcissism or of secondary identification by the self with the object following separation from it, as Freud (1914, 1917)

1. Klein was more a phenomenologist than a metapsychologist, therefore her use of the term "ego" approximates classical usage but also is congruent with the term "self," the latter of which she was to use more in her later works.
2. The whole concept of "part-object" is itself in jeopardy, since Bion's significant implications that the breast, like the penis, is a *communicating* or *linking* organ to a *whole object*, which is perceived whole, though dimly and with relatively little differentiation from the very beginning. It is always mother, not her breasts, that are of cogent importance, according to Bion (1959).

understood it. Kohut, being a phenomenologist rather than strictly a metapsychologist, seems not to make significant distinctions between the infant's experience of primary narcissism and of secondary narcissism. His term "self-object" seems to connote either or both. Giovacchini's conception of self-object representation, however, implies two different states of mind, a dual track, in which the infant is already separate enough in order to be able to re-present another experience of itself as being nonseparate, i.e., a self–object representation. A self–object (which is the equivalent of a part-object representation) is inconceivable in the absence of a separate self that experiences itself as separate enough to re-present more primitive aspects of itself.

Stated in yet another way, *sensual presentation* denotes experience; *re*-presentation denotes the experience of the experience. The two basic categories of objects are those that are sensual and those that are ultra-sensual or intuitive. The term "intuitive" is used here in the sense that Bion (1970) discusses it, i.e., as the capacity to reflect upon experiences within and experiences without thanks to the achievement of "common sense." The latter term implies that the senses have sufficiently differentiated so that they are now "willing to communicate with one another" and thus give the verdicts of internal and external experience from multiple, simultaneous vertices. A sensual object is one that is incipiently perceived as being possessed by the senses so that no separation between the infant and the object is experienced. An ultra-sensual object—i.e., an intuitive object—is a re-presentation to the consciousness of the infant of the image of the object in its absence. It has to undergo *re-creation*, which includes re-assembly of the perceived ingredients of the object in its absence. No self-reflection or intuition is conceivable without this fundamental process. This distinction between an object presentation and an object *re*-presentation is therefore crucial (Bower 1974, Condon 1977, Trevarthen 1977, Emde and Robinson 1979, Bowlby 1980, Sander 1980, and Brazelton 1981).

When an infant or child fears the experience of separation and wishes to reunite with the object, Klein believes that the infant or child may experience a phantasy of reunion, either with the external object or with the image of the object in its absence (object representation). In so doing, the object and/or object representation is transformed into a part-object presentation (not re-) and, as such, becomes an internal object. The phenomenon of projective identification makes the difference. The phantasy of invading or possessing an object renders that object no longer a representation. When a psychotic patient told me, for instance, that he was afraid of smoking in my presence for fear of turning me into a cigarette smoker, his ultimate fear was that he would have a damaged me inside him during the weekend break. Thus the term self–object representation is impossible, per se; it can only be possible as the object of speculation by an already separated self-representation existing on another track which, by virtue of its already established separateness as a fully constituted self-representation, can then reflectively regard an aspect of itself as being in a state of fusion. Only in this instance is a self–object re-presentation conceivable.

The classical concept of the self–object representation is therefore erroneous as such because, in its denotation of a state of confusion between self and object, it cannot denote a state of representation. A representation is the place where an object used to be but is no longer—and with the self's permission. Symbol formation takes its place. However, an already separated self can contemplate the representation of itself as still being in self–objecthood on another level. This would amount to a dual-track conception, one track being that of the already separated self, which has the capacity for perception and re-representation, and the other track being the experience of the self's fusion with an object.

INTERNAL OBJECTS, SELF–OBJECTS, OBJECT REPRESENTATIONS, AND NARCISSISM

The classical picture of the self–object representation, upon which the newly formed classical theory of narcissism is based, is unfortunate in yet another regard. This fused representation (and, again, there can be no such thing on its own) connotes an undifferentiated infant. How does this classical notion develop? Hartmann, Kris, and Loewenstein (1949), while exposing their concept of aggression, discussed projection and introjection of libidinal and aggressive drives from the infant as the impetus to its growth. They even pointed out that the aggressive instinct in particular is projected into an object and then re-internalized as an aggressive object, but there was no reference to Klein's already established conception of projective identification. Kernberg (1975) lists projection, introjection, and projective identification as functions of the undifferentiated self–object. How can an undifferentiated infant project or introject if it is in a state of fusion that the undifferentiated state predicates? Projection and/or projective identification imply that some separateness is already in progress. The same is true for introjection. Fusion precludes projection or introjection. This aspect of classical theory is therefore inadequate on this score.

Mahler (1958a, 1958b, 1960, 1965a, 1965b, 1969, 1971, 1972a, 1972b, 1975) has beautifully detailed the *behavior* of early, middle, and late infancy and has appended the terms "autism," "symbiosis," and "separation-individuation, hatching sub-phase". In other words, she does not seem to allow the infant in the autistic and symbiotic phases to have a *psychology* of his or her own or a mental organization that can account for experience, which Klein's phenomenology specifically does.

Erikson (1959) seems to come closer to bridging the gap between Mahler and Klein, although he too is shy on phenomenological phantasies and seems content with linear history. Mahler's concept of autism coincides with the concept of adhesive identification (Bick 1968, Meltzer et al. 1975). Adhesive identification is posited by them to be a stage of identification in which the infant seeks to develop a sense of skin boundary by apposing his or her own skin up against mother's skin so as to receive sufficient warmth, containment, and stimulation so as to establish a sense of his or her own independent skin. This stage of development corresponds to Mahler's autistic stage, whereas Klein's paranoid-schizoid position probably is to be associated more with the symbiotic stage of development in which the infant experiences himself or herself as being separate and nonseparate from his or her objects at the same time, a conception that allows for a "Siamese twin-like" nature of the symbiotic experience. It corresponds to Freud's (1900) concept of hallucinatory wish fulfillment, the capacity to conjure hallucinatorily the object in its absence. According to Klein's concept, sanity depends on the infant's capacity to hallucinate an object as a *re*-presentation of its image as a successor to an internal object, the latter of which has been released, allowed to disappear, and then imaginatively to reappear before its concrete reappearance in fact.

Basch (1981) has recently questioned the validity of all psychoanalytic formulations of early mental life and has attempted to dispel the concept of infantile hallucinatory wish fulfillment and of the occurrence of imaging of objects prior to object constancy. He bases his assumptions on Piaget's and Inhelder's well-established formulations that imaging occurs as the result of the abstraction from sensory-motor schemata at 18 months of age. These allegations seem to counter Klein's assumptions, to say nothing of Mahler's and Erikson's, that the infant can have a mental life earlier than 18 months of age. The assumptions of early mental life as developed by such developmentalists as Bower (1974), Condon (1977), Emde and Robinson (1979), Brazelton (1981), etcetera, seem to contradict this assumption. Furthermore, Piaget's and Inhelder's conclusions about mental life are: (1) based upon the testable, and therefore observable behavior of the infant whose behavioral apparatus (the neuromusculature) undergoes a slow myelination and therefore a slow development of function, which therefore may possibly mask mental activity that cannot yet be translated into behavior; and (2) seem to ignore the concept of phantasy and the activity in general of the nondominant hemisphere, which in particular does not lend itself to behavioral observations, only to phenomenological inferences.

PROJECTIVE VERSUS INTROJECTIVE IDENTIFICATION

Another feature of the difference between the classical and the Kleinian conception of objects derives from respectively different interpretations of Freud's original conception of internal objects. In his paper, "On Narcissism," Freud (1914) clearly implied that narcissism is a state that is achieved via the projective identification of omnipotent aspects of the ego into an ego ideal. Thus the clinical phenomenon of mania would be the fusion of the ego with its own ideas by a second projective identification, one that allows the ego to imagine itself once again to be one with its lost omnipotence. This paper is the birthplace of Klein's conception of projective identification (Grotstein 1981a). The classical theory of object formation seems to emphasize introjective identification in lieu of projective identification and derives its birthplace from Freud's second major paper on internal objects, "Mourning and Melancholia" (Freud 1917). In this latter paper Freud stated poetically, "The shadow of the object falls upon the ego." Klein, on the other hand, understood Freud to imply in his earlier paper that, "The shadow of the ego falls upon the object." In all probability, both are true, and the confluence of these two shadows can be called projective–introjective identification. This distinction is crucial in reading the classical and Kleinian literature. Up until recently, most classical theorists, most particularly Jacobson (1964), thought in terms of object representations and, when psychosis intervened, thought of their disintegration and repersonification into object images rather than into the internal objects.

Suffice it to say at this point that "internal object" has quite a different connotation to a Kleinian than "object representation" does to a classical person. An internal object, being the introjection of the shadow of the self upon the object, is more a reflection of the infant's *internal* world; an object representation, at least in the classical sense, is more a reflection of the infant's interface with objects of the external world. As a representation, it is in the psyche but not in the internal world per se. It is important, therefore, to make a distinction between the internal world proper and the internal representation of the external world. The Kleinian internal world is the world of internalized objects that have not yet been released in the depressive position to become object re-presentations, the latter of which are also internal within the psyche but not considered to be in the same domain as internal objects. The world of object re-presentations reflects a picture or map of the external world, whereas the internal world proper reflects the external world's mortification of the experiences of one's internal feelings. In other words, internal objects reflect more of what has commonly been called the id than of external objects, whereas the re-presentational world reflects the external world more than the id. This is the great divide between Kleinian and classical thinking.

It must be remembered that the conception of the objects of the internal world was originally brought into the so-called "classical" literature by Jacobson and by Hartmann because of the inescapable influence of the Kleinian and British middle group discoveries of object relations. It was Klein who had been publishing her works on internal objects as early as 1921. Jacobson (1964) has gone to great lengths to discredit Klein's "misconceptions" about objects of the internal world but she, Jacobson, apparently has an enormous misconception about what Klein means by internal objects. Jacobson criticizes Klein, for example, for suggesting that object representations can be projected rather than displaced. She is right in stating that object representations cannot be projected, but she seems not to comprehend that the essential distinction Klein makes between internal objects of the paranoid-schizoid position and object representations of the depressive position. Klein never believed that object representations formed in the depressive position could be projected; however, she did allow for the possibility of their being projected into secondarily by the infant who wishes to engage in a fusion or reunion with the object. Jacobson, on the other hand, dismisses Klein's internal objects as primitive object images.

In actual psychoanalytic usage an internal object corresponds to a self-object, i.e., a state of fusion between the experience of self and the experience of the needed object. An object representation, to repeat, is an object from whom separation has been achieved in the state of the depressive position of separation-individuation with rapprochement. An object that is separated from the self is now an image and no longer an object; an object that is not separated from the self is a concrete perception by the sense organs of the ego and is not an image. Klein rarely if ever referred to object representations, generally only to internal objects. When she did deal with object representations, she discussed them as objects that have been released in the depressive position. The differences between internal objects and object representations have been reviewed extensively in other contributions (Grotstein 1977a, 1978a, 1978c, 1981a).

A theoretical formulation, known as the dual-track theory, which would allow for separate, simultaneous experiential agendas of the individual so as to allow for separate states of being, has been attempted (Grotstein 1981c). This dual-track theory can account for an infant being separate, for instance, on one track and continuingly nonseparate on another track. This second track of fusion between self and object encompasses the continuation of primary identification and the development of secondary identification in statu nascendi. In times of stress, therefore, an infant may re-invade the parental object in phantasy and, thereby, transforms this external object or object representation into an internal object (self–object) by fusing with it via identification. In so doing, he or she may seem to overweigh the second track at the expense of the track of separation (Grotstein 1981c). The consequences of this are that the objects available to his or her psyche are consequently identificatory rather than separated objects, only the latter of which can help him or her to grow by offering reflections of objective mirroring from the self. The so-called mirror objects of Kohut (1971, 1977) are subjective mirroring and do not involve objective corrections, only subjective support.

Maturation and development are really the infant's processional biography from states of identification with an internal object to the release of this internal object so that the latter can then evolve or matriculate into an object representation. As a consequence of this release into an object representation, the self finds itself more confident in its sense of self-esteem and is thus able to be more effective in transforming the remaining portion of the continuing sense of primary identification into evolutional separateness. The transformation from an internal object to an object representation corresponds, in Kleinian terms, to the transformation from the paranoid-schizoid position to the depressive position. This is analogous to Hartmann's (1964) conception of the change of function that an instinctual drive undergoes to become an apparatus of secondary autonomy in the ego. In psychoanalytic practice we seek, via the transference neurosis, to re-engage states of continuing confusion with internal objects into the transference so that the transference interpretations can free up the self from its stricturing identifications with objects.

THE IMPORTANCE OF INFANTILE (PRIMITIVE) FORMULATIONS FOR KLEINIAN EGO PSYCHOLOGY

Many classical analysts have objected to Klein's emphasis on an early calendar of infant development but have overloaded the fact that her "infantile" psychology is more one of depth or of primitiveness than merely early chronologically. It is thus the verticality of her theories that has more relevance to ego psychology. For an object to become installed, it must, as previously stated, first undergo projective identification from the "infant" (primitive aspect of the person) into an object or image of the object; then this amalgam is internalized and intensified as ego objects and superego objects (and even perhaps "id objects"). These objects are gradually transformed by the maternal container in an epigenesis from part-objects to object representations. Meltzer (1967) designates this part-object transformation as the progressive relationship of the zones of the infant's body to the geography of the mother's body. In this zone-to-geography relationship, the infant's mouth is directed to the mother's breast, its anus to the mother's "toilet breast" function, including the mother's anus; its genital is associated with the mother's genital but must be renounced in favor of the father's penis, which is necessary to "wash out" mother's genital from the accumulation of the infant's harmful effects on the mother. In other words, the father's penis is necessary to repair the mother from the effects of nursing. Additionally, Meltzer states that the infant separates the mother's body into the top half and bottom half and front and back. The mother's front belongs to the objects dependent on her, the top given to the infant and the bottom to father; the backside belongs to her alone. A similar procedure takes place with the father.

Kleinians believe that all data of experience must be processed by the infant → adult according to their correspondence on the most primitive level to their relevance to these anatomic categories. Otherwise there is a zonal and/or geographic confusion that corresponds to a confusion in thinking. A female hysteric, for example, may confuse her own genital with her mouth and her father's penis with her mother's breast. This failure of proper sorting and differentiation will be reflected in mental confusion on higher levels and preclude the optimal possibility of the formation of adequate self and object representational worlds.

KLEINIAN AND CLASSICAL CONCEPTIONS OF TRANSFERENCE

The classical conception of transference is that it generally is a displacement of past object cathexes onto a present object, namely, the analyst. Projections are also possible, according to the classical conception, but include projections of the ego, the id, and the superego, not of object representations. The Kleinian conception includes the displacement of past object cathexes in terms of the representational world, but emphasizes the projective identification of all aspects of the self in the here-and-now (Grotstein 1981a). Thus the past object cathexes that classical theorists view as being "transferred" to a present object (the analyst) are themselves initial transferences in the childhood period when aspects of the child's infantile self are projected into his or her objects as permanent conceptions or even misconceptions or illusions to be carried forward into adult life. Thus displacement from the past is certainly an important aspect of transference, but the more important aspect seems to be the projective aspect both past and present. In other words, if the infant or child projected feelings into his or her parents, then he or she is likely not only to pass this on to a present object but is also likely to continue doing the same thing that he or she did then. This perhaps is a major difference between the classical and the Kleinian conception of transference.

THE KLEINIAN VERSUS THE CLASSICAL INTERNAL WORLDS

Kleinian objects, therefore, are not the same as Freudian objects, particularly at the beginning, nor is the Kleinian internal world the same thing as the Freudian internal world, as stated earlier. The first Kleinian object is the vaguely alienated, split-off aspect of the self generalized or projected outward onto the dim image of an external object and then taken back as an image of a phantom known as an internal object. The internal object, in other words, is an amalgam of split-off and reinternalized aspects of the self as well as of the external object, but initially the latter is present in the internal object experience more in terms of how it modified the projection than as an object in its own right. In other words, the internal object is a reflection of the shadow of the ego (self) falling upon the object. It is a self-reflection modified by the mirror or inchoate experience with the object. Klein refers to this as the paranoid-schizoid position.

The Freudian internal world, on the other hand, is the introjection of the external world modified to one degree or another by the instinctual endowment (Freud 1900, 1901). Kleinians accept the Freudian internal world as later evolution of the earlier internal world but one that occurs at the time of genital Oedipus complex when external objects are more knowable. Classical analysts do not accept Klein's first internal world (Greenson 1974, Kernberg 1969, Yorke 1971). Earlier the difference between the Kleinian and classical internal world was described as one between the Kleinian internal world proper and a Freudian conception of the internalization of the external world, where the latter was not properly an internal world. This may seem to do a disservice to the classical view. Actually, the classical view of the internal world is congruent with the Kleinian one in terms of drive theory; i.e., instinctual drives in the id are part of the permanent internal world that is protectively covered over by primal repression. The object-representational world, to repeat, is internal to the psyche but does not represent the internal world. Strictly speaking, however, the drive representation is part of the self representation and *does* represent the internal world, but only in that narrow sense. Thus there seem to be three internal worlds: (1) the internal world of the primary repressed, including what classical analysts call the instinctual drives; (2) the internal world of internal objects, which are the projective introjective experience of fusion with an object; and (3) the world of self and object representations, more a reflection of the relationship to the external world.

THE SUPEREGO

One of the greatest debates in psychoanalysis has been the time of origin of the superego. Its origin has been crucial in determining the onset of psychic conflict, internal guilt, and so on. Freud (1923) reasoned that the superego was due to the internalization of the parents and other significant authorities, but he was always mystified by its instinctual nature. Freud (1930) later made an addendum to his theory of the superego in *Civilization and Its Discontents* when he integrated the death instinct with the superego. He believed that the death instinct becomes housed in the superego and that the ego thereafter suffers attacks from it. Klein (1933, 1935, 1940) was able to demonstrate that the superego originates as a projective identification of libidinal, destructive, and epistemophilic aspects of the infantile ego in the following way: the infant projects his or her own invasive self into the object and reintrojects (1) the image of the object newly transformed via the projective identification, and (2) the results of the invasion. Thus a greedy infant may experience the projective transformation of his or her own greed into the image of a greedy breast, which is then internalized as a demanding superego.

Parallel to this transformation is another one in which the infant also imagines what his or her invasive attack has done to the object, i.e., mutilated it. Thus two objects are internalized via each projective trans-action: (1) a predator superego object, and (2) a victimized ego object, corresponding to Freud's (1915) melancholic paradigm of a gradient in the ego, i.e., debased victimized objects in the ego (the results of the attack) and attacking or debasing objects in the superego. Klein also made another implication that the infant moralizes his or her world by the use of his "death instinct." Although she never specifically made this link clear, it certainly seems that her concept of moralization stems from this situation in which the infant omnipotently "moralizes" his or her world through blame and crit-icism. In short, the infant uses the death instinct in order to criticize and control his or her objects in order to force them to do his or her bidding, i.e., to guarantee him or her the restoration of lost entitlement in order to ward off the experience of catastrophe. The first "moralizer," therefore, is the infantile God who condemns frustration and those responsible for it (Klein 1952). The sense of self implicit in the projection of the infant into the image of the object is split-off so that the internalized superego is then believed to be foreign or estranged. The superego now reappears as an external object that has been internalized.

Freud's (1920) use of the death instinct implied an energic tropism toward entropy and an inborn destructive drive that was directed both toward the self and toward the objects. Later classical authors seem to be unsure of the status of the death instinct and debate between primary aggression and aggression as the result of the frustration of libido. Currently, it is thought of as a drive on an equal par with the libidinal instinctual drive organization (Hartmann, Kris, and Loewenstein 1949), but as in all classical conceptions of instinctual drives, the aim is discharge. There is no narrative or purpose associated to it such as that specified above. It is the superego, however, that classical and Kleinian authors agree is the storage place of much of the destructive or aggressive instinct as well as of the libidinal instinct. (For a recent reformulation of the death instinct, see Grotstein 1981a).

There are, therefore, at least two basic components to the superego: goodness and badness. The goodness is due to the infant's satisfaction that he or she is able to create good omnipotent objects that can protect him or her. The bad superego in turn has at least two components. One of them is due to the transformation of the instinctual vicissitudes of greed and the other is due to a transformation of the instinctual vicissitudes of envy.

ENVY AND ITS RELATIONSHIP TO THE SUPEREGO

The transformation of the instinctual vicissitudes of envy follows a similar pattern. The envious infant phantasies himself or herself to have invaded the envied breast in order to destroy its goodness, the very instigator of his or her envy. Again, the result of this invasion is internalized as two separate kinds of objects: one that is mutilated and is identified with the ego, and the other, an enviously denigrating, sadistic, hostile conscience. The latter is a superego object that contains a split-off perception or identification of the envious infant but now, because of its being split-off or alienated, the qualities are associated as belonging to an internal object that is experienced as extraterritorial to the sense of "I."

In short, Klein's version of the origin of the superego is through projective identification and reinternalization of the omnipotent demands of the infant confused with an object. It later becomes modified after many reprojections and reinternalizations until it becomes more sophisticated and congruent with the Oedipal superego of Freud. By this time it has become considerably modified and diluted by external modification from realistic objects, which are overcoming the infant's omnipotent prejudices. It must also be remembered, however, that Freud himself offered the notion that the ego ideal is formed in the very early infantile period as a projective identification of the infant's omnipotence into an object that is then reintrojected. He separately discussed the origin of the superego as being located at the termination of the Oedipus complex in the late phallic phase. Klein's superego objects correspond to Freud's ego ideal objects insofar as they are primitive, omnipotent, and largely projective identifications of the infant.

Modern classical writers who have written on the superego, particularly Sandler and Joffe (1969, 1970) and Sandler (1974), seem to suggest that it is formed through projective identification into external parental objects of traits from the child, but do not assign its origin to any stage earlier than the Oedipus complex. Mahler (1971) seems to hint that the superego begins at the onset of separation-individuation with rapprochement, at which time objects are perceived as being separate and can be internalized in different gradients, e.g., as representations and as superego objects. Hartmann and Loewenstein (1962) fall into a similar category. Their explorations into the nature of the superego merely consolidate the post-Oedipal nature of it. Peto (1970), on the other hand, seems to have gone into a completely different direction when he explores the very archaic nature of the origins of the superego, especially its vestibular-forerunner origins. He therefore gives credence to the notion of a primitive origin of the superego.

Meltzer (1967) and Mancia and Meltzer (1981) have dealt with the Kleinian conception of the relationship between the ego ideal and the superego. They believe that the two terms are not synonymous. The ego ideal, according to them, refers to a protective, nurturing, and encouraging function by an internal object in contradistinction to a prohibitive and inhibitive function of the internal objects within the superego. Further, Meltzer (1967) believes:

If the sequence of events in the natural history of the psycho-analytic process is as faithful a recapitulation of early development as I am suggesting, we can see that the progress from superego to ego ideal is first and foremost a consequence of the surrendering of omnipotence by the infantile parts of the self (Mancia and Meltzer 1981, p. 243).

REPRESSION

The theory of repression also differs between Kleinians and classical Freudians. At the Jerusalem Congress of 1977, Betty Joseph (a Kleinian) alluded to "porous repression," by which she meant the achievement of a healthy repression that could allow appropriate instinctual elements into awareness. Brian Bird, Leo Rangell, and Harold Blum (all classical analysts) took issue with her conception and reminded her and the audience that repression, when clinically encountered, is pathological. The Kleinian views repression as the successful outcome of the depressive position and values the transformation it achieves on primitive and more rigid defenses. Therefore a Kleinian seems to have a more benign attitude toward repression.

If a child has confidence in his or her capacity to *re*press, then he or she can have confidence in his or her ability to *ex*press.

Klein herself was more sanguine than classical authors in relating splitting to later repression and discrimination. Thus she saw splitting as the forerunner of normal discrimination perceptually and cognitively, and also as the forerunner of normal repression defensively. Although she did not state it in so many words, it seems clear that Klein believed repression to be something like a sublimation of splitting. Repression is not generally thought of in this way by classical authors, but this formulation may have enormous importance. First, this conception changes the nature of the psychic apparatus in a way that was long ago adumbrated by Fairbairn (1940, 1941, 1943, 1944, 1946, 1949, 1951). In other words, by postulating that instincts were themselves phantasies, Klein was clearly implying (though she did not explicitly state so) that the separation between the impulsive id and the containing ego was effectively nonexistent.

Rather than a separation of formless energy and structure, which was Freud's concept, she was actually positing that energy and structure were inseparable, as Fairbairn (1952) explicitly stated, and that the impulsive character assigned to the instinctual drives by Freud was really a statement of a communication to oneself and to one's object in a communicative or transactional context. Thus a sexual impulse as posited by Freud would arise from the mucous membrances of the autoerotic zone associated with that impulse, namely, the genital zone. In Klein's thinking, a sexual "impulse" would be a phantasy that is stimulated by some frustration, whether from within or without, but not from the mucous membranes of the autoerotic zone (Klein 1929b, 1945). The stimulation of frustration immediately becomes a phantasy to the infant and, if sexual feelings are the result, these are his or her phantasied attempts to link up with the object in a way to his or her optimum benefit. In other words, the Freudian impulse theory is ultimately neurophysiological more than psychological, and the Kleinian conception is all psychological and not neuropsychological.

Splitting of the ego and of its objects has been a hallmark in Klein's conception of the infant's internal world. Classical authors were slow to develop a realization of its enormous importance. The classical literature on splitting has been reviewed in another contribution (Grotstein 1981a). Most noteworthy amongst classical authors who have emphasized splitting of egos and objects are Jacobson (1964), Kohut (1971, 1977), and Kernberg (1975, 1976). Kernberg in particular has applied Fairbairn's (1952) and Klein's (1946, 1955) conception of splitting most cogently, although Kohut was to give important emphasis to Fairbairn's distinction between vertical splitting and horizontal splitting, the former of which is primitive splitting proper and the latter of which constitutes repression. Rinsley (1981), in a brilliant critique of Fairbairn, concludes that the vertical splitting of objects involves the splitting of the ego's consciousness pari passu, whereas repression involves merely the splitting off of the content of consciousness but not of consciousness itself. Kernberg's conception of splitting ranges all the way from the splitting of egos and objects to the splitting of personalities altogether, a phenomenon that he associates with the borderline personality disorder. Mahler (1971) has also called attention to splitting of the self and of objects in early mental life during a stage of symbiosis. Thus there seems to be a developing rapprochement between classical authors and Klein's formulations on splitting and its relationship to early mental life.

THE ISSUE OF REALITY

Many commentators on Klein's work have criticized her for ignoring reality, a criticism that could equally apply to Freud since 1897 (Glover 1945, Greenson 1974, Kernberg 1969). The external world is not introjected quite so readily nor, once introjected, is the result so photographically accurate as one is led to believe. It appears, however, that Klein does not so much *ignore* reality as emphasize what she believes to be the infant's phenomenological experience of it. It is true, however, that she does not believe that the infant has a clear enough picture of reality at the beginning as to be called "realistic." The "infantile camera" is highly prejudiced, filtered, and limited in its capacity for introjection. This "infantile camera" reflects the right hemispheric organization, which is governed by the pleasure principle. Perception is therefore field-dependent rather than field-independent as it is in the more slowly developing left hemisphere. "Field-dependent" is a term that connotes prejudiced perception. Under the guidance of the pleasure principle, in other words, the right brain organization will perceive what it believes it needs to perceive on the basis of a pleasure–unpleasure cosmic causality. Hunger on the inside is associated with a frustrating object on the outside; satisfaction on the inside is associated with a satisfying, pleasure-giving object on the outside, etcetera. The assignments of these valences to these objects is done through projective identification.

Objects interpreted under the influence of projective identification and subsequent introjection become the first organizers of the psyche. As the first organizers, they determine the formation of all subsequent mental structures, which is the basis of the Kleinian principle of *genetic continuity*: these earliest internalizations of objects as the first organizer of the psyche determine the formation of the later Oedipus complex.

Thus the first internal world, according to Klein, is one that is virtually formed by a reification of instinctual projection and introjection. Its objects become organizers of further psychic development but are constantly being modified by mirroring or reality objects. The relationship between the container object and the projected content from the infant is crucial here (see Malin and Grotstein 1966). This first internal world, however, seems to be split-off and/or massively repressed and ultimately subordinated to a second internal world that arises about the time of the Oedipus complex. Conscious memory rarely goes back to the time of the first internal world, but does go back to the time of the second. As a result, patients and analysts alike are more conversant with the second internal world without realizing that it is, generally speaking, a screen memory bulwark against the feelings indigenous to the first.

Bion (1967, 1970) has greatly extended and revised Klein's concept of the relationship between internal and external reality. In his concepts of the container, the contained, and of a mother with reverie modifying the projections of the infant, Bion has brought the principle of adaptation over from classical analysis into Kleinian thinking. Hartmann's (1958, 1964) conception of the principle of adaptation, with its involvement with an average expectable environment, and Erikson's (1959) concept of the cog-wheeling of identity between the needs of the nascent infant and his or her caretaking environment link up with Bion's conception to show that the external environment effects a transformation on the internal world as well as vice versa, i.e., that the internal world helps transform the external environment, the latter being the principal emphasis of Kleinian analysis. There seems to be much more rapprochement between the two views today. "Beta element" is the term Bion has assigned to the impression upon the senses that a stimulus from external (and internal) reality inaugurates. It itself is unsuitable for thought until it has undergone a transformation, first by the sense organs themselves and then by a series of other transformational processes, until the sense data is rendered into an emotion, thought, etcetera, which can then be thought about by the mind. After it has been transformed and is suitable for storage or thinking, it is called an "alpha element."

Klein opted for the primacy of internal reality. Bion puts this into perspective by asserting that the sensory perception of reality is the most important, if not sole, stimulus for mental activity, a phenomenon he refers to as the "beta element," which is to be transformed by the receptive sensory apparatus as an "alpha element." From this explication, the newer Kleinian concept of psychoanalysis can be seen to be more reality-oriented than before.

Bion's reality addendum to Klein's theory of internal reality has important consequences for the benefit of Kleinian theory insofar as it aligns it more closely with the current theories of self-development, especially those that have been espoused by Kohut and his followers. Klein's original theory was solely a conflict theory, as was Freud's. She was better able than Freud to account for an early development of an ego state that was capable of experience, but the experience which that ego was capable of was conflictual, both within itself and with the world of objects. Kohut, following in the footsteps of Fairbairn, Winnicott, Balint, Bowlby, and others, has finally enfranchised a metapsychology of deficiency to complement the already standing theory of conflict. One of the profoundest implications of a theory of deficiency is a sense of a reality-orientation that is associated to infancy; i.e., the infant may have the dimmest capacity to perceive reality but does experience realistically assaults and intrusions into his or her privacy, empathic wounds, and deficiencies of necessary entitlement. This conception of the infant's reality-testing from the very beginning is of notable importance and, thanks to Bion's conception of the container and the contained, now allows Kleinian conflict theory based upon projective identification in phantasy from a mythical internal world to link up with realistic experiences of danger from the external world. In short, a metapsychological dual track involving a phantasied internal world and a realistically experienced external world can now be allowed to come together.

Mackay (1981), in his discussion of Klein's metapsychology, observes that Klein's theoretical formulations suffered from her too strict adherence to Freud's model of psychoanalysis. In so doing, she did not do justice to her own innovative formulations. He also points out that her point of view was largely clinical and phenomenological, rather than strictly theoretical. He believes Klein did herself a disservice by yielding to Freud's mechanistic paradigm. Her psychology stands up best as phenomenology.

Meltzer (1981) states that Klein's metapsychology is implicitly not only Platonic but also theological:

> Every person has to have what you might describe as a "religion" in which his internal objects perform the functions of Gods—but it is not a religion that derives its power because of belief in these Gods but because these Gods do in fact perform functions of the mind. Therefore, if you do not put your trust in them you are in trouble, and the trouble is the trouble of narcissism. In other words, Melanie Klein, without completely recognizing it, transformed narcissism from a theory about the nature of the libido and its attachment to the body into a conception of narcissism that is a much more social and organized one, namely the relationships of the child parts of the personality to one another, insofar as they are in competition with, or in defiance of, the internal objects, those parental figures who perform god-like functions (Meltzer 1980, p. 179).

CONCLUSION

Klein's ego psychology is more phenomenological than the classical one. It is based upon her conception of the transformation of the infant's phantasies from the paranoid-schizoid position of persecutory anxiety to the depressive position of concern for the object. In this transformation, objects that are internalized via projective-introjection in the earlier stage are then seemingly "released" into the status of separated objects, a phenomenon that corresponds to Mahler's conception of the four substages of separation-individuation and particularly embraces the concept of rapprochement. Thus Klein's internal objects follow the same pattern as Hartmann's concept of change of function. Klein therefore emphasizes the infant's capacity to author his or her own experience and to be the creator of his or her first world view before this view is amended by the arrival of the depressive position (of separation-individuation). The classical view, while still embracing the idea of the primary instinctualization of experience to a certain extent, has more and more emphasized the introjection of the external world. Thus Klein seems to be rationalistic in her world view and classical analysts seem to be more empirical. The superego likewise is formed, according to Klein, via a gradient in the ego following a projective introjection according to their predator capacity, whereas ego objects (internal objects) are formed in terms of the results of the actions of the projective identifications of the infant upon the object (prey objects). Object representations (formed in the depressive position) help transform yet remaining internal objects into object representations through facilitating the accomplishment of rapprochement with the object. Finally, an internal object differs from an object representation insofar as the former represents a concrete phantasy of the possession of an object that also possesses one at the same time. Thus the infant imagines himself or herself to be inside that object and, at the same time, imagines that object to be inside the self. An object representation is the image of an object that is no longer present but can be conceived of in its absence. Ultimately, Kleinian psychology converges with classical ego psychology in terms of change of function from the more primitive to the more representational.

REFERENCES

Balint, M. (1953). *Primary Love and Psycho-Analytic Technique.* New York: Liveright.
———. (1968). *The Basic Fault.* London: Tavistock.
Basch, M. F. (1981). Psychoanalytic integration and cognitive transformation. *International Journal of Psycho-Analysis* 62:151–176.
Bick, E. (1968). The experience of the skin in early object relations. *International Journal of Psycho-Analysis* 49:484–486.

Bion, W. (1959). Attacks on linking. In *Second Thoughts*, pp. 93-109. London: Heinemann, 1967.

———. (1967). *Second Thoughts*. London: Heinemann.

———. (1970). *Attention and Interpretation*. London: Tavistock.

Bower, T. G. R. (1974). *Development in Infancy*. San Francisco: W. H. Freeman.

Bowlby, J. (1980). *Attachment and Loss*, vol. 3. *Loss, Sadness, and Depression*. New York: Basic Books.

Brazelton, T. (1981). *On Becoming a Family: The Growth of Attachment*. New York: Delacorte.

Condon, W. S. (1977). A primary phase in the organization of infant responding. In *Studies in Mother–Infant Interactions*, ed. H. R. Schaffer, pp. 153-176. New York: Academic Press.

Emde, R. N., and Robinson, J. (1979). The first two months: recent research in developmental psychology. In *Basic Handbook of Child Psychiatry*, vol. 1, ed. J. D. Noshpitz, pp. 72-105. New York: Basic Books.

Erikson, E. (1950). *Childhood and Society*. New York: W. W. Norton.

———. (1959). *Identity and the Life Cycle*. New York: International Universities Press.

Fairbairn, W. R. D. (1940). Schizoid factors in the personality. In *Psychoanalytic Studies of the Personality*, pp. 3-27. London: Tavistock Publications and Routledge & Kegan Paul, 1952.

———. (1941). A revised psychopathology of the psychoses and pseudoneuroses. In *Psychoanalytic Studies of the Personality*, pp. 28-58. London: Tavistock Publications and Routledge & Kegan Paul, 1952.

———. (1943). The repression and the return of bad objects (with special reference to the 'war neuroses'). In *Psychoanalytic Studies of the Personality*, pp. 59-81. London: Tavistock Publications and Routledge & Kegan Paul, 1952.

———. (1944). Endopsychic structure considered in terms of object-relationships. In *Psychoanalytic Studies of the Personality*, pp. 82-136. London: Tavistock Publications and Routledge & Kegan Paul, 1952.

———. (1946). Object-relationships and dynamic structure. In *Psychoanalytic Studies of the Personality*, pp. 137-151. London: Tavistock Publications and Routledge & Kegan Paul, 1952.

———. (1949). Steps in the development of an object-relations theory of the personality. In *Psychoanalytic Studies of the Personality*, pp. 152-161. London: Tavistock Publications and Routledge & Kegan Paul, 1952.

———. (1951). A synopsis of the development of the author's views regarding the structure of the personality. In *Psychoanalytic Studies of the Personality*, pp. 162-182. London: Tavistock Publications and Routledge & Kegan Paul, 1952.

———. (1952). *Psychoanalytic Studies of the Personality*. London: Tavistock Publications and Routledge & Kegan Paul.

Freud, S. (1891). Hypnosis. *Standard Edition* 1:103-114.

———. (1899) Screen memory. *Standard Edition* 301-322.

———. (1900-1901). The interpretation of dreams. *Standard Edition* 4-5.

———. (1909). Family romances. *Standard Edition* 19:235-244.

———. (1911). Psychoanalytic notes on an autobiographical account of a case of paranoia. *Standard Edition* 12:3-84.

———. (1912). A note on the unconscious in psychoanalysis. *Standard Edition* 12:255-266.

———. (1913). Totem and taboo. *Standard Edition* 13:1-161.

———. (1914). On narcissism: an introduction. *Standard Edition* 14:67-104.

———. (1915). A metapsychological supplement to the theory of dreams. *Standard Edition* 14:217-256.

———. (1917). Mourning and melancholia. *Standard Edition* 14:237-260.

———. (1919). The uncanny. *Standard Edition* 17:217-256.

———. (1920). Beyond the pleasure principle. *Standard Edition* 18:3–66.

———. (1923). The ego and the id. *Standard Edition* 19:3–68.

———. (1924). The loss of reality in neurosis and psychosis. *Standard Edition* 19:183–190.

———. (1927). Fetishism. *Standard Edition* 21:149–158.

———. (1930). Civilization and its discontents. *Standard Edition* 21:59–148.

———. (1933). New introductory lectures on psycho-analysis. *Standard Edition* 22:3–184.

———. (1937). Analysis terminable and interminable. *Standard Edition* 23:209–254.

———. (1940a). An outline of psychoanalysis. *Standard Edition* 23:149–208.

———. (1940b). Splitting of the ego in the process of defense. *Standard Edition* 23:271–278.

Galin, D. (1974). Implications for psychiatry of left and right cerebral specializations: a neuro-physiological context for unconscious processes. *Archives of General Psychiatry* 31:572–583.

Giovacchini, P. L. (1967). Some elements of the therapeutic action in the treatment of character disorders. In *Psychoanalytic Treatment of Characterological and Schizophrenic Disorders*, by L. B. Boyer and P. L. Giovacchini, pp. 235–268. New York: Science House, Inc.

Glover, E. (1945). An examination of the Klein system of child psychology. *Psychoanalytic Study of the Child* 1:3–43.

Greenson, R. (1974). Transference: Freud or Klein? *International Journal of Psycho-Analysis* 55:37–48.

Grotstein, J. (1977a). The psychoanalytic concept of schizophrenia: I. The dilemma. *International Journal of Psycho-Analysis* 58:403–425.

———. (1977b). The psychoanalytic concept of schizophrenia: II. Reconciliations. *International Journal of Psycho-Analysis* 58:427–452.

———. (1978a). Inner space: its dimensions and its coordinates. *International Journal of Psycho-Analysis* 59:55–61.

———. (1978b). Who is the dreamer who dreams the dream and who is the dreamer who understands it? A psychoanalytic inquiry into the ultimate nature of being. In *Do I Dare Disturb the Universe? A Memorial to Wilfred R. Bion*, ed. J. S. Grotstein, pp. 357–416. Beverly Hills, California: Caesura Press.

———. (1978c). Gradients in analyzability, a discussion of Robert Langs' "Some Communicative Properties of the Bipersonal Field." *International Journal of Psychoanalytic Psychotherapy* 7:137–151.

———. (1981a). *Splitting and Projective Identification*. New York: Jason Aronson.

———. (1981b). Psychoanalysis of psychosis. Unpublished manuscript.

———. (1981c). The dual track. Unpublished manuscript.

Hartmann, H. (1958). *Ego Psychology and the Problem of Adaptation*, translated by Daniel Rapaport. New York: International Universities Press.

———. (1964). *Essays on Ego Psychology: Selected Problems in Psychoanalytic Theory*. New York: International Universities Press.

Hartmann, H., Kris, E., and Loewenstein, R. (1949). Notes on the theory of aggression. *Psychoanalytic Study of the Child* 3–4:9–36.

Hartmann, H., and Loewenstein, R. (1962). Notes on the superego. *Psychoanalytic Study of the Child* 25:401–416.

Jacobson, E. (1964). *The Self and the Object World*. New York: International Universities Press.

Kernberg, O. (1969). A contribution to the ego: psychological critique of the Kleinian school. *International Journal of Psychoanalysis* 50:317–333.

———. (1975). *Borderline Conditions and Pathological Narcissism*. New York: Jason Aronson.

———. (1976). *Object Relations Theory and Clinical Psychoanalysis*. New York: Jason Aronson.

Klein, M. (1921). The development of a child. In *Contributions to Psycho-Analysis, 1921–1945*, pp. 13–67. London: Hogarth Press.

———. (1927). Symposium on child analysis. In *Contributions to Psycho-Analysis, 1921–1945*, pp. 52–184. London: Hogarth Press.

———. (1929a). Infantile anxiety-situations reflected in a work of art and in the creative impulse. In *Contributions to Psycho-Analysis, 1921–1945*, pp. 227–235. London: Hogarth Press.

———. (1929b). Personification in the play of children. In *Contributions to Psycho-Analysis, 1921–1945*, pp. 215–226. London: Hogarth Press.

———. (1931). A contribution to the theory of intellectual inhibition. In *Contributions to Psycho-Analysis, 1921–1945*, pp. 254–266. London: Hogarth Press.

———. (1933). The early development of conscience in a child. In *Contributions to Psycho-Analysis, 1921–1945*, pp. 267–277. London: Hogarth Press.

———. (1935). A contribution to the psychogenesis of manic-depressive states. In *Contributions to Psycho-Analysis, 1921–1945*, pp. 282–310. London: Hogarth Press.

———. (1940). Mourning and its relation to manic-depressive states. In *Contributions to Psycho-Analysis, 1921–1945*, pp. 311–338. London: Hogarth Press.

———. (1945). The Oedipus complex in the light of early anxiety. In *Contributions to Psycho-Analysis, 1921–1945*, pp. 339–390. London: Hogarth Press.

———. (1946). Notes on some schizoid mechanisms. In *Developments in Psycho-Analysis*, ed. J. Riviere, pp. 292–320. London: Hogarth Press, 1952.

———. (1952). Some theoretical conclusions regarding the emotional life of the infant. In *Developments in Psycho-Analysis*, ed. J. Riviere, pp. 198–236. London: Hogarth Press.

———. (1955). On identification In *New Directions in Psycho-Analysis*, pp. 309–345. London: Tavistock.

———. (1957). *Envy and Gratitude*. New York: Basic Books.

———. (1960). *Narrative of a Child Analysis*. New York: Basic Books.

Klein, M., Heimann, P., Isaacs, S., and Riviere, J. (1952). *Developments in Psycho-Analysis*. New York: Basic Books.

Klein, M., Heimann, P., and Money-Kyrle, R. (1957). *New Directions in Psycho-Analysis*. New York: Basic Books.

Kohut, H. (1971). *The Analysis of the Self*. New York: International Universities Press.

———. (1977). *The Restoration of the Self*. New York: International Universities Press.

Mackay, N. (1981). Melanie Klein's metapsychology: phenomenological and mechanistic perspective. *International Journal of Psycho-Analysis* 62:187–198.

Mahler, M. (1958a). On two crucial phases of integration of the sense of identity: separation-individuation and bisexual identity. *Journal of the American Psychoanalytic Association* 6:136–139.

———. (1958b). Autism and symbiosis: two extreme disturbances of identity. In *The Selected Papers of Margaret S. Mahler*, vol. 1, pp. 69–181. New York: Jason Aronson.

———. (1960). Symposium on psychotic object-relationships: III. Perceptual de-differentiation and psychotic 'object relationships.' *International Journal of Psycho-Analysis* 41:548–553.

———. (1965a). On early infantile psychosis: the symbiotic and autistic syndromes. *Journal of the American Academy of Child Psychiatry* 4:554–568.

———. (1965b). On the significance of the normal separation-individuation phase: with reference to research in symbiotic child psychosis. In *Drives, Affects, Behavior vol. II*, ed. M. Schur, pp. 161–169. New York: International Universities Press.

———. (1968). *On Human Symbiosis and the Vicissitudes of Individuation, vol. I*. New York: International Universities Press.

———. (1969). Perturbances of symbiosis and individuation in the development of the psychotic ego. In *Problems of Psychosis*, eds. P. Doucet and C. Laurin. Excerpt Medica International Congress Series, Part 1, pp. 186–196, and Part 2, pp. 375–378.

———. (1971). A study of the separation-individuation process and its possible application to borderline phenomena in the psychoanalytic situation. *Psychoanalytic Study of the Child* 26:403–424.

———. (1972a). On the first three subphases of the separation-individuation process. *International Journal of Psycho-Analysis* 53:333–338.

———. (1972b). Rapprochement subphase of the separation-individuation process. *Psychoanalytic Quarterly* 41:487–506.

———. (1975). On the current status of the infantile neurosis. *Journal of the American Psychoanalytic Association* 23:327–333.

Malin, A., and Grotstein, J. S. (1966). Projective identification in the therapeutic process. *International Journal of Psycho-Analysis* 47:26–31.

Mancia, M., and Meltzer, D. (1981). Ego ideal functions and the psychoanalytical process. *International Journal of Psycho-Analysis* 62:243–250.

Mason, A. (1981). The suffocating superego: psychotic break and claustrophobia. In *Do I Dare Disturb the Universe? A Memorial to Wilfred R. Bion*, ed. J. S. Grotstein, pp. 139–166. Beverly Hills, California: Caesura Press.

Meltzer, D. (1967). *The Psycho-Analytical Process*. London: Heinemann.

———. (1981). The Kleinian expansion of Freud's metapsychology. *International Journal of Psycho-Analysis* 61:177–186.

Meltzer, D., Bremner, J., Hoxter, S., Weddel, D., and Wittenberg, I. (1975). *Explorations in Autism*. Perthshire: Clunie Press.

Peto, A. (1970). To cart away: a vestibular forerunner of the superego. *Psychoanalytic Study of the Child* 25:401–416.

Piaget, J. (1952). *The Origins of Intelligence in Children*. New York: International Universities Press.

Rinsley, D. (1981). Fairbairn's object-relations and classical concepts of dynamics and structure. In *Borderline Disorders*, eds. J. Grotstein, J. Langs, and M. Solomon. New York: Jason Aronson (in press).

Sandler, J. (1974). Psychological conflict and the structural model: some clinical and theoretical implications. *International Journal of Psycho-Analysis* 55:53–62.

———. (1980). New knowledge about the infant from current research: implications for psychoanalysis. *Journal of the American Psychoanalytic Association* 28:181–198.

Sandler, J., and Joffe, W. (1969). Towards a basic psychoanalytic model. *International Journal of Psycho-Analysis* 50:79–90.

Sandler, J., and Joffe, W. (1970). Discussion papers: towards a basic psychoanalytic model. *International Journal of Psycho-Analysis* 51:183–194.

Trevarthen, C. (1977). Descriptive analyses of infant communicative behavior. In *Studies in Mother–Infant Interactions*, ed. H. R. Schaffer, pp. 227–270. New York: Academic Press.

Winnicott, D. W. (1958). *Collected Papers*. New York: Basic Books.

———. (1962). A personal view of the Kleinian contribution. In *The Maturational Processes and the Facilitating Environment*, pp. 171–178. New York: International Universities Press, 1965.

———. (1965). *The Maturational Processes and the Facilitating Environment*. New York: International Universities Press.

Yorke, C. (1971). Some suggestions for a critique of Kleinian psychology. *Psychoanalytic Study of the Child* 26:129–155.

The Significance of Kleinian Contributions to Psychoanalysis
IV. Critiques of Klein

JAMES S. GROTSTEIN, M.D.

Some of the major critiques of Klein are evaluated. The critical points of early mental development, her attitude toward reality, and her espousal of the death instinct are emphasized. The relationship between Freud's psychoanalytic formulations and those of Klein is clarified.

KLEIN'S CRITIQUE:
INFERENCES ABOUT EARLY MENTAL LIFE

Most of the critics of Klein's contributions, including Glover (1945), Winnicott (1962), and Jacobson (1964), concentrate on her establishment of psychic life as early as three weeks of life and on her seeming neglect of the importance of the impinging effect of reality upon the infantile psyche. They criticize her in effect for adhering to Freud's (1901, 1905) second theory of psychoanalysis, the instinct theory, and for neglecting his third theory of psychoanalysis, which involved the importance of the development of the ego and the forces of repression (Freud 1923). Another source of criticism has been in her espousal of Freud's concept of the death instinct, which is elaborated by her in a way that is more sophisticated and somewhat different from Freud's concept.

Many modern psychoanalytic theorists who have approached the field of infant development have been influenced by the work of Piaget on the one hand and Mahler on the other. For example, Basch (1981) infers from

Piaget's contributions that, ". . . the infant does not have the capacity to recreate for himself a former experience, but can only re-cognize it when it occurs again. The infant therefore does not 'see' his environment in terms of figure and background differentiations that make for animate and inanimate object configurations" (p. 158). Bower (1974), who also uses Piagetian concepts and who studied directly under Piaget, observed, on the other hand, that infants of five and six months who were brought into the laboratory for a second visit often revealed that they remembered what happened during their visit and began rehearsing the responses, thus implying early memory formation. Bowlby (1980), who also uses Piaget's concepts, states as follows:

> Although the work of Piaget, and of others working the same tradition, suggests that a child is not capable of recalling and using his representational model of the world in all these more complex ways before the middle of the second year, it also shows that he is capable nonetheless of various embryonic degrees of representation throughout the preceding twelve months. Thus, it is extremely misleading to speak as though a child's representational model of his attachment figure is absent before a certain age or stage of development and present thereafter. Instead, the model is to be thought of as developing during the middle months of the first year from which time it is available for recognition and elementary search and, as the months pass, it is becoming increasingly available also for recall and for cognitive operations (Bowlby 1980, p. 429).

(See Milton Klein 1981, for an exposition and re-evaluation of Mahler's autistic and symbiotic phases. For a re-evaluation of infant development, see Condon 1977, Trevarthen 1977, Emde and Robinson 1979, Sander 1980, and Brazelton 1981, for recent revisions of "infant-mindedness" that seemingly contradict more traditional inferences from the contributions of Mahler and Piaget.)

The current thrust of infant development studies seems to suggest that infants have rudimentary mental capacity and inchoate forms of object relatedness virtually from the very beginning. What may have perhaps misled some students of infant development and psychoanalytic theoreticians has been their failure to consider the possibility that the infant may not be able to demonstrate mindedness at the beginning because of the neural immaturity of his or her behavioral modalities of expression. Behavior is the result of mindedness but is not synonymous with mindedness. It is as if the infant had an inborn aphasia or a stroke and cannot demonstrate mindedness, and this has been confused, seemingly, with the absence of mindedness rather than an inability to demonstrate it. Further, many of the "observations" about infant development were made from an empirical point of view, as the term "sensory-motor" suggests; i.e., that mindedness is the result of affective, centripetal influence (from the outside), and the infant is, by inference, a tabula rasa.

The alternative point of view, that the infant is a generator of meaning that he or she tries to ascribe to the data of experience (a rationalistic point of view of inborn givens), has hardly begun to be explored but has been hinted at by the above-mentioned infant developmentalists. On balance, it would seem that Klein's phenomenological inferences about early mental life are becoming sounder. It does no violence to her theoretical formulations to suppose that the child (and adult) is constantly trying to re-establish phantasy contact with its earliest existence. In other words, the earliest memory traces become physically worked over and become transformed into deeper psychical strata; "early" evolves into "deep."

Klein seems to have adhered to a very strict interpretation of the destructive aspects of the death instinct, whereas Freud confused the destructive aspects of the death instinct with entropy. Classical analysts have accepted the aggressive aspects of the death instinct and have so named it (see Hartmann, Kris, and Loewenstein 1949). An alternative conception of the death instinct has been delineated in other contributions (Grotstein 1977, 1978, 1981). In those contributions, the death instinct is the inherent undifferentiated defense organization that constitutes (1) the inherent warehousing of the phylogenetically honed preparation for and anticipation of the predator, in particular, and of danger and of death generally, and (2) the capacity to mobilize one's resources to meet these dangers.

FAIRBAIRN'S CRITIQUE

Fairbairn (1952), though more kindly to Klein than most, has criticized her for not clearly establishing how phantasy becomes a psychic structure and for emphasizing the melancholic paradigm based upon repression rather than the importance of splitting based upon the paradigm of hysteria. His concept of endopsychic structure, founded as it is upon this primal splitting of egos and their related internal objects, seems to be applicable to Klein's internal objects, however. What separates their theories is his emphasis on splitting and her emphasis on projection, on the one hand, and his emphasis on reality and hers on phantasy from the very beginning, on the other. Furthermore, he, like Abraham (1924), posits a preambivalent phase but one that trauma can interrupt, which he calls the schizoid position. Here the infant feels that frustration is a statement of the mother's rejection of his or her love so that the infant develops the notion that his or her love is bad. At a later time the infant develops the notion, thanks to the advent of teething, that his or her hate is bad. This corresponds to Abraham's formulations. Klein (1952a, 1952b, 1952c, 1952d), although analyzed by Abraham, chose to differ with her mentor on the issue of the preambivalent phase. For her, there is no such thing as a preambivalent phase and the badness of one's love, contrary to Fairbairn's belief, is not the issue, but destructiveness itself is. In other words, destructiveness and not preambivalence exists from the very beginning and it contaminates the infant's inchoate approach to his or her object.

Klein nevertheless is in agreement with Fairbairn on many issues, including the concept of the schizoid position. Accordingly, she renamed her "paranoid position" the paranoid-schizoid position but, in actual fact, her conception of early splitting (and therefore of "schizoid") differs somewhat from Fairbairn's because of the origin or instigation of the splitting. To Klein splitting predicates the activity of an inherent death instinct, whereas to Fairbairn splitting is instigated by a rejecting object of reality, a concept that descends ultimately into Kohut's thinking. Klein also was impressed by Fairbairn's concept of dynamic egos and endopsychic structures. However, she disagreed with him on the very important issue of identification. Fairbairn has stated that a good object need never be identified with or incorporated; only a bad object needs to be taken in and identified with because of its undependability and because the object that is bad, as well as good, is the object that is depended upon, namely, the mother. Klein believes that the ego is built upon the results of projective–introjective identifications of good as well as destructive feelings emerging from the infant. In other words, she believes that psychic structure is the result of the belief in the more permanent fantasies that have developed about the objects one contains, whether good or bad.

SOME TRADITIONAL CRITIQUES OF KLEIN

Many other authors have contributed to a critique of Klein's psychology, amongst whom are Waelder (1937), Glover (1945), Brierley (1939), Bibring (1947), Zetzel (1951, 1956a, 1956b, 1964a, 1964b, 1967), Geleerd (1963), Jacobson (1964), Yorke (1971), Greenson (1974), Schafer (1975), Kernberg (1975, 1976), and Langs (1976). Many of these critiques were made so long ago that they now seem obsolete in value (Waelder, Bibring, Brierley, and Zetzel). Some are so polemical and ad hominem that their scientific worth is in question (Glover, Greenson, and Yorke). Only four critiques are emphasized in the present paper: Kernberg's, Schafer's, Langs', and my own. First, however, one should note a more credible point made by Glover (1945), who finally criticized Klein over the issue of her choice of the terms "depressive," as in depressive position, and "paranoid-schizoid," as in paranoid-schizoid position. Apparently, his antagonism to her use of these terms had to do with his rejection of Klein's assumption that these positions were fixations for later schizophrenic, manic, and depressive psychotic illnesses. (The emphasis is on "psychotic.") Glover believed that psychosis belonged to physicians and that Klein, barely a psychologist, was linking up infantile fantasies with medical entities. Glover does have a point, although the way he stated it compromises its credibility.

Klein, like Abraham (1924), did believe that psychosis was due to fixations in the early oral period and that the paranoid-schizoid position accounted for the splitting and projection characteristic of schizophrenia, whereas the manic defenses and depressive introjections of the depressive position accounted for manic and depressive psychotic illnesses in later life. It is not possible to review here the enormous body of psychobiological literature that has emphasized hereditary and constitutional factors in psychotic illnesses; however it does seem true that Klein's assumptions of a direct correlation between her infantile stages and psychosis may very well have been an overstatement. Oftentimes, she spoke of the paranoid-schizoid position and the depressive position as comprising together the phenomenon known as the *infantile neurosis*, but at other times she seemed to imply that these positions constituted an *infantile psychosis* and that the schizoid and manic mechanisms were psychotic rather than neurotic. Furthermore, the infantile neurosis of classical analysis, namely the phallic-Oedipus complex, cannot be infantile. It is really a childhood neurosis. On this ground, therefore, Klein seems to have been quite correct in assuming that the paranoid-schizoid and depressive positions were the beginnings of the infantile neurosis. She is, however, at fault for not clearly distinguishing the infantile neurosis from an infantile psychosis. Thus she crossed boundaries and became confusing when she referred to "psychotic mechanisms" such as splitting, projective identification, magic omnipotent denial, idealization, manic defenses, etcetera. It seems that Klein confused "psychotic" with "primitive."

It was Bion who was to help Klein "get out of the woods," so to speak, by positing abnormal splitting, abnormal projective identification, infantile mental catastrophe, etcetera. In other words, Bion differentiated between Klein's infantile neurosis and the primitivism associated with it, on the one hand, and the infantile psychosis that is an abnormal transformation of the infantile neurosis, on the other hand (Bion 1967).

KERNBERG'S CRITIQUE

Kernberg (1969, 1975, 1976) has been one of the more enigmatic critics of Klein who seems to have benefited considerably from her theories and has incorporated them into classical analysis, grafting them on, so to speak, to the structural theories of Jacobson. The focus here is on Kernberg (1969), particularly on the six major critiques of Klein contained therein.

The Theories of an Inborn Death Instinct and Inborn Sexual Knowledge

Kernberg is critical of Klein's assumption of a life and a death instinct:

> . . . Melanie Klein's theory of an inborn death instinct and of that death instinct as the first cause of anxiety (1946, 1948) continue to be accepted by the Kleinian School as far as I can tell. The disregard of the criticism of these concepts, in spite of a total lack of clinical evidence in support of them, appears as an area of unfortunate dogmatic rigidity in the Kleinian group. . . . The same unwavering adherence appears to exist regarding Melanie Klein's concept (1945) of the inborn knowledge of the genitals and sexual intercourse (Kernberg 1969, p. 326).

The work of ethologists such as Lorenz and Tinbergen seems to establish the presence of a death instinct in subhuman species. Infantile observations and clinical phenomena in young child patients, as well as regressive phenomena in borderline and psychotic patients, suggest the probability of a destructive principle in early mental life. Yet, Klein did great disservice to herself in adhering strictly to Freud's drive theory. A more pragmatic and adaptive hypothesis might have stood her in better stead with classical analysts, who tend by nature to be more empirical than is the wont of Kleinian rationalism. The death instinct may be seen as an inherent, undifferentiated defense organization that is adaptively honed to the survival needs of the infant. Destructiveness, in other words, may be one of the protective devices nature has given the infant to register signs of danger communicatively to the caretaking parent. It takes the infant a lifetime to become properly acquainted with the full capacity of his or her death instinct. What troubles the infant is not the death instinct per se but the significant danger to which it calls attention. The death instinct is both the urgent communication of danger to the caretaking mother and the awareness of the danger itself (Grotstein 1981).

The Problem of Formation and Development of Psychic Structure

> . . . It is still difficult to see how fantasies are the main aspects of psychic structure. If internal objects are fantasies, and the structure of the personality is largely determined by fantasies which the ego has about itself and its internal objects, the structure in this sense seems to imply largely fantasies about fantasy and, I propose, reaffirming my analysis

of an earlier paper (1966), that this is an unsatisfactory basis for structural analysis, certainly insufficient to do justice into the psychic apparatus (Kernberg 1969, p. 327).

In this objection and in his use of fantasy, Kernberg betrays a seeming naivete about the relationship between phantasy and psychic structure. Kernberg's use of the term "fantasy" is not exactly the same thing as Klein's "*ph*antasy" in the first place. *Ph*antasy becomes a structure by virtue of the phenomenon of identification with the phantasy. *Ph*antasies are the mental presentations and re-presentations of the sense impressions from without and from within. They are, furthermore, the organizers and integrators of these perceptions. The living organism in general and the human organism in particular is inescapably affected structurally by the registration of its every perception—and, therefore, by the *ph*antasy evolving from that perception. Psychic structures are structures of the more nearly permanent beliefs (*ph*antasies) that the infant → child → adult develops about his or her psychic content by virtue of the belief that is associated to these phantasies via identification. It is identification, both projective and introjective, that is the basis of belief systems, and it is belief systems that form the basis of psychic structure. Belief systems are the result of (1) the infant's appraisals of the material *content* that he or she obtains from parental *containers*, (2) the evaluation (gratitude and respect or criticism and denegration) that the infant has given to the container source of his or her nurture, and (3) the use or deployment that the infant has made of his or her gifts that, because of the servo-mechanistic (feedback) relationship to reality, offers *correlation* from the outside of what he or she believes to be contained on the inside. *F*antasies, as distinguished from *ph*antasies, are conscious or preconscious daydreams.

Kernberg's critique is typical of other classical analysts in general and corresponds to an empirical, nonrationalistic, artificial Cartesian separation between mind and body. This phenomenon is explored at greater length in the final portion of this paper. At this juncture, however, it should be noted that structure and phantasies are identical units; they merely differ in terms of the point of view from which one is observing the phenomenon. Classical analysis seems to require two languages to describe what is described by Kleinian psychology by only one. Parenthetically, it might be added that the Kleinian understanding of phantasies, as well as fantasies, gives them a greater range of explorative possibilities than does the classical, which does not seem comfortable with *ph*antasies.

Experience modifies psychic structure and phantasy is the transmitter of that experience. Phantasy can be analogized to the cognition of the right hemisphere and contrasts complementarily, not just dialectically, to the cognition of the left hemisphere. The right hemisphere is the older and more inchoately active of the two hemispheres (Galin 1974, McLaughlin 1978). It serves as the cognitive apparatus for the infant until the cognitive capacity of the left hemisphere slowly comes to the force to achieve its hegemony.

Phantasy is the revelation of dynamic structure (biological process and perception) and is the emanation by which structures are identified. It is the biography of the dynamism of structures, i.e., it is structures in motion. The progression of phantasies is the continuing biography of the change of structures as well as the change in the relationship between existing structures. It is the "read-out" by which structures are located.

The Problem of Ambiguity and Terminology

Kernberg criticizes Klein for confusing ego and self and for confusing splitting and repression. In another publication, the present author has criticized Kernberg for advocating the concept of a self–object representation administered under the orchestration of the affects (Grotstein 1977). The only possible inference from his conception is that affects are separate from self and object. This is quite surprising for Kernberg, since he owes so many of his concepts not only to Klein but also to Fairbairn, who went to such great lengths to clarify the inseparability of instincts and ego (self). Kernberg, as many other classical authors, employs an artificial Cartesian division between self and object and self and self (Grotstein 1978). Klein, on the other hand, is vulnerable in using the term "ego" insofar as she is "copy-catting" Freud. Actually, Freud used the words "das Ich," implying "I." It may be argued that classical analysis has fallen into an epistemological trap in separating ego from self, id, and superego. It appears more logical to assume that the psychic apparatus is subjectively experienced as a composite "I" that seeks its reflection in "itself" as object in order to realize itself. This act amounts to a Cartesian artifice by which "I" can subjectively divide itself into a subjective and objective experience, one in which "I" is the former and "self" is the latter by which operational experience, subjective self-reflection, takes place. Klein need be no more penitent in this regard than other classical analysts for her ambiguous employment of terminology.

Kernberg's critique of Klein's confusion between splitting and repression is inaccurate and unfair. Klein, like Abraham (1924) and Erikson (1959), employed an epigenetic principle of the development of mental operations from the earliest and/or the most primitive to the more advanced. This concept is embodied in her principle of genetic continuity (see Isaacs 1952). The principle of genetic continuity is the epigenetic biography of all mental mechanisms and structures. In this regard repression is the sophistication of that aspect of splitting that creates a gradient or a differentiation within the self between two states of mind. The avowed or acceptable aspects are separated originally from the disavowed or unacceptable via splitting, which begins as a vertical split between two coexistent states of mind; this later develops into a horizontal splitting known better as repression, in which the coexistence changes into a subordination of the disavowed by the acceptable states of mind. The change in axes from vertical to horizontal corresponds to the topographical principle of conscious and unconscious, as well as to structural, considerations and to the simultaneous subordination of the right brain organization by a left brain hegemony.

The Predominant Focus on Primitive Conflicts and Mechanisms

Kernberg and others have consistently critiqued Klein's focus on primitive conflicts and mechanisms. Klein is at fault for not being specific about the differentiation between *early* and *deep*, a distinction that the present author has endeavored to make for her. Classical analysts tend to be more occupied with calendar events based upon a Weltanschauung that considers objects that are separated in time and space, whereas Kleinian analysts operate in a Weltanschauung that is based upon the undifferentiation between early and deep. It seems that "early" evolves into "deep" and/or primitive structuralization. Furthermore, this "early" or "deep" or both become the psychic organizers for all subsequent or successive psychic structures and mechanisms.

Although classical authors do not really mean it literally, they seem to imply that there are a series of traumata that occur sporadically from time to time that lay down memory traces that are causal or etiological in terms of the creation of fixations and/or the arrestments of developmental maturation. This is a calendar hypothesis based upon the differentiation in time and space between self and object. The appraisal of the facts presented here, which is closer to the Kleinian approach, suggests that all traumatic events, no matter when they occur, are ultimately organized totally into the psyche retrospectively as well as prospectively. Thus, for instance, a trauma during the so-called hegemony of the phallic-Oedipal stage, about age three or four, would, according to Freud, regressively activate memory traces from the oral period. These memory traces themselves have already been activated by trauma but became dormant until a later reminder reactivated them. Interpretations of this trauma that adhere to the phallic-Oedipal level are in danger not only of ignoring the earlier activations but, even more so, of neglecting the consequences of this earlier reactivation. Decompensation of mental functions would certainly seem to result retrospectively from the withdrawal of the support systems of already established systems. One sees this phenomenon oftentimes in certain autistically psychotic children, who seem to have made certain gains until about ages two or three when, because of observation of depressive illnesses in one of their parents, they dismantle their psychotic apparatus and deny their whole existence (see Mahler 1975).

The danger assigned by classical authors to Kleinian interpretations for being too deep and too early can conversely be assigned to classical analysts for being too superficial and too late. In all of the re-analyses conducted or supervised by the present author, this principle has unfailingly been the case. The criticism by classical analysts of Kleinian interpretations being too deep constitutes a peculiar confusion in the minds of many classical analysts about the topographical paradox of the term "deep." In regression, for instance, the mind does not descend into the depths, but rather the depths ascend to the surface for expression. Thus the deep Kleinian interpretation is of a deep mental phenomenon that has surfaced and seemingly demands interpretation because it is topical and cogent. Classical writers, including Kernberg, have not been able to integrate the work of Mahler and Erikson into their technique, and this failure has to do with the difficulty that classical theory has in offering a model of mind in the early narcissistic period that can account for the registration of trauma. Classical technique therefore suffers from an inability to account for very early mental traumata because it cannot account for a psychology of the early oral period; there can be no infantile psychopathology because there is no infantile psychological organization to account for it. Klein has rectified this.

The Relationship between Unconscious Fantasy and Defense Mechanisms

> The description of mechanisms such as projection as closely related to fantasies of an ejecting or incorporating kind seems clinically justifiable, although one would still wonder to what extent such a relationship holds true for later forms of projective mechanisms. The generalization, however, to the effect that all defensive operations are expressed by fantasies is questionable. Repression, intellectualization, and isolation are defenses in which it is much more difficult to accept concrete unconscious fantasies as representing these mechanisms (Kernberg 1969, p. 331).

Here is a difficult critique to answer because of its debater-point value. One can only retreat to one's own experience and ask Kernberg to do the same. Since being introduced to the work of Klein, the present author has been satisfied that all mechanisms, no matter how primitive or sophisticated, are represented and representable as phantasies. Again, it must be remarked that there is an enormous difficulty between what Kernberg and other classical writers are calling *f*antasy and what Kleinian writers are calling *ph*antasy. Kleinian phantasies are deep as well as superficial; embrace all the yearnings and urges of the infant, child, and adult; embody all the defenses and/or fears against these yearnings; and are the subject registration of experience. The most obvious example of this is the dream itself. A dream always represents the yearnings of the self and the fears of the expression of those yearnings, implying the defensive operation activated by them.

Another problem that Kernberg has not mentioned is the issue of the tools of conceptualization of paradigmatic models. Kernberg and other classical writers tend to become left brain oriented, i.e., cognitive, factual, linear, and *mechanistic* in dealing with mental phenomena, particularly of the early infantile period. Kleinians, on the other hand, tend more to be phenomenological, right brain oriented, holistic, and directed toward the inner needs of the self. They speak almost exclusively of the inner world, whereas Freudians have tended more and more to be interested in the external world as their theory of instincts has directed them. Most of Kernberg's criticisms appear to belong to a left brain contempt for right brain phenomenological experience.

Character Analysis and the Issue of Early, Deep Interpretations

Although Kernberg's criticism about Kleinian use of early and deep interpretations appears to be unfounded, his critique about character analysis appears more nearly correct. It is true that Kleinians have not written extensively about character analysis, but this is not to say that they have not written about it or that they have ignored it. It must be remembered that most critiques of Klein, Kernberg's and others, concentrate on Klein's work from 1921 through 1952. *Envy and Gratitude* (Klein 1957) constitutes a statement about the development of character, as does *Love, Hate, and Reparations* (Klein and Riviere 1964). Rosenfeld (1965) has written extensively about narcissistic, borderline, addictive, and impulse-ridden character disorders, as has Meltzer on perversions and addictions. In addition, Jaques (1970) has written extensively about work, remuneration, social justice, and their disorders from the point of view of character structure. Moreover, much of the work of Bion emphasizes character development, particularly in his study of value systems and points of view. It is true, however, that he rarely if ever uses the term "character" per se.

Kleinians appear to feel more comfortable with the term "personality" than they do with "character." Might not character be the phantasy (ph and/or f) of one's belief about one's personality and/or the belief that the outside observer has about the subject's personality?

SCHAFER'S CRITIQUE OF KLEIN

Most of the critiques of Klein by classical analysts have been either ad hominem (Greenson 1974, Glover 1945) or highly polarized and negative (e.g., Kernberg 1969, Yorke 1971), espousing, in effect, a dismissal of her contributions. Schafer (1975) is an outstanding exception in this regard. In his noteworthy critique of the Kleinian position, he takes great pains to be both fair and precise about the issues and the theoretical back-drops confronting classical and Kleinian tenets. He speaks as a classical Freudian having some understanding of where Klein is "coming from" without being totally persuaded one way or the other. He questions the Kleinian conception of early interpretations because of their violation of consideration of timing and depth. Yet at the same time he can understand that deep issues may simultaneously exist alongside superficial issues in terms of the free associations of a patient in analysis. This particular criticism derives from the misconception that many classical analysts, including Schafer too, have about maximum unconscious anxiety and deep structure. "Maximum" may denote superficial or deep. To a Kleinian, the maximum unconscious anxiety represents that aspect, which may be at any level of mental awareness, but it invariably has to do with the patient's infantile aspects, which experience the main thrust of the patient's anxiety. Usually, the maximum unconscious anxiety is triggered by the awareness of separation and the consequences of the awareness of the relationship to internalized images of the external object, the former of which represent projectively transformed modifications of that external object, via envy and/or greed, for instance, so as to turn the external object into a frightening internal one. Thus the maximum unconscious anxiety is the patient's experience of the "release" of these objects into his or her awareness as powerful, disturbing affects.

Schafer criticizes the Kleinians for exonerating the mother and yet points out that classical analysts may also go equally overboard in blaming her. At the same time he points out that Klein did at least place emphasis on pregeni-tality and the importance of the mother in contrast to Freud's emphasis on genitality and the father. The so-called Kleinian exoneration of the mother is more apparent than real, as Schafer himself is able to adduce. Because of the solipsistic, autochthonous, narcissistic, syncretistic thinking that is so charac-teristic of the infant (and the infantile aspect of the adult patient), the infant believes himself or herself to be the center of all causality. He or she must await the depressive position—i.e., separation-individuation with reconcilia-tion—before he or she can have any comprehension that there are systems of causality beyond and before his or her own.

Thus the Kleinian conception of causality tries to get to the root of the first theory of creation—how the universal infantile God believed Himself to have created the world, Himself, and His parents, Adam and Eve, before He realized that their genital intercourse created Him. What many classical analysts fail to realize is that the Kleinian conception of reality is based upon their belief of how the infant and child discover reality—i.e., in sequence, as a progression—as Isaacs (1952) has termed it, the principle of genetic progression. Kleinian analysts do not exonerate the mother. They account for *"projection into reality."* They merely lack a theory that could account for the infant's capacity to know reality. This defect in Kleinian theory has been made up for by Bion's conception of the container and the contained.

The infant is born with inherent givens and, upon confrontation with reality, experiences those impingements of reality by virtue of how and what aspects of his or her own innate equipment they stimulate. A truly bad mother will stimulate, as a rule, the awareness of the infant's destructiveness, whereas a truly good mother may very well stimulate the infant's good impulses, etcetera. At the same time, goodness, as all of us know from our life experiences, from our own analyses, from our children, and from ourselves as children, can also stimulate massive envy. The classical system appears to allow for much less individual differentiation than does the Kleinian. The Kleinian, on the other hand, does seem, as Schafer avers, to side with the mother and place the emphasis on the projective identifications of the infant and his or her descendent, the adult patient. It should be remembered, however, that the conception of projection into reality is not commonly known by classical analysts. In the depressive position, the patient must come to grips with the humanness of his or her parents. He or she must realize that these are the parents that he or she was given side-by-side with the inherent givens of his or her own internal world. In the cafeteria of experience, the patient must select those elements that he or she needs for growth and survival and must learn to eschew and avoid those that are nonrelevant in this regard.

Schafer is nevertheless correct in calling attention to a great philosophical chasm between the two schools in terms of the alleged issue of reality. Kleinians, however, do not ignore reality; they simply have a different philosophy about it than do Freudians, who appear to have returned to Freud's first theory of psychoanalysis, that of repressed traumatic reality, and have gradually eschewed his second theory of psychoanalysis, that of the biological instinctual filter that "judges" reality via phantasy.

When Schafer asks, "To whom or what is the interpretation addressed?" his question appears to be addressing the issue of the Kleinian and the classical acknowledgment of the therapeutic alliance. He is quite right in assuming that there is such a conception as a therapeutic alliance, although it is hardly a Kleinian term. Kleinians do, however, acknowledge a reality ego side-by-side with the pathological ego, and therefore do assume that there is a reasonably intact person who can accept interpretations and apply them to the right place, so to speak.

In his considerations of the relation of structure and content to interpretations, Schafer seems to understand the Kleinian predilection for dealing with metaphor, even to the point of considering all psychic structure as the consolidations of metaphor:

> As an ego psychologist, one could say that for the moment at least the ego function of writing or spelling had been deneutralized or instinctualized, had regressed, had been invaded by derivatives of unconscious impulses, or had succumbed to the primary process; but in saying only this much and in these terms, the ego psychologist would be denying that unconscious phantasies are always latent features of ordinary ego functioning, and in denying this, would be contradicting another proposition that is central to ego psychology. The formalistic concepts of *relative autonomy* and *degrees* of neutralization of structural internalization only obscure this problem (Schafer 1975, p. 20).

Here Schafer appears to be issuing a clarion call to the value of phantasy and metaphor, and is eschewing concreteness and reification, which the structural theory specifically and ego psychology generally have brought to psychoanalysis. It is now a half-an-hour till midnight on the clock of destiny of ego psychology and of the structural theory of which it is a substrate. Its contribution to technique has been minimal and its obsolescence is all too obvious. Schafer's (1976) "action language" is a new and fresh approach to psychoanalytic metatheory and seems to offer a lot of promise in reconciling many of the discrepancies in classical theory that have been alluded to in this paper. Yet this does not mean that Kleinians can go on being "wild romantics of metaphor." They too, if I understand Schafer properly, have an obligation to give structure to their endeavors and not be content with being smugly intuitive.

In his conception of the "vanishing point," Schafer calls attention to the principle of genetic fallacy that Freudians have been aware of for a long time and that Kleinians seem to ignore. This is a crucial issue. Whereas, in terms of technique, the Kleinians are probably right to assume the principle of genetic continuity, they still seem to ignore retrospectively elaborations from later stages of development. Thus the Kleinian theory of reconstruction is as yet undeveloped.

Schafer points out that any system of interpretation can produce brainwashing by virtue of the system itself. On the other hand, the very act of interpreting offers the model of a neutralized (and neutral) object relationship in which the patient's unneutralized associations can be brought from impulsive chaos into ordered containment and therefore offers itself as a model for their maturation. He also states, in effect, that resistances by the patient tend to offset the possibility of brainwashing, whereas the tendency toward identification with a parent-analyst may reinforce it in another regard. Here one is left at the mercy of the integrity of the analyst and his or her own self-corrections.

LANGS' CRITIQUE

With the exception of Schafer, Langs (1976) is virtually the only classical analyst who approaches Klein's contributions with a sound and yet balanced view, and is therefore able to place them in perspective. He states, for instance, "It is important to distinguish between issues related to the validity of aspects of the Kleinian theories about the earliest months of life and such matters as the value of their clinical observations, the nature of their formulations regarding the analytic interaction, and their technical procedures" (Langs 1976, p. 54).

His particular focus in studying Klein is on her conception of the nature of transference. He finds that Klein's use of transference is implicitly (though not explicitly) interactional and therefore more in keeping with the conception of a bipersonal field. He cites her belief that the transference underlies all of the patient's communications to the analyst and includes the present, and not just past object relationships. Thus the projective transference is more immediate and direct than the transference of past object displacements. The Kleinian employment of the tool of projective identification therefore helps to bring transference into interactional dimensions in a way classical analysts cannot.

Langs' conception of the bipersonal field, which owes its origin to Baranger and Baranger (1966), represents a new contribution to psychoanalytic theory that hopes to define the perspective of a "field of forces." In the analytic bipersonal field the patient and analyst both contribute transference (countertransference) projections. Langs is as critical of the Kleinians, as he is of classical authors, for ignoring the importance of the analyst's contribution to this force-field. He also is critical of Kleinians for their apparent disregard of the nonfantasy, or realistic, aspects of the patient's relationship with the analyst.

Langs has made a significant critique of classical technique generally and has reformulated what he believes to be a more nearly valid delineation of classical technique as a bipersonal field (Langs 1976, 1978). Although a classical analyst by training, Langs, as stated earlier, has utilized many of the conceptions of Klein and of Bion, and particularly of the Barangers, to formulate the notion of the field that is operant between the therapist and the patient. He has pursued the matter of the interaction between the therapist and the patient even more rigorously than Kohut (1971, 1977) and believes that the analyst should utilize manifest content only to develop Type Two derivatives—i.e., an unconscious, symbolic communication about the analyst by the patient—leaving Type One derivatives for unconscious aspects that may or may not be transference but are certainly not bipersonal with the analyst. Kleinians almost invariably give Type One derivatives as Langs defines them, and sometimes Type Two derivatives, whereas classical analysts seem more wont to utilize manifest content and Type One derivatives, according to Langs. Langs is especially keen, however, on pursuing the impact the analyst has on the patient via the tracing of the Type Two derivatives of every subsequent association consequent upon the analyst's intervention, whether the intervention be silence, interpretation, clarification, etcetera. Langs believes, in other words, that the analyst is always having an impact on the patient and that this impact is always implicit and/or explicit in the patient's material, particularly in Type Two unconscious symbolic derivatives.

This is another critique to which Kleinians could also well listen, though they are less "guilty" than are their classical brethren. Thanks to Kohut and especially to Langs, the days of the illusion of the analyst's neutrality are gone. The analyst may try to listen with detached understanding, but when he or she utilizes empathic understanding (Kohut) and is meticulous in pursuing Type Two derivatives, the analyst finds "daughter isotopes" of himself or herself, to borrow a term from nuclear physics, ghosts of his or her intrusion into the patient's psychical world and the patient's response to it.

Langs, unlike most classical authors, has come to realize the enormous importance of projective identification and acknowledges the importance of Klein's contribution in this regard. He is also careful to note that there has been a development in Kleinian thinking beyond Klein's earlier formulations and is able to realize some significant changes in Kleinian theory that classical authors have neglected. His criticism of the lack of importance afforded by Klein to reality is a crucial issue that many other authors, as mentioned, have offered. In answer to this criticism, it should be restated that Klein's notion of the perception of reality is based upon her belief that the infant sees reality largely, if not entirely, through the prejudiced filter of primary process and therefore constructs reality at first through projective identification long before he or she is in a position to introject it. Klein should have made some allowance for a more direct introjection of reality very early and also should have accounted for it more prominently in her theory of technique for adult patients.

Bion has corrected this defect in Kleinian theory by his conception of the container and the contained. I have tried to account for the simultaneity of phantasy and reality by the conception of a dual track that allows for the simultaneous processing of reality by projective identification on one track and by the introjection of reality on the other so that the pleasure principle and the reality principle are operative simultaneously from the very beginning and are also prominent in all analytic situations.

There is great difficulty nevertheless in the psychoanalytic understanding of reality. In the first place, reality cannot be analyzed per se; only one's experience of it can be analyzed. Thus, if a patient is subjected to a reality that is affecting him or her, it is either the patient's phantasies about that reality that disturb or the patient's inability to create enough phantasies to disguise the reality, in which case one has the traumatic state. Thus reality in analysis leaves only two options: phantasy and the repetition compulsion. If Klein is guilty, therefore, of ignoring reality, then classical analysts are guilty of exaggerating it. Yet Kohut's ability to construct a theory of psychoanalysis based upon reality deficiency, descended as it is from the contributions of the British object relations school, does seem to allow reality to be analyzable, but only through the vehicle of phantasy—i.e., by the vehicle of re-establishing self–object transferences of the mirroring and idealizing type. In other words, even though Kohut emphasizes the impact of an impinging and/ or a defective reality by virtue of defective self–objects in reality, he nevertheless deploys these self–objects in his new self-psychology in such a way so as to re-establish the omnipotence of phantasy and the phantasy of omnipotence— i.e., the vouchsafing of the exhibitionistic grandiosity of the self and the participation of the self–object in an idealizable role so as to give *phantasied* strength to the self before transmuting internalizations occur.

IMPLIED CRITIQUE FROM SELF-PSYCHOLOGY

The recent contributions of Kohut (1971, 1977) offer yet another valid criticism of classical as well as of Kleinian technique. Kohut has come to regard classical technique as one in which the analyst listens with *detached observation* (present author's term), whereas he, following in the footsteps of Harry Stack Sullivan (1953) and the latter's conception of *participant observation*, suggests *empathic observation* or *vicarious introspection*, extended by Atwood and Stolorow (1978), both followers of Kohut, to the concept of *intersubjectivity*. All these terms seem to be synonymous and to offer an even more comprehensively phenomenological technique of listening to a patient in which the patient's manifest content, his or her own experiencing of an experience, is empathically and/or vicariously validated as the experience that was experienced. To interpret the patient's unconscious to him or her is to use detached, nonempathic, nonvicarious introspection and makes use of an allegation or inference by the analyst, who is, by so doing, seemingly superior in knowledge to the patient about the patient's unconscious self. The question therefore arises as to how self psychologists understand unconscious mental life and how they approach it technically. The answer may be that patient adherence to the empathic mode of listening to the patient allows for a gradual transformation of some unconscious elements into the manifest content as the analysis proceeds, and self psychologists also interpret the unconscious but often at a point in the analysis after which empathic contact has long been established (Goldberg 1978).

The critique implied in self psychology of Klein's technique is that Klein emphasized a phenomenological approach in deciphering the inner experiences of the infant and of the patient. Klein would probably argue that her technique *was* empathic because she was describing the inner experience of the infant and/or of the patient. Kohut's answer, however, would probably be that the unconscious itself is an inference, but that manifest content is the experience that the patient recognizes as being the experience that he or she had—rather than assuming that manifest content is the encoded expressions of how the experience was experienced. Klein's premise is based upon her belief that the infant does not have a reality ego until the beginning of the depressive position. Prior to that time the infant was dominated by primary process and its vicissitudes, namely the derivatives of the schizoid mechanisms of splitting, projective identification, magic omnipotent denial, and idealization, and later by the manic and melancholic defenses against the depressive position. To Klein, that constitutes the infant's experience of his or her maximum unconscious anxieties. Thus she would argue that she too is phenomenological. It is the level of phenomenological aim that is important here. The same argument could possibly be leveled against Kohut, that he does not emphasize enough the experience of the unconscious as worthy of empathic phenomenology. This is dealt with at greater length in another contribution (Grotstein 1981).

One of the crucial offshoots of the intersubjective experience of empathic technique, however, is the stipulation that the therapist himself or herself is a participant in the experience with the patient. The therapist can, by his or her own empathic understanding (which Kohut 1981 differentiates from compassionate), can facilitate the development of a bipolar transference of the mirroring and an idealizing self-object. The mirroring transference is also associated with twinship and merger transferences, according to Kohut. Every one of these archaic self–object formations can be understood as vicissitudes of projective identification, a phenomenon that Kohut seems to ignore (see Grotstein 1981). Kohut believes that a therapist can be experienced as unempathic by the patient not only through incorrect technique resulting from countertransference errors, but also by *maintaining a correct detached listening technique.*

DISCUSSION

A critique of Kleinian analysis by anyone who has not experienced it is as questionable as a critique of classical analysis on the same basis. Having experienced both, I should like to suggest some critical points that typify Kleinian analysis and to emphasize positive and negative aspects in so doing.

At one extreme, Kleinian analysis is too object-oriented and not sufficiently self-oriented, except for the self in relationship to an object. Bion has changed this considerably in terms of his concept of the container and the contained, and one can readily see in Bion's work some of the foreshadowings of Kohut's emphasis on the self (Bion 1962, 1963, 1965, 1967, 1970).

As a consequence of the foregoing, Kleinians seldom deal with shame per se, only with persecutory anxiety, guilt, jealousy, envy, etcetera. Here, Kohut's conception of the failure of the infant to achieve sufficient grandiose mirroring from an object is of key importance—and Kleinian analysis does need this addendum. Kleinians do not emphasize some of the positiveness of omnipotence, except for Bion. Klein has placed too much emphasis on the welfare of the object by the infant and has seemingly sacrificed the right of the infant to have a "self" of his or her own and/or to have recognition of the self's needs independent of consideration of the object's welfare.

Kleinian theory has never established a definite endopsychic structure or metapsychology. It is more like the pragmatic British Constitution, agglomerative and accumulative. Kleinians are at a loss, therefore, to account for how phantasies become structures, for instance, except by relying on identification. Kleinians have a tendency to emphasize early phenomena and phantasies and to see later developmental phenomena as being reducible to early ones despite the fact that their theory does allow for later modifications of earlier phantasies.

Kleinians have tended to assign projective identification, splitting, and other schizoid mechanisms to account for the formation of psychotic states rather than seeing them as primitive neurotic mechanisms and, as a consequence of this, they often overlook the normal or neurotic aspects of splitting and projective identification. Instead, they employ the "psychotic" nature of the mechanism. Bion and Rosenfeld have tended to delineate psychosis from neurosis, however. As a consequence, Kleinians seldom talk about neuroses, only psychoses.

Kleinian analysis is superior in theory and technique to the classical analysis because of its capacity to account for an inchoate infant mental organization and a principle of genetic continuity. Thus Kleinian analysis proceeds from the beginning and is re-creative rather than starting from the surface and getting confused with realities, past and present. Their conception of phantasy → fantasy (ucs → cs) is more elaborate and more nearly complete than the classical.

Klein's conceptions of the paranoid-schizoid and depressive position and the transformations of all thoughts from one to the other are a monumental and necessary condition to psychoanalytic theory. Psychoanalysis cannot any longer be considered adequate if the study of this transformation (from the paranoid-schizoid to the depressive position) is not to be the predominant constituent of that analysis.

The Kleinian conception of reparations to the self and to the object for real and phantasied guilt conveys a more nearly spiritually fulfilling covenant with one's inner goodness and is so much more uplifting than is the mechanistic and guilt-attacking nature of classical analysis.

As I hinted throughout this series of contributions, Kleinian conceptions, like classical conceptions, are stated from a cyclopian rather than from a stereoscopic point of view. Thus, for instance, when Klein speaks of phantasy, she purposefully ignores external reality in order to focus illumination on internal reality; yet one is inconceivable without the other—there is no internal reality without external reality, and vice versa. Moreover, her use of such concepts as the death instinct, envy, and greed suggests a pejoratively instinctual point of view that lacks an adaptive context. For example, the death instinct must be seen as a potentially adaptive helper to the survival of the infant. It helps the infant to anticipate danger, the predator, etcetera, and to take appropriate steps against it. The life instinct and the death instinct are therefore but two faces of the same thing, working in harmony most of the time.

This adaptive context can be more easily visualized if one employs a dual-track theorem that allows all phenomena to be seen from at least two points of view at the same time. Thus the infant (or the patient) does not employ his or her death instinct (such as envy and its consequences) against an object just for the sheer impulsive fun of it; he or she must first perceive something dangerous in that object before employing his or her defensive armamentarium. Thus the danger that mobilizes the death instinct is really under the aegis of the life instinct's relationship to the narcissistic organization. Kohut has called attention to the separate development of the self and of object relations. This paradigm of a dual track should help reconcile many of the difficulties Kleinians and Freudians are having in comprehending each other's theories.

Langs (1976) points out that, despite the many criticisms by classical authors of Klein, there have been few, if any, Kleinian criticisms of classical theory. One of the reasons for this may be that Kleinians have remained unaware, despite classical protestations, that their own theory was in many ways so different from the classical. They seem to maintain that they accept most of the tenets of classical analysis but have simply extended analysis back to the first months of life. As has been shown in this series of papers, their conceptions are rooted in many of Freud's and Abraham's conceptions and are fundamentally psychoanalytic insofar as they hold to the tenets of basic Freudian psychoanalysis; they differ largely in areas of emphasis. A dual-track conception may help rectify many of the differences between Kleinian and Freudian ideas whereby different points of emphasis can be held to be true on different tracks simultaneously. This has been demonstrated already in the example of the dual-track conception of Klein's separated infant and Mahler's nonseparate infant as being simultaneous conceptions on different tracks. Another example would be internal reality and external reality occupying different tracks simultaneously. Instinctual drives communicating as well as discharging would be yet another.

Perhaps one of the greatest apparent differences between classical and Kleinian analysis is the Kleinian emphasis on the present as opposed to the classical emphasis on the past. Because of the Kleinians' understanding of projective identification, they are able to understand phantasies in the present that make use of day residue and historic residues of the past in order to denote present experiences. Thus Kleinian analysis seems to be more immediate and more *now*, whereas classical analysis seems more remote. Transferences are related to the past rather than to the present in the classical sense. The immediacy and "nowness" of the Kleinian emphasis allows for much greater impact of awareness.

SUMMARY

This paper has endeavored to clarify the relationship between Melanie Klein's psychoanalytic formulations and those of Freud and contemporary classical Freudians. Klein unfortunately weakened the thrust and credibility of her concepts by not differing her terms from those used by Freud. The extensions she made were in every case adumbrated by Freud and/or Abraham, but the extensions rendered her conceptualizations qualitatively different. Her concept of instinct is an extension of Freud's but, because of its more extensive application, became a significant alteration without, however, being a departure: continuity by extension persisted. Her concept of internal objects is close to Freud's concepts as expressed in "On Narcissism" (1914) and "Mourning and Melancholia" (1917). Her concept of the superego is identical to Freud's on the phallic-Oedipal level but, in the primitive oral period, involves an extension of Freud's concept of the projection of omnipotence by the infant into the ego ideal (Klein 1940).

Klein discovered projective identification in "On Narcissism" and then extended its importance. Her concept of splitting came directly from Freud's work on the subject. Her concept of the Oedipus complex also is a retrospective extension of Freud's, in which she merely added an earlier personality organizational status to the infant, a subject that Freud himself was frequently sanguine about but left undecided. Ultimately, it was Klein's use of phantasy that became the distinguishing hallmark of her conceptualizations, and phantasy was perhaps Freud's greatest gift to psychoanalysis and to Western culture.

Klein's great gift was to fill in the missing links of our origins. She, in effect, did for psychoanalysis and infantile development theory what Thomas Sherrington and Hughlings Jackson did for neurophysiological organizations —establish the hierarchy of levels of organizations of the central nervous system; there is no level of hierarchy, no matter how primitive, that does not have an organization. Klein furnished the infantile organization to antedate the childhood Oedipal organizations. The classical notion of the infant, even with the contributions of Mahler, Kohut, and Kernberg, lacks an organization because of the tenacity of the collective myth by these and other classical analysts about the undifferentiated "self–object representation." Further, Klein has completed the puzzle of genetic continuity and has shown that normal development is not so much the biography of infantile sexuality as it is the descending transformation of infantile omnipotence. Bion has brought Kleinian and Freudian conceptualizations into a newer and deeper perspective in his own metapsychological contributions and, in so doing, has brought greater meaningfulness and significance to this union. I hope that my own proposals, especially those propounded on the dual-track theory, have also contributed to this deepening perspective.

REFERENCES

Abraham, K. (1924). A short study of the development of libido, viewed in the light of mental disorders. *Selected Papers*, pp. 418–502. London: Hogarth Press, 1927.
Atwood, G., and Stolorow, R. (1978). *Faces in the Crowd.* New York: Jason Aronson.

Baranger, M., and Baranger, W. (1966). Insight in the analytic situation. In *Psychoanalysis in the Americas*, ed. R. Litman, pp. 56–72. New York: International Universities Press.

Basch, M. (1981). Psychoanalytic interpretation and cognitive transformation. *International Journal of Psychoanalysis* 62:151–176.

Bibring, E. (1947). The so-called English school of psychoanalysis. *Psychoanalytic Quarterly* 16:69–93.

Bion, W. R. (1962). *Learning from Experience*. London: William Heinemann.

———. (1963). *Elements of Psycho-Analysis*. London: William Heinemann.

———. (1965). *Transformations*. London: William Heinemann.

———. (1967). *Second Thoughts*. London: William Heinemann.

———. (1970). *Attention and Interpretation*. London: Tavistock.

Bower, T. G. R. (1974). *Development in Infancy*. San Francisco: W. H. Freeman.

Bowlby, J. (1980). *Attachment and Loss*, vol. 3. *Loss, Sadness and Depression*. New York: Basic Books.

Brazelton, T. (1981). *On Becoming a Family: The Growth of Attachment*. New York: Delacorte.

Brierly, M. (1939). A prefatory note on internalized objects and depression. *International Journal of Psycho-Analysis* 20:241–245.

Condon, W. S. (1977). A primary phase in the organization of infant responding. In *Studies in Mother–Infant Interaction*, ed. H. R. Schaffer, pp. 153–176. New York: Academic Press.

Emde, R. N., and Robinson, J. (1979). The first two months: recent research in developmental psychology. In *Basic Handbook of Child Psychiatry*, vol. 1, ed. J. D. Noshpitz, pp. 72–105. New York: Basic Books.

Erikson, E. (1959). *Identity and the Life Cycle*. New York: International Universities Press.

Fairbairn, W. R. D. (1952). *An Object-Relations Theory of Personality*. London: Tavistock Publications and Routledge & Kegan Paul.

Freud, S. (1901). The psychopathology of everyday life. *Standard Edition* 6.

———. (1905). Three essays on the theory of sexuality. *Standard Edition* 7:125–243.

———. (1914). On narcissism: an introduction. *Standard Edition* 14:67–104.

———. (1917). Mourning and melancholia. *Standard Edition* 14:237–258.

———. (1923). The ego and the id. *Standard Edition* 19:3–68.

Galin, D. (1974). Implications for psychiatry of left and right cerebral specializations: a neurophysiological context for unconscious processes. *Archives of General Psychiatry* 31:572–582.

Geleerd, E. R. (1963). Evaluation of Melaine Klein's *Narrative of a Child Analysis*. *International Journal of Psycho-Analysis* 44:493–506.

Glover, E. (1945). An examination of the Klein system of child psychology. *Psychoanalytic Study of the Child* 1:3–43.

Goldberg, A. (ed.) (1978). *The Psychology of the Self. A Casebook*. New York: International Universities Press.

Greenson, R. (1974). Transference: Freud or Klein? *International Journal of Psycho-Analysis* 55:37–48.

Grotstein, J. (1977). The psychoanalytic concept of schizophrenia. I. The dilemma. *International Journal of Psycho-Analysis* 58:403–425.

———. (1982). A revised psychoanalytic conception of the "death instinct." Manuscript submitted for publication.

Hartmann, H., Kris, E., and Loewenstein, R. (1949). Notes on the theory of aggression. *Psychoanalytic Study of the Child* 3–4:9–36.

Isaacs, S. (1952). The nature and function of phantasy. In *Developments in Psycho-Analysis*, by M. Klein, P. Heimann, S. Isaacs, and J. Riviere, pp. 67–121. London: Hogarth Press.

Jacobson, E. (1964). *The Self and the Object World*. New York: International Universities Press.

Jaques, E. (1970). *Work, Creativity, and Social Justice*. New York: International Universities Press.

Kernberg, O. (1969). A contribution to the ego-psychological critique of the Kleinian School. *International Journal of Psycho-Analysis* 50:317–333.

———. (1975). *Borderline Conditions and Pathological Narcissism*. New York: Jason Aronson.

———. (1976). *Object Relations Theory and Clinical Psychoanalysis*. New York: Jason Aronson.

Klein, M. (1940). Mourning and its relation to manic-depressive states. In *Contributions to Psychoanalysis 1921–1945*, pp. 311–338. London: Hogarth Press and the Institute of Psycho-Analysis.

———. (1952a). Some theoretical conclusions regarding the emotional life of the infant. In *Developments in Psychoanalysis*, ed. J. Riviere, pp. 198–236. London: Hogarth Press.

———. (1952b). On observing the behavior of young infants. In *Developments in Psychoanalysis*, ed. J. Riviere, pp. 237–270. London: Hogarth Press.

———. (1952c) On the theory of anxiety and guilt. In *Developments in Psychoanalysis*, ed. J. Riviere, pp. 279–291. London: Hogarth Press.

———. (1952d). Notes on some schizoid mechanisms. In *Developments in Psychoanalysis*, ed. J. Riviere, pp. 292–320. London: Hogarth Press.

———. (1957). *Envy and Gratitude*. New York: Basic Books.

Klein, M., and Riviere, J. (1964). *Love, Hate and Reparation*. New York: Norton.

Klein, Milton (1981). On Mahler's autistic and symbiotic phases: an exposition and evaluation. *Psychoanalysis and Contemporary Thought* 4:69–106.

Kohut, H. (1971). *The Analysis of the Self*. New York: International Universities Press.

———. (1977). *The Restoration of the Self*. New York: International Universities Press.

———. (1981). Remarks made at the Fourth Conference on Self-Psychology at the University of California at Berkeley, October 2–4, 1981.

Langs, R. (1976). The Kleinian concept of transference. In *The Therapeutic Interaction*, vol. 2, ed. R. Langs, pp. 53–73. New York: Jason Aronson.

———. (1978). Some communicative properties of the bipersonal field. *International Journal of Psychoanalytic Psychotherapy* 7:89–136.

Lorenz, K. (1957). The nature of instinct. In *Instinctive Behavior*, ed. C. H. Schiller, pp. 129–175. New York: International Universities Press.

Mahler, M. (1975). On the current status of the infantile neurosis. *Journal of the American Psychoanalytic Association* 23:327–333.

McLaughlin, J. (1978). Primary and secondary process in the context of cerebral hemispheric specialization. *Psychoanalytic Quarterly* 47:237–266.

Rosenfeld, H. (1965). *Psychotic States: A Psycho-Analytic Approach*. New York: International Universities Press.

Sander, L. (1980). New knowledge about the infant from current research: implications for psychoanalysis. *Journal of the American Psychoanalytic Association* 28:181–198.

Schafer, R. (1975). Freudian and Kleinian theory and technique: Some features and problems in common. A lecture delivered to the Los Angeles Psychoanalytic Society and Institute, June 26, 1975.

———. (1976). *A New Language for Psychoanalysis*. New Haven, Connecticut: Yale University Press.

Sullivan, H. S. (1953). *The Interpersonal Theory of Psychiatry*. New York: Norton.

Tinbergen, N. (1951). *The Study of Instinct*. Oxford: Clarendon Press.

Trevarthen, C. (1977). Descriptive analyses of infant communicative behavior. In *Studies in Mother-Infant Interaction*, ed. H. R. Schaffer, pp. 227–270. New York: Academic Press.

Waelder, R. (1937). The problem of the genesis of psychical conflict in earliest infancy. *International Journal of Psycho-Analysis* 18:406–473.

Winnicott, D. W. (1962). A personal view of the Kleinian contribution. In *The Maturational Processes and the Facilitating Environment*, pp. 171–178. New York: International Universities Press.

Yorke, C. (1971). Some suggestions for a critique of Kleinian psychology. *Psychoanalytic Study of the Child* 26:129–155.

Zetzel, E. (1951). The depressive position. In *Affective Disorders*, ed. P. Greenacre, pp. 84–116. New York: International Universities Press, 1953.

———. (1956a). An approach to the relations between concept and content in psychoanalytic theory. *Psychoanalytic Study of the Child* 11:99–121.

———. (1956b). Current concepts of transference. *International Journal of Psycho-Analysis* 37:369–376.

———. (1964a). Discussion of the paper by Herbert Rosenfeld, "Object Relations of the Acute Schizophrenic Patient in the Transference Situation." In *Recent Research in Schizophrenia*, eds. P. Solomon and B. Glueck, pp. 75–79. Washington, D. C.: American Psychiatric Association.

———. (1964b). The analytic situation. In *Psychoanalysis in the Americas*, ed. R. E. Litman, pp. 86–106. New York: International Universities Press, 1966.

———. (1967). Psychosis and the very young infant. Book review of *Psychotic States: A Psycho-Analytical Approach*, by H. Rosenfeld. *Contemporary Psychology* 12:126–128.

Prestructural Determinants in a Case of Phobia

M. DONALD COLEMAN, M.D.

Questions of genesis, dynamics, and treatment techniques, in what is hypothesized as the first developmental layer of agoraphobic or pan-anxious symptoms, are considered. In the patient described it was concluded that this layer of anxiety came from many inadequate ego functions brought about by a mother who could not (for reasons speculated about in her history) tolerate autonomous functioning in this child. This mother–child reality shaped the course of the patient's first four years of therapy. During this period of treatment there was more material that lent itself to reconstruction of her real world as perceived by the developing ego, while there was a paucity of fantasy material available. It is suggested that the symptom state called agoraphobia resulted from continuous stimulation since infancy from a mother making dyadic functioning appear imperative for the patient's emotional equilibrium. In similar cases, the initial phase of therapy should focus on reconstructions and clarifications of past and present dyadic relationships. This, as well as other technical interventions to aid development of attenuated ego functions, appears to be necessary as the initial and crucial aspect of therapy.

The diagnostic term *phobia* has been used in analytic literature in two different ways, which sometimes leads to considerable confusion. The first usage is the broadest psychiatric description without dynamic content: an involuntary and uncontrollable reaction of fear, out of proportion to the situation that cannot be reasoned away and leads to avoidance of the feared situation (Tyson 1978, p. 429). On the other hand, analysts have come to use *phobia* to imply basic dynamic and genetic formulations with special mechanisms (especially projection and displacement) used to defend against intrapsychic libidinal and aggressive conflicts. Freud first demonstrated this usage in "Analysis of a Phobia in a Five-Year-Old-Boy" (1909), where phallic-Oedipal conflicts were emphasized. Substantial additions, particularly concerning the role of aggression and pregenital factors, are to be found in Freud (1918), Helene Deutsch (1928, 1930a, 1930b), and others as collated by Fenichel (1945). Little that has been written since Fenichel has added to our knowledge of these "classical" phobias. Wangh's "Structural Determinants of Phobia" (1959) may be seen as presenting data complementary to the prestructural origins of phobias.

More contemporary work on child development, such as that of Mahler (1952, 1975), Bowlby (1969, 1973), and Spitz (1965) has enriched our understanding of the earliest origins of pregenital pathology, but has not been fully integrated into our understanding of phobias. One problem in integration of the new data has been a nosological one: many authors, such as A. Freud (1965) and Nagera (1966), feel that only when the structural apparatus has developed to the point where internal conflicts can be defended against by regression, displacement, and projection, can the resultant anxiety be termed a phobia. A recent effort to integrate our new developmental knowledge into our understanding of phobias has been elaborated in a paper by Tyson (1978), where he attempts to show the multiple genetic determinants of a child's phobia. These would include prestructural developmental problems as well as Oedipal pathology. Sarnoff (1970) describes the maturing psychic developments necessary to change diffuse anxiety into a phobia in a two-year-old.

This paper presents a phobic syndrome where the major symptoms appear determined by ego malformations caused by a real and continuing problem in the mother–child relationship and where recognition of this could have heuristic and technical significance. The emphasis in the case to be presented does not preclude the recognition of other dynamic and genetic determinants, but will serve as an illustration of areas that may have been overlooked previously. The designation *phobia* is used here in its original descriptive sense, although it is recognized that many analysts reserve this term only for symptoms involving later structural conflicts.

The symptomatology has a "real" basis in that it originates in some discernible flaw in the mother–child relationship which interferes with successful completion of the separation–individuation phase, and which leads to defective ego functions involving autonomy. Defenses against instinctual impulses are secondary complications to the ego dysfunctions, while the Oedipal conflict, although distinctly present, appears a relatively weak factor in explaining pathogenesis of major symptoms.

Although only one case is described in detail, the patient is representative of a group of patients who show similar clinical features and are often classified as agoraphobics. These patients have shown considerable anxiety or inhibition in venturing since early childhood, although there may have been the appearance of pleasure in exploring at other periods in development. Closer investigation of these apparent breaks with dyadic safety mechanisms would generally show some special circumstances, often involving contact with a new temporary object that permitted these exploratory phases without contributing to the development of separate autonomous ego functioning. In the case described, conflicts arising from the Oedipal period did not appear decisive in determining the major pathology, although they did result in marked increases in levels of anxiety. Overt maternal neglect is not a factor in the cases delineated in this paper.

The failure in development may be due to a physical handicap or disease in the child that promotes an overprotective type of mothering, making individuation a more frightening experience. However, most instances of this phobic problem seem to have resulted almost entirely from maternal pathology, shaped by the mother's urgent need to keep the child a functioning part of herself with obliviousness to the resultant damage to the child. Clinicians often refer to the hostility of such mothers toward their children; perhaps it would be more correct to speak of hostility toward the particular child's development of autonomous functions. Often these mothers may show less disturbance toward other siblings and in many other spheres of object relationships. The child, of course, must deal with a great deal of inner hostility toward such a mother, and since hostility would be a signal of autonomous functioning, the mother finds any manifestation of it intolerable. Consequently, so will the child. A child reared by such a mother may feel various degrees of anxiety when facing the world in anything but a dyadic situation.

CLINICAL DATA

The developmental phobia and technical suggestions for treatment are illustrated by the case of R., a 40-year-old mother of two. This patient's overt reasons for entering therapy had to do with change in her life-long pattern of anxiety unless surrounded by the familiar, e.g., when away from home she began to suffer from mild diarrhea and a fear that she would lose sphincter control in unfamiliar situations that had formerly caused only anxiety.

To friends, husband, and family, R. appeared to be a sweet, somewhat shy, retiring person, who nevertheless fulfilled her major functions in life as wife, mother, and friend, so that the extent of her limitations was largely hidden from their awareness. Actually she had no friends, only companions, and never shared intimacies with anyone. Behind her attractive facade she had made herself psychologically invisible. She lived a life of "quiet desperation," with large amounts of her energies tied up in a daily struggle to avoid situations of anxiety (almost anything unfamiliar) or to endure the anxiety of unfamiliar situations without betraying herself. Her husband had many characteristics that made him a suitable replacement for her mother, and in his presence she could generally count on being able to tolerate situations such as journeys more than a few miles from home that would be intolerable alone. This, however, meant living up to his doll-like expectations of her and never allowing any open conflict between them to develop—a neurotic bargain that she had made earlier with her mother.

The patient was the first born in a comfortable, middle-class home. Her mother had been an only child whose father had died when she was five yeras old. Despite much hardship, the grandmother had supported the patient's mother, and that mother–child relationship developed with great intensity to the exclusion of other relationships in the lives of either.

Six months after the patient's birth, the grandmother died. Little is known of the mother's mourning except as inferred by her subsequent attitudes toward this new child. The patient's father, a likeable but quiet, passive man, figures only slightly in the patient's memories as a quiet figure who offered some relief but no intervention in the mother's intense relationship with her daughter.

As the patient recalls, her mother supervised every aspect of her life, with the overt premise that she was a weak, sickly child who might at any moment be carried away by a fatal illness. As far as the patient can recall, there were no major illnesses to account for this, but it soon became a fixed point of mutual belief. It is an outstanding part of her self-image to this day, determining how she will react to exertion, and to illness or the threat of illness, whether emotional or physical. In the interest of protecting her health, her mother intervened in all areas of her life throughout childhood and adolescence, not allowing her to do the simplest tasks that most parents would encourage or require.

As an adolescent she was not permitted to pick up shoes at the shoe repair shop or perform other minor errands. Schools and gym instructors were warned of her frailty. She was not allowed to exercise her judgment in matters such as selecting clothes at any stage, and found that to differ with her mother would bring an emotional storm. To be "bad" meant to differ from mother in even the most trivial way, and she was told that God would punish this. She saw from other evidence that her mother had little consideration for others and recalled with pain the invariably rude and overbearing way her mother had with salespeople. In virtually all of her mother's recalled descriptions, the outside world was portrayed as a terrifying place, full of disasters that the patient could not possibly cope with alone.

When the patient was three, a sister was born whose treatment by the mother and subsequent development appear to be unexceptional except for her somewhat reclusive attitude as a married woman. The sister's favorite adult recreations include wilderness camping and white water rafting, in marked contrast to the patient's limited sphere of comfortable activities outside the house. There was little evidence of overt sibling rivalry, except for the lack of affective relationship between the two sisters. During the therapy the patient grew closer to her sister and found that as a young girl the sister had accepted the fact that the patient was "the favored one."

The patient's first conscious anxiety involved the separation that going to school entailed. This anxiety did not diminish with time and was not helped by her recognition that she was not like the other children and did not relate to them. Puberty and admission to a private school somewhat further from home brought an exacerbation of anxiety. She recalls feeling that her anxiety would never end and that she had no hope of ever being able to talk to anyone about it since it confirmed her self-image of being sickly and "different." However, when she was twelve she witnessed an accident to a boy in manual training. A dim perception that he was bleeding from an unknown injury created such a surge of anxiety that a pediatrician recommended that she seek psychiatric help.

This was, she felt, a turning point in her life. For the first time she found someone (a woman analyst) to whom she could describe her feelings. Details of the traumatic event remain hazy, but during her current treatment she revealed that it followed some episodes of sexual touching by her dentist. This was never revealed in her earlier therapy, which went on for once or twice a week for several years. At this point, she regrets not having been able to talk about the sexual touching, but feels it was more important to know that there was someone to whom she could describe her fears, who would take them seriously, without becoming hysterical, and who would feel that her fears had a rational explanation. She has no memories of interpretive work, but an indelible memory of the difference in character between her mother and the analyst. The implicit expectation that she could lead a normal life filled her with hope that would sustain her for many years afterwards.

The memory of this analyst's character and her method of approaching problems has guided the patient throughout her life. Although she was seen regularly for only two years, this therapeutic contact enabled her to continue in the private school and later go on to college in another city. Once there, the anxiety again became strong enough to necessitate similar contact with another woman analyst. Sexual demands from a boyfriend appeared to precipitate the heightened anxiety, but in her present therapy she recalled hasty involvement with him shortly after her first semester began to counter the intense anxiety of being away from home. She remembers quite vividly the feeling of comfort she felt in the analyst's office. Therapy at this time apparently lasted for less than a year.

She did not complete college, having met and married a well-established young man a few years her senior who was in his own successful business. He clearly wished to care for her and loved her beauty. He was never eager for a deep and introspective relationship, being more comfortable with the surface of things. In this relationship the patient bore two children, claimed she enjoyed genital sexual gratification, but suffered the daily anxieties previously described without seeking help. (Her claim that she enjoyed genital sexual gratification was modified after several years of therapy. She seldom achieved orgasm, but was pleased by the generalized body warmth and closeness.) While she had already made remarkable progress in learning to meet and overcome anxiety, I believe the decision to return to therapy was made in part because of her mother's advancing age and her concern, based on some medical reality, that her husband might die.

CLINICAL COURSE

The patient's psychotherapy has now lasted four years on a twice-weekly basis, with a very rapid diminution of the bowel problem and a marked broadening of her range of thought and action. Her material has lent itself to extensive reconstruction of the reality of her mother's relation to her from infancy to the present day and the recognition that her response to it was, as a helpless child, adaptive, although leaving her as an adult with responses that were anachronistic, and many underdeveloped ego functions, more painful to develop as an adult. During the first six months of therapy, a major problem was her fear of becoming dependent upon the present therapist, which might induce regression in giving up of hard-won positions of limited autonomy. The uncovering of this transference fear brought the relationship with the mother more clearly into focus. "Help" from Mother was always a barely disguised way to make her helpless, and she feared the same from the therapist's help. As in a case recently reported by Selma Kramer (1979), the patient needed reassurance that the therapist would not be intrusive and would let her set her own pace in therapy. During this period she made an issue of the therapist opening the door for her at the end of a session. To her it implied that the therapist thought her helpless and unable to do it for herself.

The view that her behavior was often an anachronism that once had adaptational value but no longer had, was seen to be not entirely correct in the relationship with her husband, where she came to recognize that she was adapting to some requirements of his personality that resembled her mother's.

The patient's current life was full of events that permitted constructions of her past and the effect of her perception of these events upon her ego development. For example, she would repeatedly tell her husband that a close friend and his wife were overtly hostile and cruel to her. The husband would respond that the patient's perceptions were false, even if the episode had occurred in his presence. The most overt forms of rudeness, even those fully evident to strangers, were denied by her husband.

The effect this had on shaking the patient's faith in her reality perceptions, as well as her anger and disappointment toward her husband, was discussed. Recognition of the apparent reality of her perceptions with speculation as to why her husband could not tolerate them, led to memories of her mother's unwillingness to accept any perceptions different from hers. In the case of her father's brother, whom the patient perceived as loving, Mother insisted that this was not so. This cut her off from the only living relative who might have given her some different source of love and identification. The shocking effect upon self-esteem and autonomy when a love object contradicts perceptions that appear fully documented by reality was pointed out to her. She recognized the difficulty in venturing into a world alone if one has doubts that basic perceptions about reality are valid.

During the third year of the present therapy, the patient had a trivial difference with her mother while shopping in a department store. The patient (then a 39-year-old mother of two), was threatened that if she did not stop disagreeing, her mother would leave her alone in the department store. The mother did in fact leave at this point and was later furious to find that the patient returned to her home instead of going to her mother's apartment. Discussion of this grotesque threat caused the therapist to suggest that this was her mother's way when the patient was a child and could indeed be terrified by such threats of abandonment. Of course such was the case, and this brought back a number of specific examples, as well as an appraisal of the mother's level of reality-testing in light of her behavior toward a 39-year-old daughter.

Some matters of incapacity came up that were explained to the patient as the result of lack of practice of an ego function over many years, a special kind of lack of development of ego function dictated by the many factors discussed in therapy, but for which practice would be necessary to overcome as exercise restores an unused muscle. This concept of simple lack of skill contributing to feelings of helplessness and anxiety is best illustrated by the recognition that the patient never learned to read a road map or follow road signs (these functions having been done for her). It was suggested that her fear of driving to unfamiliar places alone would have a realistic fear component until she familiarized herself with these skills at the same time she explored the dynamics of her fears in therapy.

As previously noted, the presence of the spouse, who in many ways mirrored the mother's wish to have a relationship that would preclude autonomy for the patient in return for care and protection, demanded the utmost tact as these facts came into focus. It seemed important not to create a struggle of any wider dimensions than the material being discussed at any given time; if necessary emphasizing that the conflict over autonomy was only a part of a relationship that in many ways provided mutual satisfaction, and where other modes of adaptation might be mutually possible, unlike the situation between the mother and the literally helpless child. A total struggle in all areas of the relationship seemed undesirable lest the patient and/or the husband feel that a choice was necessary between therapy and the marriage, possibly with unhappy consequences from whichever path was taken.

In her third year of therapy the patient planned and carried out a very important large celebration for family, friends, and business relationships. She reported that for the first time in her married life at one of these affairs, she felt "present," a participant, and able to enjoy the occasion. Prior to this, her anxiety would enable her to go through the forms while never feeling fully there and participating.

Reconstructions of reality, her conscious and unconscious responses to it, and the way this adaptation affected her development, appear to have been crucial in the progression of therapy. The patient began to see her life as a continuous, understandable sequence. Conflicts over Oedipal-sexual impulses were vaguely raised, but during this four year period of her therapy did not appear to have been decisive in the formation of the patient's primary symptomatology, although it was clear that conflicts over sexuality and castration anxiety twice caused the last increment of anxiety that made her seek out therapy initially. As will be reported, these higher developmental issues arose after the major ego defects found some resolution.

CASE DISCUSSION I

I would regard this case of phobic anxiety as a developmental problem subject to the same questions of usefulness of the classical psychoanalytic method for resolving them as was recently discussed by Green (1975), Rangell (1975), and A. Freud (1976). As Green (1975) indicates, the growth of psychoanalysis has helped us to understand problems such as these and that we have the capacity to make shifts in an essentially analytic model sufficient to bring more therapeutic effectiveness upon these problems.

A. Freud (1976) classifies childhood conflicts as "external, internalized and truly internal." She believes that such a classification "helps toward grading those childhood disturbances which essentially are based on conflict. So far as therapy is concerned it also explains why some cases are improved by management of environmental conditions [those based on external conflict]; why others are accessible only to internal interventions . . ." (pp. 132–133).

Later in the same paper, she describes what she calls "archaic fears":

Before children develop anxieties which are coordinate with the increasing structuralization of their personality, they pass through an earlier phase of anxiety which is distressing not only to them, but to the onlooker, due to its intensity. These anxieties are often called "archaic" since their origin cannot be traced to any previous frightening experience but seems to be included in the innate disposition. Descriptively they are fears of darkness, of loneliness, of strangers, of new and unaccustomed sights and situations, of thunder and sometimes wind, etc. Metapsychologically, they are not phobic since, unlike the phobias of the phallic phase, they are not based on regression or conflict or displacement. Instead they seem to express the immature ego's weakness and panic-like disorientation when faced with unknown impressions which cannot be mastered and assimilated (p. 161).

It seems then very likely that A. Freud would not classify this patient as phobic, although it should be pointed out that she made the preceding remarks in response to similar cases presented to her with the diagnosis of phobia. Bowlby (1973) uses the term "pseudo-phobia" (p. 260) and describes a "Pattern A" where a mother suffers from chronic anxiety and retains the child to be a companion.

Whatever name one chooses to use, the genesis and dynamics of this type of phobic-like illness should be understood to be primarily the result of separation-individuation problems unable to be overcome because of special realities created by this mother's needs. Technical considerations may then reflect these factors. A therapeutic approach that emphasizes the unseen analyst, or where interpretive work focuses on cues of the patient's fear of her sexual or aggressive impulses, would seem destined to failure. Not that these instinctual conflicts are missing in the patient's dynamics, but there is the question of relative importance, of priority. I believe that, in this case, the intrasystemic conflicts and their defensive mechanisms were less important than the ego's damage by selective crippling of autonomous ego functioning by a mother who in reality needed to do so. Such an ego will be easily flooded by anxiety from conflicts at all levels of development that may be deceptively easy to identify. However, they will not be likely to yield to interpretation until the major ego problem is identified and overcome by many years of vis-à-vis therapy with particular emphasis on reconstruction of the past reality that led to the functional malformation.

The notes of both of the excellent therapists whom she saw as a child and then as an adolescent indicate that both recognized the pervasive pathology in the maternal relationship but were, in the present author's view, essentially incorrect in their assessment. According to their notes, both felt the major issue to be mutual hostility that had to be defended against in the child–mother relationship, but they could not, nearly 30 years ago, recognize the centrality of the developmental consequences of the mother's failure to grant the child autonomy, since much of the work in this area has been done since. The conceptual framework was not available to describe that which they may very well have noted intuitively.

The lack of this conceptual framework led to some profound consequences in the way this patient was viewed and treated thirty years ago. That the mother was doing everything in her power to bind the child to her was completely unrecognized. Instead, the mother was described as distant and hostile toward the child, the child's school phobia was seen as a result of death wishes toward the mother, which were interpreted to the child. Improvement was seen as due to the uncovering of these death wishes.

In a panel on phobias at the American Psychoanalytic Association meeting in 1958, the analytic results of the treatment of phobias were reported by Weinstock (1959, pp. 187–188), from a study sponsored by the American Psychoanalytic Association. In only 6 out of 46 completely analyzed patients were all the symptoms relieved. The panelists agreed that phobias might have more varied and complex dynamics than previously thought. These dynamics included "fears of abandonment by life-sustaining objects," with one discussant (Max Schur) emphasizing "the importance of a real traumatic situation in the childhood of the phobic patient." I believe it quite likely that the diagnosis of phobias in the disappointing follow-up cases noted above may have included many patients with genetics and dynamics similar to those presented here; hence the relative refractoriness to analytic treatments based upon postulates of internal conflicts with regression, displacement, and projection.

Recognition of the problem of gaining autonomy from a mother unwilling to grant it, even in interactions with a grown woman, constitute the basis for much construction, reconstruction, and working through. As Blum (1977) states, construction is not sufficient; it must be understood in the light of its impact upon the child's ego state and experience. This task is made immeasurably less difficult when the patient's mother is still alive and interacting with the patient in ways that cause feelings of isolation from others, and where her response to the patient's autonomy can still be gauged as an adult. The department store episode with mother, and the husband's denial of her continuous perceptions of overtly hostile behavior, are representations of many examples of present interactions that had analogues in ego-weakening behavior in the past. A transient screen memory of having oatmeal poured over her head by her mother (with the nearly comic quality of the famous

Clifton Webb scene in "Sitting Pretty") became a terrifying memory of mother dashing the oatmeal in her face as the patient exercised her only prerogatives to say no—through food intake and bowel movements.

It seemed useful in the present case to be able to speculate about the events in the mother's life (relationship to her mother who died when the patient was born), not only because it gave additional dimension and credibility, but because it saved the therapist from the danger of creating a one-dimensional picture of a mother bad in all respects and without sensible motivation. From the beginning of therapy, the patient was aware of conscious hostility toward her mother and claimed no conscious conflict over these feelings. Such was not the case with her husband, where recognition of conflict would cause immediate anxiety.

ADDITIONAL CLINICAL DATA

During the third year of the therapy, the patient's husband unexpectedly died of a sudden illness. To this date the patient's complex mourning reactions and sudden assumption of responsibility for which she had had no prior preparation have progressed in a manner that would indicate a much more resourceful and anxiety-free ego than was apparent at the beginning of the present therapy. Ambivalence toward the husband has become much more conscious during the mourning process, especially as many more details have arisen that confirm most vividly the husband's desire to keep her ignorant and helpless. Currently the patient's personality has become more vivid. She can travel longer distances without anxiety. She has good judgment, is developing a surprising sense of humor, and is showing an interest in, and anxiety about, sexual matters. She has expressed a fearful but earnest interest in analysis in the future.

New material has come into therapy that suggests phobic determinants as a result of structural conflicts with which we are more familiar. The patient's interest in men has become more overt during the past year and she has been able to complete her mourning while seeing that the mourning has also been a useful device to avoid wished and feared sexual involvement. She has entered a relationship with a man where both the Oedipal and transference configurations are dramatically overt. At the same time, this experience is also something new in her life—involvement with a man who wishes to enlarge her scope of shared enjoyment, activity, and appreciation of life. With respect to these last aims of the relationship, she has disclosed that she sees this man in somewhat the position of her therapist.

Dreams have come up for the first time in her therapy. Before a trip with her suitor, which was certain to include a sexual encounter, she reported, "I was in your home. You were using a Roto-Rooter to unplug a drain. Your wife was smiling at me."

Her associations to the dream consisted of her great anxiety about the possibility of sexual intercourse on the trip. She was afraid that she would be unable to eat and would be incontinent anally. She couldn't understand the therapist's presence in the dream, but felt that the dream surely had something to do with her fears of sex. She spoke of some early memories of her mother's preoccupation with her bowels.

It was suggested to her that it sounded as though a part of her mind thought of the penis as a Roto-Rooter that would penetrate her anus. Such a sexual theory from childhood would be consistent with the degree of anxiety she felt. Her response to this was characteristic. She soberly assessed it, and allowed that it seemed reasonable and that she would have to consider it and see if it was helpful. The matter was then dropped because of preoccupation with some very complex financial problems with many ramifications in her life.

Two weeks later she reported the following dream: "I attempted to have intercourse with H. (*another suitor whom she does not care for*), but he was impotent. I went into the next room and found my mother and tried to choke her with a pillow."

There was no affect in the manifest dream or in her relating it, over the content of choking her mother. Her mother had been at her home over the weekend and had made her furious by her intrusiveness. Her mother would just barge into the bedroom when she had the door closed. She does not like H. because he is a big man who has made a remark that he could force her sexually, but she could eat with H. and had no fears of choking because she knew that nothing could happen sexually, unlike the situation with B. (the suitor whom she favors), where she wishes for more to happen.

In the next session she reported another dream. "I was on a couch like the one here and going to be cut in my leg by a man with a knife. I awoke terrified."

She was going to tell H. that she did not wish to see him anymore. She feared his response would be to hurt her or to rape her. She recalled that in the first few days of her marriage she had been relieved to find that sexual intercourse wasn't what she thought it would be. She didn't know what she expected, but it was something painful. It was suggested that she had expected the erect penis to be like a knife that would penetrate her and that, in a part of her mind, this theory was still active.

She responded with great interest. That seemed right. She gave some examples from her current life of activities that were both fearful and exciting. She recalled her previous dream of smothering her mother. It was at this point that she recalled the feeding situation with her mother pouring the bowl of oatmeal over her head like Clifton Webb in "Sitting Pretty." She said that she could feel the oatmeal stinging her face. She then remembered that her mother had flung the porridge with great force and violence in her face when she would not eat. Her mother would also go berserk over bowel movements, and she recalled her mother listening outside the bathroom door for evidence of her bowel activity. She said that she was afraid that if she used the couch she would lose control over what she was saying and the therapist would not allow her to have any secrets, as was the case with her mother. She saw the analytic situation, particularly the couch, as rendering her helpless; where she could be carried away either by her impulses or by the therapist's intrusiveness to penetrate every aspect of her mind, leaving her empty and without a self.

It was pointed out to her that she expected the therapist to behave like her mother toward her, and on this level she could keep whatever secrets she had until she wished to reveal them. On another level, however, she was afraid that using the couch would expose her to a sexual assault from the therapist, which she both wished and feared. Part of the fear must be based on an unconscious perception from childhood where the penis was seen as a cutting instrument.

The patient then recalled the episode of the boy being cut in manual training when she was twelve. She appeared very moved and announced that if she ever wanted to surmount this problem, she knew that she would have to use the couch. She wished to do so immediately but recognized that she could afford no regression at the moment, while she was engaged in certain complex financial matters that would determine her future.

CASE DISCUSSION II

This case has now progressed to the point where the patient is willing to undergo analysis, and the issues involved seem to indicate a shift toward a more formal psychoanalytic situation. It has taken the patient four years to reach this point. The case material has lent itself to theoretical formulations which might not find general agreement among analysts and which might be highlighted here in the interests of further dicussion.

First, the hypothesis of the major source of her anxiety during this time as elaborated earlier in this paper may be questioned. Given the reality described, this patient's suffering more closely approximated what A. Freud (1965) would call the legitimate distress of the (helpless) infant separated from its mother (p. 113). She had been raised to be helpless and was nearly so in fact. Hers was an ego that was shaped to function fully only in a dyadic situation. Structural conflict and signal anxiety did not, in my opinion, weigh heavily in this layer of anxiety. Only now after four years can higher structural conflicts be described as being of primary importance to her present anxiety.

Second, there would not be a general agreement about the diminished importance of death wishes against the mother as the source of her fear of separating from the mother. Conscious and unconscious death wishes toward the mother were and are present, connected with many layers of conflict. However, I do not agree that the death wishes against the mother were the primary source of what in childhood was called school phobia and what in adult life looked like an agoraphobic symptom. Again, the primary anxiety came from the recognition of an ego unable to cope with the environment's demands without her mother, a situation that her mother cultivated in every way. The almost routine assumption that a school phobia has a primary dynamic of a death wish against the mother should be more carefully assessed in each case. Similarly, the dynamics behind the phobic companion might have more complex derivations than are indicated in Deutsch's (1929) paper on this subject.

Third, many analysts might question some of the techniques undertaken in this therapy, which emphasizes reconstructions of developmental realities leading to defective ego functioning. Some reconstructions may be thought of as either too speculative, leading to life-myths, or in opposition to the centrality of fantasy in the genesis of neuroses. In relation to this problem, it should be noted that current material from the patient that makes her seem a more suitable candidate for analysis, does embrace fantasy and phallic-Oedipal material. Even her fear of more intensive therapy and using the couch can now be more fully understood in the light of sexual wishes and fears that derive from Oedipal sources. However, I believe the material supports the thesis that, before this could come about, this patient needed a long period of vis-a-vis therapy where appropriate reconstruction was a major tool toward promoting ego functions (such as reality testing) that operate more effectively.

A therapy that aims to promote ego development, and a therapy that involves actually playing the role of a good mother-therapist, may seem too close to permit distinctions. Nevertheless, it may be suggested that a distinction can be made that will be recognized by both patient and therapist. This distinction will permit the therapist to have an area of neutrality that may allow for future formal analytic treatment. The existence of such an area of neutrality will remain speculative in this case until it can be supported by future data as the patient's treatment approaches a more formal analytic model.

REFERENCES

Blum, H. (1977). The prototype of preoedipal reconstruction. *Journal of the American Psycho-analytic Association* 25:757–785.

Bowlby, J. (1969). Attachment. In *Attachment and Loss,* vol 1, New York: Basic Books.

—— (1973). Separation. In *Attachment and Loss,* vol 2, pp. 258–312. New York: Basic Books.

Deutsch, H. (1928). Agoraphobia. In *Neuroses and Character Types,* pp. 97–116. New York: International Universities Press, 1965.

—— (1930a). A case of cat phobia. In *Neuroses and Character Types,* pp. 74–83. New York: International Universities Press, 1965.

—— (1930b). A case of hen phobia. In *Neuroses and Character Types,* pp. 84–96. New York: International Universities Press, 1965.

Fenichel, O. (1945). *Psychoanalytic Theory of Neurosis,* pp. 193–216. New York: Norton.

Frances, A. and Dunn, P. (1975). The attachment–autonomy conflict in agoraphobia. *International Journal of Psycho-Analysis* 56:435–440.

Freud, A. (1965). *Normality and Pathology in Childhood,* vol. 6. New York: International Universities Press.

—— (1976). Changes in psychoanalytic practice and experience. *International Journal of Psycho-Analysis* 57:257–261.

—— (1977). Fears, anxiety and phobic phenomena. *Psychoanalytic Study of the Child* 32:85–91.

Freud, S. (1909). Analysis of a phobia in a five-year-old boy. *Standard Edition* 10:3–149.

—— (1918). From the history of an infantile neurosis. *Standard Edition*:3–132.

Green A. (1975). On changes in analytic practice and analytic experience. *International Journal of Psycho-Analysis* 56:1–22.

Kramer, S. (1979). The technical significance and application of Mahler's separation–individuation theory. *Journal of the American Psychoanalytic Association* 27 (supp.):241–262.

Mahler, M. S. (1952). On child psychosis and schizophrenia. *Psychoanalytic Study of the Child* 7:286–305.

Mahler, M. S., Pine, F. and Bergman, H. (1975). *The Psychological Birth of the Human Infant.* New York: Basic Books.

Nagera, A. (1966). *Early Childhood Disburbances, the Infantile Neuroses and the Adult Disturbances.* New York: International Universities Press.

Rangell, L. (1975). Psychoanalysis and the process of change. *International Journal of Psycho-Analysis* 56:87–98.

Sarnoff, C. (1970). Symbols and symptoms: phytophobia in a two year old girl. *Psychoanalytic Quarterly* 39:550–563.

Spitz, R. A. (1965). *The First Year of Life.* New York: International Universities Press.

Tyson, R. (1978). The analysis of a prelatency boy. *Psychoanlytic Study of the Child* 33:427–457.

Wangh, M. (1959). Structural determinants of phobia. *Journal of the American Psycho-Analytic Association* 7:675–695.

Weinstock, H. (1959). Panel on phobias and their vicissitudes. *Journal of the American Psychoanalytic Association* 7:182–192.

The Importance of "Real" Trauma on Phobic Symptom Formation

AUSTIN SILBER, M.D.

A discussion of "Prestructural Determinants in a Case of Phobia," by M. Donald Coleman, M.D. Technical questions are raised regarding Dr. Coleman's intention to continue treating this psychotherapy patient in psychoanalysis. Documentation is offered on the importance of constructions and reconstructions of real events surrounding the mother–child relationship in the analytic treatment of patients traumatized in a manner similar to the patient described by Coleman. Consideration is given to the impact on development of severe maternal pathology and the reflection of this reality upon the patient's therapy.

Dr. Coleman attempts to integrate our knowledge of early determinants of pregenital pathology with our understanding of phobias. He feels that "most instances of this phobic problem seem to have resulted almost entirely from maternal pathology, shaped by the mother's urgent need to keep the child a functioning part of herself with obliviousness to the resultant damage to the child," and that "Reconstructions of reality, [especially as they involved the patient and her mother], her conscious and unconscious responses to it, and the way this adaptation affected her development, appear to have been crucial in the progression of therapy."

Coleman thus offers a conceptual frame of reference for treating a particular type of "developmental phobia" that he feels requires a specific technical approach. He describes the delineation of the mother's need to bind her child to herself, which then prevents the completion of the separation-individuation phase of development and finally leads to the loss of specific ego functions. The importance of construction, reconstruction, and working through is emphasized.

The implication of his case report is that he has been able to undo a developmental arrest and permit this now enhanced ego to function more effectively. Autonomous ego functions, the target of the mother's animus, are freed to expand the functional efficiency of the patient's ego. Coleman hopes that, by alerting other therapists to this defined clinical entity and with requisite resort to the techniques he has described, more favorable results might be available for a significant group of patients.

As Coleman has indicated, he will feel more sanguine about his claim after this particular patient enters analysis with him. He also feels that the preliminary therapeutic work that he has done with this patient can still permit the therapist "an area of neutrality that may allow for future formal analytic treatment." He feels that the kind of reconstructive therapy he describes can "promote ego development" without his actually "playing the role of a good mother-therapist." It seems, however, that he unnecessarily complicates his task. He has done a splendid preliminary job—he has prepared a deprived patient for a more challenging task. Why does he not let someone else conduct the formal analysis that he feels is indicated? It seems that he is placing too heavy a burden on his patient. She has been too severely used by those who have heretofore managed her life. Why not let her gradually understand the clarifications Coleman has made available to her, as she freely analyzes her relationship with him, while she continues her treatment with a new analyst?

We know that she used her experience with her first analyst as a model to provide a necessary counterpoint to her bondage to her mother. We also know that the patient became able to see her mother as separate from herself, for, in contrast to the affective constriction of her childhood, she could consciously hate her mother as an adult. This meant, as Shengold (1963) might aver, the demonstration of her ability "to see and not to be" her mother. It also indicates her ability to more effectively use her autonomous ego functions.

The patient needs the time, and the setting, to free herself, not only from her mother, but from the analytic models that she so desperately required in order to free herself from the "holding environment" of her psychotherapeutic encounter with Coleman. Even a benevolent environment can be an encumbrance; she needs to develop her sense of herself (individuation) in a different setting and with a different analyst.

Coleman's role provided the same kind of essential model as that offered by her first therapist. A view of reality, free from the distortions of her mother's perception of the world (which had been internalized and experienced as the patient's own view via the obligatory pathological identifications), is now shaped instead by her shared therapeutic experience with Coleman. This configuration should be permitted to more firmly gel, for it provides the kind of ongoing psychological structure that this patient needs to counteract the initial developmental failure that Coleman felt led to her phobia formation. The constructions and reconstructions helped build a lattice-work around which her conception of an extremely significant part of her inner world could evolve. (Suggestion here provides the necessary glue to hold together a new model of reality more congruent with what really did transpire and is now observed from the vantage point of the more sophisticated, therapeutically trained adult).

Coleman notes to the patient that "she expected the therapist to behave like her mother toward her, and on this level she could keep whatever secrets she had until she wished to reveal them." This exchange came up as part of the discussion instituted regarding the possibility of the patient starting analysis with him. This promise seems to preclude the possibility of free association taking place with Coleman as her analyst. If free association is not possible, there can be no analysis. Coleman, in the above exchange is trying, correctly, to discourage the evolvement of a negative transference. The patient would not be capable of analyzing these negative attitudes in regard to him and still retain her newly constructed view of her past, which so clearly rests on her unquestioned reliance on his reconstructions. These would have for her the importance Coleman so correctly ascribes to her first analyst, namely: "The memory of this analyst's character and her method of approaching problems has guided the patient throughout her life." His constructions and reconstructions, so fundamental to his therapeutic efforts, now provide his patient with a new model of her life, derived from their collaboration, and offer a necessary vehicle for undoing the original developmental arrest. The question of this patient's eventual analyzability might very likely turn on her capacity to experience, own, and analyze her murderous wishes as these are transferred onto her analyst. This might be possible with another analyst, who could by interpretation preserve the newly constructed psychological structure, tease out the negative transferential implications involving all her previous therapist's, and permit her to "work through" all of this within the new analytic setting. The built-in blurring of the therapist's neutrality, so necessary to further the patient's psychotherapeutic progress and ego expansion, in the properly responsive therapeutic environment of her psychotherapy, would seem to preclude the same therapist from now acting as the analyst whose neutral stance invites and fosters the requisite negative transference.

The relationship between the patient and her mother that Coleman has so graphically described has been extensively documented by Fliess (1961). Dr. Fliess, drawing on his experience in analyzing adult patients whose mothers, "in the very beginning of the separation-individuation phase (Mahler 1959) . . . become compensatorily hypersymbiotic" (p. 48), bring about a veritable folie à deux between their child and themselves. Fliess goes on to state, "The hypersymbiotic mother arrests the development of the child at this phase, or so the subsequent study of his neurosis would make it appear." Fliess goes on to indicate that the child's identity fails to develop and is instead replaced by morbid identifications. At the same time, the severest distortions of the body-ego and ego, "in most cases delusory, in some illusory, and in many veiled, as it were, by excessive inhibitions preclusive of any testing of either environment, body or object world" (p. 49), take place.

Fliess seems to be describing a patient not too different from the one Coleman describes. In Fliess' technique (his patients are treated in analysis), the *reality* of the mother's illness is of necessity constructed for the patient. As this reality is further understood, amnesia removal is obtained and the patient, working with an understanding analyst, is able to remember the full extent of his or her repressed past. The amnesia removal frequently leads to memories of aggressive and sexual excess carried out by the hypersymbiotic (psychotic) mother.

Other investigators, Shengold (1967, 1971), Dickes (1965) and Silber (1979) have worked with patients severely traumatized by delusional parents. Coleman's patient's mother certainly seems to be in this category: "Mother supervised every aspect of her life, with the overt premise that she was a weak, sickly child who might at any moment be carried away by fatal illness. As far as the patient can recall, there were no major illnesses to account for this, but it soon became a fixed point of mutual belief." (Note the folie à deux that Fliess described.)

As Coleman avers, with this kind of patient, the *reality* of the mother's irrational functioning and behavior *must* be pointed out (reconstructed). Since the effects of the mother's depiction of the patient, her body, and her world become part of the patient's inner reality, these distortions can *never* be seen by the patient unless the analyst can define the reality in a different sense from that which the child (under its symbiotic bond) has been forced to perceive it. Since this type of parent fulfills so few of the child's developmental needs, the child is, paradoxically, more firmly bound to this parent. As Fliess (1961) notes, pathological identifications are substituted for a sense of identity. Embedded in these pathological identifications are the many fantasies and wishes activated within the child by the overstimulating parent. These have to be teased out and separated from the reconstructed environmental setting. In a number of the present author's patients, analyzed with the parental configuration noted above, the child's fantasies initially denied the reconstructed reality. Many of the erotic responses were integrated into masturbatory fantasies, which then evolved and were elaborated in their own unique way. It was, however, the muderous wishes, appended to erotic fantasies and organized into symptoms and dreams, that could be analyzed only as the negative transference developed and was analyzed. This frequently took place late in a lengthy analysis and took much "working through" before emotional conviction was experienced by the patient. Without this emotional reliving, bondage to this disruptive past remains.

Coleman focuses on the obliteration of autonomous ego functions as a result of this bondage. This observation is important and useful, but the critical role of the pathological identifications also needs to be more fully stressed. Unless these are undone (and they apparently were effected by Coleman's constructions and reconstructions in relation to the mother and the patient), the patient can never be free. Thus Coleman's stress on the *reality* of the mother's behavior was useful in this therapeutic quest, and it needs reemphasizing.

Ever since Freud discarded his seduction hypothesis for his more essential and valuable focus on the "truth" of fantasy—all this in the context of his discovery of the Oedipus Complex—*reality* and its consequences (as a source of trauma) have all too frequently been ignored. A traumatic event based on a "real" childhood seduction was extensively documented in a recent paper (Silber 1979). Greenacre (1956), describes her opportunity to observe the almost immediate denial of seduction or rape when experienced by young patients. In Silber (1979), the patient's seduction, taking place prior to superego development, was dealt with by denial and an increase in fantasy formation in an apparent effort to both contain and mitigate the effects of the experience. Sachs (1967) states, "There appears to be more masochism and guilt created from acts of reality than fantasy if these occur when superego formation is already well developed" (p. 421). Other analysts have reported upon the child's desperate attempt to cope with the onslaught of a psychologically disturbed parent. Fliess (1973), Shengold (1967), and Dickes (1967) have extensively documented the effects of seduction and the ensuing overstimulation of the child.

Coleman's paper focuses attention on the developmental significance of "real" events. He stresses an order of interpretation that is at variance from the more traditional approach. He is not discarding the importance of conflict in the development of neurotic illness; he is trying to set the stage for possible analytic work by first addressing a developmental arrest and attempting to repair it by requisite constructive and reconstructive efforts.

REFERENCES

Dickes, R. (1965). The defensive function of an altered state of consciousness: a hypnoid state. *Journal of the American Psychoanalytic Association* 13:365–403.

———. (1967). Severe regressive disruptions of the therapeutic alliance. *Journal of the American Psychoanalytic Association* 15:508–533.

Fliess, R. (1961). *Ego and Body-Ego.* New York: Schulte.

————. (1973). *Symbol, Dream and Psychosis*. New York: International Universities Press.

Greenacre, P. (1956). Re-evaluation of the process of working through. *International Journal of Pyscho-Analysis* 23:439–444.

Mahler, M. S. (1953). Round table: childhood schizophrenia, discussion remarks. *American Journal of Orthopsychiatry* 24:523–526.

Sachs, O. (1967). Distinctions between fantasy and reality elements in memory and reconstruction. *International Journal of Psychoanalysis* 48:416–423.

Shengold, L. (1963). The parent as sphinx. *Journal of the American Psycholanalytic Association* 11:725–751.

————. (1967). The effects of overstimulation: rat people. *International Journal of Psycho-Analysis* 48:403–415.

————. (1971). More about rats and rat people. *International Journal of Psycho-Analysis* 52:277–288.

Silber, A. (1979). Childhood seduction, parental pathology and hysterical symptomatology: the genesis of an altered state of consciousness. *International Journal of Psycho-Analysis* 60: 109–116.

REPLY BY M. DONALD COLEMAN, M.D.

Dr. Silber's thoughtful comments raise a question of great theoretical and clinical importance in contemporary practice of psychotherapy and psychoanalysis. For many complex reasons, the patients whom we see in psychoanalysis today have often followed the route of beginning treatment in psychotherapy, which then widens its scope until full analysis becomes the mutually acceptable and desirable treatment. Usually, this is with the same therapist if he or she is also an analyst, and this generally raises the issue that Dr. Silber suggests in this case: has the previous therapeutic work been conducted in a manner that would make continuation in analysis with the same therapist an impossible task?

Dr. Silber believes that there are theoretical issues that would mandate a change of therapists. The specific issues that he raises are entirely justified, although in the course of his discussion it appears that he underestimates the general analytic posture of the therapist during the first three years of the patient's vis-à-vis therapy. Some of this may be due to the manner of presentation and the need to highlight certain issues, but more specifically he raises a problem that, even after two years of analytic work with this patient, cannot be answered categorically by the present author. Dr. Silber assumes that the rage against the bad mother must ultimately come up in the transference in the course of her analytic therapy and that this will forward goals for changes that will continue beyond the time of therapy. We are in agreement here, even though I would emphasize our relative ignorance on this point.

Once this agreement is granted, however, the question would be: can this patient ever allow herself to bring up negative feelings in a situation where she would have so many reasons to feel that the transference rage would be destructive to her image of the good mother, to whom she feels bound by intense need and possibly other feelings such as loyalty and gratitude? In this estimation of the patient's difficulty in surmounting the negative transference, should we not also consider the skills of the analyst in "teasing out" elements of the negative transference, as well as his countertransference, which may help him aim toward true autonomy for the patient?

The difficulty of this question becomes particularly evident when the anlage of negative feelings arise in her work in connection with separations, conscious suspicions, and dreams. These anlagen do not seem to have been developed; in fact, our work on them appears quickly dismissed. This observation could be taken as proof of Dr. Silber's point that these issues can never be analyzed by the same person who treated the patient in psychotherapy. Nevertheless, I feel that there is sufficient justification to continue in the hope that this material will ultimately find less tentative expression and that the patient will be "freed" from her therapist.

I believe this course is correct for several reasons. First, the patient continues to make progress both in the scope of material she produces in her therapy and in her life, which is assuming a richness and complexity with a variety of resources that were not present previously. Second, there was little practical alternative; this patient was not likely to accept any conceivable reasons for a change in therapist to another analytic colleague. Third, any suggestion to change therapists might have been responded to as loss of the good mother, with the potential of creating considerable regression that might not have been easily dealt with by interpretation under these circumstances. Perhaps this last assertion reveals a countertransference that, in the end, could be as subtly stifling to her growth as her mother's fears were. Nevertheless, in a patient who has come such a long way developmentally, one should allow for a continuing capacity for regression no matter how successful her therapy might be.

However, I disagree with Dr. Silber's belief that my statement of the patient's right to withhold material until she is ready prevents any further analysis, since it frees her from the obligation of the rule of free association. I believe I was only acknowledging to her a right that she already possessed, a right that is tacitly acknowledged by analysts as inherent in the analytic situation. A patient is continually using his judgment to further the process by free association or to hinder it for whatever reasons appear compelling at that moment, although the patient knows that to do so will hinder the analytic process. If the patient understands and agrees that the full exercise of this undeniable right will hinder the process, what I understand to be an analytic process may take place. This patient had and has that clear under-standing, and so far, when coming close to material that she would prefer not to talk about, has revealed both the resistance and ultimately the material itself. As might be expected, this clarifies the reasons for her resistances, and thus furthers her depth of understanding. Disagreement with Dr. Silber on this issue in no way detracts from appreciation of the remainder of his comments, which add richness to the general thrust of the paper.

Separation-Individuation and Transitional Objects in a Four-Year-Old Psychotic Child

STAVROULA BERATIS, M.D.
ROBERT MILLER, M.D.
ELEANOR GALENSON, M.D.

A segment of the treatment of one psychotic boy in a therapeutic nursery setting is described, focusing on the therapeutic interventions that facilitated progress as well as the therapeutic difficulties in working with a nonverbal psychotic child. In the course of treatment, pathological phenomena of the separation-individuation process were highlighted. Certain hypotheses regarding both normal and distorted forms of the transitional objects and transitional phenomena are offered, particularly regarding their significance as indicators of developmental progress.

The separation-individuation process (Mahler 1968) is described as it occurred in one psychotic boy in treatment at the Therapeutic Nursery of the Albert Einstein College of Medicine, as is his concomitant development in other areas. The model of treatment, based on Mahler's (1968) tripartite therapeutic design, had been elaborated during almost ten years of experience in our own therapeutic nursery. In this contribution to the still sparse clinical literature on the psychopathology of the symbiotic and separation-individuation processes, the pathological clinical phenomena are described, and how the theory of separation-individuation helped in understanding the behavior and in formulating the treatment of a nonverbal psychotic child is demonstrated. In addition, the material presented here will be used to develop some ideas about the characteristics of normal and distorted forms of transitional objects and transitional phenomena and their use as indicators of developmental progress.

CLINICAL DATA

Johnny M. was a patient in the Rousso Therapeutic Nursery from April 1971 to December 1973. During this period he moved from a state of nearly total autistic withdrawal to one in which he was significantly more object related, self-aware, and independent in functioning.

Presenting Problem

At the time of referral to our nursery by the Infant Auditory Training Program, when the patient was two years and four months old, his parents' chief complaint was that he did not recognize them and indeed was unable to pick them out of a crowd. Moreover, he had not developed speech at all and did not attempt to imitate such gestures as waving goodbye. His father commented that his son seemed to push people away rather than go toward them. His activity was purposeless. He watched television commercials exclusively and did not point at things himself, but instead would pull his parents' hands in order for them to grasp what he wanted.

During the evaluation interviews the patient was hyperactive and showed only fleeting and tangential eye contact. No visual, kinesthetic, vocal, or other kind of contact with his mother could be observed. He used the teacher at his side in order to satisfy his needs, pulling her hand in a mechanical way to obtain things he wanted. There was a profound lack of awareness of his own body; he did not respond to physical pain, he walked over and through things, and he rarely focused manual and visual attention simultaneously on an inanimate object. When his back was turned to the examiner, he was tapped on the shoulder but he did not respond. His most substansive interaction with toys was pushing down a block tower that had been built by the teacher. His mother's reaction to Johnny's crying and screaming in the nursery was essentially one of embarrassment. The diagnostic impression was that of childhood psychosis, with largerly autistic features; whether this was primary autism or a regression from a symbiotic psychosis (Mahler 1968) could not be determined.

Past History of the Patient

Born in February 1969, Johnny was the only child of young parents in their twenties. Pregnancy, delivery, and the neonatal period were normal except for "physiologic" jaundice, which lasted for a few days. Mrs. M. had wanted a girl, and her initial reaction was to burst out crying when told that the baby was a boy. Although she had wanted to breastfeed him, she did not have enough milk, and during the first months of life, Mrs. M. frequently complained that his appetite was poor. Because of his sluggish eating, she would cry and withdraw from him or, according to the father, she would swear at Johnny and occasionally hit him because he refused food.

His parents felt that Johnny had never been a cuddly baby. He smiled for the first time at age one month, but he never developed a specific smile for his mother or father. Neither anxiety of strangers nor separation anxiety appeared during the second half of the first year of life. By one year of age, his parents were certain that he was not responding either to visual contact or to speech. At 14 months he began to eat crayons and ripped up papers. At about 16 months he began to protest and cry when he was taken out of the house, and shortly after this and continuing to 24 months, he had a very difficult time going to sleep. He would become agitated, rocking himself to sleep or standing up in his crib and moving so vigorously that his paents often thought he would break the crib. During his entire second year of life he spent a great deal of time watching television commercials. His parents thought that at 9 to 10 months he had said "mama," though this was not addressed to anybody in particular. Soon thereafter he stopped using this word, and no new words appeared subsequently. Gross motor developmental landmarks were within normal limits. Apart from occasional random ball-throwing, play activity was virtually absent.

The Mother's Background

Mrs. M. was the youngest of three children; her sister was the oldest and a brother was the next sibling. Mrs. M. had a history of separation difficulties, beginning in childhood and still present at the time that she began to attend the nursery. As a child she would cry and pull her hair whenever her mother left the house. Even as an adult she felt extremely distressed when she did not find her mother at home. From childhood on, she had preferred eating from her mother's plate. Also, beginning in childhood and continuing up to the time of the evaluation, anger at her mother would lead to a state of enraged confusion, during which she would throw her own food into the garbage can and hit walls and slam doors. Throughout her childhood and adolescence she did not have many friends and she was not particularly attached to any of those she did have.

Soon after Mrs. M. married Mr. M., when she was 20 years old, she began to feel unhappy with her husband and lost sexual interest in him. However, in spite of this, she wanted very much to become pregnant. After the birth of Johnny, they moved a little further away from Mrs. M.'s parents in order to have a larger apartment with a separate room for Johnny, and their relationship worsened. Mrs. M. continued to spend most of her time in her parents' home, and sometimes she and Johnny slept there overnight. At Mrs.

M.'s wish, Mr. and Mrs. M. separated when Johnny was two-and-a-half years old, an event that was precipitated by the confirmation of their suspicions that Johnny was not a normal child. Mr. M. moved out, continuing to see his wife and son from time to time, while Mrs. M. kept the apartment.

The Beginning Phase of Treatment

During Johnny's first year in the therapeutic nursery, a significant improvement took place. The beginning of a relationship to his therapist and increased awareness of various parts of his body emerged. He developed fairly consistent eye contact with his therapist, looked for her whenever she was not near him, and manifested anxiety at separation from her.

After Johnny had been in the nursery for about a year, he fell down a long and steep flight of stairs while playing in his grandparents' home. His mother and grandmother had been in a different room, leaving him unattended. He was hospitalized for five days, having sustained a cerebral concussion. Although there were no neurological sequelae, when Johnny returned to the nursery it was noted that he had lost most of the advances in self-object differentiation achieved so painstakingly during the prior year.

A few weeks later, Mrs. M. left New York with Johnny for the summer, and did not return, as had been planned, for the summer nursery sessions. The nursery staff felt at the time that the mother was acting out her own feelings of abandonment in response to the fact that the therapist was about to leave the nursery staff.

When Mrs. M. and Johnny returned to the nursery in the fall, S.B. was assigned as their new therapist. Both mother and child attended the nursery four times a week for two hours each session; S.B. treated the patient twice a week in the nursery with his mother present during the session, and saw Mrs. M. in individual sessions once a week outside the nursery. This paper focuses primarily on the work with the child. The patient's mother could be described as a very passive, characterologically depressed woman who spent considerable time withdrawing into a fantasy world to the extent that, at times, she was not available to interact with her son and meet his needs. At times her thinking seemed to become confused, although she did not appear to have a consistent disturbance in thinking. During the course of treatment it became apparent that Johnny's mother often became enraged in interacting with him and was unable to provide the appropriate structure for supporting the development of ego functioning. Her own primitive conflicts were stirred up, interfering with her functioning, and were discussed in her individual therapeutic sessions. Her difficulties with her own mother were also clarified to a certain extent. However, this was not effective in changing her behavior toward Johnny. Furthermore, she was not particularly verbal or psychologically minded, and it was very difficult for her to deal with her strong dependency feelings on the therapist. What seemed to have more of an immediate impact in helping her modify her behavior was the provision of concrete models of ways in which she could interact with Johnny and the structuring of tasks for her. When the therapist was not in the nursery, the rest of the nursery staff worked with the mother–child pair using the same overall orientation and approach.

At the beginning of this second year in the nursery, Johnny had reverted to the autistic level of functioning that he had demonstrated a year earlier when he first entered the nursery. He was virtually completely unrelated and lacked any capacity for focused attention, communication, or symbolic activity. He was restless and hyperactive, made only fleeting eye contact with the new therapist, and used her hand in a mechanical way to get what he wanted without indicating any awareness of her as a person. His activities were unfocused and random in nature, interspersed with diffuse tantrum-like outbursts. This severely regressed behavior was interpreted as a retreat from the real world, which was now dangerous to Johnny both because of his accident and his loss of the nursery staff and of his previous therapist in particular over the summer months. Although this seems a reasonable and parsimonious hypothesis, consistent with the dynamic model of Mahler's (1968) separation-individuation theory, it demonstrates one of the major difficulties inherent in therapeutic work with young psychotic children, namely the absence of confirmatory associative or symbolic material.

Utilizing this initial hypothesis, the new therapist considered the first goal to be that of helping the patient establish a libidinally satisfying symbiotic relationship with her, one that could be experienced by Johnny as a source of trust and reliability and could serve as his starting point for a resumption of the separation-individuation process. She decided to foster emotional contact with the patient by providing him with a consistent and gratifying sensory experience of her, much as a mother might do with a normal infant. She attempted to utilize all the major sensory routes: tactile, visual, oral, kinesthetic, and auditory. As Johnny moved without focus about the nursery, the therapist followed him carefully, blending the use of proximal and distal sensory modalities to his tolerance of her closeness. In a single session, this might involve making eye contact, then touching him, and ultimately holding him in her lap. In addition, she specifically offered him such items as a bottle with baby lotion that the previous therapist had used with him in reciprocal play, with the anticipation that an old pleasurable sensory motor schema might offer a route to investing a new object. Initially, Johnny put the lotion into his mouth, swallowing it or taking it out, but making no effort to involve his new therapist.

After three to four weeks, Johhny gave the first indication of responding to his therapist's efforts to establish a relationship. He responded to her physical and eye contact by cuddling in her lap and looking back at her for brief periods of time. Then he began to initiate more prolonged eye contact with his therapist, sitting on her lap in a cuddly way and stretching out over her by extending his back over her legs and arms. Subsequently, Johnny's first reciprocal exchanges with his therapist appeared. Johnny would put the baby lotion inside his mouth (and also soap, play dough, and food), swallowing it or taking it back out and putting it into his therapist's mouth, while at the same time looking at her and taking a deep breath. These oral activities had constituted an important part of the interaction that had taken place with his original therapist. It was hypothesized that the reciprocal from-me-to-you aspect of these sensory motor experiences had gradually been internalized during the first year of treatment and, although vulnerable to regression, were still available to him as a means of reestablishing human contact. On the basis of this hypothesis, the therapist initiated and supported these sensory motor activities, although there was no confirmatory symbolic or associative material. However, the preference the patient showed for this kind of activity and the way in which he repeated these first reciprocal interactions with the new therapist, made this hypothesis a clinically useful one.

Johnny's increasing awareness of a need-fulfilling symbiotic object paralleled his growing awareness of his own body and pleasure in physical activities. This was evident in such activities as repeatedly mounting and sliding down the slide to his therapist with an expression of joy and excitement. The therapist encouraged this activity for its kinesthetic, proprioceptive, and tactile stimulation aimed at facilitating the establishment of body boundaries, as stressed by Mahler (1965), and also for its inherent repetitious cycle of distancing from and then reuniting with his therapist.

One of the first clear indications of the patient's increasing awareness of his body was that he started looking at his reflection in the mirror. The therapist decided to incorporate this interest of his in their play, aiming to augment his awareness of himself and to expand their field of interaction. She would pose with him in front of the mirror and move various parts of their bodies. At times Johnny would move on his own before the mirror. Johnny would move his gaze back and forth between the real body part and its mirror image with an expression of pleasure on his face. This response encouraged the therapist to use the mirror to introduce the first peek-a-boo games in an attempt to reinforce the self-object distinction (Kleeman 1967). She moved him back and forth, close and away from the mirror to have their mirror-images disappear and reappear. Johnny's initial response was attentive curiosity; subsequently he manifested pleasure in the game, active partic-ipation in it, and even initiation of it at times.

In connection with disappearing and reappearing, the therapist had noticed that turning the light switch off and on in a daylit room had been one of the patient's persistent sensory motor activities. At this point in treatment, the therapist decided to associate this with a peek-a-boo game. She took the pa-tient and his mother to a small room, adjacent to the playroom, that did not have any daylight and introduced a peek-a-boo game by turning the lights off and on. After a while he started doing it himself and seemed to enjoy having his therapist and his mother disappear and reappear. While in the dark he would reach out and hug them. The therapist responded warmly by hugging him back and encouraged the mother to do the same. Through these games the therapist was attempting to reinforce awareness and mastery of boundaries between self and object. With the establishment of the symbiotic dyad, followed by signs of early differentiation between self and other, Johnny began to invest in the environment. He would watch people carefully as they moved about the nursery and try to touch them as well. He also started using his mouth to explore inanimate objects in the way that is often observed in normally developing infants.

In conjunction with these indications of advancing self-object differentia-tion, Johnny developed intense separation anxiety along with a growing repertoire of activities that were used to deal with this mounting anxiety. He began to react to his therapist's or his mother's departure by becoming agitated, running toward the door with an anxious expression, and breathing faster and more deeply. This would be followed by ingesting and then spitting out food, lotion, and soap. Subsequently, an additional piece of behavior noticed by the therapist was that when Johnny was in the process of being separated from her or from his mother, he would grab and hold certain wooden blocks. In talking with the mother, it was discovered that he had a similar set of blocks at home and that he and his mother used to play with them. The therapist supported his attempts to master his anxiety when faced with the loss of the human object by making readily available to him the items he seemed to have selected for doing so (food, lotion and soap, and the blocks). These reactions to separation were conceptualized as efforts to retain the lost object by carrying out activities shared with her when she was present. As has been shown in the work of Piaget (1962) and Werner and Kaplan (1963), early in development an action performed on an object is not differentiated from the object itself. Once again, the problem here was the absence of associative material with which to confirm the conceptualization. However, the consistency with which he used these items when he was left, and the further elaboration of mechanisms for coping with separation as therapy progressed, indicate the likelihood that the hypothesis was clinically valid.

Another way Johnny developed of coping with the anxiety associated with his growing awareness of separateness was active mastery of the event of separation. He began to push his mother and therapist out of the room, thus turning the passive experience of loss into an active one under his control. Both the therapist and his mother supported his active efforts by turning these "forced exits" into playful activities. Johnny also began to cry with tears whenever his therapist or his mother left the nursery. This was interpreted as another indication of his increased capacity to experience emotions related to separation (Greenacre 1965).

Up until this time, the patient's vocalizations had consisted of guttural, nonhuman sounding screeches, i.e., he was functioning vocally at a level lower than that of neonates, who by the first weeks of life have developed a variety of differentiated cries corresponding to different inner states (Wolff 1969). Johnny showed no such differentiation, nor did he seem to have any awareness of his own voice or that of others, although he had become aware of sound itself some weeks earlier. The first evidence that speech per se was being perceived and cathected was a shift from his previous screeching to more melodious human-like sounds of increasing phonetic differentiation and specificity, which began to appear in the weeks following his first responses to sound. It was during this same period that sobbing sounds occurred during crying, the first indication that the use of the vocal auditory apparatus was linked to an inner feeling state.

At this point in therapy, the patient seemed to have progressed well into the differentiation substage, demonstrating such characteristic elements as a specific tie to significant others, attentiveness to the environmental surroundings, interest in his own body and that of his mother and therapist, pleasure in activity, and pleasurable anticipation. The therapist decided to shift somewhat from simply fostering the symbiotic relationship to fostering some of the early processes of differentiation as well. She started this by working on his ability to cope with frustration and to substitute one activity for another. For example, when she needed to set limits for him, she offered substitute pleasurable activities, remaining involved and available to him, in spite of his angry temper tantrums. Gradually, the selection of alternative activities was taken over by him (internalized). One of the first instances indicating this involved a cabinet door that he wanted to open. When his therapist indicated to him by gesture and word not to do it, he became angry and threw various objects on the floor. This time, however, his rage state did not persist. Instead, he stopped throwing and stood quietly looking at his therapist while touching the cabinet door. Finally, he returned to his therapist, picked up a tray of water colors, and indicated that he wanted her to open the top of it. After this episode, whenever frustrated, he became increasingly able to shift his interest and derive gratification from alternative activities made available to him by the therapist, rather than discharging his rage in tantrums.

At this point, a shift in the patient's anal behavior was noted. Up until then there was nothing to suggest that Johnny attached any particular significance to defecating, much as is found in the first year of life in normal infants. Now, a typical facial expression (tensing of facial muscles and change of palpebral fissure size) accompanied his need to defecate. In addition, before having a bowel movement, he would withdraw to a room by himself, and if his mother followed, he would insist on being alone. He did not want to use the toilet or even enter the bathroom. On those few occasions when his mother put him on the toilet bowl, he protested and moved his bowels only after he had left the bathroom. Subsequently, he began to withhold his stools and defecated small amounts four to five times each day.

Anal zone behaviors such as these indicate beginnings of independence and assertiveness. In addition, Johnny's shift in anal behavior was understood to indicate an important libidinal cathexis of a body area and function and the use of these to work through conflicts of developmental progression much as it is seen in the conflicts of the ongoing separation-individuation process. Roiphe (1973) has described how the threat of anal loss resonates with early conflicts relating to object loss and how the anal area structurally lends itself to the working out of separation individuation issues; the feces standing for self and object, and the recurrent appearance and disappearance of them stimulating the fear of disintegration of both. Johnny's insistence of defecation was also understood on his terms as the more familiar use of anal functioning to work through conflicts relating to delay in gratification and compliance.

As the relationship between Johnny and the therapist became established, it became apparent that he was vulnerable to regression if he had to separate from her for more than a few days. An incident illustrating this occurred the first day after the Christmas vacation, about three months after treatment with his new therapist had begun. When Johnny entered the nursery, his therapist was not there. He was in a severely regressed state, screaming, hyperactive, and unrelated. It would seem that under the impact of separation from his libidinally satisfying symbiotic partner, Johnny was still vulnerable to regression to an autistic state as he had been in the summer. During the present separation, while at home, he was described by his mother as irritable and "lost." When the therapist entered the nursery and approached him, however, the patient recognized her immediately, and in a period of a few minutes his behavioral organization changed completely. He sat on her lap for a while, began looking around with interest, then got off of her lap and became involved with his usual activities. In the presence of the good outside object, his ego functioning became reintegrated, and cathexis in the environment reemerged. After a while he also recognized the psychologist who had tested him a few weeks earlier and whom he had ignored earlier in this session. Then he pulled the psychologist and his therapist by their hands, indicating that he wanted to go outside and led them to the psychologist's office. There he looked for a particular toy in which he had shown great interest when he had been tested.

The Second Phase of Treatment

With the above incident, a new phase in his treatment began, the phase of "the walks." The walks outside the nursery, which became the patient's main activity in the following months, presented elements of Mahler and LaPerriere's (1965) practicing subphase, which follows the differentiation subphase. Johnny showed a burst of curiosity about his environment associated with manifest delight in his discovery of and pleasure in the use of his expanding ego functions. In contrast to normal toddler behavior in the practicing subphase, however, Johnny always stayed close to his symbiotic partner on these walks. His therapist's actual presence remained necessary to support his exploratory interest except on some rare occasions. He did not show the normal relative obliviousness to the presence of the symbiotic partner. Furthermore, substitute people were not accepted by him, as is usually the case in the practicing subphase. Thus, although the patient showed advances along the individuation line of the separation-individuation process, the narcissistic thrill in the exercise of ego functions, he did not show the corresponding advances along the line of differentiation, i.e., some degree of confident expectation that would allow him to carry out his explorations on his own. The patient required constant libidinal input from the "good" object, rather than intermittant input (emotional refueling) (Mahler 1968), which is usually part of the normal practicing phase.

As soon as the therapist entered the nursery, the patient would show signs of anticipatory behavior, smiling and following her and vocalizing with pleasure while she was getting ready to take him for a walk. He would react with joyous vocalization when she referred to the pleasure they had in these explorations, even imitating the joyful affect in her tone of voice. During the walks the therapist remained with Johnny, consistently facilitating his exploratory interest by her presence and supporting his emerging ego functions, such as his striving for motoric and perceptual mastery. What a mother does intermittently and from a distance during a normal toddler's exploratory behavior had to be done continuously and in proximity by Johnny's therapist.

The therapist had to constantly provide a sense of safety and ego support. Drawing again from normal developmental theory, Johnny's constant need for the therapist's presence, in spite of his advancing individuation, was understood as an indication that the mental representations of self and object that have normally achieved some stability by the later practicing phase (Mahler et al. 1975), allowing the child to distance himself from his mother, were not stable enough so that Johnny could physically separate himself from his therapist. The patient's mother often joined Johnny and the therapist on these walks at the therapist's suggestion. While she, however, found it difficult to participate in Johnny's play and developing curiosity, she was progressively able to utilize the therapist as a concrete model for interacting with Johnny and supporting his developing ego functioning.

Johnny was distressed when it was time to end each walk and would show his feelings by crying with tears. Initially, offering him one of the objects in which he had shown interest during the walks would facilitate the return. Soon that did not suffice and he began to resist his therapist physically, the most overt display of his mounting focused aggression and opposition. A few times he even ran away without looking to see if she was coming after him. This change in his behavior, this ability to run away, was understood as a progression in the area of object relation toward a more secure representation of self and object (Mahler et al. 1975). The therapist was firm but affectionate in the process of setting limits regarding the duration of the walks. She made the conscious effort to preserve the positive affectionate element in their interaction during these times, to communicate to him that aggressive feelings did not necessarily bring the destruction of their positive relationship, and to counteract his aggression and facilitate the neutralization process. During the period of treatment in which the walks outside the nursery became the patient's main activity, he showed evidence of considerable advance in individuation. He appeared better related and able to tolerate angry feelings, as evidenced by playing with two young cousins at home, fighting with them in order to protect his toys, and also demanding more interaction with his mother and grandmother, demands that both found quite difficult to tolerate. They often ignored him or tried to involve him in activities that did not need their personal involvement, such as playing with letters or watching television. In the nursery, in relationship with his therapist, he exhibited more vitality and liveliness and a greater degree of responsiveness. However, he showed no advance as yet in his interaction with other children in the nursery and little improvement in his relationships to other adults.

He also showed signs of increasing ability to delay. For example, he pointed at objects he needed, instead of screaming; he became able to wait in order to get something he wanted; and he showed pleasure in anticipation of an event such as the walks or snack time. Soon he began to point at letters and numbers on the clock, indicating to his therapist by looking at her and by expectant waiting that he wanted her to name them. After she named them, he looked gratified, stopped pointing, and would move to another activity.

Moreover, he showed the ability to plan for something, as indicated by the following incident. Johnny had liked to play with the toothpaste by smearing it. To prevent this, Mrs. M. would put it on a high shelf, invariably making Johnny angry. One day Johnny did not protest, but when his mother was not present he pulled out a portable washer and climbed on it in order to get the paste. In addition, when he wanted to do something that was forbidden to him, he began to close the door to isolate himself from his mother, indicating that he anticipated her negative reaction.

At the onset of the period of the walks, Johnny began to produce typical infantile intonation patterns for the first time. Although they were stable and repetitive, however, these utterances did not indicate any communicative intent, such as a rising contour to indicate questioning. A short while later Johnny began babbling, and soon this became his dominant form of vocalization. Of special importance was the observation that the babbling was most pronounced when he was alone and seemed to facilitate his ability to be by himself. This was viewed as evidence for the internalization of the mother tongue and as a means of recalling the missing object in her absence (Greenson 1950). The appearance of babbling preceded the emergence of a new transitional object attachment by a short period of time, a relationship that will be taken up in a later section. Somewhat later, Johnny began to respond to simple commands such as "eat" and "come here," although it was never clear whether he was responding to verbal or nonverbal parts of the message. Later still, on occasion, he began to say "mama" while looking at his mother, but other than this there was no evidence that he was using his vocal-auditory apparatus for communicative purposes, i.e., to make requests or demands, even though he seemed to enjoy vocalizing itself. This was striking in light of his new found proficiency in pointing, which was used functionally both to indicate and to "bring an event about."

Among his newly acquired skills was his ability to turn the knob of the door in order to open it and to regulate the faucet for warm or cold water. Concurrently, signs of attempting to gain mastery over his bodily functions emerged. He became more selective and insistent in his choice of foods. An advance in attempts to control urinary impulses was indicated when he began to urinate in a corner of the room, following which he would take the mop to clean the floor (as his mother had done in the past following his urination on the floor). In reference to the anal sphere, he indicated one day to his mother that he wanted her to go to the bathroom with him. Once there, she realized that he had already wiped himself with the little towel she used to wipe him with and she could not find the dirty diaper. Also, he indicated that he could anticipate and could now carry out on his own responses that he had expected from his mother—the beginning of superego formation. For example, he did not wait for his mother to punish him by sending him to his room, but he would go there by himself when he had done something of which his mother did not approve.

During the last months of treatment, a new set of behaviors appeared. Johnny began to cover himself with a specific blanket when he was going to sleep. In addition, he developed an attachment to one of his jackets, insisting on wearing it when his mother or his therapist was not present. This use of favored transitional objects in the face of separation experiences is a relatively common event in the course of normal development and usually appears before the emergence of the exploratory practicing phase. The attachment to these transitional objects indicates an emerging capacity to symbolize, a capacity that the child uses in actually separating from the mother during the practicing phase. This had not occurred in the patient, who had not shown the ability to distance himself from the libidinal object during his practicing phase in spite of the appropriate affective development of curiosity and excitement (Mahler's narcissistic investment of self, Mahler et al. 1975). The appearance of the blanket and the jacket coincided with Johnny's capacity to run defiantly away from his therapist at the end of the walks, indicating his beginning ability to tolerate separation from her. This was the patient's level of development when Johnny had to be transferred to another therapeutic facility for older children.

DISCUSSION

Therapeutic Issues

Therapeutic work with these severely disturbed children presents significant difficulties. In the psychotherapy of neurotic children, the therapist forms an alliance with a patient who has attained a higher level of development in object relations, permitting the development of empathy in the therapist and the understanding of conflict. In autistic and symbiotic children, however, the absence or distortion of relatedness, the pervasive personality disorganization, and the deficiency of symbolic functioning challenge the therapist's capacity for empathic understanding and produce specific countertransference reactions. During the earliest period of treatment, when Johnny had regressed back to his autistic level of functioning and seemed unaware of the therapist's presence and her efforts to make emotional contact and establish a relationship, the therapist was keenly aware of persistent feelings of isolation, frustration, and disappointment. These feelings were present in the therapist in spite of her intellectual understanding that he was an autistic child. This period may be characterized as a period of "working in a vacuum." The therapist often felt emotionally drained by the absence of relatedness and emotional feedback. To be shut out, to be experienced as nonexistent, is a narcissistic blow that strikes at the therapist's primitive helpless rage and ambivalence of his or her own earliest efforts at building up object relatedness.

Another problem for the therapist may be that work must be done without the advantage of the eliciting behaviors that normal infants show in early development, as has been recently described (Lewis and Rosenblum 1974). The therapist must in effect attempt to establish the symbiotic relationship without the clear and rewarding presence of either elliciting or rewarding behaviors on the part of the child. During this initial period, the support provided by the nursery staff proved helpful to the therapist in breaking the feeling of isolation and frustration, enabling her to verbalize and understand her own reactions to the patient. The nursery staff provided the emotional contact and object relationships that the patient was unable to give.

The second phase of the therapeutic process was characterized by the emergence on the part of the patient of a semiconsistent and specific responsiveness to his therapist. The feeling of isolation experienced by the therapist was lessened considerably. The gratification and connectedness to the patient's responsiveness felt by the therapist were akin to the feeling reported by mothers as they become "hooked into" their infants' smiles. At this point the therapist needed to establish herself as an appropriate symbiotic partner. In becoming a symbiotic partner, the therapist is subject to profound regressive pulls that challenge the ability to remain therapeutically effective. It involves the therapist's capacity to identify with and tolerate states of fluctuating boundaries and at the same time maintain an observing, working, therapeutic position. It also requires a constant effort, which creates tension in the therapist and is experienced as a draining and wearing depletion. In addition, constant effort is required in order to preserve an optimal distance between patient and therapist. In working with these severely disturbed children, optimal distance is of crucial importance because any deviation from it may subject these children's fragile relatedness to profound regression.

Although Johnny moved into the differentiation and practicing phases, the relative absence of communicative skills and symbolic play continued. Therefore there was an absence of associative verbal material that would have enabled the therapist to confirm or reject the various speculations and formulate interpretations and therapeutic constructions. This period may be defined as "working in the dark," because the therapist was forced to make assumptions and inferences that could not be directly confirmed by clinical material. What proved to be helpful to the therapist's work during this therapeutic phase was the use of the theoretical model of separation-individuation (Mahler 1968) to formulate therapeutic plans and to choose play activities that would support the progress of the child along the developmental line of separation-individuation. In choosing these activities, two things were always taken into consideration: (1) the activity was related in some form to the patient's repertoire of activities; (2) if the patient was able to "catch on" to this activity, the activity was encouraged and maintained, but if the patient did not show any interest in it, it was discontinued. For example, Johnny's sensorimotor activity of turning the light switch off and on developed into a peek-a-boo game that he enjoyed and became involved with. On the other hand, when the therapist tried to introduce more advanced symbolic functioning such as certain play themes, the patient remained uninvolved and the activity was discontinued. Naming of objects by the therapist seemed to be the beginning of some interest in language, but unfortunately this remained limited and circumscribed.

An additional difficulty that characterized the therapeutic work throughout was the absence in this patient of the developmental thrust seen in a normal child. In normally developing children there is a push toward growth and mastery, which is experienced by everyone who comes into contact with them. In addition, the urge to complete development (A. Freud 1965) is a very important moving force in the therapeutic work with children who are less disturbed. The virtual absence of this moving force in cases like the one reported here deprives the therapist of an essential facilitator. In this case, the therapist, beginning with her unilateral efforts to establish symbiosis, developed the frustrating sense of pulling the patient along the developmental path rather than supporting and facilitating self-initiated developmental steps.

Intermediate Area of Experience (Transitional Objects)

Transitional Objects. The transitional object is described by Winnicott (1953) as the first not-me object of the child, the first possession. "It is related both to the external object (mother's breast), and to internal objects (magically introjected breast), but is distinct from each" (p. 97). It symbolizes fused representations of experiences of self and mother and can be used as a substitute for mother in the face of separation anxiety, having a restitutive function but also an adaptive one, being a bridge to the outer world. Among the qualities of the transitional object described by Winnicott is that it must seem to the infant that it gives warmth and has texture or some other quality that seems to show it has vitality of its own. Although it may seem to the observer to come from without, it does not seem so to the child; nor does it come from within and it is not a hallucination. In expanding on the characteristics of the transitional object, Busch (1974) describes a number of qualities attributed to it. It must be of lasting duration, it must be soothing, it is not provided by the parents but created by the child, and it is distinguished from parts of the child's body, which also can bring comfort.

The literature cites many examples of distortions of transitional object attachment. Furer (1964) describes the psychotic fetish, which he defines as a fused representation of self and other, but cannot be used as a substitute for mother because separation of self and object has not occurred. Buxbaum (1960) and Sperling (1963) write about objects that were given to the child by the mother as her substitute in toto. They are not chosen by the child and do not indicate that psychological separateness has been achieved. The infantile fetish, as it has been described by Greenacre (1969, 1970) and Roiphe and Galenson (1973), is an object used by the child less in the service of undoing separation than in the service of maintaining body integrity and reinforcing phallic representations. This is similar to the concept of the prosthetic object as described by Bak (1974). Fintzy (1971) discusses the use of several objects by the child indiscriminately. Fisher (1975) describes the use of a coke machine as a precursor of a transitional object. It was the object that helped her patient invest the outside world and move away from the exclusive relationship to her. Greenacre (1969, 1970), in her writings on transitional objects and infantile fetishes, recognizes that intermediate forms exist between the two. She suggests that when severe deprivation, frustration, and anger characterize the mother–child relationship, these objects are more constricted, less plastic in form, and more concretized in their use than the usual transitional objects.

Many of the articles cited imply that a change in object relations is reflected in the quality of the transitional objects themselves. Our patient demonstrates this theoretical proposition in regard to the choice of objects that he used in order to deal with separation experiences during this period of treatment. As his relationships improved, these objects tended to resemble usual transitional objects. Johnny's first sign of holding a particular object to allay his separation anxiety involved his use of the wooden blocks. These blocks were among the items that he used at home while interacting with his mother. It is possible that they represented this self–other experience (fusion of self and object), but their selection may also have been dictated by their hardness. Greenacre (1969, 1970) has observed that normal children, under circumstances of intense distress, may pick up certain hard objects and hold on to them for comfort. On the basis of her observations, Greenacre hypothesized that the hard object was picked due to its inherent capacity to withstand aggression, thereby offering a sense of cohesiveness. In the same way, Johnny's choice of a hard object in the face of massive separation anxiety suggests that it provided some sense of solidity and cohesiveness, which facilitated the containment of his emerging sense of self.

Subsequent to the use of the blocks, the patient developed a repertoire of activities in order to deal with separation experiences, such as oral intake of food and actively pushing his mother and the therapist through the door. With the advance in individuation, which was evidenced by his better relatedness, his increased ability to delay to plan and anticipate, increased sphincter control, some nonverbal ability to request, and the ability to distance himself from his therapist to some extent, the shift to the use of the blanket and the jacket emerged around separation experiences. Both of these objects were soft and pliable, and were related to proximal sensory modalities, as are the typical transitional objects. Also, he objected to having the jacket washed, a behavior that is very often seen in relation to normal children's transitional objects. However, the jacket was not held by the patient; it was worn by him, and thus its shape and form were fixed in contrast to the ambiguous and changeable characteristics of the transitional objects. Following Greenacre's (1970) theoretical proposition about distorted forms of transitional objects, it may be speculated that this jacket served as an outside skin that helped the patient to preserve a sense of body intactness. It seemed to represent the patient's body surface as well as the mothering person's protective arms and body, re-creating for him an experience of comfort and safety.

It seemed that there was a progression in the patient from his earlier attachment to concrete hard objects, the blocks, to the jacket, which although concrete in form and use was not hard, and then to the blanket, which often becomes the transitional object of normal children. Each more advanced form of transitional object attachment paralleled a shift in the patient's development to a higher level of self–object differentiation and body schematization, as well as an increasing capacity to neutralize aggression. On the basis of the work of others (Winnicott 1953, Furer 1964, Greenacre 1969) and of the shift seen in the present patient, it may be proposed that close observation of the different objects used by these nonverbal psychotic children, as they deal with their reactions to separation, can provide valuable material regarding the level of self–object differentiation achieved by them, their capacity for symbolization, and their capacity to neutralize aggression. This would facilitate the therapeutic work with them, which ordinarily suffers from the paucity of symbolic and verbal associative material.

Speech as a Transitional Phenomenon

The dialectical relationship between developing speech and language, on the one hand, and object relations, on the other hand, is now well recognized. On each of its levels of organization, phonetic (Greenson 1954, Rangell 1963), semantic (Werner and Kaplan 1963), pragmatic (Call 1980), and syntactic (Steingart and Freedman 1972), language development has been shown to parallel the structuring of ego functions, developing object relations, and affect differentiation. For example, Call (1980) recently described how the caretaker's smile and face serve as organizers for vocalization and for the evolution of phonemes. Through infant–mother interactions, mediated by the infant's exploration of the mother's face, specific sounds are first integrated with feeling states in mother and infant. In this way the infant advances to phonetic reciprocity with the mother, preparing the way for later use of phonemes in the composition of words. The communicative function of language appears to evolve from prelinguistic pointing as the pointing shifts from within the dyad to an area beyond it.

Along these lines, the emergence of Johnny's affectively appropriate sobbing sounds, his modulated intonations and babbling, and his pointing were understood as stemming from the establishment of a therapeutically viable symbiotic relationship and the subsequent progression of separation and individuation. In addition, however, it seemed that babbling, once established, was used as a form of transitional object to support his functioning when alone, and to foster further differentiation.

The unique self-generating and self-reporting property of the vocal-auditory apparatus has been pointed out by many (Freud 1891, Greenson 1950, Klein 1965); yet the structural qualities of the vocal auditory apparatus that lend themselves so readily to creating the illusion that there is an external reality corresponding to the infant's wish for gratification have not been described in terms of the transitional object (Ekstein 1965). Winnicott (1953) mentioned babbling as a form of transitional phenomenon, but since then there has been little exploration of this connection. As Winnicott specified for transitional objects in general, the soothing auditory illusory re-creation of mother is contributed to by both objective reality (mother's voice) and the infant's omnipotence (infant's voice). It is neither under outside control, as the real mother is, nor under magical control, like the hallucinated need-satisfying object. The place of origin, whether from without or within, is never challenged. The infant endows his or her own babbling sounds with aspects of the other's.

The general significance of the sensory modalities in the formation of a stable body has long been recognized (Spitz 1945), with special importance attributed to touch (Hoffer 1949) and vision (Greenacre 1958). No other perceptual or experiential modality available to the infant allows him or her to generate a stimulus that, as perceived by the infant, could originate from either the infant or caretaker. The vocal-auditory apparatus offers a readily accessible, body-grounded modality for working out issues of inside–outside and self–other differentiation. Furthermore, the infant can endow the sounds of his or her own babbling, as he or she does with other transitional objects, with the soothing presence of the mother, so that the babbling can be used as the mother's partial and symbolic representative until separation and individuation are consolidated. Tolpin (1971) has suggested that the transitional object, rather than "fading away" by diffusing over the whole cultural field, is internalized as a self-soothing, self-regulating psychic structure through an inherent process of transmuting internalization in which psychic structure assumes the functions of the lost object. The role of inner speech in regard to psychic functioning is well known (Isakower 1939, Katan 1961, Balkanyi 1968). Echolalia, in contrast, is an example of sensorimotor, syncretic, automatic functioning of the vocal-auditory apparatus, based on a constitutional capacity to hear, to register, and to reproduce complex sounds. The integration of the vocal-auditory apparatus as part of the ego, through which it can act to mediate between the needs of the child and the demands of external reality, may well begin in its function as transitional object. Subject to further psychic differentiation and cognitive maturation, it supports several developmental lines, such as super-ego development (Isakower 1939), drive control (Katan 1961), and verbalization (Balkanyi 1968). Vocalizations as transitional objects are not quite the same as the usual soft blanket, however. The blanket does not have a discharge function, as voice does. Vocalization as a transitional object has biological determinants that a blanket does not. For example, infants are born with the capacity to utter all known phonemes by age three or four months. The blanket is perceptually different, its substance and reality being confirmed through vision and touch. In contrast, auditory stimuli, while they can be repeated, have a fleeting and evanescent quality.

Winnicott (1953) specifically states that the transitional object should be distinguished from parts of the infant's body that may also bring comfort. While the thumb and transitional object both have soothing properties, the latter, by being outside the infant's body, leads to experiences qualitatively different from the former. The infant's vocal auditory apparatus is, on the one hand, part of his body, but on the other hand, the soothing stimulus he perceives in the form of sound waves arrives, as it were, from outside the body, whether self- or other-generated.

Winnicott (1953) also states that transitional objects do not belong to and are not chosen by the mother. Certainly the mother does not give speech in the way she might give a physical object, and the infant, in endowing his or her own vocalizations with the significance of the mother's, does go through the same creative process as is involved in endowing a blanket with soothing qualities. Yet, vocalization is shared by mother and infant in a way not found with other transitional objects, so that vocalization is not only used as a substitute for the mother's presence, but also in actual exchanges with the mother. These differences, biological, interactional, and perceptual, between the blanket and babbling, influence the developmental significance of each as transitional objects. The blanket, with its emphasis on vision, flexibility of shape and contour, and simultaneous presentation of all parts in relationship to the whole, may support the development of nonverbal thought— characterized by the unity of its elements in structure and temporal arrangement (Langer 1942, Vigotsky 1962)—play with toys (Galenson 1971), fantasy, and perhaps even dreams. Babbling, with its emphasis on audition, shared hierarchical regularities, and temporal sequence, may in contrast support the development of verbal thought—characterized by structural and temporal sequences—and communication. Qualitative differences in the nature of transitional objects are crucial in relation to their significance for development. Thus variations in the qualities of transitional objects reflect not only the level of self–object differentiation, body schematization, and capacity to neutralize aggression, but also lend themselves to different aspects of emerging ego functions. Both blanket and babbling, however, share the capacity to promote the formation of illusion, a quality that gives the transitional object its special usefulness in the process of separation-individuation.

The range of distortion that transitional objects are subject to has already been described. The extreme form of this is the psychotic fetish, an inanimate representation of a severely disturbed mother–infant relationship. It represents an attempt to restore and maintain an early unity within the symbiosis in which self and other representations are not separated and are invested with undue amounts of hostile aggression. Rigid echolalia, characterized by its evident global taking-in of vocal elements of the mother, similarly indicates fusion of primitive representations of self and other (Mahler 1968), without the flexibility implicit in stable and separate mental representations. It is here proposed that echolalia is the auditory equivalent of the psychotic fetish, not of the transitional object as has been suggested (Ekstein 1965, Griffith and Ritvo 1967). It functions to support self–other fusion rather than separation-individuation and a secure sense of self. It may be that some of the distortions of language in psychotic children, such as concreteness (Searles 1962), fragmentation (Cameron 1944), and even different levels of echoing itself (Ekstein and Caruth 1969, Shapiro et al. 1970) may be linked developmentally to intermediate forms of distortion of the transitional object, as described above.

REFERENCES

Bak, R. (1974). Distortions of the concept of fetishism. *Psychoanalytic Study of the Child* 29:191–214.

Balkanyi, C. (1968). Language, verbalization and super-ego: some thoughts on the development of the sense of rules. *International Journal of Psycho-Analysis* 49:712–718.

Busch, F. (1974). Dimensions of the first transitional object. *Psychoanalytic Study of the Child* 29:215–229.

Buxbaum, E. (1960). Hair pulling and fetishism. *Psychoanalytic Study of the Child* 15:243–260.

Call, J. (1980). Some prelinguistic aspects of language development. *Journal of the American Psychoanalytic Association* 28:259–290.

Cameron, N. (1944). Experimental analysis of schizophrenic thinking. In *Language and Thought in Schizophrenia*, ed. J. Kasanin. Berkeley: University of California Press.

Ekstein, R. (1965). Historical notes concerning psychoanalysis and early language development. *Journal of the American Psychoanalytic Association* 13:707–730.

Ekstein, R., and Caruth, E. (1969). Levels of verbal communication in the schizophrenic child's struggles against, for and with the world and objects. *Psychoanalytic Study of the Child* 24:115–137.

Fintzy, R. (1971). Vicissitudes of the transitional object in a borderline child. *International Journal of Psycho-Analysis* 52:107–113.

Fisher, S. (1975). On the development of the capacity to use transitional objects: a case study of an autistic child. *Journal of the American Academy of Child Psychiatry* 14:114–124.

Freud, A. (1965). *Normality and Pathology in Childhood.* New York: International Universities Press.

Freud, S. (1891). *On aphasia.* London: Imago Publishing Co. Ltd., 1953.

Furer, M. (1964). The development of a preschool symbiotic psychotic boy. *Psychoanalytic Study of the Child* 19:448–469.

Galenson, E. (1971). A consideration of the nature of thought in childhood play. In *Separation-Individuation*, eds. J. B. McDevitt and C. F. Settlage, pp. 41–59. New York: International Universities Press.

Greenacre, P. (1958). Early physical determinants in the development of the sense of identity. In *Emotional Growth*, vol. 1, pp. 113–127. New York: International Universities Press, 1971.

——. (1965). On the development and function of tears. *Psychoanalytic Study of the Child* 20:203–219.

——. (1969). The fetish and the transitional object. *Psychoanalytic Study of the Child* 24:144–164.

——. (1970). The transitional object and the fetish: with special reference to the role of illusion. In *Emotional Growth*, vol. 1, pp. 335–352. New York: International Universities Press, 1971.

Greenson, R. (1950). The mother tongue and the mother. *International Journal of Psycho-Analysis* 31:1–6.

Griffith, R., and Ritvo, E. (1967). Echolalia: concerning the dynamics of the syndrome. *International Journal of Psychoanalytic Psychotherapy* 6:184–193.

Hoffer, W. (1949). Mouth, hand and ego integration. *Psychoanalytic Study of the Child* 3/4:49–56.

Isakower, O. (1939). On the exceptional position of the auditory sphere. *International Journal of Psycho-Analysis* 20:340–348.

Katan, A. (1961). Some thoughts about the role of verbalization in early childhood. *Psychoanalytic Study of the Child* 16:184–188.

Kleeman, J. A. (1967). The peek-a-boo game (part I): its origins, meanings and related phenomena in the first year. *Psychoanalytic Study of the Child* 22:239–273.

Klein, G. (1965). On hearing one's own voice. In *Drives, Affects and Behavior*, vol. 2, *Essays in Memory of Marie Bonaparte*, ed. M. Schur, pp. 87–117. New York: International Universities Press.

Langer, S. K. (1942). *Philosophy in a New Key*. Cambridge, Mass.: Harvard University Press.

Lewis, M., and Rosenblum, L. (1974). *The Effect of the Infant on its Caregiver*. New York: John Wiley.

Mahler, M. S. (1968). *On Human Symbiosis and the Vicissitudes of Individuation*. New York: International Universities Press.

Mahler, M. S., and LaPerriere, K. (1965). Mother–child interaction during separation-individuation. *Psychoanalytic Quarterly* 34:483–498.

Mahler, M. S., Pine, F., and Bergman, A. (1975). *Psychological Birth of the Human Infant*. New York: Basic Books.

Piaget, J. (1962). *Play, Dreams and Imitation in Childhood*. New York: Norton.

Rangell, L. (1963). Beyond and between the no and the yes. In *Counterpoint: Libidinal Object and Subject*, ed. H. Gaskill, pp. 29–74. New York: International Universities Press.

Roiphe, H. (1973). Some thoughts on childhood psychosis, self and object. *Psychoanalytic Study of the Child* 28:131–145.

Roiphe, H., and Galenson, E. (1973). The infantile fetish. *Psychoanalytic Study of the Child* 28:147–166.

Searles, H. (1962). The differentiation between concrete and metaphorical thinking in the recovering schizophrenic patient. *Journal of the American Psychoanalytic Association* 10:22–49.

Shapiro, T., Roberts, A., and Fish, B. (1970). Imitation and echoing in young schizophrenic children. *Journal of the American Academy of Child Psychiatry* 9:548–567.

Sperling, M. (1963). Fetishism in children. *Psychoanalytic Quarterly* 32:374–392.

Spitz, R. A. (1945). Hospitalism: an inquiry into the genesis of psychiatric conditions in early childhood. *Psychoanalytic Study of the Child* 1:53–74.

Steingart, I., and Friedman, N. (1972). A language constitution approach for the examination of self/object representation in varying clinical states. In *Psychoanalysis and Contemporary Science*, vol. 8, eds. R. Holt and E. Peterfreund, pp. 132–178. New York: MacMillan.

Tolpin, M. (1971). On the beginnings of a cohesive self. *Psychoanalytic Study of the Child* 26:316–352.

Vigotsky, L. S. (1962). *Thought and Language*. Boston: MIT Press.

Werner, H., and Kaplan, R. (1963). *Symbol Formation*. New York: John Wiley.

Winnicott, D. W. (1953). Transitional objects and transitional phenomena. *International Journal of Psychoanalysis* 34:89–97.

Wolff, P. (1969). The natural history of crying and other vocalizations in early infancy. In *Determinants of Infant Behavior*, vol. 4, ed. B. Foss, pp. 81–109. London: Methuen and Co.

From Command to Request:
The Development of Language in the
Treatment of a Symbiotic
Psychotic Child

ANNI BERGMAN
MARGARET CHERNACK

A discussion of "Separation-Individuation and Transitional Objects in a Four-Year-Old Psychotic Child" by Stavroula Beratis, M.D., Robert Miller, M.D., and Eleanor Galenson, M.D. The case study of the treatment of a four-year-old symbiotic psychotic child is presented. The child is in therapy at a day treatment program at the Psychological Center of the City University of New York as part of an ongoing research program studying the relationship of cognition and object relations in autistic and psychotic children. The development of the child's language and self-concept in the course of two years of treatment is discussed. His language is regarded as an indicator of the level and quality of self–object differentiation. A distinction is drawn between the pathological symbiotic state and the normal symbiotic stage, and maturation along the lines of separation-individuation is discussed in terms of the development of dialogue.

Beratis, Miller, and Galenson's "Separation-Individuation and Transitional Objects in a Four-Year-Old Psychotic Child" is an impressive case study of the therapeutic development of a psychotic child along the lines of separation-individuation. The case study presented in the present paper supplements the one of Johnny.

Martin came to treatment at the age of four, a symbiotic-psychotic child with only the most rudimentary use of symbolic function. This child emerged from a rigid, symbiotic relationship with his mother—which did not allow him to develop further along the lines of separation-individuation—and moved toward the establishment of a firmer, more differentiated and integrated sense of self and other. His development could be discussed following the organizational principle of the subphases of the separation-individuation process, as was done in the case of Johnny and has been done by others (e.g., Bergman 1971 and Kupferman 1971). Instead, his development along the lines of separation-individuation is presented through a description of the development of his use of language as it emerged in the therapeutic process.

The choice of this method of presentation is based on several assumptions. First, it is assumed that the nature of one's self-concept and the level and quality of one's self-object differentiation are manifest in one's linguistic style. According to Winnicott (1967), cultural experience, play, creative activity, and the beginning of symbolization arise in a "transitional" or "potential space" that is neither inside/subjective nor outside/objective, but intermediate between subject and object. If one assumes that language develops in this transitional space, i.e., at the interface of self and other, then it becomes useful to regard language as indicative of previous and present successes and failures at the interface of self and other. That is, it becomes useful to regard language as indicative of the nature of self–object differentiation. Beratis et al., by suggesting that early vocalizations function as transitional objects, enrich the notion of the transitional object. They recognize that there are significant differences between "blanket and babbling," and stress that such "qualitative differences in the nature of transitional objects are crucial in relationship to their significance for development." Thus the differences between *types* of transitional objects reflect different "levels of self–object differentiation" and "lend themselves to different aspects of emerging ego-functions." However, it is suggested here that *language itself* is paradigmatic of the paradox that Winnicott sees as belonging to the transitional space; it "both joins and separates" (Winnicott 1967, p. 372) at the same time. Without some recognition of separateness there would be no need for language. The development of language already implies the recognition of an other. And language is the means par excellence with which we understand, are understood, communicate, and join with the other. The development of language (which includes preverbal communication) thus embodies the paradox of oneness and separateness and provides an avenue toward understanding the development and nature of self and object representations. Thus the description of the development of Martin's use of language also describes the construction of his self as it developed in therapy.

THE THERAPEUTIC SETTING

Martin was seen in a day treatment program as part of a research project to study the relationship of cognition and object relations in psychotic children according to the theories of Margaret S. Mahler and Jean Piaget.

The therapeutic program[1] employed three treatment modalities: (1) therapy; (2) therapeutic companionship; (3) classroom. In this setting each mother–child pair is seen by the therapist four times a week. Individual treatment sessions are conducted according to the model outlined by Mahler (1968) in her book, *On Human Symbiosis and the Vicissitudes of Individuation*, in the chapter on treatment techniques. The therapist begins treatment by acting as a bridge between child and mother, bringing them closer together in a healthy symbiotic relationship by helping the mother understand the distorted communications of the child and by helping the child respond to the care-taking of the mother. During later stages in treatment, once the child has emerged as a more separate individual, the mother is no longer required to be present in all therapy sessions. The therapist of the mother–child pair also sees the mother in individual treatment sessions. Giving support to the mother in her mothering is a very important ingredient of therapy.

In addition to treatment with the therapist, the child is also seen in individual sessions by a therapeutic companion. While the therapist attempts to make a bridge between the mother and child, the therapeutic companion attempts to make a bridge for the child to the outside world. Psychotic children are not able to approach the outside world on their own, and the actual presence of the companion in everyday life situations with the child is a very important part of treatment.

The therapeutic classroom is geared to attend to the cognitive and social development of the children to the extent that they are capable of developing in these areas. The approach is developmental, based on the unfolding of cognitive stages as described by Piaget.

THE MOTHER-CHILD PAIR

When Martin and his mother arrived at the Center, they were truly a symbiotic pair. Martin, at the age of four, could not separate from his mother, and his mother seemed to accept totally his absolute dependence upon her. Martin was incapable of functioning as a separate self. He was unable to dress himself; he drank from a bottle; when he went to the bathroom he stood passively by while his mother held his penis. In bodily contact with his mother he seemed to try to establish a total union with her by melting into her, placing his face directly up against hers, putting his fingers into her eye, placing his mouth over hers. When not joined with his mother in physical contact, he would engage in repetitive, autistic-like activities such as moving

1. The Center was originally supported by HEW Grant #02907. It continues to be supported by the New Land Foundation, by the Plumstock Foundation, and by a number of private donors. The project is directed by Anni Bergman and Professor Gilbert Voyat.

cars to and fro at eye level and putting them in and taking them out of containers. Mother impassively and helplessly tolerated Martin's assaults on her body. She engaged actively with him only when he expressed a direct need of her. When he was able to maintain himself at some distance from her, she returned to an impassive, depressive stance with sporadic and intrusive attempts to lead him back into the only engagement with her of which he was capable.

The mother's active engagement with Martin when she was directly needed, and her emotional absence when he was playing at some distance from her, gave one the impression that the mother's own feeling of being alive was dependent upon Martin's interaction with her. However, it is important to add that the availability of this mother for treatment, her unfailing concern for her son's growth, her level-headedness—in short, her strengths—were a major variable in the success of Martin's treatment.

Martin is the first and only child of a young, unmarried, West Indian woman. Pregnancy and delivery were uncomplicated and motor milestones were within normal limits. His mother claims that Martin said his first word at 6 months and had names for family members at one year. At 18 months, language dropped out and was replaced with pointing. Martin is reported to have been a healthy and playful baby. His only significant illness was a chronic middle ear infection which was discovered and treated at 3 years. Martin has always lived with his mother, his mother's older sister and his maternal grandmother. Martin's father has maintained inconsistent contact with the family throughout the years, with periods of regular visits alternating with periods of sporadic phone contact.

NORMAL SYMBIOTIC PHASE AND SYMBIOTIC PSYCHOSIS

The theory of symbiotic psychosis, as originally conceptualized by Mahler, compares the nonhatched state of the psychotic child to the nonhatched state of the normal baby during the symbiotic stage of development:

> In the symbiotic psychotic syndrome, self-differentiation from the mother during the separation-individuation phase has failed and the illusion of symbiotic omnipotent fusion with the mother is still being maintained (Mahler 1968, p. 74).

Since the time when Mahler formulated her theory of symbiotic psychosis as well as the theory of the normal stages of development, revolutionary advances in infant research have taken place. Researchers such as Brazelton (1981), Stern (1980), and others have shown that infants, even in the earliest stages of development, are capable of complex perceptual functions and affective discriminations. Furthermore, they have described the intricacy of early mother–child interaction. While Mahler and her co-workers, in their research on normal development, concentrated on the process of separation and individuation rather than on the study of the autistic and symbiotic phases that precede it, it is nevertheless clear from the point of view of their research that complex developments take place during that period. The infant, in a short span of four to five months, changes from existing in a twilight state, attuned to inner rather than outer stimuli, to outward directedness and, in particular, a state of specific attachment to the mothering partner. The symbiotic stage of development is the phase during which the infant develops a dialogue with his or her caretaker (Spitz 1965). Through mirroring and mutual cueing, mother and infant become a symbiotic dual unit.

Brazelton (1981) describes the impact of the infant on the caregiving of the mother. The infant's molding, nestling, turning the head to her voice, are all powerful messages that elicit the mother's tenderness and caregiving. Brazelton further suggests that from the beginning, the infant has a need to alternate looking and not looking at mother—i.e., to have some control over the amount of stimulation he or she receives:

> A mother must respect her infant's needs for regulation or she will overload his immature psycho-physiological system, and he will need to protect himself by turning her off completely. Thus, she learns his capacity for attention, non-attention, early in order to maintain his attention to her. Within this rhythmic, coherent configuration, she and he can introduce the mutable elements of communication. Smiles, vocalizations, postures, tactile signals, all are such elements. They can be interchanged at will as long as they are based on the rhythmic structure. The individual differences of the baby's needs for such structure set the limits on it (Brazelton 1981, p. 18).

Brazelton continues further on,

> As one looks at the richness of such a homeostatic model, providing each participant with an opportunity to turn off or on at any time in the interaction, it demonstrates the fine tuning available and necessary to each partner of the dyad for learning about 'the other' (p. 20).

It seems quite clear from this description that Martin and his mother had failed at this basic process. Both approach and withdrawal behaviors were coercive and abrupt. They lacked pleasure and playfulness. The rhythmic feedback system that provides the basis for all communication had not become established in this mother-child pair.

Brazelton describes the infant's reaction to a still-faced mother, describes the infant's attempts to bring the mother back, and his eventual withdrawal:

> If the system is violated by a partner's non-reciprocity, the infant will respond in an appropriate manner which indicates how powerfully he is affected by the disturbance (Brazelton 1981, pp. 21–22).

He delineates four stages of regulation and learning within the system of social interaction between mother and infant during the first four months, that is, during the symbiotic phase. He uses the apt term, "envelope of reciprocal interaction," in which communication between infant and caregiver takes place. In the case of Martin it was in the first stages of therapy that the therapist attempted to establish such communication with him and simultaneously encouraged it between him and his mother.

The symbiotic stage in normal development is not a fixed state of nondifferentiation and nonintegration. It is the paradox of the symbiotic phase of development that at this stage, when there is the greatest degree of attunement and thus oneness between self and other, the very fact of attunement as manifested in the preverbal dialogue between mother and baby—the "dance" described by Stern (1977)—implies the existence of the beginning of differentiation. The normal symbiotic phase, the stage of dual unity, is a stage on the way toward differentiation and separation-individuation. By contrast, pathological symbiosis is a fixed state, closed to the possibility of preverbal dialogue or "dance," and thus closed to the development of true communication.

TREATMENT

For the purpose of this paper, the word "request" is used to signify object-directed communications such as questions, answers, descriptions, and conversations. This serves to distinguish these from nondialogic utterances, termed "commands"—e.g., neologisms, immediate echolalia, the patient's nonsense language, and his early use of word names. This distinction is consonant with the intention of suggesting that there is a continuum of language development, a dialogic continuum. One end of this continuum is marked by linguistic phenomena that can be understood as indicative of a lack of self–object differentiation—i.e., the "command," the ideational equivalent of which is the hallucinatory wish-fulfillment. The other pole of the continuum is marked by linguistic phenomena that are indicative of self–

object differentiation—i.e., the "request," the ideational equivalent of which is recognition of the other and the presence of ego functions, in particular the capacity for delay.

The Command

When Martin first came to treatment, his speech was composed largely of a babbling that had all the music, the intonation, and the cadence of a language but that at this early point contained no words. He echoed words from television (e.g., "Arid Extra Dry," "Reggie Jackson") and had a few idiosyncratic word names (e.g., "taka taka" meant "Captain America"). Martin's object-directed communications were limited to pointing and a few word names such as "truck," "baseball," and "Batman." The gesture, or nominative word, was used solely to indicate that he wanted an object. The expectation that his desire would be fulfilled was absolute. When he pointed to, or named and pointed to an object, and the therapist or mother got the object for him, this did not seem to be experienced as a response to a request, but rather as part and parcel of the naming or pointing. Thus it is perhaps more accurate to regard even the apparently object-directed communications with which he began treatment as closer to omnipotent wish-fulfillments than to even very primitive forms of dialogue. The therapist's first task thus became the reinstitution of the earliest forms of dialogue. In other words, the therapist's goal was to become a need-satisfying object, to be included in the symbiotic relationship in which Martin and his mother were frozen, and thus to reopen the path toward separation-individuation.

From the first day, a baseball game was initiated. It was a three-way game. At that early point Martin was batting in his mother's arms. The therapist said, "Mommy and Martin at bat, Meg throws," at which point the therapist pitched and they tried to hit the ball. As Martin began to move from this clinging position, the ball game had its own development. "Mommy at bat, Meg throws," and Martin would run bases, run "home to Mommy," "safe with Mommy." When he tentatively ran home to the therapist as well, the litany expanded to "safe with Meg," "safe in the playroom." As he began practicing, the ball game became "Mommy at bat, Meg throws, Martin goes," and Martin would leave the playroom and then return to find us "still there," "still the same," "still playing ball." As time went on the ball game became further elaborated: "Mommy at bat, Meg throws, Martin goes," at which point Martin would invent a movement-gesture that the therapist would imitate; the ball game would then continue. As his movements became more elaborate, this gestural dialogue became richer. In the course of this baseball game, which developed over the first year of treatment, the therapist slowly came to be included within the symbiotic duo.

The previous discussion of the mother–child pair distinguished the pathological symbiotic state from the normal symbiotic stage. The therapist becomes the facilitator of the development of a more normal symbiotic relation between mother and child by becoming included in what was a rigidly defensive symbiotic state, and thus the therapist is also the catalyst for the development of a dialogue between them. In this way the path toward differentiation begins to be reopened. It is interesting to note that for Martin this ball game eventually became a stable structure into which he could integrate new experiences. For example, when Martin first ventured to play with water he next had mother and therapist play baseball, and the litany went, "Mommy at bat, Meg throws, Martin goes," at which point Martin shouted out the word "water."

In an attempt to enter into however primitive a form of interaction/dialogue with the patient, the therapist would echo Martin's many bizarre sounds. At first this could be tolerated only if they were exact echoes of his sounds. As time went on he was able to tolerate the therapist's changing the sounds somewhat, turning them eventually from harsh noises into songs.

Martin's omnipotent naming of objects provided another vehicle for the early institution of dialogue. When Martin said, for example, "truck," the therapist brought him the object, saying, "Martin wants Meg to get the truck." While satisfying the demand, the therapist puts the demand into words. While remaining at the level of a need-satisfying object, the therapist attempts further differentiation by making small and gradual changes, staying however minute a step ahead of the level from which the patient acted or spoke. This is similar to what mothers do spontaneously with their infants, always putting into words what is happening between them. Dialogue necessitates a distance between the speaker and the responder, however minute this distance may be at first. Thus even the most primitive object relation, even the symbiotic, already implies some beginning of differentiation and thus some form of dialogue.

These interventions could be successful only because the seed of development, the precursor of dialogue, is present in even the most primitive of behaviors. When Martin used word names omnipotently, this demand or order that the need be satisfied (get the truck), was also a beginning attempt at creating order in his world (that's a truck, there's a truck). The primitive sounds and simple movements called for a response that, if directed at the child's present level of development in the context of a stable and safe "holding environment," could in turn be responded to. As Ekstein (1966) notes, "The imitative aspects of [echolalia and echopraxia] can be considered a forerunner of identificatory processes . . ." (pp. 238–239).

In its earliest phases the therapeutic dialogue generally took the form of the therapist's slightly modified echoing of the patient (Ekstein's 1966 "quasi echopraxia and echolalia" p. 246). The patient's echoing of the therapist, while seen as defensive—i.e., a denial of self-object differentiation —was also regarded as a sign of a beginning attempt at, or a precursor of, identification with the therapist (e.g., Bergman 1971). After a time, Martin's immediate echolalia evolved into a delayed echoing of the therapist's approval of the smallest of his independent actions. Martin soon came to applaud himself and to say "good boy" when he succeeded at something. For a long time Martin made it clear that the therapist must echo his echo of the therapist and say in agreement, "Yes, good boy." As the identification became more stable and the internalization more possible, this became correlatively less necessary to Martin. The therapist's voice, its specific quality, as well as the words spoken, were quite important in the development of internalization and the resultant development in ego functions and self-object differentiation.

One day, toward the end of the first year in treatment, Martin began the session by looking through a set of blocks that had the names of important persons and television characters written on them. He began naming each one in a striking imitation of the therapist's voice. He came to a block that had the name of a staff member who had left the Center some weeks before and immediately put it behind his back. He stopped, thought, took the block out of hiding, and for the first time spontaneously said, "Jean went bye-bye." He then did the same with each of the blocks that represented someone whom he no longer saw. For Martin, at this point in his development, the ability to maintain this level of self–object differentiation in the face of object loss seemed directly correlated with his use of the therapist's voice. Martin's use of the quality of the therapist's voice was different than—and an advance over—his echoing of the therapist's words. In his echolalic repetition of the therapist's words, Martin repeated what the therapist said. In his imitation of the therapist's voice, Martin repeated what the therapist is. An affective component, represented by the quality of the voice, had been added.

Martin's language can usefully be regarded as a defensive maintenance of the earliest forms of object relations as well as an attempt at and difficulty with internalization. In the beginning phases of treatment, Martin would often talk with his mouth closed. He was unable to repeat a demand for something if it was not immediately understood and responded to. He would never ask or answer questions, and he tended to repeat words (and actions) over and over as if he would thus be able to drain them of all meaning. These phenomena were mainstays of the first year, and especially of the first six months, of treatment. They can be understood as attempts to maintain a lack of self–object differentiation, as primitive attempts to defend against separation. If the therapist or mother did not understand Martin's spoken demands, this signified that they were separate persons, incapable of mind-reading and incapable of omnipotent fulfillment of his omnipotent demands. To repeat himself would be a recognition, on some level, of this state of affairs. Martin's speaking with his mouth closed seemed to have a similar anxiety-reducing effect for him, as recrossing the threshold of the playroom with his eyes closed when it was time to leave. Both were attempts to deny separation. Martin's eye-closing at the threshold and reopening them outside the playroom had the additional significance of regaining him omnipotent control, since it was he who made the therapist disappear. The mouth-closing had the additional significance of trying to discover the therapist to be omnipotently able to know what he wished without his having to speak it out loud, without his having to ask.

In sum, the level of Martin's self–object differentiation, as reflected by his use of language in the early phases of treatment, is well exemplified by his early use of the single word "yes." An important variation of the baseball game went as follows: "Mommy at bat, Meg throws, Martin goes," at which point Martin shouted out the word "yes" a number of times and indicated that the therapist should repeat "yes." This joyful proclamation was sometimes accompanied by jumping or twirling motions and sometimes announced acapella. This use of *yes* preceded the development and use of *no* and was, it seemed, of a different order than the use of *yes* as a response—the *yes* that Spitz (1957) describes as developmentally following the *no*. In this case, the use of *yes* as a *response* occurred quite late in the treatment and followed the emergence of *no*. First of all to emerge, however, was the use of *yes* as proclamation and command. This is not the *yes* said to others in response to a request, but the *yes* that Martin wished others to say to him, the *yes* that represented the absence of any possible *no*, the absence of any possible boundary, limit, or difference between himself and the world, between the self and the other.

Transition

The phase in Martin's treatment that was transitional between the early command language of omnipotence, of the undifferentiated self–object, and the communicative language of self to object that is predicated upon the development of more stable internalizations and resultant self and object representations, is described through what led up to and what followed from the point in Martin's treatment at which he first came to name himself.

About six months after the start of treatment, Martin began to create situations in which he was bound to experience the loss of objects and persons. Martin, who always carried with him pictures from magazines or comic books, began having his mother cut out all the individual people in the group pictures separately. He would carry these little pieces around, inevitably losing one or another of them, at which point he would himself fall to pieces. This was understood as a dramatic repetition of a fact of life that he was first beginning to experience: that loss and separation go hand in hand. Soon, however, he seemed to be purposely creating such situations. For example, he would order his mother to throw a picture away; several hours after he saw that she had taken the garbage out, he would demand the picture again and fall to pieces when she could not supply it. He would intentionally leave an object at home when he came to therapy sessions, and then fall to pieces when it was not in the therapy room.

This is similar to the behavior of a normal toddler during the rapprochement subphase. One such little boy would ask his mother to cook some food for him. The moment the food was in the pot cooking, he demanded to have it uncooked. When he was offered the same food uncooked, he was not satisfied. He broke down into a tantrum, demanding the same food that he had asked his mother to cook, now to be given to him uncooked.

This phase of manufacturing tragic losses was regarded as a transitional phase in Martin's development toward object constancy, during which he attempted to recapture his now waning omnipotence. He commanded the toy or picture to disappear, to stay home, to be thrown away. He then attempted to command its reappearance and, when wishing did not make it so, he was devastated. That he needed to try, to wish, to make this happen clearly signified his increasing individuation and decreasing omnipotence. Previously, he would not have needed to try or to wish that others would return since, in an important sense, he never would have experienced them as having left in the first place. Previously, when he had made the therapist disappear by turning off the light, or had made a toy disappear by closing the door or leaving the session, and then turned on the light or opened the door or returned for his next session, it is unlikely that he experienced this as the person or the object still being where he left it. Rather, he commanded its reappearance, he made it present by being present again himself.

However, with the beginning of self–object differentiation, when objects and persons had begun to have an existence apart from him, when his omnipotence was no longer absolute, he desperately attempted to recapture the old state of affairs. This phase was truly transitional, progressive as well as regressive; for by setting up the situations of inevitable loss he was also attempting to master the dawning realization that others did in fact exist apart from him, in his absence. At the height of this he came to a session in an intense panic searching for one of his blocks that he had taken home with him from the playroom some days before. His mother explained that before he left he began to take the block with him, thought better of it, and put it down in his room saying, "Captain Kirk block stay." The therapist spoke to Martin about this recurrent behavior, adding that he was so afraid of losing his mommy, since then he became afraid he would lose himself too. Martin stood up quietly in the middle of the room, and after a moment announced, "Captain Kirk block home." He then indicated that he wanted to paint, and after the therapist had, as usual, signed Martin's name to his painting, Martin patted his tummy and said, "Martin, Martin, Martin."

In the months that followed there was a considerable surge of development in language as well as an advance in and consolidation of ego functions. His language progressed beyond the nominative function as if there were finally a subject to which he could attach predicates. In addition to naming objects, he now spoke of states of affairs—"put it away," "paper all gone," "paper fall down," "try again," "that's enough," "come on," "where's the boat? There it is." His body language, too, became more differentiated. He shrugged when he could not find something he wanted, put his hands in his pockets, began swinging his arms as he walked in imitation of a favorite male teacher, and began purposefully experimenting with turning in circles, walking backwards, falling down. His vocalizations became more varied as he began speaking in a squeaky little girl's voice as he played with a doll, and a gruff, rough voice as he played Batman and Robin. He began joyfully experimenting with saying a word or phrase in numerous pitches, intonations, and cadences. The correlative development of his language and self-representation was further demonstrated in his increased use of the mirror—watching himself cry, play, and rage as he had done so many times before but without awareness—and in his beginning to take pride and comfort in ownership during this period of increased language development.

As he began to become aware of objects as belonging to him, he began to take over some of the valuing of his products that had previously been left to the therapist. The therapist had always hung up or saved Martin's pictures despite Martin's apparent lack of interest in his own productions. Now Martin began admiring them, repeating the therapist's words, "They're Martin's," and began showing them to other people. He was able to take comfort in ownership. For example, under the pressure of an upcoming vacation, Martin wanted something that belonged to another child. When he couldn't have it he panicked. After calming down, he angrily banged on the floor and proceeded to enact in his play the other child taking his toys away. When the therapist commented that the other child certainly couldn't have his toys because they were his, Martin responded, "Martin's, Martin's," and was much comforted.

During this period in his treatment, the "yes" proclamation dropped out altogether and the "no" emerged. It is no surprise that, with the waning of omnipotence and the development of self–object differentiation, the "yes" as an omnipotent, absolute affirmation of perfect union should disappear. It is equally unsurprising that, with the beginning of self-awareness, the "no" should arise. As Spitz (1957) has shown, "The acquisition of the 'No' is the indicator of a new level of autonomy, of the awareness of the 'other' and of the awareness of the self . . ." (p. 129). "The child's headshaking 'no' is the visible proof of his identification with the grownup; at the same time it initiates the era of allocentric communication" (p. 59). In the case of Martin, however, "yes" as a response to a request did not follow fast on the heels of the semantic "no." In fact, for almost a year Martin went to some lengths to avoid speaking the word "yes." If he attempted to indicate that he wanted something—and it should be noted that he could not yet frequently ask for something with a question—e.g., by saying "go Pepsi," and the therapist asked, "Do you want to go to the store to get Pepsi, Martin?" Martin would not respond "yes," but instead would echo the therapist's words, "go to store," and add "okay," as if the idea had been the other's wish and not his own, but something with which he would go along.

By this point in his treatment Martin evinced some degree of self–object differentiation, internalization of the mothering principle, and the beginning development of self and object representations. The differentiation, the internalization, and the representations were not stable, however, and conflicts over separations were still of intense proportions. In saying "no," he indicated that he was able to separate himself from the other, but in being able *only* to say "no," he indicated that he could do so only if he alone commanded it. The self–object differentiation was uncertain, not stable and sure. To say "yes" at this point would threaten Martin with reengulfment. Further, it is suggested that the saying of *yes* involves a qualitatively different level of self–object differentiation than the saying of "no." To say "no" is to separate one's self from the other, so to speak, with one's back turned. To say "yes" is to do so face to face in a simultaneous, mutual recognition of each member of the dialogue's mutual separateness from the other. If Martin's original "yes" is, for the moment, regarded as a representation of sameness, and his "no" as a representation of difference, then the "yes" that was not yet available to him would be a recognition of similarity in the context of, or on the background of, difference. This last and more advanced capacity is a condition not only for yes-saying, but also for asking and answering questions and for that advanced form of dialogue, the conversation.

The Request

In some of the developments in Martin's language during the second year of his treatment, one can see the dawnings of the language of "request," i.e., linguistic phenomena that are manifestations of a differentiation of self and other.

During his second year of treatment the word "yes" re-emerged for the first time since the beginning of therapy. Along with the re-emergence of *yes* came the ability and willingness to ask and answer questions. He began to attempt to describe to the therapist and his mother what had occurred to him when they were not with him. If the therapist asked what happened in school that day, he might answer in a burst, "Helen and Gary, and no coat and run." Such a response to a question is clearly predicated on the recognition that the therapist, the questioner, the other, did not and could not know what Martin, the questioned, the self, knew because the other was not the self. Similarly, to ask a question involves the ability to recognize that the other does not know what the self wants without being told, and that the other might not satisfy the request, might say "no." Further, as suggested above, a response to a question indicates that there is an ability to reach toward the other, to join with the other to a degree, but not absolutely. To answer a question indicates an ability to join with the other at the same time as, and on the basis of, the recognition that the other is not the self. This is language as communication.

In Martin's case, three phases in the development of his communicative use of language were distinguished. These phases seem to correspond, progressively, to the degree of internalization and articulation of object and self representations. At first Martin would repeat both sides of a conversation. For example, Martin asked the therapist, "Where's Carla?" The therapist responded, "I don't know. Let's look for her." Martin says, "Okay." As they walked in search of Carla, Martin said aloud to himself, "Where's Carla? I don't know. Let's look. Okay." Somewhat later, Martin began holding conversations as if with two or more parts of himself, at which point he would say, for example, "Martin, move chair. Okay. Move it. Good." Finally he was able to hold conversations with actual others, asking and answering questions and describing events.

This section closes with some recent examples of Martin's use of language, taken from the beginning of his third year in treatment:

Martin: Meg, look you got a new table.
Therapist: Yes, I did. You noticed, and then you told me, too.

Martin: Get the toys.

Martin: (*Looking out the window*) Look, the trees, it's windy.
Therapist: (*Later that session*) Are you looking at the trees, Martin?
Martin: Yes, and the cars.

Martin: I'm hungry.
Therapist: Would you like something to eat?
Martin: Yes.
Therapist: Would you like toast?
Martin: Yes.

Therapist: With butter or jelly?

Martin: This, this, have to choose . . . I have jelly and you have butter.

Martin: It's night, where the sun go?

DEVELOPMENTS OF COMMUNICATION IN A NORMAL INFANT

The use of language as communication as it progressed in the tripartite treatment of a symbiotic psychotic boy from the age of four to the age of six has been described. Martin posed a strange dilemma, but also a special opportunity. He had words at his disposal as was fitting for his chronological age; however, he used these words not as a normal child of his age would, nor even as a child much younger, first learning to talk. Rather, he seemed to use words in the way in which a normal infant and junior toddler might use various forms of vocal and gestural communication. In other words, as is typical of a symbiotic psychotic child, maturational advances could not be used in the service of his development. Rather, in the lack of appropriate object relationships, these maturational advances become a threat rather than an asset. Some examples of interchanges with an infant during the first year of his life, interchanges that illustrate communications and thus the forerunners of verbal language, may prove illuminating; for without this kind of solid base in nonverbal communication, words seem to become encoded in bizarre, idiosyncratic, and repetitive patterns.

As an infant, Peter was sung to by both his parents, especially when they put him to sleep. Since Peter was a baby who did not fall asleep easily, his parents usually held him while sitting on a rocking chair and singing to him until he would fall asleep. Peter had favorite tunes beginning at an early age. These were not the usual lullabies. Rather, they were work songs that both parents enjoyed and liked to sing to him. After two to three months, when Peter's sounds were beginning to be more varied, they were clearly responsive to different situations. Cooing was the sound for intimate interchanges. A very distinctive screech denoted excitement. Finally, Peter would sing a "song" when he was ready to go to sleep. This song was quite different from his other sounds, a kind of hum on a two- or three-note scale, which was a very distinct signal. As soon as Peter started to sing his song his parents knew that he wanted to go to sleep. They would begin to sing to him and rock him, and Peter would quickly drop off to sleep. The "song" used in this way by baby Peter is comparable to what has been called command-type communications in Martin. The communications ceased as soon as the wish was fulfilled and Peter was helped to go to sleep. Some months later the song began to be used in a new way. Now Peter sang his song not only when he wanted to go to sleep, but also when he wanted to be sung to. When his request was met and he was sung to, he stopped singing, but started again when the song was finished and asked for another. One might say that the command (for the lullaby) had become a request, and that a dialogue ensued. Some months later still, Peter would request a song or music of any sort by bouncing up and down, looking smilingly and expectantly at the care-giver.

When Peter was nine to ten months old, now in the midst of the early practicing subphase, he discovered a new form of gestural communication in keeping with his now more mature perceptual and locomotor functions. From early on Peter's mother had enjoyed showing him pictures in books and naming objects for him. Now Peter began to point at objects and people, wishing—or rather, "commanding"—that they be named. He derived great pleasure from being carried about while he pointed at different objects, waiting for his mother to give him the name. Similarly, when he discovered objects on his own explorations, he would bring them back and show them, again wishing them to be named, acknowledged. If anyone tried to take an object that Peter brought to them, he made it clear that he did not wish to give it, that he just wanted to show it and have it named. About a month later Peter's pointing began to be accompanied by the sound, "ah." Now one had to listen to Peter's sounds to begin to understand what seemed to have moved on from the command to the request. Peter no longer wanted merely to have objects named, one now had to begin to distinguish whether he wanted something done—for example, the radio turned on, the light switch turned on and off, etcetera—or whether he wanted to have something said to him. But even what he wanted to have said was no longer simply naming. Rather, it required slightly more complex statements or explanations. By this time Peter was one year old and capable of understanding quite well what was said to him.

Peter's early screeching sounds also had a further development. They reappeared toward the end of his first year in a form that his mother said was his "love call." This love call was meant to draw attention to himself, often from strangers who were not looking at him. This could happen in the street, in a store, in a restaurant, etcetera. If he succeeded in drawing attention to himself in this way, he was jubilant. Peter's screech was comparable to Martin's "yes," a verbal communication requesting affirmation.

It is clear from the description of Peter's early "language development" that words, once they would appear—i.e., once he would maturationally be able to form them—would easily fit into an already existing, complex communication system. Martin had words to use at the time when he was developing, at a much later age, the interpersonal base for communication. On the one hand, listening to and understanding Martin's language develop-ment sensitized the present authors to a better understanding of the development of communicative powers in a normal infant. On the other hand, it is the understanding of the progress of normal development that helped decipher Martin's often strange and seemingly incomprehensible communications.

DISCUSSION

In this paper, we have discussed the development of a psychotic boy over the course of a two-year period. We have shown how the development of his language during that time serves as an important indicator of his progress along the lines of separation-individuation toward beginning object constancy and self–object differentiation. We have speculated about some of the intrapsychic developments which we have deduced from his use of language: "from command to request." By way of comparison and contrast, we have also offered a brief vignette, based on observations of a normal child and his parents during the preverbal period of development; that is, during the first year of life which, from the point of view of object relations development, would cover the symbiotic phase and extend into the practicing subphase of the separation-individuation process.

Symbiotic psychosis occurs in vulnerable children when the separation-individuation process cannot be successfully negotiated. The rapprochement crisis, in such cases, does not end in resolution with beginning object constancy and symbolic process. Instead, rigid restitutive mechanisms appear. "In the symbiotic infantile psychosis reality testing remains fixated at, or regresses to, the omnipotent, delusional stage of the symbiotic mother–infant relationship. The boundaries of the self and the nonself are blurred" (Mahler 1952).

Bruner (1974) has discussed preverbal forms of communication which eventually lead to the acquisition of verbal language. He says:

> I shall propose that the child communicates before he has language. He does so in order to carry out certain functions that are vital to the species. These primitive communication acts are affected by gesture, vocalization and the exploitation of context. There is enough that is universal about such pre-lexico-grammatical communication to support that a part of it is innate and easily triggered. There is a progressive development of these primitive procedures for communicating, and typically they are replaced by less primitive ones until eventually they are replaced by standard linguistic procedures. These progressive changes and procedural leaps are massively dependent upon the interaction of the mother and the child. Mothers teach their children to speak, however willing the children may be, and I rather take their willingness to be part of their innate preparation for language (p. 65).

It is this innate preparation for language, based on the earlier development of communication, that seems to be missing in the psychotic child. Even in those psychotic children who have seemed to develop normally to a certain point and then regressed, we must assume that the early mother–infant relationship was burdened by a constitutional difficulty in the infant to utilize the mother's care, or that the mother's care was grossly lacking in the kind of attunement which infant observers can demonstrate in normal development.

Beratis et al., discuss the difficulty of the psychotic child in the intermediate area of experience which includes transitional objects and the development of language. In the case of our patient, Martin, communicative language development was preceded by his creation of a transitional world, inhabited by all the people who became important to him. This transitional world of block people was the way by which he stayed in contact with all of the people—adults and children—who became important to him in our treatment setting. The fact that all these people came and went and were not always available to him was extremely difficult for him to accept. By creating the transitional world, he would manipulate and control that which in reality he could not. Eventually, he had to create losses in this transitional world before he could accept a measure of separateness, which inevitably entails loss of the symbiotic mother before separation. This is very different from the kind of practicing of separation that a normal infant or toddler will do in his peek-a-boo games or in his darting away, wishing to be caught up in mother's arms. In these normal games, reunion always follows a loss. In contrast, the toy which Martin had decided to leave at home was then not at his disposal. The people in Martin's transitional world were not truly symbolic as they would have been in a normal child's play. They were something in between a transitional object, a psychotic fetish (Furer 1964), or autistic object (Tustin 1981), and symbolic play. They had qualities of all these yet were also different from all of them. They were used by Martin to replay and attempt to master the absences of people which to him were so traumatic. Yet he couldn't use this play to help himself understand and accept people's comings and goings as a normal child his age would have been able to do. He experienced the losses he himself created in his play as if they were the same real losses of people which upset him. This seems to be a deficiency in the symbolic function which is characteristic of psychotic children. The space in which later symbolic play and communicative language can occur (Winnicott 1953, 1967) is missing. Therefore, separation is experienced as total and catastrophic—a gaping hole or wound (Tustin 1981). Repetitive play and language which later may develop into obsessional activities and ideation are meant to fill the hole which is created by every separation.

Why was it that all the people with whom Martin came into contact seemed to be of almost equal value or importance to him? He was like a collector of people. The loss of anyone seemed to threaten his whole existence. This is reminiscent of a seven-month-old normal infant who, for the period of a few days, was observed to cry whenever anyone walked out of his visual field without first stopping to talk to him. It was as if he were realizing for the first time that people could walk away from him. Did he displace a fear that his mother could leave, onto everybody? Or was a loss of anybody, at this particular point, a narcissistic blow to his omnipotence, as it suddenly confronted him with frightening empty space?

The same question could be asked about Martin. It would seem that Martin's need for the symbiotic partner was beginning to be extended from mother to the world outside, as this world opened itself up to him. Maybe this was similar to a normal seven-month-old who seemed to be upset by the realization that the people who inhabited the outside world could walk away from him. In the normal infant, the advent of independent locomotion, accompanied by the affect of elation, is a powerful antidote to the distress of being left. It is at this time that every new accomplishment of the infant is applauded and admired by the outside world and the infant begins to realize that his accomplishments are admired. Thus, the feeling of pleasure and affirmation arises for the infant from an inner source—being able to move and explore, as well as from an outer source—being admired. Martin, we surmised, did not experience this affirmation of his autonomous self during the important time of practicing. He could not use the maturational advent of independent locomotion for practicing and exploration, and had to first begin to have such experiences within the responsive environment created in his therapy. We believe that Martin's use of the word "yes," as it developed in his therapy, was the way in which he expressed his beginning pleasure and autonomy and wish for admiration and affirmation. Similarly, Weich (1978) points to the leap from one to two word utterance occurring at 16–19 months as a phase in which language as a transitional phenomenon occurs.

This period was followed in Martin by a kind of rapprochement crisis in which he actively attempted to come to terms with the fact of loss. In creating and then mourning and protesting situations of loss, he tried to master the loss entailed in greater realization of separateness. It was only after this had been accomplished that he began to use his name and develop a sense of ownership and agency. And it was only after that point in development that communicative language could appear. By communicative language we mean here language which needed or at least could allow for a response from the other. Enough separateness had been established so that language could be used as a bridge from self to other. This we believe was a crucial point in his development, comparable to what we observe in normal development at the point of realization of separateness. It was only then that command language, in which the answer is part of the question and the other is part of the self, could yield to request language in which the risk can be taken that the answer will not be part of the question, in which a true response from an outside other can be considered. The change described here is a structural one, denoting real progress toward object and self constancy. Nevertheless, the disturbance in the symbolic process which we described remains a characteristic of the psychotic self.

REFERENCES

Bergman, A. (1971). "I and you": the separation-individuation process in the treatment of a symbiotic child. In *Separation-Individuation: Essays in Honor of Margaret S. Mahler*, eds. J.B. McDevitt and C.F. Settlage, pp. 325–356. New York: International Universities Press.

Brazelton, T. B. (1981). The first developmental stages in parent and infant attachment. In *Emotion: Theory, Research and Experience*, vol. 2, eds. R. Pluchik and H. Kellerman. New York: Academic Press.

Brazelton, T. B., and Als, H. (1979). Four early steps in the development of mother–infant interaction. *Psychoanalytic Study of the Child 34*: 349–369.

Ekstein, R. (1966). *Children of Time and Space, of Action and Impulse*. New York: Appleton-Century-Crofts.

Furer, M. (1964). The development of a preschool symbiotic boy. *Psychoanalytic Study of the Child* 19:448–479.

Kupferman, K. (1971). The development and treatment of a psychotic child. In *Separation-Individuation: Essays in Honor of Margaret S. Mahler*, eds. J. B. McDevitt and C. F. Settlage, pp. 441–469. New York: International Universities Press.

Mahler, M. S. (1968). *On Human Symbiosis and the Vicissitudes of Individuation*, vol. 1, *Infantile Psychosis*. New York: International Universities Press.

Spitz, R. A. (1957). *No and Yes: On the Genesis of Human Communication*. New York: International Universities Press.

——— . (1965). *The First Year of Life*. New York: International Universities Press.

Stern, D. N. (1974). The goal and structure of mother–infant play. *Journal of the American Academy of Child Psychiatry* 13:402–421.

——— . (1977). *The First Relationship*. Cambridge, Mass.: Harvard University Press.

——— . (1980). The early development of schemas of self, of other, and the various experiences of self with other. Paper presented at the symposium on Reflections on Self Psychology, the Boston Psychoanalytic Society and Institute.

Stern, D. N., Barnett, R. K., and Spieker, S. (1980). Early transmission of affect: some research issues. Paper presented at the First World Congress on Infant Psychiatry, Portugal, April.

Tustin, F. (1981). *Autistic States in Children*. Boston: Routledge and Kegan Paul.

Weich, M. (1978). Transitional language. In *Between Reality and Fantasy: Transitional Objects and Phenomena*, eds. S. A. Grolnick and L. Barkin, pp. 411–423. New York: Jason Aronson.

Winnicott, D. W. (1953). Transitional objects and transitional phenomena. *International Journal of Psychoanalysis* 34:89–97.

——— . (1967). Location of cultural experience. *International Journal of Psychoanalysis* 48: 368–372.

On Speaking of Oneself by Name

DENNIS FARRELL, M.D.
MICHAEL F. HOYT, Ph.D.

Speaking of oneself by name is studied. Such behavior occurred with unusual frequency in the case of a patient with predominantly narcissistic character pathology who underwent brief psychotherapy for a stress response syndrome following his wife's suicide. A content and context analysis of this phenomenon showed that the patient would refer to himself by name as a characteristic defense in response to severe threats to his self-esteem. An object-relations perspective proved useful in clarifying dynamic aspects of this defensive maneuver, which depended for its effectiveness on the evocation of self-images negating guilt and shame. In addition to the patient's character style and the nature of the stress event, the framework of the therapy and the therapist's countertransference responses to the patient were other factors influencing the appearance of this behavior. It is concluded that referring to oneself by name reflects at least momentary disturbance in the sense of self and may be unusually prominent and frequent in narcissistic pathology. A study of the phenomenon appears to elucidate an important step in the building of self-representation from the self-object representations of the symbiotic phase: the concept of "I" becomes possible through the reconciling of a sense of physical and psychic separateness with the need for emotional relatedness to others. Where problems of this early developmental phase are reactivated in the treatment situation, the patient's relationship with the therapist is the vital bridge toward a more coherent sense of self.

A 30-year-old man came for a pretherapy evaluation interview feeling anxious, depressed, guilty, and suicidal. Five months earlier his wife had committed suicide following an intense marital quarrel. The patient, whom we shall here call Bob Smith, had this to say in describing his emotional state: "I've been resisting crying. I would not like to think that I had a very great part in Sue's suicide. I would have expected myself to cry excessively over something like this, just because it seems like I like exercising my emotions. *So Bob Smith hasn't cried as much as he would like to.*" The evaluation interview with the staff social worker was completed, and the patient was then seen by one of the authors (MFH) in short-term dynamically-oriented psychotherapy.

The patient referred to himself as if to a third person, using his proper name instead of the first-person pronoun, a number of times during the course of the therapy. There was something striking and peculiar about these occurrences, and perhaps because of their very oddity they seemed to provide a special access for understanding how the patient thought, how he construed images of himself and others, and how this influenced his response to the stress of his wife's suicide.

Fortunately, we were able to study this case in great detail. Videotapes of all evaluation and therapy sessions were made, with the patient's informed consent, as part of a research project on bereavement and response to brief psychotherapy. Using these tapes and verbatim transcripts, we collected every instance in which the patient referred to himself by name. What follows is a report of our attempt to elucidate the meaning of this phenomenon, cast within an object-relations theoretical framework.

THE STRESS EVENT

The patient and his wife had been together for several years, after he had left a previous marriage to be with her. At first the new wife had seemed to be "the one love of my life," but with time he felt that her need for him was smothering. Their relationship had been deteriorating, but it was a rather trivial event that set off their last violent quarrel. His wife had ordered him to do something with one of his plants, and when she saw him sitting and fuming at the way she had said this she added in a mocking tone, "Look at you—you can't even control yourself!" With that, he withdrew from her and barely spoke for the next two days. Then, in the evening, they began to argue. He told her he didn't love her, that he would be happier alone, and that he was going to leave her. She said she loved him and added angrily that they would be married forever. Over the next few hours, the quarrel intensified, with her alternately pleading and striking out physically at him. He shouted that he hated and despised her, and in the process of fending her off, he hit her with enough force to blacken her eye. He recalled "deliberately" letting himself go, determined to stick to his resolution to leave her. They went to bed exhausted, and he told her finally not to worry, that he would not leave right away, knowing, however, that she was not convinced, and deciding finally as additional punishment to leave her in doubt about it. The next morning he went off to work, leaving a note behind telling her not to do anything rash. She had made suicidal gestures previously by scratching her wrists and, on one occasion, grabbing his loaded gun and holding it to her head as they were driving. It had occurred to him that she might kill herself if he left her, and at work he had a premonition that she had shot herself. The accuracy of this premonition later disturbed him, especially considering that she was "a knife person," and he would have expected her to hurt herself with a knife. He had in fact disassembled his handgun before their final battle; on this occasion, however, unlike previously, he had not hidden it from her, but had left it lying on the bedroom floor. When he returned from work that day, it was apparent that she had put the gun together and had found the bullets for it, for she was lying there, horribly mutilated, having shot herself through the head. She was still minimally alive; she died a few days later in the hospital. The note that she left said that she loved him but that he hated her so that she had lost the one person on earth who had ever loved her.

BACKGROUND OF THE CASE

Because of the crisis nature of this case, a detailed history and psychiatric evaluation could not be completed before undertaking a course of brief therapy. The story of the stress event in particular, as just related, actually came out over time, in bits and pieces, in the painful process of reconstruction. From the beginning, however, there was indication of a moderately severe personality disturbance in the patient, underlying and in part determining the symptom picture. The patient was the youngest of two children. The father was described as a large, angry, powerful man, "like a machine." He was a self-centered man who dominated the family; but behind this, the patient thought, he was actually "frustrated" and "basically scared." The mother was characterized as a rather weak, sad, unhappy person; in fact, during the course of the patient's brief therapy, the mother made an attempt at suicide by overdose with psychotropic medications. The parents had never been happy together, and on occasion the father had been physically violent toward the mother. The patient could recall little of his early childhood, but did relate a significant family legend: supposedly, when he was two and still in diapers, he stood up to his father, confronting him with raised fists. The patient seemed to believe this story and, in any case, related that later on in childhood and adolescence he had stepped between his mother and father to protect his mother whenever his father threatened her. When the patient was entering puberty, an older sister underwent a "nervous breakdown" that resulted in her being sent to a mental hospital where she remained confined for many years. At about the time she was sent away, he was involved with some other boys in burglarizing the school he attended, and he was expelled from that institution. He first married in high school after his girlfriend became pregnant. The marriage, which lasted for ten years, was punctuated by occasional extramarital affairs on his part, due to his assessment that "something was missing" in the marriage. After high school, he worked at various semi-skilled jobs except for several protracted absences for injuries incurred in motorcycle accidents. He left his first wife to be with the woman who was later to shoot herself. They had been together for about four years when her suicide occurred.

The patient described having been initially attracted to his wife by her very neediness, the impression she gave of great vulnerability, which seemed to satisfy his "need to love" and protect her as he had tried to protect his mother from his very possessive, domineering, and sometimes violent father. This idea of himself as protector vis-a-vis the weak, injured woman was by far his most acceptable self-image: it rejected his father's violence and his mother's weakness; it combined his father's strength and his mother's sensitivity. But the rejected attributes were also there: he was "ten percent" of his father's violent nature and, "cast in the same mold" as his mother, he had to struggle against this weakness "not to go tits up in life." At its best, his relationship with his wife had the characteristics of the good self-object: they were like "twins." He felt they had a deep psychic connection at such times, even to the point of his experiencing and sometimes anticipating her physical sensations during menstruation. But as their relationship deteriorated, with his feeling smothered and drained by her emotional demands and challenged by her hostility, he himself became the aggressor, like Bob, his father, whose namesake he was. He wanted then to strike out at her, but usually controlled himself and then went through a cycle of remorse and renewed efforts to reinstate the image of himself as caring and protecting and loving. When his violence got the upper hand in their last battle, after he had blackened her eye in the row, he pulled away from her, out of the conviction that there was no way out of the escalating hostility between them. He knew that he would beat her again unless he left her.

After discovering his wife near death, the patient got her to the hospital and, in an initial reaction of overcontrol, efficiently managed all the things that had to be done following her death a few days later. There was a period of superficial mourning, and then the patient entered into a state of numbness, occasionally punctuated by a searing realization that "She's gone!" Scenes of their life together, their last battle, and her gunshot body would frequently intrude into his mind; he became socially withdrawn and occasionally had thoughts of his own suicide. He was preoccupied not only by the loss of his wife but by the issue of his guilt and responsibility and, given the finality of her act, by his inability to undo what had been done or to make reparation. Feeling depressed, with some loss of weight and sleep disturbance, he recognized that he was not working through this crisis on his own and sought help. He came to the Stress Clinic of the Langley Porter Institute on referral by the local Suicide Prevention Service. He was undergoing what Horowitz (1976) calls a "stress response syndrome," a state characterized by marked cognitive-affective disruptions following a stressful life event.

EVALUATION AND COURSE OF TREATMENT

The patient presented himself as soft-spoken, pleasant and cooperative, dressed casually, and in general fitting his own description of "something of the outsider . . . not exactly a member of the counterculture . . . I've never dropped out but I never quite dropped in." He seemed intelligent, articulate, and interested in therapy. He presented himself in a rather smooth manner except for a few strongly discordant notes. In the first interview, he compared the appearance of his wife's eyes after she had shot herself to "purple cupcakes." He reported feeling that he himself was "wrapped in a shroud" and that his "brain was floating, slipping in my head." The seemingly casual intrusion of such graphic statements about himself and his wife would leave the listener with the sense of him as strangely detached, almost callous in relation to his wife's death and his own experience in relation to it. Yet there was also the suspicion that such remarks may also have served the purpose of testing whether others could accept the horror of what had happened and could tolerate the pain he was anticipating having to face. He often spoke in a cool, detached manner, attempting to intellectualize and isolate in defense against intense feelings of grief and aloneness that would nevertheless occasionally break through. Controlling himself and controlling others were central issues, as captured by some of his rather unusual verbalizations: if he cried, it was because he liked to exercise his emotions; in order to experience some of his feelings he wrote a poem and "*touched me* with it"; when he felt uncomfortable around his parents, as he said, "I made myself uncomfortable." It is noteworthy that his wife's mocking remark about his not being in control of himself was the pebble that started the avalanche of hostility between them. Much of his need for control related to issues of self-esteem. His wife's suicide note had included the verdict that he was the "most selfish and spoiled person" she had ever met. He had been told "seven hundred thousand times" that he had "ego problems," and yet as he said almost plaintively at one point, "I'm not a perfect human being because there aren't any . . . I think I'm very acceptable and very likable . . . my ladies have gotten off on me, and I just don't believe that my wife killed herself because I wasn't doing something right." His self-representation seemed consistent with what Kohut (1971) calls the "grandiose self-structure" and what Kernberg (1975) describes as the pathological condensation of actual self with ideal self and ideal object. He employed defenses typical of the narcissistic personality, with splitting being particularly prominent. He spoke of the split between his heart and his head; at times it seemed to him that it was more accurate to say that he was two personalities or "one person with two different heads." He was either omnipotent with power verging on the magical—for example, causing things to happen by thinking about them— or, almost simultaneously, he was absolutely guiltless because unrelated to others, detached, "only part of the environment." Sliding meanings (Horowitz 1975) were frequently employed to ward off threats to self-esteem: frequently, any perceived external judgment was warded off with the argument that none was possible because "everything is relative;" on one occasion, he rejected the whole idea of "looking at" himself through his wife's eyes—since she was dead, he could hardly be looking through *her* eyes. In addition to the not infrequent appearance of such illogical thinking, with much reliance on splitting, denial, and sliding meanings, there were other oddities: not only were there frequent and peculiar references to himself as "Bob," but in several instances he confused whether he was speaking of "I" (himself) or "you" (the therapist). The references to himself as Bob, besides having a number of meanings to be elaborated later in this paper, were another means of distancing himself from his experience, and this was otherwise frequently expressed in terms of looking at himself from one perspective or another or even watching himself as though in a movie. In general, his defensive style and the seeming instability of self- and other-representations sometimes made it very difficult for the therapist or patient to know what the patient's true feelings were (Krohn 1974, Kernberg 1975, Hartocollis 1977, Horowitz 1977, Epstein 1979).

Considerable evidence has accumulated regarding the utility of a short-term dynamic approach in certain conditions (Sifneos 1972, Malan 1976, Horowitz 1976, Davanloo 1978, Butcher and Koss 1978), and a brief framework was indicated in this case for three reasons: (1) the patient was moving out of state in a few months, (2) he was in a crisis and could not delay treatment until he relocated, and (3) a time-limited model could be used to focus on termination and thus restimulate and make available for working through issues around the loss and mourning of his wife (Mann 1973, Hoyt 1979). A time-limited (12 session) therapy was conducted. The brief nature of the therapy necessarily limits our view of the processes at work rather than providing the extended data that would be available from long-term psychotherapy or psychoanalysis. Nonetheless, the limited or "focalized" (Balint et al. 1972, Strupp 1975, Malan 1976) goal of helping him progress in working through the loss of his wife, especially given the circumstances under which it occurred, inevitably highlighted critical issues in the patient's personality and life adjustment. Control of feelings, especially maintenance of self-esteem in the face of potentially overwhelming guilt and shame, was a major issue in the treatment. Claims of complete guiltlessness and uninvolvement in his wife's act alternated with a sense of omnipotent destructiveness, the latter linked to magical thoughts about his power to will her dead by thinking about it. He spoke of having the sense that he was both the detective trying to uncover incriminating evidence and the criminal trying to hide his guilt and remorse (Hoyt 1978, 1981). At the least, he had to conclude that he had failed his wife and in so doing had shattered the ideal image of himself as a loving and caring protector. Then, too, there were issues of now having to care for himself, a need compromised by the guilt he felt as a survivor. His anger at his wife for having killed herself, abandoning him and leaving him without hope of reparation, only increased his guilt. Horowitz (1975) underscores the need for reconstruction of traumatic life events, with clear delineation of the self-as-actor, in the psychotherapy of persons with narcissistic character styles, and he emphasizes the need for the utmost tact and concern for maintenance of the therapeutic relationship. In the case of Bob, the therapist's active focusing, helping the patient towards eventual reconstruction of the stress event, became the essential vehicle for the patient's working through a potentially overwhelming complex of thoughts and feelings in regard to the loss of his wife. The patient's response was to "use" the therapist for this purpose: he fluctuated between idealizing and mirror transference (Kohut 1971), attempting to please and placate the therapist while sometimes quite directly trying to locate his feelings and sense of self-esteem as a reflection of the therapist's responses. As a result of this process, and against the background of a basically solid therapeutic alliance, he was able gradually to tolerate and work through more painful guilt- and shame-evoking material.

At the end of treatment, the patient was more realistic in judging his role in his wife's death. He still felt responsible, although not omnipotently so, and he was somewhat less depressed and no longer thought of committing suicide. He also was more able to acknowledge and accept both his anger and love toward his wife. His sense of a separate, viable self-identity had been strengthened. His experience was now more conscious, and at the last therapy session he was continuing the working-through process (see Horowitz and Hoyt 1979). Four months later the patient returned for a routine follow-up interview with the staff social worker who had initially evaluated him. She found his symptomatic improvement to have been maintained, although, as one might expect, his basic character remained unchanged. He still seemed distant with her despite his obvious attempts to be friendly and cooperative; once during the interview, he spoke eerily of people as programmed "bio-computers," with the implication of diminished responsibility for his own actions. But he had also made clear gains. At follow-up he had formed some limited social relationships, was employed in a new city, and was continuing to mourn the loss of his wife.

BOB SPEAKS OF "BOB"

Including the one example already given from the pretherapy evaluation, Bob Smith referred to himself by name a total of 33 times over the course of the initial evaluation and brief therapy; this was, of course, in addition to hundreds of the usual references to himself as "I." Almost all (30 of 33) of the references-by-name occurred when he was specifically considering and discussing his part in his wife's suicide, and three occurred when he was speaking of his relationship to the therapist. In studying the case, we identified nine interrelated categories of meanings of the patient talking about himself by name, and then independently reviewed the videotapes and transcripts and assigned each occurrence to as many categories as its function seemed to fit. We found a high rate of agreement between our judgments, and further discussion and review easily resolved the few instances where we had disagreed.

The nine overlapping categories appear with examples in Table 1. It may be seen that the patient referred to himself in the third person most often to (1) define himself as an individual, (2) define himself as a feeling person, and (3) explicitly ward off guilt feelings for his role in his wife's suicide. These references seemed to be attempts to maintain a positive self-image. A number of the self-references express all three of these meanings simultaneously, as though the patient were saying "I am Bob Smith, the individual, personally, just himself, a lovable and loving person, a person capable of feelings, unrelated to Sue Smith and therefore not guilty." It was striking how often in referring to himself by name the patient added the words, "individual . . . himself . . . personally," as though having to underscore again and again his separateness, aloneness, and lack of relatedness to others.

The table also summarizes instances when the patient spoke of himself as though seen through the wife's eyes, i.e., as "Bob" in relation to "Sue." Here, from the perspective of the internalized Other, he has failed as the protector and he feels shame (Lewis 1971). When he thinks of himself as related to others, he is often unable to avoid a negative self-image; this, too, is "Bob," but a Bob who needs to emphasize his capacity for deep feelings, for feeling guilt about his wife's death.

There were also instances when he spoke *to* himself, as in saying, "Come on, Bob, you can say it." These references are of a different nature (and generally are a more common bit of verbal behavior) than those in which he speaks *about* "Bob." In this case, however, they occurred with unusual

TABLE 1. Occurrences of the Patient ("Bob Smith") Speaking of Himself by Name

Categories	Number of Occurrences*	Examples
Asserting a Positive Self-Image		
Bob as an individual	12	"One of the things that distresses me personally, just Bob Smith himself, individual, I feel so much that Sue is irreplaceable."
Bob as a feeling person	9	"Bob Smith as I know him has not reacted emotionally to this whole occurrence anywhere near the point where he's capable."
Bob warding off guilt feelings	8	"Bob Smith the individual, not related to Sue, allows himself to be human and he doesn't think of himself as a terrible person relative to others."
Bob as a protector	5	"Christ. I was just thinking of Bob Smith when Sue was alive. I was just thinking of myself as a centurion, as a guard of some sort, guarding this woman's life from herself."
Bob as loving, giving	5	"I think that Bob Smith would rather just plain love than need to love."
Bob as lovable	2	"Yes, so in a sense, Sue cared for Bob very much, as much as Sue could" *and* "I could see where I could get involved with Bob if I were Michael" [the therapist].
Asserting a Negative Self-Image		
Bob as failing in the protector role	3	"If her ghost or something was standing here, being as critical to Bob as Bob is being critical to Bob, the ghost would say, 'Well, you didn't do what you needed to do. You didn't do what I needed you to do. You just blew it and I'm dead'."
Bob as seen through others' (Sue's) eyes	3	"Bob Smith, as related to Sue, really fucked up, and it seems like I'm looking at me through my eyes and looking at me through Sue's eyes."
Talking to Himself		
Bob talks *to* Bob	6	"I thought, Bob, uh, Sue is very dead. You're not gonna make things better by thinking your way out of it."

*Totals more than 33 since one occurrence might have several meanings.

frequency and may also express the patient's lack of clear self-integration and need to evoke a stabilizing other (Andreson 1980, Horowitz et al. 1980). All 33 times the patient referred to himself by name he used either an admonishing or consoling or exhorting tone. He spoke once of "stroking Bob" in this way, and on another occasion he referred figuratively to his tendency to slap his own hand when he made a mistake. In every instance, it was as though someone outside himself—and here one imagines the parent of a small child—scolding or soothing or attempting to encourage one of two "Bobs": the Bob who is just himself, unrelated to anyone else, and the Bob who is connected to and involved with other persons.

Understanding of this self-reference-by-name phenomenon can be enriched by considering the adaptive contexts (Langs 1976, 1978, 1979) in which it occurred. First, there were special parameters of the therapy: the patient was well aware not only that treatment was time-limited, but that he was both a patient receiving treatment and a research subject completing questionnaires and being videotaped. These violations of absolute confidentiality may have increased the patient's sense of himself as a *dramatis persona*, intensifying the tendency to refer to himself in the third person. It is important to note, however, that, as he later commented, he also spoke of himself by name at other times, specifically when he was aware of having made "a mistake." In this instance, his sense of guilt and moral culpability—recall that he referred to feeling like both a "detective" and a "criminal"—often led him to speak of himself in the third person in the manner of a prosecutor and a defense attorney, each sifting the evidence pertaining to the defendant, "Bob." Inevitably, the therapist would become for him both judge and jury, and there may also have been a few instances in which, in a countertransference response to the patient, the therapist intensified this aspect of the interaction. For example, on one occasion, the therapist inquired unnecessarily about the exact date of the wife's death; in that instance, this "legalistic" approach seemed to have prompted the patient's referring to himself as "Bob." Several times the patient spoke of himself and the therapist as "Bob and Michael" (without having been invited to use the therapist's first name), apparently in an attempt to create an image of a friendly Other in order to stabilize, via the mirror transference (Kohut 1971), a positive self-image.

At other times he would critically test the therapist's ability to tolerate him, offering lurid and grotesque details of his wife's death and then keenly watching the therapist for signs of rejection. The importance of the "holding function" (Langs 1978) provided by the therapist was attested to when the patient, in the last therapy session, commented that he had felt reassured early on when the therapist, having heard his story, did not run out of the room screaming.

AN HYPOTHESIS AND SOME FURTHER EVIDENCE

We believe that each time the patient spoke of himself as "Bob," he was doing so mainly to invoke and assert an ideal self-image in defense against what was at that moment a too painful threat to self-esteem. The use of his name also served as a distancing device, helping him to disown his role in her death, saying in effect "it was Bob, not I" who had failed vis-à-vis her needs and demands (*see* Globus 1980). It should be emphasized that he usually spoke of himself in the ordinary manner, using the pronouns "I" and "me"; it was especially under the acute pressure of his sense of failure and of wrong-doing that negative self-images would threaten to emerge and he would slip into speaking of "Bob" in order to get away from the image of himself as evil. A further significant finding was that, as the patient's trust in the relationship with the therapist grew, he gained the strength to face more directly his guilt feelings and shame about himself; and as this developed, the frequency of his self-references by name dropped off sharply over the last few hours of the treatment.

Fortunately, we were able to test the hypothesis that a question bearing directly on the issue of the patient's guilt would produce the phenomenon of his referring to himself in the third person. At the time of the patient's four-month follow-up evaluation, we enlisted the assistance of the social worker (who had also done the pretherapy evaluation). We requested that she ask the patient about his part in his wife's suicide, and question him then about the use of his own name, if in fact it did occur. A special feature of this challenge would be the lack of an ongoing therapeutic situation to offer the patient support against his characteristic defenses. If the behavior occurred as we predicted, we hoped that the patient's associations might be able to contribute some understanding regarding this peculiar form of self-reference.

Our hopes were confirmed. When the interviewer asked what came to mind concerning "the specifics of the events that led up to Sue's death," the patient gave the following response:

Hmmm. Jeez, most of the relationship, um, is still pretty clear, and I can still remember what happened immediately before, ah, my telling her that ah, um, hmmm (*pause*) *come on Bob, you can say it* —ah, that I felt so confined in the relationship that she was ah heavy on my life, she was ah making demands on me that I didn't want anymore and ah, that I couldn't feel love for her anymore, that these things all um, were input for Sue to use to upset herself and shoot herself. Ah, I remember arguing, I remember um, ah, my pushing her around, my hitting her, her hitting me back, um just a general bad scene.

The interviewer then remarked on the patient's seeming to get "stuck" and noted that he had called himself by his first name. She then asked a series of tactful but persistent questions about the patient's thoughts and feelings regarding calling himself by name. He first responded that he was telling himself "to go ahead and think about it," that is, to think about what made him feel so uncomfortable. He then went on:

I think when I am aware of what I consider a personal error, I do it, when I think I've made a mistake and I'm ah talking to somebody else about it. (*Pause.*) Um, I'm just beginning to wonder now if, if I was looking at me through your eyes when I was talking to Bob, if I was talking to Bob perhaps for you, perhaps for somebody else that I'm around.

Later in the interview they returned to the topic of the patient's role in his wife's death. At first he disavowed any responsibility or influence, then gradually shifted to looking more critically at his role. His comments addressed the question of his self-image:

I, my behavior ah, not only d-direct immediately before she killed herself but through a lot of our relationship, frequently my behavior wasn't ah ah what I would paint as ah an image of, an ideal image. I was the typical fallible human being. I wasn't Superman. Ah, but you know, that's okay, I'm not Superman. I don't really know what else to say about it, Janice, except that if I had an image of perfection for myself I didn't live up to it. But it seems ridiculous to me now to even expect it; it just doesn't happen. I don't know anyone who's perfect, and um people appear to be so relative to each other and myself, too, and just so relative to everyone else that ah it's pretty easy for me now to accept that I was not perfect.

DISCUSSION

Other writers have noted a relationship between the development of self and other representations and the self-reference-by-name phenomenon. Students of language development, such as Piaget (1929), Gesell et al. (1940), and Lewis (1963) have observed that children first refer to themselves by name, then usually pass through an intermediary stage of calling themselves "me," and finally begin to use the pronoun "I" to refer to themselves at about 18–24 months of age. Mahler et al. (1975) followed children "from the twilight state of symbiosis to a point where they emerged as individuals in their own right, with a definite sense of 'I', 'me', and 'mine', with a sense of who and where they are, even if this sense was still to an extent dependent on a syncretic context and subject to many distortions" (p. 220). Autistic children usually do not ever make the transition to using the pronoun "I," but rather persist in speaking of themselves by name or even as "you," indicating their severely confused self- and other-differentiation (Bettelheim 1967; *also see* Pine 1979). References-by-names in older children and adults are usually associated with seriously disturbed self-representations. Bleuler (1911) discussed schizophrenics speaking of themselves in the third person, and Schilder (1928) cited the case of a schizophrenic woman named Pol who maintained that she knew a "Miss Pol" about whom she was maliciously critical (p. 39). Whitaker (Haley and Hoffman 1967), Forrest (1973), and Searles (1977) also describe instances of patients revealing confused self- and other-representations through their peculiar selection of pronouns.

This phenomenon of self-reference-by-name has not been studied as an occasional expression of transitory narcissistic disturbance in relatively healthy people and as a frequent finding in narcissistic personalities. In another case treated by one of the authors (DF), in which narcissistic and borderline features were prominent, the same phenomenon occurred on occasion. This patient, a strikingly beautiful young woman, had as one of her main symptoms a recurrent image of herself as fat, ugly, and grotesque. This was true to such an extent that she was at times ashamed to leave her apartment and go out in public. Once, in attempting to describe her sense of this and to reconcile this self-image with what was only minimally persuasive intellectual knowledge that others did not see her this way, she said, "The way Ann sees Ann, unrelated to anyone else, is a lot different from the way I think others see me." She explained this usage as an attempt to be "objective" about herself. Here, again, there was the sense of a self-image totally "unrelated to anyone else," an image therefore more or less cut off from the possibility of correction by realistic perceptions of self and others. This example, too, illustrates the adaptive use of self-reference-by-name as an attempt to grasp cognitively and to reconcile discordant self-images.

Mahler's findings in her work with disturbed children clearly implicate traumatic experiences during the separation-individuation phase in the creation of such narcissistic "defect." The child's difficulty differentiating from the mother correlates with the tendency toward fragmentation of self-images under stress (Mahler 1968). Presumably, in narcissistic persons, especially those "borderline" cases without a coherent sense of self, this tendency is unusually strong and persists throughout life. The form such self-splitting will take should, in a given case, depend upon the specific nature of the defect and the stress inducing the regression. These considerations have, for us, justified the detailed study of a small, though pathognomonic, bit of behavior in a single case.

CONCLUSIONS

A content and context analysis of the patient's speaking of himself by name during the entire course of brief therapy revealed a clear correspondence between this behavior and his attempts to ward off intolerable feelings of guilt and shame concerning his wife's suicide. The stress was extreme and came in the especially traumatic form of overwhelming guilt and shame about the loss of a woman with whom he had had an almost symbiotic relationship. In the therapy, in the context of a basically good therapeutic alliance and by means of narcissistic transference to the therapist, he was able gradually to work through the traumatic material. He was then able to experience and mourn the loss of his wife. As his feelings became deeper and more genuine, he virtually ceased referring to himself in the third person. Later on, in a follow-up interview with another person, without the support of the therapeutic relationship, he responded to the stress of a question regarding his role in his wife's suicide as predicted, with a reversion to speaking of himself by name.

We viewed the phenomenon of speaking of oneself by name as an indicator of a tendency toward self-splitting. Such behavior may occur on occasion in anyone under certain conditions, not necessarily with pathological implications. But the patient reported doing this habitually, at times when he felt he had made a "mistake"; and following the severe stress of his wife's suicide, this behavior became unusually prominent and seemed to point to a particular vulnerability of his sense of self.

The form this splitting took was also of interest. In this patient, response to loss and to potentially severe feelings of guilt and shame was not only along the lines of splitting into good and bad self-images (Sandler et al. 1962). When the good self-image—himself as basically loving, caring, and protecting —could no longer be maintained, a more primitive self-image emerged. In this state he was *unrelated to others*; and he was innocent, since neither hurting nor being hurt is possible without a relationship. This was the third-person "Bob" at its most extreme.

A. Freud (1965) has pointed out that ego regression reveals in reverse the path or line of ego development. We submit that the ego regression that occurred in this patient may suggest a crucial step in the transition from the self-objects of the symbiotic phase to more mature self-representations, especially where narcissistic pathology is prominent in the later personality. That this regression should occur in the context of traumatic separation and potentially overwhelming guilt-feeling suggests that development occurs by the reverse process—first, of reconciling a (pathologically hypertrophied) sense of physical and psychic separateness with the need for emotional relatedness to others; and only then, of resolving the problem of love and hate for the same object—so that then the "I" comes into being. Some support for this formulation comes from child development studies. For instance, Mahler comments on the case of Teddy (Mahler et al. 1975) at about age three: "At this time, when Teddy seemed to be so preoccupied with who was good and who was bad, *who was to blame* and *who was hurt*, he added two important new words to his vocabulary—'yes' and 'I'" (p. 181, emphasis added).

In the later personality, after the "I" has for the most part been well established, how can we conceptualize a splitting of the self? The use of the term "splitting" as an active verb (Lichtenberg and Slap 1973) to describe a mode of defense (Freud 1938, Sandler et al. 1962, Lustman 1977, Kernberg 1976, Masterson 1976, Volkan 1976) has been challenged by Pruyser (1975) and Dorpat (1979), who suggest that the phenomenology of patients presenting contradictory and fluctuating self- and other-images reveals an initial failure to achieve self-cohesion rather than an active and self-reflexive ego splitting. "Who or what splits?" is thus replaced by "How is integration achieved?" We regard both uses of the term as relevant to our conceptualization of the present case.

When a weakly consolidated sense of self, a defective "I," as it were, is subjected to intense stress, the patient may attempt to defend himself against guilt and pain by recovering a positive self-image; this may include regression to a more infantile state, with activation of such mechanisms as splitting of the self, the invoking of superego precursors, and a dependence on a witness and judge (in this case the therapist) in the external world. In our patient, where relatedness had such magical implications of omnipotence over the narcissistic object, perceived as part of the self, further transitory regressions occurred with splitting of the self to a level bordering on complete detachment from object-relatedness. It would not be surprising if persons with such deficits are especially in need of an on-going positive relationship (and perhaps the actual physical presence of another person), such as can be had with a therapist, for them to be able to progress in the work of mourning. With Bob, it seemed that active grieving occurred mainly during the sessions; late in the therapy, he told the therapist, "You have replaced her." Through the therapeutic relationship, persons such as Bob may be able to re-experience the infantile state of mourning, to risk the loss of the ideal self-object with its magical omnipotence and vulnerability, and finally, to achieve a more real self, the self that is individual and unique and *yet* related to others. As Buber (1970) put it, "The basic word I-You can only be spoken with one's whole being."

REFERENCES

Andreson, J. J. (1980). Why people talk to themselves. *Journal of the American Psychoanalytic Association* 28:499–518.

Balint, M., Ornstein, P. H., and Balint, E. (1972). *Focal Psychotherapy.* London: Tavistock.

Bettelheim, B. (1967). *The Empty Fortress: Infantile Autism and the Birth of the Self.* New York: Free Press.

Bleuler, E. (1911). *Dementia Praecox, or the Group of Schizophrenias.* New York: International Universities Press, 1950.

Buber, M. (1923). *I and Thou.* New York: Scribner's, 1970.

Butcher, J. N., and Koss, M. P. (1978). Research on brief and crisis-oriented psychotherapies. In *Handbook of Psychotherapy and Behavior Change: An Empirical Analysis* (2nd ed.), eds. S. L. Garfield and A. E. Bergin. New York: Wiley.

Davanloo, H. (1978). *Basic Principles and Techniques of Short-Term Dynamic Psychotherapy.* New York: Spectrum.

Dorpat, T. L. (1979). Is splitting a defense? *International Review of Psycho-Analysis* 6:105–113.

Epstein, L. (1979). The therapeutic use of countertransference data with borderline patients. *Contemporary Psychoanalysis* 15:248–275.

Forrest, D. V. (1973). On one's own onymy. *Psychiatry* 36:266–290.

Freud, A. (1965). *Normality and Pathology in Childhood: Assessments of Development.* New York: International Universities Press.

Freud, S. (1938). Splitting of the ego in the process of defence. *Standard Edition* 23:275–278.

Gesell, A., Halverson, H., Thompson, H. et al. (1940). *The First Five Years of Life.* New York: Harper & Row.

Globus, G. G. (1980). On "I": The conceptual foundations of responsibility. *American Journal of Psychiatry* 137:417–422.

Haley, J., and Hoffman, L. (1967). The growing edge: an interview with Carl A. Whitaker, M.D. In *Techniques of Family Therapy.* New York: Basic Books.

Hartocollis, P. (1977). Affects in borderline disorders. In *Borderline Personality Disorders*, ed. P. Hartocollis, pp. 495–507. New York: International Universities Press.

Horowitz, M. J. (1975). Sliding meanings: a defense against threat in narcissistic personalities. *International Journal of Psychoanalytic Psychotherapy* 4:167–180.

———. (1976). *Stress Response Syndromes.* New York: Jason Aronson.

———. (1977). Cognitive and interactive aspects of splitting. *American Journal of Psychiatry* 134:549–553.

Horowitz, M. J., and Hoyt, M. F. (1979). Book notice of David Malan's *The Frontier of Brief Psychotherapy. Journal of American Psychoanalytic Association* 27:279–285.

Horowitz, M. J., Wilner, N., Marmar, C., et al. (1980). Pathological grief and the activation of latent self images. *American Journal of Psychiatry* 137:1157–1162.

Hoyt, M. F. (1978). Secrets in psychotherapy: theoretical and practical considerations. *International Review of Psycho-Analysis* 5:231–241.

———. (1979). Aspects of termination in a brief time-limited psychotherapy. *Psychiatry* 42:208–219.

———. (1982). Concerning remorse: with special attention to its defensive function. *Journal of the American Academy of Psychoanalysis.* (In press.)

Kernberg, O. F. (1975). *Borderline Conditions and Pathological Narcissism.* New York: Jason Aronson.

———. (1976). *Object-Relations Theory and Clinical Psycho-Analysis.* New York: Jason Aronson.

Kohut, H. (1971). *The Analysis of the Self.* New York: International Universities Press.

Krohn, A. (1974). Borderline "empathy" and differentiation of object relations. *International Journal of Psychoanalytic Psychotherapy* 3:142–165.

Langs, R. (1976). *The Therapeutic Interaction,* 2 vols. New York: Jason Aronson.

———. (1978). *The Listening Process.* New York: Jason Aronson.

———. (1979). *The Therapeutic Environment.* New York: Jason Aronson.

Lewis, H. B. (1971). *Shame and Guilt in Neurosis.* New York: International Universities Press.

Lewis, M. M. (1963). *Language, Thought, and Personality in Infancy and Childhood.* New York: Basic Books.

Lichtenberg, J. D., and Slap, H. (1973). Notes on the concept of splitting of representations. *Journal of American Psychoanalytic Association* 21:772–787.

Lustman, J. (1977). On splitting. *Psychoanalytic Study of the Child* 33:119–154.

Mahler, M. S. (1968). *On Human Symbiosis and the Vicissitudes of Individuation.* New York: International Universities Press.

Mahler, M. S., Pine, F., and Bergman, A. (1975). *The Psychological Birth of the Human Infant.* New York: Basic Books.

Malan, D. H. (1976). *The Frontier of Brief Psychotherapy.* New York: Plenum.

Mann, J. (1973). *Time-Limited Psychotherapy.* Cambridge, Mass.: Harvard University Press.

Masterons, J. F. (1976). *Psychotherapy of the Borderline Adult.* New York: Bruner/Mazel.

Piaget, J. (1929). *The Child's Conception of the World.* London: Routledge, Kegan Paul.

Pine, F. (1979). On the pathology of the separation-individuation process as manifested in later clinical work: an attempt at delineation. *International Journal of Psycho-Analysis* 60:225–242.

Pruyser, P. W. (1975). What splits in "splitting?" *Bulletin of the Menninger Clinic* 39:1–46.

Sandler, J., Kawenoka, M., Neurath, L. et al. (1962). The classification of superego material in the Hampstead Index. *The Psychoanalytic Study of the Child* 17:107–127.

Schilder, P. (1928). *Introduction to a Psychoanalytic Psychiatry.* New York: Nervous and Mental Disease Publishing Company (Monograph Series No. 50).

Searles, H. F. (1977). Dual- and multiple-identity processes in borderline ego functioning. In *Borderline Personality Disorders: The Concept, the Syndrome, the Patient,* ed. P. Hartocollis. New York: International Universities Press.

Sifneos, P. E. (1972). *Short-Term Psychotherapy and Emotional Crises.* Cambridge, Mass.: Harvard University Press.

Strupp, H. H. (1975). Psychoanalysis, "focal psychotherapy," and the nature of the therapeutic influence. *Archives of General Psychiatry* 32:127–135.

Volkan, V. D. (1976). *Primitive Internalized Object Relations.* New York: International Universities Press.

Self-Naming

MARDI J. HOROWITZ, M.D.

A discussion of "On Speaking of Oneself by Name," by Dennis Farrell, M.D. and Michael Hoyt, Ph.D.
Drs. Farrell and Hoyt are to be complimented for a careful effort at intensive case study. Their paper indicates that a semi-quantitative approach can be used to check out the prevalence of an apparent pattern. Their counting approach provides a useful buttress to their clinical impressions. They have taken on a difficult topic and illuminated it. Two salient questions to such self-naming are addressed: (1) In what context is this phenomenon most frequent? (2) In which people is this phenomenon most likely to occur?

Farrell and Hoyt have used a careful, systematic approach, made possible by their review of a video-recorded 12-hour therapy. They found 33 instances in which the patient, instead of saying "I" or "me," used his first name and sometimes both his first and last names. It was possible to examine the context of these 33 instances of self-naming, and to compare them with other contexts when the usual first-person pronouns "I" or "me" were used. These usual episodes numbered in the hundreds. Most of the unusual episodes, thirty of the 33 instances, occurred while the patient was discussing his part in his wife's suicide, and three occurred when he was speaking of his relationship with the therapist.

Farrell and Hoyt divided up their classification into times when the patient, Bob Smith, was asserting a positive self-image and times when he was asserting a negative self-image. They found that he called himself Bob rather than "I" or "me" more often when he sought to define himself as an acceptable individual, a feeling person, and when he was warding off guilt feelings about his role in his wife's suicide. The authors believe that he used the self-naming when a special type of distancing or assertiveness was required. In effect, he was saying to the listener, "I am this Bob Smith and not that Bob Smith"; i.e., that he was the good Bob Smith and not the bad self.

The authors note that in each of the 33 instances in which self-naming occurred, he used an admonishing, consoling, or exhorting tone of voice. In their words, "in every instance it was as though someone outside himself . . . was scolding or soothing or attempting to encourage one of the two Bobs." Thus the authors see this verbal behavior as an effort to stabilize a relatively more ideal or competent self-image and to help ward off the threatened activation of a more defective, guilty, and worthless self-image. The exhortation was an effort to preserve self-esteem in the face of an excessively painful threat.

The authors developed a test for the validity of this explanatory hypothesis. It was carried out in the evaluation interview conducted four months after the end of the brief therapy. They had predicted that when the evaluating clinician asked specifically about the death of his wife, Bob might then address himself by name. They found that, indeed, this did happen. At that precise moment, as prompted by the suggestion of the authors, the evaluating clinician asked Bob directly about the meaning of this phenomenon.

His response to the direct inquiry of why he addressed himself by name was to wonder if he was "perhaps looking at himself through the eyes of the interviewer." One reason, then, for addressing himself by name may be that he is introjecting the critical role usually assigned to the interviewer as part of his transference potential. There is another phenomenon that may be associated to this. He uses the first name of both his therapist and the evaluating clinician. This custom is not invited, and patients usually address the clinician by a more formal title, such as Dr. Jones. This may be part of Bob Smith's effort to establish a social alliance in order to ward off the potential of the transference in which the therapist would be seen as a critic of his past "bad behavior."

The authors suggest that the more frequent context for addressing himself by name is "an attempt to grasp cognitively and to reconcile discordant self-images." It may also be an attempt to contour self-concepts into encapsulated forms. When he calls himself Bob or Bob Smith he is trying to segregate some of his attributes; in a way he is saying "I am only this whole Bob, not that one who has bad traits."

One may also explore this phenomenon by asking about the impact of naming on another person. When one addresses a companion by his or her first name, one is saying that one recognizes that one is intimate with him or her. One is saying "I know that it is *you* who I am with, you are particularly the individual named Bob." One uses a first name rather than the pronoun "you" when one means to say "I know that you are someone in particular named Bob, not just anybody I might be talking to." Use of the first name alerts the other. It does so because it repeats an event, calling a name that orients the person toward the source of pending communication. One calls out a first name when one wants to get attention from that specific person.

How does this differ from the phenomenon of the person addressing *oneself* by name? In a similar manner, it may produce alerting, orienting arousal in both the subject and the object. The companion is alerted, since expectancy is for first-person pronouns rather than the name. Within the self, the use of the name may act as a kind of reminder, an orienting arousal that aids self-stabilization. This follows the reasoning suggested by Drs. Farrell and Hoyt. But paradoxically, within the subject, self-naming also seems to be a compromise between closeness and distance. In terms of distance, the person takes the stance of a reflecting object rather than a subject. This distance is less than that seen in pathological defenses in which the person disavows his identity. Yet it is not so close as an acceptance of self-attributes. When the patient said, "Bob Smith, the individual, not related to Sue, allows himself to be human, and he doesn't think of himself as a terrible person relative to others," he was discussing his own potential affects and memories of behaviors in a distant manner. He was not going so far away as to disavow them by saying, "I don't feel terrible" or "I did not do bad things."

Using his own name, Bob Smith was identifying with an external critic without completely locating the blame attribution function outside the self. By saying his name, he took the position of an introject of potential criticism: neither himself nor another. He occupied an ambiguous space. The self-naming represented a partial and incomplete externalization.

PERSONS WHO MOST LIKELY USE SELF-NAMING

Following this reasoning, the people in whom the phenomenon is more likely to occur are those who most need to use some type of externalization in order to extrude blame or any badness from their self-concept; i.e., people with pathological self-concepts and narcissistic vulnerabilities would be more likely to exhibit this phenomenon. However, those without such vulnerabilities might also do so in situational contexts where their sense of vulnerability was heightened by loss of self-esteem or self-cohesiveness.

The activation of latent self-images during the course of pathological grief has been discussed by Horowitz et al. 1980. In the cases they summarize, the regressive alteration of self-concept is to neurotic level conflicts. Regression may also involve activation of more primitive self-concepts, in which conditions bordering on dissociations or loss of object-relatedness occur (Kernberg 1975). Drs. Farrell and Hoyt suggest that their patient may provide a clinical instance of this phenomenon, with compensatory grandiosity and a mirror transference instituted to stabilize self-concepts otherwise vulnerable to fragmentation (Kohut 1972).

REFERENCES

Horowitz, M., Wilner, N., Marmar, C., and Krupnick, J. (1980). Pathological grief and the activation of latent self-images. *American Journal of Psychiatry* 136:1157–1162.
Kernberg, O. (1975). *Borderline Conditions and Pathological Narcissism.* New York: Jason Aronson.
Kohut, H. (1972). *Analysis of the Self.* New York: International Universities Press.

Mary Shelley's *Frankenstein*: Creativity and the Psychology of the Exception

WAYNE A. MYERS, M.D.

The genesis and importance of the fantasy of being the exception is detailed in the life history of Mary Shelley, as well as in the character structure of the monster in her novel, *Frankenstein*. The justification for her fantasy, based as it was upon her feeling of having suffered inordinate parental (especially maternal) deprivation, is seen to parallel the justification offered by the monster in *Frankenstein* to explain his own malevolent behavior, i.e., his being an exception to the rules. The impetus given to Mary Shelley's creativity by the fantasy is discussed, as is the ultimate dissolution of the fantasy under the impact of a series of blows in reality. Mary Shelley's famous gothic horror tale, *Frankenstein*, is reexamined from a different vantage point than has been attempted in prior analytic studies of this subject. Specifically, the importance of the fantasy of being the exception in the life history of the author and in the character structure of her infamous creation in the novel, the monster, is described to illustrate the impetus given to the author's creativity by her possession of the fantasy. The problem of validation in the absence of a "patient" is dealt with in two ways: (1) by describing the frequent expressions of, and the significance attached to, the fantasy of being the exception in the life of the author and in the personality structure of the monster, the specific character in the novel with whom Mary Shelley most identified; and (2) by focussing on the specific psychodynamic needs that were met in the author's life by her writing of the novel. The latter approach, suggested by Baudry (1978), implies that the final creative product may be viewed (albeit in a limited sense) as being somewhat analogous to the associations of the patient in the psychoanalytic situation. These means offer a further increment of confirmation for the speculative hypotheses of this paper.

THE EARLY LIFE OF MARY SHELLEY

Mary Shelley was the daughter of two famous authors. Her father, William Godwin, was a nonconformist Calvinist minister whose most famous work, *Enquiry Concerning Political Justice* (1793), was a book that described governments as corrupt and most social institutions as worthless.

He saw man as yearning for perfection and virtue, and felt that such heights could only be reached by use of man's intellect, once man was rid of superstition and emotionalism.

Mary's mother, Mary Wollstonecraft, a brilliant, rebellious woman, had already given birth to one child out of wedlock, Fanny, by a prior liason with an American adventurer, Gilbert Imlay. She was rescued from a suicide attempt after the rupture of the affair, and later met and became enamored of Godwin. Prior to their meeting in 1792, she had published a remarkable feminist tract, *On the Vindications of the Rights of Woman*, that advocated equal opportunities in the rearing and education of men and women, and characterized marriage as not being essential for happiness. When she became pregnant by Godwin, she forsook these convictions and married him. Young Mary was born in August 1797. Mary Wollstonecraft died of sepsis following the retention of the placenta some ten days after young Mary's birth.

After the tragic death of Mary Wollstonecraft, Godwin became quite depressed and was unable to meet his infant daughter's need for warmth and love. He began an urgent search for another wife to take over the burden of raising the two young babies whose fate was entrusted to him. A cousin, Miss Jones (see Grylls 1938), who aspired to become the second Mrs. Godwin, and who was responsible for whatever maternal input Mary received during the first three years of her life, was rejected by him. Godwin ultimately settled upon a widow, Mary Jane Clairmont, whom he married when young Mary was three and a half years old. Mrs. Clairmont is described by a number of Mary Shelley's biographers (Grylls 1938, Bigland 1959, Gerson 1973) as the prototypical evil stepmother, a woman who heaped physical and mental abuse upon her stepdaughter's head. She favored her own two children, a son Charles, and a daughter Mary's age named Claire. Another child, young William, was later born to grace the union of Mrs. Clairmont and Godwin when Mary was four years old.

Mary Shelley's biographers (Grylls 1938, Bigland 1959, Gerson 1973) and a number of the prior analytic commentators on *Frankenstein* (Bond 1973, Hirsch 1975, Moers 1974, Rubenstein 1976) have emphasized the extraordinary impact that Mary Wollstonecraft's death had upon Mary Shelley's life. We are told how she immersed (perhaps buried would be the better word) herself in the reading and rereading of her mother's works from her late Oedipal years until her late adolescence, committing many of them to memory and dreaming of the day that she too might be as great a writer as her mother and father. Gerson (1973) further notes how much of her reading occurred at the mother's gravesite at St. Pancras Churchyard. There she would read the "sacred" books, eat her meals, and fall into a peaceful slumber on the buried bosom of her dead mother, only to be carried home in her father's arms over the objections of her stepmother.

One may speculate here that Mary was attempting, on the one hand, to ingest the essence of the warm, loving mother she had only heard of and fantasied about, and on the other to become one with her mother's creativeness in order to win over the affections of her brilliant but distant father from her sadistic stepmother. It also seems likely that the early loss of the real mother became combined in fantasy with the loss of the surrogate mother-cousin (Miss Jones) during the early Oedipal period.

During her early latency years, Mary's extraordinary literary proclivities began to attract the attention of her father and of the remarkable circle of fellow writers gathered about him, including Coleridge, Wordsworth, De Quincey, the Lambs, Hazlitt and Southey. To a person, Godwin's circle detested Mary's stepmother, Mrs. Clairmont, and loudly proclaimed her vices to young Mary, as well as extolling the virtues of her real mother, Mary Wollstonecraft. Godwin encouraged his young daughter to read both his own and his former wife's highly unorthodox socio-political tomes. According to her biographers, Mary seems to have viewed her father as being her own property. Interlopers, such as Mrs. Clairmont, who had no primal marital or blood relationship with the great man, were thus consciously seen as having no valid rights upon his time and affections. Attitudes such as this, along with Mary's popularity with Godwin's peers and her reading of her parents' works, led to a considerable increase in the friction between Mary and her bourgeois stepmother, as well as to an ever heightening intensity of the level of maternal deprivation she experienced.

In this setting, Mary and her stepsister, Claire, incessantly pursued an interest in the occult. They were initially abetted in this endeavor by De Quincey and later by Percy Shelley, whom Mary had met at her father's house when she was about 15 years of age. Her interest in the occult took the form of reading books on spirits and spiritualism (particularly the ones dealing with the raising of the dead) and of participating in seances. Much of her reading on this subject took place at her mother's gravesite, so it seems quite clear that the spirit she most wished to commune with was that of her dead mother.

Godwin sent the 15-year-old Mary off to Scotland to visit family friends, whom he felt might be better able to provide her with the love and warmth he was unable to give. There Mary fell in love with the maternal force of nature and let her creative fantasies come to the foreground. She secretly began to commit her thoughts to paper and only divulged her ideas to her constant companion, Isabel Baxter, whose happy family provided the model for the Frankensteins and Clervals in her later novel.

Isabel Baxter was perhaps the first woman (with the possible exception of Miss Jones) with whom Mary had an unambivalent relationship. Her older sister, Fanny, had been of little solace to her, being a depressed woman who ultimately committed suicide. Her stepsister, Claire, was frequently a rival for her father's and stepmother's attentions, and, as noted before, young Mary was constantly at odds with Mrs. Clairmont herself. The happy sojourn to Scotland thus served to highlight for Mary the intensity of the parental (especially maternal) deprivation that she had suffered during the preceding 15 years.

On her return to England, Mary became romantically involved with Percy Shelley. The young poet had become an admirer and disciple of Godwin's, and in his brilliance and rebelliousness, he clearly served as a surrogate for her emotionally distant father. He alone was allowed to share her sacred sanctuary at her mother's gravesite in St. Pancras Churchyard. In his encouragement of her interest in the occult and in their shared communion with her dead mother, whose works they read together, an indissoluble bond was born. This led to Shelley's abandoning his wife, Harriett, and to his elopement with Mary. Claire accompanied them on their honeymoon, amidst a storm of scandal and rejection by both of their families and by society at large. Godwin only maintained a distant contact with Shelley in order to borrow money. A tentative rapprochement between the lovers and Godwin was only achieved when Mary and Percy married after Harriett's suicide, some years later.

Mary gave birth to a baby girl out of wedlock soon after the elopement, a blatant imitation of her mother's rebellious early life. The child died some 12 days later, a dramatic reversal of her mother's loss after her own birth. A year later, Mary gave birth to a son, also out of wedlock who died in childhood. Shortly thereafter, she began to write her epic novel, *Frankenstein*.

The major thesis of this paper is that Mary Shelley conceived of herself as an exception to the rules. The data thus far presented indicates that Mary sensed herself as an individual who had suffered unjustly by virtue of her real mother's death. Her sense of ownership of her father, which derived from this idea, was in part responsible for the ever-present friction with her stepmother, Mrs. Clairmont. The encouragement given her in her hatred of her stepmother by Godwin and his peers, and their reinforcement of her sense of loss vis à vis Mary Wollstonecraft's death, abetted her feelings of herself as an exception, a person apart from all others, one who had suffered inordinate early deprivation for no reason of her own making, and one who thus deserved exceptional indemnification from life. The meeting with Percy Shelley provided both the impetus and the sanction needed by Mary for the living out of the fantasy of being the exception. In eloping with Shelley, she exhibited an utter disregard for his marriage to another woman, a serious contravention of the rules of the society in which she lived. In this exceptional action, she was abetted by Shelley's own scorn of the formal rules of society. By virtue of his being so transparently a surrogate for her father, she also clearly flew in the face of all of the usual Oedipal strictures. Through Shelley's encouragement, she in essence became her mother-writer, adventurer, adultress, and bearer of bastards.

The crystallization of Mary Shelley's fantasy of being the exception occurred during her adolescence. Jacobson (1959) observes in this regard that, ". . . at some phase of our life, especially during adolescence, not only women but probably all of us, may wish or even feel to be exceptions, and expect to be granted special privileges" (p. 136). Mary's wish for special privileges included the taking of another woman's husband, the bearing of children out of wedlock, and the recognition of her own creativity as being on par with that of her illustrious mother. Additional facets of the living out of the fantasy become clearer in the discussion of Mary Shelley's mood during the period in which she wrote *Frankenstein*.

SYNOPSIS OF *FRANKENSTEIN*

Frankenstein is constructed as a Chinese-box narrative within a narrative. The framing stories, at the beginning and end of the book, are written in epistolary form by the explorer Walton to his sister in England. The tales of Victor Frankenstein and the monster are contained within Walton's letters.

Victor is the beloved elder child of a Genevese nobleman, and a mother left an orphan after her own father's death. His happy childhood is spent in the company of his orphaned cousin, Elizabeth, and his friend Henry Clerval. In midadolescence, he becomes interested in the study of the occult, which upsets his father. Shortly before he is to depart for the university, Elizabeth contracts scarlet fever and Victor's mother becomes infected with the disease and dies. On her deathbed, she joins the hands of Victor and Elizabeth, who by this time are affianced, and commends the girl to take her place.

At the university, Victor relinquishes his interest in the occult and begins to study natural science. He soon surpasses his professors in knowledge and learns the secret of creating life. He then fashions a gigantic man out of dead tissues and animates the creature with an electrical spark, but is instantly revolted by the grotesque being he has created and wishes it were dead. With this thought, he falls into a fitful slumber and dreams of embracing his fianceé, only to have her turn into his dead mother. The creature, meanwhile, disappears.

On awakening from his dream, Victor flees from his lodgings into the comforting arms of the newly arrived Clerval. Henry nurses Victor through a long and near fatal "nervous disease." On his recovery, Victor learns of the murder of his younger brother, William, and hurries toward Geneva. As he nears his home, an electrical storm illuminates the landscape, and he sees his hideous creature in the distance and immediately becomes convinced that the fiend has murdered William.

A servant girl, Justine, who was abandoned by her mother as a child, is accused of the murder, since she was found asleep near the scene of the crime and in possession of a locket that had been on the dead boy's person. Victor cannot bring himself to confess his complicity in the crime (in the sense of being the creator of the monster) and falls into another depression as Justine is executed.

Victor later confronts the creature atop an Alpine glacier, and the monster relates his history to him. He tells Victor of how he hid himself in a shed near the cottage of an exiled French family, the Delaceys. Through spying on them, particularly as they instructed an orphaned Arabian girl in their tongue, he mimicked their sounds and acquired language. From a discarded cache of books by Milton, Goethe, and Plutarch, he learned to read and became conversant with the history and philosophy of mankind. When he finally exposed himself to the blind Mr. Delacey in order to win his friendship, the Delacey children appeared and rejected him on the basis of his horrific appearance. He then wandered toward Geneva, having learned of Victor's origins from some papers he had stolen from Victor's rooms. Arriving there, he encountered William, and when the child spurned his friendship and then identified himself as a Frankenstein, the fiend murdered him and planted the locket on Justine.

With his various laments to Victor about his prior rejections, the monster temporarily arouses his creator's sympathy. He then entreats Victor to create a female mate for him. Victor consents and postpones his marriage to fulfill the request. Nearing the moment of the woman's creation, Victor reneges on his promise and destroys the new creature, once more depriving the monster of a chance for happiness.

The monster vows to be with Victor on his wedding night and then kills Clerval. Victor marries and has his wife's life snatched away from him by the monster on their unconsummated wedding night. Victor's father dies soon thereafter, and Victor sets out in pursuit of the monster. In the Arctic wastes, near death, he encounters Walton, a failed poet turned explorer. Walton seeks the warm heartlands he envisioned as existing at the pole, a pursuit specifically interdicted by his father before the father's death.

The monster is encountered again, and Victor dies of his infirmities, ambivalently urging Walton on to kill the fiend. The monster returns and guiltily mourns his creator's death and promises to immolate himself as an act of atonement. Walton then gives in to the entreaties of his crew and, renouncing his vainglorious pursuit of fame, returns to port as the book ends.

PRIOR STUDIES OF *FRANKENSTEIN*

A number of authors have offer critiques of *Frankenstein*, but only a few of these are analytically oriented. Graubard (1967), for example, describes the book in terms of man's ambivalence about knowledge and power. Rieger (1967) points out Mary Shelley's identification with her father and notes the similarity of *Frankenstein* to Godwin's novel, *Caleb Williams* (1794), in which the insatiable curiosity of the servant, Caleb, leads to the mutual destruction of both him and his master, Mr. Falkland.

Kaplan and Kloss (1973) stress the Oedipal derivatives in *Frankenstein*, particularly Victor's intense curiosity about where babies come from. The monster is seen as his Oedipal child with his mother, and Victor's horror at his creation is seen as representing his guilt over realizing his incestuous desires.

Small (1973), in an elegant, scholarly tome, sees the monster as possessing the potentialities of a child for happiness and virtue, very much in keeping with Mary's father's views in the *Enquiry Concerning Political Justice* (1793); but because the monster is rejected and miserable, he becomes a fiend. Small notes how much of the essential spirit of Shelley is contained in the character of Victor, and he relates the monster's loneliness to Mary's own. He further recognizes that the monster's claim for emotional nutrients belies Godwin's hypothesis that food and shelter were a child's primary needs. Victor's inability to finish the female creature is linked with the death of Mary's first-born daughter. Victor and the monster are seen as the conscious and unconscious aspects of the same individual, and the book is viewed as an Oedipal drama, with the monster as the guilt-provoking child of Victor's wished for incestuous union with his mother.

Bond (1973) notes Mary's wish to represent her dead mother in the book and hypothesizes that the fear of the mother's retaliatory rage against Mary's Oedipal procreative urges are responsible for Victor's fateful failure to create the female mate for the monster. He, too, notes her incestuous longing for her father.

Moers (1974) sees *Frankenstein* as a birth myth, a "phantasmagoria of the nursery" (p. 28), influenced by Mary's just having become a mother for the second time, after her first child had died. The book deals with the "trauma of the afterbirth" (p. 25) and the fear, guilt, and depression that follow.

Victor's preoccupation with changing dead tissues into a live person is linked with Mary's wish to reanimate her dead baby, and the rejection of the monster-child by Victor is connected with Mary's mother's death ten days after Mary's birth.

Joseph (1975) writes about Frankenstein's dream after creating the monster and being reviled by it, in which he embraces his fiancee, and she turns into his dead mother. The dream intimates a connection between Victor's disgust for his creation with the revulsion he feels toward both his beloved and his mother, "doubles of one another in sexual counterpoint to Frankenstein and his double (the monster)" (p. 101). The monster is seen as Victor's repressed sexuality, and the family romance themes apparent in the text are stressed.

Hirsch (1975) conceptualizes the story in terms of what he sees as Mary's feelings of inferiority because she is a woman, i.e., in terms of penis envy. Victor is described as focussing on Oedipal sexual curiosity, and his activities are seen as masturbatory in nature, leading to guilt and to feelings of inadequacy and castration, a feature paralleled by the feelings of the monster about himself. The monster blames Victor for his ugliness and rejection as a girl blames her mother for her castration, and the retaliation against Victor is seen as a revenge against the castrating mother.

Rubenstein (1976) sees *Frankenstein* as a parable of motherhood. He views Mary as being preoccupied with her own mother's sexuality and equates the novel with Mary's first dead baby girl. In the monster's narrative, Rubenstein takes a seemingly irrelevant description of the Arabian girl's dead mother as standing for an allusion to Mary's own and sees this search for the dead mother as the central theme of the book. The shifting of participant-observer roles in the various narratives is likened to the shifting active and passive wishes engendered in the observer of the primal scene. Rubenstein also highlights Mary's ambivalence regarding the wished-for return of her dead mother because of her Oedipal competetive procreative desires.

DISCUSSION OF *FRANKENSTEIN*

Mary Shelley's *Frankenstein* offers the psychoanalytic student a plethora of interesting themes to pursue. The present paper is primarily concerned with the character of the monster, where significant aspects of the psychology of the exception are most clearly exhibited. The monster's story may be read as a parable of child development and as an indictment of the Godwinian method of education (stressed by Mary's father) with its emphasis on intellectual rather than emotional nutrients for a child (Small 1973).

The creature's life is barren of parental emotional nutrients from the outset, as he is immediately rejected by his creator, Victor Frankenstein. In his lament to Victor after the murder of William, the monster describes how sad, confused, lonely, and abandoned he felt after the overwhelming rebuff by his maker at his birth (feelings shared by the author during her own lonely childhood). He ascribes this initial rejection, and the subsequent ones he encountered at the hands of the other human beings with whom he interacted, to his horrific appearance. His tale of woe is related to Victor atop an Alpine glacier known as La Mer de Glace—a name that puns upon the word mother in a manner icily calculated to describe the quality of the parental deprivation that the monster feels has been his lot.

Instances of parental abandonment or rejection abound throughout the book. Victor's own mother was orphaned as a child, and she was raised by her father, as were Clerval and Walton. Elizabeth's mother died in giving birth to her, and Justine's mother surrendered her up to servitude in the Frankenstein household because of unwarranted hatred of her own offspring. Mary Shelley's feelings concerning her own mother's death, coming so soon after her own birth, seem to be clearly mirrored in this theme so repetitively encountered in the lives of the characters throughout her novel.

The eloquence of the monster's words, as he voices his anguished feelings of rejection, opens the reader's heart to the poor maligned creature. His suffering has been unjust, particularly since he did not begin his life as an evil, angry, murderous fiend. On the contrary, he has literally cried out to those around him for love and acceptance, only to be rebuffed repeatedly because of his appearance, an aspect of his being over which he has never had any control. His ugliness may serve, in part, as a metaphor for his anger, another aspect of his being for which he is not really responsible. This is a feeling that the author very likely may have wished to feel about her own rage toward her stepmother (and perhaps toward her real mother as well). The monster's sense of being guiltless and of having been unjustly imposed upon by fate, in the guise of his parental creator, is highly reminiscent of Freud's (1916) description of the psychology of certain individuals who saw themselves as exceptions to the rules by virtue of the congenital deformities that had caused them inordinate suffering.

The initial rejection by his creator, and, later, reading Victor's laboratory papers dealing with the experiments leading to his own conception, are utilized by the creature as his rationale for stealing. The subsequent rejections by the Delaceys and by Victor's youngest brother, William, are offered as the explanation for the creature's turn toward malevolent behavior, in particular for the murder of young William.

Another aspect of the monster's sense of despair and deprivation is depicted in the events immediately following this crime. The fiend finds a locket upon the dead child containing a picture of Victor's mother. The portrait of a mother softens his anger momentarily, as the beauty of the sleeping Justine (a surrogate for Victor's mother) shortly thereafter arouses him sexually. He becomes enraged again, however, when he contemplates that he is ". . . for ever deprived the delights that such beautiful creatures should bestow . . ." (p. 39). Parental love (here described primarily in maternal terms) and sexual love have been denied to him forever by virtue of his innate ugliness.

The monster berates his rejecting parent, Victor, in a series of remarkably poignant passages, which eloquently exclaim his feeling of having been unjustly treated. These passages provide his basis for later proclaiming himself an exception to the laws of society and serve as an apologia for his murder of William.

In one such passage, he says,

Oh, Frankenstein, be not equitable to every other, and trample upon me alone, to whom thy justice and even thy clemency and affection is most due. Remember, that I am thy creature: I ought to be thy Adam; but I am rather the fallen Angel, whom thou drivest from joy for no misdeed. Everywhere I see bliss, from which I alone am irrevocably excluded. I was benevolent and good; misery made me a fiend. Make me happy and I shall again be virtuous (p. 95).

In another passage, he says,

When I looked around, I saw and heard of none like me. Was I then a monster, a blot upon the earth, from which all men fled and whom all men disowned? (p. 116).

He compares his lot in life with that of other beings and observes,

But where were my friends and relations? No father had watched my infant days, no mother had blessed me with smiles and caresses; or if they had, all my past life was now a blot, a blind vacancy in which I distinguished nothing. From my earliest remembrance I had been as I then was in height and proportion. I had never yet seen a being resembling me, or who claimed any intercourse with me. What was I? (p. 117).

Surely these passages reflect Mary Shelley's feelings about her own early parental deprivations.

With this as a preamble, the monster turns to his justification of his crime against young William. He describes his attempt to befriend the lad and his second rejection at the hands of a member of the Frankenstein clan. Once again, he invokes the horrific appearance for which he is not responsible as the presumed cause of the rejection. At this juncture in his history, the monster voices no remorse or guilt. Instead, he exultantly voices his sense of triumph in the discovery of his malevolent powers:

> I gazed on my victim, and my heart swelled with exultation and hellish triumph; clapping my hands, I exclaimed, "I, too, can create desolation; my enemy (Victor) is not impregnable; this death will carry despair to him, and a thousand other miseries shall torment and destroy him" (p. 139).

In the recognition of his power to destroy Victor's happiness by his blatant contravention of the rules of a civilized society, the monster achieves a sense of purpose, a murderously "creative" identity as an exception.

As the book progresses, the monster gains co-equality with, and even ascendency over, his creator. The two become more like twins or siblings on the one hand, and depriving mothers or parents on the other. This is particularly apparent in the crucial sequence of the novel, where Victor reneges on his promise to create a female mate for the monster, thereby sealing his own (and Elizabeth's) doom. Both Victor and the monster are forever left abandoned and bereft of any hope for love in both the maternal and genital sexual senses.

After the murder of Elizabeth, the monster assumes the upper hand. Although Victor, now reduced to a lonely orphan, pursues him to the frozen Arctic wastes, he is clearly unequal in the competition with his creature against the elements. When he finally perishes, however, a remarkable transformation takes place within the monster. He suddenly becomes over-burdened with feelings of guilt and expresses the desire to immolate himself in order to atone for his crimes against his progenitor. Victor comes to be regarded with a near reverential aura. Here we see the monster's maladaptive attempts at dissolving his fantasy of being the exception, as he attempts to ward off the reality of Victor's loss. Having been responsible for his maker's demise, the long denied guilt surfaces and overwhelms him.

Victor's idyllic depiction of his own early life and education makes a striking comparison to that of the monster's. Victor's narrative literally bursts forth with evidence of an abundance of parental love. His later deviant interests in the occult and in monster making seem inexplicable, as does his instantaneous rejection of his hapless creature, unless one invokes the Oedipal rivalry with his father (and his professors) over who shall be allowed to procreate with the mother. But it is Victor's inability to success-fully deal with his guilt feelings that proves to be his undoing. Although he continuously attempts to project his guilt onto the monster, his defenses frequently break down, and his guilt either erupts directly into consciousness or is loudly suggested by his frequent bouts of depression. Victor is an exceptional being by virtue of his having created life, but he cannot invoke the idea of being an exception, cursed by fate, as the monster does. He succumbs to his depressive despair and embarks upon his suicidal sojourn in order to revenge himself upon his malevolent creature.

Walton's tale provides an illuminating counterpoint. Walton, too, had been abandoned by his mother (through her death) when he was a young child. He had been raised by a stern, prohibiting father, whose dying wishes interdicting Polar exploration were rejected when Walton undertook his voyage of discovery in pursuit of the warm, maternal heartlands that he imagined to be nestling at the Pole. The parallel between Walton's early life and that of the montser, with regard to the subject of parental deprivation, is quite interesting. One significant difference exists, however: Walton has a beloved sister in England, to whom he writes the remarkable tale of the exceptional beings he encountered in his forbidden voyage of discovery. Having received love from at least one source (his sister), Walton does not seem to qualify as blatantly as does the monster, to wear the mantle of the exception. As the action of the novel ends, Walton responds to the desires and pressures of his crew (perhaps an externalization of the paternal superego) and to the lessons garnered from the morality tales of Victor and the monster. In so doing, however, he surrenders his creativity and a portion of his individuality. He has become a conformist, rather than an exception, to the rules.

THE CIRCUMSTANCES LEADING UP TO
THE WRITING OF *FRANKENSTEIN*

Mary Shelley's first child, a girl, was born out of wedlock in 1815, a little more than a year before the book was written. Mary was seventeen-and-a-half years old at the time and living amidst a storm of scandal with another woman's husband, Percy Shelley. As mentioned earlier the baby died 12 days later, a seemingly fateful reversal of her mother's loss after her own birth. Undoubtedly, this was one of the determinants of Victor's rejection in the novel of his own grotesque creature. On March 19, 1815, some two weeks after the child's death, Mary wrote in her journal,

> Dream that my little baby came to life again; that it had only been cold, and that we rubbed it before the fire, and it lived. Awake and find no baby. I think about the little thing all day. Not in good spirits (p. 41).

The reanimation of the dead baby by the fire and the electrical spark of life breathed into the inanimate creature by Victor Frankenstein both illustrate Mary's wishes to rejuvenate her own dear dead.

Mary suffered a brief period of depression after the loss of her child, certainly a natural reaction under the circumstances. However, Asch (1978) suggests that Mary's postpartum depression may have been related to guilty fantasies (or even to some actual crime in reality) about having murdered her own infant. Although little hard evidence exists, this shockingly bold speculation is lent further support by another circumstance. In the year preceding the actual writing of *Frankenstein*, Mary's journals detail the constant reading and re-reading of her parents' books. Unfortunately, the journal entries from May 14, 1815 until July 20, 1816, the period covering the actual writing of *Frankenstein*, are lost. During this period, Mary's first-born son, William, was born (in early 1816), shortly before she began writing the novel. The shocking speculation concerning Mary's possible crime against her first-born girl is lent credence when one considers that the monster's first victim in *Frankenstein* is Victor's younger brother, William. It is a rather exceptional thing for a mother to so clearly represent murderous feelings toward someone bearing the name of her own infant son in a novel. While William was also the name of Mary's father and of the half-brother born to Godwin and Mrs. Clairmont when Mary was aged four (against both of whom she may also have harbored murderous impulses), the presumably conscious filicidal fantasies are most clearly in keeping with the hypothesis of this paper—that Mary Shelley viewed herself as an exception to the rules.

At the time of the writing of *Frankenstein*, Mary and young William, and Mary's ever present half-sister, Claire (who, in a rivalrous fantasy with Mary, had contrived to become pregnant with Byron's child) were in Switzerland, near Geneva (the birthplace of Victor in the novel). She found herself in the company of the two literary giants, Shelley and Byron, and the latter's physician (also a writer), Polidori—a repetition of the circle of great writers gathered about Godwin during her childhood. In essence, a reenactment of her early life situation with her father and his literary circle was much in evidence during the rainy days at Lake Geneva that spawned *Frankenstein*.

In order to while away the wet weather, the assembled group responded to Byron's suggestion to read some ghost stories. One tale concerned an inconstant lover who, in reaching to embrace his fiancee, finds himself holding her pale ghost instead. The duplication of this tale in Victor's dream about Elizabeth turning into his dead mother after the creation of the monster is apparent. Another tale dealt with the saga of a father, whose fate it was to involuntarily destroy all of the younger sons of his household as they blossomed into manhood.

Mary had, needless to say, blossomed into womanhood and was capable of imitating the creativity of her mother, both with respect to having babies and to writing books. The stories resonated so acutely with her earlier life and conflicts, and provided a significant impetus for the creation of *Frank-*

enstein (Baudry 1978). Such creativity seemed to carry with it a concomittant confusion in the sense of her sexual identity. As Rubenstein (1976) notes,

> For Mary Shelley, authorship and motherhood were equivalent aspects of the same urge toward realization and expression of the self. As such, they were the inheritors, and in a way, the victim of what Mary Shelley took to be her mother's legacy. There was, for her, conflicted fusion of creative with forbidden sexual forwardness and masculine prerogatives (p. 168).

Byron then proceeded to read Coleridge's unfinished poem, *Christabel* (probably inspired by the lives of Mary Wollstonecraft and Mary Shelley). This work deals with a girl who lost her mother at birth. The mother had announced on her deathbed that she would return for her daughter's nuptials, and the action in the poem occurs as Christabel is engaged to marry. A woman of beautiful exterior and deformed interior aspects, Geraldine, appears and the reader anticipates that a sexually destructive liaison between her and the young Christabel is about to occur. Rubenstein (1976) aptly captures the poem's meaning:

> In transmuting Coleridge's lines into Frankenstein's nightmare Mary captured the essence of her own conflict. The dead mother, hideous and ghostly, returns at the moment of symbolic inauguration of creative and sexual life to take the lost child in her arms and to return with her to the grave. The mother's return, the fulfillment . . . of an old wish, is precipitated by the child's daring to aspire to motherhood and becomes instead a punishment for audacity and rivalry (p. 186).

Mary's ambivalence regarding the wished for resurrection of the dead mother, and her guilt and self-loathing over possessing such feelings, are neatly expressed in Victor's speech after his immediate repulsion at the monster he has created: "A mummy endued with animation could not be so hideous as that wretch" (p. 53). Here, in Mary's pun on the nursery word for mother, she speaks to both her feelings for the dead mother and for herself. She also clearly betrays her identification with the monster in this and other passages in the novel.

From what has been described of the setting in which Mary Shelley began her epic novel, it might seem quite amazing that she ever completed her task. Her unconscious competitive wishes with the dead mother and live stepmother seem remarkably close to the surface. In addition, her previously well defended guilt feelings had also surged once more to the foreground. It appears that two concomittant fantasies must have allowed her to mitigate her guilty feelings and to proceed with her act of creativity. One involved a fantasy of disavowal of her actual competitive, creative desires, accomplished by crediting her male companions, Byron and Shelley, with providing her with the inspiration for her work. In other words, she informs us that she has been passively "impregnated" with the ideas that gave birth to the novel, and thus need not assume any responsibility for her guilt-provoking desires.

In her account of the events leading up to her commencing work on the story, she speaks of feeling blocked initially, and then of how, after the others had engaged in a conversation about experiments wherein Erasmus Darwin had applied electricity to dead tissues in an attempt to reanimate them, she had her famous waking dream. In it, she envisioned a man infusing life into a creature he had put together from dead tissues. He then shrinks back in horror from his creation and wishes that it would die. The scientist in her dream then falls into a sleep and is awakened in horror to see his hideous creature hovering over him. With this dream, she began to work upon the novel.

The second fantasy that allowed Mary to write her epic horror tale is that of being an exception to the rules. Only under the sway of such a fantasy could young Mary have allowed herself to live out the remarkable flaunting of societal rules in which she was then engaged. The elopement with Shelley, the giving birth to children out of wedlock, and the blatantly murderous filicidal impulses find their parallel expression in her remarkable novel *Frankenstein*, most particularly in the character with which Mary most identified, the monster.

MARY SHELLEY'S LIFE AFTER THE WRITING OF *FRANKENSTEIN*

Following the writing of *Frankenstein*, Mary Shelley's most blatant depiction in print of her fantasy of being an exception is seen in her second novel, *Mathilda* (1819). The story devolves about a young girl, Mathilda, who, like Mary, has lost her mother in infancy. She is cared for by a cold-hearted aunt (a shade of Mary's stepmother) in the absence of her father. Daughter and father are blissfully reunited when Mathilda is sixteen. The father is initially attentive and then becomes cold to her until she forces him to admit his incestuous desires for her. The sense of the work is that this passion is both expected and desired by Mathilda, and is also not perceived of as an unthinkable possibility by her. In other words, there is little conscious guilt in the work. The unconscious carries the day, however, as her father commits suicide, and Mathilda succumbs to consumption after meeting a young poet modelled after Shelley.

This drama, which contains a theme of reunion with a lost loved one (the fusion of the incestuous union with the father and the earlier wished-for reunion with mother) was, like *Frankenstein*, written at a time of mourning for lost children—Mary's recently deceased children, Clara and William. The revival of old wounds (the infants' deaths recall the death of Mary Wollstonecraft and the idea of having suffered unjustly) most likely allowed Mary to once more invoke her feelings of being an exception and to baldly expose her incestuous desires for her father and her wish for reunion with the lost mother (via the medium of identifying with the mother's creativity).

Other lesser works followed. By Mary's early 20s, four of her five pregnancies had ended either in death in infancy of the children or in their miscarriage. Only her son Percy Florence survived. Mary's half-sister, Fanny, had committed suicide when Godwin coldly informed her that he was not her real father.

Finally, in July 1822, Shelley drowned. At this juncture, Mary's interest in reunion with lost loved ones once more surged into the foreground. This is especially in evidence in her journals and letters after the time of Shelley's death. In a letter to Maria Gisborne (an early choice of Godwin's to replace Mary Wollstonecraft, and a subsequent target for an intense adolescent idealization by Mary Shelley) dated shortly after Shelley's death, August 27, 1822, Mary writes, "How long do you think I shall live? As long as my mother? Then eleven long years must intervene . . ." (p. 189). In a journal note addressed to Shelley, October 7, 1822, again shortly after his death, she writes,

> . . . you will be with me in all my studies, dearest love! Your voice will no longer applaud me, but in spirit you will visit and encourage me: I know you will. What were I if I did not believe that you still exist? . . . I believe that we all live hereafter . . . (pp. 182–183).

And in the final entry of her journal (June 1, 1840), read at her funeral nearly eleven years later, she observes,

> . . . God and good angels guard us! Surely this world, stored outwardly with shapes and influences of beauty and good, is peopled in its intellectual life by myriads of loving spirits . . . Whether the beloved dead make a portion of this company, I dare not guess, but that such exist I feel . . . (p. 209).

Mary devoted the rest of her chronically depressed later life to the publication of Shelley's works and let her own creativity slip away from her. As she grew older, she grew more ambivalent toward her famous novel, *Frankenstein*, referring to it as her "hideous progeny." This ambivalence was paralleled by a growing ambivalence toward her dead mother's image, although she was loathe to admit this directly.

One of the few negative references to her mother is encountered in a journal entry dated October 21, 1838. Here Mary explains her rejection of the feminist ideals espoused by her dead mother:

> I was nursed and fed with a love of glory. To be something great and good was a precept given me by my father: Shelley reiterated it . . . since I had lost Shelley I have no wish to ally myself to the radicals (the feminists her mother had allied herself with) . . . They are full of repulsion to me (pp. 205–206).

Here it is Mary who is the rejecting one and not her mother. Curiously, this entry is almost contemporaneous with Mary's contracting a minor case of smallpox in Paris. She described herself as looking like a "monster" at that time. So the anger at the real mother for rejecting her, and the consequent identification with Victor's rejected creature, seem close to the surface here and are dealt with by the rejection of the dead mother's ideals and the acceptance of the bourgeois morality embodied by her stepmother.

As with Walton's surrender to the demands of the crew at the end of *Frankenstein*, Mary's acceptance of her stepmother's standards lead to the loss of the creativity associated with the identification with her real mother. Here, as in the monster's actions at the end of *Frankenstein*, is a final maladaptive attempt to dissolve the fantasy of being the exception and to resolve her chronic later-life depression. This was accompanied by the surrender of much of her sexuality and creativity, as she never married again and had few relationships with men. The blows from fate had been too much for her, and the dangerous creativity was sacrificed as the price for warding off her recurring feelings of depression. For Mary Shelley, the Promethean pleasures of creativity and sexual fire (*Frankenstein* is subtitled *The Modern Prometheus*) had been more than balanced by the Promethean pains; hence she castrated her creative gifts rather than let the vultures do it. Her fire was returned to the Olympian Gods (her parents) and she became their simple, unexceptional handmaiden.

PRIOR STUDIES ON THE EXCEPTION

At this juncture, it behooves one to consider the concept of the exception in greater detail. Freud (1916) points out how some patients are unwilling to renounce the desires for immediate gratifications in their treatment, expressing the idea that they have suffered enough, and that they would "submit no longer to any disagreeable necessity, for they are exceptions" (p. 312). He saw their neuroses as resulting from suffering in early childhood secondary to congenital deformities or early illnesses of which they know they were *guiltless* and which they look upon "as an unjust disadvantage imposed upon them" (p. 313). As a result of these early injustices, they became rebellious.

In the paper, Freud comments on another literary "monster," Shakespeare's *Richard III*, who, because of his congenital deformity and ugliness, proclaims in the opening soliloquoy his desire to be an arch villain. Freud notes that the true meaning of the soliloquoy is that,

> Nature has done me a grievous wrong in denying me the beauty of form which wins human love. Life owes me reparation for this and I will see that I get it. I have a right to be an exception, to disregard the scruples by which others let themselves be held back. I may do wrong myself, since wrong has been done to me (pp. 314–315).

The obvious parallel to the monster's laments in *Frankenstein* is quite striking. Freud ends his paper by stating that women, feeling themselves to be congenitally damaged (castrated), tend to regard themselves as exceptions. He sees them as often voicing bitter reproaches against their mothers for bearing them as women, i.e., without a penis. Hirsch (1975) follows this idea in his conceptualization of the monster as a woman who rails at its mother (Victor) for its feeling of having been born ugly (deformed and castrated).

Jacobson (1959) did not agree with Freud that the woman's sense of castration has the same impact on her as do realistic physical afflictions. She observed that Richard III was hated and despised by his own mother from birth, i.e., denied the love of women, hence he could not love women. In all of her own cases, she saw the denial of maternal affection as leading to a "dangerous masochistic need for punishment" (p. 139). This early dyadic root of the fantasy of being an exception is the one that is defensively emphasized in the apologias of both Mary Shelley and the monster in *Frankenstein*. It serves to defend against the blatant Oedipal fantasies harbored by both Mary (in her relationship with Percy Shelley, an obvious surrogate for her father) and the monster (in his sexual arousal by Justine, a surrogate for Victor's mother).

In explicating the difficulties suffered by one of her patients, a woman born with a congenitally paretic leg, Jacobson notes that,

> . . . her profound unconscious need for punishment and her angry, spiteful rebellion against the power of her own superego were nourished

by her parents contradictory emotional attitudes: their seductive behavior coupled with unfair, reproachful hostility (p. 141).

The patient's mother had particularly blamed her for her illness, as if it were the result of a moral affliction, which made the patient guilty but also rebellious, thus covering over ". . . her self-contempt and her desperate cry for maternal love and acceptance" (p. 141). Jacobson further stresses the narcissistic and aggressive nature of her patients' Oedipal strivings,

> their rebellious, ambitious aims and claims, their resistance to accept the Oedipal laws, their spiteful denial of their own conscience, the victory of their unconscious self-destructive trends and underneath it all, their desperate cry for a love they never received (p. 143).

If one examines Mary Shelley's life, one may note the contradictory emotional attitudes on the part of her parents and apply Jacobson's material. Mary's father was seductive with her and obviously was desirous of moulding her in the image of his lost wife. Her stepmother, on the other hand, saw in Godwin's pretty daughter the incarnation of the dead woman she detested, the woman-child who impeded her own position (and that of her children). Mary was treated by Mrs. Clairmont as a moral leper and was blamed for her very essence and existence on the one hand (elements over which she had no control and was not responsible for), and for her Oedipal interaction with her father on the other. Mary felt guilty but justified in her rebellion against this feeling because of the deprivation of the maternal love she so ardently desired.

One other comment of Jacobson's is of interest with regard to the thesis advanced here. She refers to persons of genius and observes that, ". . . the biographies of great men suggest that their psychology has much in common with that of women marked by extraordinary beauty [the psychology of the exception]" (p. 147). As noted earlier, Mary Shelley spoke of being reared for greatness by her father, a man who also seemed to regard himself as an exception to many of the usual rules of morality. He like Mary's real mother, suffered early parental deprivation. In Mary's identification with her father's and mother's attitudes, another impetus for her later abrogation of the moral laws of her society was provided.

SOME CONCLUDING THOUGHTS

Mary Shelley's feeling of being an exception to the rules was one of the important factors in allowing her to overcome her inhibitions about being creative (most likely related to her unconscious feelings of guilt because of her very actions and thoughts). In so doing, the fantasy helped her in the writing of the novels *Frankenstein* and *Mathilda*.

Sachs (1942) and Kris (1952) both note how the successful literary production helps the writer to overcome strong feelings of guilt associated with unacceptable sexual and aggressive wishes. Too intense feelings of guilt, however, are likely to lead to blocks in creativity of the kind initially experienced by Mary Shelley in the prodromal period at Lake Geneva before she began *Frankenstein*. With the mobilization of her fantasy of disavowal of her active (pro)creative desires and her fantasy of being an exception to the rules because of her unjust early suffering, she was able to overcome her inhibitions and to create her masterpiece.

After suffering an inordinate series of reality blows, Mary apparently attempted to dissolve the fantasy of being the exception and the concomitant identification with the creativity of her mother, Mary Wollstonecraft. The dissolution of the fantasy and the surrender of her creativity seemed the necessary price to pay to ward off a serious depressive syndrome; although she did continue to suffer from low-grade depressive symptoms throughout her life. She concentrated her remaining energies on the immortalization of her late husband, Percy Shelley. Without these efforts, his works might never have achieved the exceptional fame that they have attained. For this, we are much in her debt; although we must regretfully mourn the resultant curtailment of her own very significant creativity.

It seems appropriate to end this paper now with a final passage from *Frankenstein*. The lines are the monster's, as he prepares to immolate himself after Victor's death at the end of the book:

> I shall collect my funeral pile, and consume to ashes this miserable frame, that its remains may afford no light to any curious and unhallowed wretch, who would create such another as I have been. I shall die. I shall no longer feel the agonies which now consume me, or be the prey of feelings unsatisfied, yet unquenched. He is dead who called me into being; and when I shall be no more, the very remembrance of us both will speedily vanish (p. 220).

Here the monster informs us that he and Victor will soon be forgotten. How wrong he was! *Frankenstein* has never been out of print since its first appearance in 1818. To have remained with us throughout so many generations, Mary Shelley's infamous creature must have touched exceptionally resonant chords within us all. One of the many that reverberate in our memories and fantasies is the one struck whenever we, too, desire to be exceptions to the rules and wish to right the wrongs the cruel fates have unjustly imposed upon our lives.

REFERENCES

Asch, S. (1978). Personal communication.

Baudry, F. (1978). Discussion of an earlier version of this paper at a meeting of the New York Psychoanalytic Society, January 17.

Bigland, E. (1959). *Mary Shelley*. New York: Appleton-Century-Crofts.

Bond, D. (1973). The bride of Frankenstein. *Psychiatric Annals* 3:10–22.

Coleridge, S. T. (1962). *Poetical Works of Samuel Taylor Coleridge*. ed. E. Coleridge. Oxford: Clarendon Press.

Freud, S. (1916). Some character-types met with in psychoanalytic work. I. The "exceptions". *Standard Edition* 14:311–315.

Gerson, N. (1973). *Daughter of Earth and Water: A Biography of Mary Wollstonecraft Shelley*. New York: William Morrow & Co.

Godwin, W. (1793). *Enquiry Concerning Political Justice*, ed. K. C. Canter. Oxford: Clarendon Press, 1971.

———. (1794). *Caleb Williams*. London: G. Routledge & Co., 1853.

Graubard, M. (1967). The Frankenstein syndrome: man's ambivalent attitude to knowledge and power. *Perspectives in Biology and Medicine* 10:419–443.

Grylls, R. (1938). *Mary Shelley*. London: Oxford University Press.

Hirsch, G. (1975). The monster was a lady: on the psychology of Mary Shelley's *Frankenstein*. *Hartford Studies in Literature* 7:117–153.

Jacobson, E. (1959). The "exceptions": an elaboration of Freud's character study. *Psychoanalytic Study of the Child* 14:135–154.

Joseph, G. (1975). Frankenstein's dream: the child as father of the monster. *Hartford Studies in Literature* 7:97–115.

Kaplan, M., and Kloss, R. (1973). Fantasy of paternity and the doppelganger: Mary Shelley's *Frankenstein*. In *The Unspoken Motive: A Guide to Psychoanalytic Literary Criticism*, pp. 119–145. New York: The Free Press.

Kris, E. (1952). *Psychoanalytic Explorations in Art*. New York: International Universities Press.

Moers, E. (1974). Female gothic, the monster's mother. *The New York Review of Books* 21:24–28.

Rieger, J. (1967). *The Mutiny Within: The Heresies of Percy Bysshe Shelley*. New York: Braziller.

Rossetti, W. (1911). *The Diary of Dr. John William Polidori*, ed. W. M. Rosetti. London: Elkin Matthews.

Rubenstein, M. A. (1976). "My accursed origin": the search for the mother in Frankenstein. *Studies in Romanticism* 15:165–194.

Sachs, H. (1942). The community of daydreams. In *The Creative Unconscious*, pp. 11–54. Cambridge, Mass.: Sci-Art Publishers.

Shelley, M. (1818). *Frankenstein*, ed. J. Rieger, New York: The Bobbs-Merrill Co., 1974.

———. (1819). Mathilda. ed., E. Nitchie. *Studies in Philology, Extra Series* 3:1959.

———. *The Letters of Mary W. Shelley*. ed. F. L. Jones. Norman: University of Oklahoma Press, 1944.

———. *Mary Shelley's Journal*, ed. F. L. Jones. Norman: University of Oklahoma Press, 1947.

Small, C. (1973). *Mary Shelley's Frankenstein: Tracing The Myth*. Pittsburgh: University of Pittsburgh Press.

Wollstonecraft, M. (1792). *A Vindication of the Rights of Woman*, ed. M. B. Kramnick. Great Britain: C. Nicholls & Co., 1975.

Problems in the Application of Psychoanalysis to Mary Shelley's *Frankenstein*

FRANCIS D. BAUDRY, M.D.

A discussion of "Mary Shelley's Frankenstein: Creativity and the Psychology of the Exception," *by Wayne A. Myers, M.D.*

The most challenging pitfalls facing the analyst who wishes to deal with a work of literature concern the possible misuse of the analytic method in a field alien from the one for which it was designed. Another challenge is the establishment of rules of inference and the search for adequate data to bolster one's hypothesis.

As much of Dr. Myers' thesis rests on the assumption that Mary Shelley considered herself an exception, the basis for this hypothesis must be examined:

First we encounter Mary's undeniable sense of herself as an individual who had suffered unjustly by virtue of her real mother's death. . . . The encouragement given her [Mary] in her hatred of her stepmother by Godwin and his peers, and their reinforcement of her sense of loss vis-à-vis Mary Wollstonecraft's death, abetted her feelings of herself as an exception, a person apart from all others, one who had suffered inordinate early deprivation for no reason of her own making, and one who thus deserved exceptional indemnification from life. The meeting with Percy Shelley provided both the impetus and the sanction needed by Mary for the living out of the fantasy of being the exception. In eloping with Shelley, she exhibited an utter disregard for his marriage to another woman, a serious contravention of the rules of the society in which she lived. In this exceptional action, she was abetted by Shelley's own scorn of the formal rules of society. By virtue of his being so transparently a surrogate for her father, she also clearly flew in the face of all of the usual Oedipal strictures.

One would feel more comfortable if Dr. Meyers could supply more direct information about Mary's inner life (diaries, letters, and the like). Not everyone who looses a mother in the early days of life feels like an exception or that they have suffered unjustly. Likewise, not everyone who takes another woman's husband, marries him, and begets a child is acting out the fantasy of being an exception. That is, the behavior presented is consistent with the existence of the fantasy but not quite sufficient. Is it possible, for example, that Mary was looking for a mother surrogate? Considerable caution must be exercised in using manifest content and drawing certain inferences about it without clarifying the basis on which the conclusions are reached. What about the role of guilt in Mary's case? The exceptions claim they have suffered enough and can, therefore, flout the laws obeyed by other mortals without paying a price. There is no direct evidence to either support or contradict this in the present case.

Do we know how Mary looked on her marriage to Shelley? Were any letters to her father saved? How was the decision to elope reached? A more thorough search of the author's nonliterary writings and evidence presented by biographers or contemporaries would be of considerable assistance in this regard.

A recently published edition of Mary Shelley's letters (Bermet 1980) gives this author the impression that her life theme resembles more that of the fate neurosis described by Alexander (1930) than that of the exception. An unusual onslaught of calamities seems to have befallen her—deaths, losses, financial reverses. Her chosen husband, Shelley, was always falling in love with someone else; he suffered from tuberculosis and experienced frightening hallucinations. Yet Mary's attachment to him was exemplary.

In a letter dated September, 1822, to the widow of Edwards—Shelley's friend who drowned with him—Mary writes:

> I was never the Eve of any Paradise, but a human creature blessed by an elemental spirit's company and love—an angel who imprisoned in flesh could not adapt himself to his clay shrine and so has flown and left it— and I feel as poets have described those loved by superhuman creatures and then deserted by them—impatient, despairing—and resting only on the moment when he will return to me (Holmes 1980).

GENERAL PROBLEMS OF METHOD

The analyst who wishes to devote himself or herself to the study of literature must in some way tackle several problems. First, the analytic situation is dependent on an interaction, a process involving forces and exchanges between two individuals developing a relationship with each other and attempting to resolve problems in that relationship. As Ricoeur (1977) notes:

> Psychoanalysis as an investigatory procedure gives preference to relations of meanings, while the method of treatment gives preference to relation of forces between systems and the theory attempts to integrate these two aspects of psychical reality. Interpretation of a dream means both assigning a meaning to it and inserting it into a chain of other mental acts as a link having validity and importance (pp. 845–846).

What does interpretation of a work of art really mean in psychoanalytic terms? The work of art is a finished product, inert, with no forces and no relationships. What avenues are then open to the psychoanalytic investigator who wishes to use his or her instruments in the study of literature.

One can, as Dr. Myers has done, decide to some degree to endow the characters in a novel with a life of their own, study their relationships to one another, and behave as though the characters were responsive to each other, possessing a past, and feeling, acting and reacting. Problems arise, as Dr. Myers is aware, as speculations made are difficult to anchor, and evidence is hard to come by to buttress hypotheses of a psychological nature.

A second approach, also chosen by Dr. Myers, would be to use the work of art to illustrate some psychic mechanisms or psychological hypothesis—in this case, the psychology of the exception. This same approach is, of course, the one Freud (1907) used in Gradiva.

A third approach might be to isolate certain aspects of analytic theory dealing with symbols and their translation as applicable to a text. One might try, for example, to study the nature of the metaphors and to identify certain unconscious fantasies or underlying themes. This method would entail looking at the novel a bit like a text to be deciphered and drawing inferences from its imagery and structure. Arlow (1978) has done this very successfully in a paper on the primal scene in Mishima. This is a search for meaning.

A fourth approach might consist of painstakingly reconstructing traces and elements of a dynamic object relation that in fact exists both in the present and in the past. In the present, a form of relationship is established between the reader and a text. The data derived from elements of this empathic relation have to be evaluated in the context of other data, as the data derived in the analytic situation by the analyst's empathizing with the patient also require evaluation and assessment. The second form of relationship, existing in the past and liable to some degree of reconstruction, is the relationship between an author and his or her work. It is possible by careful sifting of data to assess the dynamic meaning of a

particular character to an author, and also to describe the detailed circumstances of the composition of a work so as to assess something of the
meaning of the creation to its author. What dilemmas were confronted, and
what problems did the author try to resolve through its composition?

CIRCUMSTANCES OF THE NOVEL'S COMPOSITION

The circumstances of the novel's composition and the psychological situation of its author must be reconstructed from available data, with the level of
inference remaining relatively close to the data of observation. This approach
is illustrated through an examination of *Frankenstein.*

In Geneva, Mary, Byron, and the latter's physician, Polidori, were together
for a rainy summer. The atmosphere was charged with sexual innuendos, as
Claire, Mary's half-sister, already pregnant with Byron's child, was also
present. Mary's concern about loss and disaster must have been increased by
an eminent physician's pronouncement in the Spring of 1815 that Shelley
was rapidly dying of consumption. The group of three men and Mary
resembled the childhood situation in which Mary was the witness of the
adult's literary productions in her father's house. In addition, she was urged
by Polidori, Byron's physician, to seek her own literary reputation. His
urgings may have been accompanied by some more passionate persuasions.

Many of the day residues that led to the novel's composition are available.
This may allow us to reconstruct some of the significant antecedents to the
process of composition and writing—an attempt that will enrich Dr. Myers'
work. Some of the sources for this thesis include Mary Shelley's own
introduction to the novel and the diary and correspondence of the various
protagonists of that summer, especially Polidori. The search through these
materials is for connections between the content of the novel and the act of
writing itself.

Mary had eloped with the still married Shelley and had lost a girl-child in
1815 about a year before the novel. Her second child, William, was born
in 1816 shortly before the composition of the novel began. In the introduction
to the novel Mary Shelley mentions the ghost stories that were read by the
assembled group that summer and that made a particular impression on her.
One story was of the inconstant lover who, when he thought he was clasping
the bride to whom he had pledged his vows, found himself in the arms of the
pale ghost of her whom he had deserted. Another tale dealt with the sinful
founder of his race whose miserable doom it was to bestow the kiss of death
on all the younger sons of his ill-fated house just when they reached the age
of promise. His gigantic shadowy form clothed like the ghost in Hamlet was
seen at midnight. The shape was lost beneath the shadow of castle walls, but

soon a gate swung back, a step was heard, the door of the chamber opened, and he advanced to the couch of the blooming youth cradled in healthy sleep.

One does not have to be an analyst to see potent reminders of Mary Shelley's past life and conflicts in these stories. The similarities with the novel are obvious. The first story is duplicated in Victor's dream after the monster's birth. Consider the guilty feelings of the adulteress and young mother whose cruel first loss must have been seen both as a punishment for her crime and a reversal of the loss of her mother, a retribution of fate. Possibly out of some sadistic urge, Byron read Coleridge's poem *Christabel* to the assembled group—a horror tale written probably around the death of Mary's mother and dealing with a ghost:

> Then drawing in her breath aloud
> Like one that shuddered, she unbound
> The cincture from beneath her breast:
> Her silken robe and inner vest
> Dropt to her feet, and full in view
> Behold! her bosom and half her side,
> Hideous, deformed and pale of hue,
> A sight to dream of, not to tell!
> And she is to sleep by Christabel.

According to Polidori's diary (Rossetti 1911), the storm raged unabated, and Byron related to the assembled how he saw a tree spun into life by lightning. The discussion continued on reanimation of corpses. "After some silence," Polidori writes:

> Shelley suddenly shrieking, put his hands to his head, ran out of the room . . . I threw water in his face and after gave him ether. He [Shelley] was looking at Mrs. Shelley and suddenly thought of a woman he had heard of who had eyes instead of nipples. When Shelley's hallucination had abated, Byron proposed, "We will each write a ghost story." Byron and Shelley quickly lost interest in the process (Florescu 1915, p. 118).

"The illustrious poets, annoyed by the platitude of prose, speedily relinquished their uncongenial task," writes Mary in the introduction to *Franken-stein*. Mary herself struggled: "I thought and pondered vainly. I felt that blank incapability of invention which is the greatest misery of authorship when dull Nothing replies to our anxious invocations, 'Have you thought of a story?' I was asked each morning and each morning I was forced to reply with a mortifying negative" (Shelley 1818, p. 9).

After several days of sterile effort, she reported a frightening fantasy in a hypnopompic state, the core of the novel—the scene of creation of the monster. She writes:

> his success would terrify the artist; he would rush away from his odious handiwork, horrorstriken. He would hope that left to itself the slight spark of life which he had communicated would fade. He sleeps but he is awakened. He opens his eyes, beholds the lurid thing standing at his bedside, opening his curtain and looking on him with yellow, watery but speculative eyes (p. 9).

For the purpose of this exposition, it does not matter a great deal whether the waking dream was a daydream, a fantasy, or a completely artificial construction resorted to by Mary Shelley as a device to disown the plot origination from some conscious effort. It would indeed be a trap to consider this literary dream as the equivalent of a daydream or night dream.

The waking dream, as Mary Shelley recalls it, frightened her so that she decided to write a story about it. "I could not so easily get rid of my hideous phantom, still it haunted me. I must try to think of something else. I returned to my ghost story . . . oh, if I could only contribute one which would frighten my reader as I myself had been frightened that night" (p. 10). It would seem likely that the frightening incident referred to could well have included Shelley's hallucination and bizarre behavior. In a final section of the introduction written in 1831 (after Shelley's death), Mary Shelley refers to the novel as "my hideous progeny, I have an affection for it, for it was the offspring of happy days when death and grief were but words which found no true echo in my heart" (p. 10). Would the theme of monstrous progeny be congruent with the plea of the young child burdened by many guilty feelings about the miseries her birth caused? Notice the line by Milton introducing the novel—"Did I request thee, maker from my day to mould me Man, did I solicit thee from darkness to promote me?"

FORM AND CONTENT IN THE NOVEL

One may propose that the writing of the story was psychologically equivalent to the content (i.e., the creation of the monster); the writing served several purposes including the mastery of the multiple traumata that preceded it. The similarity with the ghost stories suggests that the "nightmare" expressed the guilty dread that anything she created would wreak destruction. There is clearly an aura of doing the forbidden, "for supremely frightful would be the effect of any human endeavor to mark the stupendous mechanism of the Creator of the world" (p. 10). In contrast, Mary writes about

Byron: "He was the only one among us who put his thoughts upon paper. These as he brought them successively to us, clothed in all the light and harmony of poetry seemed to stamp as divine the glories of heaven and earth whose influence we partook with him" (p. 6).

If the creation of the novel and that of the monster are psychologically similar, we can learn more about Mary's inhibition by carefully reading that part of the novel detailing Victor's reaction after the creation. Interestingly enough, it takes the form of a dream:

> I thought I saw E. in the bloom of health walking in the streets of Ingolstadt. Delighted and surprised I embraced her but as I imprinted the first kiss on her lips, she became livid with the hue of death, her features appeared to change and I thought that I held the corpse of my dead mother in my arms. A shroud enveloped her form. I saw the grave worms crawling in the folds of the flannel (p. 58).

The paragraph ends with Victor bemoaning and fearing each sound as though it announced the approach of the demoniacal corpse to which he had so miserably given life. The similarity between this dream and the manifest content of the first ghost story is evident. This dream is, of course, the reverse of the creation of the monster. It is followed by the appearance of the dreaded creature at Victor's bedside. The scientist then flees just as Mary was trying to escape from her nightmare. If one considers the manifest text at this point of the novel, the dream stands out like a sore thumb. Its content is precise, gripping, and not accounted for by the previous development and sketching out of the main character. The author's inner world seems to have intruded. This remarkable passage suggests many new meanings. The monster and the book could represent a fantasy of its creator bringing back to life the dead mother, embodying both a wish and a fear of Mary Shelley's. However, the manifest incestuous fantasy also suggests a reversal, representing Mary's bond with her father. There is evidence that incest played a consider-able role in her fantasy life—the manifest plot in her second novel *Matilda* deals with a story about incest; in later editions of *Frankenstein*, Mary Shelley, responding to editorial pressure, changed the semi-incestuous bond existing between Victor and Elizabeth by abolishing the "cousin" relationship and making them into friends; and finally, as Dr. Myers mentions, selecting as a husband a poet who was already married to someone else at the time also suggests a living out of a derivative of an unconscious fantasy which includes incest in its content. It is also known that Mary had been haunted ever since childhood and adolescence with thoughts about joining her mother and bringing her back to life. What would mother be like if she could be disinterred? The novel then is an outgrowth of such fantasies.

The inhibition about writing the book would be consistent with Mary's fear of being overwhelmed by her inner feelings about the dead mother, i.e., creation threatens the suppression of many troublesome thoughts and conflicts about Mary Wollstonecraft.

INTRUSION OF THE AUTHOR'S LIFE IN THE NOVEL'S CHARACTERS

How can one approach the meaning of a character to an author? A character in a novel is an artificial construction, a bit like a screen memory in which elements of the past and the present fuse in a highly complex vehicle. A character in a novel is, of course, much more subject to conscious secondary elaboration and is also responsive to certain external aesthetic criteria being inserted into a tradition or genre, in this instance, a gothic novel.

It may be possible to surmise which aspects of the author's personal psychology are relevant to one or another aspect of the character by examining the aesthetic distance or stance the author assumes. Does the author appear tender, ironic, critical, or detached? Can some of the motives impelling the author to write about his or her characters be reconstructed by comparing known facts about his or her personal life with the circumstances in the novel? Is the author reliving certain moments of happiness, trying to master certain traumata, or perhaps taking revenge? These are, of course, familiar motives to be found in the day-to-day work with patients.

In Mary Shelley's case, certain themes seem to recur as leitmotifs in the author's life—her overwhelming solitude, a sense of loss, and a wish to be reunited with her dead mother. The many lengthy sojourns by herself on her mother's grave would suggest that when she is writing about the monster's solitude, she is writing from her own experiences. She is, so to speak, inside her character, and the passages dealing with the issue of solitude are indeed written in a very empathetic manner. One feels sorry for the poor creature.

In a subplot, the monster himself becomes the narrator of the story of the Delacey's. Felix, the son, is sad and depressed, searching for a lost love. As Felix and his sister, Agatha, see the monster for the first time:

Agatha fainted and Sofie, unable to attend to her friend, rushed out of the cottage. Felix darted forward and with supernatural force tore me [i.e., the monster] from his father to whose knees I clung; in a transport of fury he dashed me to the ground and struck me violently with a stick. I could have torn him from limb-to-limb as the lion rends the antelope.

But my heart sank within me as with bitter sickness, and I refrained. I saw him on the point of repeating his blow when overcome with pain and anguish and I quit the cottage and in the general tumult escaped unperceived to my hovel (p. 135).

This scene mirrors the infantile situation of Mary Shelley in many ways—her attempts to get close to her father, and her relationship with her nasty, difficult stepmother who preferred her own children and made Mary's life at home nearly intolerable. Scenes of physical abuse have been described. At this point, the character of Felix could be the carrier of Mary's relationship to the father, but also of the stepmother who came between her and her father. To take another example, Mary lost her mother a few days after childbirth, hence the way she depicts the relation of children to their parents, particularly mothers, will be an important area to study, and one might then trace out certain transformations of her early history. Consider the story of Elizabeth, the daughter of poor peasants, yet different from her brothers and sisters; she had been adopted by peasants following her mother's death in childbirth. At age 17, shortly before Victor is to leave and study at the university. Elizabeth contracts scarlet fever and causes the death of Victor's mother, whose last words are, "I will indulge a hope of meeting you in another world" (p. 43). At this point then, Elizabeth, not Victor, is the cause of the mother's death. Reactions to the grief may represent the author's inner experience, and the manifest content may also suggest that Mary felt responsible for her mother's death. Is it an accident then that Elizabeth dies at the hands of the monster on her wedding night? The moment when the monster kills Elizabeth, might represent Mary's need for punishment. At the time, of course, Mary was living in sin with Shelley, Harriet Shelley still being alive in England.

The monster, or any character in a novel, stands for multiple aspects of the author's psychic life. These aspects shift at different points in the novel. As a final example, the monster's reaction to his creator's death is to mourn guiltily, refer to himself as an abortion, to be scorned and promise to immolate himself. At this point, an identification between Victor's and Mary's mothers may be suspected, with the monster as the carrier of Mary's guilt.

CONCLUSION

The cautious use of certain aspects of psychoanalytic theory may preserve the integrity of a literary text as a text. If one wishes to respect the structure of the work of art, one must not transform it into a case history. To do so would be to lose the very essence of the object of the analysis. It is possible to study some aspects of the process of transformation of the author's inner world into a work of art by paying close attention to the main affective trends and object relations between the characters of the literary work, comparing these to what is known or can be reasonably inferred about the author. The concept of aesthetic distance would allow one to judge the narrator's (or author's) attitude towards the work and could provide one with additional data.

REFERENCES

Alexander, F. (1930). The neurotic character. *International Journal of Psycho-Analysis.* 2:292.

Arlow, J. (1978). Pyromania and the primal scene: a psychoanalytic comment on the work of Yukia Mishima. *Psychoanalytic Quarterly* 47:24–52.

Bennet, H. T. (1980). *The Letters of Mary Wollstonecraft Shelley.* Baltimore, Maryland: John Hopkins University Press.

Florescu, R. (1975). *In Search of Frankenstein.* Boston: New York Graphic Society.

Freud, S. (1907). Delusions and dream in Jensen's *Gradiva. Standard Edition* 9:7–93.

Holmes, R. (1980). Review of the letters of Mary Wollstonecraft Shelley, ed. B. T. Bermet. *New York Times Book Review*, May 18, p. 8.

Ricoeur, P. (1977). The question of proof via Freud's writings. *Journal of the American Psychoanalytic association* 25:833–870.

Rossetti, W. (1911). *The diary of Dr. John William Polidori, 1816.* London: Elkin Matthews.

Shelley, M. (1818). *Frankenstein or the Modern Prometheus.* London: Oxford University Press, 1969.

Some Sources of Conflict within Psychoanalytic Societies

STANLEY E. GREBEN, M.D.

Societies and associations of psychotherapists have special problems that lead to conflict amongst members. The psychoanalytic society is taken as an example. Such societies have had considerable conflict and eruptions since psychoanalysis was first developed. The sources of these disturbances are examined, and suggestions are made for changes that might be helpful in preventing or alleviating some of these conflicts.

Societies of psychotherapists display certain characteristics, including tendencies toward conflict and discontent amongst members. Ideological differences often serve personal intrapsychic competitive strivings. Idealizations of psychoanalysis and of analysts account for much conflict. A two-tier system of "training" and "ordinary" analysts is a major source of difficulty. The autonomy of societies and institutes, with no real responsibility to higher authority, readily encourages a "closed shop" system, with attendant "guild" attitudes. Since this author's experience as a psychoanalyst has been specifically within the psychoanalytic movement, this type of society will be used as a model in order to examine this general area of functioning of psychotherapists.

The material presented comes from the author's experience during psychoanalytic training and practice, as well as from informal discussions with analytic colleagues. These discussions have been highly personal and are attended by very strong feelings. In more recent years the colleagues have included highly competent and experienced psychoanalysts who were prepared to share privately their concern with these matters and, as a result, their concern for organized psychoanalysis. Because of the sources involved, the material warrants the serious attention of psychotherapists, including psychoanalysts.

HISTORICAL BACKGROUND

Throughout the history of psychoanalysis, there have existed very strong conflicts amongst its adherents. In the earliest days, disagreements arose between Freud and some of his first and principal colleagues (Freud 1914). Since then, psychoanalysis has spread as a discipline throughout the world. Today it has organizations at the local, national and international level. This paper is concerned mainly with those conflicts that arise within local societies.

One of the main goals of psychoanalysis is to help those who are analyzed to live more fruitfully and realistically. It might therefore be expected that psychoanalytic societies, made up as they are of members who have all had long psychoanalyses, would be models of harmonious human functioning. Barring that, one might hope to find them relatively conflict-free or capable of readily resolving issues that inevitably arise. In fact, this does not appear to be the case. On the contrary, psychoanalytic societies in general seem to show a relatively high degree of both conflict and strife and a poor capacity to adaptively resolve such strife.

The conflicts are, first, personal, arising out of attitudes of individual members; second, vocational, arising out of stresses imposed by the work itself; third, organizational, having to do with certain characteristics of such societies; and fourth, ideological, having to do with clashes over theoretical matters.

The history of psychoanalysis has always been marked with explosions and eruptions (Glover 1969, Rangell 1974). This paper examines the nature of the conflicts that exist within our societies, studies their sources, and considers possible ways of avoiding or reducing them.

THE SOURCES OF CONFLICT

1. *Unavoidable conflict.* This arises in all human groups, based upon innate aggressiveness, rivalry and acquisitiveness. It may be assumed that there is some irreducible minimum below which humans cannot go and, ipso facto, even the individual psychoanalyses of the group members cannot eliminate or prevent it.
2. *Conflict of a general nature that is psychoneurotic in origin.* This will be less in some psychoanalytic groups and more in others, depending on the individual composition of those societies. Some colleagues point to the presence in certain societies of well-established senior members who, for many years, stand in the way of compromise or change. One colleague related that the same three analysts had "held sway" in his society for two decades, discouraging all attempts to modify the society. Since many of

their colleagues had been either their analysands or their supervisees, they readily intimidated the younger colleagues. Of those who disagreed, some fell silent, some chose to be inactive in society affairs, and some sullenly waited for the authoritarian triumvirate to retire or to die. Clearly in this instance a very large effect was brought about by these few persons, whom the group found it impossible to either dislodge or work around. A more extreme example of this category is the colleague who is not just difficult, but truly emotionally disturbed. A psychoanalyst whose stance was highly suspicious and even paranoid kept one society disturbed over a period of years, according to another colleague. No one found a way to intervene to insist that this man needed to be relieved of responsibility and, indeed, required treatment.

3. *Conflict due to theoretical or ideological differences.* Some such difficulty will presumably always exist as any discipline makes its way between the need to preserve its present position and the need to develop further. This was seen in Freud's early conflicts with his original students and colleagues. It can lead to difficult divisions that are impossible to heal (Fleming 1977). Divisions of societies on the basis of ideological difference continue to occur today.

4. *Conflict due to special demands placed upon the practitioner of psycho-analysis by the nature of the work itself* (Greenson 1954, Greben 1975). This includes (a) long hours of deprivation involved in maintaining a neutral psychoanalytic posture; (b) constant exposure to disturbing material in analysands; (c) idealization of and disillusionment with the analyst on the part of analysands; (d) frustration (for the good of the analysis) of the natural wish to take excessive gratification from analysands (this reaches its zenith with the reality that the analysis must end with the analyst suffering separation from the object to whom he or she has for so long been closely attached); (e) practice in isolation, where the analyst is the authority, so that giving himself or herself over to a group authority is difficult or impossible.

5. *Conflict arising out of how candidates in psychoanalysis come to be selected, and how they are then trained.* This includes the effect of the idealization of the profession by its candidates, as well as the idealization of their analysts. It also includes the disillusionment that in so many instances supervenes.

6. *Conflict resulting from certain features of all or most psychoanalytic societies.* These include (a) that most members have once been the analy-sands of other members, which leads to residual ties, both positive and negative, that continue to influence them; (b) that the analysis of each member has been a "training analysis" (i.e., the analyst has had not just the analytic relationship to the analysand, but another one that can

influence his vocational future), which undoubtedly compromises most, if not all of these analyses; (c) the existence of two "classes" of analysts in the society, those who are training analysts and those who are not; and (d) the attitude that change means being heretical (members are always on guard that the "truth" should not be abandoned or diluted). Since it is very difficult to know what the "truth" is, a very conservative atmosphere develops, and difference is treated with a high degree of suspicion. In this regard psychoanalysis is related to as though it were a religion in which final truth has already been revealed, rather than as a science, where fuller truth is always being sought and skeptical attitudes are encouraged.

Conflict Due to Theoretical or Ideological Differences

The fact that psychoanalytic societies continue to divide and separate suggests that some inherent problem is thereby being expressed. In part such divisions are due to the alliances that are based upon who has been analysed by whom. In part they are the result of unconscious fantasies that resist change.

Candidates share the fantasy that the body of theory in psychoanalysis has been more verified than in fact it has been. All theoretical positions remain basically incomplete. The infantile expectation that the parent knows the truth and will reveal it to the child continues despite analysis. This expectation is encouraged by the conviction with which teachers present theories and formulations as though they were proven and accepted facts. Thus psychoanalysis becomes doctrinaire. The son wants the father to be omniscient and defends the father's faith to bolster himself against his own doubts. Shades of difference assume an importance that they do not deserve.

Some new societies break off because the old society is too "traditional." Some break off for the opposite reason, that is, that too much tradition has been put aside and must be recovered. In each case the theory is treated as holy revelation.

The battle for supremacy between the father and the son may be played out in this way. The father takes all that is in the realm of established theory as his own. The son feels that he can achieve his own separate identity only by a massive break from the father.

Those who disagree about theory may deal with each other with great bitterness. An analyst who considers himself "purely Freudian" dismisses another as "merely Kleinian." Another, hearing a colleague's report of a case condescends to the presentation as "no analysis at all, merely psychotherapy." An experienced analyst gives a long and detailed account of the analysis of a case and is suspiciously asked by a colleague, "But what interpretations did you make to analyse the infantile neurosis?"

Whereas these examples come out as differences in theoretical opinion, behind them lie rivalries and competition for ascendency, which personal psychoanalyses have not prevented. The question of who will know the truth becomes a vehicle for posturing that basically has much more to do with who will have power.

Conflict Arising out of Idealization of the Analyst, the Profession, and the Society

In any psychoanalysis, one of the most difficult challenges faced by the analyst is the tendency to split objects into two portions, one denigrated, the other idealized. In theory, the tendency of the analysand to overvalue should have been well resolved in the long analysis of the candidate who has become a psychoanalyst. Overidealization of the analyst and analysis is a problem in every psychoanalysis (Greenacre 1966, Lampl-de Groot 1976). In the psychoanalysis of candidates the tendency to leave the idealization of the analyst unchallenged is a common shortcoming (Greben 1975).

There is considerable evidence of this continued idealization in psychoanalysts. Admission to membership in the society very often continues to have about it the air of a rite of passage (Arlow 1951, 1970). Members of societies continue to treat their proceedings as so important that great care must be exercised in choosing who may be witness to them. There is caution that candidates should not be present at scientific meetings before they are "really ready." Much sober thought is given to which guests might attend society scientific meetings, requiring that any guest would be highly likely to make a scientific contribution, whereas many of the members themselves do not appear able to make such a contribution.

The following incident concerned a psychiatrist who is internationally accepted as an authority on some aspects of psychoanalytic theory and who has himself been psychoanalyzed, but is not, in fact, a psychoanalyst. A senior analyst, hearing that this person might come to visit the city in question, wondered whether he might be asked to read a paper to the local society. After a moment's thought he asked, "Is he an analyst?" "No," he was told. "Then I don't think there would be much gained by inviting him." In this instance, not only are those who are invested with the psychoanalytic mantle idealized, but reciprocally, those who are not thus invested are automatically underestimated or denigrated. Such thinking rests on the fantasy that the psychoanalyst has reached, simply by virtue of *being* a psychoanalyst, some idealized state that all seek and only a few achieve.

In the training situation, the training analyst starts with the fantasy of his own superiority over his more ordinary analytic brothers. The candidate is accepted for psychoanalysis and is grateful for his acceptance. The majority of candidates have come to psychoanalysis via medicine and psychiatry. In each of these two professions their teachers have carried on the fantasy of the omnipotence of the qualified practitioners. This fantasy is not challenged sufficiently by the training analyst, who covertly feeds upon his idealization by the candidate.

The countertransference of the training analyst makes him see the analysand as a favored child who elects to follow the path of the father. The training analyst should encourage the analysand to question the analyst's omnipotence and to overtake and, in some ways, surpass the father-analyst. Many training analysts do not do this because of the unconscious fantasy of being devalued and destroyed by the son. Instead the analysand is rewarded for compliance, agreement, and admiration.

Both analyst and candidate resist the realization that whereas analysis can accomplish a great deal, there is a very great deal that it cannot accomplish. The analyst tries to manage his envy of the candidate's youth and vigor by keeping himself in the favored position, always ahead. He avoids his own disappointment with how much he is able to achieve through his work by denying its limitations through the continued idealization of the profession.

In reality, not *just* our professional potency, but the society itself, is disappointing; something the new analyst comes to recognize once he has graduated and has been admitted to membership. Van der Leeuw (1968) puts the issue as follows:

> It is my impression that our attitude toward the Society is greatly influenced by our need to idealize. Because we are continually occupied by our patient's unconscious impulses, we wish to have an ideal community life and accordingly expect to find it in our own society. Disappointment is inevitable, and it is difficult not to go to the other extreme and direct our resulting hostile feelings against this very society (p. 163).

At one level we are herein seeing the child's view of the adult world. At a deeper level, the society is seen as the "holy of holies" or the inner sanctum, precisely as the parental bedroom is viewed. Something occurs there that fills the child with fascination and awe.

The problem is not only that this tendency to idealize is insufficiently dealt with in the training analysis, it is compounded by the continued treatment of society and institute matters, by many if not most analysts, as though some secret knowledge or power lay therein.

For example, a psychoanalyst, about 50 years old, had been an energetic enthusiastic society member. He found his colleagues ordinary, but friendly, and was able, in the first ten years of his analytic career, to assimilate gradually the recognition that the analytic society and its members were not special in ways he had once expected. He decided to apply for membership in the institute. He was treated coldly and critically and, although his skills were at least equal to those of the average institute member, he was rejected for unconvincing reasons. He could not accommodate such behavior within the scope of what he saw good analysis to be. He withdrew from the society to his own practice, which he continued to enjoy, but never again participated in any society meetings, business or scientific. He was left permanently disillusioned with the quality of behavior of his colleagues, as well as profoundly angry and hurt. This is not uncommon.

Many psychoanalysts, although not driven as far as a complete divorce from the society, assume a sardonic and cynical view of society matters. One analyst, who is considered sufficiently gifted by his colleagues that they will turn to him for help when a friend or close relative becomes overtly disturbed, rarely if ever attends society meetings. Rather than being bitter, he is philosophical. He feels that the quality of personal interaction is such as to make attendance valueless. Compared to the analyst in the above example, this one is less unhappy about his experiences. In good part this is due to his having had what this author considers a more effective analysis; for the training analyst of this second analyst had, even though the analysand was then a candidate in training, a very balanced and realistic view of the limits of psychoanalysis and psychoanalytic societies. This allowed this candidate to work through his potential idealization and emerge as a more flexible and less vulnerable psychoanalyst.

Conflict Arising out of the Way Candidates for Psychoanalysis Are Selected and Analyzed

Two aspects of the selection of candidates for training must be considered: one that pertains to the candidate and the other that pertains to the institute. The candidates who tend to be selected by institutes appear to display more of certain qualities than are displayed in a random sample of the general educated population. It is not an easy matter to become a psychoanalyst. The career lines of those involved are long and difficult. Much self-denial is required, much single-minded goal-directedness is necessary. The emotional, intellectual, and economic demands are very great. As a consequence, psychoanalytic institutes select from among gifted and ambitious candidates. Very often psychoanalysts have trained themselves to control well or to sublimate their aggressive ambitiousness; but very often they have simply learned to cover it with an air of apparent agreeableness or even passivity. So psychoanalytic societies are composed of energetic, determined, and ambitious people.

In other professions, the same might be said. Yet, strangely, the meetings of these ambitious people, if they are physicians, or if they are engineers, or if they are town planners, are likely to be more open in the expression of what they really think than if they are psychoanalysts. When one attends meetings of the Medical Advisory Council of a general hospital, one finds its members often openly angry or openly derisive, but at any rate tending to say what they think at the time when an issue is being discussed. At a psychoanalytic meeting one is more likely to find an excessive degree of selection and "discretion" in what is said. Without exception, it is only afterwards, in the corridors outside of the meeting room, that the greatest frankness about the members' true opinions is expressed. Somehow the atmosphere of the society militates against such directness as would give full enough expression to the drives and needs of its members.

Psychoanalytic institutes often lean toward potential candidates who are not likely to be challenging. In this way, as well as through the training analysis, which invites the regressive position for so long a period, conformity is rewarded and difference is penalized, at least by many senior training analysts.

This combination is a highly frustrating one. Ambitious energetic people are penalized for just those qualities whose expression would most satisfy them. To complete their analyses and their training, they become more agreeable and compliant. Later, as graduates and as society members, they do not have, when they form a group, good ways of dealing with their frustrated aggressive drives.

Another quality that is found in a very large proportion of candidates, and hence in psychoanalysts, is obsessionality. At a meeting of an institute committee, two hours were spent, at the insistance of one member, in devising a set of rules to cover all aspects of one question related to the selection of candidates. One member leaned over to another and said with cynical chagrin, "A perfect obsessional document."

Societies must, compared to other associations, have a relatively high number of "perfect obsessional documents." However, an even more important problem arises amongst obsessional psychoanalysts. Discussions amongst members are careful, wordy, exacting, dry, and legalistic. A need to protect oneself is so apparent that it becomes palpably an air of mistrust. Were societies comprised of emotional, hysterical members other problems would exist. By and large, it is the problems that groups of obsessionals have in working together that tend to trouble or even plague psychoanalytic societies.

An eminent psychoanalyst of international reputation was invited to spend a half hour at an annual meeting responding to questions of members about his work. The format was intended to be a free exchange, and he was asked to make only a few introductory remarks and then have open discussion with the colleagues in the audience. Despite several insistent reminders from the arrangements chairman, he brought "introductory" notes that took 25 minutes of the allotted time.

The problem of this characterological tendency becomes increased in the candidates' training analyses and in their subsequent work as analysts. Obsessional analysts serve as models for obsessional candidates. The inherent message in "generations" of transactions is that the intellect is to be prized and that emotions are to be studied and suspected. This attitude seems to run as a main thread through much psychoanalytic work.

The limits of what psychoanalytic therapy can achieve have been a consistent concern (Freud 1937, Wilson 1971, Guntrip 1975), but perhaps we still expect too much of the analysis of our members who, despite years of intense analytic treatment, still exhibit a disappointingly large residuum of pathology displayed through rigid self-interest and self-service. The manifestations of this narcissistic residuum are well evidenced in the conflicts within a psychoanalytic society.

We must ask ourselves whether this is typical of all analyses, or whether, indeed, society members are at a marked disadvantage as to the quality of their personal training analyses. There is reason to think that the latter may, to some degree, be the case. The candidate knows that his analyst has a connection with his vocational future. Some analysts attempt to minimize this effect through a nonreporting posture, and this represents some protection. Nevertheless, the analysis is limited to some degree by the training connection. A fuller and more satisfactory outcome would arise were the analysis seen as entirely therapeutic.

A significant number of psychoanalysts, once they are graduated and have been admitted as members of a society, later resume personal psychoanalysis. In this author's experience, such analysts usually choose a different psychoanalyst from their former training analyst. When one colleague was asked why he had taken such a course, he replied, "I learned early on that there was a great deal I was not going to accomplish with him. However, my training was at stake, and I decided to get through it as quickly as I could. But now I've picked someone I can be more open with, and I'm getting a great deal more out of it."

Even short of conflict amongst members of psychoanalytic societies, it appears as though true closeness or friendship does not occur in the majority of instances among analytic colleagues. Van der Leeuw (1968) observes, ". . . I have the impression that there are few true friendships amongst our members. Only now and then do our inter-relationships develop into real friendships" (p. 163).

Rivalries of an intense nature govern this observed phenomenon. The majority of analysts make their friends among those whose work is different, and where comparisons and rivalries are less intense. Also, many analytic colleagues appear to start out as friends, but the painful and powerful struggles and divisions that characterize their societies often lead to broken friendships. The feelings aroused in analysts about their work are sufficiently strong to destroy what had up until then appeared to be true friendships.

A part of this phenomenon appears related to the lines of cleavage that exist in societies based upon who has analyzed whom. There are two principal directions in which unresolved transference and countertransference feelings may show themselves. A former analyst and analysand may always side together on issues, deferring to one another and supporting one another. Here the mutual dependency that was developed in the analysis is insufficiently resolved. Or the two may always appear on opposite sides of any issue—the former analysand may still be acting out of his need to break free of his analyst's influence. The former analyst may still be demonstrating that he is the powerful and all-knowing one. The newer analyst may remain convinced that his former analyst needs to keep him a child. The older analyst may continue to see his former analysand as a rebellious upstart who refuses to give him the credit due to him and threatens to take away his hard won advantages. Too often it appears that these residual transference and countertransference issues remain unresolved over many years of society inter-relationships. In the training analyses rivalrous and deeply critical feelings were left unexplored because their exploration would have put the candidate's vocational future too much at risk.

Conflict Arising out of the Existence of Two "Classes" of Psychoanalysts

The task of training new members for the profession of psychoanalysis is traditionally assigned by a psychoanalytic society to its psychoanalytic institute. Some members of the society then have to become members of the institute—i.e., training analysts. Of the three functions that are part of training (analysis of candidates, supervision, and teaching), the first is the most important, and the most painful feelings develop from it. It is a good principle to try to provide the most effective analysts available for candidates. Unfortunately, no successful means has been found of selecting such analysts. When the selection is made by those who are already training analysts, a closed self-serving system develops. Rivalries and envious self-protectiveness become all too apparent. Choices are rationalized, but make no sense to those on the outside. Some institutes require a paper to be read and voted upon. The skills needed to write a paper are not those required to conduct a good psychoanalysis. When the voting is widened from the members of the institute to all members of the society, this is one step better, as it eliminates the "closed shop" phenomenon; but still one is left with the strong feeling that choices are made on purely personal grounds, and most members remain unconvinced that a rational system of selection has been utilized.

There is no way to conduct a rational evaluation of "ability to conduct a good psychoanalysis." In some societies, members who were rejected felt terribly humiliated because of the basic inequity of the system of choosing. Favoring of friends, protecting economic interests, and acting out of omnipotent fantasies all enter into the choosing. Many authors have pointed out the damage that is done to societies by the existence of this two-tier system of analysts (e.g., Arlow 1972, Van der Leeuw 1970). In the view of McLaughlin (1978), "The question of who is to teach and train, in the broadest sense, always has been the primary source of tension and friction in the analytic community. The damage done by these conflicts is impossible to assess, but it has been considerable" (p. 8).

Of the three functions involved in training, the most important is the personal analysis. It is also the function that every analyst probably feels he is most capable of performing. There is no way of fairly and objectively measuring analytic capacity and performance that would allow us to differentiate two groups of psychoanalysts in terms of such abilities. It has already been brought out that, for the needs of the candidate's analysis itself, it is best to have the personal analysis as divorced as possible from the educational business of the institute. For the good of psychoanalytic societies, a two-tier, hierarchical system should be abandoned. Any psychoanalyst who is certified as a member in good standing of the society (i.e., whom is felt to be able to analyze members of the public), should, after achieving some minimal period of experience as an analyst, be able to analyze candidates. The choice of analyst would be made by the candidate from among these experienced analysts. Of course, candidates are in a better position to make some critical judgment about potential analysts than are most members of the public, since they inevitably make use of their own private grapevine in deciding on the choice of their analyst. As for the necessary experience, this author suggests that it should be a minimum of five years of analytic experience following graduation, with analytic work filling at least half of the analyst's time.

This is a rather simple proposal, but it would have very important effects. The Royal College of Physicians and Surgeons of Canada accredits any medical practitioner to be a specialist. (Psychiatry is one of those specialties.) From its inception, the College had maintained two levels of accreditation. One examination led to a Certificate, which was the ordinary level of specialization. Another more demanding examination led to Fellowship, which was needed, for example, for certain hospital or teaching posts. The same sense of hierarchy existed among the specialists. After much consideration the College decided to abandon the system and award all specialists the Certificate upon graduation. Any such specialists could then, by simply applying for it, be given the Fellowship. At the time of the proposal, great fears were expressed that the standard of specialist competency would drop drastically, but the change was made. To this author's knowledge no problem has resulted. Certainly, the matter is rarely if ever discussed, and the sense of a discriminatory differentiation among medical specialists has disappeared.

The most destructive effect of the two-tier system occurs in the minds of members, who recognize its irrational aspects. Keiser (1972) points out how the prestigious implications of the title of training analyst work against a free academic environment. The most destructive aspect of the system is that all concerned recognize how such designations cannot be made in fair and rational ways. This then erodes the confidence of members in the integrity of the society and brings feelings of helpless disillusionment with the society and with one's fellow members.

There is another ill effect of confining the analysis of candidates to a limited number of training analysts. This situation means that a smaller, rather than a larger number of analysts has analyzed the members of the society. If one senior analyst is conservative and even rigid in his views, this is passed on to many members of the society. Numerous authors have written about the place of neutrality in psychoanalysis (e.g., De la Torre 1977, Dorpat 1977) and how some analysts have extrapolated that neutrality far beyond what is optimal, even to the point of being unnecessarily depriving of analysands (Greben and Lesser 1976). Societies have often faced the problem in which the analysis of many of their members by constricted and excessively depriving analysts has led to many members who, deprived in their own analyses, have discontent among one another as one unavoidable end product.

Thus another reason for enlarging the number of analysts who may train candidates is to avoid the situation in which a few training analysts have analyzed a large number of the societies' members. Greater variation in personal analytic experience is more likely to lead to a capacity for change and freedom in members, rather than in a stereotype that carries on for "generations" of analysts.

Conflict Due to the Nature of the Psychoanalytic Work Itself

Psychoanalysts are members of a profession that uniquely studies the effects that the work has upon themselves. Working long hours, alone with patients, the analyst has pressures upon him that are regressive in nature. He is constantly confronted with primitive material in the patient's productions and in his own. He is alternately idealized and denigrated by analysands. He is deprived of a natural balance between listening and talking, giving and taking, being passive and active. In its overall effect, psychoanalytic practice is both very rewarding and very depriving. That deprivation makes many of its practitioners draw back, be nonparticipants, and not develop the skills and capacity to compromise necessary for functioning as a member of a group.

A. Freud, on this point, has said, "An analyst who practises in isolation runs the risk of becoming depressed, which is bad, or omnipotent, which is worse" (Davie 1970). There is no simple solution to this problem, since doing good analytic work requires being exposed to these deprivations. Greenson (1954) points to the necessity for analysts to provide outside their working hours for those emotional needs that are neglected during the course of the work.

It would probably be best if most analysts did some work other than psychoanalysis during part of their week. This view is of course controversial, for many analysts hold the opposite view, namely that in order to be the most competent in this work one needs to devote oneself full-time to it for years. Very few colleagues who have done so have flourished either personally or as society members, however. On the contrary, those members who only did analytic work seemed in society work to be the most unyielding in their views. Some might see this as a strength, but this author sees it as a deficiency.

A number of psychoanalysts who, later in their careers, changed from full-time practice to part-time practice, adding hospital or university duties to their analytic work, have changed both their personal attitudes and their capacity to work with others. This is the not surprising result of a more balanced and hence less depriving professional life.

Conflict Arising out of the Organization of the Psychoanalytic Society

In most academic or professional organizations, as one goes higher in the organization, there is a further authority to whom one is responsible. A good example of this is a university, where faculty are responsible to chairmen of departments, who in turn answer to the deans, who report to a president who is responsible to a board of governors, and so on. An opposite model exists in fraternal organizations or private clubs, where members create a situation in which they are responsible only to themselves. The former, or open system, functions quite differently from the latter, or closed system. The closed system encourages the fantasies of specialness of its members. The myth of superiority is fostered in the minds of those who are within the charmed circle. Those outside, confronted with the irrationality of the rites of admission, feel impotent rage.

Despite the supposed responsibility that the local psychoanalytic society has to its national and international associations, it usually functions as responsible only to itself. Even more serious, an institute often becomes entirely autonomous, answering to no senior agency that might have some influence on its decisions, and keeps to itself, as do private clubs, the power to decide who will join it in membership.

To correct this latter problem, the institute must not be autonomous unto itself. It would be best to have the institute, if it exists at all, be the administrative vehicle whereby the society, the senior and umbrella organization, discharges its training and educational responsibilities. If the institute were indeed only the educational committee of the society, with no autonomy of its own, then many of our current problems would be avoided.

As for the society itself, the organizational problem is more difficult to solve. Attempts to make psychoanalytic societies responsible units within universities have had limited success. This may be, in part, because of the specific personalities of those who have thus far attempted these arrangements. It may also be that because analysts are used to having autonomous societies, the idea appears too constrictive to them, and they fear that they will lose too many degrees of freedom of choice. In the end it appears best that psychoanalytic societies become part of accredited institutions of higher learning. Otherwise, they run the risk of continuing to be guilds rather than academic associations. It is the guild atmosphere that has led to the academic poverty and lack of creativity of most psychoanalytic societies.

Several years ago the society of which this author was a member was struggling with a problem of organization. This author telephoned a colleague in a large American city that has an eminent society and institute. He is a senior academic psychiatrist and psychoanalyst who writes broadly on psychoanalytic matters. When asked what the current approach was in his society, he replied to my surprise that he didn't know. "I have no idea what they are up to," he said. "I gave up on them years ago. I practice psychoanalysis with pleasure. I write about what interests me. I get my academic and intellectual stimulation in the hospital and the university."

Such disillusionment is not at all uncommon. The loss of such people to organized psychoanalysis is a great loss. Changes must be made in how societies function if our best people are to choose to remain connected to organized psychoanalytic effort.

RECOMMENDATIONS

Some of the sources of conflict within psychoanalytic societies have been presented. It is proposed that improvement could come about by following some or all of the following suggestions:

1. The designated status of training analyst should disappear. The analysis of candidates should be entirely personal and removed from the educational process. Such analysis could be undertaken with any member of the society who has had five years experience (at least half-time) since graduation. (In some localities, the limitations on the number of psychoanalytic patients available may require a reduction in the optimal half-time requirement.) There should be no contact between personal analyst and the institute, except perhaps to confirm that the analysis has occurred and to report its frequency.

2. The analytic society should be the only autonomous organization. If the institute continues to be designated as such, it should simply be the educational committee of the society and responsible to it. The institute should in no way be autonomous.

3. The function of supervision should be open to all these same experienced analysts. Other teaching should be done by any appropriate analyst. As in any educational institutions, selection of teaching and supervising personnel would be undertaken by chairmen appointed to be responsible for the educational task.

4. More psychoanalytic societies should explore the possibility of affiliation with universities, probably in the form of multidisciplinary departments responsible to the university rather than the faculty of Medicine. This would provide an administrative line of responsibility that would diminish the omnipotent sense of total responsibility that many societies have had. A greater measure of academic expectation of members is needed, accentuating the professional rather than the guild side of the organization. (Some professional organizations—for example, medical associations— have achieved a degree of autonomous function without becoming as mired down with conflict as have psychoanalytic societies. It may be that the other suggestions, if implemented, would lead to a workable result without the implementation of this one.)

5. Discussion should be provided for and encouraged both among society members and candidates about the covert tendency toward idealization of psychoanalysis and of its practitioners. This should take place in seminars that would be part of the society's scientific program, as well as in the teaching of seminars of candidates. Members should be made aware of the necessity of dealing with this idealization in the analysis of candidates.

6. Selection committees for candidates should be careful to avoid selecting out challenging and intellectually critical potential candidates.

7. Society meetings and proceedings should be, as much as possible, open to others. Members should make a conscious effort to avoid the mystification of analytic societies, seeing them more as meeting places of academically oriented professionals and practitioners, rather than as inner sancta where special mysteries occur and awesome special knowledge exists.

8. In scientific meetings, younger members should be encouraged to speak critically and constructively, rather than to feel that deviation is heresy. A more openly challenging attitude toward psychoanalytic theory needs to be fostered.

9. New psychoanalysts should be encouraged to consider varied careers, rather than exclusively psychoanalytic ones. Those who pursue only psychoanalytic work should be made aware of the literature that discusses the need to provide, outside of the consulting room, gratifications that the analyst needs but cannot derive from psychoanalytic practice.

Psychoanalytic societies fill several important roles for their members (Waelder 1955), but much of their potential value is lost through the conflicts that have been described. Psychoanalysts must give serious consideration to making essential changes within their societies if those organizations are to be satisfying rather than frustrating ones, meeting the needs of members, rather than creating more problems in themselves.

REFERENCES

Arlow, J. A. (1951). A psychoanalytic study of a religious rite: bar mitzvah. *Psychoanalytic Study of the Child* 6:353–374.

———. (1970). *Group Psychology and the Study of Institutes.* Chairman's Report, Board of Professional Standards, Annual Meeting. American Psychiatric Association, San Francisco.

———. (1972). Some dilemmas in psychoanalytic education. *Journal of the American Psychoanalytic Association* 20:556–566.

Davie, J. M. (1970). Personal communication.

De la Torre, J. (1977). Psychoanalytic neutrality: an overview. *Bulletin of the Menninger Clinic* 41:366–384.

Dorpat, T. L. (1977). On neutrality. *International Journal of Psychoanalytic Psychotherapy* 6:39–64.

Fleming, J. (Chairman). (1977). Report of the Ad Hoc Committee for Los Angeles in Bulletin of the American Psychoanalytic Association. *Journal of the American Psychoanalytic Association* 25:498–502.

Freud, S. (1914). On the history of the psycho-analytic movement. *Standard Edition* 14:7–66.

———. (1937). Analysis terminable and interminable. *Standard Edition* 23:211–253.

Glover, E. (1969). In praise of ourselves. *International Journal of Psycho-Analyses* 50:499–502.

Greben, S. E. (1975). Some difficulties and satisfactions inherent in the practice of psychoanalysis. *International Journal of Psycho-Analysis* 56:427-434.

Greben, S. E., and Lesser, S. R. (1976). The question of neutrality in psychotherapy. *American Journal of Psychotherapy* 30:623–630.

Greenacre, P. (1966). Problems of overidealization of the analyst and of analysis: their manifestations in the transference and countertransference relationship. *Psychoanalytic Study of the Child* 21:193–212.

Greenson, R. R. (1966). That "impossible"profession. *Journal of the American Psychoanalytic Association* 14:9–27.

Guntrip, H. (1975). My experience of analysis with Fairbairn and Winnicott (how complete a result does psychoanalytic therapy achieve?). *International Review of Psychoanalysis* 2:145–156.

Keiser, S. (1972). Report to the board on professional standards. *Journal of the American Psychoanalytic Association* 20:518–539.

Lampl-de Groot, J. (1976). Personal experience with psychoanalytic technique and theory during the last half century. *Psychoanalytic Study of the Child* 31:283–296.

McLaughlin, F. (1978). Some perspectives on psychoanalysis today. *Journal of the American Psychoanalytic Association* 26:3–20.

Rangell, L. (1974). A psychoanalytic perspective leading currently to the syndrome of the compromise of integrity. *International Journal of Psycho-Analysis* 55:3–12.

Van der Leeuw, P. J. (1968). The psycho-analytic society. Presidential Address, 25th International Psycho-Analytical Congress. *International Journal of Psycho-Analysis* 49:160–164.

———. (1970). Four years' presidency: a personal view. *International Journal of Psycho-Analysis* 51:49–54.

Waelder, R. (1955). The function and the pitfalls of psychoanalytic societies. *Bulletin of the Philadelphia Association for Psychoanalysis* 5:1–8.

Wilson, C. P. (1971). On the limits of the effectiveness of psychoanalysis: early ego and somatic disturbances. *Journal of the American Psychoanalytic Association* 19:552–564.

Psychoanalytic Societies and Their Discontents

JOHN KLAUBER, B.M. B.Ch. Oxon., F.B.P.S., F.R.C. Psych.

A discussion of Dr. Greben's courageous paper on the discontents that undoubtedly exist in psycho-analytical societies. Conflict has always been inevitable owing to the imprecise nature of the work, but with the degree of diffusion of style and doctrine that exists today it seems even more so. Frances Gitelson's study of the actual history of splits in psycho-analytical societies emphasizes the personal factor of the leaders, as groups organize round a charismatic personality; but these personalities can surely only crystallize something in the needs of the led. These include a revolt against the conservatism that an inevitably lengthy training and the consequent hierarchical structure of psychoanalytical societies seem unavoidably to induce. Dr. Greben is bitter at the intensity of political infighting, but ideas are important to people and psychoanalysis does not transform human nature. It is inevitable that psychoanalysts use political means to try to implement their ideas. The attempt to liberalize psychoanalysis also has its dangers, as training procedures sometimes degenerate into superficiality. The history of the British Society shows that originality has been allowed to flourish in analysts who have first displayed their basic competence.

Dr. Greben tackles an important subject with courage. The only suspicion of an understandable funk comes at the beginning when he starts to talk about psychotherapeutic societies, though these are not in his title. I know little about such societies, and think that in many cases their problems cannot be identical. For the most part, however, the conflicts that Dr. Greben describes are easily discernable in psychoanalytical societies and strongly merit discussion.

This is especially so today when the identity of the psychoanalyst world-wide is so diffuse. Few psychoanalysts are full-time psychoanalysts. In Europe it has been estimated that more than 70 per cent are also engaged in other work. Considering the admixture of psychotherapy in most psycho-analysts' private practice, this is probably an underestimate. And regional differences of style in psychoanalysis are immense. How differently analysts set about their task in the United States, in South America, in England, and in France!

It was for such reasons that the International Psychoanalytical Association held a small conference on the identity of the psychoanalyst in 1976. Its proceedings have so far been published only in French (*L'identité du psychoanalyste* Presses Universitaires de France 1979). This is unfortunate, as they contain an experienced discussion by Frances Gitelson (formerly Secretary of the IPA) of the subject that concerns Dr. Greben in its most acute form: an analysis of the causes of splits in psychoanalytical societies as she has understood them.

Dr. Greben does not seem to know this work, but one of Gitelson's conclusions is somewhat similar to his. Rival groups organize themselves around personalities who always possess qualities of leadership and may possess charisma. They are often characterized by unanalysed residues of pathological narcissism that prevent them from reaching constructive compromises. Ideology is not the prime cause of the split. She thinks, in fact, as Oliver Cromwell did of the Civil War in England: "Religion was not at first the thing contended for, but God brought it to that in the end."

Dr. Greben expresses disappointment at the ineffectiveness of analysis to enable analysts to live at peace in analytical societies. Neither Greben nor Gitelson is wholly convincing in this respect. To take Gitelson first, it seems a mistake to overvalue the person of a leader: Leaders come to prominence because they catalyze and express the needs of the led; the revolt against conservatism, whatever other meanings it may have, being one of them. Of course, it usually takes a good quotient of narcissism in the personality to become a leader. In politics, indeed, it often seems as though only pathological narcissism verging on insanity could prompt a man or woman to believe so strongly in his or her power to influence events; but the pathology, which is the other pole of leadership, is something other than the reasons for the direction that the leadership takes.

This brings us back to Dr. Greben's arguments: Psychoanalysis aims at personal development, but it does not seek to alter human nature—there he expects too much of it. People believe in their ideas, and political in-fighting is bound to occur as groups of psychoanalysts seek to extend the influence of their ideas by gaining control of key positions in an institute. Dr. Greben rightly draws attention to the difficulties of the psychoanalytic life, but if so many analysts are disillusioned with psychoanalysis something must have gone wrong with their training.

Dr. Greben points to the failure of some training analysts to tackle the idealized transference, so that their candidates float into the analytical profession on a wave of omnipotent fantasy. He is also obviously correct in his emphasis on the effect of transference and hierarchy in maintaining conservatism. However, his description of the way in which "conformity is rewarded and difference is penalized" is grimmer than is warranted in this author's experience of his own society. Perhaps this experience has been happier because it is one that managed to compromise instead of splitting. One can certainly visualize being very unhappy in some psychoanalytical societies, but originality has always been welcomed in those psychoanalysts who have first demonstrated their competence in understanding basic principles and technique: after all, the British Society has successfully tolerated such intellectual individualists as Ernest Jones, Melanie Klein, Ella Sharpe, Clifford Scott, W. R. D. Fairbairn, and Wilfred Bion. (Of course, it took a long time to recognize some of them, but arousing resistance often goes hand in hand with originality in any sphere.)

Dr. Greben has clearly been brave enough to say what he thinks in fundamental matters in spite of the resistance he knows he will stimulate. He approaches his critical task constructively, ending with a number of recommendations, not all of which will fundamentally alter the situation, not all of which are practicable, and with not all of which one can agree. He has gone to some of the roots of our difficulties and emphasized the central role of struggles over training and the consequences of the division of psychoanalytical societies into an elite of training analysts and an enraged remainder. There is a great deal in his criticisms, but the picture of a psychoanalytical society that he paints is too depressing. Furthermore, he fails to acknowledge that to become a psychoanalyst takes a lot longer than five years of half-time practice.

There is of course the view, said to be supported by some distinguished analysts, that anyone can be a training analyst, even a student. The important thing in this view seems to be the stimulation of the analytic process and not the internalization of a technique that may be oppressive. And there is the other point that to expect even as much as half-time psychoanalytic practice may in many societies be idealistic. To open the field of training analysts would certainly enable societies to increase the entry of candidates, but it remains to be established that those countries that have relatively inexperienced training analysts and a large student entry are improving the standard of psychoanalysis. It is difficult enough to train students under any part-time system—to refer to Dr. Greben's suggestion, not easy to implement satisfactorily, of links with Universities—but to use analysts who are still struggling to master the technique (or should be) is a doubtful remedy. Theory, philosophy, and applied analysis may flourish, sometimes with some new ideas; but the standard of clinical psychoanalysis often tends to be superficial.

Dr. Greben's remark about the qualities required in a psychoanalyst reinforces the feeling that we may not see eye to eye on one fundamental question of training (perhaps the question that lies behind many of the splits): "The skills needed to write a paper are not those required to conduct a good psychoanalysis." There are certainly many good psychoanalysts with writing inhibitions, but the skills involved in the conceptualization of a paper are also highly important for doing good psychoanalysis.

The Training Analyst Concept:
A Superego Problem

Z. ALEXANDER AARONS, M.D.

The concept of "training analyst" is a controversial issue, with those colleagues who are training analysts arguing for its legitimate place in psychoanalysis, and colleagues who are not training analysts more likely to question the concept. This paper discusses the issue solely on its merits, for to take sides on the basis of "vested interests" is not a scientific approach.

Training analysts are appointed by constituent institutes for their training jurisdiction, with such appointments seldom, if ever, rejected by the Board of Professional Standards of the American Psychoanalytic Association. Even though standards are set by the board, it must ultimately rely upon what information is supplied to it by the educational committee of the institute recommending appointment. This procedure would seem practical enough if it were not for the uneven development among institutes and the arbitrary and judgmental attitudes that prevail in educational committees. Once ensconced in the position, one becomes entrenched in it (even though it is renewable). In short, educational committees perpetuate themselves. On the basis of expediency, to promote and facilitate analytic training, a selection is made from the given group of qualified analysts. The implication is that those selected are the "better" analysts. Many of them, however, might not be selected by older and "mature" institutes. In the final analysis, "qualifications" may be minimal, relative, and arbitrary. It is simplistic to argue that the faculty position an appointment entails is a *task* to be performed for training purposes. It is a position that carries with it the connotation of "superiority."

To what extent respect may be largely made up of fear is a question asked in relationships in which authority and decision-making are vested in some and withheld from others; but this mitigates against the establishment of peer relationships. The deference accorded the training analyst may or may not be warranted; the position he occupies, nevertheless, commands it. The distinction between being authoritative and authoritarian is often blurred. It is agreed that in any field of scientific and professional endeavor the position of authority should be in the hands of those who are authoritative, but it all too often happens that one occupying a position of power and prestige is more authoritarian than authoritative, and by virtue of being the former succumbs to the delusion of thinking of oneself as being the latter. The protection that some may have against being taken in by such a delusion is a well-developed critical faculty together with the courage of one's convictions. Less experienced analysts, especially students, find themselves in a milieu in which awe and reverence (attendant with a degree of unconscious ambivalence) are displaced onto training analysts; fulfilling, as they do, parental roles of acceptance or rejection. This state of affairs is a hangover from the period of candidacy, turning "fratricidal" among colleagues competing for the achievement of training analyst status. At first (among candidates), it is expressed by a belief in the myth of infallibility of one's training analyst, then, among colleagues, to the competition (among the brothers) for succession to the hierarchy.

Ultimately we may question whether "official recognition" of authority is necessary. Sooner or later it will carry itself by its own weight. Freud's creativity is ample testimony to this. The motivation underlying the need for recognition should be subjected to scrutiny in one's own analysis. It is not enough to leave it as a benign and natural wish to be acknowledged for one's work and contribution. From Freud's biography we may remember when, during his early days in Charcot's clinic, he complained of being disregarded by his colleagues. His remark in a letter to his fiancée was that although he did not find himself "ambitious," he felt that his work should be "acknowledged." Also in point is the recent issue of official status in the American Psychoanalytic Association for qualified lay analysts in supervising and training positions at constituent institutes. Aside from the broader issue of medical versus lay analysis, the intrinsic necessity for any "special" or "official" recognition for these colleagues was questioned by some members.

It may be argued that their authoritative position would remain the same regardless of how they may be categorized within or related to the Association. The work and reputation of the Waelders and Eriksons as active lay members, the Krises and Bornsteins as guest participants, or the Loewensteins, Hartmanns and Lewins as active medical members (to reach for a sampling in each category) has not depended upon their designations. Although these were among the original colleagues in the heyday of psychoanalysis of the forties and fifties, their authoritative position in the elucidation and development of psychoanalysis was not connected, except incidentally, with the training positions they held. Is it the case that after retirement or demise of the fathers, the sons, too eager to wear the crown (Henry IV, Part 2) are not as authoritative as the masters were, and consequently place primary emphasis upon obtaining a status position—the trappings in lieu of the substance?

With an increase in the number of psychoanalysts and institutes, a degree of mediocrity is creeping upon us. This may be inevitable, carrying with it arbitrary and exclusive rules and regulations for acceptance for training, formalization of meetings and promotion of "public relationship." Analytically, it may be argued that these conditions are the "realities" to which one must adapt. Some may contend, however, that efforts should be bent in the direction of making the kind of reality that facilitates analytic expansion in all its scientific aspects. A decade or two earlier more analysts were known to each other, as were the creative and expository thinkers among us. Now that geographic penetrations are sought for psychoanalysis, like the screening and testing in candidate selection, sponsoring institutes often require further scrutiny and review for prospective training analysts, rationalized as a safeguard for standards, but which often subordinates freedom to pursue analytic work to procedural requirements. Sometimes it seems that in concern over selection the individual is sacrificed for the rule; clinical evaluation and the discovery of motivation cease to be paramount factors. The best of rules and procedures may be a defensive screen for the justification of prejudices by offering a semblance of objectivity.

Institutes are "spotty," although there is a formal declaration of adherence to basic principles, placing emphasis upon the internal psychic state of the individual, the role of conflict, repression, defense and the unconscious, as well as adaptational reactions; nonetheless, there is much aberrance. Training analysts cultivate coteries of "followers," inevitably so, because the transference, no matter how well the infantile neurosis may have been resolved, leaves a sequela of an affiliation bias favoring adherence to one's analyst in which what is accepted as authoritative in psychoanalytic development becomes so by virtue of the authoritarian role invested in the training analyst. If he does speak and write authoritatively, well and good, but an outside reviewer might see it the other way around; the bias due to the libidinal investment creates the authority, whether he is authoritative or authoritarian. Sophisticated as it may appear, there is, to put it bluntly, a blind following of training analysts (seen most clearly at institutes in the "provinces") who have attained positions of leadership and thereby perpetuate their authority status, which can be done, seemingly impersonally, through the educational committee, appointing training analysts who carry on the rule of an entrenched hierarchy. This criticism may appear fraught with animosity, and to an extent it is. Perhaps it would be better to say that there is discontent engendered in competition for the position of training analyst, which has become a status symbol of achievement among us; and being regarded as such, it is divisive.

There has been much discussion in our literature of the proper role and function of the training analyst toward his student-candidate analysand in regard to evaluating and reporting, and of the complications that may be introduced as a result of the training analyst's dual role—his relationship to institute and analysand. Specious identifications often arise in the training analyst–analysand relationship, and other complicating factors engender resistance and surreptitiously defy analytic penetration. Relatively little has been written in regard to the necessity for the training analyst position as such and, if it is necessary and valid as a psychoanalytic institution, what the *desiderata* in selection are. Factors operative in a training analyst appointment seem to parallel many of the considerations and factors that enter into the selection and evaluation of candidates. Whether, in the application of criteria, "objectivity" or arbitrariness prevails in either selection process is a serious question. McLaughlin (1974) ties the two together in his concluding comments on Shapiro's (1974) paper (reporting a Columbia Institute survey indicating a "symptomatic" reaction that makes it mandatory to investigate the "status" of training analyst):

> For better or worse in most of our analytic groups the status of training analyst has become the ultimate symbol of recognition of professional worth. This evidences itself in the striving for this position, the anger and the depression which so often follow the realization that one is not going to be successful in this quest, and the tensions which arise in societies and institutes between those who "belong" and those who do not.

Limentani (1974) specifically questions the role of the training analyst and its attendant analytic problems. It is interesting to note that, in the discussions of his paper at the Fifth Pre-Congress Meeting on Training (28th International Congress), it was agreed that the main point should be the "difficulties in the training analysis," seemingly to avoid or relegate to a secondary consideration the point inherent in Limentani's paper—the validity of the training analyst concept. Pfeffer (1974) did, however, squarely raise the issue in his summary.

Bearing in mind, then, that the *raison d'etre* of the training analyst concept and function should be subjected to scrutiny, several issues raised or implied in the discussion at the pre-congress meeting are pertinent to our subject. Limentani is of the opinion that "the differences and similarities between therapeutic and training analyses . . . are considerable in number and quality" (p. 72), but indicates that this issue would require a separate paper and discussion. In this author's opinion, it should have been given preference because of the increasing discontent over selection and the animosities engendered among our colleagues. Of the three parts of analytic training (personal analysis, supervision, and seminars), the student's personal analysis is of first importance, not only for the resolution of neurosis, but for heightening the awareness of problems when they arise. Being aware of one's problems has a parallel in the physical sciences of knowing what questions to ask in clearing the path to an answer. By knowing himself, the analyst is empathic, aware of countertransference reactions, and alert to the nuances of transference manifestations in his patients. This shorthand formula applies to the requisite ability to analyze and must obtain in every analyst-analysand relationship, whether the analyst is or is not a training analyst, and whether the analysand is or is not an institute student. In other words, there is no intrinsic difference between a therapeutic analysis and a so-called training analysis. As Stone (1975) stated:

. . . any colleague of some experience knows that the latter's distinction from therapy is fictive. It is usually a prolonged therapeutic analysis in which the professional aspiration is a special and complicating condition (p. 353).

Perhaps the neutral term should be the "personal" analysis, which would not prematurely commit the analyst to an assessment of the analysand's therapeutic potential. The proper question is that of analyzability. An analysis is an analysis or it isn't; or we may speak of whether an analysis is successful. We cannot contend that a training analysis is or should be more thorough than a nontraining analysis. This is one of the questions dealt with by Freud (1937), who showed that qualitative as well as other analyzability factors enter every terminable analysis. In the present context, "more or less analysis" is meaningless. (There is a distinction between having found out more about oneself and having been analyzed.) Is the analysand analyzable or not, and can the analyst analyze him if he is analyzable? When it comes down to this formulation, what difference is permissible between a training and a nontraining analyst? What makes sense is whether the analyst is a "qualified" analyst, and this must be defined by unprejudiced empirical evaluation. The term "qualified" may be reserved to distinguish an experienced analyst from a student learning to become an analyst or a recent graduate. From these discursive remarks, one may conclude that if there are nonanalysts, student and recent graduate analysts, and qualified analysts, there is no need for a category of "training analysts."

Sometimes one hears the argument that it is more difficult to analyze candidates because they present "characterological" problems, whereas noncandidates have plain neuroses, psychoses, or various mixtures of the two. A corollary of this argument is that character problems, in order to be ferreted out, require a training analyst. Such an argument is empirically nonsensical, i.e., no such dichotomy exists. Suffice it to recall Ernst Kris' remark at one of the founding sessions of the Kris Study Group that it is an illusion to think that there are any easy analytic cases; all are fraught with resistances, and the analyst must learn how to overcome them.

Limentani asks:

> Are we justified in perpetuating the existence of an elite called "training analysts" or would it help if we were to regard the term quite simply as a title or label of quality? An aspirant analyst would not necessarily choose the holder of such a title for his personal analysis (p. 72).

In reply we might pose two questions: Why shouldn't a candidate choose for his analyst one of "quality" (whatever the term means)? The important question, however, is: what need motivates an analyst to seek "a title or label," or why must a qualified analyst (analyst of "quality"?) be dubbed with a title? More seriously, to speak of an analyst of "quality" implies that there are analysts devoid of quality, and one may suspect that this is the main contention. By the same token, then, this must as well apply to training analysts. Moreover, who is to make this evaluation, and would it not in any event, positive or negative, be subjective and judgmental? The answer may be that no one person or group should in all good conscience take upon itself the prerogative of selecting training analysts. This has nothing to do with an educational committee overseeing that standards are maintained.

The issue, however, is moot if we hold that the category of training analyst is unnecessary. If standards for qualification are not minimal, but maximal, then all analysts are (or should become) qualified. To have to further qualify some analysts as of "training" caliber may superficially seem reasonable. Inequality in endowment and skill is a reality, but let us not fall prey to specious reasoning! It is not pertinent to speak in terms of virtuosity, but rather in terms of whether an analyst has the ability to analyze, and if not, then it would be better to question our training itself. This may sound like espousing an ideal (and indeed it is, in aim at least). Under the best of training facilities, it is conceivable that a dullard may get through a course or a genius become handicapped. The matter may be simplified, viz., that it serves psychoanalysis to concentrate on maintaining the highest possible standards for qualification, and to leave the selection of personal analyst to the student, who, if motivated less by career considerations and more by his scientific and libidinal investment in psychoanalysis will be attracted to a personal analyst by the weight of the latter's authoritativeness. This has been shown in the past (the 1940s and 1950s), when students gravitated to analysts who demonstrated in their work their devotional interest in teaching and elucidating psychoanalysis. It is true that many of these teachers grew up with the later development of our science, but their dedication surpassed "career" or "elitist" motivations. If left to candidate selection, impressionistic as it may sometimes be, chances are that a "natural selection" of the most knowledgeable and inspiring of analysts would be sought.

Pfeffer (1974), in the summary of the pre-congress conference cited above, draws attention to the close parallel between acting-out on the part of the student and the "power-endowed group of training analysts" (p. 82). An obvious conclusion is that unresolved narcissistic needs are carried over into the training analysts' reactions, seldom subjected to "peer review." The students find themselves often subjected to countertransference reactions in the training analyst's "compulsion" to produce successful and grateful sons and to become surrounded by disciples, even though, as Pfeffer admonished in one of his summary statements, "the student [must] not be used to satisfy the training analysts's unconscious needs" p. 83. It is also this author's impression (from student days) that there may be much condescension and suppressed aggression that the training analyst has to restrain while with his analysands, but which he can let out on his supervisees. The tact, forebearance, and patience that should become cultivated in his art and skill, if the analyst has developed a sense of empathic responsiveness, may well put a training analyst to the test with his "captive" students. Invectives are not intended here, nor is the object to indulge in recrimination, but bold and challenging statements may sometimes be in order to bring an insidious situation to attention.

Pfeffer (1974) summarizes the thinking of another of the subgroups into which the conference was divided. Acting-out on the part of the training analyst may appear "in an attempt to keep other analysts out of the power-endowed group of training analysts" (p. 82). This group's statements (preceding the remarks of McLaughlin cited above) directed attention to the "hierarchical structure in institutes, and to the fact that many analysts feel that they had not fully succeeded professionally if they did not go on to become training analysts" (p. 82). Drawing a parallel, it stated, "There are also narcissistic disappointments on the part of students about status in their search for fantasy power," and finally, the group "discussed ways in which the status of training analysts might be deidealized" (p. 82). (It sounds like a diehard suggestion, instead of reconsidering the validity of the position itself.) Again, the question presented is whether the training analyst occupies his position by securing a status or by supplying a need that can't be fulfilled by any other qualified analyst. The conference gave "considerable thought to the motivations for wishing to become a training analyst" (p. 84) and mentioned that "an experiment has been made in one society which has recently abandoned the concept of training analyst and replaced it by 'experienced analyst'."

If there were validity in the training analyst concept, assuming that it could be defined accurately in terms of its evaluation in psychoanalytic theory and practice, not being a training analyst would probably not engender adverse reactions. At any rate, the position has become something other than that for which it was allegedly intended, lending itself to extraneous motivations. Furthermore, if it may so easily yield to nonanalytic rationale, it is contrary to the analytic principle of motivational candor.

The institution of training analyst, as it appears in recent criticism, has tended to foster rather than resolve defects in character, and again may fit into what Rangell (1974) terms "compromise of integrity" (so prevalent in our times). As analysts we may be guilty of this compromise, either by aspiring (for ulterior motives) to the position of training analyst or, if opposed, by not taking a stand against the need for it. What honesty is there in going along with it if it is divisive, causes animosity, reinforces a feeling of failure, and is a factor in producing society "splits"?) The American Psychoanalytic Association *Newsletter* of June, 1975, concluded that the "mitosis" approved of in one of our oldest societies was the result more of personality than idealogical differences.) Should our endeavor be to "smooth over" and bring about "acceptance"? To succeed in this would create a division in our midst between those who are "passive" and those who are "active," with schismatic recruits from both (the one seeking to be on the team and the other to make all the moves).

In an important sense we are dealing with a *superego* problem, viz., its role in the development of character, which determines, obviously, the analyst's attitude toward himself and his relation to psychoanalysis. The vicissitudes of narcissism and aggression displayed in seeking power over one's peers and succumbing to opportunism in furthering one's ambition are a violation of "psychic integrity" (a basic superego principle, essential for collaboration with colleagues, as it is in the practice of psychoanalysis itself).

Resentment and negative feeling left unexpressed are indicative not only of the lack of courage of conviction, but a "passive dishonesty," thereby allowing something to continue, constituting in effect a co-conspiracy with what one, in all good conscience, disapproves—a form of betrayal of an ego-ideal. On the other hand, passivity in this instance may be an unconscious recognition of inadequacy or inferiority, and the attendant depression would amount to an admission of inability to overcome the deficiency. In other words, if "professional worth" is predicated on being a training analyst, and this goal is not achieved, a negative (passive) reaction would indicate a punitive superego and a helpless ego; if, however, one is actively opposed to the training analyst category on the grounds that it impedes analytic training, development, and coherence, a positive ego-ideal governs one's thinking. To put it simply, where do our values lie, in self-aggrandizement or in accumulating our knowledge of human behavior and perfecting the art of elucidating it?

What is a solution to the problem? Is maintaining the category of training analyst necessary? The dissension that it has caused should cast a serious doubt. The external pressures on psychoanalysis—e.g., its role in our medical school teaching of psychiatry, which in many situations compromises basic principles (witness the confusions in regard to the application of psycho-analysis to psychiatry)—and the election by analysts to accept patients for psychotherapy when psychoanalysis is indicated (presumably bowing to expediency), present problems better solved if basic principles are understood and if aspirations for academic posts or greater financial gain are minimized. A rationalization often heard, and sometimes true, is that training analysts, by virtue of preempting candidates, have a monopoly on analytic cases. To what extent, then, is the spread into psychiatry by nontraining analysts felt necessary because of this "monopoly"?

Rangell's (1974) address to the 28th International Congress addresses this issue:

> Psychoanalysts in training capacities, or in administrative positions of responsibility, dealing as they do in the evaluation of others, are frequently in tight and delicate situations, subject to crises of character of their own, caught in conflicts between independent judgment and group pressures, attachment to charismatic or even just dominant figures, with the variety of attendant gains or the same need "to be a member of the team" . . . may often cast the deciding influence (p. 10).

Unfortunately, sibling rivalry affects analysts as much as it does any other professional group. Their fratricidal nature is manifest in a totem status symbol with the totemic (training) analyst, given to omnipotence and an authoritarian attitude toward students and peers; whereas other analysts, in a beholden position to the totem, are beset with envy, animosity, and disappointment, more conscious than unconscious.

The weight of evidence shows that fratricidal rivalry is universal, and repressed ambivalence toward the father emerges into consciousness as fratricidal rivalry. No group is free from this instinctual-like ambivalence, perhaps because, biologically, our species is predatory upon itself as no other is (overly documented, from cannibalism to human sacrifice, to war). This may be man's curse; although it may also be his privilege to sublimate his species-predatory "instinct." (It is interesting to note that the "split" between Freud and Jung occurred around the time of Freud's discoveries in *Totem and Taboo*.) Fratricidal rivalry may, however, be sublimated. Given a personal analysis without the complications engendered by having an analyst encumbered with a dual role, fratricide may be neutralized (very much as other destructive aggressive drives), and the need to achieve to the hierarchy may be decathected, with its energy channeled into scientific activity.

Any procedure as unobjective as the selection of training analysts— judgmental and fraught with questionable ulterior motives as it is—is a violation of psychic integrity; in a word, uncandid. The analytic model of incorruptibility does not hold in the selection of training analysts. It may be argued that it is not possible to avoid being arbitrary, impressionable, and prejudiced in the matter. If so, that's all the more reason to do away with "training analyst." If there were exclusive emphasis upon training qualified analysts, a major concern in institutes need not revolve around the selection of training analysts. The only psychoanalytically valid distinction is whether one is or is not a qualified and experienced analyst. The first comes with exacting and thorough training, the second with time and experience in the practice of psychoanalysis (not psychotherapy). This position may be summarized by Stone's (1975) statement in his critically constructive comments on psychoanalysis today:

> . . . thoroughly trained analysts with a certain number of years of clinical experience should be automatically qualified to conduct analyses of candidates, if no important ethical or other professional misbehavior or inadequacy is validly demonstrated in relation to them. This last step in the prolonged initiation ordeal . . . should be available to the colleague of mature years on the basis of interested and conscientious work, rather than on the basis of unclear intangibles. This would be to his and to the psychoanalytic community's advantage (p. 342).

CONCLUSION

This paper questions, first, to what extent any hierarchical system is a manifestation of mastery in the achievement of scientific goals or suborned to an expression of rivalry of a nonconstructive nature. Second, how much are factors intrinsic to the scientific pursuit of psychoanalysis compromised by emphasis upon secondary gains? Furthermore, if seeking the position of training analyst is motivated by the need to be successful over sibling rivals, sublimation is little more than a deceptive displacement and would indicate a narrow narcissistic gratification as compared with that derived from the intrinsic nature of analytic work itself.

The zeal and preoccupation, including ensconcement of a bureaucracy attendant upon the training analyst's position in our institutes have provoked this discussion. Our colleagues should not lack the courage to express their disaffection and anxiety in regard to a usurpation of power that is psychoanalytically as well as morally unwarrantable. That a protest may come from the disenfranchised does not mitigate its merit.

REFERENCES

Aarons, Z. A. (1974). The application of psychoanalysis to psychiatric training. *International Journal of Psychoanalytic Psychotherapy* 3.

Bernfeld, S. (1962). On psychoanalytic training. *Psychoanalytic Quarterly* 31:453–482.

Bibring, G. (1954). The training analysis and its place in psychoanalytic training. *International Journal of Psycho-Analysis* 53:169–173.

Freud, A. (1950, 1938). The problem of training analysis, in *The Writings of Anna Freud, Vol. 4.* New York: International Universities Press, 1968.

Freud, S. (1937). Analysis, terminable and interminable. *Standard Edition* 23:216–253.

Greenacre, P. (1966). Problems of training analysis. *Psychoanalytic Quarterly* 35:540–567.

Limentani, A. (1974). The training analyst and the difficulties in the training psychoanalytic situation. *International Journal of Psycho-Analysis* 55:71–77.

McLaughlin, F. (1974). Discussion of the paper by Daniel Shapiro. *International Journal of Psycho-Analysis* 55:307–309.

Pfeffer, A. A. (1974). The difficulties of the training analyst in the training analysis. *International Journal of Psycho-Analysis* 55:79–83.

Rangell, L. (1974). Presidential address: a psychoanalytic perspective leading currently to the syndrome of the compromise of integrity. *International Journal of Psycho-Analysis* 55:3–12.

———. (1975). Psychoanalysis and the process of change: an essay on the past, present and future. *International Journal of Psycho-Analysis* 56:87–97.

Shapiro, D. (1974). The training setting in training analysis. *International Journal of Psycho-Analysis* 55:297–306.

Stone, L. (1975). Some problems and potentialities of present-day psychoanalysis. *Psychoanalytic Quarterly* 44:331–370.

Training Analyst Selection: The Need for Criteria

ROBERT M. DORN, M.D.

Training analyses are not the same as other analyses. Simultaneously analyzing and educating complicates matters. Historical events in psychoanalysis confirm this; modest recommendations regarding non-reporting met significant resistance. Training needs and psychoanalysis needs overlap and merge rather than remain distinctly separate. Powerful professional identifications exist, evoking a sense of "parents' rights" and privilege within the training analyst and Education Committee, and abrogation of candidate privilege. Historical cultural factors in the training schools served or serve as social reinforcers, perpetuating pressures to share data. Democratization of training analyst appointment procedures denies manifest training complexities. After graduation, clearly defined steps toward training analyst status should be outlined. These should include criteria for selection, encouragement to apply step-wise procedures to aid further development and sophistication regarding issues described, and dilution of power among many well-qualified training analysts.

TRAINING ANALYSES AND THERAPEUTIC ANALYSES

Simultaneously analyzing candidates and dealing with training school education creates unique pressures for the candidate and analyst. It is more stressful. The nontraining analyst should not imagine it is "simply like any other analysis." By reviewing the struggle to develop nonreporting about the candidate-analysand, one gains some sense of the historical and contemporary factors within the training school that make the syncretistic life (analyzing and teaching) so complex.

Dr. Aarons' paper suggests there is no intrinsic difference. He quotes Stone (1975) in support:

. . . any colleague of some experience knows that the latter's distinction from therapy is fictive. It is usually a prolonged therapeutic analysis in which professional aspiration is a special and complicating condition (p. 353).

Dr. Aarons believes that this special and complicating condition does not warrant a special category of analyst. Instead, he suggests we should shift our focus to the candidate-patient and ask, "Is he analyzable?"

This question ignores a most important variable. It is less complex to simply inquire of analyzability of the candidate-patient, but as pointed out in a paper on psychoanalytic education (Dorn 1969), the analysis of the candidate takes place in the context of the training situation. It is unique and not ideal. In many instances, training analysts have exercised *real power* over the candidate-analysand, contributed to it being perpetuated, and actively participated in control of and decisions relating to the lives of candidates they were currently analyzing.

A. Freud (1950), as reported by Kairys (1964), succinctly highlights these differences. She points out how nonanalytic the training situation becomes: the analyst accepts patients from his immediate social environment, mutually sharing interests, and even, on occasion, openly expressing biases, where the analysand-patient may hear them. He can be seen criticizing, judging, and even actively intervening in peoples' lives. His own beliefs are evident (p. 486). If these are observed early in the candidate-analysand's training, or if the analysand has personal needs to utilize these observations for premature or characterological splitting (into "good" and "bad"), the training analyst apparently has provided the opportunity and reasons.

Ideally, transference should grow out of a relatively "uncontaminated" experience. That is the reason for a period of analysis before attending professional meetings of the Society where senior members actively participate, and before beginning the didactic course work at the Psychoanalytic Institute. For the majority of analysts-analysands, as couples, this appears to work satisfactorily, and they settle down to the primary task: analyzing (together).

TRAINING ANALYST REPORTING

Yet, as the literature confirms, there is a long history of the analytic compact of confidentiality being broken. Reasons "sound" and "rationalized" have been provided to explain why reporting was essential. Kairys' (1964) critical review of the training analysis literature concludes with the recommendation that the training analysis be conducted totally apart from the training school and that the educational arm of the Institute respect the same requirements of privacy and confidentiality as any other analysis (p. 506).

However, Kairys fails to ask why it took so long for many analysts (including respected senior analytic scholars) to agree with his recommended, more "analytic," nonreporting arrangements. Does not the perpetuation of apparently "anti-analytic" behavior suggest forces at work within the individual, irrespective of seniority, reinforced and abetted by the group, and rationalized in the patients' and organization's interests?

Psychoanalysts may wish to examine the unpleasant evidence that an authoritarian position has been consistently perpetuated in many training rules and regulations. Training analysts have been pulled, all too often willingly or "unwittingly," into the role of judge regarding ostensibly reality issues. Omnipotent fantasies and wishes are powerful seducers. Rigorous examination, discussion, and ongoing attention by each generation of analysts are essential as the most likely antidotes to these inevitable forces within each of us, especially when offered organizational sanction and encouragement.

Dr. Aarons is not alone in recommending democratization of training analysis. He joins Bernfield (1962), Limentani (1974), Stone (1975), and Greben (this volume), who also wish to simplify procedures based on appropriate graduation and postgraduation experiences as a member in good standing of the psychoanalytic society. Weigert (in Dorn 1969), in her discussion of this author's paper (Dorn 1969), also agrees with them (p. 258). However, she hedges somewhat, emphasizing that a student's competency as a psychoanalyst requires many years of assessment by teachers, supervisors, and peers. She recommends therefore, that consideration for membership in the American Psychoanalytic Association be made only after colleagues and teachers see how the student deals with successes and failures. Thus, in practice terms, she postpones full acceptance as a peer for some relatively lengthy period postgraduation. Urges to infantilize others are not always solely in the service of the conscious analytic ego and the analytic process.

Other discussants (Grinberg, Kairys, and Horowitz in Dorn 1969, pp. 261, 264, 267) are even more cautious, pointing to numerous complications born of the syncretistic dilemma: analyzing/judging. A growing awareness emerges that psychoanalysts, who are training analysts, could give up reporting. By 1969, several institutes had indicated nonreporting procedures were in operation. Methods had to be developed by these training schools to determine candidates' readiness for progression without recourse to the training analyst. As a member of one of these Institutes, this author can attest to the pressures brought to bear by at least some colleagues, who continued to insist on the essential need to break confidentiality, and also, to the occasional pressure a training analyst feels within himself to break confidentiality and voluntarily report.

An example may help the reader feel a little of these pressures. A candidate in training decided unilaterally to interrupt his analysis after four years. Two years later, a supervisor of one of his cases noted his inept handling of sexual material and parts of transference and resistance. Direct inquiry of the candidate by the supervisor brought out the facts. Rather than only dealing directly with the candidate and the Candidate Progress Committee of the Education Committee, the supervisor, a highly respected senior analyst, chose also to attack the training analyst for being unwilling to discuss the candidate and events with him. Scathing and sarcastic comments were made in public about the training analyst for adhering to patient privilege and confidentiality. The supervisor had been told by the training analyst that all essential facts seemed available and without evident need for the training analyst's participation. The supervising analyst nonetheless made an insulting report about the training analyst to the Education Committee regarding his unwillingness to publicly discuss details of the candidate's analysis. This example is perhaps unique in its stridor. Nonetheless, the insistence on intrusion as a right has been extensive and historically complied with routinely, as custom.

Even if the ideal of nonparticipation in any aspect of the analysand's analytic life were to be accomplished one day, the historic fact that such experiences occurred routinely commends us to inquire as to what "appeals" they represent. How did senior analysts rationalize intrusiveness of this magnitude, accompanied by a sense of righteousness?

As a child psychiatrist and child analyst, this author has observed and experienced similar forces in parents and in their children working to establish more appropriate body and thought boundaries, as the children grew older and changed. Oftentimes it is a struggle for adult, or child, or both to relinquish a sense of parents' rights and/or needs to intrude. Such symbiotic and controlling behavior is inappropriate as a part of an adult's psychoanalysis and represents pathology. It can be transference acting-out, countertransference, or both.

These self- and group-rationalized distortions of the analytic compact speak forcefully. They provide evidence that a training analysis evokes powerful parenting-like forces, with an associated sense of self-righteousness, rationalizing intrusiveness, and a need to know about colleagues' inner lives. Thus experienced psychoanalysts succumbed to training school pressures from colleagues and acquiesced to reporting.

APPOINTMENT CRITERIA

Training reality and authority issues do not facilitate analyzing. They may impair the psychoanalytic process and irrevocably damage it. Also, in some institutes at least, authority issues continue to control training organizations and make [the method] of appointment to the position of training analyst unclear [as to method,] and sometimes less than democratic. Psychoanalytic educators have tried to be all things to all people: administrators, teachers, and psychoanalysts. Once again the seductive attraction to "high achievers" is to the role of training analyst, the "ultimate accolade" deserving a peer approval, admiration, and understandably, but unfortunately, envy. Needless to say, power and financial reward also come with it. Relatively little has been done to reward administration and teaching equally; they continue to be treated as stepping stones to becoming a training analyst.

Some analysts would deal with this vigorously and cleanly. In discussions, some colleagues have suggested that certification by the American Psychoanalytic Association should serve as the sole qualification to do psychoanalysis with either candidates or noncandidates. They say selection of analysts should be the "free choice" of the analysand. However, almost invariably, these colleagues begin to delineate requirements, albeit, at times, loosely stated stipulations. Greben (this volume), who would do away with the classification "training analyst," continues to make some requirements such as five years experience, at least half-time. Aarons (this volume) voice similar beliefs, referring to experience and measurements as "exacting and thorough training," and "time and experience in the practice of psychoanalysis," emphasizing its difference from psychotherapy. Moving these criteria from generalities to concrete statements will require answering such questions as: if half-time psychoanalytic practice is required, and at least five years of such experience is essential, what specific skills are being developed by the graduate psychoanalyst during this time frame? Is it not possible for us to be more specific? Can the more senior analyst who is particularly interested in training issues spell out for the younger colleague some of the particular post-graduation issues to be addressed? I will try to point out some of the answers in a later section of this paper.

Inevitably these factors become essential concerns of any analytic organization that can be held responsible for the quality of its training. Note Stone's (1975) position when he states: ". . . thoroughly trained analysts with a certain number of years of clinical experience should be automatically qualified to conduct analysts on candidates . . ." (p. 342). Note how he begins to talk of criteria ". . . mature years on the basis of interested and conscientious work . . ." (p. 342). Is this not evidence that he has concrete recommendations to make that will require criteria differentiating who can, and who cannot, analyze candidates?

Analyzing candidates requires specific experience with the complications and conflicts aroused by analyzing in an educational setting. Dedication, a predominatly psychoanalytic practice, and four or five years of postgraduate experience with analyzable patients, should be minimal requirements to start *consideration* for training analyst status. Cases need be once again reviewed with senior teachers, preferably from a nearby, but different institute. If this can be arranged, it will help deal with some of the inevitable problems that arise when promotion to training analyst status become a reality consideration. Once accepted as a training analyst, first cases should be followed with a senior training analyst to facilitate noting differences between character problems of the usual patient, and those who, as future colleagues, have chosen to also become "like us" professionally.

TRANSFERENCE AND COUNTERTRANSFERENCE ISSUES

Dr. Aarons' conclusion concerns a critical two-part question. When a person is appointed a training analyst, to what extent is it evidence of mastery (of the psychoanalytic method) and sublimated ego capacities relevant to this accomplishment? To what extent is it actively or potentially politicized, (re)aggressivized, and (re)libidinized? It is politics, self-serving, or clique-serving? These are very fair questions and can be asked for each institute and appointee-aspirant for training analyst consideration. Also, the answers to these questions can be acquired relatively easily, provided the membership agrees to seek answers.

Greben (this volume) deals with similar issues in terms of character and conflict. He points out four potential problem areas that may subsequently emerge in the candidate as training analyst:

1. Conflicts occur. Idealization tendencies ensue and analyses fail to deal with disappointments and rage by way of transference and genetic precursors. Defenses of displacement to the organization take place. (See point 4.)
2. Character problems are not eliminated. Greben describes ". . . well-established senior members who, for many years, stand in the way of compromise or change," and "Obessional analysts [who] serve as models for obsessional candidates."
3. Training and graduation arrangements foster infantile postures and magical attitudes. These arrangements include perpetuation of control over candidates' and oftentimes graduates' lives.[1] Admission to training-analyst status remains a key issue for at least some analysts. Who will

---

1. To the extent that members of the Society truly need candidates to practice psychoanalysis (as contrasted to psychoanalytic psychotherapy), this is a serious reality issue. To the extent the Society member aspires to the role of training analyst as evidence of self-worth, the accolade "training analyst" represents a potential identification, defense, and resistance to analyzing an intrapsychic conflict. This primarily requires and deserves careful analysis.

analyze candidates remains heavily charged with potential for continuing to live on with unresolved infantile aspirations and feelings of denigration, if not fulfilled, until fulfilled, and even after fulfillment.

4. Vocational hazards exist, secondary to forced isolation or due to preference for isolation. The psychoanalytic group serves self-needs rather than training and organizational needs. Lack of accountability regarding individual and organizational work perpetuates individual and fraternal goals without opportunity for resolution.

Most of us can attest to these as accurate. Each represents a potential pitfall or opportunity for further analysis. If instead of analyzing and gaining insight, one or another character problem finds positive reinforcement and perpetuation (despite analysis), it behooves us, as a group of concerned analysts, to clarify issues and deal with them.

Examples may help. Some of us tend by nature to be "loners" (point 4). Analyzing is a one-sided arrangement and puts the analyst "at risk". Graduation from an institute represents a potential time of fulfillment and rite of passage, symbolically and experientially (Arlow 1970). Oftentimes, however, initial joy and excitement are followed by profound feelings of depression. Optimally these depressive experiences become appropriately related to transference and genetic precursors (point 1).

Unfortunately, other outcomes occur. Some graduates complain about lack of referrals from more senior colleagues. Some abandon plans to practice primarily psychoanalysis and gradually withdraw even more from active roles inside the professional group. In some, abandonment, bitterness, and disillusionment spread from colleagues to method. A common outcome is a perpetual living on the fringe, or a substitution of ritual participation for a working through and freeing up of collegiality and organization for adult, conflict-free, and object-related purposes.

One group of candidates who anticipated these possible outcomes, dealt with their "graduation" in an anticipatory and "phase-specific" way. At a meeting of the Committee on Postgraduate Education of the American Psychoanalytic Association, Wallsh (1976) described how a group of five members of the fourth-year class of the New York Psychoanalytic Institute met to consider development of a study group. They discussed the facts of impending graduation, realities of separation from candidate status, and anxieties about the solitary role of the graduate analyst. Each was still in training analysis. Ensuing discussions included considerable attention to whether the creation of such a group constituted resistance to termination of analysis or personal hurts and disappointments with the results of analysis. Each person decided to deal with these issues within the individual analysis. Meanwhile they decided to form a group. It continued unchanged for two years. One person moved at that time. The remaining four continued together, and at the time of reporting were in their fifth year.

The group's focus was mainly clinical. Wallsh described how support and encouragement for each other was followed by feelings of deep trust, in addition to comradery and respect. Members grew more open (". . . less protective of themselves . . ."). Issues of "countertransference" regarding each other ensued, with illuminations of blind spots not evident from personal analyses. Some had finished analysis; others had not. To avoid displacement of issues to the group, findings were pursued individually and not as part of the group process. The group became increasingly aware that "postgraduate" group process could help with personal analytic work and raise it to a cognitive data level. For example, one member presented personal anniversary reactions to the termination of his training analysis. It also substantiated how fragile and in need of support one's beginning as an "independent" psychoanalyst can be.

Such groups could easily document how analytic training provides a professional developmental line from "family" to organizational participation. Each participant has need to deal with phase-specific issues if the organizational participation is to remain relatively conflict-free and uncontaminated with transference–countertransference problems, displaced from personal life to organizational action. Ideally, it would be the other way around—professional analytic development would enhance personal insights.

POLITICS AND PSYCHOANALYTIC ORGANIZATIONS

Political activities are an essential part of all organizations. In his discussion of Greben's paper (this volume), Klauber (this volume) deals with leaders and followers and propensities of followers to idealize and overvalue leaders. He helps us focus on certain critical issues. Do we overidealize leaders in the psychoanalytic group for such unconscious reasons as rebellion against conservatism? Is it therefore inevitable for one group of psychoanalysts to defend "the faith" against an equally inevitable group who must attack it? Is it in the service of "influence" and "gaining control" as primary motives and only secondarily rationalized as "new," "innovative," and "unique" ideas that supersede the "old" and "out-moded"?

It is inherent in the nature of human beings to get caught up in situations that lend themselves to splitting mechanisms. Psychoanalysts, as introspective individuals through professional training, know well the regressive potential group behavior provides. Candidates in their training analyses are expected to be experiencing regressive phenomena, predominantly (one hopes) as part of a transference neurosis and in the service of gaining personal insight. It takes time and much postgraduation working-through to disentangle cognitive psychoanalytic education and interpersonal experiences of studenthood from personal motives. Only then can one talk about a relatively apolitical role for psychoanalysis within the healthy politics of a psychoanalytic society. This state has clearly not arrived.

It also takes time after graduation, and experience with one's own analytic style to determine if we have the interest and qualities of chartacter to urge us to deal with these additional variables, knowing they will inevitably contaminate our psychoanalytic field and stir up transference/countertransference issues. It takes time and in-depth work over several years. As Dr. Klauber notes, it takes a lot longer than five years of half-time practice to become a psychoanalyst, comfortable and competent to work creatively and constructively on behalf of one's patients, oneself, and the *science* of psychoanalysis (this volume).

Stone (1975) writes regarding the training analysis that it is a special and complicating condition (p. 353). Klauber reminds us to look at both analyst and analysand (leader and follower). The present author (Dorn 1969) concurs, when describing how generations of analysts and former analysands, now members of the same training institute committees, agree to allow ". . . *real power* to continue, with resultant serious consequences of control and decision over lives of candidates . . ." (p. 243). Collusion may be conscious or unconscious, and politicization of psychoanalytic ideas is an everpresent temptation.

A psychoanalytic society should be a place where new ideas are welcomed. However, ideas are not necessarily facts. To the extent that new ideas are not welcome, we lack the potential to encourage creativity. To the extent that ideas are not vigorously tested and treated as hypotheses, we lack the fundamental requirements of science. As potential progenitors of new ideas (hypotheses), and as aspirants seeking to insure psychoanalysis will enjoy a reputation as a science, we must assiduously know the difference between the two and equally firmly insist that basic fundamentals be followed to facilitate and enhance *each*.

The analytic society is the place to present new ideas and "research" in progress. Hypotheses can be shared and discussion encouraged. The psychoanalytic institute is the training arm where facts, which have stood the test of time, can be shared with the future generation of psychoanalysts. Training takes place simultaneously with the personal psychoanalysis. Where regression is not limited to the psychoanalytic transference process and where schisms exist among Society members and faculty, especially around new ideas, regressive forces infiltrate the Institute and Society, with countertransference issues affecting training and trainees. Recruitment of cohorts, convoying of candidates, splitting into "we" versus "they," are evidence of regressive group phenomena, affecting learning and future practice. Descriptively they suggest "family problems." As such, they belong in personal analysis of self and object representations. Displacements to the "family" of psychoanalysts on the Education Committee and in the Institute, as training school, reflects group psychopathology.

In a proposed talk on the psychoanalytic process and the psychoanalyst's quest for scientific certainty, the present author (Dorn 1981) addresses the discomfort felt as one moves from so-called knowledge, objectively measurable, quantifiable, and replicable, to less certain states of exploration. As "scientists," psychoanalysts examine clinical findings for data. The analyst and his patient have opportunities to work together collaboratively, each learning how the psychoanalytic process will permit them, over a period of time, to collect into the transference process such materials as action, pre-verbal derivatives, possible projective identifications representing self and others, and developmental editions that are partially sublimated in later phases of development. Inasmuch as these will be reconstructed in the here and now (accurately, one hopes), eventual placement developmentally in sociobiologic and intrapsychic languages will be helped by ongoing professional conversations with other researchers sharing interest in early psychic development. Data provide hypothesis-testing opportunities. Hypotheses need assessment, testing, and retesting over time.

Psychoanalysts, as others bent on "cure" and scientific research-stature, swing emotionally from hope and optimism when hypotheses appear substantiated, to depression, anger, and even despair, when hopes for discovery (and possible immortal fame) are dashed by failure of hypotheses to become fact. Rigorous reality-testing and honesty are critical in science. Freud (1954), with his scientific honesty, changed his original seduction theory and set each of us a significant example. As he wrote Fliess, ". . . the hope of fame was so beautiful. . . . Now I can be quiet and modest again . . ." (pp. 217–218). Freud recognized his serious flirtation with grandiose and omniscient fantasies. His rigorous scientific attitude protected him from the premature leap from hypothesis to claims of fact. He was willing to question his findings. He did not have to opt for premature closure to support a wish-system of fame or fortune. These can be powerful motivators affecting outcome.

Psychoanalysis, as a science using the clinical field as its laboratory, is clearly vulnerable to premature substitution of hypothesis and wish for rigorous testing and replication. Therefore, like other clinical sciences, it too should prefer to seek for linking and generalizing frameworks that allow for collaborative assessment and dialogue from related sciences. The analyst and analysand in the two-person field, where ideas of infantile transference/

countertransference can be evaluated over time, can then check findings with workers in infant and child development, who also examine dyads.

What Klauber (this volume) describes as the ability of the British Psycho-Analytic Society to *contain* differences provides pale description of the so-called intellectual individualism and quarrels that swept British psycho-analysis in the 1940s. Feelings ran high at Society meetings. Differences were ostensibly around critical scientific issues, but reactions of training analysts were not only cerebral. We might ask, what data did the British leaders in their second and third generation "innocence" provide analysands that today we might view as potential for primal scene displacements and nonanalyzing of personal meaning? How much remained unanalyzed or unanalyzable, never finding its way back into individual intrapsychic representations? It is painful to confront history, but preferable to a new set of screen memories about psychoanalysts as people and potential contributors to a developing science. Here one deals with consequences, not with motives.

As Klauber asserts, no one should hold his analyst and teachers accountable. They have been the product of their generation, and probably in most instances did a commendable job despite the syncretistic dilemma. As with our parents, our growth and maturation should evoke understanding without the need to overidealize or denigrate. Where our analysts and/or teachers provided us with "ammunition" and/or countertransference screens, rather than with opportunities to analyze our fantasies if displaced onto their action, so be it. It is up to the current and next generation of psychoanalysts to deal constructively with both sets of issues as each emerges in personal analysis and in the analytic society. Meanwhile graduate analyst and candidate have ample opportunity to work collaboratively in institute and society for personal growth and scientific clarity of ideas.

TO BE ANALYZED, TO BE EDUCATED

In earlier sections, the inevitable stresses and intrusions complicating the training analysis were addressed. Questions of reporting and breaking confidentiality were described.

Greenacre (1966) points out how rapidly career aspirations may appear, intruding ". . . the shadow of the Institute . . ." on student and analyst. Wishes to graduate and to receive the title "psychoanalyst" often gain ascendency and priority over the psychoanalytic process. As Greenacre believes, there is an inevitable conflict between these aims. The training analyst also may experience conflict between his analyzing concerns for his patient and his involvement and possible investment in his analysand-student's career-line (p. 722).

In training analyses, both analyst and candidate are involved in narcissistic identificatory, competitive issues (career aspirations coincide). Intrusions of reality (active social and professional relations) will occur, which may easily fall into mutually agreeable "acting out." *If* the analyst is sophisticated and keenly aware of the "acting in" meaning that has, one hopes, found only "temporary" mutually acceptable displacement into the training situation, and *if* this gets analyzed rather than rationalized, it can be resolved analytically. However, training and professional career lines are seductively enhancing of rationalized living-out and require additional insights beyond graduation.

Greenacre (1966) cautions that ". . . the analyst may be quite unaware of the nature and extent of his own cooperation in such acting out, or in fact that it is an acting out at all" (p. 729). She describes these as becoming "encapsulated" and as "strangulated transference problems." Therefore they are not available to analysis, and ". . . it makes for future trouble in the personal and professional life of the student."

Additional countertransference problems can be described, but details are not particularly germane at this time, in this context. Suffice it to say that special attention to these countertransference issues is essential. Special training experiences would help aspirants to training analyst status. These are potential countertransference problems. They are subtle, often occurred in the previous generation, and can easily have escaped notice and discussion. Careful preparation for obtaining training analyst status and ongoing experience provide the best potential for additional insights into one's own conflict areas with candidate analysands.

Drs. Aarons' and Greben's wish to improve the quality of the training analysis deserves attention. They wish to eliminate a distinction between the dedicated analytic graduate and the training analyst by relatively simple means. However, problems reside in four and/or five generations of analytic institute cultures and structure, and detailed attention will have to be given to issues of training wherein syncretism has resulted in "archaic remnants" that remain deeply embedded in prevailing traditions.

Aarons and Greben wish to eliminate a distinction between the two classes of analyst-graduates by relatively simple rule changes. The present author emphatically recommends a continuing postgraduation dialogue between aspiring training analysts-to-be and the Education Committee to develop an active pool of qualified training analysts and a very small number of candidates for each. Attention to complexities due to the *real* differences must be made conscious, specific, and concrete. The analyzing environments are different when one is "simply" a patient and when one is both patient and candidate. Graduates interested in adding further to their fund of knowledge regarding these differences should request opportunities to participate.

Education committees and training-analyst representatives from the Institute should both encourage graduates to get this further training experience and provide ongoing opportunities for these member-graduates to have appropriate training opportunities. Attention by analyzing participants to these two different environments is the way to begin another lengthy but essential process.

A new generation of candidates, well-apprised of the humanness and understandable foibles of their predecessors, "forefathers" and "mothers," can construct a training school environment more capable of dealing with wishes and aspirations, especially if the primary goal is to have as insightful a personal analysis as possible within the training situation. Probably, periodic recertification of training analysts will also be essential. Planning for retirement is another important issue.

The critical questions and answers will deal with action and persistent facilitation of action by displacement into psychoanalytic groups. These are the organizational areas that need careful attention. Kairys, Greenacre, and others are to be commended for posing the critical questions, although answers to date approach the problem obliquely and not forthrightly. We can understand this. Graduates, primarily practicing psychoanalysis, with continued interest in becoming training analysts, and Education Committees made up of training analysts prepared to deal with these issues constructively, can find ways to address them, describe complexities, and provide workable solutions.

REFERENCES

Arlow, J. A. (1970). Group psychology and the study of institutes. Chairmen's Report of Professional Standards. San Francisco: American Psychoanalytic Association.

Bernfeld, S. (1962). On psychoanalytic training. *Psychoanalytic Quarterly* 31:453–482.

Dorn, R. (1969). Psychoanalysis and psychoanalytic education: what kind of journey? *The Psychoanalytic Forum* 3:239–274.

———. (1981). Early psychic development as reflected in the psychoanalytic process: objectivity/subjectivity and a quest for certainty. Proposed joint meeting of the Los Angeles Psychoanalytic Society and Institute and the Southern California Psychoanalytic Society.

Freud, A. (1950). Problems of the training analysis. In *Max Eitington in Memoriam*, pp. 80–94. Jerusalem: Israeli Psychoanalytic Society.

Freud, S. (1954). *The Origins of Psychoanalysis: Sigmund Freud's Letters*, ed. M. Bonaparte, A. Freud and E. Kris. New York: Basic Books.

Gitelson, F. (1979). Discussion in *L'identitité du psychanalyste*. Paris: Presses Universitaires de France.

Greenacre, P. (1966). Problems of training analysis. In *Emotional Growth*, vol. 1, pp. 718-742. New York: International Universities Press, 1971.

Kairys, D. (1964). The training analysis. *Psychoanalytic Quarterly* 33:485–512.

Limentani, A. (1974). The training analyst and the difficulties in the training psychoanalytic situation. *International Journal of Psycho-Analysis* 55:71–77.

Stone, L. (1975). Some problems and potentialities of present-day psychoanalysis. *Psychoanalytic Quarterly* 44:331–370.

Wallsh, R. (1976). The use of a study group in post-graduate psychoanalytic education. Presentation, American Psychoanalytic Association, Workshop on Postgraduate Education. December 16, 1976.

The Rat Man Revisited:
Comments on Maternal Influences

K. H. BLACKER, M.D.
RUTH ABRAHAM, Ph.D.

Freud's case study of an obsessive young man, published in 1909, has provided the foundation for the psychoanalytic understanding of obsessive illness. Freud reported the case in Oedipal terms, viewing the patient's symptoms as arising from his fear of castration by his father as punishment for his sexual desires. Freud's working notes on the case, however, contain much material about the women in Lorenz's life not included in the published case or in Freud's formulation. Careful review of this data suggests that important aspects of Lorenz's obsessive disorder harken back to conflicts in his relationship with his mother. This reexamination of Freud's classical case suggests that these questions concerning the genesis of obsessive dynamics should be further explored.

Freud's (1909) case study of an obsessive young man, titled "Notes Upon a Case of Obsessional Neurosis," has provided the foundation for the present psychoanalytic understanding of obsessive illness. The wealth of information contained in this report has been further expanded by the availability of Freud's working notes of the case. Portions of these notes, found in his London apartment after his death, have been published in *The Standard Edition* (1955), and a complete set of notes has been published in French and German (1974).

Relatively little has been written about this fascinating analysis. The reports by Zetzel (1966), Grunberger (1966), and Holland (1975) focused on broadening the understanding of the psychodynamic issues in Paul Lorenz's life. Sherwood (1969) utilized the published case to demonstrate the nature of psychoanalytic evidence and to illustrate the construction of psycho-

The authors wish to acknowledge the contributions of Samuel D. Lipton's comments in the preparation of this final version.

analytic theory. Muslin's (1977) interest lay in documenting Freud's 1907 conceptualization and utilization of transference phenomena. In addition, several authors (Kanzer 1952, Morgenthaler 1966, Biegler 1975, Lipton 1977, and Langs 1978) have written on the technical aspects of Freud's treatment method. Among this group there is a lively dispute as to what were the curative factors in Lorenz's treatment and differences as to which of Freud's interpretations and interventions can be considered proper psychoanalytic technique.

Freud's sensitive and graphic description of the ambivalences, the rituals, the defenses of doing and undoing and reaction formation, and the magical thinking of his patient, Paul Lorenz, are classical and remain as true today of obsessive patients as they were 70 years ago. The present authors feel, however, that Freud's narrowly paternal interpretation of Lorenz's psychodynamics needs re-examination.

The working notes in particular contain much material about the women in Lorenz's life. They are significant both in terms of the number of references and their power and graphic quality, most of which Freud did not carry over into his published case history. In the present paper, evidence is presented to suggest that Lorenz and his pathology can be more adequately and completely understood by taking into account this material, and by recognizing the powerful influences exerted on him during his development and adult life by his mother and other women.

In comparing and contrasting the content and quality of the published case with that of the working notes, it is discovered that Lorenz's associations in the working notes concentrated heavily on his mother and other women, yet there is a remarkable absence of this emphasis in the published case. Many references to women may be traced out in both sets of material, but whereas the mother is mentioned in the working notes a total of 41 times, she appears in the published case only 8 times, and only in passing, never as a major reference point. She is reduced to a shadow of herself as compared to the full-bodied, dominating figure found in the working notes.

With the father, the situation is reversed. Lorenz mentions him far fewer times in the working notes (42) than he is referred to in the published case (62), and in the published case two-thirds of the references to him are exclusively Freud's. Women dominate the working notes as men dominate the published case. What happened to these women? Can it really be that they proved unimportant to Lorenz's pathology?

A careful compilation and review of biographical information from both the published case and the notes (see Abraham 1977) suggests that Freud may not have fully appreciated the individual personalities of Lorenz's parents and the nature of their influence on him and on his development. The following brief descriptions of Lorenz and his parents have been constructed entirely from the case material as presented by Freud. They include some inferences that follow naturally from the facts. By organizing the material in this way, the true situation in the Lorenz household becomes more apparent, and the argument for the mother's central role in Lorenz's pathology achieves a solid historical and contextual underpinning.

THE FATHER

Herr Friedrich Lorenz was a military man in his younger years and a business man in his later years. Under most circumstances, he had an easy and pleasant temperament. He was a fond parent and, as Lorenz emphatically states, he was his son's best friend. He confided the vicissitudes of his life to his children and made them his confidants. He had humor and kindly tolerance, and liked to share his little failures and misfortunes with them. He also had a loving relationship with his wife, although a tendency toward raw language and a habit of breaking wind in public drew some chastizement from her. He was a "good old boy" and rather a spendthrift to his wife's frugal way of thinking. He was unable, for instance, to refuse friends who were in financial need, and for years he secretly made up the difference between what a boarder in their home could afford and what he was actually expected to pay.

On occasion, Lorenz's father displayed a hasty and passionate temper and was capable of violence. When the children were small, there were spankings and punishments that made the boy very much afraid, even though he was the object of physical rebuke only once: when he was three, his father beat him for biting his nurse, or "some such naughtiness."

Friedrich Lorenz was a man of impulse, somewhat immature, and lazy. It appears that he allowed his wife to handle the financial affairs of the family. He was also given to petty dishonesty, sometimes coaxing young Lorenz to steal small change from Frau Lorenz's purse. He was fond of cards, especially with army friends, and he once appropriated a certain sum of money while gambling, which he may never have repaid.

He was a virile man, fathering seven children (five girls and two boys), but he was in despair after each new birth, presumably because of the burden on the family's finances. He liked having his permission asked, enjoying the feeling that everything came from him, so his frustration at not being consulted about the new child, of being the helpless recipient of a new responsibility, undoubtedly played its part. Although he was a handsome man who had no cause to mistrust his wife's loyalty, he was once possessed by jealousy and doubt to the extent that he made his wife swear on her children's lives that she had not been unfaithful to him—and this after 33 years of marriage. He seems to have been relatively loyal to her also, though there were times in the financially lean years of their marriage that he was seldom at home, and his wife made a sort of family joke about the possibility of his philandering.

The picture is of an agreeable but ineffectual man with somewhat adolescent attractiveness and fits of temper, a man who gave up a poor girl in order to marry into a more financially promising situation.

THE MOTHER

Frau Lorenz was Fredrich Lorenz's first cousin, and she seems to have been a woman of a more practical and controlling disposition than her husband. She seems to have handled most of the monetary and the moral affairs of the family. She was shown to grant or refuse money, advice, and permission on frequent occasions. She appears to have been a somewhat harassed woman who reacted more compulsively than hysterically to her situation. For instance, she was strict in ways of cleanliness, reprimanding her son about his dirtiness, and even attempting to wash "the little pig" herself once, though he was a strapping ten-year-old and was much ashamed by the procedure. She was consistently strong-willed, perhaps intimidating, as is evident from the fact that when he wanted something from her, like a few bits of small change, the preferred course for Mr. Lorenz was to steal it rather than to ask for or demand it. His assistance to the needy boarder also had to be done secretly, rather than simply telling Frau Lorenz (as would be expected from a Victorian husband) that the boarder would only be paying so much rent.

There is evidence that Frau Lorenz was sharp-witted and given to outspokenness. She could chide and tease her husband in a way that did not break the peace but made her irritations and disappointments perfectly clear. Her derogatory reference to his philandering seems an example, as was her habit of chafing him for his temptation to marry a butcher's daughter when it was so obviously to his monetary advantage to marry her instead. She implied that he would certainly have been a fool to do it, and there seems an unspoken judgment that, though he did have enough sense to marry her, he was fool enough even so.

Frau Lorenz used to complain about her husband to her son; yet she was fond of him and lamented his death, chastizing his physician for not persuading him to stop work earlier and thus prolonging his life a little. She felt that he had squandered a great deal of her money, and she swore (or at least said that she had sworn) to economize once he was gone, and to try to rebuild some of her capital. She seems to have held to this plan firmly, for she doled out her son's inheritance, which he had turned over to her for management, with a lean hand.

As with most obsessives, Frau Lorenz's fastidiousness was sometimes broken by displays of crudeness, "dirtiness," and sexual suggestiveness, of which she seemed curiously unaware. She had the habit of burping at the table, for instance. And in her later years she had a genital odor (caused by an infection) about which she complained, but which she could not "afford" to eliminate. When Lorenz was very young, she once reached under her dress in his presence and brought out a yellow jelly-like substance that was fascinating to him and yet gave him a horror of feminine secretions that persisted into adulthood.

WOMEN AND PAUL LORENZ

In relation to women, the picture of Lorenz is a full and complicated one. As a young boy, he had already developed specific desires for women along with the intention, and to a large extent, the opportunity, to carry them out. Overtly seduced by his nurses, and perhaps covertly seduced by his mother, he wished, and in fact had a tormenting need, to see women naked. And it can be inferred that before he had isolated his desire in the visual sphere, he had the need to touch women and explore them tactily. The boy was, as Freud remarked, a little sensualist. Lorenz was in an environment that afforded him intense sensual stimulation. He had around him a large group of girls and women—nursemaids, housemaids, sisters, aunts, cousins, and of course, his mother. From the day he was born until he was grown, he lived in familial proximity to no less than eight women.

He learned early that women meant sensual delight, but he also learned early that they meant abandonment and death. The death of his older sister, Katherine, when he was five, was one of the major traumatic events of his early years. An obsessive concern for the adult Lorenz was the women who could not be induced to come close to him, or to care enough for him, or to be persuaded to commit themselves to him. He had around him many women, but he felt deserted nonetheless, left alone, and disregarded by the women who counted for him—the very ones bound to discourage him. The "lesser" women who wanted him, he humiliated and rejected. The most pronounced ambivalence centered on women. Women gave sensual delight; they also gave the pain of abandonment. Women were worthy of devotion and tenderness, even worshipful sacrifice. They also had mysterious secretions and infections, were ill, were perhaps syphlitic, and perhaps prostitutes.

They were, in any case, mysteriously tainted and often digusting. What ailed Lorenz? For one thing, he was obsessed with the idea of women, trapped by his conflicting concepts of them, and trapped by his overwhelming need for and fear of them.

THE CASE

With the foregoing as a descriptive account of Lorenz and the influence of women in his life, the focus shifts to an examination of specific case material. In the initial interview with Freud (for which both the published account and the working notes are available), and in the first seven sessions, there is a wealth of material on the influence of the mother. The importance of this early material cannot be underestimated. It is often in the first weeks of analysis that the core conflicts are revealed. Some clinicians go so far as to say that the answers to the whole analysis can be found in the material of the opening session. Freud claimed that the key to the analysis of Lorenz was in the solving of the rat obsession, and that this was discovered later in the work, but it is clear that he considered the first eight interviews to contain critical material, as a considerable part of his published case is devoted to these sessions.

In the opening interview an important piece of information is learned: Lorenz was unwilling to engage Freud for analysis until he had consulted with his mother. This was apparently the final statement in the hour, a parting remark that, strangely, Freud failed to mention in the published version of the case. In the published version of this initial interview, Freud stresses a first appearance of the paternal transference by reporting that Lorenz was willing to engage him not after consulting with his mother, but because he was impressed by one of Freud's own works.

THE PSYCHOPATHOLOGY OF EVERYDAY LIFE

One reason Lorenz needed to consult his mother about the analysis was because she controlled his money. Without his mother's approval and co-operation, this 29-year-old man could not have paid Freud's fee.

In these opening sessions, too, a piece of pathology emerges that recurs throughout his analysis: a conviction in the omnipotence of his own thoughts and the harm they might do. He was beset by obsessive fears, one of which was that something dreadful would happen. When Lorenz was induced to give an example, his reply "that my father might die," seemed to Freud no mere example, but *the* major fear—that his persistent thoughts of seeing women naked would surely result in his father's death—and this despite the fact that his father had already died some time before. Upon this delusional fear—that his thoughts would kill his already dead father—Freud bases much of his argument for the father–son conflict in the case.

It is interesting to note, however, that the infantile genesis of the uncanny fear of his own thoughts was when he showed his *mother* an erection, a childish display of his desire and also perhaps his defensive, hostile aggression. He was perhaps seducing his mother, as he had already seduced a mother-substitute (his nurse), and was perhaps also responding to his mother's own seductions. Although he was, as Freud says, a little sensualist, it was clearly the big sensualist, his nurse, who had been the actual seducer of the child. This overt, and his mother's probable covert, seduction was responsible for his exaggerated sexual interest—and, it may be postulated, for his exaggerated fear as well. One may speculate how his mother could fail to seduce him when, until the age of six, he was known to have slept in her room? He apparently spent a good deal of time in her bed, for he told Freud that he had seen her buttocks while lying with her and had conceived an elaborate idea of marriage being a fusion of these parts between husband and wife. The child had very good reason to be torn between fear and desire, to be, as Freud points out, already ill. But where Freud would say the fear was of the father, it may also be said that he believed his mother was dangerous. His sister Katherine, he well remembered, had died shortly after she had been in the parental bed. Perhaps Lorenz could see that to be in the marriage bed, or close to mother, was fatal. Katherine had sworn (Lorenz reports) that if he died, she would surely kill herself. His death would mean her death, and she was dead. Did the boy also ask himself if her death, then, would mean his death? Had she died from sexual desire, and would his desire, his erections, also be the death of him? Who was it, ultimately, who killed little children? Mother was desirable, but perhaps she was deadly. She certainly showed signs of it, by producing something nasty, something yellow from under her skirt, which both fascinated Lorenz and gave him a horror of women's secretions, of things female and sexual. He perhaps feared that she was tainted and dangerous, and that her charms were diseased and deadly. He had another reason to fear her: she clearly seemed magical to the boy. She gave life and she took it away. No sooner was Katherine dead than Julie was born. But Lorenz seems to have had some question as to whether Katherine was really dead. Was she not stuck up on Mother's hat in the form of the stuffed bird of which he tells Freud he was so afraid—the stuffed bird that seemed to stir uncannily in his hand, giving him the fright of his life? (Later the idea will be explored of children, including Lorenz being part of Mother, namely her penis, which it was necessary to cut off in order to be free, and yet dangerous to cut off since it might mean death, either through retaliation or lost nurturance.) Was it Mother who killed little children; or was it angry Father; or was it lustful Lorenz, jealous Lorenz? In fact, it had been Father who carried Katherine away ill and scolded her, and then Katherine died. Wasn't it Father who killed children? In so far as Katherine and Lorenz were identified, will Father kill Lorenz? But *was* it Father who killed children, or was it Father who obeyed Mother, acted as her lieutenant, and carried out her wishes, who lived on her money and stole small change out of her purse? Was it not the controlling Mother who was really responsible?

From the critical early sessions, the source of the above reconstruction and speculations, it is also learned that the reality of Lorenz's father's death— the death Freud documents as central to Lorenz's breakdown—was not fully faced by him until 18 months after the fact. But only in passing does Freud mention it was the death of a female family member, his aunt, that brought the truth home to him. Freud maintains the catalyst to Lorenz's feelings was a remark by the aunt's widowed husband, "Other men allow themselves every possible indulgence, but I lived for this woman alone!" (Freud 1909, p. 175), and that Lorenz heard this as a slight on his father and a questioning of his fidelity to his wife.

But of what did Lorenz reproach himself? He seemed to reproach himself with having been away from his father when he died, of not being responsive to his last call. What was the connection between these reproaches (which he shared with his mother and sisters) and his sensitivity to his uncle's infidelity remark? Freud does not tell us. The only clue to Freud's thoughts on the matter is his mention of Lorenz's identification with his father at the time of the "Rubensky marriage plan." This identification, Freud says, caused a paralysis of will in Lorenz, an inability to work or make plans, a refusal, in other words, to follow in his father's footsteps and marry for money (although he was tempted by the well-to-do Rubensky girl). All this took place the year before the remark of the widowed uncle and a short time after the father's death. So, Freud would probably say the reason Lorenz was struck so hard by his uncle's remark was because he was guilty for not obeying his father's wishes that he leave his respectably poor "lady" Gisela and marry the Rubensky girl. He would be guilty then of infidelity in terms of his father's desires for him, and would therefore see his disobedient self in his uncle's remark, and see that his father's death was the result of this kind of infidelity.

Fortunately, this important but unelaborated incident of the aunt's death, followed by the uncle's remark and Lorenz's reaction of guilt and remorse, is described in greater detail in Freud's working notes (Freud 1909, pp. 274-275). Lorenz heard his uncle's remark, but he did not take immediate notice of it. It impressed itself upon him only some days later, and his first action was to ask Gisela about it. Why would he ask Gisela? What could she know of the matter? A good deal, if Gisela was identified in Lorenz's mind with his mother. His mother had remarked cryptically about the father's philandering and lack of sense. In identification with his father, was it being suggested that he, Lorenz, was *not being faithful to mother*? Here perhaps lay his great sensitivity. He identified with his father, and the remark touched a sore spot in him, not because his faithlessness is concerned with disobeying his father's wishes, but because it is concerned primarily with a rebellion against his mother's wishes. Lorenz was at that time "philandering" with various young women (including some sex play with his own sister). His mother knew this very well and had reprimanded him for it. Lorenz was playing the libertine. He was certainly dishonoring a parental wish, but it was clearly Mother's wish. For as shall be seen, it was not his father who was pushing him into marriage with the Rubensky girl, but his mother.

There is another point that can be clarified through access to the process notes: the importance of the dead aunt whose husband made the bitter remark. This aunt was actually Gisela's grandmother, and Lorenz had earlier felt a serious suicidal/murderous impulse toward the old woman. For him the woman was highly cathected. He was morbidly drawn to her. Once he had a dream of Gisela showing him the woman's beautiful youthful body, though she was old. He was obviously fascinated by her final illness. He was described by his family as behaving like a "carrion crow," and was maddened when he was forbidden access to her when she was ill. She appears to have been a great many of his female images rolled into one: she was beauty, she was disease, and she was on her death bed, succumbing to things anal (she was suffering from a disease of the rectum). If the assumptions presented here about Lorenz's ambivalence toward women are correct, one can imagine that he was torn by love and hate, loathing and desire, that the death of such a highly cathected, highly symbolized woman figure might shake him to the point of an outbreak of neurosis and the response to the father's death might in fact be a further ramification of his response to this primary death-of-the-woman. The aunt might be anything but the accidental catalyst that Freud presents in his published case.

THE RUBENSKY PLAN

Freud says quite unequivocally, "After his father's death, the patient's mother told him one day that she had been discussing his future with her rich relations, and that one of her cousins had declared himself ready to let him marry one of his daughters . . ." Freud calls this the "family plan," and says that Lorenz's conflict was "whether he should remain faithful to the lady he loved in spite of her poverty, or whether he should follow in his father's footsteps and marry a rich well-connected girl. . . . This conflict, which was in fact one between his love and the persisting influence of his father's wishes, he resolves by falling ill and thus doing neither" (Freud 1909, p. 198). In support of his conviction that Lorenz was conflicted over a *father's* wish, Freud cites a transference fantasy in which Lorenz "experienced, as though it were new and belonged to the present, the very episode from the past . . ." He met a young girl on Freud's steps and imagined that the only reason Freud was kind to him was that he wanted Lorenz for a son-in-law. He dreamed "he saw my daughter in front of him; she had two patches of dung instead of eyes. . . . He declared he was marrying my daughter not for her 'beaux yeux' but for her money" (Freud 1909, pp. 199–200).

However, when these situations are examined in the working notes, a good deal more information emerges, much of it pertaining directly to the mother's influence in the matter. For one thing, the plan was clearly an old one of his mother's and was described as her "scheme" (p. 292). It is also learned that though the young lady in question was lovely, the Rubensky family was not—for "his mother was brought up by (them) as an adopted daughter, but was very badly treated." And then there was a son who was a sadist and cut off chicken's heads ("it excited him very much"), and once "koshered" a cat by "baking it in an oven and then skinning it" (pp.290–291).

This cruelty had a strong effect on Lorenz. He confessed to Freud that everything bad in his character came from his mother's side of the family. Lorenz reflected further that he once saw a cat beaten in a sack and immediately thought of his father. Although he doubtless hated his father for having given himself up to a Rubensky plan of his own, he obviously saw his father as a victim of his mother's economically practiced "cruelty" as well. He saw his father as more weak than tyrannical, and his mother as calculating. "He was convinced, from a remark which his mother let fall to the effect that her connection with the Rubenskys was worth more than a dowry, that his father had married her and abandoned his love for this material advantage. . . . This made him detest the poverty which drives people to such crimes. In this way his low opinion of his mother found satisfaction . . . he hands over all his money to his mother because he does not want to have anything from her; it belongs to her and there is no blessing in it" (Freud 1909, p. 197).

As for Lorenz's response to Freud, his "transference" to him just prior to the unfolding of the Rubensky plan is remarkable for its violence, its crudeness, and its almost exclusive concentration on women. At one point Lorenz reports a dream that Freud's mother had died, and upon offering his condolences he was afraid he would break into an impertinent laugh. Freud asked him "Hasn't it occurred to you that if your mother died you would be freed from all conflicts, since you would be able to marry?" (p. 283). This is a startling statement to hear from Freud, since he so consistently asks this question in terms of the father. Only in the working notes is the question asked in terms of the mother. Lorenz's response is also startling, and more violent than any other responses heard from him: "You are taking revenge on me," he said to Freud. "You are forcing me into this, because you want to revenge yourself on me," and he walked about the room for fear he would get a beating, and all the while he beat himself. The response seems to us to contain a guilty and enraged (projected) reaction to a murderous impulse against the creator of the Rubensky plan, the mother. (For an examination of other interesting aspects of Lorenz's "transference" responses to Freud, see the discussion of Freud's own responses to Lorenz and some resulting examples of therapeutic "misalliance," in Langs 1978, pp. 255–272).

As part of this intense preoccupation with women, spanning the sessions from November 21 to December 8, Lorenz had a dream in which he defecated into the mouths of some children and Freud's son licked off the fecal matter with relish. This brought on a fantasy of Gisela defecating into the mouth of a "badly behaved" female cousin, whereupon the cousin turned around and similarly insulted Gisela. "Pride and high-minded regard lay behind this," Freud says. Lorenz was accusing Gisela of being too good for the common people, in fact a snob like Lorenz's mother, who set great store in manners and position and money (Freud 1909, p. 186). In his dream, his too fastidious woman received the same kind of insult that she tended to give—an anal one—from a common cousin, someone in fact like Lorenz's father, who was a low person in his wife's eyes, a person who used low words like "ass" and "shit." Lorenz then remembered his mother's washing him, her calling him "the little pig." He remembered his outraged curses and his mother's surprising defense of his profanity before his father. Lorenz mentioned that his father and mother were first cousins (the only time we hear of their close blood tie), the same kind of tie that existed between Lorenz and Gisela. The dream seems to say that Gisela (identified with the mother) and Lorenz are both capable of hurling the same kind of insults, are filled with the same "high-minded" dirtiness. They are too good for low people like the father, yet they "get it" from them and they even like it (lick their mouths), and defend their dirtiness (the mother's defense of her son's obscenities). For Lorenz, clean is at the same time dirty. Pure and high-minded Mother is also dirty and lascivious Mother, and Mother and Son are very much alike.

Also part of Lorenz's obsessive preoccupation with the clean and dirty, the high and low woman, was his a fantasy of laying back-to-back with Freud's daughter and having intercourse with a piece of feces hanging from his anus. He associated this to his sister Julie, to whom he once said, "nothing about you would disgust me." The fantasy is also connected with his "conflict" of whether to marry Gisela Fluss or Freud's daughter.

It is only after this barrage of primarily anal, sadistic associations involving women that he reveals to Freud the whole complex of issues around the Rubensky marriage plan (Freud 1909, p. 292), his mother's "scheme." And he follows the telling of the plan with some gross abuse of Freud, accusing him of picking his nose, of being a swine, of being unmannerly, and of being "too intimate" with him. As Langs (1978, pp. 161–165) points out, Freud had, in fact, inadvertently encouraged Lorenz's hostile productions by a "deviation" in technique—the sending of a cordial postcard—an act that may have signified to Lorenz not only a homosexual approach by Freud requiring a hostile, panicky retreat, but also a manipulation, and a seduction by Freud as a maternally perceived figure, resulting in a response that illuminates the ambivalent attraction and repulsion he felt toward his mother.

In the whole range of Lorenz's responses, there is evidence of rage at the weak, low-minded father who could abandon his love, and also rage at a high-minded but nevertheless money-conscious and calculating mother. When he says to Freud that Frau Freud should "lick his ass," and that Freud's daughter has two patches of dung for eyes, this may be perceived as, among other things, a projected response to a mother who has an "eye for money," who is, in a phrase, "ass-licking" and full of "unclean" motives. As he perceives his mother, so too he perceives Gisela, his analyst, and, of course, himself.

GISELA: HER IDENTIFICATION WITH FRAU LORENZ

Gisela, Lorenz's lady, has a strikingly different emphasis in the working notes from the one Freud develops in the published case. What is noteworthy in the working notes is that Lorenz frequently equates Gisela and his mother in his remarks. The two are often tied together in his mind. In Freud's published version, this integral link has been eliminated. Gisela is seen by Freud as a yearned-for prize, a desired object, but not a subject of conflict in herself, and not the surrogate figure she appears to be from the working notes. In the published case, Freud argues that she stands out of Lorenz's reach only because of the prohibitions of his father, a stance in striking contrast to the impression of her in the notes, as a subject of excruciating ambivalence, arousing in Lorenz all the love and hate, desire and avoidance that probably originated from his relationship with his mother.

In the working notes, for instance, Lorenz felt exactly the same way toward his mother and Gisela each time he had sexual contact with another woman. With Gisela, his "lapses" were at first guilt-laden, but were later transformed, as the analysis progressed, into acts of defiance against her influence.

With his mother, the same trend may be observed. After the revelation to Freud of his mother's Rubensky marriage plan, Lorenz dared for the first time to openly criticize his mother. It was at this time that he began to care for a dressmaker with whom he had been having sex for some weeks. He openly compared the dressmaker with his mother, and was amazed that she did not have revolting secretions as he suspected "all women" had (Freud 1909, pp. 295–296). He was able to be with the dressmaker and not be too obsessed with contaminating Gisela. He was able to visit the dressmaker and not worry overly much about his mother's ideas of cleanliness, though both with Gisela and with his mother he continued to perform protective acts. For instance, he made sure that he did not touch Gisela's cigarette case with the fingers that touched the dressmaker (Freud 1909, p. 191); and he showed exaggerated consideration for his mother in deference to "her educational strictures," especially about his dirtiness (p. 296). Nevertheless, he felt free enough to tell Freud that he found his mother's burping at the table disgusting, and he was in other ways defiant and critical of her (p. 296).

A fantasy of Lorenz's that serves to illustrate the identification in his mind between Gisela and Frau Lorenz, and that actually makes them mother and daughter, or "one flesh," is that of the whore who carried Gisela around inside her. (Lorenz often thought of both Gisela and his mother as whores.) In this fantasy, the genitals of the whore and of Gisela inside her were juxtaposed, so that when the whore had intercourse, Gisela also benefitted. Gisela then blew herself up until she burst the whore (p. 312). Though this fantasy clearly lends itself to various interpretations, one is that Gisela was produced, or given birth to, by Frau Lorenz, and was her heir, her flesh, in fact, herself.

Paul also had notions that whatever he did to injure himself would in turn injure both Gisela and his mother. For instance, he vowed that he would never commit suicide, "even if he was unlucky in love," because of the effect it would have on his mother. And he refused to have a tooth pulled once because somehow his pain would also damage Gisela.

Freud also stresses Lorenz's magical thinking, his fear that his thoughts could harm others. Lorenz felt that he was omnipotent in this way, and the above fears may be seen to include the wish to do harm—cause pain—to his mother and lady. But the feeling of omnipotence perhaps involves not only a belief in one's power, but also a conviction of one's helplessness. If his thoughts could harm others, if he was so closely connected to others that his thoughts (wishes) could have this intimate effect on people, then they were also intimately linked to him.

THE MATERNAL TRANSFER TO FREUD

Thanks mostly to the working notes, it is possible to take a fascinating look at Lorenz's transferences to Freud, "those unconscious fantasies about, wishes toward, and reactions to the analyst that reflect some intrapsychic alteration or distortion of the prevailing realities" (Langs 1978, p. 515). These notes reveal many of the themes mentioned in this reformulation.

A number of these transference phenomena are brought by Freud into the published case and identified as such. They are interpreted by him as mostly paternal. Very few of them seem exclusively so, however. Many of the very powerful transferences seem to be maternal.

An example of Freud's tendency to view himself as a powerful male, a recipient for the projection of male transference fantasies, and of his failure to recognize the presence of mother-infant fantasies and maternal conflict, occurs in the opening session (Freud 1909, p. 255). When Freud tells Lorenz his fee, Lorenz responds to the "fatherly-authority" by holding to the image of his mother. "He said he must consult his mother." As already noted, Freud did not publish this statement. Instead he concludes the published record of this session with a testimony to his own masculine influence: "He had been turning over the pages of one of my books . . . [and] had decided to put himself in my hands" (p. 159).

The "pour condoler" dream, in which Lorenz feared he would respond inappropriately to Freud's mother's death, has already been described as Lorenz's hostile feelings toward his mother, transferred onto Freud. The basic element is Lorenz's wish to be free of his two powerful controlling mothers—his real mother and his transference mother, Freud. In another example, Lorenz refers to Freud's house as a "house of joy" or a "Freudenhaus-Madchen" (house of prostitution) (Freud 1909, p. 284). This image is almost certainly a reflection of his attitude toward his own women-dominated house, with his mother viewed as the Madame who charges her fee. "For each krone a rat for the children," Lorenz thinks in relation to the analytic charge. Freud as mother extracts his price for the analysis and gives a dubious return, a rat (Lorenz's rat obsession involved his perception of them as seductively intrusive).

THE TRANSFERENCES AROUND THE FEEDING SESSION

Freud calls forth a barrage of maternal transferences when he serves Lorenz a meal during an analytic session. This meal has been commented on by many psychoanalytic writers. Sharp differences exist among them, ranging from Lipton's (1977) view that, given the setting and culture, Freud's feeding of Lorenz was consistent with proper psychoanalytic technique, to Biegler's (1975) statement that the feeding was an intrusive disruptive act, "a breach of the analytic barrier . . . (and) a source of over stimulation" (p. 274). Other writers have seen it as an error in technique, a "misalliance" (Langs 1978).

This issue of whether the feeding was in this case proper psychoanalytic technique may be overshadowed by the clinical data that emerge in the rich and lengthy series of associations produced by the event. Freud's only reference to his feeding of Lorenz appears in the working notes (Freud 1909, p. 303), though many of Lorenz's reactions to it are mentioned in the published case and a number of them are analyzed by Freud. They are analyzed, however, without reference to the act of the feeding itself, an act maternal in nature, and certainly the direct stimulus of his productions. "He was hungry," Freud reported, "and was fed." Freud records as the content of that session Lorenz's account of his slimming compulsion at Unterach, an account that had begun the session prior to the feeding session, but was broadened and intensified by the feeding itself. At Unterach, Lorenz reported, he ran wildly about, trying to lose weight, and only ate a portion of his meals (he had eaten only a portion of the meal served him by Freud). It sounds as though he was running off the effects of the nourishment (influence) he was subjected to, running away, one may venture to say, from the most basic of maternal acts, the giving of food (symbolic of herself). He said he felt he had become too fat. Was he hostilely dependent on and too close to an ambivalently perceived, intrusive, and controlling mother (as called up by the too intrusive Freud)?

Freud interpreted the losing-weight compulsion as a jealous response to Gisela's attentive English cousin, Richard, a losing of "dick" (fat). It was, according to Freud, an attempt to do away with a male (paternal) rival. Though one must thoroughly respect all Freud's interpretations, this material may well warrant the additional interpretation of a flight from mother, both because of its timing in relation to the feeding episode and in light of other material that appears to have been stimulated by the "feeding hour" (Freud 1909, pp. 303–306).

First of all, Lorenz was very angry with his mother at Unterach (the dieting summer) and was defending his anger with an array of reaction-formations and magical acts. He told Freud of his compulsive social chatter to his mother. He told him of various obsessions experienced in regard to her. In her presence, for instance, he counted between thunder and lightning flashes. He felt the need to protect her "as though he had a command that nothing must happen to her," and told of an obsession of understanding "every syllable spoken to him."

He was in deep psychological distress on this vacation with his mother and Gisela. He told Freud he had the uncanny feeling that he would never get back from Unterach alive. He wrote a friend that he thought the interlude would be the death of him. In fact, he made a suicide gesture there, but told Freud of his vow not to injure his mother by such an act, a vow already discussed in terms of his wish to harm her (see p. 19). He had the conviction that his mere thoughts could inflict such harm, and his frantic attempts to control these thoughts are evident here.

He seems to have wanted to break away from his mother (and Gisela). He would have liked to shake himself free from her influence. His impulse (obsessively defended against) was in fact to murder her. Only once did he make a harmful gesture toward anyone but himself, however. The gesture is significant, hostile. The importance of it is underscored by the doing and undoing ritual that accompanied it. In the last revelation of the "feeding hour," he described how he had removed a stone from the path of Gisela's carriage, lest she come to harm, and then was compelled to replace it, thereby undoing his harmful thought.

Lorenz seems to be telling Freud exactly how he felt about being fed. It is likely that these transference reactions were stimulated both by the immediate feeding and the unconscious fantasies relating to women, primarily his mother and her surrogate, Gisela. What he told Freud is that he felt trapped and helpless, murderous, guilty, and eager to flee from the situation. In the analysis he acted out his wish—he did flee. He did not return to analysis for two or three sessions, "owing to the illness of Dr. Pr.," says Freud. (As an aside, the date on which Lorenz returned—January 2?—Freud erroneously records as December 2 [Freud 1909, p. 307], thereby eliminating the missed sessions, and indeed all of the maternal sessions that have just been reviewed here).

This was by no means the end of Lorenz's responses to the maternal act of feeding, however. When he returned to analysis, he brought a significant dream, which Freud recounts in these words: "Between two women—my wife and my mother (Freud's)—a herring was stretched, extending from the anus of one to that of the other. A girl cut it in two . . . All he could say at first was that he disliked herring intensely; when he had been fed recently, he had been given a herring and left it untouched. The girl was one he had seen on the stairs and had taken to be my daughter." (pp. 307–308).

One thing about this dream seems clearly possible: he "disliked intensely" what he had been fed—the herring— and viewed it as dirt, more precisely womanly fecal matter. He seems to be saying that it is this dirt or excrement that women have in common, which the Mother (as represented by Freud's mother) and Gisela (as represented by Freud's wife) have between them.

To carry the interpretation a step further (on the basis of Lorenz's own later associations), if Mother's nurturance is a piece of feces, it is also a penis, and therefore her aggressive and intrusive control over him. When the girl (nee Lorenz?) cuts the piece of feces, an act of castration is performed and his mother's domination is symbolically cut off. Castrating the Mother has another consequence as well, that of cutting off Lorenz himself from his mother. The feces-penis is also Lorenz himself, for marriage, it may be remembered, was to young Lorenz an affair of the behinds, and children were consequently a product of the anal tract. Such a separation or cutting off from the mother most likely would be a source of intense ambivalence for Lorenz.

To castrate Mother, to be free of her, was perhaps to castrate oneself and lose one's own life. His strong dependence on her and his identification with her were intimately involved in his rage toward her. The issue of his money is illustrative: financially he was in her hands, as she controlled his inheritance. By giving his mother his money to control, he gave up his adulthood, his independence, and gave her control over his destiny in general, and over his masculinity specifically. It is his own train of associations that links money ("filthy lucre") to feces, and which links feces to penis, to self.

Also illustrative is another memory in response to the "feeding hour," the memory of the stuffed bird from his mother's hat that seemed to come alive in his hand. According to Lorenz, this was "the greatest fright of his life." The memory is probably a screen for a number of deeper issues. Grunberger's (1966) interpretation of the boy's anal sadistic wish to castrate the phallic mother's penis concurs with the interpretation presented here, and it is given additional merit by a further association dealing with Lorenz's voyeuristic fantasies, suggesting a search for the hidden female phallus (Freud 1909, pp. 160–161). The great fright most probably would represent, along with the above fear of loss of the dependent relationship, both the wish to castrate and the fear of the mother's retaliation.

Additionally, it is possible that this train of memories and associations contains a deeply negative self-image of Lorenz-made-of-feces, or dirt; of Lorenz as a stuffed appendage on his mother's hat. The idea of his identification with the helpless bird-as-Katherine was discussed earlier. In other words, the "feeding hour" reopened deep feelings of ambivalence toward the mother and pointed, by the way of powerful images and impulses, to issues of helplessness, sexual degradation and dependence, and fears of loss of identity, and of engulfment. These issues have been seen before, but are especially clear here.

Freud explores much of the above material in the published case, interpreting it for the most part as a manifestation of the paternal conflict. A recognition of the maternal character of many of the transference manifestations, with their indication of a deep conflict with the mother, is an important contribution to a fuller and more complete understanding of the case.

A NEW LOOK AT THE OBSESSIONAL FEAR OF RATS

Freud felt that all the elements of Lorenz's illness were present in the rat obsession, and this certainly appears to be the case. The obsession took hold of Lorenz while he was away with his troop on annual maneuvers, and after his "cruel" captain told him of a terrible torture using rats. Greatly condensed and highly symbolized, the rat obsession *was* Lorenz's illness. Freud (1909, p. 214) details the various meanings rats had for Lorenz: as carriers of infectious diseases they meant *syphilis* and aroused Lorenz's fear of having contracted it, and his doubts about his father's life in the army (this is a disease, one may note, that is transmitted to the child via the mother). Rats also meant the *male sex organ*, since it is the penis that carries syphilis (and Lorenz's possible fear of the mother-with-a-penis has been noted); rats also meant a *child's penis* (and therefore, as has been seen, the child himself); rats meant many *things anal*, since they feed on excrement and live in sewers (the ambitious mother with her eye-for-money was a "thing anal"); rats meant *prostitutes* via the statement "so many rats so many florins" (Lorenz tended to see both his mother and Gisela as prostitutes, therefore rats); rats meant *intercourse per anum*, "which could not fail to be especially revolting to him when brought into connection with his father and the women he loved" (Freud means his fantasy of the sexual abuse of Gisela; here the abuse *by* Gisela and by the phallic mother are seen as well). Rats meant *marriage*—"heiraten" means "to marry"; and finally and most importantly, rats meant *children*, a meaning Freud says became clear when Lorenz made a key association to a fictional character called the "Rat-wife."

"(In)spite of all this wealth of material," says Freud, "no light was thrown upon the meaning of his obsessional idea until one day the Rat-wife in Ibsen's *Little Eyolf*, came up in the analysis . . ." (1909, pp. 214–215). The Rat-wife provided Freud with an important analytic insight, which led ultimately to his full interpretation of the rat obsession. Freud's assessment of this obsession is also of critical importance to the understanding of Lorenz's mother conflict, and it also confirms the present emphasis on the mother.

THE RAT-WIFE

It cannot be known how deeply Lorenz was affected by the image of the Rat-wife, but it may be assumed that he (and probably Freud) was more than cursorily familiar with the play in which she appears, since he told Freud he often went to the theatre. Ibsen's *Little Eyolf* was first performed in Vienna in February, 1895, when Lorenz was 17 years old. Perhaps he saw the play then, at an impressionable age. It had several revivals in subsequent years.

Ibsen's character, the Rat-wife, was a kind of Pied Piper, hired by the community to lure rats out of their hiding places and, with the aid of her dog, to lead them down to the sea where they were drowned. "(E)very blessed one," she says, "(a)nd there it is all as still, and soft, and dark as their hearts can desire, the lovely little things. Down there they sleep a long, sweet sleep, with no one to hate them or to persecute them any more" (Ibsen 1894, p. 25).

It is not surprising that Lorenz should bring the Rat-wife into his analysis. The Rat-wife's business was to kill, even though she killed out of "love." She led rats back to the sea (universally symbolic of the womb) and drowned them there out of "pity" for them, yet she also hated them. She had started her trade by drowning her lover, her first "rat." It was said that the old woman turned into a werewolf at night. If any situation was created to point up Lorenz's ambivalence around the mother relationship, it would be that of the Rat-wife. The play, it seems, is very much like the rat image, a multi-faceted condensation of Lorenz's conflict.

The Rat-wife gave Freud the much needed identification of rats/children/ Lorenz. Freud then leaves the play, drawing no further inferences from it. Nevertheless, the identification leads quite naturally and compellingly to further meanings, for instance, it seems that Lorenz is identified with the character in the play who becomes a "little rat" and who is seduced by the Rat-wife to his death. The character is Little Eyolf, the crippled son of a mother and father largely caught up in their own egotistic concerns. As an infant he was crippled as a direct result of his parent's love–hate relationship, the power struggle between them that led to his father's being fatally lured to the bed of his wife, a jealous and possessive sensualist, when he should have been caring for the child. The father had married for money, while continuing to love a poverty striken half-sister whom he hoped, with romantic generosity, to help by the wealthy connection. (The parallel to Herr Lorenz's "romanticism" is striking.)

Eyolf's mother was seriously conflicted over her son. On the one hand, she felt that her husband had come between herself and her son. "I cannot endure to share anything with anyone! Not in love," she says (Ibsen 1894, p. 90). She did not love generously and empathically, but narcissistically and from a sense of emotional deprivation.

Little Eyolf was a victim, a child both parents would unconsciously have liked to dominate or to get rid of. When the Rat-wife came to the house to rid it of its vermin, Little Eyolf, in a suicidal renunciation, gave himself up to her. He knew where his destiny lay, surrendering to one who he knew was a lure to engulfment and death. This kind of surrender to death could not resolve his insoluble conflict, however. It was an end to his life, yet to Little Eyolf, for whom everything in life was uncertain and doubtful, it was at least sure. As Freud (1909) says concerning the obsessional's need for death, "these neurotics need the help of the possibility of death chiefly in order that it may act as a solution of conflicts they have left unsolved" (p. 236).

It is postulated that Lorenz unconsciously identified with Eyolf and his plight. His own "Rat-wife" was Frau Lorenz, a woman who had led him into a state of unending ambivalence and conflict, a psychological state of doubt, or longing and fear, love and hate, from which he seemed helpless to escape.

In Ibsen's play, the Rat-wife has many qualities of the primitive pre-Oedipal mother. She offers warmth and security, and control and death. It may be speculated that Lorenz's identification as a rat also indicated that his mind contained this "vertical split" of his mother's image. This suggestion is supported by the many primitive maternal transferences documented in Freud's notes.

Freud (1909) writes that when the riddle of the obsessive fear of rats was solved, "the patient's rat delirium disappeared" (p. 20). Freud's interpretation, based on the Oedipal father–son conflict, may have contributed to Lorenz's cure, but it was incomplete. The issue stressed here is that along with, and often behind, the ambivalence and anger toward the father stood the ambivalence and anger toward the mother. More than the solution of the riddle by means of a key interpretation, the therapeutic success achieved in the treatment can best be explained by the total experience of the patient in the analysis (Lipton 1977). One important experience was the relationship to the parental figure of the analyst. About this Freud would have no argument. However, the major emphasis that Freud places on the *paternal* transference, and his exclusion of the *maternal* transference and the conflicts with the mother that these transferences reveal, limits the scope and inhibits theoretical formulation of the case. There is a wealth of evidence, in the working notes especially, to support the position that a very complex and active process occurred in which the figure of the mother was central.

Freud's 1909 formulation of the Rat Man case history and of obsessive symptoms was heavily influenced by his recent discovery of the Oedipus complex. His discovery of the web of rivalry and love between father and son had been stimulated by the death of his elderly father and identified through his self-analysis. He apparently never explored in a similar fashion the nature of his relationship to his mother, who was 20 years old at Freud's birth, and who lived a long, full life to the age of 95, a life almost concurrent with that of her son (Jones 1953). His continuing close relationship with his mother and a series of almost uncanny similarities between Freud and the young man he treated in this analysis may have contributed to Freud's reluctance, or inability, to give appropriate emphasis to the mother–son issues in Lorenz's analysis. (For a discussion of Freud's own mother-conflict and his defensive maneuvers around this conflict, which included the re-casting of the conflict into the paternal sphere, see Abraham 1979a and 1979b.)

The evidence suggests that Freud failed to deal with the role of the mother in the development of Lorenz's obsessional disorder. Others, and indeed Freud himself (1905, p. 142), have pointed out his failure to recognize the importance of the maternal conflict in several of his key cases, for instance, the Wolf Man, Little Hans, and Schraber. Of special importance is the fact that this case history, interpreted by Freud in terms of father–son rivalry and fear of paternal castration, has significantly influenced the psychoanalytic conceptualizations of the obsessive patient. Study of this pivotal case suggests that the present understanding requires re-evaluation.

SOME PRELIMINARY THOUGHTS

The genesis of obsessive neurosis is no simple matter. Freud viewed this neurosis as arising from the need to fend off libidinal demands of the Oedipus complex, coupled by a regression to a fixation at the anal-sadistic stage and the ego's and superego's reaction to this aggression. An excellent review of the psychoanalytic literature and of the conceptual issues regarding obsessive neurosis has been done by Nagera (1976). Blacker and Levitt's (1979) paper draws attention to the frequent clinical error of automatically diagnosing a patient with obsessive symptoms as an obsessive neurotic, and discusses the problem of clearly identifying an obsessive-compulsive neurotic syndrome.

The genesis of obsessive neurosis is thought to arise from two sources: constitutional factors, such as precocious ego development (Freud 1913, 1916, 1926), and psychological factors, primarily the deep ambivalence at the core of the obsessive's personality, i.e., the eternal struggle between love and hate. According to the Oedipal paradigm, these opposites are caused by a son's love for and fear of his father, the hate being generated by a father's prohibition of a son's sexual striving and ambitions. In this model, castration anxiety serves as the motivating force that inhibits the son's normal genital development and precipitates the regression to an anal stage of functioning.

Recently, Mahler et al. (1975) have provided psychoanalysts with a deeper appreciation of the role of the mother in a child's development. She has described the vicissitudes of the powerful attraction that a child experiences for its mother, and the equally powerful desire a child has to escape from the maternal orbit. In the light of her observations and theories, some forms of obsessive ambivalence might be seen to harken back to a conflict in the dyadic relationship with the mother. Issues of autonomy and control that have long been recognized as central to the psychoanalytic treatment of ob-sessive patients, and which psychoanalysts have typically considered as signs of defensive regression from Oedipal sexual conflict, might be seen as an arrest in the development and separation process from the mother. A child's concurrent love of the mother and need for mothering and his or her need to assert autonomy and loosen the dyadic bond may, in the face of conflict, initiate a neurotic dilemma that sets the stage for certain kinds of obsessive conflict. A series of obsessive-neurotic men whose transference reactions were clearly tied to a maternal figure and revelatory of deep mother conflicts has been described. Maternal transferences of this sort have been described by Blacker (1977). Zetzel (1966) and Holland (1975) have touched on these same issues in relation to the case reviewed here. They have pointed out Lorenz's unresolved ambivalence toward his mother, as well as his need to keep control of himself and his great fear of being controlled by another.

Awareness that obsessive dynamics may represent dyadic (mother–child) as well as triadic (Oedipal) struggles may enable a clinician to be more precise and exact in his or her formulations and interpretations. The misidentification of a struggle for autonomy and independence as a competitive rivalry will confuse, not cure. In addition, father figures, both genetic and as revealed in the transference, may be used as surrogates for the mother, and the conflict may be acted out with this often safer "heir" to the primal parent. There is evidence of the surrogate mother in many aspects of the Lorenz response to his father and to Father-Freud.

Correct formulations and interpretations can only be made after careful and complete examination of a patient's associational patterns. This re-examination of Freud's classical case and the preliminary suggestions for broadening the psychodynamics of obsessive neurosis may encourage further exploration of work with obsessive patients. In this manner a more complete understanding of obsessive illness may evolve.

REFERENCES

Abraham, R. (1977). Freud's Rat-man case: a look at the maternal conflicts in the analysis of Paul Lorenz. Unpublished Master's *Thesis*, University of California, Davis.

———. (1979a). Freud and "mater." Unpublished Doctoral Dissertation, University of California, Davis.

———. (1982). Freud's mother conflict and the formulation of the Oedipal father. *The Psychoanalytic Review*.

Biegler, J. S. (1975). A commentary on Freud's treatment of the Rat-Man. *Annual of Psychoanalysis* 3:150–165.

Blacker, K. H. (1977). Frightened men: a wish for intimacy and fear of closeness. *International Journal of Psychoanalytic Psychotherapy*, 6:269–288.

Blacker, K. H., and Levitt, M. (1979). The differential diagnosis of obsessive compulsive symptoms. *Comprehensive Psychiatry* 20:532–547.

Freud, S. (1905). Fragment of an analysis of a case of hysteria. *Standard Edition* 7:7–122.

———. (1909). Notes upon a case of obsessional neurosis. *Standard Edition* 10:153–318.

———. (1913). The disposition to obsessional neurosis. *Standard Edition* 12:311–326.

———. (1916). Introductory lectures on psycho-analysis. *Standard Edition* 15–16.

———. (1926). Inhibitions, symptoms and anxiety. *Standard Edition* 20:77–123.

Grunberger, B. (1966). Some reflections on the Rat-Man. *International Journal of Psychoanalysis* 47:160–168.

Hawelka, R. E. (1974). L'Homme aux Rats. *Journel d'une analyse Sigmund Freud.* Paris: Presses Universitaires de France.

Holland, N. (1975). An identity for the Rat-Man. *International Review of Psycho-Analysis* 2:157–169.

Ibsen, H. (1894). *Little Eyolf. Collected works of Henrik Ibsen* vol. 11. New York: Charles Scribner's Sons, 1910.

Jones. E (1953). *The Life and Work of Sigmund Freud, Vols. 1–3.* New York: Basic Books.

Kanzer M. (1952). The transference neurosis of the Rat-Man. *Psychoanalysis Quarterly* 21:181–189.

Langs, R. (1978). *Technique in Transition.* New York: Jason Aronson.

Lipton, S. D. (1977). The advantages of Freud's technique as shown in his analysis of the Rat-Man. *International Journal of Psycho-Analysis* 58:225–273.

Mahler, M. S., Pine, E., and Bergman, A. (1975). *The Psychological Birth of the Human Infant.* New York: Basic Books.

Morgenthaler, F. (1966). Psychodynamic aspects of defense with comments on technique in the treatment of obsessional neurosis. *International Journal of Psycho-Analysis* 47:203–209.

Muslin, H. L. (1977). Transference in the Rat-Man case: the transference in transition. Presented at the Annual Meeting of the American Psychoanalytic Association, Quebec, May, 1977.

Nagera, H. (1976). *Obsessional Neuroses: Developmental Psychopathology.* New York: Jason Aronson.

Sherwood, M. (1969). The psychoanalytic narrative. In *The Logic of Explanation in Psychoanalysis*, pp. 185–257. New York: Academic Press.

Zetzel, E. R. (1966). 1965: additional notes upon a case of obsessional neurosis: Freud 1909. *International Journal of Psychoanalysis* 47:123–129.

·

A Reply to Dr. Elmhirst's Discussion of "Primitive Defenses: Cognitive Aspects and Therapeutic Handling"

LESLIE S. GROH, Ph.D.

"Primitive Defense: Cognitive Aspects and Therapeutic Handling," by Leslie S. Groh, Ph.D., and the discussion paper by Dr. Elmhirst appeared in volume 8 of this journal.

The central difference between Dr. Elmhirst and the present author concerns the weight one ought to give to reconstructions based on clinical material as opposed to observational research carried out at the age being considered in the development of genetic theory. While my clinical work has been deeply influenced by Melanie Klein's writing, I am also aware that the youngest patient she treated was two years old, and consequently the timing of the paranoid-schizoid and depressive positions that she so brilliantly described was by necessity speculative. Another issue is that Klein never concerned herself with cognitive development, which is critical if we are ever to develop a psychological explanation of thought disorder. It has been clear for many years that cognitive processes in psychotic patients regress only partially (or sometimes completely, but only in a certain conflict-ridden areas). Thus Cameron (1938, 1939) has shown that when the logical processes of schizophrenic patients are studied, some of their solutions are based on normal adult logic, some other solutions use the logic typical of children between three and five years of age, and some are very primitive and disorganized, and appear to have logical structures stemming from below 18 months of age.

The line of reasoning of "Primitive Defenses," that cognitive development should have a relationship to mechanisms encountered in severely regressed patients, appears to have revived the long-standing argument between the Kleinians and their critiques concerning early development and the relative importance of reconstructions made from psychoanalytic material and direct observational studies. The paper goes even further by suggesting that the depressive position is brought about by development in the infant's cognitive organization.

The depressive position as a transitional stage between a schizophrenic and a neurotic organization is the most important contribution of Melanie Klein, in that it bears directly upon the understanding and treatment of psychoses. The clinical usefulness and validity of this concept is increasingly recognized by non-Kleinian clinicians. Thus Sonnenberg and Miller (1970), treating schizophrenic patients within an ego psychology framework, reported that all patients who recovered went through a series of depressions. Spotnitz (1976), working with schizophrenics, discovered that after initial severe withdrawal is penetrated, patients exhibit a severe struggle to protect their therapists from their destructiveness. This is, of course, what Melanie Klein called depressive anxiety. All this points out the need to understand the relation of the cognitive, representational aspects of the split-off parts of the self and its objects and how merging split-off segments affect cognitive processes, which the paper tried to do.

The pitfalls inherent in mixing clinical work and genetic reconstruction is well illustrated, which made Dr. Elmhirst conclude that the paper equated all mental processes with defenses. During therapy one is forced to look at primitive mental mechanisms and defenses, for they have not been replaced by higher level mechanisms precisely because of the material defended against. Whether thinking processes found during the course of treatment of schizophrenics are exactly the ways these patients thought when the fixation had occurred is an open question. The same dilemma is raised by the widespread observation that psychotic patients produce enormous amounts of sadistic material and relatively little libidinal material during therapy, which led Spotnitz (1976) to believe that during the pregenital period sadism dominates over eroticism, while beginning with the phallic phase the reverse is true. Here again it is a moot question whether this clinical observation indicates regression or the increase in destructive drive strength brought about by constitutional factors or unfortunate infantile experiences in people who later become psychotic.

Dr. Elmhirst appears to misunderstand the use of the word "symbolism." In the paper symbolism meant the conscious or unconscious equating of one thing with another, such as taking a mound of sand as a symbol of the breast. As the paper stated, Piaget's studies show that this kind of mental activity does not appear before nine months of age. This is not to say that no object relations exist before that age, nor does it deny that people are recognized and reacted to in certain ways. What it does imply is that the infant cannot react to people in their absence. This means that both the "good" and the "bad" mother exist only when the mother is present. When she is absent, only the sensations derived from external and internal sources in the here-and-now exist for the child. A mother who does not exist cannot be lost; this is why a permanent mental representation of her is necessary to enter the depressive position.

Piaget's work has firmly established that cognitive development consists of a gradual decrease of dependence on external and internal sensory support of cognitive processes (as opposed to perceptual ones). This gradual transition from the here-and-now determination of thinking to reflective internal thought starts shortly after birth and is completed by eleven or twelve years of age. The clinical parallel to the lack of internalization of thought in early life can be seen when the interpretation of splitting and other mechanisms as applied to people other than the therapist has no effect but produces results when the transference is interpreted.

Dr. Elmhirst is correct in saying that dismissing disturbed patients' communications as psychotic drivel, as practiced by the self-psychology group, is a real barrier to the successful treatment of these people. One must, however, add to this Kernberg's criticism of Kohut for ignoring the destructive material that such patients produce. During the treatment of borderline and psychotic patients, dealing with sadistic material and the defenses erected against them is a crucial aspect of successful treatment.

REFERENCES

Cameron, N. (1938). Reasoning, regression and communication in schizophrenia. *Psychological Monographs* 50: No. 1.

———. (1939). Deterioration and regression in schizophrenic thinking. *Journal of Abnormal and Social Psychology* 34:265–270.

Sonnenberg, S. M., and Miller, J. B. (1970). Depression in resolving schizophrenia. *Psychotherapy: Theory, Research and Practice* 7: No. 2.

Spotnitz, H. (1976). *Psychotherapy of Pre-Oedipal Conditions.* New York: Jason Aronson.

Index